740

PARK

740 PARK

THE STORY OF
THE WORLD'S RICHEST
APARTMENT BUILDING

MICHAEL GROSS

BROADWAY BOOKS

NEW YORK

PUBLISHED BY BROADWAY BOOKS

Copyright © 2005 by Michael Gross

All Rights Reserved

A hardcover edition of this book was originally published in 2005 by Broadway Books.

Published in the United States by Broadway Books, an imprint of The Doubleday Broadway Publishing Group, a division of Random House, Inc., New York.
www.broadwaybooks.com

BROADWAY BOOKS and its logo, a letter B bisected on the diagonal, are trademarks of Random House, Inc.

Book design by Marysarah Quinn

Title page: Front door, 740 Park Avenue. *(Photograph by Nancy Adams Gillon.)*

Library of Congress Cataloging-in-Publication Data
Gross, Michael, 1952–
    740 Park : the story of the world's richest apartment
    building / by Michael Gross.
    p.   cm.
    Includes bibliographical references.
    1. 740 Park Avenue (New York, N.Y.)—History. 2. Park
Avenue (New York, N.Y.)—Social life and customs. 3. Apartment houses—New York
(State)—New York—History. 4. Apartments—New York (State)—New York—History.
5. Rich people—New York (State)—New York—Biography. 6. Park Avenue (New York,
N.Y.)—Biography. 7. New York (N.Y.)—Biography. 8. New York (N.Y.)—Social life and
customs. 9. New York (N.Y.)—Buildings, structures, etc. 10. New York (N.Y.)—
Economic conditions. I. Title: Seven forty Park.
II. Title.
    F128.67.P3G76 2005
    974.7´1—dc22   2005050127

ISBN-13: 978-0-7679-1744-5
ISBN-10: 0-7679-1744-8

PRINTED IN THE UNITED STATES OF AMERICA

10 9 8 7 6

FOR BARBARA

This is New York, skyscraper champion of the world,
where the Slickers and Know-It-Alls
peddle gold bricks to each other.

—**BEN HECHT**, Nothing Sacred

The real values of life are not purchasable
with money. You can't buy peace and good will.
If you could, the problems that face us would be simple.
All you can do, at most, is to help provide a setting,
a scaffolding, an atmosphere, a soil perhaps,
where these values can have at least some chance
to grow.

—**JOHN D. ROCKEFELLER JR.**

CONTENTS

740
PARK

Architectural rendering of Candela and Harmon's 740 Park Avenue
(Drawing courtesy Steven Candela)

INTRODUCTION

SOMETHING DRAWS THE EYE TO THE COUPLE WALKING INTO AN ITALIAN restaurant on the fringe of Manhattan's Gold Coast—the Upper East Side rectangle formed by Fifth and Park avenues between Fifty-ninth and Ninety-sixth streets—the man is hunched, halting, and stout, and the woman, stately and sylphic-thin. "Pride goeth before destruction, and a haughty spirit before a fall," says the Book of Proverbs. The former plutocrat Saul Philip Steinberg and his third wife, Gayfryd, seem to embody that adage.

It is clear as they maneuver their way to their table at Sette Mezzo that Saul Steinberg still suffers from the effects of a devastating stroke he had a decade earlier. So Gayfryd gently guides him, holding one of his arms, the left one, the one that seems partly paralyzed. And as they pass their fellow diners, many of them members of the same super-wealthy clique the Steinbergs once led, friendly greetings are murmured aloud, while silently prayers are said—and not necessarily for Steinberg's health. Rather, they tend toward sentiments like, "There but for the grace of God go I."

Saul Steinberg's stroke was followed by catastrophic financial reverses that upended his life at the turn of the millennium. Steinberg hit bottom on May 11, 2000, when his troubles drove him from his home of twenty-eight years, a sumptuous duplex apartment, previously owned by John D. Rockefeller Jr., atop 740 Park Avenue. Steinberg bought the place for $225,000 after Rockefeller's widow died in 1971, and sold it twenty-nine years later for approximately $30 million. It may have been the best investment in a life full of them. Yet it was not cause for celebration. Rather, it was a harrowing admission of defeat. Saul, friends say, is getting over the bouts of spontaneous sobbing he suffered after the stroke. But Gayfryd still cries over the hand fate has dealt them.

Once, Steinberg was the boy wonder of Wall Street. In 1961, fresh out of Wharton, the baby-faced business phenomenon opened a computer-leasing company that became one of the highest fliers in that decade's go-go market. Trading on the inflated value of his flash-in-the-pan technology stock, Steinberg swooped in on unsuspecting companies and bought large positions in their stocks. The first time he did it, in 1968, he conquered Reliance, a 151-year-old Philadelphia insurance company. Not yet thirty, he used its millions in cash reserves to reinvent himself as a swashbuckling corporate pirate who would soon attempt more takeovers of such iconic American companies as Chemical Bank, Walt Disney, and the New York Times.

After Reliance, Steinberg rarely succeeded, but that may have been beside the point. He usually raked in a fortune, either by selling when his moves goosed stock prices or by getting paid what became known, post-Saul, as greenmail.¹ Corporations paid greenmail to foil takeovers—buying back their shares at a substantial premium over market value to make the likes of Steinberg go away. Quaker State paid him $10 million, Penn Central, $8 million. Then he turned on Disney. The house that Walt built paid him $60 million to go away, but in the process they also replaced their chief executive with a new one, Michael Eisner, who turned the vulnerable studio into a media colossus. No one thanked Saul Steinberg.

In 1981, forty-two-year-old Steinberg and his family controlled a $100 million fortune, according to the Forbes 400 list of the richest Americans. By 1983, that stake had doubled. And in 1984, the magazine doubled its estimate again, to $400 million. His holding company, Reliance Group, was worth $3.7 billion. Steinberg's personal net worth peaked in September 1987 at about $660 million, then dropped by a third in a stock market crash. In the early 1990s, Reliance stock was still sinking and it owed $650 million in junk-bond debt, but *Forbes* pegged Saul's personal fortune at $330 million, plumped up by the sale of Reliance's stakes in United Air Lines (for $100 million) and Days Inn ($765 million).

Steinberg always used his money as if trying to live up to a boast he'd made after raiding Reliance. "Like the Rockefellers, I'll own the world," he'd said. Entertaining in imperial style, cultivating a fearsome public reputation, and a private one that blended charm with intelligence, while giving millions—both his own and Reliance's—to museums, libraries, and universities, he was deemed lordly. But that wasn't enough for him. A sign in his office read, in both English and Hebrew, "On the eighth day, Saul rested."

Perhaps the hubris finally did him in. After his 1995 stroke, Steinberg fell off the Forbes 400 list of America's richest—and his life fell apart. He was even sued by his own mother. But the worst part was losing his home at 740 Park Avenue, for it was the apartment of his dreams. He'd bought it from the richest man in the world, the son of the greatest capitalist of the industrial age, the same son who'd overcome the family's rotten, bloody, grasping reputation to become the reigning paragon of American wealth. Saul had planned to repeat the accomplishments of Rockefeller father and son in a single lifetime.

Instead, he was forced to abdicate their throne as well as their apartment.

THE HOME THAT LINKED STEINBERG TO THE ROCKEFELLERS, APARTMENT 15/16B at 740 Park, was the most extraordinary apartment in New York City. Its magnificence is hard to overstate. Writing about 740 in *Town & Country*, Steven M. L. Aronson waxed lyrical over its "imperially vast, insolently self-contained apartments [that] embody what V. S. Pritchett called 'the glamour of wealth and respectable certainty.' Unbudgingly supreme, they are not only New York's but the world's best addresses." Steinberg's was the best of them all.

It was "a Manhattan residence of unsurpassed elegance, tradition, location, and proportions," a real estate agent would later say. Boasting more than twenty thousand square feet in a city where seven-hundred-square-foot studio apartments were the norm for thirty-two-year-olds, it had, depending on who was counting, anywhere from twenty-three to thirty-seven rooms, the discrepancy caused by such questions as whether one included hallways and foyers the size of ballrooms, servants' quarters, and the fourteen bathrooms.

The entrance gallery alone was 56 feet long and 13 feet wide, larger than many New York living spaces. The 40 x 23 living room boasted eastern and southern exposures and a terrace overlooking Park Avenue. The 23 x 33 dining room had another terrace, which could also be accessed from a small den that Steinberg converted into a breakfast room. The pine-paneled library was 21 x 27. Steinberg quickly decided to turn a 17 x 22 bedroom and dressing room next to it into a billiard room. It was paneled, too. Across the hall was a mirror and black lacquered bar. The fifteenth floor also had eleven closets, three bathrooms, and fifteen-foot ceilings. Tucked away in a corner behind the dining room were the vast service quarters, a pantry, a porcelain storage room, a kitchen, a servants' dining room, and a laundry.

Up a stair outside the kitchen was the servants' mezzanine—a low-ceilinged half floor with a half-dozen servants' bedrooms, a storage room, and two baths; Steinberg later combined several of the maids' rooms to make them larger. Another servants' area was directly above on 16. Originally, it had four bedrooms, two baths, and a sewing and pressing room. Steinberg turned it into a two-bedroom apartment for a domestic couple, with seven closets and a kitchenette.

After Steinberg's first renovation, the private rooms on the sixteenth floor would feature an astonishing thirty-two closets, seven bathrooms, three master bedrooms with attached dressing rooms, two lesser bedrooms, a sitting room, a second kitchen, a study, a gym, and a 26½ x 18½ playroom. And then there were the several more terraces on both levels, eleven working fireplaces, his-and-hers saunas, a precision-engineered steel entrance gate with a lacquered wood door beyond, a private elevator and dumbwaiter connecting the two main floors, state-of-the-art air-conditioning, quadraphonic speakers in every room—even bathrooms and dressing rooms—museum-quality art lighting, a customized inlaid parquet gallery, custom-designed tile floors in the kitchen and pantry, and catering-hall-quality appliances, including an eight-burner stove and a three-door refrigerator. (In a later renovation, Steinberg would add a screening room and steam bath.) The $6,528 monthly maintenance was high, but it was also 43 percent tax-deductible.

Steinberg lived there with all three of his wives. During each of his two divorces, he put the place on the market to ensure he wouldn't lose it to an ex, but just as quickly snatched it off. Women came and went, but 740 was a prize he could not let go of easily.

Saul's first wife was his high-school sweetheart, Barbara Herzog. They'd met in Brooklyn, where Saul grew up, the older son of the owner of a factory that made kitchen and bathroom products, dish racks, and skidproof bath mats. Saul and Barbara married, had three children, and began raising them in a mansion on the water in one of Long Island's Five Towns, an affluent, mostly Jewish suburb. Then came Saul's bold bid for Chemical Bank.

The banking establishment, astonished by the cheek of the twenty-nine-year-old whiz kid, took its gloves off and fought like street gangsters, using not knives and guns but power and influence and white-shoe lawyers and the Federal Reserve Board, a Senate committee, and a raft of other politicians, most notably New York's governor, Nelson Rockefeller, one of John D. Rockefeller Jr.'s sons. The massive retaliation seemed somehow personal, which inevitably led to suspicions that the mostly gentile bankers were driven by anti-Semitism. What's certain is that Steinberg was rejected as a foreign body and branded a pariah for what he thought was commendable ambition and his enemies considered immense gall.

So Saul savored the irony when he bought Nelson Rockefeller's father's apartment a little more than two years later. He knew exactly what it meant—he'd arrived—and what it said about him. "I'm not a Rockefeller; this wasn't handed to me," he'd later tell a reporter, sitting with his feet up in his den, beside a Matisse.

IN THE 1970S, WHILE BARBARA RAISED THEIR KIDS, SAUL STARTED RAISING hell, "having," as a very close friend puts it, "his midlife crisis in his thirties." He probably needed the distraction. That decade was hard for

Saul Steinberg. You can only be rookie of the year once. Reliance fell deep into debt; by 1975, it owed $500 million, and its stock price had fallen from $100 to $10. Saul's fortune sank to $9 million from a high of $60 million. What to do? Give in to the temptations the world offers a young man with millions, of course. He'd hurried from school into business, then spent a decade getting rich. Now he was set to enjoy it, and Manhattan was happy to open its arms to a new kid, particularly one who was articulate, informed, erudite, and, sometimes, hilarious.

Inevitably, he began having an affair. His lover was a passionate, beautiful Italian P.R. woman, Laura Bordoni Sconocchia Fisher, whom *Vanity Fair* dubbed "a major party girl." It was the disco era, and the two indulged a taste for the latest party favor, cocaine. Steinberg divorced the mother of his children, had a fourth child with Laura, and then, after she converted and became a Jew, married her in 1978.

Saul's arrival at 740 Park Avenue had been a watershed event. When he bought into the building, New York was in deep trouble, financially and socially; real estate values were severely depressed, and apartment towers full of huge, expensive-to-maintain residences were seen as white elephants. In other buildings, such grand apartments were routinely cut up into lesser ones or literally given away if someone came along who could afford the monthly payments. Some no doubt thought Saul a sucker to buy one, but to 740 Park he was a godsend. Less than a decade later, with the city rebounding and the value of apartments rising steeply, Saul, remarried and reinvented as a swinger, began to be seen in a different light.

In March 1980, Saul was forty when he and Laura landed their prestigious building on the front page of the *New York Post*—the kickoff of a full-fledged tabloid scandal. They'd been having major marital problems and Laura had moved out, but that night she invaded the apartment and barricaded herself in the master bathroom as lawyers, policemen, and hired goons stood outside, arguing about whether she had a right to be there. The standoff ended when one of Steinberg's lawyers performed a citizen's arrest and Laura, draped in a floor-length mink, was hauled out of the building by a grinning New York policeman. *FLASH!* With that memorable page-one photo, Steinberg's rep as the quintessentially of-his-time tycoon was sealed.

In the weeks and months that followed, the public lapped up every detail of Steinberg's travail. And almost every account mentioned the famous Rockefeller apartment. Though it was sometimes called a duplex, sometimes a triplex, sometimes a penthouse, once even a quadruplex, and room counts ranged from twenty-five to ninety, the details didn't really matter. The affair pulled back the limestone curtain that had long kept 740 Park in shadows. Once a wealthy fortress, it became an advertisement for what wealth can buy.

JUST LIKE A STAR WHO ONLY NEEDS ONE NAME, A HANDFUL OF SUPERSTAR New York apartment buildings are known only by a number. Number one among those is 740. It was the childhood home of Jacqueline Bouvier Kennedy Onassis; the urban castle that kept Princess Henry XXXIII of Reuss, and now Countess Marie Douglas, the second wife of United Technologies chairman George A. David. Seven forty has long been a sort of safe-deposit box for brand-name heirs to the fortunes of Standard Oil, Gulf Oil, Anaconda Copper, New York Central, Havemeyer Sugar, International Harvester, Seagram, Campbell's soup, Chrysler, Marshall Field's, Gimbel, Bonita Banana, Pullman, Friendly Ice Cream, Avon Products, Milliken, and, currently, Mosler Safe, Time Warner, Loews, Estée Lauder, and TV Guide. And it's the trophy today's tycoons—Steinberg, David, Ronald Owen Perelman, Henry Kravis—have all called home.

It was conceived in 1929 as the most expensive, the most exclusive, simply the best apartment house in the world. More than that, it was going to be the richest in every way, built of only the most expensive materials, filled with only people of the greatest wealth, half from New York's old aristocratic class, the rest members of the new moneyed elite, bankers and industrialists enriched by the 1920s bull market. Construction began in September 1929, a month before the great stock market crash. The architect was Rosario Candela, designer of the best Gold Coast buildings (fifty years later, a "Candela apartment" became a Greed Decade status symbol even more potent because of its rarity). The ultimate Candela apartments are at 740, which, at the epicenter of the Gold Coast, is also well possessed of those three necessary attributes for valuable real estate, as defined by the developer William Zeckendorf: location, location, location.

Unfortunately, 740 opened its doors in October 1930. The Great Depression and World War II quickly followed, and the building became a financial sinkhole, remaining one for almost fifty years. The democratization of American culture by the war made upper-class enclaves like 740 Park obsolete. Family names, dynastic fortunes, and the quasi-religious institutions of old money lost their confidence, their allure, and their power. Once, old school had cohabited with new rich; beginning in the 1950s, it became an endangered species.

At the dawn of the 1980s, lively, sometimes raucous new money reinvigorated the old forms of wealth and reinvented the notion of a social elite that had been abandoned by the previous generation. With that, 740's fortunes reversed. The last tattered remnants of the *oldveau* crowd did their best to bring a rearguard action against those newcomers, like Steinberg, who were at odds with the neighborhood's carefully cultivated and genteel patrician image, but it was futile. Ever since, the newly enriched have sought to plant roots at 740, and the prices of apartments have climbed until they are among the highest in the world, ranging from $20 million to more than $30 million per apartment.

In its seventy-five years, 740 Park has been a mirror to the changing face of the Gold Coast. Since that population is drawn from the wealthiest families all across America, and they come to New York to take their place on the nation's stage, 740 also reflects the inevitable, relentless evolution of American wealth as social standing and consanguinity give way to brute wealth (so long as it agrees to become less brutish), inheritance gives out or is squandered, technology replaces industry, debt becomes desirable, and the ability to successfully manipulate money trumps even the skill required to make it from nothing.

In that grinding ritual of social advance and retreat, a building like 740 Park is a necessary abrasive, for 740 is also a club: you have to be admitted. Some clubs will have you just because you want in. Self-selection doesn't cut it on the corner of Seventy-first Street and Park Avenue. So the raging desire to live there helps uncut stones become diamonds. Of course, a few zircons slip in, too. More than a few. Blood, brains, wealth, and power drive the story of 740. But so do excess, greed, scandal, and extravagant folly.

BECAUSE 740 PARK OFFERS WHAT F. SCOTT FITZGERALD'S CHARACTER Nick Carraway calls "the consoling proximity of millionaires," the building is also a community, and a particular one at that. It is one of New York City's cooperative apartment houses, and they are a breed unto themselves. Formally speaking, cooperatives are corporations that own a building and issue stock. Each owner has exclusive occupancy of his or her apartment, but does not own it. Rather, they own a portion of the whole building, represented by shares of stock in the cooperative corporation. Those shares are sold in blocks proportional to the size and perceived value of the apartment (so an apartment with a skyline view will often have more shares than a dark one of the same size on a lower floor). In 740's case, the owners collectively own the building and its thirty apartments and four doctors' offices. When Saul Steinberg "bought" his apartment, he actually acquired 3,355 shares out of a total of 48,350 outstanding shares of the 740 Park Avenue Corporation, representing the proportional value of his apartment compared with those of his fellow shareholders. The next-best 740 residence, George David's, is allotted only 2,300 shares. Most 740 apartments are worth well under 2,000 shares. A document known as a proprietary lease is inextricably tied to those blocks of shares and gives each shareholder the right to live in a particular unit. So the owners of cooperatives are both tenants and, collectively, the equivalent of the landlord in a rental building.[2]

Co-ops were invented to allow little groups of like-minded people to buy and control communal homes. In a real sense—they were invented by a socialist—co-ops are communism for capitalists. Co-ops even have Soviet-style politburos, called boards of directors, who have legal authority to run the co-op, set the rules, decide the size of monthly maintenance payments (that's co-op-ese for rent), and, most dramatically, decide who is and who is not allowed to buy shares and thus gain possession of a proprietary lease and an apartment. The board can reject an applicant for almost any reason aside from outright discrimination. Because co-op boards generally operate in secret and with complete autonomy, the process is often assumed to be arbitrary and sometimes is. But usually it isn't arbitrary at all.

One prerequisite of admission is sacrosanct. You have to be able to pull your weight financially. Maintenance charges for a typical 740 apartment are now about $10,000 per month. You also need the resources to deal with whatever comes. In 1990, the average 740 stockholder paid a onetime charge of more than $250,000 to repair the building's aging facade. Steinberg's share was about twice that. So the 740 board has let it be known that applicants must have a liquid net worth of $100 million to even be considered for admission to the co-op. That number is actually elastic, but it is used to intimidate the wrong sort of buyer.

Saul Steinberg got into 740 Park Avenue when standards were looser, but even then finances were paramount. In 1971, both the building and the American economy were on the ropes. Seven forty needed him as much as he needed to live there. But when he put the building at the center of a front-page scandal just as apartment values began rising from a long swoon, Saul became a liability. The board couldn't get rid of him, at least not easily, but it could and did begin cracking down, not only stiffening its standards generally, but specifically rejecting two of Steinberg's business associates and others it deemed equally worrisome.

It is commonly thought that co-op rejections are based in religious or racial prejudice, and the rarity of black shareholders in Gold Coast co-ops is an observable fact. There are no black shareholders at 740. In one almost indiscernible way, 740 is also a monument to what's called social anti-Semitism. Formally speaking, half of 740's tenants live at 71 East Seventy-first Street, a side entrance of the same building with the less ostentatious address that's favored by some of the more discreet patricians in residence, those who have long considered Park Avenue addresses too—well, sorry, but it has to be said—Jewish.

But 740 Park is not a "restricted building" or a "good building," both euphemisms for a building that does not allow Jews. Indeed, half its current tenant-shareholders are Jewish, several are Asian, and only one is in the *Social Register*. It is, rather, a rich building (six of *Forbes* magazine's 2004 list of the richest New Yorkers, all billionaires, either live or have lived there). And even more than that, Saul and Laura Steinberg's stay there notwithstanding, it styles itself a bastion of *quiet* wealth. So

Ronald Jeançon, a past board president, once had to let Barbra Streisand's broker know that the board would not even consider her because she was an actress and, worse than that, a singer. And Streisand is in good company. Others who have not made it into 740 include Joan Crawford, the late agent Ted Ashley, Neil Sedaka, the Daimler-Benz heir Friedrich Christian "Mick" Flick, the junk-bond tycoon Nelson Peltz, and, most recently, a Russian plutocrat, Leonard Blavatnik.

For every rejection, there is a shareholder who wants . . . needs . . . to cash out and leave, but is held hostage by a difficult co-op board. And even when an applicant has passed the board, there are still more hurdles to get over. Cooperative ownership, clearly, has its drawbacks. The board at 740 also mandates that renovations be limited to summer months. In New York, the wealthy often leave town for the summer; this simple rule ensures that they will not be annoyed by the sights and sounds of construction.

So Stephen Schwarzman, the financier who bought Steinberg's apartment, and David Koch, a Kansas oil billionaire, both had to wait more than a year to occupy their apartments, because their renovations stretched out over two summers. But there are compensations. One is that others share the financial pain when something goes horribly wrong in the building. Another is the joy of picking and choosing one's neighbors. They are not only partners in a significant investment; they are fellow members of a secret society. Tenancy at 740 constitutes proof of membership in America's ruling class.

For years, 740 Park was a silent sanctum. But after Saul Steinberg, many more moved in who hoped to hide in plain sight. They wanted it known that they could afford to, and had been allowed to, live in the highest-profile low-profile building in the world. They wanted others to look up at it and envy them. So nowadays, anytime someone moves in or out, it causes a frisson in the wired-in worlds of Manhattan society, money, and media. Yet very little else leaks out, and only some of that is accurate. "It's the most tight-lipped building in the whole city," says Roger Erickson, the senior managing director of Sotheby's International Realty. Then, like most realtors who either sell apartments there or simply hope to, he refuses to say another word.

The neighbors also try to be discreet, but they're as fascinated with the lives of 740 as the rest of the world, acutely aware of which hedge fund operator is under investigation by authorities, which prominent family man is keeping an equally prominent mistress in a town house nearby, which young wife is struggling to get pregnant. Their current financial faux pas and sexual foibles are bush-league, however, compared with the ones that have been hushed up in 740's glorious past. Truth be told, 740 Park has never been entirely respectable. But its merry widows and jolly Rogers have had at least one thing besides an address in common with their starchy socialite, industrially fortunate, and money-managing neighbors: they have all had access, even if only briefly, to serious fortunes.

IN 1995, SAUL STEINBERG SUFFERED HIS LIFE-THREATENING STROKE. And by 1999, he had lost a nearly unfathomable amount of money. The insurance business as a whole had hit a cyclical recession. Steinberg's Reliance Group was rocked by a series of disasters on top of that. An insurance pool Reliance was part of collapsed, leaving it exposed to $170 million in losses. Then claims started pouring in on risky new policies the company had issued to bolster revenues—$250 million worth of claims—causing the stock to plummet 20 percent. Saul tried to sell more debt and failed. He tried to offer stock on a profitable unit of the company—and failed again. Late in 1999, facing an annual loss of more than $300 million, he agreed to sell those profitable subsidiaries and, in November, fired his own brother, who'd run Reliance since Saul's stroke.

Saul's personal fortune was dwindling along with his company's. At year's end, Sotheby's started cataloging the contents of the apartment at 740 Park, preparing to auction off the Steinbergs' furniture. In January 2000, with Reliance's vital credit rating in doubt, Steinberg finally gave in to Gayfryd's advice and agreed to see what price the apartment would bring. It was never formally listed; instead, he hired his brother's ex-wife, Kathy Steinberg, who worked at one of the city's ultra-high-end realtors, and she quietly reeled in an offer of $30 million. Saul accepted, and his dream of becoming his generation's Rockefeller officially ended.

Saul's nightmare was far from over, though. A few days after the sale of the apartment, regulators stopped the million-dollar dividend payments Reliance had continued paying to Saul and his family and stripped him of his multimillion-dollar bonus. He stepped down as chief executive (although he remained as chairman). A month later, his art collection went on the block. Within eighteen months, the authorities would take over Reliance and reveal the extent of the rot: more than $5 billion in cash, equity, and loan payments had, as *The Philadelphia Inquirer* put it, "vaporized during the company's final 24 months [in] the biggest insurance company failure in U.S. history."

At the end of 2000, after Reliance announced a quarterly loss of half a billion dollars and defaulted on $538 million in debt, its stock was delisted. Permanent overseers were appointed, and they filed for bankruptcy in June 2001. The company had $3 billion in claims it was unable to pay. In the wreckage of Reliance, investigators found clues to its collapse. Steinberg and his family had taken $150 million out of the company in pay, bonuses, dividends, and stock options in the 1990s alone.

It is unclear how much Saul has left. He certainly had the proceeds of the sale of the 740 Park apartment. He also earned $12.5 million from that auction of his furniture and possessions and more from art sales, although *Vanity Fair*, which covered his fall as assiduously as it had his rise, reported that he'd borrowed repeatedly against both his stock and his art collection—and continued to do so after leaving 740, pledging most of his holdings as collateral. Still, despite lawsuits (including one by Saul's eighty-three-year-old mother, later settled, claiming he'd reneged on a debt), clamoring lenders, and swarming regulators, Saul and Gayfryd remain financially secure by any normal standards. "Very secure," says his close friend. "Saul and Gayfryd are rich people. Of course, in today's world, if you don't have $500 million . . ." She drifts off. They are not in that world anymore, the world Saul Steinberg longed to conquer.

IN NEW YORK'S DARWINIAN SOCIETY, THE PREVAILING ATTITUDE toward those who fall combines public pity with private schadenfreude. But Society with a capital *S* seems to feel differently about Saul Steinberg. Once they took his caviar and champagne. Now they offer him praise and sympathy for keeping his head down, not complaining, and getting on with his life. He is no longer at the epicenter of the linked worlds of finance and society, but he has a wife who loves him and whom he loves, and good relationships with his children and grandchildren. Finally, in adversity, they say, Saul Steinberg has achieved what long eluded him, even in his heyday: dignity. "He treated adversity with the same grace he treated success," says Reinaldo Herrera, a socially prominent New Yorker whose family has occupied the same *finca* outside Caracas, Venezuela, since 1590. "I think that is the sign of a true gentleman."

Steinberg disproves both of F. Scott Fitzgerald's famous dictums about the rich. They are *not* always so different from you and me, even if they misbehave in larger apartments. And there *are* sometimes second and even third acts in American life. People will tell you Saul Steinberg is a bad man who deserved what he got. But it isn't that simple. Neither is the story of the apartment building that meant everything to him.

PART ONE

OLD MONEY

J. Watson and Electra Havemeyer Webb's dining room, eighteenth floor (1931–60)

(© Shelburne Museum, Shelburne, Vermont)

1

AT THE END OF THE ROARING TWENTIES, SMALL CONSPIRACIES OF THE powerful—many of them members of high society—formed investment pools to manipulate stock prices. Among them was Albert Wiggin, the chairman of the Chase National Bank. In 1927, business was booming when President Calvin Coolidge declared that America was "entering upon a new era of prosperity." That March, pool operations peaked, as did Cadillac sales in New York City. In May, trading volume hit a new high. Brokers' loans to speculators shot up to $4.4 billion at interest rates of between 10 and 12 percent. Then, on June 13, 1928, the stock market collapsed. It quickly recovered, but the plunge was a sign—one that few people read.

The market cratered again on March 26, 1929, sending interest rates on loans to speculators soaring to 20 percent. But loans were still being made; it seemed that nothing could end the mad speculation. The Federal Reserve Board urged bankers to stop handing out money. Immediately, one bank announced a fresh $20 million available for loans—and the stock market recovered again.

"In such circumstances, one might have expected bankers, at least the most important, prestige-laden, and supposedly conservative among

them, to lie low, to accept quietly the profits that flowed to them so ef-
fortlessly," John Brooks wrote in *Once in Golconda*, his classic tale of Wall
Street's ruination. Instead, men like Wiggin were anything but circum-
spect. Through holding companies formed to conceal trades and minimize taxes, he played the market, frolicked in pools, and even speculated
in Chase stock to the tune of millions of dollars. Only in the summer of
1929 did he start to worry.

Though the economy was showing signs of weakness, the stock market was still soaring, volume hitting records, new fortunes being made.
On September 3, the market's averages hit all-time highs—highs that
would stand for the next twenty-five years. Though he kept touting Chase
stock, Wiggin also started selling it short—borrowing forty-two thousand
shares and selling them, expecting to buy them back later for less—effectively, dishonorably, despicably, really, betting that his own company's
market value as set by the price of those shares would drop. Which it did.
Then he bought the shares back with a loan from the Chase.

That's when the house of cards fell in. Stock prices started dropping
on Wednesday, October 23—and the next day, later known as Black
Thursday, they collapsed. A third precipitous plunge followed on October
29—it would be known as Black Tuesday. Get the feeling things were
black? John D. Rockefeller and his namesake son, who was called Junior,
tried to brighten the outlook by announcing that they, at least, were buying stocks, but their virtuous stand had no effect on the economy. Within
a few weeks, $30 billion worth of equity—more than a third of the mar-
ket's value—had vanished. The Great Depression was on.

A year later, apple sellers appeared on street corners for the first time.
In December 1930, the Bank of the United States closed its doors—the
most significant in a wave of failed financial institutions. By 1931, stock
prices stood at less than half their 1929 highs. Unemployment rose in in-
verse proportion. In just two months in the fall of 1931, another eight
hundred banks went belly-up. Building ceased. Life went on, if barely,
for most.

And what of Wiggin of the Chase? After the crash, he toted up winnings of just over $4 million for selling his company down the river—
profits he hid offshore to avoid taxes. That said, his dealings were not
only legal but perfectly respectable—at least according to the era's busi-

ness mores. After Wiggin retired in 1933, the bank awarded him an annual pension of $100,000 for life. But that same year, when he was hauled before a Senate banking investigation, he "asked" the bank to stop the payments, a request with which it "complied," according to *The Wall Street Journal*'s 1951 obituary. Wiggin nonetheless managed to leave a $3 million estate.

History has judged him more harshly, even as it has repeated itself. "[Even if] they had done nothing actually criminal, [they] had treated their own stockholders and the investing public as so many sheep to be fleeced by whatever means the ingenuity of accountants and lawyers could devise," wrote the stock market historian Charles Morris.

This is the backdrop as the curtain rises on the story of the most prestigious apartment house in the world, 740 Park Avenue.

A BRIEF LESSON IN NEW YORK LIVING ARRANGEMENTS IS IN ORDER. Throughout the 1920s, developers began putting up buildings like 740 Park, full of grand apartments with the proportions of fine, freestanding homes—mansions stacked one atop the other, designed as suitable replacements for the private homes that had led society's march uptown and become obsolete within a single generation.'

In the middle of the nineteenth century, Manhattan's social elite, the Knickerbockers, who were descendants of the original Dutch settlers of New York, the English colonists who followed them, and, finally, the American revolutionaries who tossed the English out, went to bed at night exclusively in private houses. The location of those homes had moved inexorably uptown over the years. In the eighteenth century, the city's genteel residential district was a tiny enclave at the southern tip of Manhattan island: south of Chambers Street, clustered around Trinity Church and St. Paul's Chapel, lower Broadway, Bowling Green, and the Battery.

Driven north by fire and yellow fever epidemics, social life first alighted in what is now Tribeca, then, in the 1830s, skittered east to a new district surrounding the intersection of Lafayette Place and Bond Street in today's NoHo. John Jacob Astor, the richest man in America, lived there, as did his son William's future wife, Caroline Schermerhorn, who would become known as "The" Mrs. Astor. Their district's heyday was brief. By the middle of the century, the center of aristocratic gravity shifted again, to Washington Square, from whence society began a slow, steady progress up Fifth Avenue. That march was led by a Knickerbocker, Henry Brevoort, who built a house on Fifth Avenue and Ninth Street in 1834, on what had previously been farm and grazing land, and gave a fancy dress ball there in 1840 that was considered the best party of its era. It was eighty more years before the town-house era ended, years in which new money poured into New York faster than derogatory names for the arrivistes could be coined. According to one historian, by 1929, 98 percent of "respectable New Yorkers" occupied apartments. The reasons for this sea change were as many as the multiple dwellings that had risen all over town. The American economy and New York's population boomed after the Civil War. Public life took on new allure, and public spaces for entertaining replaced private ballrooms.

Then there were income taxes, introduced in 1913. Running a private house got expensive. And there was something called "the servant problem"—the inability to find good help. It was all compounded by the automobile, which got rich folks thinking they could split their time between sprawling country houses and smaller city residences.

"Apartments gave you choice," says Andrew Alpern, who has written extensively on the history of luxury apartments. "You could lock your door and go away and you had a great deal of security with doormen and elevator men and guards." Some of the new buildings even boasted service departments, "from which servants can be procured by the hour," The New York Times pointed out helpfully, "about as easily as taxicabs can be picked up on Broadway" so that "when Mr. Croesus contemplates returning to his city apartment for a brief sojourn . . . when he arrives he finds his domicile adequately staffed."

Multiple dwellings weren't new. They'd been common in Europe for centuries; "the earliest were Roman tenements," says Alpern. They arrived in France in the eighteenth century, and grand, imperial apartment houses became fashionable when Paris was reconceived in the mid-nineteenth century by the urban planner Baron Georges Haussmann. But they remained a rarity in America.

Tenements had housed New York's lower classes since the 1830s, but the city's first luxury apartment house wasn't built until 1869, when Rutherfurd Stuyvesant, a descendant of New York's first governor, Peter, erected one at Eighteenth Street and Irving Place.

Stuyvesant was a member of New York's elite, the clans who formed the city's first capital-S Society. But his innovation—derided as risqué "French flats"—was declared folly by his peers. They soon changed their tune. By the 1870s, John Jacob Astor and August Belmont (both relative upstarts who'd arrived on the social scene at the start of the nineteenth century) were investing in apartments, too, and buildings like the Dakota, erected in splendid isolation on the west side of Central Park in 1884, began making apartments chic. The Dakota was just as exuberantly ostentatious and lavishly tricked out as the single-family mansions on Fifth Avenue, but it was conceived to let the less wealthy live on a similar scale—even allowing tenants to enter their apartments directly from the (then-novel) elevators. They could imagine the show was theirs alone. But the Dakota was a rental; its tenants had no sense of ownership. And its West Side location was odd, almost antisocial, so it didn't attract the elite, who were sometimes called the bon ton.

THE FIRST COOPERATIVE APARTMENT BUILDING IN NEW YORK, CREATED to be owned by its occupants, was erected in 1880 by a French architect, Philip Gengembre Hubert, backed by a syndicate of artists.[2] Soon, Hubert was building more and more luxurious co-ops, and other developers followed suit. When the huge Spanish Flats, which was built as a co-op on a block fronting on Central Park, failed, its shareholders lost their investments, and the co-op movement stalled. But the conceptual foundation for co-ops had been laid. Ironically, it was their vaguely socialist intention that would prove enticing to the upper classes. Hubert's Home Clubs, as they were called, held out the promise that birds of a feather— "gentlemen of congenial tastes . . . occupying the same social positions in life," as the *Real Estate Record* put it—truly would flock together.

First, though, came the age of the urban château. These Gilded Age monstrosities were erected by men who'd made fortunes in the post–Civil War era. They were symbols not just of success but of a new kind of social potency based on astonishing bucks instead of hoary old bloodlines.

Until the Industrial Revolution, social status and wealth stemmed from ownership of land. Old money didn't need to be big money. But the expansion of urban mercantile wealth in the first half of the nineteenth century, and the creation of industrial fortunes in the second, changed all that—and old-line society threw up demarcation lines.

Between 1870 and 1880, more new money flooded New York and, at least at first, was greeted as a tidal wave of trash. Mere wealth didn't guarantee acceptance. Substance and ineffable qualities of culture and grace mattered as much. Initially rejected by reigning society, ambitious nouveau-riche families like the Vanderbilts (the Astors had squeaked under the wire and were considered old money; the Jewish-born Belmonts, who'd arrived from Germany in the 1830s, didn't quite measure up) redefined the terms of social engagement, making themselves celebrities with their showy châteaus and the huge parties they held in them. The press used the rich to entice the hoi polloi. The floodgates had opened.

In the face of this dire threat, the Old Guard closed ranks, inventing exclusionary groups such as the social arbiter Ward McAllister's Patriarchs (in 1872), lists like the social leader Mrs. Astor's Four Hundred and more expansive successors like the *Social Register* (in 1887), exclusive enclaves for the right people like New York's Tuxedo Park and Georgia's Jekyll Island, and hereditary societies like the Daughters of the American Revolution, Sons of the Revolution, Colonial Dames, and Society of Mayflower Descendants. They sought to exclude, but it was in vain.

New people with new money set a new standard. One's home was no longer one's castle but one's calling card. Fifth Avenue turned into Show-Off Row. Famously, the Vanderbilts, the newest richest family in the world, could not win Mrs. Astor's approval. "Railroad people!" she called them. But Willie Vanderbilt, grandson of the Commodore, and his wife, Alva, finally gained entry to an Astor ball in 1883, just after their limestone château rose on Fifth Avenue and they gave the latest party of the decade there. Railroad money might not be old money, but given time to mature, it proved acceptable. Mrs. Astor ended up moving to Fifth Avenue and Thirty-fourth Street in the 1860s, and then, in 1893, to Sixty-fifth and Fifth, where she lived in a sixteenth-century-style limestone château until her death in 1908.

New York absorbed its outer boroughs in 1898 and was inching toward a new role as a world-class city, second only to London, and beginning to reach for the sky. Nothing was permanent in this new New York, least of all living arrangements; the famous skyline was created as thousands of new apartment buildings and grand new office and public buildings rose in Manhattan and redefined fashionable life. The wealthy couldn't help but notice as entrepreneurs sought land on which to raise the new behemoths, and private homes fell victim to their ambition and the unquenchable demand for new housing.

The east side of Central Park was dubbed the city's emerging "aristocratic residential section" in 1906 by the *Real Estate Record*, which also pointed out that thanks to Park Avenue's width, it was well suited to large buildings. The first apartment house to gain favor with New York's elite (indeed, the first to rise among the mansions of Fifth Avenue) was 998 Fifth Avenue, at Eighty-first Street, designed by McKim, Mead & White and completed in 1912. An Italian Renaissance palazzo based on Rome's Farnese Palace, incredibly luxurious yet restrained, with a subdued limestone, granite, and marble facade, an elaborate terra-cotta cornice, and a huge iron-and-glass marquee over its side-street entrance, it was billed as the most expensive and exclusive apartment house in the city. Its seventeen simplex and duplex apartments, including two full-floor units of ten thousand square feet apiece, featured every modern convenience—even jewelry safes for each bedroom, a large silver vault in each kitchen, an ice-making plant and individual refrigerated wine cellars, and private laundry rooms in the basement.

These were the first of the sorts of apartments that, eighty years later, inspired the fictional one created by Tom Wolfe for Sherman McCoy, the hapless lead character in the novel *The Bonfire of the Vanities*: "the sort of apartment the mere thought of which ignites flames of greed and covetousness under people all over New York, and for that matter, all over the world."

The first renters at 998—attracted by a lavish hardcover brochure—included a granddaughter of Commodore Vanderbilt; Levi Morton, U.S. vice president under Benjamin Harrison; the former secretary of state and war Elihu Root; John Jacob "Jack" Astor V, who moved in after surviving, in utero, the sinking of the *Titanic*; and Murray Guggenheim of the mining Guggenheims. Root, who had been a leader of society's move uptown when he built a private house for himself at Seventy-first Street and Park Avenue, was offered a cut rate to sign a lease at 998. Morton, who was the governor of New York from 1895 to 1897, followed.

Their building "aroused not only interest but considerable agitation among the old time dwellers" of the city's most fashionable quarters, wrote *The New York Times*. In 1915, two more large buildings followed, and the locals issued a call to arms, decrying developers as vandals determined to ravish their virgin landscape. Their châteaus and town houses threatened, they banded together and sought restrictions on the height and bulk of new buildings. "The city will die of its greatness," warned *Vanity Fair*.

Briefly, in 1921, Fifth Avenue mansion owners managed to limit building heights to seventy-five feet—but they were reactionaries trying to hold back the tide. After a protracted legal wrangle, led by the architect James Edwin Ruthven Carpenter and a property owner who wanted to sell her home for development, a court overturned the restriction in 1924, raising the value of the obsolete mansions. Before World War I and with greater speed after it, tall apartment houses, conceived to attract the wealthy and worldly, with commodious public rooms, large foyers, servants' quarters, and other amenities already familiar from freestanding houses, as well as novelties like elevators, refrigerators, telephone and central vacuum systems, and laundry rooms, began marching up the avenue. The row houses fell like dominoes. "The parallel to the 1990s is amazing," says Alpern. "Money kept making more money and nobody thought it would end."

In 1926, *The New York Times* reported that thirty large apartment buildings—$100 million worth—had been erected on Fifth in a two-year period. The same was happening on Park, which began evolving from a polluted, inhospitable industrial corridor to a grand residential street after the New York Central Railroad electrified its tracks in 1907, buried its sprawling rail yards, and erected the current Grand Central Terminal just to the south. Before that, nobody with serious money would have lived on Park.

A 1927 advertisement for the new 812 Park made the economic advantages clear. A four-story house, it said, would cost $125,000 plus a $100,000 mortgage plus yearly maintenance (for taxes, mortgage interest, heat, and operating costs) of $13,000. An eleven-room duplex at 812 sold for only $66,000 and cost only $6,600 annually.

Many of the best buildings on Park were designed by J. E. R. Carpenter and elaborated on McKim, Mead & White's 998 Fifth. To its standard of vast rooms and restrained luxury, Carpenter added a signature innovation: apartments with clearly defined entertaining, sleeping, and service areas, all designed around a grand entrance gallery. Though the Dakota offered separate service and living areas, and the 1907 Langham featured a foyer-based plan, Carpenter perfected the combination, creating the modern high-end residence.

Contemporary critics were unkind—the *Times* dismissed the 1924–26 buildings as "dignified and massive" yet "disappointing"—but that harsh judgment would alter with time. Years later, the architecture critic Elizabeth Hawes would write that the Gold Coast builders had in fact "offered a new and revised version of well-to-do urbanity; [that] spelled out how the modern aristocracy intended to live now: lavishly, privately, but also cooperatively and efficiently, well served and well serviced . . . The city encircled, but it did not encroach."

2

CAROLINE KENNEDY SCHLOSSBERG REFERS TO HER MATERNAL GREAT-grandfather as Grampy Lee. "Grumpy" Lee would be more apt. A portly, gruff man who chomped a dozen cheap cigars a day, he didn't speak to his wife for years, disinherited several grandchildren, and died with no company but his Oriental manservant.

Today, James Thomas Aloysius Lee is best known, if at all, as Jacqueline Kennedy Onassis's grandfather. But he was also one of New York's most adventurous real estate developers. And he built the greatest apartment building in the world.

Lee's grandparents immigrated to Newark, New Jersey, from County Cork, Ireland, in 1852—refugees from the potato famine. Lee's father, also James, a teacher, a medical doctor, and a school superintendent, married in 1875 and produced his first child in 1877 in an Irish neighborhood on New York's Lower East Side, which, though near the city's social districts, was practically a million miles away. Young James would be joined by five sisters before he entered the City College of New York in 1892 as a fifteen-year-old engineering student. An overachiever like his father, Lee moonlighted as a $6-a-week law clerk and earned extra money running adult-education lectures for the Board of Education.

Lee earned a master's degree in political science and economics at Columbia in 1897 and a law degree there in 1899. After representing several developers at the dawn of the twentieth century, he began dabbling in real estate himself, buying land along the route of the Seventh Avenue subway, then selling it at triple the price. He invested his profit in stocks, building a fortune of $2 million before he turned thirty. But he lost it all in the 1907 stock market panic.

A die-hard Republican, Lee always wore a three-piece suit. Though he loved sailing and swimming as a young man, says his granddaughter LeeLee Brown, even at the beach "he usually had on white flannels, a vest, a jacket, a Panama hat, and a pair of white and brown wing-tipped Fred Astaire shoes. But he was formal and serious to others, not to his grandchildren."

Or perhaps not that grandchild. Another describes Lee as "crotchety, difficult to understand, difficult to get along with. He had a big superiority complex or else treated everyone—at least his grandchildren—as not very intelligent, which I guess was possible. But he was hard to relate to." So standoffish and mysterious was he that in East Hampton, where he began spending summers in the mid-1920s (second homes had become de rigueur in the 1880s), he was rumored to be Jewish and to have changed his name from Levy. "His name *was* changed," Brendan Gill, the *New Yorker* writer, once insisted to the Kennedy biographer Edward Klein. "There was never anybody named Lee."

Lee prided himself on being tough and determined. He'd married another child of Irish immigrants, Margaret Merritt, a teacher, and they'd had three daughters: Marion, born in 1905; Janet, in December 1907; and Winifred, in 1913. Lee wanted them to rise in society. So after losing his fortune, he went back into real estate, partnering with a wealthy Columbia classmate, Charles R. Fleischmann, of the yeast-making family. Charles's brother Raoul also worked with them and would soon become a key financial backer of *The New Yorker*. Charles and Lee built an apartment house named for Peter Stuyvesant at Ninety-eighth Street and Riverside Drive, not far from where Lee lived in a row house at West End Avenue and Ninety-third Street. Then, in 1910, their partnership, the Century Holding Company, knocked down a row of frame houses and spent $2.5 million to build McKim, Mead & White's 998 Fifth Avenue.

After he developed several office buildings between Grand Central Station and Times Square, Lee stopped practicing law and became a full-time developer, operating from his latest building at 25 West Forty-third. Lee was formal—always referred to as Mr. Lee or James T. Lee, never Jim—and full of energy; he'd stop work to spar with a boxing instructor in his office once a day. "He was a powerful, two-fisted man," says a real estate operator who knew him.

Lee also liked to shoot and kept a wall of gun cases in his paneled office. "He was looking out the window one day when he saw a pigeon hawk circling across the street," says his granddaughter LeeLee Brown. "He loaded a shotgun, shot the hawk, called the super, and had him get the bird and bring it to his office. He had it stuffed. Imagine doing that today in midtown!"

After World War I, Lee began developing apartment buildings again. In 1922, he opened 420 Park at Fifty-sixth Street and moved his family in. That year he negotiated to buy a block of Park between Sixty-third and Sixty-fourth streets and failed, but in 1923 he bought a plot at Sixty-fifth and Park and hired J. E. R. Carpenter to build 620 Park, with twelve full-floor apartments. That year *The New York Times* said he was worth $23 million, and he was profiled as "The Master Builder of Uptown New York" in *The New York World.*

Lee wasn't only ambitious in business; he had strong social ambitions, and having moved to Park Avenue, he started to fulfill them. It wasn't easy. Lee may have been better off had he been Jewish. Jews were able to operate as equals to Protestants on Wall Street (Kuhn, Loeb & Co. was J. P. Morgan's only significant rival in investment banking), despite a deep, lingering anti-Semitism in the banking community. Most of the city's other clubs remained closed to them. But Irish Catholics like James T. Lee were even more excluded from the centers of financial and social power by the Anglocentric American elite, who were predominantly Episcopalian. In their book *The Power of Their Glory*, Kit and Frederica Konolige described this elite as America's ruling class and coined the term "Episcrats" for them. Irish Catholics were cops, firemen, and bartenders, not gentlemen. "You couldn't get anyplace unless you were of pure Anglo-Saxon stock," says Raymond O'Keefe Jr., president of the James T. Lee Foundation, whose father worked for Lee. Old money still mattered.

That year Lee rented his first summerhouse in East Hampton, driving out on weekends to join his wife and children. He also formed a second real estate firm, Shelton Holding Company, to build a twelve-hundred-room hotel on Lexington between Forty-eighth and Forty-ninth streets, designed by Arthur Loomis Harmon, who'd left McKim, Mead & White to go out on his own. The Shelton, at thirty-four stories, was the tallest hotel in the world and, thanks to its visually arresting set-backs, won several architecture prizes and rapt praise from critics.' The artists Georgia O'Keeffe and Alfred Stieglitz lived in a top-floor suite and painted and photographed cityscapes from their windows. "He was very proud of the Shelton," says LeeLee Brown. "He was a frustrated architect. That was his first love. Whenever he could, he put his two cents in. He liked the technical part, the aesthetic part. I don't think he got that thrill from banking."

In January 1925, Lee did his biggest real estate deal yet, teaming up with Carpenter (in his role as speculator and developer); Eliot Cross, the patrician architect who'd developed Sutton Place and co-founded the real estate giant Webb & Knapp; and Robert E. Dowling, the son of a California gold-rush mine owner and another major real estate operator. They bought two of the most valuable parcels of land on Park Avenue, the sites of Presbyterian Hospital on the full block between Seventieth and Seventy-first streets between Park and Madison avenues and the hospital's nurses' residence on the north side of Seventy-first Street.

The two properties were part of the former Lenox Farm, thirty acres bounded by Fifth and Park and Sixty-seventh and Seventy-fourth streets, put together in 1818 for $6,920 by Robert Lenox, a Scot who'd come to New York just after the Revolution. In the years after his death, Lenox's son and heir, James, a philanthropist and collector of rare books, slowly sold or gave away much of the farm. His Lenox Library was one of the collections that merged to form the New York Public Library, and its site became the private house that is now the Frick Collection.

In 1868, Lenox founded Presbyterian Hospital with a gift of land and $100,000. By 1880, when James Lenox died, his remaining land was worth $10 million (more than $175 million today). That year his family sold the property across Seventy-first Street from the hospital. Twenty years later, the hospital bought it and built a nurses' residence there. But by 1925, Presbyterian had outgrown the site and wanted to move uptown.

It would be three years before that move was accomplished, though, and in the meantime Lee kept busy. He merged his Shelton Holding Company with four other hotel and real estate firms, creating a $20 million company that owned nine hotels in the United States and Canada. In 1926, Lee joined the board of Morris Plan, an investment bank; built the Farmers' Loan and Trust building at Forty-first Street and Fifth and the Central Savings Bank at Broadway between Seventy-third and Seventy-fourth streets, modeled after the Pitti Palace in Florence; and joined Chase National Bank as its real estate adviser. His first assignment was assembling a building site and developing a new Chase headquarters at 20 Pine Street.

That year Lee leased a five-story English-style house at 750 Park Avenue, fully furnished, from Theodore Douglas Robinson, the assistant secretary of the Navy. Lee moved in with his wife and their daughters. His mother-in-law lived with them, but she was never allowed downstairs when guests came to visit, for fear that her old-country brogue and manners would offend in the circles in which Lee had begun to move. His new home was just around the corner from the Presbyterian Hospital property. His next-door neighbor was George Brewster, a descendant of Elder Brewster, leader of the Plymouth Colony.

Brewster had built a limestone mansion on Seventy-first Street and Park in 1911.² "There were so few houses in that area that Father was told he could choose any house number he wanted, so he chose 71 and we had 71 East 71," recalls his daughter, Katharine Brewster Whipple.

The next January, *The New York Times* reported on the fuss surrounding the marriage of Lee's daughter Marion to John J. Ryan Jr. of Troy, New York. The Lees gave the couple a pre-wedding dinner dance at the Hotel Pierre, and then hosted a reception at their new home. This, though Lee considered Ryan a little . . . common. With his father and four brothers, Ryan ran a firm that bought and sold cotton.

Despite the public display of domesticity, Lee was rarely home, and when he was, he was hardly a loving homebody. Surrounded by adoring women—five sisters and three daughters—he was less than an adoring or adored husband. According to several of Jacqueline Onassis's many biographers, Lee pushed his wife, Margaret, to the sidelines of his life; they slept in separate bedrooms, avoided each other, and communicated only through their three girls. "He was very fed up with my grandmother," says John Ryan III. "She was too talkative. An enormous talker. You could put the phone down, pick it up, and she'd still be talking."

Enter John Vernou Bouvier III. At age thirty-six, Bouvier was sixteen years older than James T. Lee's middle daughter, Janet; he was also a bit dim and lacked ambition. But he was well dressed and perma-tanned and had dark, lacquered looks, blue eyes, and a dapper mustache that won him the nicknames Black Jack, the Black Sheik, the Black Prince, and the Black Orchid. "He was powerful, wealthy, exotic, and undeniably, darkly attractive," says Kathleen Bouvier, who married Black Jack's brother's son.

Jack seemed made-to-measure for Lee, whose ambitions were shared by his Spence-educated daughter. Black Jack Bouvier was in the *Social Register* and through a distant relative was a member of the Society of the Cincinnati, descendants of George Washington's officers in the Revolution. Michel Bouvier, his great-uncle, had come to America from France in 1815 and had worked as a cabinetmaker in Philadelphia, where his clients included Joseph Bonaparte, Napoleon's brother. Thanks to fortuitous marriages to prominent Philadelphia families, the Bouviers attained social status within a single generation; John V. Bouvier Sr., Jack's grandfather, had founded a stock brokerage and was listed in the very first *Social Register*, as was his brother, Michel Charles, who lived with their three unmarried sisters, all buoyed by a fortune of $10 million. Jack III, born in 1891, grew up in New Jersey—first in a rented house in Nutley, then on an estate known as Woodcroft—indulged and entitled and disrespectful toward and envious of his wealthier uncle Michel. His mother would blame his undisciplined behavior on "bad French blood."

Graduating from Yale in 1914 at the bottom of a class that also included his lifelong friend Cole Porter, Black Jack was known for his panache and his parties. He began his career with a brother-in-law's brokerage firm, but left in 1917 to join the Navy. Finding it tough, he switched to the Army and spent his stint in uniform in "honky-tonk back alleys and brothels . . . waiting for this dirty little war to end," as he put it. In 1919, Bouvier bought a seat on the New York Stock Exchange with a $115,000 loan from his uncle, joined the Racquet and Tennis and University clubs, and, defying the odds, did well investing for clients mostly gained through his family connections. Jack had several broken engagements on his romantic résumé when he met Janet Lee at the snooty Maidstone Club in East Hampton. Bouvier's father was a member, and James T. Lee had joined, too, after he bought a house in the summer community in 1925. The next summer Janet graduated from Spence, debuted at Sherry's, and, while attending college at Sweet Briar, segued from palling around with Jack's younger twin sisters to dating their much-older brother.

Jack's proposal of marriage offered an escape from her parents' control—and their unhappy household. Her father had his doubts, despite Jack's social position. Relatives warned that Jack was after the family's money, spent more than he made, was a gambler and a plunger, and was deeply in debt. But Janet had inherited her father's fierce determination to rise socially, so despite Lee's feelings, she married Jack in East Hampton in July 1928. Predictably, father and husband had a vicious argument at the wedding reception at Lee's place on Lily Pond Lane. The next day, aboard a cruise ship for their honeymoon, Jack got drunk before the friends who were seeing them off had even disembarked, then annoyed Janet by flirting with teenage Doris Duke, the tobacco heiress, and gambling incessantly throughout the trip. "He went to the casino and came back very depressed because he had lost everything," Jackie Onassis would later tell friends.

Back in New York, the newlyweds moved into 790 Park, two blocks north of Lee's house. Jack's parents lived between them at 765 Park. In keeping with his lifestyle, Jack bought stocks on margin and took huge chances, but so did everyone in the fall of 1928. He spent his inevitable market winnings wildly, even buying the car of the moment, a custom-built Stutz Bearcat, with a driver. Janet enjoyed the money and the life it let them lead, but the charm that Jack employed to bamboozle others wore thin for her. Inside, she seethed at her husband's infidelities and drinking, his gambling, spending, and borrowing, and only felt better in East Hampton, where they summered at an estate owned by Jack's grandfather and she could ride away her anger on the horses they kept there.

3

JAMES T. LEE AND HIS PARTNERS SOLD THE PRESBYTERIAN HOSPITAL properties in April 1927 for a reported $7 million. The buyers announced their intention to take down the hospital on the south side of the street and build a prestigious co-op on Park Avenue and another apartment building with retail shops on the ground floor on Madison. Three days later, they sold the nurses' residence site on the north side of Seventy-first Street—which had frontage on neither Park nor Madison—for a mere $40,000. The buyer was James T. Lee.

In April 1928, just as the hospital properties were emptying out, Lee was named to the board of the Chase Bank by Albert Wiggin; a year later, he'd be made a senior vice president. Founded in 1877, the Chase, as it was called, was named after Abraham Lincoln's secretary of the treasury, Salmon P. Chase, and was originally a wholesaler, a banker's bank, or, as the *Times* put it, "guide, philosopher and friend" to banks in the untamed West.

Albert Henry Wiggin, a driven, energetic, bespectacled banker with a thick brush mustache, had joined the Chase in 1904 and become president in 1911. A quick success, he solidified his position by appointing many top corporate executives to the Chase board and joining dozens of boards himself. Wiggin established the Chase Securities Corporation in

1917. By 1929, this investment banking and brokerage business had become a major player on Wall Street and beyond—Chase Securities had offices across the country and in Europe. In 1919, the Chase entered the trusts and estates business, too, becoming the trustee of choice for patrician American fortunes. By 1921, the Chase had become the third-largest bank in America, but Wiggin was just getting started.

The Chase tripled in size in the 1920s, taking over five other banks by merger. In 1928, Wiggin's son-in-law, Lynde (pronounced *Lindy*) Selden, head of the Chase Bank's foreign department, had the idea that by acquiring American Express, the bank could become an instant player in international finance—until then, its operations had been limited to the domestic front. Founded as a package carrier in the days of the railroads, American Express by the 1920s had morphed into the company it remains today, issuing traveler's checks and running a travel business in offices around the world. With huge loads of cash on hand, all those offices, and passive management, American Express was ripe for a takeover. That summer Wiggin decided to attempt one secretly. By autumn, he controlled 40 percent of the company's shares.

In April 1929, Wiggin went public with a tender offer, backed by the top executives of American Express. By summer, the Chase controlled 97 percent of it, and it became a subsidiary of the bank. Wiggin had already managed to get himself elected to the American Express board of directors and had engineered an expansion of its board from eleven to thirteen directors. Both of the two newly appointed directors also held seats on the Chase board. One of them was Frederick Hudson Ecker, the president (and later chairman) of Metropolitan Life Insurance Company. Ecker was a good man to have around, even when he was in the shadows. Which is where he was when James T. Lee's Shelton Holding filed plans to build 740 Park on March 13, 1929. A few months later, Ecker would issue his Chase board colleague a hefty mortgage to pay for the building.

COOPERATIVE APARTMENT HOUSES ARE THE MOST EXCLUSIVE FORM OF what are commonly called multiple dwellings. Invented for artists, they flourished in the beginning of the twentieth century because common was precisely what they were not. The great appeal of co-ops in the early

1920s was that they allowed shareholders to live among their own. Co-ops were like private golf courses and gated communities, their own worlds, little clubs for people with lifestyles and social standings in common. One Sutton Place, a neo-Georgian co-op with its own yacht landing on the East River, had been built by and for the Phipps family, for example. But by the middle of the decade, speculation in real estate had become as popular as plunging on Wall Street. So instead of being financed and constructed by groups of wealthy friends, associates, or relatives, co-ops were as often strictly business ventures financed by the sale of apartments. Seven forty Park would prove to be a somewhat uneasy combination of the two.

The public record offers not a clue about whom, if anyone, 740 Park Avenue was built for, but it does reveal that behind the scenes, Lee had formed another syndicate, much like the one that first bought the hospital properties, this one called the 71 East Seventy-first Street Syndicate, membership unknown, managed by Lee. It is certainly no coincidence that its address was 20 Pine Street, the headquarters of the Chase. Nor that sprinkled among the names of the first apartment buyers at 740 were several with significant ties to the bank: Albert Wiggin's colleague and son-in-law, Selden, and Charles S. McCain, who became president of the Chase that year when it merged with National Park Bank, where he'd been president. James T. Lee, of course, managed all of the Chase's real estate interests.

Seven forty would symbolize not just James T. Lee's arrival at a peak of power and influence but these apartment buyers' arrival as well, for none of them could claim to be from old money or old families. McCain, the son of an Arkansas lawyer, had begun his career as a bank cashier in a roped-off enclosure in a general store serving a town of one hundred. Wiggin, the son of a Unitarian minister from Massachusetts, had started out as a bank cashier, too. Despite that, Wiggin's daughter, an amateur singer named Muriel, "never felt she took second place to" her Selden in-laws, says a grandson, Paul Selden, even though *they* could claim descent from mid-seventeenth-century settlers of central Connecticut, local religious and political leaders, and even a Revolutionary War soldier. Her husband, Lynde Selden, still worked for Wiggin.

Now they would *all* live as equals—even better, as next-door neighbors—to American aristocrats like George and Eleanor Brewster. Buying their house between his and the nurses' residence was Lee's most audacious move, for it made 740 a place where blood and money would cooperate for their common good.

Brewster's lineal ancestor "Elder" William Brewster, born in England in 1567 and jailed for his Pilgrim religious beliefs in 1607, had traveled aboard the *Mayflower* to the Plymouth Colony of Massachusetts in 1620. George Brewster was the son of Benjamin Brewster, who joined the California gold rush in 1849 and returned east in 1874. A mutton-chopped, bushy-eyebrowed eminence, Benjamin built the famous Rock Island Railroad and was one of the founders and trustees of the Standard Oil Company, part of the great monopoly run by John D. Rockefeller. Brewster was the president of the Keokuk and Des Moines Railroad, too, and owned a mansion at Fifty-fifth Street and Fifth Avenue when he died in 1897. In 1905, his son George married Eleanor Grant Bosher, the daughter of a Confederate officer, a tall, cultured blond beauty from Richmond, Virginia. George had ridden crew at Yale and worked as a banker, but mostly invested and gave away his family's money. In 1909, he filed plans to build his five-story stone mansion house on the corner of Park Avenue and Seventy-first Street, costing $200,000. It was the new fashionable neighborhood. When a banker named Oakleigh Thorne bought a corner two blocks to the north a few months later, the *Times* took note of the "new order of things," a "colony of fine dwellings on the crown of Lenox Hill."

Brewster initially agreed to sell Lee's syndicate his house, but at the last minute his wife made him renege. "Mother said she was very comfortable where she was, thank you," says Katharine, Brewster's daughter, who was born in that house in 1915. "So poor Mr. Lee had a terrible time, and he finally, in desperation, said if she and Father would sell him the house, he would get her any kind of apartment that she wanted in the new building." Eleanor Brewster agreed and "got what she wanted, something pretty large," says Katharine. She deeded their house and land to the Shelton Holding Company in May 1929. In exchange, the finest residence in the building would be built to their specifications.

Such deals were typical, if not quite commonplace. "People sold their houses in exchange for money plus an interest in the project plus an apartment," says Andrew Alpern. Developers who coveted the land beneath Mrs. E. F. Hutton's town house at 1107 Fifth Avenue acquired it only after promising her that they would not only re-create her fifty-four-room mansion in a triplex atop their new apartment house but also give her a private entrance with her own triple-arched driveway and a private elevator to reach the largest apartment ever created in the world (and a rental at that).' Other swells made similar deals. When Mrs. William Vanderbilt II purchased a maisonette within 660 Park, *The New York Times* gave the event feature treatment, reporting the dimensions of her new living room (46 feet x 22 feet) and the number of master bedrooms (seven). "Low-ceilinged living rooms have always been a drawback in modern city apartments," the story went on. "They were ill-adapted to entertaining. Their walls did not offer sufficient space for tapestries. Pictures in heavy frames looked out of place in them, as did carved Italian mantels. In the last word apartment, this difficulty has been eliminated. The ceilings in the living rooms of Mrs. Vanderbilt's triplex will be 18 feet high." In the end, Mrs. Vanderbilt never moved in.

Along with his expertise, and the nurses' residence, James T. Lee contributed not just one but two houses, his own at 750 Park and 752 Park next door, which he'd bought that month from William H. Woodin, president of American Car and Foundry Company, a maker of railroad cars.

THE BUILDING THAT WAS ABOUT TO REPLACE THEM ALL HAD BEEN WELL thought out in the preceding months. Lee hired Hegeman-Harris Company as his general contractor. Then enjoying its best year since its founding, the company already had the Harvard School of Business, the Tribune Tower in Chicago, and New York's Beekman Tower, Bryant Park Hotel, and Daily News and American Radiator buildings to its credit, and it would shortly build the main unit of Rockefeller Center. Lee had hired Rosario Candela as lead architect and Arthur Loomis Harmon, who'd designed Lee's Shelton Hotel, as an associate architect. Harmon, who'd joined Shreve & Lamb, architects of the Empire State Building, that year, was hired to design 740's streamlined exterior elements (which subtly echo the Art Deco styling of his Empire State Building) and the public spaces within. But 740 Park would eventually come to be known as a

Candela building, indeed, *the* signature Candela building, and the crew-cut Candela would emerge as the greatest apartment designer in America.

Born in Sicily in 1890, Candela, the son of a plasterer, came to the United States at nineteen, somehow gained entrance to Columbia University's School of Architecture ("How, in God's name?" asks Alpern. "Architecture was an elite thing. He may have convinced them with his skill with a pencil. The talent was obvious") and graduated in 1915. Christopher Gray, the leading historian of New York real estate, reports that Candela was already so sure of his talents that he placed a velvet rope around his drafting table to keep other students from copying his work. "He really was a genius," says his granddaughter Jackie Candela. "He was very arrogant and knew his talents."

Candela began his career working for several fellow Italians, Michael Paterno and Anthony Campagna, the most significant luxury-apartment-house developers of the time. Candela started small, with apartment houses on the West Side of Manhattan, but in the mid-1920s, with two dozen completed buildings on his résumé and the economy bubbling like fine champagne, he began planning the buildings that would become, half a century later, the most lust-inspiring real estate in the world.

The inevitable trend toward taller apartment buildings on Park Avenue played to Candela's strengths. "He did the crossword puzzle in ink," recalls Patricia Candela MacLeod, a granddaughter. "We're all very strong in the math department. It's a gene. My brother is a math genius. Rosario clearly was." He discovered he was expert at fitting different-sized and -shaped apartments together like puzzle pieces *inside* his buildings.

His early architectural efforts were mostly flat-topped and sedate. Then a landmark zoning law passed in 1916 allowed buildings to rise higher if they incorporated setbacks—a requirement that above a certain height, buildings be set back a certain distance from where their walls stood at street level so that light and fresh air would reach streets and neighboring buildings that would otherwise be submerged in darkness. By varying the lines of these setback buildings, urban planners created the jagged vertical modern skyline, and gave the Jazz Age and Manhattan their visual signatures. Lee and Harmon's Shelton Hotel had been the first great work of architecture formed by the new law. They all proved to be the right men in the right place at the right time, perfectly positioned to make the most of the moment, using setbacks to symbolize the sky-piercing ambitions, the soaring imagination, the heedless glamour, the wild, crazy overreaching of the times.

In 1927, *The New Republic* reported that Park Avenue had surpassed Fifth as the address of choice for the plutocracy. Park Avenue, it said,

> is the end of the American ladder of success. Higher one cannot go . . . The street lays acknowledged claim to the most stupendous aggregation of multimillionaires which the world has ever seen . . . massed along this harsh stone canyon—the winnings from oil, steel, railroads, mining, lumber, motor cars, banking, real estate, moving pictures, foreign trade, speculating, the manufacturing of widgets, the marketing of toothpaste, the distribution of the assets of button kings. The art treasures of Europe and the East—paintings, frescoes, paneling, tapestries, jewels, period furniture—have been imported by the shipload to make these dollars manifest . . . There are no more worlds to conquer. If America has a heaven, this is it.

The first great co-op sales record was set at Candela's 960 Fifth Avenue, built by Anthony Campagna. It opened in 1928 on the site of the huge mansion of Senator William Clark. A jigsaw puzzle of one- and two-story apartments, it contained one especially sparkling gem—the apartment of a widower, Dr. Preston Pope Satterwhite, with a dining room and library each thirty feet long flanking a double-height fifty-eight-foot-long living room that contained a crisscrossing double staircase up to Satterwhite's bedroom, which had a balcony overlooking the grand parlor. Satterwhite reportedly paid $450,000 for the place when it existed only in plans. Though the apartment was later subdivided and the grand living room is now gone, the building remains and still boasts an in-house chef, maid service, and the Georgian Suite, a pair of dining rooms and a kitchen that can be rented by residents for private parties.

Nine sixty Fifth was the first of a Babe Ruthian string of home runs for Candela. In 1929, 720 Park Avenue, designed by Candela and Lee's former partner Eliot Cross, was completed. That year the *Times* predicted that 1929 would be "the greatest of all building construction years," and a new multiple-dwelling law went into effect in New York, allowing apartment houses to rise to nineteen stories. In a mere eight months, Candela would design and file plans for six more buildings— 740, 770, 778, and 1220 Park Avenue and 834 and 1040 Fifth Avenue— that are "the most magnificent assemblage of extraordinary apartments ever produced by any architect," according to Andrew Alpern, "the final display of fireworks before the Depression descended."

Candela's innovations, listed singly, may seem mundane, but they added up to something extraordinary. As the architectural designer David Netto has noted, Candela thickened walls to hide columns, structural framing, plumbing risers, and building mechanical systems. In his buildings, protruding radiators disappeared beneath deep windows, and rooms and windows were re-proportioned, "endowing [them] with a feeling of greater space and balance."

The architect Donald Wrobleski, who has made a lifetime study of Candela and is writing a book on the architect, praises his use of visual axes, diagonals that "produce a panoramic view upon entering" a Candela apartment. "This gives complete orientation of the sort that one might expect in a great country house," Wrobleski writes. "These all seem like solutions to a puzzle. The puzzle being how to produce the ingredients of a great house in a severely limited space." Thanks to Candela's genius, windows are perfectly framed in doorways, daylight is maximized throughout, and not only the public rooms but also the hidden sleeping quarters on the second floor of the duplexes are immediately perceived as elements of an integrated whole. Yet uncannily, privacy is maintained.

Carpenter had first proposed a building-full of gracious duplexes for his award-winning 812 Fifth Avenue, but Candela gave the idea a stunning new intricacy at 740. And he was continuing to refine what Netto considers his greatest innovation: those terraced setbacks that were, in reality, the children of necessity. In order to build higher than one and a half times the width of the street, architects had to create setbacks above the eleventh or twelfth stories of their buildings—and that, combined with the newborn cachet of penthouse living, gave Candela an opportunity to stretch his talents, as well as the definition of what constituted luxury urban housing. Anyone looking up at the tops of his buildings on Park Avenue will see that Candela was a leading voice in the architectural choir that was re-creating New York's image by reaching, magnificently, for the sky.

THERE WERE TWO BLESSED EVENTS IN JAMES T. LEE'S FAMILY IN THE summer of 1929. A granddaughter, Jacqueline Lee Bouvier, Janet and Black Jack's first child, was born on July 28, 1929. A few days later, in early August, the 740 Park Avenue Corporation was born.

The new corporation entered into a $4 million mortgage (the equivalent of $43,478,000 in 2004 dollars) with the Metropolitan Life Insurance Company, run by Lee's Chase board colleague Frederick Ecker, on August 6, 1929. Construction costs were estimated at $2,225,000 ($24 million in 2004 dollars)—the highest amount per square foot ever spent on a residential building in the city's history. Installment payments of $40,000 would be due semiannually beginning on June 1, 1932. Interest on the loan would be 6 percent while the building was being erected, then drop to 5.5 percent for ten years and 5 percent after that. The principal on the loan would not come due until December 1949—a long way off. Lee and his partners would be responsible for the rent on any unsold units, but would control the board of directors until half of them were sold.

The handsomely printed prospectus for 740 Park made Lee's audacity clear. He'd set out to build a stack of mansions, four triplex maisonettes and another twenty grand duplex apartments, most with between ten and thirteen spacious rooms, galleries, conservatories, and loggias, all designed to offer maximum sunlight and cross-ventilation. It was a beehive of apartments, each fit for its own queen.

Candela proposed a 506-room fortress occupying twenty-two thousand square feet covering half a block on Park Avenue and most of a block on Seventy-first Street (the rest was occupied by St. James Episcopal Church, which had its entrance on Madison Avenue). The exterior of the building would be brick, terra-cotta, and portland cement, but unlike most apartment buildings, where limestone hid the brick for a floor or two, 740 would be clad entirely in expensive ashlar-patterned Indiana limestone with a marble base. Exterior walls were to be 2 ½ feet thick; floors 1 ½ feet thick. The plans specified that the ground floor would hold a superintendent's apartment, nineteen small bedrooms for servants, and three maisonettes—triplex apartments with their own entrances, one on Seventy-first Street and two on Park Avenue.

Instead of one entrance, 740 would have two, one on Park Avenue, where the primary address was carved into the granite slab topped by finials that surrounded the doorway, and a second on Seventy-first Street. Each entrance featured large marble halls and ornamental ceilings. They were going to be connected with a long carved-wood-paneled hallway floored in Belgian and travertine marble. The apartments, the managing agent, Douglas Gibbons, promised in a letter describing the "points of excellence of this outstanding cooperative building," would also be "splendidly planned" to include "the most spacious rooms and galleries ever designed for a New York apartment" and have gracious ceiling heights (between ten and twelve and a half feet for public rooms, between nine and eleven feet on bedroom floors).

The building would contain four lines of apartments, known by the letters *A, B, C,* and *D.* Three would be anchored by triplex maisonettes (on floors 1–3) with their own entrances on the street, and above each of them would be five similar duplexes (four per floor on floors 4–13). The C line would have a doctor's office on the first floor and six duplexes above. The fourteenth floor would house two one-floor apartments, each stretching across two lines, and above each of those would be two grand duplexes, one occupying the entire Park Avenue frontage, the other running all the way down Seventy-first Street. Above the Park Avenue duplex would be another simplex and, above that, a duplex penthouse. On Seventy-first Street, a smaller duplex penthouse would rise from the seventeenth floor.

Apartments in the A and B lines, which would be accessed from the

740 Park entrance, were larger. The A line would look out on Park Avenue, the B line both east and south. The Seventy-first Street apartments in the C line were going to be the smallest and, except on the higher floors, would lack views; 730 Park, across the street, blocked them. The D-line apartments would be quite desirable because they would have sweeping views to the south, the north, and the west. The higher floors would look out over the steeple of St. James Episcopal Church and the Frick mansion and across Central Park.

Candela's setbacks were ingenious, utilizing a legal loophole in the rules to create spacious libraries on the upper floors—and avoid a pyramid effect. The rules also mandated that the building shrink partway down narrow Seventy-first Street, where setbacks had to begin at a height of 90 feet instead of the 150 feet allowed on wide Park Avenue. "They didn't violate the rules," marvels Donald Wrobleski. "It's a very graceful transition. Looking at the building, you're not aware of the problem. And there's very little waste, very little space that could have been used but wasn't."

Each apartment was to have its own private marble-floored vestibule, so owners would never have to fumble for their keys in front of neighbors. Then, once inside their doors, they'd enter Candela's signature travertine entrance galleries. They were not created equal, however. The largest apartments—realtors put the range at eighty-five hundred to ten thousand square feet—were in the B line; their public rooms opened onto both Park Avenue and Seventy-first Street. The next best were the D-line apartments that looked south and west. On floors that cleared St. James Church, the western views were stunning. The least-coveted apartments, the C line, were smaller and on lower floors, darker compared with others in the building. All except the two fourteenth-floor simplex apartments had "artistic winding marble" staircases. The triplex maisonettes were going to have two staircases each, and all-marble ground-floor entrance galleries to boot.

Candela planned kitchens with glazed-tile walls, porcelain sinks, ash drain boards, chromium-trimmed eight-burner gas ranges, plate warmers, metal cupboards and pantry sinks, and two solid porcelain refrigerators, one large and one small. Behind the walls would be only "highest quality" brass pipe. Each apartment would also contain a housemaid's closet with four feet of tiled wainscoting, an enameled-iron slop sink, and a tile floor.

All master bathrooms came with marble floors and wainscoting two feet eight inches high, marble-faced, enameled-iron tubs, and separate showers. Other bathrooms would boast marble trim and faience tile. Sinks and water closets were to be made of vitreous china. Many of the servants' bathrooms would boast similar high-quality fixtures. Windows in the masters' rooms were all to be double-hung with rattle-proof frames made of solid bronze, as were all the casement doors leading to the many terraces on the setbacks. The roofs and terraces were going to be covered with multicolored slate, and the flashings, gutters, skylights, and leaders would all be made of sixteen-ounce copper.

Most apartments would feature several wood-burning fireplaces, although only iron dampers and smoke chambers were included in the purchase price. The fireplace surrounds were unfinished, without mantels, facings, linings, or hearths, which purchasers would have to install. Masters' rooms would all come with triple-coated plaster walls. Servants' rooms would have two coats of plaster. All public rooms and master bedrooms and bathrooms also came complete with molded cornices or coves and gold-plated doorknobs and key plates. All other hardware was bronze. Master-bedroom closets had built-in electrical outlets and shoe shelves. Every apartment contained a locking cedar closet. Bedroom floors were made of strips of quartered oak, those in the public rooms of teak planks (although many of the original owners upgraded the teak floors to parquet de Versailles in the main reception rooms). Terrace railings, Douglas Gibbons boasted, would be "artistic," "very handsome," and "most attractive as viewed from apartments."

Because one could hardly be expected to yell for a servant in such an elegant atmosphere, all masters' rooms were outfitted with call bells that rang in the servant quarters, and each apartment was connected to a house telephone system that let owners call either of the entrances as well as the four high-speed, self-leveling, gearless Otis passenger elevators (one per apartment line), the chauffeur's waiting room, the superintendent's office, and the thirty-two extra servants' rooms tucked into the rear of the ground and third floors. (Servants, of course, were going to have a separate entrance, via an alley on the west side of the building between 740 and St. James Church.) Connections for still-new telephones and radios were also provided in all apartments. One window shade was furnished for each window. Additional, uniformly colored shades were available for purchase.

Luxurious though the building was, the apartments were sold raw, with all refinements beyond plaster and a primer coat on the interior trim left up to the initial purchasers. While the building was going up, buyers could request layout changes—and did. Candela understood their needs. "He swung with a pretty upscale crowd," says his grandson Steven. Some of them, at least, hired Candela to help them; among the scant number of original documents still available are his plans for two apartments, the homes of the Lynde Seldens and of J. Watson and Electra Havemeyer Webb. For the former, Candela created a neo-Georgian scheme. For the latter, he added a third floor to their penthouse, grafting on several rooms from the simplex apartment directly below, giving them a total of 8,340 square feet of space plus another 710 square feet of terrace.

Candela also worked on the Brewster apartment—adding an oak dumbwaiter, for instance, just before the family took occupancy (they'd moved to a sublet at 1 Sutton Place when their mansion was demolished). He was unable to give Eleanor Brewster one thing she wanted, though: an elevator that would travel not just from one floor to another but from one end of the apartment to the other, even turning corners. "Father explained that it could not come up here and then go over there," recalls Katharine Whipple.

"But that is *very* inconvenient!" Eleanor Brewster groused.

Candela was still rearranging rooms in James T. Lee's new duplex next door to the Brewsters as late as July 1930. Years later, Candela's son told Christopher Gray that his father's commissions from designing interiors were lucrative enough that in good years, those billings alone covered his annual overhead.

Besides the oak-paneled super's office and the chauffeur's waiting room (which had its own entrance and bathroom), the building's public spaces included a mailroom, a baby-carriage room, and, in the glazed-brick-wall basement, individual tiled twelve-by-twenty-foot laundries (each with three washtubs and gas stoves and dryers), individual locked seventeen-by-fifteen-foot storage cages (with trunk shelves raised three inches off the floor), and separate vaults with combination-lock steel safe doors, all refrigeration-ready for any tenants who required wine cellars and a refrigerated garbage room ("so as to be free from insects or vermin"). A gymnasium and steam room were also planned, though left uncompleted. Over the years, tenants would install their own, including a workout room in the basement. Finally, two Otis service elevators were installed, running between the A- and the B-line and the C- and the D-line apartments, respectively, accessible through doors off the servants' quarters.

4

In September 1929, Candela filed his final plans with the Department of Buildings, and excavation of the site began. A new-building permit was issued on October 14. Simultaneously, Albert Wiggin was named chairman and chief executive of American Express. But by the end of the month, he had been forced to turn his attention elsewhere. On October 24, the stock market crashed, and in the tense days that followed, Wiggin was among the group of financiers who labored mightily to right the listing economy—pledging more than $200 million to a banking pool set up to stabilize the market by buying stocks for which there would otherwise be no takers.

Wiggin's actions weren't entirely altruistic. He felt the market collapse represented a buying opportunity and in the next few weeks ordered American Express to invest its surplus funds in stocks. Confident, for the moment, in the economy, Wiggin made himself a spokesman for optimism, committing another $300 million in Chase funds for loans to customers who needed cash, and won a reputation as the most popular banker on Wall Street.

For the moment at least, 740 Park seemed to be flying over the wreckage of the market. Just as building commenced, the first buyers were announced: Bayard Cushing Hoppin was a member of a grand old Knickerbocker family that controlled a large swath of the east side of Manhattan known as the Beekman Estate and a longtime friend of the George Brewsters and of Jack and Janet Bouvier. He took an apartment shortly after selling one seventeen blocks south. Not long afterward, his brother Gerard Beekman Hoppin bought another.

As the building rose, more names would be released. Lee and his managing agent, Douglas Gibbons, were using the announcements to help market the apartments. In those days, such transactions made the papers as a matter of course. *The New York Times* had regular columns like Manhattan Transfers, chronicling real estate purchases. Most of the purchasers were either captains of industry, society folk, or both. They had the funds to cushion them from the immediate effects of the crash. And at the time, like Wiggin, most Americans, and particularly wealthy Americans, believed that prosperity was a birthright and would inevitably and quickly return. The hit song "Happy Days Are Here Again" was first released in October 1929.

IN YEARS TO COME, 740 PARK AVENUE WOULD BECOME KNOWN AS A Rockefeller building, supposedly built by John D. Rockefeller, who turned ninety in 1929, for his son and heir, John D. Rockefeller Jr. But the elder Rockefeller had nothing to do with 740, aside from knowing George Brewster, and Junior didn't move in until 1938. As the building was still rising, he did become involved, though, at least peripherally. The network that got 740 off the ground was about to merge into one that was even more powerful.

Rockefeller Sr. was a man of controversy. The creator of the Standard Oil monopoly that controlled 90 percent of American oil, and owner of the world's first billion-dollar fortune, he'd been reviled by muckrakers and trustbusters who accused him of practicing, if not inventing, every dirty trick in the capitalist playbook. He became a symbol of all his late-nineteenth-century counterparts, the first industrialists, mostly men from the Midwest involved in heavy industries like steel, fuel, and railroads. Like many of them, Rockefeller became a philanthropist, and among the assets he gave to the world, the most significant may have been his son, who was stunned by the legacy, wealth, and opportunity that had been handed to him and determined that, after him, the Rockefeller name would stand for good works, not monstrous, or even banal, moneygrubbing. Junior was on the verge of accomplishing that end when the market crashed in 1929.

Not long after that, the sudden death of one of Albert Wiggin's competitors—another master of banking mergers—brought the family of the founder of Standard Oil into 740's orbit. On December 13, Chellis Austin, the newly named fifty-three-year-old president of Equitable Trust, the Rockefeller family bank (John D. Rockefeller Jr. became its largest shareholder in 1911'), gave a speech defending his fellow bankers to a convention of the Association of Life Insurance Presidents at New York's Astor Hotel. Austin asserted that "the danger is over," hailed "the extraordinary strength which the banks revealed," noted that neither banks nor brokerages had failed after the crash, and claimed, "We have passed the stage in our national history when even the worst speculative excesses could affect the fundamental base upon which our economy rests, namely, our banking system." Those would prove to be his ironic last words.

Following the afternoon speech, Austin returned home to Montclair, New Jersey, ate dinner, and went to bed early. At 3:00 A.M., he woke up in excruciating pain, then collapsed as his wife called for a doctor. He died of angina pectoris just as one arrived.

Junior led the thousand notables who attended Austin's funeral the next day. Winthrop W. Aldrich Jr., a lawyer whose sister Abby was married to Junior, was an honorary pallbearer, as were Albert Wiggin and Franklin d'Olier, whose son would later marry James T. Lee's youngest daughter. It was a very small world that the very rich inhabited. It was about to get smaller.

Aldrich, a child of the former senator Nelson Aldrich of Rhode Island, was about to become Lee's boss. He'd graduated from Harvard Law School and won a job at a law firm called Murray, Prentice & Howland in 1919, after Junior recommended him. Founded in 1866 by the son of an Episcopal minister, the firm represented wealthy families like the Vanderbilts and the Goulds. George Welwood Murray, who became a partner in 1888, won the Rockefellers as clients after meeting Junior's father through their Baptist church. He became a close adviser. When Junior's sister Alta married Ezra Parmalee Prentice, a steel company lawyer, in 1900, Prentice joined the firm, which promptly added the name of its best client's son-in-law to the door.

Winthrop Aldrich, who wore a pince-nez and custom-made John Lobb shoes, was to Junior what first Murray and then Prentice had been to his father. In 1921, he became a name partner and head of the law firm and in 1922 was made chief counsel for Rockefeller's Equitable Trust, its largest client. Four years later, William Hale Harkness, scion of another family with ties to Standard Oil, and a friend of George Brewster's family as well, joined the firm, and in 1929 it merged with Webb, Patterson & Hadley and became Murray, Aldrich & Webb. Harkness, his new partner Morris Hadley, and their partner Vanderbilt Webb's brother, J. Watson Webb (both of them great-grandsons of Cornelius Vanderbilt), would all buy apartments in 740 Park. So, just a bit later, would Junior.

MEANWHILE, WINTHROP ALDRICH WAS AT JUNIOR'S RIGHT HAND WHEN he orchestrated a proxy fight that forced the chairman of Standard Oil of Indiana, one of the tent poles of the Rockefeller empire, out of his job after he vexed a Senate committee investigating the oil industry. "Father had very strong moral convictions, and when he was involved and other people were doing things that he thought were wrong, he would stand up against it," says Junior's youngest son, David Rockefeller, who was then in college.

Aldrich had hired Chellis Austin—a mere three months before his unexpected death. In order to get him, Equitable had had to merge with a rival, Seaboard National, which Austin ran. Now, with Austin dead, Junior asked Aldrich to take over Equitable. He agreed on condition that he be allowed to seek a merger with another bank.

To replace Aldrich as his chief lawyer, Junior turned to a college friend (and another honorary pallbearer at Chellis Austin's funeral), Albert Milbank, who'd also done legal work for the family. When Milbank declined out of loyalty to his firm, Masten & Nichols, Junior engineered *its* merger with Murray, Aldrich & Webb. Partners in both firms were furious, but such was the power of the Rockefellers: their wishes were commands. The merged firm became known as the Rockefeller law firm, and that proved very good for the lawyers. Though it took years for them to successfully integrate the two parts, eventually the combination became "the law firm for anybody who was well off," says Leila Luce, a friend of partner Morris Hadley. Milbank would eventually develop the largest trusts and estates practice in the country. One partner was said to disdain using the telephone book; all he needed was the copy of the *Social Register* he kept on his desk.

A few years later, Milbank, Tweed, Hope & Webb would take on the 740 Park Avenue Corporation as a client—and keep it for decades (and Hadley would move in, too). But first Winthrop Aldrich and Albert Wiggin engineered the merger of the Chase, America's third-largest bank, and Equitable Trust, which had become the fourth-largest, in March 1930. The result was the world's richest financial institution, with $2.7 billion on deposit.

THE NEW CHASE NATIONAL BANK EMERGED THAT MONTH, JUST AS A plan of organization, prospectus, and price list for apartments at 740 Park Avenue was issued—officially putting them on the market. Douglas Gibbons and Brown Wheelock: Harris, Vought & Co., two of the companies that handled the very best buildings for New York's aristocracy, were named as selling agents. Gibbons would also manage the building for $10,000 a year. Buyers were asked to put 25 percent of the purchase price down upon joining the cooperative, another 25 percent when the steel frame of the building was topped off, 25 percent more when the plasterwork was completed, and the last quarter upon issuance of the certificate of occupancy.

Typical apartment prices ranged from a low of $72,000 for the building's smallest duplexes, twelve-room apartments with five bathrooms on low floors in the C line, to $215,000 for a grand terraced duplex with eighteen rooms and eight bathrooms on the twelfth and thirteenth floors of the largest line, the B apartments. A maisonette in the second-largest A line—containing fifteen rooms and six bathrooms—cost $136,000. The largest penthouse, above the B line, was priced at $205,400. The large simplex apartment on the Park Avenue side of the fourteenth floor, which boasted sixteen rooms and seven bathrooms, was priced at $185,000, making its next-door neighbor, which ran down Seventy-first Street, with only twelve rooms and six baths, a bargain at $130,000. An even bigger bargain was the building's smallest apartment, the seventeenth-floor penthouse on the D line, with only nine rooms and three baths. Despite its staggering views, that little bijou was priced at only $120,000. Additional servants' rooms downstairs were selling for between $2,100 and $2,900.

Included with the prospectus was a financial plan projecting annual income from maintenance (which paid for overhead, mortgage interest, and taxes) at $472,500 a year, representing $10 per share of stock on 47,250 shares. Out of that would come real estate and corporate taxes; mortgage interest of $220,000 a year; just over $35,000 in annual labor costs (for the salaries of a super, twelve elevator men, four doormen, four carriage men, three porters, a handyman, two relief men, and one night hall captain); insurance premiums; and payments for electric light and power, steam heat, water, repairs, supplies, and administrative costs. James T. Lee predicted that this budget would throw off a surplus of just over $9,000 a year—presumably extra cash for emergencies. That would prove a tad optimistic.

THE NEW APARTMENT HOUSE ROSE QUICKLY THAT WINTER AND THE FOL-lowing spring, proof, if any were needed, that a mere stock market correction couldn't stop progress. Steelwork had been completed by January 1930. Roof riveting commenced the day after Valentine's Day. Bricklayers and masons had begun working on the penthouse by April Fools' Day. Interior walls were completed in April, plumbing fixtures were installed in July, and general finishing work proceeded through the summer.

In September 1930, construction ended, the building was inspected and found to conform to city codes, and a certificate of occupancy was issued to Rosario Candela for his latest eighteen-story building topped with a penthouse. The critics approved. *The Architectural Forum* praised its "conservative expression of contemporary freedom . . . not at all in a classical or traditional manner."

"Here is a pleasant, simple design, limestone throughout, with the fluted panels of the lower floors and the low-relief vertical and horizontal bands of the shaft ingeniously arranged," wrote the pseudonymous T-Square in *The New Yorker*. "The Park Avenue entrance, trimmed with a beautiful purplish marble, is most attractive. In fact, the whole building has great dignity; one feels that thought and skill have gone into the making of it."

The building and $15,000 in working capital were turned over to its tenant-shareholders on October 8. On the ninth, the *Times* announced the building had opened and published a list of the owners. Aside from the Chase Bank executives and the Brewsters, they were an extraordinary if not terribly diverse group.

Beekman Hoppin was named the co-op's first president, with Lee as his vice president, positions they would hold for a decade. The first purchasers were Frances W. Scoville, the widow of a *Mayflower* descendant whose family's fortune came from railroad car wheels; the Vanderbilt scion J. Watson Webb (described simply as "polo player" in the *Times* announcement that he'd bought a twenty-one-room, nine-bath apartment) and his wife, the former Electra Havemeyer, whose family controlled the Sugar Trust; Mrs. David Carlisle Hanrahan, the wife of a Navy captain and a great-granddaughter of Moses Taylor, one of the wealthiest bankers of the Gilded Age (a niece of hers had just married Ralph Pulitzer Jr., who besides being a grandson of Joseph Pulitzer, the publisher, was also a nephew of J. Watson Webb's); Bertram Harold Borden, whose family produced Lizzie Borden and also owned the Fall River Iron Works and American Printing companies, the latter the world's largest cotton manufacturer and printer; Landon Ketchum Thorne, one of Wall Street's most successful bond dealers, whose family had come to America in the seventeenth century; and William Nelson Davey, who was the least accomplished and pedigreed of the lot, merely the chairman of a large insurance brokerage.

George Brewster's apartment was the most extraordinary and expensive of all—a twenty-three-room double duplex on the fifteenth and sixteenth floors of the building. Because it encompassed both the A and the B apartment lines, the two largest, it ran all along the building's Park Avenue front and around the corner onto Seventy-first Street and had that mezzanine level above the service area of the apartment with seven servants' bedrooms, for a total of ten.

"We had a good many in help," Katharine Whipple says. "A butler and two what they used to call footmen and three in the kitchen, and a parlor maid, a chambermaid, two drivers, laundresses. I don't know where they all came from!" There were thirteen servants in all.

Eleanor Brewster had visited the apartment when it was still raw with a decorator whose name has been lost in time, and decided to panel their new library and furnish the living room and foyers comfortably but elegantly. George Brewster was induced to give up the bear rugs he'd had in his mansion in favor of carpeting. But he had his own breakfast table, where he could eat by himself and read his newspaper. Because it faced east, the apartment was full of light and "very darn big," Whipple says. "The decorating didn't take too long, but my sister, Franny, and I were at school, so we weren't so conscious of what was going on."

In fact, it took longer than expected. The Brewsters moved in before it was finished, and so their two girls, away at Foxcroft, missed the first reported crime at 740 Park Avenue. In the middle of the night on December 8, 1931, just after the Brewsters returned from a performance of *La Traviata* at the Metropolitan Opera, a thief opened a wall safe in the apartment and made off with $75,000 in jewelry: two sapphire-and-diamond bracelets, three sapphire-and-diamond brooches, a diamond ring, and two diamond stickpins. At 7:30 that morning, the family butler, Henry Thurley, was setting the tables where the family ate breakfast when he spotted a red jewelry case on the floor. When he saw it was empty, he had a maid wake Eleanor, who opened her safe in an alcove between the master bedroom and bath and discovered it was empty.

When detectives arrived, they found that the combination dial had been wiped clean of fingerprints, and there were no signs of forced entry. The robbery occurred at the end of a nine-month-long crime spree on Park Avenue, and sixty detectives had been assigned to the neighborhood. Four days after Brewster was robbed, *The New York Times* headlined the arrest of the "Park Av. Gem Thief," an "acrobatic Negro" who'd dressed as a chauffeur in order to enter fancy buildings and steal $500,000 in jewelry. But that thief had nothing to do with the Brewster heist, as police learned a few days later during routine questioning of an assistant who'd been in the apartment hanging curtains for the Brewsters' decorator.

Frederick Potter, seventeen, gangling and badly dressed, confessed almost immediately, saying he'd seen Brewster open the safe after consulting a card in his desk. When his workday ended, Potter hid in a closet, slipped out hours later, checked the card, and popped the safe. Only later, on his way back to his Bronx home—or so he claimed—did he realize what he'd grabbed and panic, wrapping his booty in a newspaper and leaving it with a restaurant owner, claiming it was a Christmas present. The restaurant owner and Potter's half brother, who'd been to prison for burglary, were arrested, too—and most of the jewels were recovered.

Potter pleaded not guilty, then switched to guilty in a courtroom session that included a plea for mercy from Eleanor Brewster. "He is only a boy of 17," she said. "I communicated with his employer and found the boy had a splendid reputation and had worked for him three years." Potter was convicted nonetheless and placed in a reformatory—and the legal system appears to have made the right choice. Two years later, he was in the news again, arrested for attempted extortion after he demanded $200 for the return of documents stolen from a safe in an apartment a few blocks from 740. He later accused the police of giving him "the third degree"—a sound beating—when they arrested him for the felony. "That really is disappointing, isn't it?" says Katharine Whipple. "You make a big effort to make everything go straight and it goes crooked again. I'm still glad [Mother] did it."

Upon their return from Foxcroft, the Brewster girls were wowed by their new digs. "The house had been pretty big, but we'd never seen this before," Whipple says. "My sister and I had a very, very good suite, a bedroom and a bath apiece, and between us we had a very nice sitting room. It was very impressive."

But people like the Brewsters were reserved, they downplayed their importance, they didn't seek to impress. Whipple describes her father as "informed, distinguished-looking, tall for those days, and very, very modest. If you asked him a question, he never gave a quick answer. He would be a little vague, so he wasn't showing off." They rarely entertained, although the children often had friends over and there were regular Sunday lunches. Dinner was served promptly at eight o'clock each night. "We didn't go out to restaurants very much," says Whipple. Aside from the Beekman Hoppins, who came for those Sundays, neighbors rarely visited. And truth be told, the Brewsters were only there from late September until mid-April of every year.

They didn't travel abroad, as many in their set did; after a trip around the world on their honeymoon, George Brewster vowed he would never leave America again—"and he never did," says Whipple. Instead, in the spring, the whole household—and some of the servants—moved en masse to Fairleigh, their summerhouse in Oyster Bay on Long Island, built in 1915. Brewster cousins ran the Brewster Carriage Company, which made horse-drawn carriages and, later, cars. "So we had Brewster cars," says Katharine Whipple, "that were very elegant-looking but couldn't get up hills. I don't know what kind of engines they had. I think there were squirrels in there or something. So we had an old Lincoln and an old Pierce-Arrow to get us back and forth to the country."

The family also went to Jekyll Island, Georgia, for a little more than a month every February. A tiny private island club off the Atlantic coast, founded in 1888, it was known as the resort of the "100 Millionaires"—a hundred members with names like Morgan, Vanderbilt, Rockefeller, Baker, Goodyear, Gould, and Pulitzer, who, it was said, together controlled a sixth of the world's wealth. George Brewster was its vice president.

JAMES T. LEE MIGHT HAVE LIVED ON LILY POND LANE IN EAST HAMPTON, but he was not a member of the Jekyll. Neither was Lee's apartment, also a double duplex encompassing the C and D lines, nearly as extravagant or expensive as Brewster's, the Webbs' penthouse, or even the larger duplexes in the B line. With sixteen rooms, seven of them baths, it was priced at $185,000, making it only the fifth-most-valuable dwelling in the building. Winifred Lee "was the youngest [child] and she lived there with her mother and father," says LeeLee Brown, her daughter. Although she'd sailed to Paris on the day of the stock market crash to attend school for a year, on her return in 1930 nineteen-year-old Winifred came home to the apartment high above Seventy-first Street. "She always talked about the fantastic views," her daughter says.

From the elevator and entry hall, Winifred would have stepped into a spacious marble-floored gallery that opened onto a bedroom and a paneled library. To the right, a marble staircase with a wrought-iron handrail curved up to the sixteenth floor. Just past it, she could see straight through the living room (31 feet x 22 feet) to a sunroom beyond, with views over the steeple of St. James Church to Central Park. Lee's grandson John J. Ryan III, who visited a few times as a boy, remembers the apartment as "immense" and the living room as a ballroom. "The ballroom just boggled me," he says.

South of the living room was a huge terrace and, to the north, a dining room large enough to seat dozens of guests. The service area of the apartment was beyond. It contained a pantry, a kitchen, a large hall, and a maid's room with its own bathroom. One floor up were bedrooms for four more servants, hidden away from the Lees' private quarters, which encompassed another long gallery, a master bedroom with a dressing room, and a second large bedroom with a west-facing terrace and views of the brand-new Empire State Building, thirty-seven blocks to the south. Down a hall were two more bedrooms, with large closets and their own bathrooms.

Despite the presence of the Irishman Lee, there were no Jews in 740, as there were no Jews in most of the better co-ops that lined the west side of Fifth Avenue and the east side of Park Avenue. Jews, no matter how rich, were not welcome, which is how the two buildings just south of 740, its closest neighbors, came to be erected. Jesse Isidor Straus, the Jewish president of R. H. Macy & Co. (and later, U.S. ambassador to France), aware that he couldn't buy into a *good*—i.e., a Jew-free—building, decided like Lee to build his own. He bought a large piece of the Presbyterian Hospital land fronting on Park Avenue between Seventieth and Seventy-first streets and had Candela design a co-op on the southern half of it, topped by the seven-bedroom duplex that Straus occupied. With its terraces, forty-foot foyer, and thousand-square-foot library with a baronial stone fireplace, the Straus home instantly ranked as one of the best apartments in New York when 720 Park opened in mid-1929 just as the excavation for 740 began.

Though several of Straus's descendants deny it, New York real estate aficionados say that even though Straus was Jewish, 720 immediately became the most restrictive (that is, anti-Semitic) co-op in New York. Among the "group of gentlemen who are erecting the building for their own use and that of the few who are so fortunate as to recognize the unusual when they meet it," as an advertisement for the building put it that May, Straus and his wife, Irma, and their daughter, Beatrice Straus Levy, and her family were the only Jews.

The Straus family was also behind the building next door, 730 Park Avenue, which simultaneously opened as a rental, it is said, so that the family's Jewish friends would have somewhere to live.[2] That building would remain a Jewish sanctuary, while 720 remained restrictive into the 1980s. Anti-Semitism, racism, and other restrictive policies in co-ops were commonplace long after Jesse Straus's death in 1936. His grandson Jerry Levy says that when he tried to buy into a co-op on East Seventy-second Street in 1999, "we were turned down because the board felt they already had enough Jews." And a current apartment owner at 720 says that even today, Jews are allowed to buy apartments there "only when someone can't unload one." Compared with those buildings, 740 Park was a progressive bastion—long before the first Jew moved in.

5

In the spring of 1930, the stock market plunged—again—and the worst was *still* to come. That fall, with the economy sinking and unemployment rising, rumors flew that the Bank of the United States, established in Philadelphia in 1791, was failing. On December 7, crowds of depositors clamoring for their money formed outside its branches. Over the next four days, $20 million was withdrawn. On the morning of December 11, the bank shut its doors as mounted policemen kept furious, frustrated customers at bay. The bank's operations were taken over by state officials. The tsunami set off by the failure flattened more banks.

James T. Lee, like most of his fellow developers, started canceling projects. Park Avenue's limestone cliff dwellers were having trouble making their rent and their maintenance payments. Though no one knew it yet, the age of the great luxury apartment had ended. In years to come, the word "prewar" would be invested with market power; prewar—pre–World War II, that is—apartments were quality apartments. But they should correctly be called "pre-crash" apartments, because construction of these buildings slowed considerably with the advent of the Depression and had stopped long before the war began.

"It was a very special moment in time," says the apartment historian

Andrew Alpern. "Coming together were imaginative architects, imaginative builders, a change in lifestyle that made sites available, an economy that made money available, and an optimistic population who enabled it—until this incredible bubble burst and it all stopped in its tracks."

Rosario Candela designed twenty-six apartment buildings in 1929. More than half were never built. Though apartments still sold in recently opened buildings, in 1930 Candela had but two commissions for new ones, in 1931 only one. "Who would build when he could not eat?" the architect would ask. Luckily for Candela, who had been so well paid for so long, he could eat. Steve Candela inherited receipts for major pieces of jewelry his grandfather bought in 1928 and 1929, as well as a number of worthless stock certificates. "I think that's where his money went," he says. "He suffered the loss of half a million to a million dollars," agrees Candela's daughter-in-law Gertrude. His granddaughter Patricia MacLeod jokes, "If Rosario had left us just one apartment, we'd all be better off."

The work picked up again eventually. "He never lost money except in 1933," says Steven, "and he was able to continue until the war" designing private houses, theaters, New York's Fort Greene Houses, and smaller apartment buildings. But his heyday as a luxury-apartment architect was behind him. "His career waned because he couldn't build the way he wanted to and he was unwilling to cheapen up." Luckily, Candela's native abilities helped him find ways of keeping busy. He'd always loved puzzles, and he had a secretive streak. "My uncle told me he never signed his name the same way twice, for some idiosyncratic reason," says Patricia MacLeod.

Between jobs, Candela loved to read, and in the midst of the Depression he happened to pick up *The American Black Chamber*, a classic work on cryptography by Herbert Yardley, who headed the Army's code-breaking effort in World War I, and found himself intrigued. Cryptography and architecture had crossed before; Leon Battista Alberti, a fifteenth-century architect, was a pioneer of ciphers. Both fields dealt with mathematics, spatial relationships, and elaborate puzzles. Candela "credited the crash for his interest in cryptography," says MacLeod. "He wouldn't have had the time otherwise."

"He was a student, an intellectual," says his daughter-in-law Gertrude. "He was a perfectionist who pursued things prodigiously. He spent hours." When Candela broke some previously unsolved cryptograms, "the first thing I knew *I* was the great expert," he recalled for *The New Yorker* in 1943, in the staccato Italian-accented voice his students loved. At the time, he was teaching night classes in cryptology at Hunter College and heading the New York Cipher Society, where he went by the code name Iskander. Though it's been written that Candela cracked the Japanese military's codes during World War II, experts on cryptography dispute that. He did help set up and briefly worked for a secret counterintelligence unit in the research and analysis branch of the Office of Strategic Services called FBQ—the letters stand for Foreign Broadcast Quarterly—charged with intercepting and interpreting foreign codes and ciphers, but it was shut down in October 1942 due to interagency rivalries. Candela, says David Shulman, one of his students, was left frustrated; he was on the verge of breaking Italian military codes.'

Regardless, after the war, the indefatigable Candela kept going full speed, writing a third book, a massive study of cryptography, but finally his work was cut short. Overweight, suffering heart problems and the ill effects of a three-pack-a-day cigarette habit—he smoked Lucky Strikes—Candela died of a heart attack in 1953 at age sixty-three. Two days after his death, one of his daughters-in-law recalled, several CIA agents appeared at his Westchester home, cordoned off his top-floor studio, and took all his papers, which his family never saw again. Nor have living members of his family been able to see his best work, even though in the 1980s the rising prices of New York's finest apartments made Candela's name, previously unknown, into a designer brand. Steve Candela has repeatedly tried to visit 740 Park Avenue—to no avail. "Every time I go, I get thrown out," he says. But Candela understands. "The tenants there are pretty illustrious."

THEY ALWAYS WERE. GERARD BEEKMAN HOPPIN AND BAYARD CUSHING HOPPIN were, like the Brewsters, colonial-era aristocrats, descended from Wilhelmus Beekman, who came to New Amsterdam from Holland with

Peter Stuyvesant in 1647. A son, Gerardus, doctor and landowner, owned two farms downtown and a third bounded by the East River and Second Avenue, Forty-ninth and Sixty-first streets. Beekmans became New York politicians and intermarried with the wealthy and equally distinguished Livingstons, Fishes, and De Peysters.

The Beekman manor house on the East River at Fiftieth Street was seized by the British and used for the sentencing and execution of the Revolutionary War hero Nathan Hale. Some of the land remains in the family's possession today, though the 109-year-old mansion was demolished in 1874 to make way for Beekman Place.

Gerard, who was called Beek, was born in New York in 1870, his brother Bayard in Oyster Bay in 1888. Both graduated from Yale and worked on Wall Street, and together they ran the Beekman Estate, the corporation that held the family's properties. Beekman "was a nice little man, terribly polite, and really pretty good fun," says Katharine Whipple. "He was about as upright as you can get," adds Frederick Hoppin, a great-nephew. "He was a man of integrity. It oozed out from him."

Though Beek had contracted polio as a child, which left one leg shorter than the other, family legend has it that he was one of Theodore Roosevelt's Rough Riders in the Spanish-American War, then commanded an infantry company during World War I, where, the legend says, he was wounded or gassed but survived to ride a white horse in the Fifth Avenue victory parade in March 1919. "He was always at the front, a plucky, pugnacious guy, small in stature but very confident, a real leader," says a lineal descendant who asks to remain anonymous; the family has always avoided publicity.

Though Bayard Hoppin attended Groton, the famous Episcopal preparatory school, under the legendary educator Reverend Endicott Peabody, though he rowed crew at Yale and was an Army captain in World War I, he was a disappointment to his family. After the war, he and Beek co-founded Abbott, Hoppin & Co., a New York Stock Exchange brokerage. But Bayard lost his fortune in the crash of 1929, whereas Beek got his money out in time. "Bayard lost a bundle," says the relative. "He was pretty much wiped out."

Bayard's wife, Helen Lispenard Alexandre, the granddaughter of a Civil War general, inherited more than half a million dollars in 1930, but their marriage was troubled. In the spring of 1932, they disagreed over whether to adopt a child: Bayard was for it, Helen against. That October, Helen Hoppin sublet the apartment to William Hale Harkness, the Murray, Aldrich & Webb lawyer and Standard Oil heir. By the time he and Helen divorced a few years later, Bayard was living in a rental.

Beek sold his seat on the stock exchange and retired just before a three-year-old crime involving the Hoppins' brokerage was solved in San Francisco. Though no connection was made at the time, it was the only wrinkle in the brothers' otherwise seamless existence. In July 1929, nineteen hundred shares of stock in a company called American Superpower, worth $130,000, disappeared while en route to Abbott, Hoppin & Co. Curiously, American Superpower's co-founder Landon Ketchum Thorne was another of the original apartment owners at 740 Park; along with Bayard Hoppin, he'd helped found a new golf course in Islip, Long Island, near their respective country homes. All but one hundred of the Superpower shares were returned anonymously a few days later. But it wasn't until August 1932 that the remaining shares turned up in San Francisco—where local police launched an investigation, the results of which have been lost to history. Two years after that, Abbott, Hoppin closed; the Hoppins and one of their former partners opened Hoppin Brothers & Co., while twelve other partners split off and formed a firm of their own.

"Beek came out of retirement to give his brother a job," says their relative. "He was always rescuing people. Bayard was not as smart and capable as Beek was." Not as rich, either. Beek, too, had married well, though much later than his brother; his engagement to Rosina Sherman Hoyt, who was fifty, was announced in 1924, when he was fifty-four. The Hoyts were another old, hugely wealthy family; Rosina was a grandniece of the Civil War general William Tecumseh Sherman. "She was at the very pinnacle of society," says Michael Barker, a family historian. "She would have thought Mrs. Astor a parvenu." Rosina's wedding to Beek was one of the significant social events of the season, "being a union of families for many generations associated with the history of New York and the United States," said The New York Times.

The bride's parents were patrons of the arts who lived in an Italianate palace in Southampton designed by Stanford White, whose firm built

998 Fifth for Lee. Rosina's mother brought William Merritt Chase to nearby Shinnecock, where he established the Shinnecock Summer Art School in 1891. Two decades later, Rosina hired Grosvenor Atterbury, an associate of White's, to renovate an old storage building on acreage owned by her family in Montauk at the eastern tip of Long Island and turn it into a house. Published reports claim the still-unmarried Rosina, an amateur poet, used the building, known as the Stone House, for romantic trysts. Local gossip embellishes these tales. "She didn't get on with her family," says Anthony Ingrao, who bought the Stone House in 1987. "She had a love interest that was unacceptable. She was supposedly a lesbian."

"Completely ridiculous," scoffs Barker. "She didn't have a poetic bone in her body. But she was the sort of woman who did what she wanted when she wanted to do it. She was quite a lot like Elizabeth Sherman Cameron, her first cousin once removed." Cameron, a Washington hostess unhappily married to a hard-drinking millionaire senator from Pennsylvania, carried on a decades-long flirtation with the author Henry Adams.

Rosina "was very good-looking and formidable, an independent woman who followed her own passions and who was rich enough and perhaps narcissistic enough to insulate herself against the consequences of poor judgment in her personal relationships," Barker says. "I suppose that sort of behavior could be interpreted any number of ways. She may have entertained lady friends out there, but it's just rumor. We all assume from family anecdotes that Beekman carried a torch of sorts for her for many years."

Rosina's fortune—she'd inherited $960,000 from her parents ($19.2 million in 2004 dollars)—would have insulated her and her husband quite well from the vicissitudes of the economy. "I tend to think she paid for everything," Barker says—including a forty-five-acre estate, Four Winds, with a Georgian house surrounded by statue-filled gardens in Oyster Bay Cove, Long Island. When they were there, Beek would commute to Wall Street by boat; a butler on board served drinks.

"If they were ever hurting," says the relative, "it didn't show."

The Beekman Hoppins stayed at 740 until 1942. Their apartment, 10/11D, was "magnificent," says the relative, who attended a magic show there every Christmas along with three dozen other cousins. "They were friends of Saint-Gaudens and had a lot of his bronzes, a lot of paintings, terrific furniture, beautiful Oriental rugs, an awful lot of stuff." Since neither brother had children, much of it ended up with Michael Barker and his wife, another Rosina, after Beek died at eighty in 1950. Bayard followed in 1956. Rosina Hoppin lived on in another Candela building, just around the corner at 19 East Seventy-second Street, and in their estate in Oyster Bay until she died at ninety-one. Hoyt women are renowned for their longevity.

All survived long enough to shepherd another relative into 71 East Seventy-first Street. E. Farrar Bateson Jr. and his wife, Rosina Hoyt Otis, Rosina Hoppin's niece, took an apartment there in 1945. Relatives are sure the Hoppins had a hand in that move. "The Hoppins are very tribal," says Barker, whose wife is one of the Batesons' five children. "She wears a ring Beekman gave his Rosina after their thirty-year courtship, with three enormous diamonds. Her sister said that was one rock for every decade she kept him waiting."

THE HOPPINS MAY HAVE GOTTEN TO 740 PARK FIRST, BUT ANOTHER FAMily has the claim to being the oldest Americans in the building, beating even the Brewsters. In 1943, applying for admittance to the National Society of the Colonial Dames in the State of New York, Edith Scoville traced her ancestry back to Richard Warren, a passenger on the *Mayflower*'s first trip to America in 1620. Warren was the twelfth signer of the Mayflower Compact and a founder of Plymouth, Massachusetts. One of his descendants married a Scoville in 1783 in Salisbury, Connecticut, a Dutch town where the family were among the earliest settlers. Scovilles were farmers, politicians, and owners of one of the famous local pig-iron mines.

In 1860, Nathaniel Church Scoville and a brother moved to Buffalo, where they opened a foundry making railcar wheels and made a fortune that allowed Nathaniel to return to Salisbury in 1880 and augment their family's property, ending up with a thousand acres.[2] Scoville died in 1890, at fifty-eight, leaving behind his wife, Frances, two sons, and four daughters. In 1905, Frances bought a six-story marble-and-limestone mansion, complete with elevator, on Fifty-second Street just off Fifth Avenue and lived there for twenty-four years as all but two of her children, Grace and Edith, married and began their own lives. A month after Black Tuesday, she sold their house for cash and invested the proceeds in apartment 4/5B at 740.

Though their family was famous in Salisbury, where they gave the town its library and its town hall, the Scovilles were only quietly known in New York, where they made donations and attended benefits with the likes of Albert Wiggin, the Hoyts, Harrimans, Carnegies, Roosevelts, Auchinclosses, Warburgs, and Pratts. Edith was a music lover. Grace helped the needy. Their two brothers, one a stockbroker, the other a lawyer, both died in the 1930s. Their mother followed in 1944, and the next year the two girls moved to a smaller apartment, 8/9C, at 71 East Seventy-first Street. Grace died in 1959. Edith sold their apartment the following year and moved to 570 Park, where she lived until 1970, when she, too, died, at eighty-nine.

"In those days, there were many more maiden ladies," says Ann Scoville, one of the last Scovilles in Salisbury. "I did hear about one person Grace might have married . . . but the family discouraged it."

MARY TAYLOR MOULTON HANRAHAN BOUGHT THE D-LINE TRIPLEX maisonette in October 1930. She, like the Scoville sisters, was "very proper," says Lynn Royden of her great-aunt. "She'd scare the wallpaper off a wall."

An Anglophile and collector of English porcelains, Mary Hanrahan always wore a hat and gloves and loved gardenias and angel food cake. The wife of Captain David Carlisle Hanrahan, USN, the commander of the USS *Omaha*, she was the great-granddaughter of Moses Taylor, who started his career as a sugar broker, became the first president of the National City Bank, and owned a controlling interest in the Delaware, Lackawanna & Western Railroad and its affiliated coal and iron company.

When Taylor died in 1882, he left $40 million (about $702 million today). When Mary got her share on the death of her mother in 1925, the fortune was smaller but still considerable. She was named a co-executor of the estate, along with a brother and the Rockefellers' Equitable Trust bank. Less than half a year later, she married Hanrahan in a surprise ceremony that lacked bridal attendants, a best man, or ushers at her new fourteen-room apartment at 510 Park Avenue.

Both the bride and the groom had been active in World War I, she organizing relief efforts, he commanding a bombing squadron in France and the steamer *Santee*, which was torpedoed off Ireland in 1917. After the war, Hanrahan was the port officer at Danzig, where relief supplies entered Poland, and later the naval attaché in Warsaw. After running a department that sold off captured German cargo ships, he returned to active duty in 1923 and was given command of the newly commissioned USS *Omaha*, a light cruiser. He retired just before their wedding.

Taylor relatives owned châteaus in Europe and were social figures in Newport and Palm Beach, prone to hosting elaborate parties with hundreds of guests. But like the Scovilles, the Hanrahans were quiet sorts who rarely rippled society's surface. Hanrahan, a sportsman, loved England as much as his wife did, went grouse shooting with the royal family in Scotland, and treasured the set of Purdy shotguns he'd been given when he retired from the Navy.

Recalled to active service in 1941, he was named commandant of the Iowa Navy Pre-flight School in Iowa City, and the couple left 740 to move there in 1942. Mary Hanrahan spent the war knitting sweaters for British sailors. Her husband died in Iowa in 1944 at sixty-eight, and she returned to New York, where she died in 1953.

"She was the oldest thing I'd seen in my life, dressed in black lace," says her nephew Lloyd Aspinwall III, who met her before she died. "One of the few women my mother was afraid of, and she wasn't afraid of much."

THE SHERBURN MERRILL BECKERS, SENIOR AND JUNIOR, TOOK TWO apartments, the B-line maisonette and 12/13C, in March 1931. The elder Mrs. Becker was from the colonial family that gave its name to Garrison-on-Hudson, New York. Descended from a soldier in the Continental army and Thomas Danforth, a colonial official in Massachusetts, the Beckers, from Wisconsin, worked in railroads, ran a shipping insurance company, and ended up in banking.

Known as the Boy Mayor of Milwaukee, Sherburn senior was renowned for fighting corruption after his election in 1906 at age twenty-six. "He liked going to fires," says his granddaughter-in-law Marion Becker, so he had an alarm installed in his bedroom. "He rigged a carriage in his house so harnesses could be dropped on his horses, which his wife did not appreciate very much." Becker Sr., who was called Sherb, had come to New York in 1908 to join a brokerage house. In 1924, he was running it when he bought a four-story house on East Sixty-first Street, on the edge of the former Beekman estate. He also owned a home called Windlyn in Southampton. Three years later, his son was named captain of the Princeton varsity crew team, right after the family returned from Europe on the *Île de France*. Not shabby.

A year later, fresh out of college and set to join the family firm, Sherburn junior, known as Sherbie, married Mildred Barclay Vander Poel, the daughter of S. Oakley Vander Poel, a descendant of early settlers of Albany, like the Schuylers and Ten Eycks. That was on her father's side. On her mother's, she descended from the first rector of the seventeenth-century Trinity Church in lower Manhattan, where John Jay and Alexander Hamilton worshipped.

Mildred's mother had been one of the Barclay sisters, a Gilded Age version of the twenty-first century's Hilton sisters. "My mother-in-law came out in 1926, and in those days New York society was a very restricted kind of thing, so of course she knew Black Jack Bouvier and Janet," says Marion Becker. "Nelson Rockefeller wasn't a beau, but he was her escort at deb parties. What I'm saying is, they all knew each other."

Sherbie met Millie on board an ocean liner en route to France. "He was terribly glamorous," says Becker. "He had a raccoon coat and drove a Duesenberg." Their full choral wedding at St. Thomas Church featured selections from *Lohengrin* and a bride wearing a cap of antique lace and a cream satin gown with three bustle ruffles covered with a veil of tulle on its long round train. A thousand guests attended. Millie was three months pregnant.

After a four-month cruise in the Mediterranean, with visits to King Tut's just-excavated tomb in Egypt and to Damascus, Syria, the couple were to return to a house on East Sixty-third Street. But before they'd even reached Europe, Sherb's father, the Milwaukee banker Washington Becker, died, leaving his son $7 million. A few months later, in March 1931, father and son took their luxurious new apartments at 740, the former, the Park Avenue maisonette, the latter, a Seventy-first Street duplex, just in time for the arrival of Sherburn III, who was born that fall. "Sherb wanted the dynasty to continue," says Marion Becker.

The Beckers did not want for anything; they waited until 1933 to sell their former home to Allen Dulles, the future CIA director. They kept the carriage house next door for their driver, who was called Mortling.

Sherb's brokerage ended up "merging" out of existence, just like the Hoppin brothers' Abbott, Hoppin & Co. In 1936, it was swallowed up by Fahnestock & Co.,[3] and a year later Sherb retired. In 1937, Sherbie and Millie moved to 521 Park Avenue. In 1939, the elder Beckers left 740, too, for a smaller duplex at Candela's 19 East Seventy-second Street, the building where 740 people go to downsize. The day Pearl Harbor was bombed by the Japanese, Sherbie left a baseball game to enlist. He was made chief intelligence officer on the USS *Ticonderoga*. Sherb died in 1949, Sherbie in 1993, tragically, seven years after *his* son, Sherburn III. Mildred Becker followed in 1995.

Marion Becker and Lynn Royden, Mary Taylor Moulton Hanrahan's niece, both think it was no accident that their relatives lived in James T. Lee's building. The Moses Taylor trusts had moved to the Chase when it merged with Equitable. And the Becker family trusts were there, too. "Everybody banked with the Chase," says Royden. "Everybody still banks with the Chase. They were the friendly family bankers. Every family had someone who'd taken care of them forever. The money is still there—what's left of it."

"Oh yes, it was all Chase," says Marion Becker. "It's a very small world. It's like a passport, like the Mafia. They all knew each other. Sherbie heard through somebody or other that Jimmy Lee was doing this building. My guess is, somebody said, *'Have I got a deal for you.'*"

6

THE WORLD THAT WAS ONCE 740 PARK'S REMAINS A SMALL ONE, AND now it is secluded but very much still there. Marion Becker lives in Rumson, New Jersey, where another of the Beckers' 740 neighbors, Bertram Harold Borden, had his principal residence, a twenty-two-room house on six acres with its own deepwater dock on the Navesink River. His fourteen-room apartment at 71 East Seventy-first Street, 4/5C, was just a city pied-à-terre. "He could have known the Chase people," says a second cousin, Linda McKean. "They all traveled in the same circles."

The Bordens arrived in America in 1635. John Borden, born in Portsmouth, Rhode Island, in 1640, began acquiring land in New Jersey, Pennsylvania, and Delaware. His son Richard and a brother bought a mill stream and its water rights in Fall River, Massachusetts, and built a large lumber and grist mill. It was seized by the British during the Revolution, and another, later, Richard Borden was taken prisoner, but he survived and reclaimed his land, which passed to Bertram Borden's grandfather, who called himself Colonel Richard Borden. The colonel sold his rights to the stream and invested the profits in a cotton mill and a blacksmith shop, which became the Fall River Iron Works, which threw off more profits, which he invested in more cotton mills and cotton printing plants, steamboat and railroad lines, water and gas companies, a coal mine, and banks.

The colonel's fifth son, Matthew Chaloner Durfee Borden, attended Phillips Academy Andover and Yale, before moving to New York City and greatly expanding the family businesses, helped in no small part by a contact made at Yale. His roommate there had gone on to become an adviser to the Rockefeller family.

Matthew Borden left control of his companies to his eldest, Bertram, on his death in 1912, along with a quarter of his fortune, estimated at $8 million (and including $1 million worth of old master paintings). Father and son had been next-door neighbors on West Fifty-sixth Street off Fifth Avenue.

Borden touched all the bases: he served as a director of the Manhattan Bank, married the granddaughter of one of the founders of Brooks Brothers in 1896, and, according to the 1916 *Encyclopedia of Biography*, was "a staunch Republican" who gave his time "solely to his business" and was "quiet and dignified in manner and upholds the best New England traditions," carrying "well the large responsibilities of the business interests he represents." Paul Birdsall, who married a niece, agrees. "He was a gentleman of the old school. He wasn't particularly bluff or boisterous, though he was used to having his own way." Linda McKean remembers him as "a marvelous creature," round-faced and cheerful, but also all business. "He and my grandfather ran the company," she says. "They didn't do anything else."

In 1918, Bertram inherited another $1 million from his father, who'd disapproved of his son Matthew's marriage and prohibited Matthew's wife and children from sharing in his estate. When Matthew died, Bertram and his remaining brother split the extra fortune. Bertram spent some of the proceeds on a yacht, *Oriole*, which he raced, and another $84,000 on his new city apartment. Borden didn't really need the city apartment; he, like Beekman Hoppin, was one of the city's most-privileged elite, who commuted to their jobs on Wall Street aboard private boats. In the summer of 1930, when most New Yorkers were worrying about where their next meal was coming from, Borden and his wife were just back from a world cruise when he and his ilk were written up in a *New York Times* article headlined COMMUTATION DE LUXE DEVELOPS FOR THE WEALTHY:

> There is no more picturesquely busy place
> on the Island of Manhattan than the New
> York Yacht Club between the hours of 9
> and 10, on a clear morning. Through the
> Sound and down the East River glides a
> jaunty procession of sleek boats, all more
> or less of a size, dapper in their coats of
> polished wood . . . The roar of the city rises
> to greet the slim craft. Briskly, the sun-
> bronzed men and women (the latter in the
> minority) cross the gangplank and the
> landing, making their way to automobiles
> and taxis. The masculine contingent is
> ready for the first news the ticker tape
> may bring.
>
> Commutation de luxe has become an art.
> The business man times his trip to town
> with precision . . . A few men stride across
> their lawns to their private docks, bathrobe
> fluttering about their shins with the noncha-
> lance of a Roman senator's toga. On board
> efficient valets have laid everything in readi-
> ness, and in the galley there is the sound of
> rattling plates and clinking silver . . .
>
> Cabins and salons are furnished in good
> taste. Wood paneling is carefully chosen;
> colorful sun-fast fabrics are made into
> curtains to frame the panorama of blue
> water and green shores. Wicker furniture
> for decks and upholstered cabin chairs are
> as carefully selected as if they were to
> grace the sun room of a Fifth Avenue
> apartment . . .
>
> To name those who use the New York

Yacht Club in the Summer months would
be to skim the Social Register, picking out
the captains of industry. Among the most
ardent commuters are . . . Mr. [George]
Baker, whose Little Viking is well known
on the Sound, J. P. Morgan's Navette . . .
Bertram Borden's Alida . . . Otto H. Kahn's
Oheka II, and dozens of others in the same
class.

The Depression was happening elsewhere. "He wouldn't have noticed," says Borden's grandniece. But that didn't insulate the residents of
740 Park from the outrageous exigencies of fortune. There were some
problems money couldn't solve. In July 1933, Borden's *Oriole* was dis-
masted in a strong wind while leading the first point race of the Rumson season. The Bordens promptly took off for Europe. But three months
later, a few weeks after their return, Mary Owen Borden checked into the
hospital and died, aged sixty-two, from complications of acute appendicitis. She left her husband more than $2 million, and $2,500 to Alma An-
derson, one of her maids ($35,000 today).

Bertram Borden soon left 740 Park Avenue, moving to Rumson full-
time and subletting his apartment to Harriet Schermerhorn, the daughter of the inventor of the Pullman railroad car and widow of a scion of
an old Knickerbocker family. Borden died childless at age eighty-seven in
May 1956 and left his fortune to a foundation he established in his late
wife's name.

TOWERING OVER EVERYONE AT 740 PARK WERE THE J. WATSON WEBBS.
Unsatisfied with the mere duplex penthouse Rosario Candela planned
for the building, the Webbs added a third floor—even though there were
several triplex Candela penthouses already for sale on Park Avenue. They
wanted one built just for them.

The Webbs weren't rich; they were dynastic. Webb's mother was a
granddaughter of Cornelius Vanderbilt. His family had been in America
for eight generations when the Commodore, as he was known, made his

fortune, but despite his colonial roots, he was deemed too vulgar for society. Lila Webb was the youngest daughter of the Commodore's eldest son, William Henry, who inherited his father's steamship and railroad fortune—the largest cash stash in the world—and promptly doubled it.

Like his father, William Henry could cock a snoot at society. His famous quip, "The public be damned!" permanently stained his reputation, even though it was likely taken out of context. He didn't need to care. He had more money than the cash reserves of the United States. Lila and her siblings each inherited huge, untouchable trust funds in addition to another $10 million they could squander as they chose. They were the first Vanderbilts in society and built palaces appropriate to their position. Their decadence and diminishment were a public spectacle. James Watson Webb's father, Dr. William Seward Webb, lived a private version.

The Webbs were a colonial family; their grandfather General Sam Webb led the minutemen up Bunker Hill and held the Bible when George Washington was sworn in as president. Seward Webb gave up a career in medicine at his father-in-law's urging to become the president of a private railroad car company owned by Vanderbilt, and later a railroad financier in competition with the Vanderbilts. Gentlemen were not doctors, so he became a gentleman and lived the life. His son Watson grew up between their mansion at 680 Fifth Avenue—built by Lila's father—and a fifteen-hundred-acre farm on the shores of Lake Champlain in Vermont, where Seward Webb dreamed of running America's greatest horse-breeding operation.

Shelburne Farms was country life at the pinnacle: a 110-room house, a 117-foot steam yacht, an immense horse barn and stud farm, and the country's first private golf course. The family was served meals in a marble dining room by six liveried footmen and a steward hired away from Blenheim Castle. They entertained dozens at a time, importing a private social life that, unlike the balls of New York, never made the newspapers. Admiral Dewey, Teddy Roosevelt, Jack Astor, and the Duke of Marlborough all visited as Watson grew up. And when they weren't at one of their homes, the Webbs were traveling in private railcars. In 1893, the whole family, two nurses, a piano, and a pack of friends boarded a private six-car train for a nine-week twelve-thousand-mile trip across America,

Mexico, and Canada. Tracks were cleared ahead and behind so they could travel at top speed and stop when they pleased.

At the dawn of the twentieth century, spade-bearded Seward suffered a series of business reverses—his horsey hopes were dashed by the automobile. He developed devastating migraine headaches, staved them off with morphine, and became a respectable junkie. Seward took to bed, attended by a doctor and his valet. All through Watson's young adulthood, his mother kept up a facade of respectability while his father dwelled in twilight, emerging impeccably tailored to go to dinner parties or ride around in a carriage. Seward remained in his netherworld until his death in 1926. His three sons burned his stash of opiates.

Dr. Webb's addiction left the family financially pinched. Luckily, then, Watson's wife, Electra Havemeyer, was from a family less well known but somewhat more solvent. The Havemeyers had come to America in the late eighteenth century and started a bakery. Eighty years later, Henry O. Havemeyer created the Sugar Trust, consolidating the business to control prices and costs. The Havemeyers kept the government from regulating their monopoly until 1922, fifteen years after Havemeyer's death, and even then, the family dominated sugar for years.

Henry Havemeyer's second wife was Louisine Waldron Elder, whose family had raised him after his own mother's death. The niece of his first wife, Louisine was from a sugar-refining family, too, and was raised in a world of connoisseurship. A lifelong friend of the painter Mary Cassatt and a supporter of women's suffrage once jailed for picketing the White House, Louisine started collecting art in Paris before she was twenty and made her first purchases from Edgar Degas and Claude Monet. When she married her late aunt's husband, he became interested, too, and the resulting collection—including sixty-five works by Degas, thirty Monets, seventeen Cassatts, forty-one Courbets, twenty-five Manets, and thirteen Cézannes, as well as canvases by El Greco, Ingres, Renoir, Daumier, Corot, Rembrandt, and other old masters—was incomparable. Asked once why she bought paintings, Louisine eyed the questioner's jewels and said, "I prefer something made by a man to something made by an oyster."

The Havemeyers spent summers in the same Long Island social circle as the Thornes and the Hoppins. Their daughter Electra was born on

the Great South Bay in 1888. She inherited her mother's passion for collecting and many of her paintings (the rest, two thousand artworks in all,
went to the Metropolitan Museum of Art). But Electra preferred folk art;
her first purchase, at eighteen, may have been a Goya of a child with a
flower, but her second was a cigar-store Indian.

In 1910, she married J. Watson Webb, a handsome, six-foot three-inch
family friend and Yale graduate. Webb had spent a year working as a
railroad clerk after college. Back home in the fall of 1909, he spoke to a
reporter—from the comfort of his private railroad car—of the "tough
work" he'd done.

"I know how to lay a track, how to make a flying switch and a thousand and one other things," he said. "The men with whom I worked
were princes. They didn't know who I was and they took me right in for
my own sake and were calling me by my first name in a week. Just as
men to men they have no superiors on earth. Their word is their bond.
Furthermore, their life is simpler. They do not get divorces every few
months." Electra must have been glad to read that. They were affianced
two months later in what the *Times* described as "one of the most interesting engagements of the year." They spent their honeymoon foxhunting in England.

After a year in Chicago, where he continued his railroad apprentice-
ship for $75 a month, Webb returned to New York and joined Marsh &
McLennan, the insurance brokers. After a stint in France as an Army
captain in World War I (Electra drove ambulances on the home front), he
spent his career in insurance but was far better known as a polo player.
The only left-handed ten-goal player in polo history (ten goals is the
maximum handicap), he'd started playing in 1904, before southpaws
were banned. Webb was known for hitting hard and true and won the
U.S. Open six times; he played against England on the 1921, 1924, and
1927 world championship teams, known as the Big Four, and quit the
sport in 1927 at forty-two.[1]

In the next twenty years, the Webbs had five children and accumu-
lated that many residences. Shortly after her son's marriage, Watson's
mother sold her Fifth Avenue mansion to John D. Rockefeller Sr. for $1
million and became one of the society types moving into Park Avenue
apartments—a rental. At the same time, the J. Watson Webbs moved to

Long Island, ending up in Old Westbury, the center of the Long Island polo scene, in "a typical New England white frame farmhouse," according to their grandson Sam junior. "Typical" may not be the word for the sixty-five-room house with a swimming pool, a skeet range, and a garden of flowers and privet hedges behind it, all tended by an English gardener, Pete Connor. Past a pinewoods and grape arbor was an indoor tennis court that was used as a set for the Humphrey Bogart–Audrey Hepburn movie *Sabrina*. And then there were the stables and outbuildings and cottages and a farm where they raised chicken, sheep, cattle, and horses and produced fresh milk, cream, and butter. A chauffeur would drive dairy into Manhattan daily.

There, the Webbs lived first at Sixty-sixth Street and Fifth Avenue in a house connected by a tunnel to Louisine Havemeyer's on one side and adjoining the house of Electra's brother Horace on the other. They also owned a second country home in Vermont, where they'd taken over and renovated an unoccupied Georgian brick farmhouse on the five-thousand-acre Webb estate in Shelburne. The Brick House sat on Lake Champlain and had a majestic view across the water to the Adirondack Mountains. The elder Webbs had wrapped it in a thousand acres and given it to their son and daughter-in-law as a wedding present. It included Seward's breeding barn, his pride and joy and for forty years the largest unsupported indoor space in America.

When Electra's mother died in January 1929, Watson and Electra decided not to take over her New York mansion. "It was too big," said their grandson Sam Webb Jr. "They wanted their own place." They could afford it. Electra had already inherited $4 million and a third of her father's trust fund upon his death twenty years earlier. Now a third of her mother's fortune, less only what the Metropolitan Museum of Art's director described as "the most magnificent gifts of works of art ever made by an individual to a museum," would be added to that pile. A few months later, the Havemeyer children leased the site of their three contiguous Fifth Avenue mansions to a co-op syndicate for $25 million—a third of it Electra's. But even before that, the Webbs took the plunge and bought an apartment.

They began looking in the winter of 1929 and by the spring had bought the sprawling twenty-one-room, nine-bath penthouse at 740

Park. They moved into a suite in the Hotel Delmonico (redecorated to the tune of almost $10,000) to use as a pied-à-terre until their palace in the sky was ready for occupancy. That would take about two years. At almost the same time, Watson joined an insurance firm owned and run by S. Oakley Vander Poel, the father-in-law of 740 Park's Sherburn Becker Jr. "Nothing is a coincidence," says Marion Becker, who married Sherburn junior's son.

WATSON'S KIDS CALLED HIM "L&M" FOR LEAN AND MEAN. "HE WAS A cool customer, a pretty distant guy, very much a product of that period," says John Foreman, who befriended him while writing a book about the Vanderbilt family. Electra was "warm and accessible and lovely," but also fearless, a necessary trait for dealing with her elegant but aloof husband. She could keep up with him; she would often go hunting alone, staying out all night with no company but a guide. She was so proficient a hunter that once she'd gutted a deer with a can opener. Clambering over the steel beams of their penthouse in-process—which they'd bought as a shell—struck her as a walk in the park. Her son didn't feel that way when she took him with her to decide where an antique paneled room her decorator had found would go within; it was going to be custom-built so the disassembled panels would fit perfectly.

"Most of the memory is fear, going up in that elevator that the workmen worked on," Watson junior said. "They carried the cement up on it. There were no outside walls yet on the building. And you were just going up on the steel girders. They said, you cannot change any outside walls, but you can change any inside walls in any way that you want them." The rooms had to be built to fit the paneling. "And so she went. I just remember being quite scared. I might have been fourteen. But even so, eighteen floors and no outside walls, and it was kind of scary. You couldn't walk around a great deal. It just would have been too dangerous. But you know, she could talk her way into anything, particularly back in those days."

Existing records indicate the apartment was her project, not her husband's, and it's likely, given the state of their finances, that she paid for it, too. Watson also left her in charge of creating the place. Well aware she couldn't decorate a New York penthouse with the arts-and-crafts gewgaws and bits of Americana she so loved and sprinkled around her country homes, Electra hired the Schmitt brothers, George and Charles, Madison Avenue decorators and dealers of English antiques, to do the place with her.

"She went to Europe—and also had her antique people go to Europe," Sam Webb Jr. recalled. "She had about four or five art dealers who did nothing but go to auctions for her and look at things and present them in terms of whether or not she'd be interested in acquiring them. Most of the time, she did." The Schmitts were teachers and Electra their student. They taught her that English pine paneling was superior to American because the knots in the wood were smaller. So the Webbs paid $28,500 for two rooms' worth of old pine paneling, one from Redcliffe Parade in Bristol, England, and a second from Cocken Hall in County Durham.

"I didn't know enough then," Electra would tell her son Watson junior, who added, "She was a hell of a pupil."

The great bulk of the apartment was on the eighteenth floor, where the elevator opened into a foyer floored with green marble taken from the old Havemeyer mansion. Downstairs, there were two bedrooms, two baths, and a sitting room—which they'd annexed from the seventeenth-floor apartment below the original Candela penthouse. Up a steep circular staircase were two more bedrooms and bathrooms, a sewing and ironing room, and a roof terrace. On the main floor were the public rooms, the Webbs' bedrooms and bathrooms, another couple of bedrooms, and the servants' quarters. The Webbs had also bought four servants' rooms on the first floor of the building.

The Schmitts' first decorating estimate was enormous, and the costs escalated as work proceeded. The Webbs changed their mind about paint colors, and then added touches like eighteenth-century balusters, marbleized bathroom fixtures, extra closets, a makeup table and pink-glass medicine cabinets for Electra, special towel bars in the powder rooms, and bordered linoleum tile in the servants' quarters.

Their daughter Lila's room and a room for her governess, Mademoiselle, on the seventeenth floor cost over $4,000 and featured paneled doors, antique wallpaper, and decorative painting. The hallway leading to it, with a carved frieze and antique pewter and glass lights over the doorways, was $2,600. More antique wallpaper went into the vestibule on the eighteenth floor, which led to the green-marble gallery through carved and painted antique doorways, with similar antique pilasters and skirting beyond (another $7,000). Directly ahead was the thirty-four-by-twenty-foot living room, which sat on the corner of Park and Seventy-first Street. All white, it contained a piano, several seating groups, and lots of paintings.

Next door, with a view over Park Avenue, the library boasted antique leather walls removed from the Havemeyer mansion, renovated with canvas backing, patched, and remounted with the original brass nails ($1,300); ebonized holly trim; secret cupboards; elaborate-shaped bookcases topped with arches; a marble mantel and hearth; and suitably masculine pilasters, cornices, and hardware ($6,900). Initially, the columns were faux-painted to match the marble in the gallery, but the effect displeased Electra, so she had them covered in leather, too. An entire new hide was bought, and whenever the walls needed patches, they were cut from it. Down a hallway to the north was the twenty-by-twenty-two-foot dining room, where the Schmitts created cupboards and Palladian doorways and windows to complement the Monets and the antique paneling (just under $13,700).

Long hallways led down Seventy-first Street to the family wing. Their daughter Electra's suite, decorated with bookcases, moldings, and ornamental plaster, cost just over $3,500. Watson's eighteenth-century pine bedroom with carved mahogany doors and windows was $6,300. The hallway off Watson's room, which required painting, minor woodwork, and a closet, cost $1,100. Electra's neoclassical bedroom was a seventeenth-century Robert Adam–style room removed from Wenvoe Castle, Glamorgan, Wales, with two new door frames, thirteen shutters, carved skirting, two pedestals with fluted columns, window architraves, and a carved pine chimney piece ($9,500). Her bathroom boasted molded trim, antique wallpaper, and triplicating mirrors on three walls (a bargain at $900). "You'd walk in and see yourself fifty or sixty times in every direction," marvels her granddaughter Kitty Harris. "It was incredible." A guest bathroom cost a mere $1,700, but two paneled stairway halls—one to go up to the boys' rooms, the other, tucked back in the family quarters, to go down—were $9,100. Up on the roof was a small—and quite likely illegal—two-room suite, where Watson and Harry would share one room and Sam would have the other, all faux-painted to resemble a pine room, at a cost of about $6,000.

The modern woodwork alone cost more than $66,000; the antique wood in the master bedroom suite another $11,000. The total estimate, including incidentals like painting the service quarters tucked behind the dining room with glossy paint, came to just over $95,000. That's the equivalent of $1,173,000 today. The bills were all sent to Electra, who noted when she paid them in her rounded hand.

Early in 1931, Electra turned her mind to furnishings; she would eventually mix English, European, and Asian furniture and objects with artwork: an English pier table topped by two Degas bronze racehorses, Qing dynasty watercolors and wallpaper, Greek terra-cottas. Her "white" living room, with three windows facing south, had an eighteenth-century feel, and three Manets, another Monet, a Corot, and two old masters. She paid $2,000 for a pair of white Chelsea swans, circa 1760, $525 for a fireplace grate, $1,285 for eighteenth-century rose damask curtains.

A bill for curtains of taffeta, silk voile, and chintz, window shades, upholstery, and reproduction furniture for the children's rooms, issued in February, added $5,746. Another, for re-covering chairs and sofas, making slipcovers and bookcase doors, and adding the odd antique here and the Venetian blind trimmed with special colored tape and cords there, raised the total another $11,000. The Schmitts tossed in an antique door outside Electra's bedroom for free "as we feel the work is not satisfactory," or so they said on an invoice. Still, they weren't finished; the Schmitts returned after the Webbs took residence in 1932 to redecorate, fiddle with woodwork, change doors, and move wall switches, at a cost of $1,162. And by 1933, they'd apparently made so much money off the Webbs that they began offering them discounts. A $4,700 mahogany coffer bought that year was marked down to $2,465, an antique oak cabinet from $800 to $435.

The Schmitts' influence was strong enough that Watson junior credited them with the decision to hang four Monet paintings—of ice floes in the Seine, grain stacks in Giverny, a church in fog, and London's Charing Cross Bridge—on painted pine panel walls in their new dining room, instead of using the red damask they first chose. "Electra had never shown any great interest in Impressionism," Watson junior recalled, but she came to love the Monets she'd inherited from her mother.

What of the setting? "You look at the fancy molding, the fancy doorways, and then how crude the wood is, it doesn't make any sense," said Watson junior, "and I bet it was Schmitt's idea. He was a brilliant decorator with brilliant ideas." The Schmitts placed all seven of Electra's works by Degas in a French-inspired guest room that doubled as a sitting room; they called it the "green" room. The horse and foxhounds paintings and animal bronzes in the library, and the English sporting paintings in Watson's bedroom, on the other hand, were definitely chosen by Watson. "He liked them," said their son. "She tolerated them." As she probably did his polo trophies, which he kept on his mantel.

The family used the dining room daily. "If there were two or three for breakfast, that was rather nice to have breakfast in front of the Palladian window," said Watson junior. And the Webb children and grandchildren particularly loved one sculpture. Sam Webb Jr. recalled how he and the other children would walk by Edgar Degas's bronze statue of a ballerina, *Petite danseuse de quatorze ans*, in the marble foyer, "and the boys always picked up her tutu to see what was underneath it, but it was pretty well wrapped."

It was the home that Electra, not her husband, loved best. "It *was* home," said their son. "She loved her time at 740."

The family finally moved into the apartment in the winter of 1931 while Junior was at Groton. He came home to 740 that Christmas. "I was a little disappointed. I had shared a room with Sam [on Fifth Avenue], and then I shared a much smaller room with Harry at 740. Why Sam got the big room to himself I don't know. But he was the oldest son."

Senior had more to worry about than his son's happiness. On May 21, 1931, as a cold Depression winter gave way to spring, he'd been in despair over his market losses. "I hope we shall not live through such depressing times again," he scrawled in his diary. "It is heartbreaking and everyone everywhere is very discouraged. We can only hope and pray for a change before long or we'll all be broke." Four months later, on September 28, just back from two months in Alaska, he returned to his theme. "Big selling continues and no sign of a letup. I have mighty little left now. Had I sold before leaving for Alaska I would have come out pretty well." As he and his family moved from the Hotel Delmonico to 740 Park that December, his gloom deepened. "A collapse of everything is possible," he told his diary.

From the outside, the Webbs' troubles were invisible. "They never had to suffer, I promise you that," says their nephew Harry Havemeyer. "They have a certain position to maintain, and certain expectations are built in," says the Vanderbilt chronicler John Foreman. "They'll pay their club dues, keep the grooms, and let the grocery bills go on forever. Certainly, they'll redecorate."

Their spending on the apartment also took its toll on the Webbs' finances. The following spring they were forced to economize after the stock market began its ninth distinct decline since 1929 and the real severity of the Depression began to hit home. Previous depressions, pundits noted, had been limited to five to seven of these so-called liquidating moments. By April 14, 1932, when the market finally bottomed again, 84 percent below its value in September 1929, $65 billion had vanished.

That spring, the Webbs cut the salaries of their large staff. The paycheck of their butler, Charles, dropped from $215 to $165; of Mademoiselle, the governess, from $200 to $160; of their cook from $160 to $130; of the parlor maids from $85 to $75; of Electra's maid, Mary O'Connor—who'd been with her since she was fourteen—from $90 to $85; and of their least-paid kitchen helper from $50 to $45.

"You can see we couldn't reduce her more," Electra wrote to her mother-in-law in April on her new stationery engraved 740 Park Avenue. "Not a complaint from anyone. Things are getting worse and worse all the time. My own income last year was ¼ of what it was before. Heaven knows if we will have enough next year to keep up the way we have. Well, the apartment goes first. We have decided on that. I don't care as long as we can stay happy and well and if only Watson doesn't get too depressed. That is what takes the joy out of life."

In 1933, Watson founded Webb & Lynch, his own insurance brokerage. "My father and his pals used Webb & Lynch," says Harry Havemeyer. "Watson wasn't the kind of person who worked a forty-hour week." It's not clear if he was doing better, or living off Electra, but he remained tight about money throughout his life. The words TURN OFF

LIGHTS were carved into the wall above the light switch in one of his bedrooms. Dundeen Bostwick Catlin, a granddaughter, remembers him as "more cautious about money than grandmother." Watson once gave her father a necktie wrapped "in dirty paper with a rubber band and a note," she recalls. The note asked for the return of the rubber band. "He saved ribbon at Christmas, too," Catlin says.

However tight things may have gotten, that didn't stop the Webbs from spending. The day Electra wrote that letter about staff pay cuts, Watson and his son Sam were at Nehasane, Seward Webb's seventy-thousand-acre camp in the Adirondacks—his railroad had a little spur that ran there. Electra was heading to Shelburne after seeing *Madama Butterfly* at the Metropolitan Opera in Gertrude Vanderbilt's box. The Webbs' daughter Electra was planning a June wedding to Dunbar Bostwick, the grandson of an early officer of Standard Oil. When their son Watson was hospitalized near Groton with appendicitis, Watson senior set an air-speed record flying into Boston from Shelburne, while Electra got there on another plane rented near their home in Westbury.

In July 1935, Electra, Harry, and Watson junior flew to Anchorage, Alaska, en route to the upper Kuskokwim River, "where they will fish and hunt and take motion pictures," reported the Associated Press of a trip so extravagant it made headlines. They returned by steamship to Seattle in September, according to a later report, "with two splendid moose heads, one with an antler spread of seventy-two inches."

The Webbs' Depression wasn't as depressing as most.

HOUSEHOLD FINANCES WERE USUALLY HIDDEN FROM UPPER-CLASS CHILDREN. "We never heard boo about them," says Frederica Webb Gamble, a niece of J. Watson Webb's. But a nation's financial distress couldn't be. "There were breadlines at the churches, and as you drove or walked around town, you were conscious of people selling apples," says Katharine Whipple. Though her father, George Brewster, issued "a good many complaints about the market," says Katharine, "I don't think we were ever, ever pinched in any way. I remember Mother saying to him he should stop complaining. We were very, very, very fortunate."

So were most of the residents of 740, where apartments continued to sell, albeit slowly. Not long after the Beckers bought in, the Social Register Association helpfully declared 740's block the social focal point of New York, based on a study of the location of addresses in the register.

"It is a recognized fact that real estate is the last to suffer in a business depression," said James J. Sexton, head of New York City's Department of Taxes and Assessments, when he announced that the taxable value of 740 Park had risen from $1.45 million to $5 million when it opened its doors. But all was not well on Park Avenue.

"Foreclosure actions took the place of normal real estate transactions," wrote Timothy N. Pfeiffer in his privately published book, *Milbank, Tweed, Hadley & McCloy* (the title reflects the firm's name after 1946). "Corporate reorganizations and bankruptcies seemed endless . . . In 1932, defaults began and soon there was a flood of foreclosures, with valuable properties going for a fraction of their previous worth."

David Milton, the husband of John D. Rockefeller's sister Abby, known as "Babs," acquired Rosario Candela's 778 Park with a partner in April 1931 after its mortgage bank seized it in mid-construction and it stood unfinished for nine months. After bidding $2,000 more than the mortgage debt of $2.1 million to get it, Milton (who'd previously built 1 Beekman Place on land owned by Bayard Hoppin, with a mortgage issued by Milton's brother-in-law Junior) negotiated a reduction of 778's mortgage and reduced the asking prices of apartments there. It was one of three big Park co-ops that had suffered a sales slump that year. In August, 895 Park went into foreclosure after a year in which only two apartments were sold; the building owed $2.8 million.

Real estate types put the best face on it, claiming the slowdown would allow demand to catch up to supply. Some co-ops filled up by renting apartments at discounts; some income was better than none. But rents nationwide had fallen 32 percent: for those few who still had funds sufficient to afford them, apartments had become a bargain.

The pace of foreclosures and forced sales continued steadily from 1932 through 1934—sixteen buildings were offered in foreclosure sales on February 24, 1933, alone, another twenty that April 18—and Lee's lender, Metropolitan Life, was among the companies bringing foreclosure actions, but Lee and his managing agent, Douglas Gibbons, put the best face on their predicament, continuing to refer to 740 as a "100 percent cooperative" building. Truth be told, it was struggling, too. Building Department files give a clue as to what was happening. In 1931, Lee filed plans to cut up one maisonette, turning an empty triplex apartment into an eminently more rentable doctor's office with a smaller, standard duplex above. The work was completed in December, and the office soon rented, giving the co-op much-needed income. (In years to come, the other two maisonettes would be broken up, too. By September 1940, they were gone.)

Lee filled another apartment with relatives. In October 1931, *The*

New York Times announced that Black Jack Bouvier had bought an eighteen-room, six-bath duplex. According to the prospectus, 6/7A was worth $138,000. But the fact is, Black Jack merely occupied his new apartment; he didn't own it and didn't even pay the $13,800 annual rent. The apartment was a gift from his father-in-law—"Old Man Lee," as Jack called him now—and one that came with strings attached.

Black Jack Bouvier's fortunes had ridden a roller coaster of reversals and recoveries in the two previous years. His beloved brother William "Bud" Bouvier had died at age thirty-six of acute alcohol poisoning a few days before the 1929 stock market crash. Jack initially kept his money in play. But after taking a profit on the crash—he'd shorted the market—Bouvier proved too smart for his own good. By November, when 740's steel skeleton had risen four floors aboveground, Bouvier was ruined. His reaction would have made Albert Wiggin proud. He started borrowing. And kept drinking. And, according to one biographer, beat his wife, who went riding to escape him and threw things at him when she couldn't. When his wealthy uncle only came across with $25,000, a quarter of what he'd asked for, Bouvier, furious, turned to his father-in-law, James T. Lee.

According to Janet Lee's biographer, Jan Pottker, Lee responded with a four-hour lecture. In exchange for an apartment at 740, Lee demanded Jack give him a detailed monthly accounting of his spending and give up three of his four cars. He refused to pay Jack's club or tailor bills. Lee's granddaughter LeeLee Brown thinks he probably paid the maintenance, and an allowance to Janet as well. Worst of all, Lee would pop in unannounced, much to Jack's unhappiness. "Remember, you're living in my house!" Lee would roar. Bitter and resentful, Jack responded to Lee's graceless generosity with charming ingratitude and a fierce determination to keep up appearances. So he constantly broke his promises, beginning by decorating the until-then-empty apartment and installing fancy paneling, a new kitchen, a gym with a portable sauna, and gold-plated fixtures in the master bathroom. He paid for the work with more loans from his own family.

Janet and young Jacqueline escaped to East Hampton for the summer, where they lived in a rental called Rowdy Hall paid for by Jack's parents. Janet wouldn't have heard of giving up her string of seven hunters, jumpers, and ponies—Danseuse, Pas d'Or, Stepaside—all stabled at Lasata, the East Hampton estate of Jack's grandfather. Jack, who joined them on weekends, would stay in the city during the week, showing off his tan, which he acquired sitting nude in front of Candela's perfectly placed windows, while squiring other women around town.

Predictably, the Bouviers' fights grew more vicious, with Janet complaining that her father was the family provider and Jack improbably blaming Lee for his womanizing. By the next summer, Janet was pregnant again, and their second daughter, Caroline Lee, now Lee Radziwill, was born in March 1933, the day before Franklin Delano Roosevelt was inaugurated president of the United States. Her middle name, like her older sister's, spoke volumes about who was the alpha male in the Bouvier household.

Roosevelt's election—and the dramatic emergency measures he put in place in his first days in office—caused a brief surge of optimism. Jack did better that year, too, making $2 million on the market and ratcheting up his spending accordingly, but he promptly lost it all when stocks fell again that fall. Janet was ready to kill him.

On the surface, Jackie and Lee had a blissful life, doted on by servants in a Park Avenue apartment, each with her own room and a playroom besides. "I lived in New York City until I was thirteen," Jackie later recalled. "I hated dolls, loved dogs and horses, and had skinned knees and braces on my teeth for what must have seemed an interminable length of time to my family. I read a lot when I was little, much of which was too old for me. There were Chekhov and Shaw in the room where I had to take naps and I never slept but sat on the windowsill reading, then scrubbed the soles of my feet so the nurse would not see I was out of bed. My heroes were Byron, Mowgli, Robin Hood, Little Lord Fauntleroy's grandfather, and Scarlett O'Hara."

But the girls couldn't ignore Jack and Janet's constant battles. In East Hampton, Jacqueline had her horses for distraction, but in New York she would sometimes sneak out in the huge hallway at 740, standing silently, listening. "All they do is scream at each other—scream and yell," she complained to her cousin John H. Davis. But it wasn't all they did. Jack also cheated, every chance he got. And Janet—"a fine horsewoman," according to *The New York Herald*—rode away her anger and frustration and "relentlessly" trained her daughter in horsemanship, says Davis, in the jumping ring on the grounds at Lasata. Jackie, a strong horsewoman, learned to vent on horseback, too.

Janet couldn't ride far enough. In 1934, the *Daily News* ran a photo of Jack holding another woman's hand at a Tuxedo Park horse show while Janet sat, apparently oblivious, right next to them. Humiliated, she decided her only course was divorce, but James T. Lee wouldn't hear of it. The Bouviers stuck it out five more miserable years.

Marital misery was familiar. After all, James T. and Margaret Lee had barely spoken in years, but nonetheless made it clear they would not separate, let alone divorce, as long as their youngest daughter, Winifred, remained unmarried. Not only did Winnie ignore the pressure; with Janet out of the house, she'd even stopped playing the game. Her niece Mary Lee "Mimi" Ryan Cecil remembered Winnie finally telling her parents that she would no longer play intermediary, would never again ask either of them to pass the salt—unless it was she who wanted it. "That's the end of that!" she cried.

LEE'S BOSS AT THE CHASE, ALBERT WIGGIN, ALONG WITH THE BANK'S chairman, Charles McCain, and its president, Winthrop Aldrich, were still in denial about the market crash. They bought Harris, Forbes, an investment banking house, while Lynde Selden, McCain's 740 neighbor, cooked up a plan to absorb American Express into Chase. But all went awry when Germany threatened to default on its foreign loans, shaking the world economy—and the similarly tenuous reputation of the world's bankers. The Chase lost $5 million in 1931. And the banking business kept getting worse as more countries, cities, and corporations went insolvent.

Wiggin announced his retirement at the end of 1932, left the bank with a $100,000-a-year pension ($1.37 million in 2004 dollars), and was succeeded by Aldrich, who must have rued the day he'd left his law firm. "He was pretty much on his way back into the practice of law when everything fell apart," says David Rockefeller, who would take over the Chase many years later. "Father no longer wanted to deal with [Wiggin]. He did nothing illegal, but he certainly had done a number of things that were amoral and unethical."

Toward the end of his term in office, President Herbert Hoover asked the Senate Banking and Currency Committee to investigate the pre-crash securities business. Hearings began in February 1933 and quickly uncovered the existence of stock pools. Simultaneously, runs on banks became commonplace. Hoover's successor, Franklin Roosevelt, declared a national bank holiday, temporarily closing all banks, immediately after his inauguration in March. When they were allowed to reopen on March 13, thousands didn't. The Chase rescued some of the rest by advancing them funds.

Aldrich, aware that Wiggin's role in the pools was about to be exposed, made a series of public statements distancing himself from his predecessor, disavowing many of Wiggin's accomplishments, and admitting that the "intimate connection between commercial banking and investment banking almost inevitably leads to abuses." He proposed that investment bankers such as those at J. P. Morgan be banned from becoming directors of commercial banks, and then put Chase's securities subsidiary, which owned American Express, up for sale.

In the meantime, though, Wiggin appeared before Congress, and his (and Chase's) market manipulations were exposed. In addition to his stock pools, Wiggin had set up half a dozen companies devoted to avoiding taxes. The inevitable uproar led Wiggin to renounce his pension; when he and 135 other Chase directors were sued for $100 million by stockholders, he left its board of directors, too.' In 1934, Wiggin traded his Chase stock for the securities company that by then had shrunk to little more than American Express. He would never again take a public role, content to collect art, manuscripts, and books until his death in 1951. He left a $3 million estate ($21.5 million today).

Lynde Selden left the Chase to head American Express in 1936, successfully guiding it through World War II before he was kicked upstairs to the post of vice chairman in 1941; he remained with the company until 1965 and died in 1972. He'd left 740, too, briefly subletting his apartment to Frank Gould, the grandson of the robber baron Jay Gould. The Seldens removed ten mahogany doors from the 740 apartment, which are now in the home of their daughter Muriel "Mimi" Paris in Greenwich, Connecticut, built on property first acquired by Albert Wiggin. But wait. "It was 71 East Seventy-first, *not* 740 Park," she says. "Somehow it was more discreet."

Mimi Paris was a schoolgirl when the investigations were going on, and a private detective would sometimes walk her and her sister to Miss Hewitt's School. There were kidnapping threats. "My English teacher was very against Wiggin and made it known in our little class that he was a crook," she says. "It was kind of a blow." Such things weren't spoken of at home, where the children "led very separate lives," she says.[2] "We ate in the dining room, but early. We never ate with the family." No surviving Seldens know anything about the family's dealings with James T. Lee or the 740 Park Avenue Corporation. "They just would not have discussed business," says Muriel "Muggins" Badgley, a granddaughter.

Lucky thing. Because the Selden children and grandchildren are also unaware of their family's falling-out with Charles McCain, who "was great friends of my family," says Mimi Paris.

ALBERT WIGGIN "WAS A SON OF A BITCH WHO WAS LUCKY NOT TO GO TO jail," snorts Charles L. McCain, a grandson. "The evil Mr. Wiggin—[the family] blamed him for the whole thing." The whole thing was McCain's financial ruination in 1933, his expulsion from the Chase and from 740 Park Avenue, and his exile to Chicago, with his reputation in tatters and himself deep in debt, all thanks to Wiggin.

Charles McCain had arrived in New York in 1927; the city's youngest bank president, he was just forty-three. He moved from Arkansas to Rye, in Westchester County, and *The Wall Street Journal* announced that he was a Presbyterian, a Democrat, and one of the city's "coming banking leaders." "In a room of fifteen strangers, by the end of the night, he'd know everyone's name," says his surviving son, Charles junior. Two years later, he merged his National Park Bank, a conservative commercial bank, with the Chase to create a giant with the most capital funds in the country. Despite his politics, McCain echoed Wiggin late in 1929 when he praised the Republican president, Herbert Hoover, and declared that the economy would survive the crash undiminished.

His view was certainly undiminished when he moved into a high-floor apartment at 740 Park Avenue a year later. His younger son Charles junior, who was seven, was first put in a maid's bedroom, where he could hear the wind whistling at night, an eerie, portentous sound. Later he

shared a larger room with his brother, William. Their maternal grandmother, Grace Dodge Walker, lived there, too, as did a chauffeur, a maid,
a cook, and a butler.

By 1933, with the national and local economies considerably diminished, McCain was one of the bankers laboring to prop up the invalids.
But that didn't stop him from vacationing in Arkansas in May, motoring
through Maryland and Virginia en route to the social spa Hot Springs,
where many of his 740 neighbors were regulars. The kids stayed at home
with their grandmother.

It was the calm before the storm. Two weeks later, the Chase cut its
board in half and announced its immediate departure from the securities
business. Among the divorced directors were Albert Wiggin and James T.
Lee, though Franklin d'Olier, Winifred Lee's father-in-law, and Frederick Ecker remained.

In September, the McCains were back in Hot Springs; he was steel-
ing himself for December, when he was hauled before the Senate committee investigating the market collapse. McCain was interrogated about
sweetheart loans, his salary and bonuses, and his borrowing from the
Chase (he owed the company more than twice his $128,000 salary). He
was challenged on charges as petty as taking advantage of a single "old
lady in a tight place" in a stock deal and charged with political corruption, specifically an intimation that he'd bribed the populist senator
Huey Long with a breakfast of eighteen oysters, a sirloin steak, French
fries, and vanilla ice cream. Long shot back that McCain had eaten a
dozen of the oysters, all the fries, and half the ice cream, and then stuck
him with the check.

"You rarely get the best of these birds," the senator sneered.

Long did not describe the night he came to the banker's apartment as
it was being readied for a full-dress dinner party. At that meeting, he
tried to persuade McCain to invest in Louisiana. Afterward, he planted
himself in the drawing room, making calls all over the world, then
stayed, uninvited, for dinner.

In January 1934, McCain abruptly quit the Chase and 740 Park to
move to Chicago and take over the United Light and Power Company, a
huge public utility. The Chase owned 42 percent of it. "It was Mr. Wiggin who—how shall I be tactful?—caused Father to resign," says Grace

Heidt, one of the McCains' two daughters. "He said no officers should be in debt. He said no officers should sell Chase stock. But Mr. Wiggin did both those things. He was always alone at his club at lunch because nobody would sit with him. People said he was the most hated man on Wall Street."

Wiggin had asked McCain not to sell his stock as the market sank and he found himself in great debt. "He went to the bottom," says Heidt. "Wiggin ruined a lot of his directors," adds her brother. "Dad refused to jump out of the window." Instead, he went through hell, "but he never gave up."

McCain's mother died in April 1934; a cousin, a vice president at Chase, was in a car crash a few months later; and one of McCain's brothers died in 1935. All through these trials, he was wrangling with the new Securities and Exchange Commission,[3] which was forcing United Light to register as a holding company and begin consolidating and simplifying its operations. He was also a witness in a trial seeking recovery of $2 million in lost deposits from Chase, Bankers Trust, Chemical, and several other banks. The government held the officers of those banks responsible for the collapse of the Harriman National Bank following the 1933 bank holiday and alleged that they had looted Harriman before it was shut down.

In 1939, though, Charles McCain staged a triumphant comeback, returning to New York finance as a partner in Dillon, Read & Co., the stockbrokers. When Clarence Dillon offered him the job, McCain refused, saying he'd have to pay his debts first. Dillon lent him $1 million to pay his creditors, "and he paid back every cent," says McCaw's daughter, despite Dillon's attempts to forgive the debt. "And then he was able to make another fortune." When Dillon, Read's president, James Forrestal, resigned to become Franklin Roosevelt's administrative assistant in the White House, McCain stepped into the job, where he remained until he retired in 1951. Finally, weakened by two heart attacks and a stroke and suffering from Parkinson's disease, McCain died in 1957.

Meanwhile, all those bank failures and hearings led to significant legislation to reform the financial industry. The Banking Act of 1933, or the Glass-Steagall Act, erected a wall between banks and brokerage houses, established the Federal Deposit Insurance Corporation, insured people's bank accounts, and made banks choose between accepting deposits and underwriting securities. Henceforth, only commercial banks could offer checking and savings accounts, and only investment banks could underwrite new securities issued by corporations and sell them to the public.[4]

The Securities Act of 1933 regulated the sale of securities for the first time and sought to ensure that investors were well informed about the companies selling stocks and to punish deceit, misrepresentation, and fraud in the sale of securities. The Securities Exchange Act of 1934 created the Securities and Exchange Commission and gave it broad authority over the securities industry. It outlawed manipulative and abusive practices in the issuance of securities and required the registration of stock exchanges, brokers, dealers, and listed securities and the disclosure of certain financial information and insider trading. The Public Utility Holding Company Act of 1935 put interstate public-utility holding companies under federal control. A holding company was defined as an enterprise that directly or indirectly owns 10 percent or more of stock in a public utility engaged in retail electricity or natural gas distribution.

All those reforms would bear fruit in years to come. But many, particularly at 740 Park, thought the fruit was poison and Franklin Delano Roosevelt a class traitor. Sherburn Becker Sr. called him that.[5] So did Landon Ketchum Thorne, although he'd have the last laugh, and several more after that.

8

LANDON THORNE WAS SOMETHING NEW, AN AGGRESSIVE NEW GENE THAT put some sting back into wealthy Waspdom. Thorne's family was old; his money wasn't. William Thorne sailed from England to Lynn, Massachusetts, in 1638. That May he was made a freeman, one of the four hundred people in the Massachusetts Bay Colony (population approximately ten thousand) entitled to vote. That wasn't enough to keep him in the Puritan colony or the Puritan fold, though.

"William was clearly in tension with the Anglican hegemony and seems to have been a guy that had vision and determination," says Landon Ketchum Thorne III, an investment banker in South Carolina. "He probably figured out that he was never going to 'fix things' in Massachusetts, and if you got too wrapped around the axle there, you could find yourself in the brig. Thus, in the true American way, he moved and became a civic activist in Flushing [Queens, New York]." In 1657, Thorne, who'd married a Quaker, signed the Flushing Remonstrance, a protest by village residents against an order banning Quakers, issued by Governor Stuyvesant. The remonstrance is considered a precursor to the Bill of Rights.

Thorne's grandson Isaac built Thorndale, an estate in Dutchess

County, New York, in 1725. Thornes have lived there ever since. Isaac's great-grandson Jonathan Thorne moved to New York's Washington Square, married into a family that sold fur and leather, made a fortune selling boots to the Union during the Civil War, branched out into insurance, banking, lighting gas, railroads, and coal, and founded the Society for the Prevention of Cruelty to Children, then returned to Thorndale. "Jonathan lived highly," says David Thorne, another grandson of Landon's.

Over the next two generations, Thornes ran coal companies and banks, gave to museums and cultural institutions, and bred a stable of trotters and one of the most valuable herds of bulls in the world. "They always had a knack for making a buck," says Landon III. "There's a merchant gene in us." That, says another grandson, Peter Thorne, may be why family members left the Quaker church and converted to Episcopalianism. "Quakers believed in the simple life and not materialism," he says. "I'm sure it was more complicated, but on a certain level that's what was happening in New York society at the time. Quaker kids came to New York and didn't want to go back to Millbrook, wear black, and live in simple homes. It's hard to be a pacifist when you're clothing the Union army."

Landon's father, Edwin, chairman of the Central Hanover Bank, interrupted the family's idyll when he had a nervous breakdown and retired young. "He had psychological problems. But we were never told that, because no one in that generation talked about things like that," says David Thorne. So Landon, born in 1888, didn't have the head start in life he might have. "He had to work his way through college," says Landon III. "He busted his chops." But when his father died in 1935, leaving an estate of $3.7 million, Landon was by far the wealthiest Thorne.

Landon graduated from Pomfret, a Connecticut prep school, then divided his time between Yale and the New York debutante scene, where he was a popular escort. At Yale, he befriended Alfred Loomis, a fellow student, and in 1911 married Loomis's sister Julia in Tuxedo Park, where Julia's mother, a descendant of a Revolutionary family, lived.

Julia's sable-bordered, rose-brocaded bridal gown was "perhaps the most notable wedding gown in existence in this country," wrote the

Times when she wed. Made in 1778, it had been worn by seven generations of brides in her mother's family. The wedding party included Harrimans, Burrs, Van Rensselaers, Morgans, and Rosina Hoppin's niece. Another guest, Alfred and Julia's cousin Henry Stimson, held the family's flag in government; a former U.S. attorney, he'd been named secretary of war under William Howard Taft after a failed run for governor of New York. But Julia was socially insecure.

Her parents' divorce had left the family ostracized. "Julia wanted to be part of society, but she was batting with a sticky wicket," says Betty Loomis Evans, a niece. Even before Julia's father died in 1909, her mother, "a formidable woman with a big bosom draped in pearls who ordered everyone around," made a new life for herself, "traveling to Europe with her black chauffeur," says Evans. But Julia "felt that because of her father's reputation as a ladies' man, certain families wouldn't invite them. Aunt Julia wanted to be up there."

In marrying Thorne, "Julia was certainly not going down," says her grandson David. "She was established. Landon was going up a bit in terms of New York society." He would prove a perfect mate, and not just because, within a few years, no less an arbiter than the gossip columnist Cholly Knickerbocker would describe them as "socially consequential." Thorne and Julia's brother were about to change the face of finance—and earn the funds that allowed Landon to personify the new archetype of wealth, a man who neither owned land nor built industry but manipulated money with consummate skill. Landon Ketchum Thorne *was* what 740 Park Avenue would come to.

Thorne was well connected; his success "was more about social alignments than business alignments," says David Thorne. At Yale, Thorne rode his cousin Brink's coattails; Brink was captain of the football team. But Landon also rowed crew and graduated with an engineering degree. Out of school he clerked at his father's bank, then took a job at Bonbright & Co., a Civil War–era investment house, before going to fight in Europe in 1917 as a captain in the Army. "You go to war and your confidence changes," David Thorne says. "You come back and you say, 'I am going to try something completely different.' "

Thorne was gregarious, and as aggressive as Bonbright was sleepy. "He was a young man with prospects," says Landon III. "He connected the dots very quickly." Initially, he didn't know that his success selling bonds (he brought in half the firm's profits—more than all its partners combined) was keeping Bonbright afloat. His brother-in-law Alfred Loomis, working for a cousin's law firm, was Bonbright's attorney, so when Thorne was invited to become a partner, they pored over the Bonbright books together. Thorne, though only thirty-one, was already a master salesman, and Loomis was a mathematical genius. They realized how precarious the firm's finances were and decided that if they worked together, they might turn things around.

Thorne had a vision: Bonbright would have a bright future underwriting bonds to finance and centralize the new electric utilities powering America. Two years after Thomas Edison formed the Edison General Electric Company in 1890, Charles Coffin, a former shoe manufacturer, had merged his electrical equipment company with Edison's to form General Electric. In the years that followed, private electric companies consolidated and evolved into public-utility monopolies, replacing local plants with interconnected networks that generated not just power but huge profits.

After World War I, holding companies were formed to make interstate connections more profitable and efficient. Sophisticated financiers with engineering backgrounds were in a unique position to aid the nation and make a fortune by planning and financing the expansion of the country's electrical systems. Thorne and Loomis, who'd also been a captain during the war and worked with electrical armament engineers, were perfectly cast for the parts. And Bonbright, which had already financed one of the biggest electric holding companies, was an ideal stage.

With backing from GE's Coffin, they took over Bonbright. Loomis quit the law; they set up a private investment company and began secretly buying the firm's shares; and within a matter of months "the Bonbrights vanished from Bonbright." In 1921, Thorne was made its president and public face; Loomis operated behind the scenes, shaping the transactions that made them both wealthy beyond their dreams. Under their direction, Bonbright became one of the so-called Big Six Wall Street investment banks.

One of Thorne's uncles had helped finance the takeover after his father refused to. "He wants to make a play, but his father does not back him," says David Thorne. "He is determined. He thinks electric power is a good idea. He persuades Alfred this is a cool thing to do and we can make a lot of money, and then Alfred, who was always the brains figuring out the percentages and the legal structures, figures out a way to take over Bonbright, and the other guys there are happy to cash out and let these Young Turks drive the boat. And then it was the twenties and they were financing bonds, financing electric power plants, all over the world." Soon they'd forged ties with every power in the power business, raising the money that funded the industry's expansion.

"He was the Michael Milken of the twenties," says Peter Thorne, comparing his grandfather to the junk-bond king of the 1980s who also made a fortune and changed the world by financing what seemed like risky new technology.

In the fall of 1924, Thorne and Loomis engineered the creation of United Light and Power, merging utilities in nine states into a $34-million-a-year colossus—and also revealed that they'd secretly organized the American Superpower Corporation, which had acquired ownership interests in some of the largest power companies across the country. "It owned stocks," says David Thorne. "It wasn't a company that did anything." But congressmen were soon charging that it was a power monopoly.

When American Superpower issued its first annual report in March 1925, Thorne, its president, promised it would never seek "to exercise dominion or control" over the companies it invested in. Instead, it would be a clearinghouse for ideas that would advance the power industry. "Landon was on every board there ever was and had influential friends all over the world," says Betty Evans. Loomis knew everyone in science. "But nobody knew who they were!"

Generally, Thorne's holding companies did own only minority stakes, but their web of influence was tantamount to control. And investors, who could spread their bets across a diversified group of power companies and regions, loved them. Between 1924 and 1929, Bonbright issued $1.6 billion in securities representing 15 percent of all utility financing in America. Thorne and Loomis, said *Fortune*, were "the most potent forces in shaping the present and future organization of America's huge, complex power and light business." Many credit them with creating today's Eastern Seaboard power grid.

"They did very many good things," says William J. Hausman, Chancellor Professor of Economics at the College of William & Mary and an electrical utility historian. "They sometimes cut corners and were not entirely upright, but others were far more notorious. The bottom line was making money for the owners. The industry was consolidating; it was still relatively new and had a voracious need for capital. The holding companies raised capital by issuing bonds. The proceeds were used to buy equity in the operating companies and thereby control them. In good times, the return on equity was very high."

Thorne was doing the same all over the world. He financed power companies in Japan and in 1927, with Italy's premier, Benito Mussolini, formed the Italian Superpower Corporation in concert with General Electric, with Bonbright financing $38 million in stocks and bonds. Marshall Field, the retail heir who would soon move into 740 Park, was one of its founding directors.

Loomis and Thorne's market machinations continued in 1929, when they teamed up with J. P. Morgan and Drexel & Co. to form a new holding company, United Corporation, which was part-owned by American Superpower. United made $50 million that year on assets of $225 million. Those assets consisted of the utility holdings of the banks and of American Superpower. "United, in 1929, was the single largest multistate holding company and the largest utility in the United States," says Professor Hausman. "It controlled 21 percent of total electrical output."

A few months later, the duo created Commonwealth & Southern Corporation, merging three holding companies that owned power plants in Tennessee, Ohio, Pennsylvania, Alabama, Georgia, and South Carolina. More than half of American Superpower's investments were in United and Commonwealth & Southern. Through these entwined companies, and a third formed in 1930, Niagara Hudson, the Thorne and Loomis influence extended from Massachusetts to the Gulf of Mexico. They were "decried by those who fear the 'power trust,' but . . . viewed with high approval by those who think that power problems should be worked out by harmonious cooperation," *Fortune* said.

Thorne sold most of his stock holdings in the spring of 1929, cashing out near the market's peak. "Getting out at just the right moment was the most blatant move of all," says David Thorne. "But he just got it, that this was crazy, way crazy overvalued." So even in the straits of November 1929, the Thornes could afford to party like it was 1928, giving the first dinner dance of the debutante season at the Colony Club and dining with President Hoover at the home of Henry Stimson, who'd become secretary of state.

They also played: the Thornes headed to Southern Pines, a North Carolina winter resort colony popular with the equestrian set. And Landon, in a then-rare feat for an entrepreneur, personally financed and managed the syndicate building an eighty-seven-foot J-class yacht—one of only ten of the largest, most opulent racing vessels ever built. It was called *Whirlwind* and would compete in the America's Cup the following September, against, among others, a yacht backed by Winthrop Aldrich and Harold Vanderbilt, and another backed by J. P. Morgan. Thorne and Loomis also funded an oddly quaint foundation; it designed and built a fleet of trucks to take groups of college students and young businessmen on six-week camping trips to factories across the country.

There was always time to make more money. The same week *Whirlwind* was launched, Thorne joined a syndicate that bought 7 percent of Bankers Trust from John D. Rockefeller. The $30 million deal had been forced by the Rockefeller takeover of the Chase. The chairman of Bankers Trust announced that Thorne and the others had invested personal funds, believing that "the outlook is bright" for the bank.

Thorne obviously thought the outlook was bright—for Thorne. In November 1928, he'd bought a huge parcel of land totaling 230 acres on the Great South Bay in Bay Shore, Long Island, and begun building Thorneham, a sprawling estate there. The Thornes had all lived in a row of Victorian homes in Islip. This was Landon's breakout. "He said, I have all this money and I am going to flaunt it, and he did," says David Thorne.

A Yale classmate was Thorne's architect. Ferruccio Vitale and Umberto Innocenti were his landscape architects for the project, which took six years to complete and was considered a modernist masterpiece. Thorneham eventually boasted fields for pheasant hunting, a croquet court "like green glass," says Evans, an indoor tennis court, indoor and outdoor swimming pools that Thorne used daily, a canal giving boat access to the bay, a bay boat named *Julia*, and a thirty-room Tudor manor house, surrounded by man-made lakes "stocked with trout and all those goodies," lawns, terraces, and gardens, all reached by way of a long paved *allée* lined with birch trees. In the city, the Thornes had lived at 950 Park, but in June 1930 Landon bought apartment 14A/B at 740 Park. It was a fifteen-room simplex with six staff bedrooms, and it ran the length of the Park Avenue side of the building. The public rooms looked out over Seventy-first Street, the living room and four bedrooms had narrow terraces on Park Avenue.

"They really cruised through the Depression," says a nephew, Francis Thorne. Landon had discovered that he liked to spend money—and it could buy so much more when most had less. "You could buy almost anything if you had some cash," says Landon III. "It's amazing what liquidity will do for you. It's an engine of great social change."

Thorne's homes and yachts were only part of it. "There were fabulous parties," says David Thorne. "Images of the great Gatsby loomed." Landon bought his wife a Bentley, a red sports car, flashy jewelry, even Romanov emeralds to wear at the splendid parties they hosted. Julia Thorne knew how to spread her feathers. Loomis relatives, who didn't entirely approve, tell tales of her ostentation, her gold dinner service, the jeroboams of champagne poured by the butler, John Bucket. But Julia also played concert piano and treasured rare manuscripts and first editions. Her William Blake collection, which she would donate to the Morgan Library, was considered among the finest in existence. "For a woman born in the nineteenth century," says her grandson Landon, "she was in her way enormously independent."

"My grandmother was a very interesting woman, very smart and very beaten down by him, I think," says David Thorne. "He was a very strong personality, and she was always trying to find her way. She liked spending money, but she was very smart about it and bought interesting things like first editions of Marcel Proust. Was she a princess? Well, yeah, she certainly wasn't out there doing good work."

Neither was Thorne, who had a reason to buy his wife whatever she wanted. "He had lots of girlfriends," says Betty Evans. "Julia wasn't easy and outgoing, and Landon was. He was so good-looking." Relatives suspect he had an affair with Diana Tate, half of the interior design team of Tate and Hall, who decorated the Thornes' apartment with Oriental rugs, classical statuary, and Julia Thorne's collection of family portraits and Americana, passed down by the Boudinots. Their dining room was painted white and had white curtains, Chippendale chairs covered in emerald green damask, and a black-manteled hearth. They paneled the living room in pale green antique boiserie and filled it with eighteenth-century French furniture and a white Chinese lacquered screen, all sitting on a white, gold, and pink Bessarabian rug. The library was hung with hunting pictures, and pride of place belonged to a Hamilton clock with wooden works, now in the Metropolitan Museum of Art.

Thorne installed another of his suspected paramours in a house near Thorneham, and sometimes took relatives by to meet her because "he wanted her to know he wasn't ashamed of her," says one. Ultimately, Julia took to touring Europe with her piano teacher, "a very proper, pristine, priggish, socially adroit gay guy," says Landon Thorne III. "The perfect traveling companion."

WHIRLWIND WAS A RARE FAILURE FOR THORNE. IT WAS TECHNOLOGI-cally advanced and "very pleasing to the eye," said a witness, "the stem sweeping down to the keel in a very sweet line. And to a man who, like myself, believes that a pointed stern is a logical ending for all vessels, her stern is a joy to behold." But despite Loomis's gadgets belowdecks, the oversized sloop placed third in its first trial off Newport in the summer of 1930, and last in the final one. Difficult to steer, even when someone more experienced than Thorne was at the helm, it wasn't chosen to defend the cup (Winthrop Aldrich's *Enterprise* was, and went on to win). *Whirlwind* was scrapped in 1935. It was a harbinger.

In 1932, American Superpower failed to pay dividends when the corporation's capital fell below the value of its preferred shares, which represented the assets the partners had put into the company. Thorne assured investors it was in no danger and shortly afterward began exchanging its preferred shares for those of the United Corporation, allowing it to pay dividends again. But United wasn't doing well, either. Its stock holdings had done nothing but dwindle in value, and a few years hence both its common and its preference stock would be worthless.

The holding companies "made the stocks and bonds more marketable, but they became very highly leveraged," says Professor Hausman. "When things turned down, the dividends stopped, the bond payments stopped. You can see in retrospect that it wasn't sustainable."

Nonetheless, early in 1933 Thorne was named to the board of the Baker family's First National Bank (today's Citibank), which needed, according to the *New York Journal*, "a man of Thorne's proven ability" to guide its securities affiliate, which was millions of dollars in debt. When Thorne and Loomis quit their executive jobs at Bonbright in April 1933, banking was touted as their future, and one newspaper predicted they would soon rival the Rockefeller and Morgan banking interests, placing them at the pinnacle of finance. Through Henry Stimson, they'd even been advising President Hoover on the economy. "They were wired with the Republican Party and had been for a long time," says David Thorne.' "They hated Roosevelt, and so did many other rich people."

But then Hoover lost the election, Roosevelt came into office, and those pesky congressional investigators were everywhere. After a meeting with the new president and Winthrop Aldrich, Loomis stayed behind, says his biographer Jennet Conant, to warn Roosevelt of a public rush to judgment against bankers. But the public was fine; it was the politicians who were rushing—to catch up.

The Tennessee Valley Authority, created in May 1933 as a government agency providing low-cost power to the South, was a direct threat to Commonwealth & Southern. Loomis and Thorne resigned from its board, and Wendell Wilkie was named its president. Wilkie quickly became the chief spokesman of the electric utility industry, and chief critic of Roosevelt's New Deal policies, which positioned him to run for president in 1940.² Meanwhile, businessmen became public enemies. In June 1933, the Senate Banking and Currency Committee looked into the "preferred lists" of investors who'd gotten the first chance to purchase stock in United Corporation, and whether politicians were among them. That fall, complying with the Glass-Steagall Act, Thorne and Loomis quit the board of Bonbright, and news reports said they'd chosen banking over investment banking. But then, early in 1934, Thorne quit the First National board, too, and Loomis resigned from Bankers Trust.

The two men sold all but their United Corporation stock, and Loomis turned his stake over to Thorne to manage and, reading the public mood, "without so much as a backward look, quit Wall Street for good," his biographer Conant wrote, "shaken by the imputations of self-serving dishonesty." Loomis had decided to leave it all behind and devote himself to his first love, science. His Tuxedo Park laboratory would soon produce radar systems and research that led to the atomic bomb. Conant says that henceforth Thorne did much better than Loomis. "He ended up with $50 million," Francis Thorne confirms. But as usual, Loomis was on to something. Had Thorne become anathema? It seemed so in February 1934, when a House Interstate and Foreign Commerce Committee report singled him out in a list of men who ran interlocking corporations, part of a study of the power exercised by the holding companies he and Loomis had pioneered. Yesterday's geniuses were now villains—and 740 Park housed lots of them. Thorne was revealed as an officer or director of eight separate power systems, Loomis of six. Chase Bank had twenty-two directors and officers involved with thirty-one different power companies.

Thorne took his partner's instincts seriously; in the months that followed, he, too, quit almost every bank, utility, and holding company board he served on, staying on only at United and American Superpower. "It appears they are concentrating their activity," said *The Wall Street Journal*, rather than "becoming inactive."

The *Journal* was wrong. At age forty-six, Landon Thorne was retiring, too. And just in time. A few months later, the Public Utility Act defined American Superpower as a holding company, and it began selling off shares. In December 1934, with the market value of its assets underwater—they'd dropped from $41 million to $28 million in just six months—Superpower again suspended dividends and announced a plan to buy back its preferred stock, repaying the major shareholders who'd set up the company. It was the beginning of a slow denouement that would last eighteen years and effectively reduce the onetime superpower to an empty shell.

Landon and Julia Thorne spent that spring in Southern Pines, giving dinners and riding, then journeyed to Bay Shore, where Landon, ever the sportsman, raced several new boats, before returning to Southern Pines with the ten horses they would ride in the upcoming foxhunting season. Landon was on the board of Southern Pacific, which put a private railcar at his disposal for trips to Mardi Gras in New Orleans. Landon and Loomis also started going to Hilton Head, South Carolina, for about a month every year to shoot game. Once a paradise for wealthy Southerners, it was sold to freed slaves after the Civil War on an order of Rosina Hoppin's ancestor General William Tecumseh Sherman. Aside from hunting season, the ex-slaves had the island to themselves. Thornes had hunted and owned plantation properties in the South Carolina low country for years. Loomis and Thorne bought tens of thousands of acres for $120,000 in 1931, and more over subsequent years (including the eight-hundred-acre site of the Confederate Fort Walker, bought from the government for $12,600), until they owned most of the island, except for a few small sites owned by descendants of slaves.

"Landon was the instigator," says Betty Evans. "It was always Uncle Landon. Alfred never would have thought of buying it." Conant describes the implausible grandeur of their shoots: the black men in livery setting tablecloths with china, grilled quail, and oysters in the shell and full-dress dinners. Through the 1940s, Loomis, Thorne, and their families and friends like the banking Bakers, the social Livingstons, and the Chubbs of Chubb Insurance would come to hunt, fish, and sail. They finally sold their island in two parcels in 1949 and 1950 to timbermen who went on to develop Hilton Head as a resort. Thorne and Loomis got about $1 million for about nine thousand acres on the south end of the island and another $1 million a year later for eleven thousand acres to the north and west.

Thorne also loved to fish off Long Island: he had a fifty-three-foot deep-sea fishing boat called *Twister* and another named for his wife. "Fishing was his passion," says David Thorne. In 1936, he caught a 195-pound broadbill swordfish off Montauk after a half-hour fight. A few months later, the Thornes arrived in London en route to the wedding of Landon junior to the daughter of the tenth Baronet of Stobs, Sir Gilbert Eliott of Wolfelee, Hawick, Roxburghshire, Scotland, a descendant of James Boswell, Samuel Johnson's biographer. (The marriage would end in a Reno divorce and Landon junior's remarriage five years later.) After a brief stay at Claridges, the Thornes returned to America, where Landon made a quiet argument against "undue taxation" of profits and dividends at a public hearing of the Securities and Exchange Commission, where it was revealed that Bonbright had made more than $18 million in profits on American Superpower stock, atop nearly $3 million in underwriting fees.

Six months later, it was rumored that Thorne would come out of retirement to replace his friend George F. Baker Jr., chairman of First National Bank. Baker had died of peritonitis aboard his yacht *Viking* while cruising near Hawaii with Thorne, among others. "The question is not of his qualifications but whether he would accept it," reported the *Evening Journal.* "He has all the money he will ever want or could possibly spend . . . [but he] likes to hunt and fish and travel. And he has gotten out of the habit of being tied down to a desk." Instead, Thorne, a major stockholder in the bank, chose to serve out Baker's term on its board.

Likely a wise move. Thorne remained a target. "There were a lot of people pissed off at Grandpa because he kept all his money and he hadn't kept anybody else's money," says David Thorne. In 1938, the Supreme Court upheld the government's right to regulate public-utility holding companies, and Commonwealth & Southern and United both stopped fighting and registered as such with the SEC. That, says Professor Hausman, "was the death sentence" for holding companies. "It didn't happen until the late forties, but they had to be broken up."

Thorne promptly resigned from United's board. But SEC investigations continued, and late that year United announced the largest writedown of asset value in the history of the utility industry: in eight years, $434 million had gone up in smoke. By 1940, *The Wall Street Journal*'s investment advice column would sound grim when discussing American Superpower. "Aspects of the situation leave much to be desired," the paper wrote. "Common stockholders appear doomed to drastic treatment." In the mid-1940s, Superpower, too, wrote down losses totaling upwards of $53 million. And in 1948, the corporation finally admitted that its common stock was worthless. Even holders of the preference shares were out two-thirds of their investment. (By 1950, though, the market value of the shares had risen sufficiently that the company—at that point run by the father-in-law of one of Thorne's sons—paid its first dividends since 1932.)

United fared even worse. It had succeeded in laying the groundwork for the creation of the Eastern Seaboard electric grid. But by 1942, when its shares had fallen to $.31 from their high of $75, the SEC called it a "multi-tiered monstrosity" and a "corporate screen" protecting the bankers who created it, and recommended it be liquidated and shut down.

Though distracted by his weapons research, Alfred Loomis "was devastated by the hearings," says Betty Loomis Evans. "Alfred had to protect cousin Harry [Henry Stimson, who'd joined Roosevelt's cabinet] at all costs." Landon Thorne handled that, just as he continued handling investments for Loomis. "Landon kept working, buying and selling for their accounts, going to his office on Wall Street." He spent weekdays at 740 and weekends in Bay Shore when he wasn't traveling. And ultimately he survived all the investigations and calumny.

During World War II, little is known of Thorne except that he worked for the Red Cross and sometimes carried correspondence to England on behalf of Stimson. "I remember meeting Admiral Halsey as a four-year-old," says David Thorne. "This big mucky-muck came to the estate and went out on the boat one day."

Big mucky-mucks were regular visitors to the Thorne household, even in war. In August 1945, Stimson dined with the Thornes at 740 and announced over dinner that the next day America would change the world. The next day America dropped the first atomic bomb on Hiroshima, Japan. Seven forty wasn't the White House, but its access to power was nearly the same. In the mid-1950s, Thorne and Loomis split up their winnings, and each walked away with about $15 million. Thorne put the proceeds into trust for his grandchildren, and though he subsequently financed Fisher Electronics after Loomis introduced him to Avery Fisher in 1959, his business career was ending.

Apparently content at the center of his world, Landon Ketchum Thorne barely made the papers the last fifteen years of his life, much of it spent as a member of the board of directors of 740 Park Avenue, a post his wife inherited when he died. "In the '50s, there was some entertaining, but not a lot," says David Thorne. "The lifestyle became less, they had less energy, they lived less high on the hog, but my grandfather would take trips and treat us to things. There were still Bentleys and chauffeurs, a lot of staff. There was still property and they were maintaining it, but there used to be horses, and then there weren't. You just got a sense that things were winding down."

Thorne developed heart disease, had a heart attack, and died in 1964 at seventy-six. Julia Thorne lived on at 740 almost ten years. Her living relatives say she blossomed in the absence of her colorful, domineering spouse. "That was when we grandchildren got to know her as an individual," says David Thorne. "And she was just such an interesting character, much less a princess, much more a flesh-and-blood person. She would tell her stories about dealing with Grandpa and how she'd try and get back at him. She was much more real after he left the scene."

The family's last brush with notoriety came in 1969, when a granddaughter, Julia Stimson Thorne, married Lieutenant Junior Grade John Forbes Kerry at Thorneham shortly after his return from Vietnam, where he'd earned a Silver Star. The bride wore the famous family wedding dress. Just like her grandmother before her, she'd been introduced to the groom by her brother David, a classmate of Kerry's at Yale. After having two daughters, the couple separated in 1982 and divorced six years later. The Thorne family remained close to Kerry, though, and David was a key member of Kerry's kitchen cabinet when he ran for president in 2004. Although his grandson's affiliation with the Democrats would probably not have pleased him, Landon Ketchum Thorne would likely have been proud that his family was still in a position of influence.

After the first Julia Stimson Thorne's death in 1973, Thorneham was sold to developers for a mere $1.2 million. Much of the Bay Shore property had already been donated to the Episcopal Church and to the Nature Conservancy. The 740 apartment was also disposed of for next to nothing—about $200,000—by Julia Thorne's executors. Also worth very little was Thorne's United Corporation stock, which he'd always refused to sell. It ended up in family trusts, says David Thorne. "I always wanted to know exactly what it was and never got a very clear answer." United fought back against the regulators, and eventually its shares recovered. It merged with D. H. Baldwin & Co., the piano manufacturer, in 1977, when United still had $130 million in assets, and Baldwin-United went bankrupt in 1983, $1 billion in debt.

9

PRINCESS HENRY XXXIII OF REUSS, THE FORMER ALLENE TEW OF Jamestown, New York, was the last, but hardly the least, original apartment owner at 740, buying 10/11C in March 1931, just before sales ground to a halt and James T. Lee began renting his vacant apartments. She'd soon divorce the prince, marry Count Paul de Kotzebue, a Russian nobleman, and move to the larger 6/7B. Though they could not have been more different—one upright, the other a bit bent—she and Mrs. Marcus Daly Jr., the former Lele von Harrenreich of Vienna, Austria, one of the very first renters at 740, are inextricably linked by a shared taste for Russian royalty, both real and fake, and by their multiple marriages.

Princess Reuss turned Countess Kotzebue would stay in the building more than twenty years until her death on the Riviera, famous every step of the way. Mrs. Daly would only last a few years at 740 and would die much later, disgraced, in obscurity. They were just what Depression New York needed, making madcap headlines as they married their way through five—count 'em, five!—husbands apiece.

. . .

ALLENE TEW'S FAMILY APPEARED IN NEW ENGLAND IN THE EARLY EIGH-
teenth century. The first Tew in Jamestown, New York, was George
Washington Tew, and he rose from tinsmith to lawyer to bank president
before he died. Allene's grandfather William H. and her father, Charles,
followed in his footsteps as presidents of City National Bank. The family
owned one of the finest houses in Jamestown, they employed the first
African-American there as a coachman, and one of Charles's brothers
married the sister of the tire maker B. F. Goodrich. Allene Tew would top
them all.

"There's something of a perennial Cinderella about the Countess
Kotzebue," her friend Maury Paul, writing as the gossip columnist
Cholly Knickerbocker, once said. Born around 1872—her exact birth date
is unknown—the blue-eyed blonde with defiantly arched eyebrows married charming, rakish Theodore Rickey Hostetter in 1891. Ted was a
grandson of Jacob Hostetter, a doctor in rural Pennsylvania who'd invented Hostetter's Bitters, a concoction of cinchona bark, quinine,
calumba, and gentian root. Supposed to cure colic, constipation, and
fever, it was 47 percent alcohol masquerading as medicine. A fierce believer in advertising, Jacob's son David created the Hostetter Stomach
Bitters company in Pittsburgh, made a fortune selling the stuff to the
Union army as a cure for diarrhea during the Civil War, spent the profits promoting the name, and was soon selling half a million bottles a
year.

Ted, a vice president of the bitters maker, set his new wife up in a
twenty-five-bedroom redwood mansion on 265 acres on the Ohio River,
where she had three children, one of whom died young. After that,
Cholly Knickerbocker later wrote, Hostetter turned into "a gay Lothario,
as reckless as he was handsome—and the victim of 'too much money.' "

For a time, this was fine with Allene, who gloried in the "glittering
paradise" Hostetter created for her, Knickerbocker wrote. "Jewels were
hers for the mere hint and money flowed like a veritable Niagara. But society, always fearful of Ted's wild ways, never bothered much about his
pretty blond young wife." Allene finally tired of his gambling and phi-
landering and left him. Ted died of pneumonia in 1902, at age thirty-
four. A few months after his death, Allene was sued for $115,000—and
the extent of Hostetter's gambling was revealed.

They called him "The Lucky Plunger." LOST A MILLION IN A YEAR, said *The New York Times. The Washington Post* said he'd "mowed one of the widest swaths known to the sporting community along Broadway." Tod, as he was known at Canfield's, New York's top casino, where the "best chair at the best table" was his for the asking, was renowned for betting on anything: which way a fly would turn after landing on a table, whether the date on a coin would be odd or even. Tod's bête noire was roulette; though he won at everything else—even $1,000 coin tosses—he always lost when playing the wheel. Generous to a fault when winning, he expected the same in return when losing. At the time of his sudden death, his gambling debts were said to total over $800,000. Allene reportedly settled. She could afford it; despite his losses, and their separation, Hostetter left her millions.

A few months later, Allene met Morton Colton Nichols, who worked at J. P. Morgan & Co. and was a member of all the right clubs, including the Union, which his father had helped found. A yachtsman and a banker, the elder Nichols had been a member of the New York Stock Exchange since 1856 and was very wealthy. His son had been engaged once before, to President Ulysses S. Grant's granddaughter, but five years on, when he met Allene, they still hadn't made it to the altar, and Nichols's father, on his deathbed, pleaded with Allene to marry his son so he could attend the ceremony.

Wed in December 1904, they divorced in Paris less than a year later, and it was said that her fortune had been "largely augmented by her alliance with the Nichols family." Nonetheless, when Nichols remarried, Allene petitioned a court to allow her to be a Hostetter again, arguing that the presence of two Mrs. Morton Colton Nichols in New York social circles was a problem. Nichols committed suicide in the Hotel Pierre in 1932. Leaving nothing to chance, he hanged himself after taking cyanide and inhaling chloroform. Family members said he was in despair over acute sinus pain.

Allene had long since moved on. In 1912, she'd married Anson Wood Burchard, who was secretary to the president of General Electric. But her third passage to wedded bliss wasn't smooth, either. When Burchard applied to be married in a London church, permission was refused because of Allene's divorce. A front-page article in the *Times* quoted Allene, described only as Tod Hostetter's widow (clearly, Allene preferred that her marriage to Morton Colton Nichols disappear; divorce was still a disgrace), saying they might not marry after all, and then she deferred to Burchard. "At midnight," the paper continued meaningfully, "Mr. Burchard, who it is understood had been spending the evening with Mrs. Hostetter, stated that nothing definite had been arranged."

Wed they were, though, just a few weeks later, and together they raised her two surviving children by Hostetter in Birchwood, their home in Locust Valley, New York. Burchard rose at GE, first to vice president, then to the board of directors. All was well until tragedy struck again in 1918, when Allene's son, Ted, who'd joined Britain's Royal Flying Corps, was killed in action two weeks before his twenty-first birthday. A month later his sister died, too, pregnant with twins, in the influenza epidemic that swept the world after the war.

In 1923, Burchard was promoted to the presidency of International General Electric and the vice chairmanship of its parent, jobs that made him a regular commuter between New York and Europe. As GE's stock price soared through the 1920s, Burchard stepped back to become chairman of International GE and bought a mansion on Park Avenue and Sixty-ninth Street, and Allene began a concerted but unsuccessful assault on the inner circle of New York society. Her past taste in husbands stood in her way, and so did the hand of fate, which snatched husband No. 3 from her in 1927, when Burchard died at age sixty-one after an attack of indigestion at lunch at the home of Mortimer Schiff of the famed investment banking family that ran Kuhn, Loeb.

Allene inherited about $3 million. Because Burchard himself was childless, Seth Rosewater, an eighteen-year-old nephew whose father had owned the *Omaha Bee*, changed his name to Burchard shortly after his uncle's death and inherited some of the remainder.

Already accustomed to the high life of London and Paris, "the richest and saddest of New York's socially celebrated widows" found solace in those cities, even bowing before their Britannic Majesties at Buckingham Palace. She bought the home of a *comtesse* in Paris and in January 1929 chartered a houseboat, the *Indiana*, to take a monthlong sail up the Nile from Cairo with a party of seven. Among them was Prince Henry XXXIII of Reuss.

Henry's complicated, obscure, yet very grand name had an equally complicated and obscure history. Until 1918, his family, one of the oldest reigning royal houses in Europe, had ruled two tiny German principalities near the Polish border. At the end of the twelfth century, when a Prince Henry married a relative of the Holy Roman Emperor Henry VI, he decreed that henceforth all his sons would be called Henry. Two factions of the family followed suit ever after, using different numbering systems, one beginning afresh each century, the other renumbering once they hit one hundred.

Henry XXXIII was the widower of a Hohenzollern princess and had fought in World War I on the Russian front, where he was wounded. He then became a diplomat. He was also a distant heir to the throne of the Netherlands through his mother, the Grand Duchess of Saxe, granddaughter of the sister of the king of Holland. But all wasn't crowns and jewels; the Reuss line also had thorns.

Henry was broke and, as Cholly Knickerbocker put it, "anxious to exchange his ancient title for a luxurious life that only a rich wife could provide." Then there was the matter of the Reuss reputation. Henry XXIV was made "deaf, dumb, imbecile and blind" by his own mother, *The New York Times* reported in an article on the family's "tainted stock," not long after the princes abdicated after Germany's defeat in the war. His mother had insisted on holding him during a minor operation, then twitched in horror, causing an oculist to plunge a lancet into the child's eye. His father, an ascetic autocrat, had insisted on personally caning any misbehaving schoolchildren in his principality and on living in a "palace" without running water.

Henry's engagement to the widow Burchard was announced with great fanfare, and they married in the spring, making Allene the most entitled American in history, with the possible exception of Wallis Simpson, the Duchess of Windsor. The Reusses sailed to England and New York for a series of celebratory dinners. During their trip, they saw the electric chair at Sing Sing and attended the grand opening of the St. Regis Roof. The government even gave them a wedding present: a tax refund of $257,000 on Anson Burchard's estate. Allene gave it right back by endowing an Anson Wood Burchard Chair in Electrical Engineering at his alma mater, the Stevens Institute of Technology. Henry, a society column declared, was "not at all bad looking," "somewhat more youthful than his wife," and "apparently not displeased with the concern his presence incited" at parties.

Another column was less fawning, noting that Allene's Paris staff had refused to wear the Reuss family livery because of its "Germanic origin and design." For the next two years, the prince and his new princess commuted between Paris; an apartment in Rome; Henry's palace in Reuss; his family's winter palace, Castel Mare, in Cap-d'Ail on the Riviera; her New York mansion; and Allene's latest purchase, the Château des Suisnes, a seventeenth-century estate near Fontainebleau, France, built for the maître d'hôtel of Louis XIV and later owned by the explorer Bougainville.

In March 1931, Allene sold her New York house (she'd disposed of Locust Valley in the spring of 1930) and bought her first apartment on the Seventy-first Street side of 740 Park. She hung *A Landscape*, her 1778 Gainsborough, and decorated her silver and gray dining room with murals of Versailles. It was said she sometimes went into the kitchen herself to whip up a batch of doughnuts.

LELE DALY SHOULD HAVE BEEN IN MOURNING AS THE PRINCE AND Princess of Reuss moved into their new home. Her husband, Marcus Daly Jr., had died mysteriously a few months before. He was said to have had a heart attack while hunting on the shores of the Chesapeake Bay. But members of his family suspected he'd killed himself and blamed his wife.

Born in 1893 in Austria, Lele von Harrenreich was the daughter of Alois von Harrenreich, a retired lieutenant colonel with the cavalry of the Eleventh Dragoons of the court of the emperor Franz Josef. At nineteen, Lele, a saucer-eyed, bow-lipped brunette, married William Henry Young, the twenty-two-year-old son of a real estate man from Tuxedo, New York, after meeting him in Switzerland. They divorced six years later, and less than four months after that Lele married thirty-six-year-old Marcus Daly Jr.

Daly's father had immigrated to New York from potato-famine Ireland at age thirteen and in 1861 went to California to seek his fortune in its gold mines. He became a foreman at Nevada's famous Comstock Lode, then ran silver mines in Utah. When his bosses sent him to Montana to investigate their claims there, he bought one and sold it for a profit, which he used to buy a small silver mine, the Anaconda. Anaconda turned out to contain a huge amount of copper—at its peak it produced $17 million worth a year—and as his operations grew, Daly bought coal mines to fuel his furnaces, forests for timber, and power plants to run the mines and added smelting, banking, newspaper publishing, politics, horse breeding, ranching, real estate development, and feuding with his rivals to his portfolio of interests. In 1899, by then known as the Copper King, Daly sold Anaconda to Standard Oil interests shortly before he died at age fifty-eight, leaving a widow, three daughters, and a son.

Though her principal residence was the Daly Mansion on fifty acres in the Bitterroot valley of Montana, with twenty-five bedrooms, and seven fireplaces, the elder Mrs. Daly also kept a Fifth Avenue mansion. She could afford it: Daly left an estate variously estimated at $20 million to $100 million. It was in trust for his children, "to guard against fortune hunters seeking marriage with his daughters," said the *Los Angeles Times*, citing Daly's "bitter hatred of such" and "suspicion as to their motives." He probably also should have worried about his son.

Two of Marcus junior's sisters had married well—one to a former American ambassador to Germany, another to a Hungarian count— when their brother walked down the aisle with Lele in 1919. Though his sisters' weddings had attracted scores of social figures—Vanderbilts, Belmonts, and Rockefellers—only the immediate family attended the wedding of Lele and Marcus. After a Palm Beach honeymoon, they moved into an apartment on upper Fifth Avenue and soon had a son, Marcus III, by a then-rare Cesarean section performed by a professional wrestler turned doctor.

Throughout the 1920s, the Dalys lived the social life, summering in Southampton and Cap d'Antibes, fishing in Canada, hunting gorilla in the Congo, buying land in the Bahamas, attending lavish parties and balls, sailing for Europe, attending the races at Longchamp, often in the company of Lele's future neighbors at 740 Park, but as often as not traveling separately.

In February 1930, Marcus left for Cuba with his brother-in-law for a six-week visit, and while he was away, Lele sailed for England. That summer Marcus checked into a Southampton hotel alone. But by September, the couple were en route home from Le Havre together on the *Île de France*. Then Marcus took off for his fateful duck-hunting trip to Virginia, and on Monday, November 10, word reached New York that, though in good health, he'd died of a heart attack. News reports said he'd left a friend and a guide in a duck blind at the Holly Island Club, a private hunting preserve on an island off Wachapreague, Virginia, when he felt ill and went for a walk. When he didn't return, they found him slumped by a tree next to his gun, which was still fully loaded. On his death certificate, the cause was given as "probably heart disease . . . fell down while duck shooting."

What really happened? It was "known amongst family and servants" that Marcus junior killed himself, says Bob Notti, Marcus III's best friend in college. A Daly housekeeper told Notti the boy "would cry and cry and cry," he says. "That was one of the reasons he became estranged from his mother. He blamed her for driving him to suicide."

At the Daly Mansion in Hamilton, Montana, now a museum and tourist site, curators and volunteers have struggled for years to piece together the story of Marcus junior's fate. They believe he and Lele had separated. However Daly died, it was immediately obvious there was bad blood between Lele and his family. Tellingly, the *Los Angeles Times* report of his death mentioned his son but not his wife, while the *New York Times* death notice placed by Lele didn't mention any of the Dalys. And shortly after his death, they all got into a tangle over his $7 million estate, with Lele charging that the brother-in-law who'd been named executor was taking excessive fees. Marcus's sister sued for control of a building left jointly to her and Lele. Luckily, the will contest wasn't resolved until 1933, for by then the value of the estate had increased considerably. Lele was left the income from half the fortune and given control of the other half until their son turned thirty. On her death, Marcus III would get her half as well. Her sister-in-law paid Lele for her half of the building, and the brother-in-law got his fees after all.

Seven forty Park Avenue received no publicity when it ceased to be a "100 percent cooperative." The last announcement of a sale had come with the Bouviers in the fall of 1931. And in that case, it was James T. Lee, not Jack Bouvier, who'd bought the apartment, so it likely amounted to no more than a bookkeeping entry, since he'd bought it from himself. By early 1932, with $40,000 due on 740's mortgage every six months, Lee began offering rentals. The first taker was Lele Daly, who rented an apartment just before marrying George Jamhar Djamgaroff.

Djamgaroff described himself as a former officer in the White Russian army during the revolution, but he was more pertinently a former interior decorator who'd been taken up by Landon Thorne's mother-in-law, Julia Stimson Loomis. She'd organized an Opera Club in 1923 to raise money for Russian exiles and made Djamgaroff its secretary. He also sold cigarettes and rugs, according to a Russian officer who pegged Djamgaroff as an Armenian who'd never been an officer. He had been a busy boy, however, evolving from a social gadabout into a spokesman for exiled Russian royals and then a fervent anti-Soviet propagandist, testifying before Congressman Hamilton Fish's committee investigating Communists in 1930, then forming a news service specializing in exposés of American Communists.

Djamgaroff wore homburgs, carried a gold-topped cane, and had a taste for rich women. In 1930, he'd sued Ganna Walska McCormick, a light-opera singer, actress, and, lately, wife of the head of International Harvester, for hundreds of thousands of dollars in fees he claimed he'd earned as her press agent. Shortly afterward, he met Lele through the socially connected representative Fish. They married in a London civil ceremony in July 1932.

Their wedding announcement gave Lele's father, who'd died in 1917, a promotion to general. The story it told of Djamgaroff's past was equally questionable; the couple claimed he'd been a cadet at a military school when the Russian Revolution broke out, fought against the Bolsheviks, and had come to America in 1920, a refugee from Communist suppression of the bourgeoisie. It didn't say that he'd bluffed his way into America with a fake passport. After a honeymoon in Brittany, the couple returned to 740 Park for a round of wedding dinners.

The Djamgaroffs sailed to Europe to spend the summer of 1934 with the czarist grand duke Cyril, whose wife was a friend and client of Djamgaroff's, then returned to 740 for the winter. The next summer they rented an estate called La Lanterne in Brookville, Long Island. Lele, who'd taken up portrait painting, showed her work there. It's unclear what Djamgaroff was up to, but in October, instead of going to Europe as planned, Lele hied to Reno to establish Nevada residency for a divorce in which she charged her husband with cruelty. She wanted to be rid not only of him but of his name as well. Needless to say, she wasn't planning on going back to Harrenreich. Djamgaroff moved out of 740 and started planning an anti-Communist convention.

By 1937, both Lele Daly and her ex had been linked with others in gossip columns, but no weddings were in the offing, and she lived on at 740 Park for several more years. Djamgaroff resurfaced in 1942 as a "Russian mystery man" in a grand jury probe into pro-Nazi sedition. It emerged that he'd worked as a registered agent for the Dominican dictator Rafael Trujillo for $50,000 a year. So had Representative Fish, but he'd kept his payments a secret.

Outside the grand jury following one of his eight appearances, Djamgaroff denied he was a mystery of any sort and said the Nazis had offered him $200,000 to be their publicist in 1934, an offer he'd refused. He also denied a charge that he took money from his wealthy ex-wife and produced a statement from her to that effect. He then expounded on his desire to work for an undersecretary of state he claimed had a grudge against him. Later, Djamgaroff worked as a fixer for a group of isolationists opposed to the war against Germany and did P.R. for the Argentine strongman and demi-fascist Juan Perón. He spent the last years of his life running A.B.C. Publications, a lobbying group for Latin American newspaper publishers, and died in an apartment at the Plaza Hotel in 1951.

Lele had long since moved on. In 1941, she married Roe Wells, whom she'd met in Palm Beach. She'd gone from the Copper Prince to a dapper, mustachioed, white-haired man known as the Donut King; Wells was the president of the Doughnut Corporation of America.

Wells had a colorful marital history himself. In 1938, he was fifty and already twice-married; his first marriage had ended in Reno; he married a shipping heiress two months later, only to get divorced again. That year he eloped with Emily F. Gilchrist, seventy, who'd inherited $2 million from her previous husband, a timberman from Chicago. Three years later, $675,000 in jewelry and cash was reported stolen from her home on Star Island near Miami, and then found beneath a mattress. More was in the hands of a lawyer in New York. Why was never explained.

That was in February. Emily Gilchrist Wells filed for divorce in July—and cut Roe Wells out of her will—then died suddenly in September. Within sixteen days, Wells was married to Lele Daly and embroiled in a court battle with Emily's relatives: a second, photostated will had appeared leaving him 80 percent of her estate. Coincidentally, Lele's primary family antagonist, the real Mrs. Daly, Marcus's mother, had died that same June, leaving Marcus III, then at school in Missoula, Montana, a quarter of her $12 million fortune. Wells, fifty-three, finally received a $500,000 payoff from his late wife's estate.

This time Lele moved fast when she realized her marriage wasn't working. After she was foiled in an attempt to get a Florida divorce and a New York annulment a mere twenty months later, Lele demanded a financial accounting, accused Wells of making $225,000 disappear, had her lawyer call him to say "she doesn't want to live with you anymore," and then divorced him in Chicago, where she told the court she'd been living. She said that Wells had struck her during arguments over money. The first assault occurred thirteen days before the quickie divorce; she said he smashed her hand with a telephone. The next day, she claimed, he struck her in the face. Those details would prove important; they were all false.

The divorce was revealed one day after Lele's fifth engagement was announced in *The New York Times*. Her latest victim was Richard Franklin Ford, a balding Standard Oil executive and the great-great-grandson of Gideon Wells, Abraham Lincoln's secretary of the Navy. Ford was "no spring chicken" and was famed for his "marital elusiveness," according to *The American Weekly*. They married the very next day at Shadow Cliff, the forty-three-room Upper Nyack, New York, estate of Ford's mother. Lele wore gray organza and a shocking pink feathered hat.

The day after that, Lele von Harrenreich Young Daly Djamgaroff Wells Ford became a political football in Chicago. Illinois divorce law allowed a nonresident to sue for an instant divorce based on acts of cruelty committed during a visit. Because Lele asked for neither attorney's fees nor alimony, a lawmaker charged, she'd clearly colluded with her husband. Within a week, a lawsuit to vacate her divorce was filed by the same judge who'd granted it. Investigators had learned she'd never been to the apartment where she'd allegedly been assaulted; indeed she'd only rented it the day before the "assault." A "Negro maid," as the papers put it, who testified she'd seen Wells hit her, had never lived at the address she gave in court.

In October, Lele was ordered back to Chicago, and when she failed to appear twice, it was ruled that her fourth marriage was still valid and her fifth one was adulterous, leaving her subject to arrest for bigamy. Early in 1944, the marriage to Ford was annulled. A few months later, the order vacating her Chicago divorce was reversed on a technicality, but she still couldn't breathe easy. That June she was charged with divorce fraud again. And in July, she was back in court in New York, suing a twenty-two-year-old playboy, the heir to a tinplate fortune who'd sublet her apartment, for breaking a chair and getting lipstick on her rug while playing Jonah and the Whale, a game in which he was tied into a chair and blindfolded while women romped around him until he caught one. Finally, that fall, Lele won one, when her divorce from Wells was declared valid.

One press report had it that she promptly married Richard Ford again. But when Ford died in 1967, no wife was mentioned in his obituary. And Lele had long since dropped from public view. After fifty years in the public eye, she disappeared for the rest of her life. When she died, unnoticed, a month after her last husband, she was living in the Lowell Hotel on East Sixty-third Street in a suite that rented for $825 a month.

Lele, it turned out, had gone to Charlotte Amalie, St. Thomas, the U.S. Virgin Islands, where she wrote a last will and testament in 1953 in which she left her entire estate—worth $470,000 (about $2.6 million today)—to a close friend. None of her husbands was mentioned in it. Though she left nothing to her only child, whose trust funds from his father had long since made him wealthy, Marcus III arranged her funeral and allowed his mother to be buried in the Daly family mausoleum in a

New York cemetery. But he "hardly ever mentioned her," says his best friend, Bob Notti. "They had been estranged for years. He didn't care for her. He referred to her in very derogatory terms."

Lele left a poisoned legacy. Though Marcus III had been with his mother when she married Djamgaroff, he was soon sent away to boarding school and spent every summer with his grandmother in Montana. When he got married at eighteen to the daughter of a founding family of Santa Barbara, California, his grandmother was there. His mother, who was in Austria as World War II began, did not return for the wedding. At the Daly Mansion, many of the employees believe that by then, the first Mrs. Daly had bought her grandson from his mother.

Marcus III met Notti in a photography class at Montana State University in 1940, when Daly was a freshman and Notti a junior, and they became fast friends. Notti saw that Marcus was already wealthy—he drove a Cadillac and had a cook—and Notti would later hear that his friend had inherited about $28 million, some of it apparently released early from his father's trusts.

After the war, Marcus was running an auto dealership in Missoula when a couple who were old friends of his wife's turned up in Missoula and became inseparable friends of the Dalys. So inseparable, in fact, that they soon divorced, switched spouses, and remarried, all on the same day in the same courthouse, albeit by different judges. A year later, Marcus moved to Las Vegas and was divorced and remarried again, to Kay Little, a former showgirl with flaming red hair. "I'm going to end up like my mother," Marcus joked to Notti.

A few years later, Daly induced his friend to move to Las Vegas, and Notti realized that despite their luxurious circumstances—Marcus owned a photo shop and a Mercedes dealership, they lived in one of the finest houses in the desert gambling town and kept a yacht on Lake Mead—they were both alcoholics, and Kay Daly was belligerent when drunk. Her condition worsened over the years, particularly after Marcus and Kay adopted a baby girl, Candice, in the early 1950s. Marcus was her biological father, though that was never said aloud. Her mother was another showgirl, who "gave her up under duress," according to Sue Wild, who'd meet Candice years later.

In 1961, Marcus and Kay were divorced, and he married a waitress named Juanita from the Showboat Hotel. Nine years later, Marcus
Daly III died at age fifty from complications following surgery on
a broken hip. "He lived a very bad life, drinking all the time,"
says Notti. Meanwhile, Candice Daly had left home, gone to California
like so many teenagers of that era, and ended up an alcoholic, too,
living on a ranch outside Carmel, California, in the 1970s with a
biker husband named Buddy Lamb and a son they'd named Marcus.
Juanita Daly was one of many who sometimes took care of the child.
"Candice would just take off," says Juanita's current husband. "That
poor kid."

Candice Daly's fate is something of a mystery. Sue Wild describes
her as an unfaithful alcoholic who "had relationships with Hells Angels outside the marriage" and fought with her husband often. "They
destroyed furniture," Wild says, "and drove over each other's cars.
There was all this money—at least $4.8 million—but she couldn't re-
member to pay the electric bill." Candice's first husband died in 1979 after their last fight; she'd handed him a large check in exchange for a
divorce, but it bounced. When he learned that, he "roared off on his motorcycle and crashed within five minutes," according to Wild. Candice remarried and moved away, but didn't change. Lynn Perry, a childhood
friend, heard she was a passenger in a car that hurtled off a pier. "She
was either killed or she's in witness protection after testifying against the
Hells Angels," says Wild, repeating a story she's heard. In another, Candice tried to use her ranch to bail an Angel out of jail. If she really did
die, then she is buried next to Buddy Lamb in a grave on the Monterey
peninsula.

Marcus was three when his mother vanished, and he became the object of a three-way custody battle between Juanita Daly, Buddy Lamb's
family, and the lawyer who'd won Candice her share of the Daly family
trusts after her father's death. The trust lawyer won ("They wanted to
grab the money," says Juanita's husband, "and they grabbed every
penny") and raised Marcus IV. Today, in his early twenties, he lives quietly in a western state where he coaches a college baseball team. He
didn't request anonymity, but certainly deserves it. He first learned
who he was when he was nine or ten, he says. "I always knew there was

something different about me. It's a mess. But everything turned out okay. It's something you can't really explain."

"It's a very colorful family," says the eighty-eight-year-old Daly cousin Sumner Gerard.

"It's an American tragedy," says Rhonda Johnson, who worked for the Daly Mansion. "This family was hell-bent to destroy themselves."

10

As a rental, 740 finally filled up, but the process was slow, indeed excruciating for James T. Lee, who was responsible for the mortgage and the maintenance on all the unsold apartments. Now even the wealthy were feeling the effects of the Depression. All the luxury apartments that had gone up in the bubble of 1929 were glutting the market. Lee left no records and no diary and never discussed his obvious business problems with family, friends, or the press, but he was in trouble and doing anything to make a buck, just like most of his fellow Americans.

Luckily, people still needed a place to live, and some of them could still afford to rent nice ones. In the spring of 1933, Blanche Brownell Grant, who'd just concluded a friendly divorce with the twenty-five-cent-store mogul W. T. Grant, leased the penthouse at 71 East Seventy-first Street, the smallest, least expensive, but perhaps most exquisite apartment in the building. A month later, Clarence J. Shearn, a former state supreme court justice, signed a four-year lease to rent a simplex above the Brewsters. Around the same time, Clifford Hendrix, a stockbroker just back from six years in Europe, rented 6/7B, next door to the Bouviers. "We didn't pay much for it," reveals Clifford junior, who was paying attention, though he was a child at the time. "It was desperation on [Lee's] part."

There were some renters who were just plain rich. In September, Robert Thurlow Vanderbilt, a chemical, mineral, and drug manufacturer, rented apartment 12/13A. Unrelated to the famous Vanderbilts, he was married to Mildred Bedford, the daughter of one of the Bedford brothers. Like the Brewsters, the Bedfords were a founding family of 740 Park Avenue. They were also founders of Standard Oil. Three generations earlier, before the Civil War, the Bedfords had gone into the oil business in Brooklyn. In 1879, the family business was sold to Standard, and henceforth Bedfords would run various aspects of what was known as the Octopus and serve as its rulers, even after its monopoly was broken. The Bedfords were the most powerful family in Standard after the Rockefellers. Although Mildred and her husband were rather colorless, relatives would cause fireworks to light up 740 soon enough.

In May 1934, Lee and Douglas Gibbons finally gave up on discretion and advertised "a few apartments now offered for rent" in "one of the finest co-operative apartment buildings ever erected." This open admission of failure must have rankled. Nobody was writing newspaper profiles of the great builder Lee anymore.

But the ads worked. That September, Mrs. Walter Phelps Bliss, a widow, rented apartment 8/9B. Though she could still afford 740, her story reflected the declining fortunes of America's ruling class. Walter Bliss was the grandson of a common laborer who'd died insane. Walter's father went to work at age eight and eventually became a banker under Levi Morton, the future governor of New York and vice president of the United States. Walter inherited a small fortune—approximately $15 million—and was a Yale graduate, like so many at 740 Park. In 1897, Walter married Katharine Baldwin, the daughter of a governor of and senator from Michigan. Walter's Yale classmate William Rockefeller, John D.'s nephew, was his best man. On his father's death, Walter retired and spent his remaining years managing family investments, serving on railroad, mining, bank, and insurance boards, and working as treasurer of Grace Church. But there weren't many remaining years. Bliss died at fifty-three in 1924, slumping in his seat on the Lexington Avenue subway as it pulled into Brooklyn Bridge station.

Three years later, Sibyll, the second of the couple's four daughters, married Gouverneur Morris Carnochan, a direct descendant of Lewis

Morris, who signed the Declaration of Independence. Four years after that, the family's fortunes began to decline—and not just because Katharine Bliss kept her money in stocks, although that didn't help matters.

In 1931, Carnochan, a stockbroker, turned one of his partners in to the police for forgery and the theft of $32,500 from the firm. As things turned out, that was the least of it. The precise circumstances were hushed up, but the embezzlement left the firm bust. "The partners had to make good, the Carnochan patrimony vanished overnight, and what had been an ordinary life, as rich lives go, turned into a kind of elegant wreckage," Bliss Carnochan, a grandson who grew up at 740, writes in a family memoir, *Momentary Bliss.* Shortly after his mother-in-law rented her eighteen-room apartment, Gouv, as he was called, was forced to move his young family in with her. He and Sybill shared a bedroom with a view of Park Avenue across the hall from her mother. As the youngest of three children, Bliss got the room closest to the servants' quarters.

Until the move to 740, the Bliss family had known the sort of wealth that few can contemplate: their pre-income-tax fortune had paid for a 240-foot yacht; a splendid summerhouse, Wendover, in New Jersey hunt country, where they raised cattle; and the sprawling duplex Mrs. Bliss rented after moving out of the house on Eighty-seventh Street just off Fifth Avenue where she'd spent winters with her husband. Mrs. Bliss still kept both residences staffed, but by the mid-1930s the cattle were gone, and "the fanciness disappeared," says Bliss. As time went on, the staff shrank, too, until there was just West, the stately, balding English butler; a Scottish nanny who'd never be let go, even after the children were grown; Johnson, the plump housekeeper; a part-time chauffeur; and a cast of Irish housemaids.

Though their apartment was large, the Bliss family's circumstances didn't allow them to furnish it properly. They usually gathered in the library, hung with a seventeenth-century Dutch painting of exotic birds. The living room was "huge and formal," Bliss recalls, "with a piano that nobody played." A smaller sitting room featured purple chintz and Chinese wallpaper printed with more birds.

Bliss went to school at Buckley. Coming home each day, he'd jump to see if he could touch the green awning as Pat Owen, the heavyset Irish doorman, encouraged him. Like many kids in the building, Bliss knew the staff better than he knew his neighbors. "It was like living in your own private empire," he says.

Though he made friends in school, he never brought them home. "I was embarrassed by luxury and by (comparative) penury all at once," he wrote. "None of my friends lived in such grandeur, though many lived on Park Avenue, but neither did they and their parents live with their grandmothers . . . It was a matter of not enough and far too much, all at the same time."

Then there was the embarrassment of being forced into the Knicker-bocker Greys, a battalion of prepubescent boys from good families who performed military drills at the Park Avenue Armory and, once each spring, paraded up and down Fifth Avenue in full-dress regalia.

Meals in the Bliss household were served with military precision—lunch at 1:30, tea at 5:00, martinis at 7:15, dinner half an hour later—but Bliss usually ate alone. "I wasn't allowed to eat with the grown-ups," he says. His early memories are of listening to the radio: he was terrified by Adolf Hitler's speeches and remembers being in his 740 bedroom in December 1941, listening to a Redskins football game, when "they broke into the broadcast with the news of Pearl Harbor." Otherwise, the war barely intruded. Bliss remembers blackout curtains, but as "a joke," he says. "I don't think anyone seriously expected the Germans to arrive in New York." The war did hit home, though, when Bliss's father, who'd reenlisted at age fifty as a lieutenant commander in the Navy, was killed in an airplane crash in what was Dutch Guiana and then his brother died as well, two years later in 1945, in the Battle of the Bulge.

At eighteen, Bliss came home drunk one night, and a doorman took him to the basement to wash his face before allowing him to go upstairs. At that point, Bliss was a visitor, not a resident, going from St. Paul's to Harvard. "Once you've left New York," he later wrote, "you aren't a New Yorker anymore."

Infirm and bedridden Katharine Bliss remained at 740 until she died in 1961. A few years later, Sibyll Carnochan, who'd taken care of her mother for twenty-five years, moved out and the apartment was sold. "Seven forty Park Avenue in the 1930s and 1940s was a comfortable, in-sular world," says Bliss Carnochan. "I look back at life there with wonder, doubt (did it really happen?), ambivalence, and no little nostalgia. But I'm sure of one thing: even if that world, like Rome, was bound to fall, it had a measure of dignity."

MORE TENANTS TRICKLED IN. MOST WERE LINKED TO 740'S MATRIX OF family influence. May Forsyth Wickes, from an Old Society family, was the daughter of Edward Allen Wickes, a Union army captain in the Civil War who rode with Rosina Hoppin's grandfather General Sherman. Her brother, Forsyth Wickes, worked at Masten & Nichols, John D. Rockefeller Jr.'s lawyers. Selina Riker married into an old Dutch family in 1900. Abraham Rycken was given several Dutch land grants in Manhattan, including today's Rikers Island. Samuel Riker was held prisoner by the British during the Revolutionary War. His great-grandson Charles left $3.5 million in trust to his widow, Selina, who used some of it to lease apartment 4/5D at 71 East Seventy-first Street. She and her sister-in-law, another Riker widow, lived there until 1953.

Nora Borden Baldwin, a niece of Bertram Borden's, landed at 740, too, after she divorced her stockbroker husband, Peter, for cruelty in Reno in 1935. Francis Patrick Garvan married money—his wife, Mabel Brady, had a $12 million trust—but also earned his own. The son of a Connecticut paper manufacturer and a graduate of Yale and New York University Law School, he got a job as an assistant district attorney in New York, was soon named the city's top homicide prosecutor, and gained a certain fame by losing the most sensational murder case of the early twentieth century: two trials, held in 1906 and 1907 (the first ended in a hung jury), of the Pittsburgh mining and railroad millionaire Harry Kendall Thaw for murdering the architect Stanford White of McKim, Mead & White. Thaw shot White, who was known as a libertine, at the opening of a musical at Madison Square Roof Garden. Thaw's young wife, a former artist's model named Evelyn Nesbit, had told him she'd been drugged and raped and had lost her virginity to White at age sixteen—and then proceeded to have an affair with him. When rumors spread that White was seeing her again after she married Thaw, the alleged cuckold shot the architect three times.

Thaw's mother spent $900,000 on his successful defense. One of his lawyers, Clarence Shearn, who would later move into 740, called Garvan's boss, the district attorney, "a human hyena," in the spirited trial. "It was the first time temporary insanity was used as a defense and [my father] lost!" says Marcia Garvan Coyle. "To lose a trial where a person was shot in full view of a roomful of diners—"

Mrs. Coyle's husband, Frank, interrupted, "Is not easily done!"

Garvan's career hardly suffered, even when he failed in an attempt to keep Thaw locked up in an asylum. In 1909, it was said that Garvan might run for district attorney, but instead, seeking to earn more money, he went into private practice. In 1910, the blue-eyed Celtic charmer married Mabel, the daughter of Anthony Brady, an Albany millionaire whose business interests ranged from tea to New York City's streetcars; one of Mabel's brothers, an executive of New York Edison, was married to one of Garvan's sisters.

After the United States entered World War I, Garvan was named chief of the U.S. Bureau of Investigation and then alien property custodian in charge of all German assets in America. In that job, he discovered that nearly every chemical patent in the country was held by foreigners, who controlled the American dye industry. That discovery set him on the career path he would follow for the rest of his life. He seized the German patents, sold them to Americans, and then, after the war, successfully defended the move against an attack by the Hoover administration, which was trying to damage the reputation of Hoover's predecessor the Democrat Woodrow Wilson, who'd appointed Garvan. He later founded the Chemical Foundation to promote innovation in chemistry and ran it the rest of his life.

In the mid-1920s, Mabel Garvan and a sister, represented by Garvan's law firm, charged that their two brothers, the executors of their father's estate, had mismanaged the fortune. Garvan's brother-in-law testified that his father had structured his estate so it would not fall into the hands of "such persons as the husbands of these contestants." After a year of bad publicity and $500,000 spent on legal fees, the case was referred to an arbitrator. Finally, in 1924, the executors were forced to give Mabel and her three sisters millions in dividends earned by the trusts. The Garvans were suddenly rich, or rather, Mrs. Garvan was. Her husband sold his house on the corner of Fifth Avenue and Seventy-first Street (the asking price was $600,000), and they and their six children moved to a Tudor-style thirty-five-room estate called Roslyn House on Long Island and took an apartment in Manhattan's Carlton House.

Their hard-earned fortune didn't last long. Hurt by the market crash, the Garvans were forced to borrow (Harry Payne Whitney lent Garvan $300,000 in 1930), and in the spring of 1936 they downsized, moving from the hotel into one of the unoccupied apartments, 6/7C, at 71 East Seventy-first Street. The move was a natural one; they were part of the building's society, friends with the Webbs, the Brewsters, and the Princess of Reuss.

MORRIS AND KATHERINE HADLEY MOVED INTO APARTMENT 6/7D IN 1935. Hadley came from 740's legal matrix. He'd founded Webb, Patterson & Hadley in 1922 with Watson Webb's brother Vanderbilt and remained through all the firm's mergers. Hadley was a third-generation Yalie. His grandfather was a Yale graduate and professor; his father, Arthur Twining Hadley, a Yale student, too, joined its most exclusive secret society, Skull and Bones, married the daughter of a governor of Connecticut, and served as Yale's president for twenty-two years.

When World War I ended, Morris, twenty-three (who'd joined Skull and Bones, too), was the youngest major in the U.S. Army. He married Katherine Blodgett, the granddaughter of a millionaire Michigan lumberman, soon afterward.' After the wedding, Hadley headed to Harvard Law School, where he chaired the *Law Review* and was a favorite student of Felix Frankfurter's. He was said to have a mind that could cut to the heart of a problem intuitively. His long, successful, yet virtually unpublicized career at Milbank, Tweed, the stodgy, white-shoe law firm, was a testament to both his brilliance and his conservative style.

The Hadleys moved to 740 shortly after their fourth child was born. Hadley's career was on the upswing. He was a partner in the law firm that represented the Rockefellers and the Chase and had spent ten years on the board of Vassar and was its chairman from 1939 to 1941. During the war, he was also deputy director of the quaintly named Office of Facts and Figures in Washington. As if that weren't enough of a résumé, Hadley played a crucial role in the history of 740 Park Avenue. His firm represented the 71 East Seventy-first Street Syndicate that put together the deal to build it. But even before that, as 740 Park was still taking shape, Morris Hadley was part of the team buying up land for an even more thrilling Depression-era real estate development, Rockefeller Center. Which turned out to be good, very good, for 740 Park.

PART TWO

OIL MONEY

John D. Rockefeller Jr.'s dining room, fifteenth floor (1938–71)

(Photograph by Bob Wands, courtesy W. Kelly Simpson)

11

THE FIRST ROCKEFELLER CAME TO AMERICA FROM GERMANY IN 1723. More than a century later, John Davison Rockefeller was born in a small town in western New York, the son of a bigamist and his pious wife. Growing to manhood after the Civil War, Rockefeller was the right man at the right time to create Standard Oil, the most powerful monopoly in a world full of them. At its peak, Standard refined and sold 90 percent of America's oil and was public enemy number one for muckrakers and investigators who accused it of every form of predation.

By then, of course, Rockefeller had become the richest man in America.

ROCKEFELLER WAS FORTY-FOUR WHEN HE MOVED TO NEW YORK FROM Cleveland, the seat of his empire, in 1883. He'd been visiting the city in summer, staying in hotels before returning to Ohio, but was finally convinced to relocate by George Brewster's father, Benjamin, a Standard director. Brewster barked that a two-headed calf belonged in the circus, not in business. "You can't have one head in Cleveland and another in New York," he said, insisting Rockefeller choose.

So in 1884, when Junior, his youngest child and only boy, was ten,

Senior moved his family and ten servants—among them Nesmith, the housekeeper, and William Johnson, the butler—to a modest, dignified four-story brownstone mansion off Fifth Avenue on West Fifty-fourth Street, purchased, fully furnished, from the mistress of a railroad mogul. Next door was a garden and beyond, near Fifth Avenue, a two-story carriage house. The only changes Rockefeller made were to add a massive, menacing double iron fence with spear-pointed pickets and to level the garden so it could be turned into an ice-skating rink in winter.

Rockefeller was surrounded by men he'd made fabulously wealthy—"a colony of company directors," wrote his biographer Ron Chernow. Catty-corner on Fifth Avenue was Henry Flagler, with William Rockefeller across Fifty-fourth Street and Brewster right next door. Mrs. Seward Webb lived just around the corner on Fifth Avenue. Junior was raised by his religious yet progressive mother, Laura Celestia Spelman Rockefeller, to follow the Baptist religion in every way, to always be pious and decent. He was largely unaware of his father's place in the world, at least according to his hagiographer, Raymond Fosdick. But he probably knew more than he let on: all his life, he suffered from awful nerves and devastating headaches, and twice as a boy he was shipped back to Cleveland—once for a year—to recover from emotional collapses.

"You can never forget that you are a prince, the son of the King of kings," his mother warned, "and so you can never do what will dishonor your father or be disloyal to the King." He grew up under that fearsome spell in a suite on the fourth floor of the house on Fifty-fourth Street. He told his diary that Rockefellers "did not enjoy prodigality and shunned display." His family vacationed at Yellowstone, not in Europe. If he told his mother what he wanted for Christmas, she made sure he didn't get it.

Junior went to Brown University, where he was known as Johnny Rock, but he shied away from others; he was an unsociable teetotaler. Abby Greene Aldrich, his future wife, met him in the summer of 1894. Back at Brown, he took her to dances and vespers and was wowed by her. She was bold and inspiring, had savoir faire, and wasn't put off by his wealth or his name. She had her own: a descendant of good, old Elder Brewster of Plymouth, Abby was the daughter of Senator Nelson Aldrich of Rhode Island, one of the most powerful men in American politics. Formally, Aldrich represented his state, but he really represented monopolists and robber barons. Lincoln Steffens, the muckraker, called him the Boss of the United States. William Randolph Hearst's *Cosmopolitan* described Junior's and Abby's fathers respectively as "the chief exploiter of the American people" and "the chief schemer in the service of their exploiters."

In 1900, after dating for several years, they decided to spend six months apart to test their love. Their relationship passed the test, so they got engaged. After a honeymoon at New York's Plaza Hotel, they spent a month at the Rockefeller estate at Pocantico, north of the city, then moved into Senior's Fifty-fourth Street house while building their own across the street. In 1908, they moved to No. 13, just to the west of Junior's father's house; in 1913, they moved again to a new, palatial ninestory limestone mansion at No. 10. At 102 feet, it was the tallest private home in New York City, estimated to have cost $200,000, with another $100,000 spent on interiors. With its bronze doors, barred windows, and an infirmary, solarium, and fenced-in playground on the roof, all watched over by private guards, it became a tourist attraction. In the summer, the Rockefellers went to the Eyrie, Junior's eleven-thousand-acre, 107-room estate in Seal Harbor on Mount Desert Island off the Maine coast, which he'd bought in 1910.

Outgoing Abby helped socialize her shy, obsessively orderly husband by encouraging him—to spend, in order to balance his stinginess, and to mingle with others, rather than withdraw—and by strategically denying him: she categorically refused to keep careful financial records and wouldn't go to church on command.

Junior had gone to work at 23 Broadway, the Standard Oil building, in the office that managed his semiretired father's finances and investments. He had experience. Beginning at age thirteen, he'd diligently kept track of every penny he made and spent, right down to the two cents he was paid by his parents if he killed a fly. By seventeen, he was the family's travel agent and ran its stable—the family still traveled by carriage—on Fifty-fifth Street. At Brown, he'd managed the football team. His passion for exactitude was noted by his father, who put him in charge of maintaining the family's homes and managing its real estate, negotiating leases and sales, an expertise he put to good use assembling Colonial Williamsburg and, later, Rockefeller Center.

Junior was passionate about construction. For the rest of his years, he would carry a four-foot folding ruler in his pocket for measuring plans and construction sites. He had less luck as an investor, losing $1 million on Wall Street in 1899 and turning to his father for cash to make good. He never trusted the market again.

Despite his losses, Junior was extraordinarily rich. By 1922, when his father finished transferring his wealth ($200 million to charity, $475 million to his children, most of it to Junior), he was richer than anyone in America. That grubstake expanded to $995 million in 1928 (just shy of $11 billion in 2004 dollars).

"Your fortune is rolling up, rolling up like an avalanche," his father's top adviser, the former clergyman Frederick T. Gates, roared. "You must keep up with it! You must distribute it faster than it grows! If you do not, it will crush you and your children and your children's children."

Gates was charged with teaching Junior business—and lured him into the business of philanthropy. The pressure almost flattened him; Junior was not only plagued by nervous breakdowns, but by mundane ailments from bronchitis to shingles. After meeting him, Mark Twain described Junior as "a plain, simple, earnest, sincere, honest, well-meaning, commonplace person, destitute of originality or any suggestion of it."

The sad fact was that, by Junior's own admission, some of the practices of Standard Oil "sickened" him, and though he defended his father's creation in court, on corporate boards, and in the court of public opinion, at thirty-six he'd finally accepted the fact that the company that had enriched him was the cause of his emotional illness. So Junior found his natural outlet and devoted himself to improving the family's image via philanthropy.

In 1910, a year after his father funded the Rockefeller Foundation with $50 million in Standard Oil stock, Junior resigned from almost all his corporate positions. He spent the rest of his life giving away the family's money, inspired as much by Senior's long-standing but unpublicized devotion to charity (he gave away 6 percent of his income long before he was rich) and his mother's fervent Christianity as by his unhappy relationship to the oil monopoly.

The one board Junior stayed on was Colorado Fuel & Iron. When its workers went on strike in September 1913, seeking union recognition, Junior held out for an open shop, telling a CF&I official he was fighting "a good fight." The following April, striking workers at the company's mine at Ludlow were evicted from their company-owned homes and attacked in their tent colony by an overwhelming force of state militiamen, company guards, private detectives, and strikebreaking goons who shot and burned to death twenty people, thirteen of them women and children.

It became known as the Ludlow Massacre.

Junior at first dismissed the debacle as an "outbreak of lawlessness," but after the socialist writer Upton Sinclair penned an open letter calling *him* a murderer, picket lines formed outside his office and the thirty-three-hundred-acre family compound at Pocantico, and a bomb meant for 10 West Fifty-fourth Street exploded before it got there, killing several people. Junior was blamed personally and underwent a profound conversion.

"I should hope that I could never reach the point where I would not be constantly progressing to something higher, better—both with reference to my own acts and . . . to the general situation in the company," he told an investigating commission. "My hope is that I am progressing. It is my desire to." Shortly after that, he traveled to Ludlow without bodyguards, spoke to workers, let them unionize—and in the process found himself. "For the first time in his life, Junior had taken an independent step," Daniel Okrent wrote in *Great Fortune*, his book on the creation of Rockefeller Center. "After Ludlow, Junior was the Rockefeller who mattered."

IN 1929, JUNIOR LED A PROXY FIGHT ON BEHALF OF SHAREHOLDERS IN Standard Oil of Indiana to remove its board chairman, who'd been less than candid when questioned by a Senate committee. His father had been the ultimate symbol of private wealth. Junior now epitomized its opposite, the public citizen. "Giving interests him more than getting," wrote *The New York Times* in a 1930 article on the men who ruled America.

In the 1920s, when he wasn't dealing with his aging but still-feisty father, Junior launched a mind-boggling array of philanthropic endeavors:

studying prostitution, saving ancient artifacts in Palestine, restoring Versailles, supporting colleges for African-Americans, financing the Tuskegee Institute and Margaret Sanger's efforts to advance birth control, promoting roadside beautification, and creating the Rockefeller Institute for Medical Research (now Rockefeller University). His good works would grow grander over time: he helped preserve the forests at Yosemite; his land donations made possible the Acadia, Grand Teton, Great Smoky Mountains, and Shenandoah national parks; he created Colonial Williamsburg and built International Houses for foreign students. In New York, he built Riverside Church, what became the Memorial–Sloan Kettering Cancer Center, and the Cloisters in Fort Tryon Park, which sat on land he'd donated to the city. In all, he'd give away more than $1 billion between 1917 and 1960.

In his Tudor-paneled, antiques-filled office at 26 Broadway, the seat of the family's power—at least when he wasn't in one of the sanitariums where he was still frequently treated for nerves—Junior commanded the Rockefeller empire. And he was about to embark on the greatest adventure of his life, building Rockefeller Center a few blocks south of the family's little village on West Fifty-fourth Street.

Society's steady crawl northward was threatening this family redoubt; they defended it by buying up lots and buildings and fighting attempts to re-zone to allow businesses on their streets. In 1928, Otto Kahn, the partner in the investment bank Kuhn, Loeb who'd helped the Rockefellers buy Equitable in 1911, approached Junior with an idea. Kahn's alliances were many: he was a member of the Jekyll Island Club (where he wintered with the Brewsters), and, like Rockefeller, he was represented by the publicity man Ivy Ledbetter Lee. Another of Lee's clients, Walter Chrysler, was negotiating to lease land for a new headquarters on Forty-second Street and Lexington Avenue—evidence of a phenomenon: as New York's patricians moved north, and their houses were replaced by skyscrapers, the commercial value of midtown land was spiking.

Kahn ran the Metropolitan Opera Company, which needed a new home. Columbia University was looking for a way to squeeze more revenue out of land it owned between Forty-seventh and Fifty-first streets, from Fifth Avenue almost to Sixth, where an elevated train ran above a dark, unappealing corridor. It and the streets south of the Rockefeller houses were blighted by brothels, speakeasies, and shabby brownstones and rooming houses. Kahn decided to build a new opera house there, and Ivy Lee thought Rockefeller might acquire the land. Not only would the opera help protect his home; it would create an incentive to clean up the neighborhood, a notion calculated to appeal to Junior, who was a staunch prohibitionist.

Rockefeller's advisers, led by his brother-in-law Winthrop Aldrich of Murray, Aldrich & Webb, saw a greater possibility—for profit—and encouraged him to lease Columbia's entire property for $3.3 million a year. He did so in January 1929.

The stock market crashed eight months later. The opera company, pleading poverty, then asked Junior to donate not just the land but half the cost of its building, too. He refused.¹ "It was clear that there were only two courses open to me," he recalled years later. "One was to abandon the entire development. The other to go forward with it in the definite knowledge that I myself would have to build it and finance it alone . . . I chose the latter course."

Junior was already a poorer man: the stocks he and his father bought after the crash had gone down like everyone else's; his net worth had sunk from almost $1 billion in 1929 (the equivalent of $10.8 billion today) to less than $500 million in 1934, and then to $379.6 million in 1938 (or $5 billion in 2004 dollars). The center was a huge undertaking, and in the end he would spend $125 million on it, paying out more than $10 million a year for a decade—all of it from his $15 million annual personal income and stock sales. And he would recoup less than half his investment and never see income from the venture in his lifetime. But he was still better off than most or, rather, *all* of his fellow Americans. And Rockefeller Center, which would ultimately succeed, would finally be seen as his crowning achievement.

The first task for the Rockefeller interests was to buy out the existing leaseholders to acquire the handful of parcels Columbia did not own and as much frontage along Sixth Avenue as they could get their hands on. And it all had to be done without Rockefeller's name involved, because that was sure to raise the cost of doing business. Morris Hadley was one of the lawyers who pulled off that coup.

. . .

ON THIRTY-FOURTH STREET, THE EMPIRE STATE BUILDING WAS RISING, just the sort of folly that had seemed like anything but a mere few months before. The *Empty* State Building, as they called it post-crash, was financed with a $27.5 million mortgage from Metropolitan Life. Yet Fred Ecker, the chairman of Metropolitan Life, was in a generous mood in the spring of 1931, when Thomas Debevoise ran into him at a golf club on a South Carolina plantation. Debevoise was Junior's in-house lawyer (they'd met as students at Yale) and had come to ask Albert Wiggin, Ecker's host, for advice about Rockefeller Center. All three men were on the Chase board. Soon a deal was struck. If Junior would personally guarantee the loan, Metropolitan Life would issue him the largest mortgage ever made by an insurance company, a $65 million line of credit at 5 percent interest, enough to pay for half the development costs. Junior "was quite unhappy about it," says his youngest son, David. He felt the interest rate "was very high," that Ecker "had pressed for a very stiff bargain," and he "never really forgave him." But his advisers saw no other way out.[2]

Junior promptly had another nervous breakdown. But now, nothing could stop Rockefeller Center. Work had stopped on buildings, roads, and bridges all over New York, but in the center of Manhattan men were employed by the thousands, and buildings, if not hope, were on the rise. In 1933, Junior moved his antiques-filled office into the all-new office of the Messrs. Rockefeller in Room 5600 on the fifty-sixth floor of the RCA Building, the heart of Rockefeller Center.

By 1936, Rockefeller Center, the majestic symbol of the family's accomplishment, was nearing completion, Riverside Church had opened, the Cloisters were ready for occupancy, and Colonial Williamsburg was a reality (though work there would never cease), where the Rockefellers had finished work on their own estate, Bassett Hall, an eighteenth-century house on 585 acres.

Abby, too, had completed the largest-scale project in a lifetime of good works. Junior had been collecting art since 1915, when he'd bought J. P. Morgan's collection of Chinese porcelains—which spoke to his passion for detail—after the banker's death. He then branched out into traditional paintings, Oriental rugs, and the set of French Gothic Unicorn tapestries from the fifteenth century that now hang in the Cloisters. Having inspired him to do that, Abby began her own collection, using money from Junior to buy European and English porcelains and her Aldrich fortune to pay for paintings by German Expressionists and Postimpressionists, American folk art, and modern woodcuts. These so offended her husband—who detested modern art—that he gave her a floor of their town house as a private gallery where he could avoid ever seeing them.

With some like-minded friends, Abby decided to found a museum for contemporary art. Though Junior was indifferent, if not hostile, to her taste and intentions, one week after the crash of 1929 he accompanied her to the opening of the institution she'd co-founded, the Museum of Modern Art, in its first home, six rooms in an office building at Fifth Avenue and Fifty-seventh Street. It soon moved to Rockefeller land on Fifty-third Street.

BY THE MID-1930S, THE ROCKEFELLERS WERE A VASTLY DIFFERENT FAMily from the one America had feared and loathed at the turn of the century. They were still standard-bearers of wealth: Rockefeller and his son took first and second place on a list of real estate assessments in New York published in 1932.[3] But their old image as vampiric monopolists had been upturned. By the time Rockefeller Sr. died in his sleep just before his ninety-eighth birthday in 1937, they'd come to epitomize all that was best about capitalist accumulation.

Junior continued to call himself Junior for the rest of his life. Yet his children were already grown up—David, the youngest, turned twenty-one in 1936 and was at Harvard that year—and Rockefeller had already begun the process of transferring his father's fortune to them.[4] In 1934, he'd set up trusts before new estate and gift taxes were imposed, giving them the income from $102 million (about $1.4 billion in 2004 dollars).[5] The handoff begun, his nest emptied, his work mostly done, Junior thought about moving.

"They had decided that with all of the children gone, it didn't make sense to live in a nine-story house by themselves," says David, the only one of their children who would even have a bedroom at 740. "So they decided to move. The Museum of Modern Art didn't have a place to go, and [my mother] persuaded Father, even though he didn't like modern art, to give it the whole piece of property, not only 10 West, but also 4 West, which had belonged to my grandfather, 12 West, and the intervening spaces, from Fifty-fourth to Fifty-third, back where my aunt had a house." It was David who persuaded his aunt to leave her double-width mansion to the museum. MoMA still sits on that land.

It was natural, once he decided to move, that Junior would look at 740. The Brewsters were a Standard Oil family, as were the Bedfords, the family Robert Vanderbilt had married into. Rockefeller controlled Chase (which meant that, practically speaking, Lynde Selden and James T. Lee worked for him), and Morris Hadley's law firm represented it. Not only that, William Hale Harkness, the Hoppins' subtenant, was a Standard Oil heir *and* had worked with Watson Webb's brother Vanderbilt at Murray, Aldrich & Webb.

ROCKEFELLER COULDN'T HAVE ENTERED JAMES T. LEE'S ORBIT AT A BETter moment. Lee had sold seventeen of the thirty-one apartments at 740, but he still owned a majority of the co-op's shares, giving him control of the building but also crushing financial responsibilities. Though he'd rented all but six of the empty apartments (two of which he and the Bouviers occupied), he still wasn't making enough to service 740's debt. In the relentlessly declining economy, the building was hopelessly overfinanced. And its balance sheet was increasingly unbalanced: there was a $208,000 deficit at the end of 1933, and it was growing. Then Charles McCain, who'd only laid out a $30,000 deposit for apartment 8/9A and still owed $116,000 to the 71 East Seventy-first Street Syndicate, quit the Chase Bank and stopped paying rent, and Lee's losses accelerated.

Lee "was a very shrewd, smart, tough real estate man, who had a very high reputation for his skills and knowledge," says David Rockefeller. Yet all around town, businesses were failing—and the 740 Park Avenue Corporation was one. The depth of Lee's problems would never be revealed, and only a handful of 740's tenant-owners would become aware of them, but in the spring of 1935 the board began a series of momentous meetings at the dusty, Dickensian offices on Fifty-seventh Street of the managing agent Douglas Gibbons.

James T. Lee was well aware that his Chase board colleague Frederick Ecker, the chairman of Metropolitan Life, hated to foreclose on loans. Mortgages were the secret of Ecker's success. He'd joined MetLife, as it is now known, as a sixteen-year-old office boy in 1883 and won his first promotion because he was the only employee who knew how to use the then-new telephone. A clerk in the real estate department—mortgages represented 60 percent of the company's investments—Ecker impressed executives by spending nights studying real estate law and the property market. When a financial panic brought a wave of foreclosures in the 1890s, Ecker began renovating and selling properties. At thirty-one, he was named head of the mortgage department.

By the time the Depression sank to its low, MetLife was the world's largest investor in real estate, with a portfolio still worth $1.34 billion, four times the assessed value of Atlanta. Ecker, by then the chairman, had decreed that despite tens of millions of dollars in back interest owed to the company, if property owners acted responsibly, the company would not foreclose on mortgages; it would forgo principal payments and rene-gotiate loan terms to let people keep their homes. "He made a point of showing off his integrity," says Debbie Ecker, a granddaughter. "He didn't keep it under a barrel." He helped businessmen in trouble, too: MetLife canceled $4 million in mortgage interest debts on the Empire State Building, which was only 25 percent rented in 1933, in exchange for concessions.[6]

Ecker was not only a colleague but also a friend of James T. Lee's. And the rest of 740's tenants were the folks they ran into at the opera, fellow captains of industry, colleagues on the Chase board. Ecker lived a few blocks south at 660 Park. So he well understood that the 740 Park Avenue Corporation's troubles threatened all of them. Two years earlier, he'd allowed it to pay only 4 percent interest on its mortgage (instead of the 5 percent owed) and to forgo principal payments altogether. Notwith-standing the assertion in Lee's 1968 obituary that "in spite of the Cassandra-like predictions of his friends, the venture proved successful," 740 was anything but.

"It was an inopportune time for people to move into fancy buildings," says Lee's granddaughter LeeLee Brown. "They were jumping out win-dows!" Indeed, several dozen brokers and speculators made news in the early 1930s by killing themselves in all sorts of ways—jumping out windows and off bridges, drinking poison, inhaling gas, carbon monoxide, and chloroform, shooting and slashing themselves (one even hung himself at the stock exchange). There is no record of a 740 tenant committing suicide, but given the times, it's likely such thoughts occurred in its echoing, under-furnished parlors.

On January 15, 1936, the board president, Beekman Hoppin, sent a few of his neighbors a memo outlining a proposed reorganization of their cooperative. It came from Lee, who "asks that the matter be kept confidential among a small group of which you are one," Hoppin wrote. He and another of the original apartment purchasers, insurance executive William Davey, had met with Lee two weeks earlier and found his attitude "most co-operative." He hoped they could discuss it all at a meeting at Hoppin Brothers on the morning of January 22.

The memo could not have made happy reading for the tenants of 740. It opened with a breakdown of shares in the corporation. Though more than half the apartments had been sold, more than half the shares still belonged to Lee. When Charles McCain's shares were added in, the sponsoring syndicate held 25,893 shares, the tenant-shareholders only 21,357. The memo was blunt about Lee's syndicate, saying it wasn't a syndicate at all, but rather "J.T.L. personally with no other participants." But it also referred to "a number of other creditors" with an interest in the $116,000 loan that had allowed McCain to buy his apartment. Those creditors, the silent and invisible partners in the syndicate, obviously didn't want their role made known.

McCain, who'd long since left for Chicago, not only owed the syndicate that sum and accrued interest; he also owed the corporation $11,599.99 in back rent. For its part, the corporation owed MetLife almost $4,000 in principal and $156,800 in interest. Lee reported that carrying the unsold apartments had already cost him $920,085. And he owed the 740 corporation a bit more than $114,000. He pointedly mentioned that anytime he wanted, he could give the empty apartments to "an impecunious relative"—that is, a penniless one—and be free from his financial obligation. He had not done that yet.

It's unlikely that a copy of the memo went to Jack Bouvier.

"J.T.L. feels that he has reached the limit of any *moral* obligation to continue to pay the carrying charges upon the unsold apartments and that he must terminate his legal obligation," the memo continued. Lee suggested that the co-op become a rental and the tenant-owners become minority partners in the corporation and assume a proportional burden of its losses. Once that was done, he would offer MetLife $170,000 cash if they would reduce the loan principal and let the interest rate remain at 4 percent. Lee hoped that MetLife would forgive the outstanding interest debt, so the shareholders would need to raise only $15,000 more than the building's cash on hand to pay down the mortgage. Lee offered to turn all his unsold apartments over to the corporation for rental and to give it the right to toss him out on a month's notice. The seventeen owners would be guaranteed the right to rent their apartments for $10 per share a year or could, if they chose, move out and let the corporation rent them at market rates.

The memo ended with a vague threat. Lee's proposal, it said, was based on the assumption that the owners wished to keep their equity and their homes "in the belief that future value in this equity is well within the realm of probability." The alternative? Let MetLife take the building and do what it pleased.

The tenant-owners were horrified. They doubted Lee's figures, distrusted his ability to bargain with MetLife, and felt sure they'd get stuck with the $170,000 payment, which worked out to $3.60 a share atop rent increases of $1.80 a share. They also argued that rents of $10 a share, equal to the maintenance payments set in the pre-crash offering plan, were "far in excess of today's rental values," that they'd be subsidizing the majority shareholder (Lee), and that they would be left without any working capital. They surely did the arithmetic, too. Under Lee's plan, the Webbs would not just lose their right to sell their apartment, but with 2,060 shares they would be on the hook for more than $11,000 of the money due MetLife and an annual rent of $20,600 besides. Even Bertram Borden, who held only 840 shares, would have to pay more than $4,500 on the mortgage and $8,400 rent. An outrage!

Their counterproposal showed they could play hardball as well as Lee. Turn the building over to MetLife or file for bankruptcy, they told him. Then they would rent their apartments back for market rates—that is, less than they were currently paying. "There seems little doubt" they could do that, they said. As an alternative, they agreed to modify the corporation as Lee suggested and seek to negotiate the interest rate on both deferred and future payments, but only if they could forgo the $170,000 payment or have it paid by all pro rata, so that Lee paid the most. And they wanted to be guaranteed that $10 per share rent, with Janet Bouvier and Lee paying the same.

The committee of owners, calling themselves the 740 Group, hired a lawyer at Davis Polk to negotiate with his counterpart at Milbank, Tweed (the successor to Murray, Aldrich & Webb), representing Lee. Refining their position over the next week, they asked that any profits from rents be repaid to the tenant-owners, that MetLife be paid its $170,000 from the corporate account only if it agreed to waive the deferred interest due and reduce its interest rate to 4 percent through 1938, and that there be no further assessments against their stock. They also demanded that all principal reduction payments, whether past due or new through December 1938, be deferred until the loan matured in 1949. Janet would get to keep her apartment. Lee would have to move out. And a new bylaw would set strict rules about the eligibility of future rental tenants, "so that the high standard of the building may be maintained."

Lee countered that he would make up any deficit owed to MetLife as well as any operating deficits with loans and would personally guarantee interest payments through 1938, but he insisted that lease-renewal options end in 1949 and that his total loan obligation to 740 be capped at $450,000. He also produced a revised budget that showed the building's deficits dropping to $12,000 within two years.

What happened next isn't clear. MetLife's in-house historian can find no records of the 740 Park loan. All the record shows is that in 1935, the 740 Park Avenue Corporation (G. Beekman Hoppin, president, James T. Lee, vice president) disappeared from Polk's corporate directory, the standard reference, without explanation, and in March 1936 Lee filed papers with New York's secretary of state that formally turned 740 Park into a rental building for all, even shareholders of the 740 Park Avenue Corporation. All the owners turned over their leases, which were marked "surrendered" in bright, flowing red script, effective at midnight on the last day of 1935.

The high hopes of 1929 had turned into dashed hopes in seven depressing years. Each of the original owners—the Brewsters, the Mc-

Cains, the Bordens, Davis, Davey, Countess Kotzebue, the Hoppins, the Beckers, the Scovilles, the Webbs, the Hanrahans, the Seldens, and the Thornes—became minority partners in a money-losing enterprise. Seven forty Park, which rose to symbolize their reach, had turned out to be their folly. It was now just another rental building, albeit a very expensive one. So Lee needed to hook a whale, the sort of tenant other tenants followed—even into troubled buildings like 740 Park. John D. Rockefeller Jr. was the kind of catch he dreamed of.

IN YEARS TO COME, GOSSIP COLUMNS WOULD COVER 740 AS IF IT WERE A Hollywood starlet collecting ever-larger paychecks while enjoying ever-more-tempestuous love affairs. And they would repeatedly say it was built by a Rockefeller (though they disagreed on which Rockefeller) and owned by a Rockefeller. But the truth is, 740 had a checkered past, and Rockefeller was hardly an owner. He arrived as a mere sub-lessor, an understudy stepping into the starring role in an unacknowledged flop.

At age sixty-seven, on March 11, 1936, George Brewster dropped dead of a heart attack at the Jekyll Island Club, three days before the "Plan and Agreement of Readjustment of 740 Park Avenue Corporation"—formalizing the deal between Lee and the owners—was sent to the printers. "I suspect that my grandfather's heart attack might be connected with the loss of his investment," says Christine Farrington. Yet he never said a word about it to his family. "Father never spoke of it," says Katharine Whipple, who'd just turned eighteen. "Nobody ever mentioned it. I'd have thought it would have bugged him a lot."

Eleanor Brewster immediately decided the apartment was too big and too expensive. "My brothers didn't live there; they had moved to their own places by then, so we were really a pretty small group," Katharine says. She remembers coming home one day not long afterward to find John D. Rockefeller Jr. measuring the walls of the sitting room she shared with her sister with his fancy folding ruler. "We asked him why, and he said to make sure it was big enough to have dancing lessons," she says.

Late in April 1936, Junior's lawyer and friend Thomas Debevoise had had two meetings with Frederick Ecker, who held the mortgages on both

Rockefeller Center and 740 Park Avenue. By June, Debevoise and Vanderbilt Webb of Milbank, Tweed were negotiating for Junior to sublease the massive apartment built for Brewster, his wife's relative, the man on whose land 740 Park stands.

The Brewsters were paying $25,000 a year for the apartment. Eleanor's lease was for three years, ending in September 1938, with options to extend to 1949. She could no longer sell it and recoup the capital her husband had traded for it. But she could ask Rockefeller to pay $40,000 a year—the extra $15,000 representing 5 percent interest on the $250,000 purchase price. "Some of those Southern belles were pretty bright," Whipple says of her mother. "I suppose she must have talked it over with the boys, but she did it."

Rockefeller was the answer to everyone's prayers, so every effort was made to close the deal. "There are three or four vacancies in the building which will be promptly filled Mr. Gibbons confidently believes as soon as it is announced that you have taken an apartment in the building," says a letter from an unknown sender in Rockefeller's files. Once those apartments were rented, it promised, the $25,000 carrying charge would likely decrease.

Still, Rockefeller dickered. He wanted a five-year lease with two five-year extensions. Instead, the Brewsters offered him possession on July 1, 1937, and a lease running through September 1945 with an option to extend through 1949. The deal was finalized on June 19, 1936. Four days later, Rockefeller telegraphed from the SS *Europa*, en route to Europe, still negotiating: he'd changed his mind and wanted the lease to run twelve years with two five-year options. Gibbons gently reminded him that the Brewsters didn't have the right to do that, but would agree to renew if they were allowed to. Two days later, the Brewsters' lawyers clarified: after 1949, it would be up to James T. Lee. That was okay; Lee worked for Junior.

As was his habit, Junior went over his lease with a flea comb once he returned to Maine and produced a five-page single-spaced list of questions for Debevoise, leaving spaces after each question for answers. Mostly, it revealed his ignorance of rental leases.

Junior wanted to ensure that he could have guests, that he would not be tossed out in the event that Lee failed to pay his mortgage, that he would be protected if the building were condemned or found to be flawed in some awful way, and that the Brewsters would be obligated to pass along any credits against the carrying charges.

Allowing that the Brewsters' lawyers had been "overzealous, not intentionally insulting," Junior's lawyer assured him that all the lease provisions were typical and the best a renter could hope for and that a building like 740 was unlikely to have hidden defects that would cause it to be condemned.

So Junior signed the lease at the Eyrie on August 24, 1936, and Vanderbilt Webb wrote from Shelburne Farms to say he expected the deal to close within a week, assuming the leasing committee gave its approval. But two members were out of town, so Junior had to wait until September 22. Then he had to wait again, until the twenty-fifth, when Webb said the sublease had been "submitted to Mr. Lee" and "meets with his approval."

Two weeks later, Rockefeller's plan to move made national news—confirmed on the front page of *The New York Times* after several days of rumors. It was declared the end of the era of the urban elite living in private houses: fully 90 percent of Manhattan's wealthiest now occupied apartments. But this, this was the ultimate apartment, as the *World-Telegram* made clear when it helpfully printed a picture of 740 with the huge Rockefeller residence highlighted by a dotted line under the headline ROCKEFELLER, JRS., TAKE TO AERIAL LIVING.

Time called it, simply, "the most notable lease of the year."

12

WITH JUNIOR IN RESIDENCE, 740 PARK BECAME KNOWN AS A STANDARD Oil building. But it had always had a Standard Oil contingent. The Harknesses, best known as Ohio retailers, had branched out into distilleries and grain before the Civil War, then gone into banking and real estate afterward. Junior's new neighbors were original shareholders in Standard Oil—their stake was second only to the Rockefellers'. In 1918, when *Forbes* printed its very first "Rich List," it named a Harkness the sixth-richest man in America, after John D. Rockefeller Sr., his brother William, Henry Frick, Andrew Carnegie, and George Baker.

William Hale Harkness was born in 1900, the son of a financier and yachtsman whose $100,000 *Gunilda* was the flagship of the New York Yacht Club until it hit a shoal and sank in Lake Superior in 1910. Harkness *père* was so rich he just walked away. When he died in 1919, Harkness left an estate worth in excess of $54 million, a quarter of which went to his son William Hale immediately (he would receive another $3.5 million on his mother's death in 1947). A graduate of Yale, William quit the law in 1930 to manage his investments and in 1932 married Elisabeth "Buffy" Grant, the cousin of an Alabama senator. Harkness went to Europe with the Army Air Force as a lieutenant colonel during World

War II, winning a chestful of medals. "Everybody had them, so nobody wore them," says his irreverent daughter, Anne Harkness Mooney. "He flew a desk."

The couple's marriage didn't survive the war, and they were divorced in 1945 shortly after his return from Europe. "They knew it was going to happen," says Mooney. "I didn't, but why would I?"

A year later, Harkness married a divorcée, Rebekah West (who became an arts and dance patron), and moved across Seventy-first Street to 730 Park. His ex kept up a busy social life as Mrs. Grant Harkness, induced her sister to move into an apartment at 71 East Seventy-first in 1947, and lived on there herself until 1949, when Anne went to Miss Porter's School. "She stayed because it was where I'd grown up, and when I left, she moved," says Mooney. The next year Mooney's mother married the movie star Robert Montgomery and began a second life. William Hale Harkness died of a heart attack at fifty-four in 1954. Elisabeth Grant Montgomery lived till age ninety-three. Another daughter was Elizabeth Montgomery, the star of the television show *Bewitched.*

Not every tenant had a Rockefeller connection. Some were merely wildly wealthy, just like the oil clan. And unlike more typical 740-ites like Harkness, they weren't always quiet about it.

In April 1936, as Thomas Debevoise was meeting with Frederick Ecker on Jekyll Island, Marshall Field III was leasing apartment 12/13B from Lee. Field could easily afford the sprawling spread; he was one of the richest tenants yet at 740. Also, the most politically outré. The millionaire grandson of Chicago's most famous retailer was about to become an outspoken, and very controversial, supporter of the class traitor Franklin Roosevelt.

Field had just married his third wife, Ruth Pruyn Phipps, a descendant of Dutch settlers from the Hudson Valley and the ex-wife of Field's sportsman friend Ogden Phipps, who was the grandson of a Pittsburgh steel man. The couple, along with the youngest of Marshall's children and Ruth's two young sons, divided their time between their new apartment and Field's glorious Long Island estate, Caumsett.

Field's grandfather, the first Marshall Field, was a farm boy who went to Chicago to seek his fortune before the Civil War. As John D. Rockefeller eliminated rival oilmen, Field did the same to small storekeepers in Chicago, made Marshall Field & Co. Chicago's preeminent department store, and amassed a fortune, albeit one a tenth the size of Rockefeller's.[1]

Field wasn't as successful with his family. His wife suffered from neurasthenia, a vague condition that might have merely been boredom or a version of chronic fatigue syndrome. Their son, Marshall junior, was born delicate. His son Marshall III was born in 1893. A sickly child, he was thrown from a horse at ten and developed rheumatism. He was twelve and recovering from measles when, he would later say, he heard a gunshot and his father cry out and fall, wounded, in his bedroom. Marshall junior died a few days later. Rumors circulated throughout Chicago that he'd botched a suicide attempt at a local brothel. The family insisted that he'd died at home while cleaning a gun, but the whorehouse story lived on, and a postmortem comment made by his widow didn't help matters: "American wealth is too often a curse."

Marshall Field Sr. was crushed and died within weeks.

Senior's twenty-thousand-word will, filed a few days later, was iron-clad and uncompromising; its premise was to keep his fortune intact, and it eventually withstood nine legal challenges. His $118 million fortune (worth $2.36 billion in 2004 dollars) was left to his two male grandsons, but the bulk of it was tied up until they turned fifty. Marshall III's mother promptly left America for England with her three children, re-marrying two years later. She and her husband, Maldwin Drummond, a London banking heir and friend of Marshall junior's, provided the children with an idyllic life at his ancestral home in southern England. Marshall III grew up "a very keen, committed Anglophile," says Gilly Drummond, a step-granddaughter. At twenty-one, Field was handsome and pleasant, with a distinct English accent.

After studying at Eton and Cambridge, with side trips to France on his stepfather's yacht, young Marshall married just as World War I broke out. Before enlisting, he fathered Marshall IV. While he was in the service, his brother died, and he became sole heir to the Field fortune, though he only had access to half the interest until age forty-five.

Back in New York at the start of the 1920s, he went to work at a brokerage firm, built a $3 million house in the city, acquired a thirteen-thousand-acre quail-hunting property in South Carolina, and spent

$6 million creating Caumsett, a nineteen-hundred-acre replica of the Drummond estate in England on Long Island's North Shore. It was designed by John Russell Pope and boasted fifty-six rooms, stables, a polo field, a private hunting preserve, a golf course, tennis courts, a private beach, a boat landing (like Bert Borden and William Hale Harkness, he commuted by water), an airstrip, its own fire department, and twenty-five miles of private roads—all tended by a staff of eighty-five. His neighbor Watson Webb's polo teammates Devereux Milburn and Tommy Hitchcock were frequent visitors.

Marshall was more successful in business than he was as a husband and father. Floating bonds for power and light companies, he greatly increased his fortune, but in 1925 his marriage failed. Separated in 1928, he and his wife divorced in 1930 (in Reno, of course; she charged him with desertion and won a settlement of $1 million a year). The children were devastated, even more when their father remarried two weeks later and took off on an African lion-hunting honeymoon on his private airplane. His daughter Barbara would later claim her subsequent mental illness began at that moment.

Wife No. 2, Audrey Coates, was a wealthy and frivolous widow, one of the glamorous Bright Young Things who inspired Evelyn Waugh's fiction, a goddaughter of King Edward VII, and a former girlfriend of both the Prince of Wales and Rudolph Valentino. At first, she and Marshall continued to live richly, even as the Depression darkened the horizon for most Americans, commuting between Caumsett and an apartment at River House, where Marshall piloted his boat into the private dock. But then Marshall Field & Co. started hemorrhaging millions. Though he began the Depression a conservative Republican, Marshall fell under the sway of Franklin Roosevelt's New Deal.

A second divorce was inevitable, and when it happened in 1934, Marshall began seeing a socialist psychoanalyst who catered to Manhattan's liberal upper crust. Under his daily care, Field's progressivism flowered; he quit banking, married wife No. 3, Ruth Phipps, who was pregnant by him, and moved into a pastel-painted eighteen-room apartment at 740, decorated by the society interior designer Sister Parish. Ruth's two boys by Phipps, Marshall's youngest, Bettine, and their new baby, Phyllis, all moved in, too.

The family was well cared for, even before Field inherited $93 million—the remaining half of his grandfather's estate—in 1938. They had thirty-two servants; sixteen were day workers and the rest lived in the building. The staff was run by an English butler named Hider, who had "the manner and appearance of a bank president" and used "the British form of understatement," according to Helen Worden in her book *Society Circus*. Formerly the butler for the Duke of Westminster and chief officer in England's Ministry of Food, Hider was a sort of socialite himself. He headed the Butlers Ball, invented by the second Mrs. Field, who thought it amusing to let servants dance and masters serve them. All for charity, of course.

The dining rooms of 740 went dark that night. "It's impossible to give a dinner in your own house the night of the Butler's Ball," James Haslam, Field's chauffeur, said. "The staffs are too busy with their own engagements." The children called Haslam, who drove the family's "town car," Uncle Jimmy.

Even in the depths of the Depression, butlers like Hider were necessary to run great apartments, managing staffs that typically included a chef and an assistant, a laundress, a footman, two to four maids, and one or two chauffeurs at minimum. A Mrs. Crush was in charge of Field's bathhouse and tennis courts at Caumsett. Field had three chauffeurs—the second was called Riseboro, the third, Sturmer—two secretaries and a valet, a pilot for his seaplane, and a captain and crew for his yacht.

Only those who'd made their fortunes before 1913, when the Sixteenth Amendment authorized the federal government to levy income taxes, could afford such extravagances. But they were the very sort of people attracted to 740 Park and attractive to its financial overlord, James T. Lee. When country homes, hunting lodges, and yacht crews were added in, household payroll could run as high as $1,000 a month. That was on top of the cost of a yacht (proper ones began at $500,000), its interior ($25,000 to $1 million), running it ($250,000 to $1 million), yacht club dues ($150 a year), and keeping a shooting lodge (anywhere from $50,000 to $1 million). The top tax rate in America rose steadily from 1 percent to 7 percent to 77 percent during World War I; it dropped to 25 percent afterward, and jumped again to 91 percent during

World War II—a rate that remained in effect until 1964. You had to be *very* rich to live at 740.

ELINOR DORRANCE WAS. "MOTHER AND DADDY MOVED IN RIGHT AFTER it opened; there were a lot of empty apartments," says Dorrance Hamilton, the daughter of Nathaniel Peter Hill and Elinor Dorrance, who rented apartment 10/11B in 1936. "The Bouvier girls and I would practice tennis in the empty apartments, driving the supers and the nannies wild, roller-skating on the marble floors. That didn't go over well at all. The balls left horrible marks on the walls, and eventually they collared us and said, 'No more of this.' "

Nathaniel Hill's grandfather and namesake was a chemistry professor turned mining entrepreneur who pioneered the smelting of gold from rocks and was elected Colorado's U.S. senator in 1879. Elinor's father, Dr. John T. Dorrance, invented condensed soup in 1897 at age twenty-four and turned a small canning company named for a fruit merchant into one of the great American brands. Dr. Dorrance eventually bought out the founders of Campbell's Soup to become the sole owner of a company worth $50 million in 1926.

That fall, Elinor, eighteen and just back from the Sorbonne in Paris, took a thirty-cent-an-hour job peeling tomatoes at the Campbell factory in Camden, New Jersey. "I see so many flapper daughters today whose only thought seems to be teas, dances, drinks, cigarettes and theaters, that I think a girl should be given lots of credit who really wants to work," her father said. "She intends to learn each of the departments of the plant in turn."

"Why shouldn't I want to work?" Elinor added. "Isn't that my business?"

A year later, though, she was engaged to Hill, a stockbroker who'd once made the papers for stepping behind the bar at his friend George Djamgaroff's New Year's Eve party to pop the corks on champagne bottles; that was work for some. Their first child, a daughter, Dorrance, whom they called Dodo, was born ten months later, and their second, Hope, known as Happy, followed in 1934. In between, Dr. Dorrance died, leaving an estate of $200 million to his five children. The Hills moved to an apartment at 740 Park, where they knew the Harknesses and Countess Kotzebue.

The Hill children preferred the doormen, who took them for rides on the elevators and helped them find empty apartments to play in. "The children were allowed to run the elevators," says Hope van Beueren, "though there were not a lot of children. Nobody knew anybody. That's why we loved New York."

Work was no longer Elinor Hill's business. The Hills "thought they were social," though they didn't really entertain a lot, says Dorrance. "Daddy was always going downtown to Wall Street and to the Knicker-bocker Club. Mother played bridge and volunteered a lot. They had dinners. There was always great consternation about what silver, linen, and china to use. She loved porcelain. She always talked about how food would look on what china."

Hope remembers place settings coming out of the combination-locked silver vault near the pantry and then watching the grown-ups from the top of the stairs "because children were never allowed downstairs," she says. "The table was French; it sat about twenty-four. Everything was hugely Louis XIV."

Menus were traditional: roast beef and Yorkshire pudding, oyster stews and lemon pudding on Sundays. "In those days, people didn't drink wine," says Hope. "There was a lot of drinking before dinner. It was martinis, cocktail hour, a tray was set up, lemon peel was brought out. Daddy made his own, always, shaken not stirred. Everything was silver. I had to go to bed at seven, when they went into dinner, but I'd go to the bar and take the top off the shaker and lick it, and then I'd run upstairs. It was a ritual."

Like their neighbors, the Hills employed a large staff—"thousands of them," says Hope van Beueren. "I remember the door to the back of the house where they were. I was always in the kitchen. I guess they liked me." Chefs came and went; Hope remembers one who taught her to make spun sugar. The staff had a cook of their own who filled in for the family's chef on his days off—every Thursday and alternate Sundays.

"Mother had a maid, there was a butler [named Orlando] and a downstairs maid, a cook, and a tweeny who cleaned up the kitchen and helped wherever it was needed," says Dorrance Hamilton. "There was a waitress, a parlor maid, an upstairs maid, and a nanny for the two of us." The girls never dined with their parents—eating off trays alone instead. Before the war, Dorrance attended Brearley nearby, but after the fighting started, she was shipped to Foxcroft and spent holidays with her grandmother in Pennsylvania. Hope remained in New York, attending Brearley with her best friend, Anne Harkness, who lived at 71; the two girls would sleep over at each other's apartments.

Those apartments were darker during the war: both remember blackout shades on all the windows. The Hills spent summers in Newport, first in rentals, then, after 1941, at a "cottage" originally designed by Charles Platt for William Fahnestock. It was called Bois Doré. The 740 apartment would be closed, the furniture covered, the chandeliers wrapped, the rugs rolled for cleaning. "We'd sit on the library floor, Mummy, Daddy, and me," says Hope. "One whole wall was leather books. We'd wax all the books, fold them in newspapers, and stack them. The house was totally put to bed, and we'd stay a few days in a hotel while the staff went ahead and opened the house, and then we'd move to Rhode Island." They returned to New York in September, when "the house was opened again," says Hope. "But I don't remember undoing the books."

After the war, the party culture of Newport revived—and the Hills were often photographed at balls by magazines like *Vogue*. In 1946, Dorrance debuted there, and three years later she married the grandson of a locomotive manufacturer. Hope, too, debuted in Newport in 1952, was photographed for *Vogue,* and married two years later.

Bois Doré was the scene of an infamous jewel theft—Newport's largest—in 1963. The Hills were at a party when, after a week surveilling the house from up a tree, two thieves climbed a rope to a balcony and found an open safe with $300,000 in family jewels within, including a diamond necklace by Jean Schlumberger. Margaret, Elinor's maid, blamed herself. That night, feeling ill, she'd neglected to lock the safe after her mistress chose her jewelry for the party. One of the thieves, Allison Williams, admitted forty-one years later, while serving a life sentence for murder, that he'd pulled off the long-unsolved crime. "They don't wear that kind of jewelry anymore," he told a reporter.

Nathaniel Hill died in 1965. Two years later, his widow went back to work as a board member of Campbell under her brother, who was its chairman. A year after that, she married Vice Admiral Stuart Howe Ingersoll, former commander of the Sixth and Seventh fleets and superintendent of the United States Naval Academy at Annapolis, whose first wife had died. "He was very bright, very much the admiral," recalls Hope van Beueren. "He was a nice companion for Mom. In those days, you had to marry rather than move 'em in." Ingersoll had his own bedroom, "a secondary bedroom," says someone who saw it, "with a sign that said 'The Admiral.' "

Elinor Hill Ingersoll died in January 1977. Her second husband lived until 1983. In 1989, Elinor's daughters, Dorrance and Hope, who controlled 17 percent of Campbell stock, began lobbying to sell the company—and in 1991 sold two million of their eighteen million shares, netting about $155 million. Subsequently, the family's fortunes declined along with the company's share price, but in 2004 Hope and Dorrance were still on the Forbes 400 list of the richest Americans, with fortunes estimated at just under $1 billion.

Theirs remains a small world. Hope van Beueren and her husband recently bought a new house at Brays Island Plantation in Yemassee, South Carolina, once the six-thousand-acre home of Francis Breese Davis, the chairman of U.S. Rubber, a subsidiary of E. I. du Pont de Nemours and Co., who bought apartment 8/9C in 1931 and lived there until 1942. Davis bought Brays Island in 1937 but went broke, and the place was sold at auction; it is now a mansion community where Landon Ketchum Thorne III also lives.

13

James T. Lee's youngest daughter, Winifred, aged twenty-five, finally left her unhappy home a few weeks after the readjustment negotiations were concluded. In April 1936, she married Franklin d'Olier. "As soon as they walked down the aisle, everyone moved out; they got separate apartments," says her daughter LeeLee Brown, who is called Big LeeLee to differentiate her from *her* daughter, who is also named LeeLee—further proof, if such is needed, of the shadow the builder cast over his family.

Lee moved out of 740 shortly after that and Belle Ledyard took over his double duplex, next door to the Brewsters. Belle was the daughter of a Louisiana lottery millionaire, the granddaughter of a racehorse breeder, and the widow of Lewis Cass Ledyard, the most famous lawyer of his age. As a child, just after the Civil War, Belle lived in Germany and France and studied piano under Franz Liszt, then returned to New Orleans, where her family was taken up by society and she served as Mardi Gras queen. She met Ledyard in 1897 when he represented her in a divorce (her husband of ten years had cheated on her with an actress). They married nine years later after Ledyard's wife died.

After twenty-six years of marriage to Belle, the great lawyer died in

1932, leaving $2 million to the public library, half that to his wife (along with an additional $1.1 million in trust and a Constable painting of Salisbury Cathedral), and most of the rest to his son.

Belle stood five feet tall and, although ailing, had presence as well as charm. She read a book a day and had total recall, says Jarden Guenther, who married one of her granddaughters in 1945.

The apartment was perfect for Belle. For one thing, she was great friends with the Garvans. For another, she needed a place large enough to hold her nine servants, including Minnie, her personal maid of thirty years, and Chisby, her tall, dour butler, "who put the fear of God in my daughter," says Frances Ferry Dennison, another granddaughter. "Oh, he was very fierce." None of her grandchildren would ever go anywhere near the servants' rooms, "kept out by orders," says Guenther. Adds Dennison, "I was much too afraid of Chisby."

Despite its lofty position high atop the building, the apartment was gloomy. But Belle herself was a light source: she often entertained and, despite her small size, was usually the center of attention. "I'm going to live forever," she'd say, "so I will have to have young friends or I won't have any friends left."

"She would sail into a large party and be the only person you saw at that moment," says Guenther. "She had stage presence."

"The belle of the ball," agrees Dennison. "My brother described her as having spiritual sex appeal." Shortly after she moved into 740, the cast of characters at those parties changed. Belle opened her sprawling home to Allied military officials; the designers of the artificial harbor built at Arromanches, France, just after D-day, stayed there while they toiled on their creation. "She was very grateful to me because I had friends who were young and beautiful, and even though I was married, I produced them to be sociable," says Dennison. "Hundreds of people came to see her all the time." Important people, like General Dwight D. Eisenhower. So meals were elaborate, "millions of courses, and afterwards, she'd say, 'Oh, is that all we're having?' "

After the dinner with Eisenhower, Belle summoned everyone on her staff to meet him. But she could also be a snob, says Louis Auchincloss, the lawyer and author of books on patrician society, who claims that it was at her instigation that the Seventy-first Street entrance to 740 Park was given its own address, 71 East Seventy-first Street. "She insisted on it," says Auchincloss. "Mrs. Ledyard was very grand. She thought Park Avenue was a Jewish address—and it is. It always has been."

"I believe it!" says Dennison. "Park seemed crass. It had a name!"[1]

UPON HIS DEPARTURE, JAMES T. LEE INSTALLED HIMSELF IN HIS SHELton Hotel and eventually rented an apartment at 580 Park, where he lived out his days alone except for a manservant. But 740 still had Jack Bouvier, who, let's face it, was a lot more fun.

Jack's troubles were mounting and his fortunes falling. In 1935, he'd spent $5,000 more than he made, and in 1936, due to new SEC restrictions on specialist brokers, he lost twice that amount. When Michel Bouvier died in 1935, he was the longest-tenured holder of a seat on the New York Stock Exchange. Though the "Wall St. Dean," as his obituary was headlined, only left Jack a token bequest, Black Jack inherited many of his great-uncle's brokerage clients. And the following summer, when his father took over Lasata, Jack moved into Wildmoor, his father's six-bedroom clapboard house on ten East Hampton acres, which he could occupy rent-free. A good thing. His net worth had plummeted from $750,000 to $100,000, yet, his cousin John H. Davis marveled, Jack nonetheless managed to keep three pedigreed dogs, six Thoroughbreds, and two grooms to care for them.

"Jackie," Jack told his seven-year-old daughter, "you never have to worry about keeping up with the Joneses because we are the Joneses."

Only their parents' fights intruded on the idyll of that Depression summer for the beautiful Bouvier girls. According to Davis, Janet was increasingly prone to "uncontrollable rages" over Jack's extramarital intrigues, which typically began at the Polo Bar of the Westbury Hotel, a block from his New York apartment, and then continued in the duplex, which rarely failed to impress his pretty prey. Jackie's nurse would later testify to a horrific scene that fall when Janet tried to slap little Jackie, and the nurse stepped between them, caught the blow, and promptly returned it. Only when Jack moved out of 740 on October 1, 1936, the beginning of a formal six-month separation, did the fights stop. Even Lee had come to realize a divorce was inevitable.

Jack agreed to pay Janet half his income in support and maintenance during the separation, but his great-uncle's estate began pressing him to repay the money he'd borrowed, and the government was after him for back taxes. Even the Bouviers began to criticize his reckless ways. Old enough to know that something was wrong, Jackie turned inward, angry and sullen and, as another household staffer would later testify, "high-strung [and] difficult to manage."

Her little sister, Lee, though she was too young to be conscious of what was happening, felt the pressure, too. "I remember almost jumping out the sixth-floor window," she recalls sixty-eight years later. "My sister rescued me and my mother spanked me." Child guards were promptly installed on the windows "after my stupidity," she confesses. On another occasion, Lee decided to run away and headed east, "across the Triborough Bridge in my mother's heels," she recalls, with her shaggy dog, Caprice, at her side. "I hadn't a clue where I was headed, and it was more than me or my Bouvier des Flandres could handle. I decided I couldn't make it, so back we trotted."

What brought on the urge to flee? "I always liked the idea of escaping," she says wistfully.

Jack's financial situation did have one upside for the Bouvier girls; he couldn't afford to finish furnishing their apartment, so they got to play in it. The year she turned six, Lee says, she learned to roller-skate in the vast living room. "Everyone laughed about the fact that they were given this apartment but didn't have enough furniture," says her granddaughter LeeLee Brown. "So the girls rode tricycles around the apartment."

Despite it all, the girls preferred their Bouvier relations to the Lees. Grampy Jack, their paternal grandfather, was Jackie's first close adult friend. James T. Lee, on the other hand, could barely abide them. Lee Radziwill once called him "a very severe man, a miser. He didn't have much warmth or charm." And time has not softened her view. "We disliked him so much, my sister and I," she flatly declares of Old Man Lee. Almost as much as they loved their wayward father, who indulged them, indeed worshipped them in return.

"He influenced his daughters profoundly," said John Davis, "transmitting certain qualities to them that they would one day project to the entire world. One of these was a sense of style . . . elusive individualism was another."

Jackie and Lee influenced their father, too, or at least so he claimed in a desperately manipulative letter he sent to his father-in-law, in which he called the separation "a situation that is so vital to both Janet and myself and our two kiddies that it has almost reached staggering proportions. Of course, at the minute, Janet has not very much feeling for me." Referring to one of their fights, he continued, "Insane was what I was. After what Janet's always been to me and stood for, I'm the ashamed one. I may deserve to lose Janet because I haven't been much of a husband. But I still love her and adore her, certainly now more than ever, and I'm not letting her break up our home as long as there's a fighting chance of preventing it. I tell you, Mr. Lee, if there's a chance that she may resume, say even for the kids, I'll make a go of it. Jacqueline and Lee suggest that we forgive and forget and even give them a little dual control for a change."

Hope springs eternal. The Bouviers reconciled in the spring of 1937, and Jack rented a cottage in East Hampton for the summer. But within a week, relations between Jack and Janet were, in the words of their daughters' governess, "strained and irritable" again. Jack had charmed the governess as he'd charmed his daughters; she would later testify that Janet ignored her husband and seemed indifferent to her children when she wasn't spanking them or getting irritated with them "for no reason that I was able to see."

Back at 740 that fall, Jack moved into the apartment briefly but soon returned to the Westbury Hotel and the charms of its Polo Bar. Janet would later testify that the last straw was when he began making vicious remarks about Old Man Lee, owner of the roof over his head. On January 22, 1938, the *New York Journal* reported:

> Their friends were happy to learn of their
> reconciliation—but it was a short-lived
> one, and lately the Bouvier marriage seems
> to be on an "off-again" keel, giving every
> indication that the separation is a perma-
> nent one this time. Janet is never so happy

> as when attired in riding togs and showing
> her azure-blooded thoroughbreds in a
> tan-bark arena—and while "Jack" is also
> interested in matters equestrian, one
> wonders if it wasn't a case of too much a
> "horsey" life for him to take. With [Jack's
> sister] Michelle and [her husband] Henry
> Scott, Janet and "Jack" Bouvier and Janet's
> parents, the James T. Lees, all reported
> separating—it does look as if the Bouviers
> and the Lees have attained little marital
> happiness.

The governess would later swear in a deposition in the couple's divorce that Janet stayed in bed until noon and filled her afternoons and evenings with social engagements, leaving the children to their own devices, turning jealous and violent whenever they asked to see their father.[2] He would sneak over to see them when he could, and on weekends, when he was allowed to see them under the terms of the latest separation, life was a mad whirl of toy stores and sundaes, the zoo, the racetrack, and romps in Central Park.

Returning to 740 was like climbing off a cloud; the two girls would weep copiously. Not even the pet white rabbit that Jackie kept in her bathtub could console her for very long. It was more of the same the following summer, when the girls spent an unhappy July with Janet and then August with Jack in East Hampton. But their pleasure in their father's company couldn't arrest the family's meltdown.

James T. Lee took over. He'd decided that the Bouviers' free ride at 740 Park had come to its end. In 1939, Lee moved Janet and the girls uptown into another Candela building, 1 Gracie Square, near the East River, and sublet their apartment (which, after the divorce, ended up in Janet's name, not Jack's). One Gracie had opened as a co-op in 1929 and had just become a rental, but unlike 740 it had been foreclosed and taken over by its mortgage lender. Many nights, Lee and his daughter would dine together there and plot strategy: two years after Black Jack Bouvier's infidelity went from private matter to public disgrace, Janet Lee Bouvier and her father had both had enough.

Though she could have just gone to Reno, where divorce was time-consuming but relatively neat, when Jack accused her of me-too infidelity in another letter to Lee, an incensed Janet decided to drag her husband's name through local mud first. Because the only legal grounds for divorce in New York was adultery, Lee sent her to a lawyer at Milbank, Tweed, who hired a private detective, who had no trouble getting the goods on Jack, and in January 1940 the New York newspapers carried the news that Janet was suing her husband for divorce, alleging not one but multiple adulteries.

CALLS MATE A ROVING CASANOVA, said the *Journal-American*, which wrote that Bouvier's wife was "accusing him of covering several hundred miles of territory . . . in his love-making to other women . . . in a succession of blitzkrieg romances." SUED AS LOVE COMMUTER, screamed the *Daily News*, which said Janet's "complaint indicated that Bouvier had spent most of his time since the Summer of 1936 galloping from one siren to another . . . so many women she had been unable to get more than a line on most of them."

Jack struck back with depositions from the household staff that painted him a doting dad and Janet a violent child beater. After that, it only took the Bouviers six months to hammer out a settlement and get divorced in Reno. The grounds Janet claimed, cruelty, seemed fair enough. "Women," Jack groused in a press release he issued, "are all the victors in my generation."

Two years later, Janet would achieve the dream she'd failed to find with Jack when she married a Standard Oil heir, Hugh Dudley "Hughdie" Auchincloss Jr., a member of a vastly social family of Scottish descent that had a knack for making auspicious marriages. The writer Gore Vidal, a stepson from one of Hughdie's earlier marriages, recalled Janet as she left 740 Park as "a financially desperate 'social climber' " working as a saleswoman in a department store and claiming to be one " 'of the Virginia Lees' . . . until the real Lees ordered her to shut up."

Jack Bouvier and James T. Lee would continue to despise each other all their lives. "It was a schooling that would stand [Jackie and Lee] in excellent stead when they eventually entered the marital wars themselves against far bigger game than their beleaguered parents had had to contend with," their cousin John Davis wrote: "the Radziwills, the Kennedys, Onassis."

Black Jack got drunk before Jackie's 1953 wedding to the handsome, roguish Massachusetts senator John F. Kennedy, and never made it to the church to give his daughter away; he died four years later, an impoverished alcoholic. Lee, an archconservative, used the wedding to make his disdain for the liberal Kennedys clear. As the first head of the Securities and Exchange Commission, Kennedy's father, Joseph, had made life miserable for the sorts of folks who lived in Lee's buildings.

Lee did not attend Kennedy's inauguration as president in 1961. Nor did he remember either of his Bouvier grandchildren in his will. "I am fully aware," he wrote, "that I have not provided equally for all of my grandchildren. This is deliberate on my part and is the result not of any difference in my affection for them" but of his conclusion that disinheritance was "appropriate in view of other resources available to those grandchildren."

Lee did have a continuing influence on his granddaughter Jackie, though. "From him, she got a strong sense of the importance of striving for excellence," said her cousin Mary Lee "Mimi" Ryan Cecil. "Being strong, being tough, setting his mind with determination to accomplish things—that was his greatest influence on Jackie," added her half brother Jamie Auchincloss. Brendan Gill, the writer and chairman of New York's Municipal Art Society, who met Jackie when she volunteered to help the organization save Grand Central Station from the wrecker's ball, sourced her love of great buildings to James T. Lee.

"He was a very important influence on Jackie's life," Gill said in an interview with the journalist Edward Klein. "Whether consciously or unconsciously, she imbibed some notion, even as an adolescent, of what buildings meant."[3] Seven forty obviously meant a lot to her; in years to come, she would often return and ask permission to walk down the long hall connecting 740 to the Seventy-first Street entrance. "Everyone remembered her," says Patrick O'Connor, then an elevator man. "I'd say, 'Welcome, First Lady,' and the Secret Service would say, 'Which way did she go?' And I'd say, 'That-a-way.' "

Someone once asked her why she returned. "A lot of memories," she whispered.

14

FRANCIS AND MABEL GARVAN MARRIED OFF ANOTHER DAUGHTER IN OC-
tober 1937. Then, in early November, Garvan fell ill with pneumonia and
died in his apartment at 740 at age sixty-two. Two days later, a solemn
High Mass was said for him at St. Patrick's Cathedral. Among his pall-
bearers were the former governor Alfred E. Smith and J. Edgar Hoover,
who ran the Federal Bureau of Investigation, which Garvan had helped
found.

"Father had died, so Mother naturally wanted to move," says their
daughter Marcia Coyle. "So we moved around the corner to the apartment owned by Mrs. Bouvier." James T. Lee had lots of reasons for moving Janet Bouvier and her girls out of 740, but it didn't hurt that his
daughter could make some money subletting the apartment. Marcia apparently got little Lee's room: she still remembers the bars on the windows. "She really must have made a great effort to climb out that
window," Coyle says. "There was a radiator in front of it!"

Compared with the C line, their new apartment, which they rented
partly furnished, was a palace, "beautifully appointed with murals in the
entryway, paneling, and a lot of rugs Mrs. Bouvier left behind, which was
very nice. We were crazy about her taste in rugs." Once the Garvans

moved in, the place seemed fuller, too, since they had no problems furnishing it from their antiques collection.

"It was my sense the building was full," Coyle says, "but it wasn't making money. It was in trouble. They all talked about it. But what was trouble? Everything was in trouble to some extent. Who was going to tear it down?" Coyle graduated from high school in 1940, and then went to Manhattanville College, so she spent the war years in New York. Her memories are mostly of rationing. "Sugar, meat, gasoline. You got four gallons of gasoline a month. If you wanted to go anywhere, forget it. We raised pigs in Roslyn so we got some ham."

The upside? "The town was full of servicemen," Coyle says, smiling coyly.

Mabel Garvan worked at the Red Cross blood bank; her friend Electra Webb ran it. "The building was incredibly charitable if someone who lived there was personally involved," says Coyle. "My mother collected substantial sums for the Red Cross during the war. And she was so kind to some of the servicemen. Some of them were very badly hurt—I remember one had been blown out of a minesweeper—and they'd come and stay with her."

Marcia did volunteer work, too, at a Red Cross facility near New York's downtown courthouse district, where her father had once toiled. "My brother was a prisoner of war," she recalls. "We sent packages of cigarettes, chocolates, bacon, and Spam to them. We sent fifteen hundred the first day. At the end, we were sending eleven thousand packages, one a month to every POW, but the Germans would grab them."

ELEANOR BREWSTER REMAINED IN HER APARTMENT UNTIL JULY 1937, but Junior immediately threw himself into planning his move. "I have had made quarter inch scale drawings of our new apartment giving each room with floor and adjacent walls on a sheet," he wrote to Wallace Harrison, the architect of Rockefeller Center. "I want to have thick paper or very thick card board cut to the same scale, representing the dimensions of the pictures, tapestries, rugs and pieces of furniture." Each sort of object, he went on, should be a different color, and every one needed a caption. Junior planned to create his apartment with precisely the same obsessive care, and the same top talent, with which he'd built Rockefeller Center.

In November, Junior began getting letters seeking work on the renovation. But he'd already hired his team, led by Mott Schmidt, who'd made his name renovating and building the row of understated town houses and mansions on Sutton Place in conjunction with Elsie de Wolfe, a former actress turned decorator and tastemaker. In 1922, Schmidt had married one of de Wolfe's protégées, Elena Bachman, who (with an assist from the future film director Vincente Minnelli) designed the decor for the Rainbow Room in Rockefeller Center in 1934, bringing the couple into Junior's orbit.

On April 2, Junior wrote a memo to his head of security addressing his concerns. He'd already asked Schmidt to design and install a bronze grillwork door outside the apartment's mahogany entrance so that "whoever answers the doorbell could talk to a caller without opening the grille until the propriety of admitting the caller had been established." But he wondered about extra locks, about protecting the elevator, and particularly about how to protect against someone entering via the back stairs or elevator. Junior also asked for proposals on burglar alarms and grilles or gates on all the windows.

Junior wrote to the Brewsters' son Edward to say he didn't want to keep three of the original mantels and eleven chandeliers; Edward asked that they be put into storage. Five days after that, Gibbons told Junior that changes to the apartment would have to be approved by the building corporation, not the Brewsters. Those changes, Junior noted in a letter to his builder, Marc Eidlitz (whose résumé included the Metropolitan Opera House, St. Regis Hotel, J. P. Morgan Building, and Rockefeller Institute), were "mostly small, fussy things"—though they'd have been major for most—like replacing Candela's main staircase, installing a private elevator between floors, relocating fireplaces and flues, and moving doors and walls.

There was so much to do, and Junior delighted in the detail. Schmidt wanted to replace key locks with "thumb latches" in the servants' rooms. Junior said no—he didn't want servants opening their doors for each other or friends. He erected a cork-lined temporary storage cabinet in a warehouse for his porcelains and discussed extra servants' rooms with

Gibbons (he already had seven on the mezzanine and three more below, behind the kitchen). He wrote to Landon Thorne, asking permission to access Thorne's servants' hall for the elevator installation. "We are expecting to make this apartment our home from now on indefinitely," he said, adding that he was "looking forward to the pleasure of coming to know you another winter as one of our neighbors." From Bay Shore, Thorne wrote back that he was "delighted to accede" and had alerted his caretaker.

Eleanor Brewster and her two daughters had decided to move to Candela's 19 East Seventy-second Street, just a few blocks away. The day before they moved, Gibbons let Junior know that Lee had approved his alterations, and Junior hired the Brewsters' caretaker, Gabriel Samalens, to remain in the apartment through October 1 and supervise the work at $75 a month. Rockefeller would provide simple furniture and housewares, but Samalens had to buy his own food. Rockefeller added that he was counting on "your loyalty and your complete respect to see that the apartment is properly cared for." Then he wrote a note to Eleanor Brewster, thanking her for her courtesy and consideration in what "might in some cases have been a difficult and unpleasant task."

Rockefeller headed to the Eyrie while his workers toiled through an oppressively humid New York summer, installing call buttons in every room, library lights, a radio antenna, steel grilles and fences on the terraces, and a flower closet. Endless letters covering every detail flew between Maine and the Schmidt and Eidlitz offices in New York. More went to Gibbons when some windows sprang leaks and Rockefeller asked that the building pay to fix them; negotiations went on for months and finally Rockefeller paid, but kept arguing. In the process he learned more of 740's tangled history, eked out in grudging tidbits by Gibbons, who was forced to explain that although it was a rental building, 740's rules were those of a "customary co-operative," and so, when Rockefeller added screens and grilles to his windows, any resulting problems became his responsibility. Junior wasn't so sure and kept insisting that the building return his outlays. His persistence would ultimately pay off; in June 1940, he was finally reimbursed.

His security expert had recommended that existing steel-and-glass terrace doors be supplemented with steel-grilled screen doors; floodlights be installed on all terraces with "switches strategically located in master bed-rooms" and near watchmen's stations; all the windows be wired with bur-glar alarms set to go off if a window was opened more than seven inches; and a steel bolt, a chain, and an alarm trigger be added to the doors at the service stair and elevator, which were generally left unlocked throughout the building, and an extra light fixture be installed there as well.

Fall arrived and, with it, the electricians, come to wire that alarm sys-tem, complete with electric eyes, annunciators, emergency buttons, and sirens. The installation cost $7,716; an alarm monitoring service would be an additional $43.25 a month. Realizing that work would continue for some time, Rockefeller revised his move-in date and extended Gabriel Samalens's term as caretaker. The power had already been switched to his name; an aide had to write to Consolidated Edison, asking that it cor-rect the spelling, which was rendered as "Rockerfellow" on his first bill. "We are indeed sorry," groveled a Con Ed minion.

Rockefeller's passion for detail sometimes overcame him. He worried about the placement of a cedar closet for out-of-season clothing and was skeptical when the Schmidts suggested that steel doors be installed and painted to resemble wood. "I have never seen anything of the kind," he wrote, asking if the technique had "sufficient precedent to warrant its adoption." Schmidt responded with a book on Georgian homes that showed precisely what he wanted to do. Woodwork was ordered, and mir-rors and duct and tile. Plans were laid to move mantels and the safe in the Fifty-fourth Street house to 740, along with the floor of the dance room. Parquet was ordered to match that floor, and velvet for inside the porcelain cabinets. In the midst of micromanaging, Junior got truly manic about those cabinets. "We must insist on the velvet being in bet-ter condition," he wrote to the contractor.

In November, he groused about the slow pace of painting, then apol-ogized to Schmidt for an "unjust" complaint against the painter Anton Sattler. "Exonerate the painter, as well as everyone else, from blame in the matter," he wrote on the same day a note went to Elena Schmidt hag-gling over the painter's bill. Sattler wrote back and detailed jobs large and small, everything from decorative painting and faux-marbleizing to painting medicine chests and switch plates, in what certainly appears a defensive gesture.

By that point, the storage room in the basement had filled with discarded material: marble, stair rails, radiators, mahogany doors, three wall safes, medicine cabinets, and squares of parquet from the long-demolished Brewster mansion. Junior wrote to Edward Brewster, asking if the family wanted any of it. There is no record of a reply.

Late in 1937, the final preparations began. With nine floors full of furniture on Fifty-fourth Street, the Rockefellers had more than enough—and had a minion say as much to a dealer who wrote, asking to sell him rugs. But in fact, they were still buying: a 1785 chest of drawers in Sheraton style, inlaid with rare wood and veneered in rosewood, for instance, came from Wentworth Castle and cost $3,550. But Junior and Abby's concerns were elsewhere: Where to hang the Botticelli? The Veneziano? The two Duccios? The Madonna and Child from the collection of Ludwig I of Bavaria? The Goya, the Chardin, the Thomas Lawrence portrait of Lady Dysart? Hopper's Judith Beresford? Benjamin West's Benjamin Franklin? The codicil of San Giorgio, Piero della Francesca's *Crucifixion*? The van der Weyden, Nattier, Uccello, and Fragonard? The busts by Verrocchio and Laurana?"

Junior contacted the Frick Collection to ask about picture lights for John Singer Sargent's portrait of his father, which he'd hung in the entry gallery, his mother's portrait, and another of Abby that went up in Junior's bedroom. Years later, he'd give his two busts to the Frick in thanks.

Years later, too, the apartment would be photographed, a visual record made, even of the private spaces. Mrs. Rockefeller's sitting room had a fireplace and two exposures; it was big enough for several seating areas and a little desk. Bedrooms were austere, decorated with porcelains and family portraits. Long hallways were filled with old rugs, mirrors, tapestries, and candelabras. A bust of George Washington sat atop a marble mantel in a reception room. The library had knotty-pine paneling and old master paintings. A headless classical statue sat beneath the winding stair between floors.

On January 19, Junior wrote to Landon Thorne, thanking him for putting up with the noise and alerting him that they would move in in about ten days. Five days later, the builders turned the keys over and the move commenced. Finally, on February 8, 1938, the telephones were disconnected at 10 West Fifty-fourth Street and the phone numbers

(BUtterfield 8-1760 and BUtterfield 8-1761) transferred to 740. Those numbers were actually listed in the telephone book for six months before Junior had them removed. In June, two days after scaffolds went up and the wreckers began breaking windows and tearing down doors at No. 10, the family made official what had been rumored, that both Junior's old house and his father's had been given to the Museum of Modern Art.[2]

Several years later, the Brewsters would be invited to the Rocke-fellers' for the first and only time. They particularly liked what their sub-tenant had done in the library. "They had really very fine Dutch paintings all around, beautifully lit," says Katharine Whipple. "It was really lovely." Abby Rockefeller was talkative over dinner. "Mother was pretty chatty, too!" Whipple says. "And, of course, Mrs. Rockefeller kept on saying, 'It was much more beautiful when *you* were here, Mrs. Brew-ster.' And Mother said, 'Everything is lovely *now*,' and back and forth, back and forth."

THAT SECOND WEEK OF FEBRUARY 1938, JUNIOR ENTERED THE LOBBY OF 740 one day, walked to the elevator, and rode upstairs with Janet Bouvier and her daughters, Jacqueline Lee and Caroline Lee. What was said on the ride to the sixth floor is lost—only Lee Radziwill, then five, remains alive, and she doesn't remember—but what followed is preserved in the Rockefeller Archives.

The next day, Valentine's Day, the girls left a commercial greeting card for Junior, wishing him "double joy," signed in awkward childish letters: "From the three girls who came up in the elevator with you."

"Keep," Junior wrote on it, and personally typed a reply, which he sent to Janet Bouvier that day along with valentines and a note asking her to pass the enclosures on to the girls. One said:

TO MY THREE FRIENDS WHO CAME UP IN
THE ELEVATOR WITH ME

> I love the valentine you sent me and thank you many times
> for it. It is the only valentine I received.
>
> When we came up in the elevator together the other day, I
> had just left my home where I have lived for a long time and

felt very lonely going up to my new home in your building.
But when your valentine came the next day, I was no longer
lonely for it assured me that I already had friends in my new
home. I am glad we live in the same building and I shall hope
to see you again some day.

**FROM THE MAN WHO CAME UP IN THE
ELEVATOR WITH YOU.**

Attached to a carbon copy and Janet's note of thanks that came in return
("Your letter has been read and re-read a thousand times") is a small
scrap of paper on which is typed "Keep as letter establishes approximate
date of Mr. and Mrs. R. taking residence at 740 Park Ave."

The Rockefellers had decided to road test their apartment before they
finished decorating. Their back door remained a huge concern, even
though Gibbons promised Debevoise that the super, John Powers, would
"be sure no mistakes were made" and would "find out the business of
anyone who came and who might loiter in those halls."

They were also very concerned with aesthetics. Junior wrote the
Frick to say its picture-lighting experts had gotten the light "about
right" on the Sargent in the hallway and asked if they'd like to tackle another portrait of his father at Pocantico. And he first ran afoul of the
building when he laid new parquet in several rooms without approval,
then learned he'd have to delay completing the job until summer, because the defunct co-op's rule limiting renovations to summer (when the
building was empty) was still in effect.

The Rockefellers were gone, too, when the work recommenced. In
June, they sailed to Europe for an antiques buying spree, mostly for Colonial Williamsburg, but also for 740. In London, they checked into Claridge's and bought a Hepplewhite bureau (£400), an eighteenth-century
mahogany table, a Chippendale chest, George I candlesticks, a 1785 sat-
inwood side table from Dupplin Castle in Perth, dessert plates, door
knockers, a 1790 sideboard (£325), and lots of porcelain.

After a brief side trip to Holland, they went on to the Crillon in Paris,
where Junior bought an Empire portrait of a woman and another of the
Marquise du Plessis-Bellière (Fr 20,000); a gilded Regency mirror (Fr
12,000); a gilded Louis XV candlestick from the Château de Sablé

(Fr 40,000); a Roussel chest of drawers (Fr 28,000); three Louis XV commodes (Fr 22,500, Fr 72,000, and Fr 45,000); another signed Boudin (Fr 30,000); a gilded Regency mirror (Fr 12,000); and two little violet veneer-over-marble Louis XV corner cabinets (Fr 13,300). Even when he sent things back, Junior got thank-you notes. And Abby never forgot to request discounts for cash.

When he returned home in July, his private elevator jammed, and his office reminded Junior that he hadn't signed a service contract with Otis. He refused and asked Otis to show his staff how to maintain the elevator. Because of the window leaks, the apartment continually needed repainting, and Junior fought with Lee over that for a decade. Holmes, the burglar alarm company, was called three times for false alarms, and Junior agreed to pay them $21.50 a month if they'd come by twice a month to adjust the system. But he disconnected from central monitoring in 1939. And then there were the bars and locks on the china cupboards in the pantry. Why on earth were forty locks ordered, when a third that number would have been overkill? "A frightful nuisance to handle," Junior grumbled.

Then 740 gave Junior a housewarming present. Thanks in large part to his presence, the building finally turned a profit in 1938, and $10,371.58 was being rebated to the tenant-owners. Junior would get a taste of that—$2,926.50 to be exact. Which would pay $\frac{1}{100}$ of the total renovation bill, which Junior, ever his detail-conscious father's son, carefully noted: $290,075.19 (or $3.8 million in 2004 dollars).

LILA OSGOOD VANDERBILT WEBB DIED IN JULY 1936 IN SHELBURNE, Vermont, and her many homes were split up among her children. Watson and Electra Webb, who already owned one at Shelburne, which they'd named Southern Acres, took over Nehasane, the family camp in the Adirondacks. Vanderbilt Webb inherited the main house at Shelburne and the northern acreage. As the Depression continued, he decided he would have to tear the mansion down. Only the cost of demolition stopped him.

In January 1937, all was well for the Watson Webbs. "There is no family deriving more pleasure from their country homes," a newspaper reported. Watson detested New York City and was rarely at 740 more than a few months a year. "I'd rather be a trapper alone in the woods," he'd told his diary in 1935. "I'd like to leave this d——d city for good. There is nothing I like about it except a party once in a while and seeing one's friends. Corrupt government, terrific taxes, dirt, rush and worry is what it [word illegible] to me, but Electra likes it and there you are!"

They'd spend Septembers in New York, getting the kids settled at school, then head to Shelburne in October and November for foxhunting. Hunting was Webb's primary passion, breeding horses for hunting a close second; he served as president of the Masters of Foxhounds Association for many years. "They would have nonstop friends coming up to hunt with them, and the kids all had tutors," Sam junior recalls. After Thanksgiving, it was back to New York, where they opened the apartment and spent winters. "She'd do charity work, and during the war she was head of the blood bank, she was president of the Colony Club; always very active, very busy," says Sam junior. "Collecting, museums, on the board of the Met."

"Their regular migration, amidst baggage, private railroad cars, and suites aboard ocean liners and in great hotels and houses, was as measured and grandiose, and even as inexorable in its way, as the passage of the seasons," wrote John Foreman and Robbe Pierce Stimson in *The Vanderbilts and the Gilded Age*. It was the end of that era.

In the early 1940s, the Webbs joined Okeetee, a hunting club in South Carolina founded in 1894 by Samuel Thorne, Landon Thorne's grandfather. They bought a winter plantation nearby so they wouldn't have to abide the club's limit on the number of quail a member could shoot. In the spring, they would go to Westbury and 740, then to Shelburne in May, and in August they'd go exploring in northern Canada or grouse hunting in England, bear hunting on horseback in Alaska, or to Nehasane in the Adirondacks, returning there in the fall from Vermont to shoot deer. In later years, they leased a Scottish lodge as a base for grouse hunts and went pheasant hunting on Long Island.

During the war, Watson's diary records many dinners at 740, but beyond dashed-off comments like "quite a crowd" they give no indication that he cared a whit about them. In January 1940, Tyrone Power, the actor, who'd become an intimate friend of Watson junior's, came for a visit, but other than noting his arrival and a dinner with him, the laconic Webb had nothing to say about the movie star or the homosexual relationship Power was having with Watson junior, who would become a Hollywood film editor. He did note the arrival of Power's first wife, the French actress Annabella, for a stay at the apartment in June.

Two weeks after the Japanese attack on Pearl Harbor, Douglas Gibbons alerted the tenants of 740 of the need for a plan in the event of an attack on New York. After considering and abandoning the idea of jamming tenants and servants into an empty apartment on a middle floor facing the St. James Church courtyard, Gibbons wrote to all asking that those living below the fourth floor and those above the twelfth floor arrange with a neighbor in between to take shelter in his or her apartment. The Webbs and the Rockefellers immediately made plans to go to the Garvans, who were on the sixth and seventh floors; the families would use the public rooms, while the servants huddled above.

"There is never very much time between the warning siren and the all clear, and I believe we can work it out along those lines," Gibbons wrote Junior in late December 1941. "I believe that we will have everything so organized that there will be no confusion in the event of an alarm. I feel that the building will give a very good account for itself in the event of an explosion, because it is really well built. May I take this opportunity to wish you and Mrs. Rockefeller a very merry Christmas, as merry as it is possible to be in the times we are going through."

In May 1942, Watson noted a blackout in his diary and in March 1943 the blaring of an air-raid siren. "E. slept through it," he wrote.

The Webbs' grandchildren were more observant than sound-sleeping Electra, and several of them lived at 740 during the war. When John and Lila Wilmerding's father went off to fight, and their mother, Electra's eldest daughter, fell ill and was hospitalized, they moved into the apartment for a year. In later years, John would overnight at 740 when he was in boarding school and college. "It was such a convenient location, and after all the children were married and had their own apartments, there were frequently bedrooms available, and we all had rooms assigned. I stayed often on the lower floor."

While Dundeen Catlin's father was in England, she lived with her grandmother, too, sleeping in the "green" room and often using Electra's bathroom, where she loved the triplicating mirrors. "I went to my first day of school from the apartment," she says.

Electra kept several poodles. "A dog walker took them to Central Park," says Catlin. "I wasn't allowed to do that, they were too special." Plus she was only five years old. But she did take the dogs out on the nineteenth-floor terrace. Catlin also visited the service rooms of the apartment—but only once. "I was told that was not something you needed to do," she says. "I thought, 'Darn.' "

After the war, Webb's diaries refer to 740 with ever less frequency, although he did note that Admiral Halsey came to dinner in January 1946. The war over, their solvency was restored along with the economy. In 1948, Electra earned $425,000 from the trusts left to her by her parents, and another $65,000 in interests and dividends, the equivalent of $3.8 million today. Half of that went to taxes. She spent about $80,000 that year on household expenses, another $36,000 on country homes, $3,000 on their cars and horses, $5,000 to go bear hunting, $2,500 on legal bills and accounting, $8,500 to run her office, and another $3,000 on miscellany, according to her handwritten records. In 1947, she gave $29,000 to charity, but cut that to $8,000 in 1948, leaving her with a $19,000 surplus at the end of the year.

A decade earlier, they'd had to cut the salaries of the household staff, but they never really cut back. Catlin recalls two waitresses; a couple of maids; the cook, Augusta ("She let us in the kitchen, which was a no-no"), and an assistant; a driver, Edward ("But he did everything"); and Electra's personal maid. "I wondered what the heck she did," says Catlin. "She lined up the closets, neat as a pin, zipped her dresses, and ironed her clothes."

There was also Electra's secretary, Elsie Schoonover, who'd entered the Webb household during the war, when she was a civil defense worker for the Red Cross blood bank, and Mademoiselle Giannoni, the children's governess, who stayed on even after they left home. A housekeeper stayed in the apartment all summer, so the Webbs could let friends and family use "one of the finest hotels in New York City," as Sam junior calls it. "She would never say no to anybody, and it was just laid out for them. It was a constant array of characters; you never knew who you were going to run into." Says Wilmerding, "I used the apartment without them there, and I never paid attention to anybody."

After Watson Webb retired in 1946, he became withdrawn. They made Vermont their regular residence, and Electra devoted herself to establishing the Shelburne Museum. "Grandfather stood aside and, with awe and amazement, watched her do it," says Wilmerding. Beginning as a home for Seward Webb's collection of carriages, it grew into a sprawling museum of Americana, with thirty-seven mostly historic buildings spread over forty-five acres, housing Electra's collection of about eighty-thousand folk art and crafts objects, and even the 220-foot side-wheeler the SS *Ticonderoga*, which the family had used as a pleasure boat before it was put into permanent dry dock as an outdoor exhibit.

Still, each year the Webbs returned to 740 for a lunch on Christmas Day. Their granddaughter Dundeen Catlin remembers them as formal occasions where everyone dressed up, Electra in "something you'd wear to a dance," Watson in a dark green jacket and tuxedo pants. The children were "always made to eat early," she says. "Grandfather was very disagreeable and stiff. He said children should be seen and not heard. Children were a bother. He was considered dashing and handsome, but I found him quite scary." "He'd sit sourly, barely conversing, barking orders," remembers Wilmerding.

Catlin remembers Electra as "a cozy person" in sensible shoes and cotton dresses. "Grandfather let her take the stage, and she was clearly the more warmhearted person." Sam junior agreed, recalling his grandfather as "a little crotchety." His grandmother "made up for it because she bubbled all the time."

Sam found the apartment formal, too, as was the strict schedule whenever the Webbs were in residence. "Tea was served every afternoon in the white living room," he said. "If there weren't more than six or seven for dinner, we'd always have cocktails in the Leather Room before dinner." Electra sat on a sofa and drank one and a half sidecars. "That was all she ever drank. Then she would have dinner, and after dinner she would have her one Chesterfield cigarette of the day, which she—believe it or not—did not inhale. But she would puff it."

In the early 1950s, Watson announced that he had decided to live in Shelburne full-time and his wife "either could come along, or not. Didn't matter to him," said Sam junior. Over the next several years, Electra dismantled the Westbury house and finally sold it.

But they kept 740 and had dinner parties, coming-out parties, wedding parties, and a fiftieth wedding anniversary party there that attracted guests from around the world. Once a year, a group of big-game hunters would meet at the Museum of Natural History, and afterward Electra would give a huge party for what she called the "heads and horns" crowd. "Of course, she was very preeminent in there," recalled Sam Webb Jr. "The only woman, naturally. But she had better trophies than anyone."

Typically the Webbs would hire a pair of musicians and serve what today would be called comfort food. "Granny was not what you would call a gourmet," said Sam junior. "She was real meat-and-potatoes—all of them beautifully served on the finest china and silver and glass, but it was very simple, excellent food": shrimp cocktails, turkey, ham, poached salmon, roast beef, Yorkshire pudding, roast potatoes, and, for dessert, chocolate cake or floating islands and little dishes of chocolate-covered orange peel and caramels. Electra's Swedish cook, Augusta, who'd been with her for years, was especially beloved for her oatmeal cookies.

Because the apartment had no ballroom, Electra would sometimes take over the one at the St. Regis Hotel, but only for white-tie dinner dances. "She loved to dance," said Sam junior, "and the old man loved to dance." Then there were the annual all-night parties in Shelburne, held at first aboard the *Ticonderoga*, then in the Brick House.

Watson Webb died at seventy-five in March 1960 at 740. Electra died in Vermont eight months later at age seventy-two, two months after suffering a stroke. Her will left six of the rooms from 740, including paintings and furnishings, everything but the floors and ceilings, to the Shelburne Museum. Today, anyone can visit those rooms, which have been painstakingly re-created.

In the years that followed the Webbs' deaths, the Havemeyer branch of the family (the occupants of Southern Acres) were often at odds with the Vanderbilt side, the descendants of Watson's brother Vanderbilt, who'd inherited the northern acreage and the hundred-room "big" house. The rift began because Electra did not get along with Vanderbilt's wife. "It's worth a gothic novel," says Wilmerding. "Strange cousins, odd marriages, misdemeanors, nasty squabbling, and all the rest. They were an overpowering family, a burdensome legacy. With someone as strong and accomplished as my grandmother, there's an intimidating power and it's still there. All that land, all that money."

After Electra's death, it took a year to dismantle and vacate the penthouse. It was stripped to the bones by the time it was sold in the spring of 1961. Electra Webb Bostwick was the last Webb to see it. She went with Sister Parish, who'd been hired as a decorator by the new owner, Edgar Miles Bronfman, head of the Seagram liquor empire. "She didn't want the rest of us to see it," her daughter Dundeen recalls. "It was down to wires hanging. It was closure for her."

For J. Watson Webb Jr., closure was harder to find. He is credited with completing the Shelburne Museum after his mother's death. But in 1996, when its board decided over his protests to sell twenty-two works of art to raise funds for its endowment, he resigned. The sale brought in $32.8 million, nearly $12 million from the sale of the Degas ballerina alone. In retaliation, when he died in 2000, Watson junior left various nonprofit groups, including Shelburne Farms, $11 million, but gave nothing to his mother's Shelburne Museum. He also left a bed from 740 Park, which he'd inherited, to the farm and not the museum, even though it had been his mother's plan that it would go to the latter. "He gave it with the explicit proviso that it could be *lent* to the museum," says Wilmerding. "It was an act of matricide."

WATSON WEBB'S POLO BUDDY MARSHALL FIELD III WAS BECOMING more and more an odd man out at 740 Park. Most of his neighbors were politically conservative or at least conservative about expressing nonconformist views, but Field was so outspoken that some in his social circle deemed him anti-American. He began to earn such enmity when, in 1937, he invested $200,000 in the dream of a young editor named Ralph Ingersoll: a progressive New York daily newspaper called *PM*, that would carry no advertising. Field's psychiatrist had urged him to give back, and he'd chosen to do so not only through the new Field Foundation, funded with $11 million, but also by becoming a publisher.

PM had a glorious start. Marxism had a certain outlaw glamour in those days, and Ingersoll brought in Dashiell Hammett, Lillian Hellman's lover, to hire the paper's staff. The mystery novelist and his playwright girlfriend, who had also been a girlfriend of Field's, were both committed leftists, as were many of their hires. *PM* launched in 1940, just after the start of World War II, and was an interventionist voice in an isolationist country. When it immediately faltered, Field bought out his fellow investors at twenty cents on the dollar and became the sole owner, inviting vicious attacks from the right. The rich already hated FDR and now worried he would take the country into Europe's war. The *Chicago Tribune* columnist Westbrook Pegler called *PM* variously "a hive of Communists" and "a nest of fellow-travelers . . . distinctly reminiscent of the Nazi press."

In early 1941, Field took the offensive, selling a large block of Marshall Field stock and rapidly expanding his publishing business. First he backed *Parade*, a new Sunday supplement; then he started a Chicago daily newspaper, the *Sun,* to provide an alternative to the fiercely anti–New Deal *Tribune*. Its first issue was published three days before Pearl Harbor brought America into what had become the world's war. The *Tribune*, suddenly pro-war, was still anti-Field. It attacked him as a "hysterical effeminate" and a coward for not going to war himself.

"I came of age today," Field told a dinner party in his apartment the night he turned fifty in 1943 and finally inherited the remainder of his grandfather's fortune—an additional $75 million.

During the war, several members of his stepfather's Drummond family had been evacuated from England, and Field sheltered them at 740 and Caumsett. Maldwin Drummond, who was eight in 1940, remembers Field with "great admiration and affection," he says. "He was a quiet man with a sense of humor and determined ideas but with a kindness that radiated throughout all his relationships."

Despite his liberal politics, Field had been accepted in New York society, where he sat on the boards of the Metropolitan Opera and the Metropolitan Museum, the twin towers of the city's cultural power. But he remained controversial. Shortly after the war ended in 1945, the Cold War began and anti-Communism sentiment rose. *PM* had already lost $5 million, when it was accused of being Red. Field sold the paper, and it soon closed.

He didn't leave publishing, though. He bought the *Chicago Times* (and later merged his two papers into one), then bought Simon & Schuster and Pocket Books, magazines and radio stations, and *The World Book Encyclopedia*. In the summer of 1947, he was invited to join a planeload of media magnates on the first around-the-world airplane flight. Also aboard was Gardner Cowles, another progressive publisher.

Field was ending his run. He gave his newspaper to his son Marshall IV in 1950, just before a congressional committee brought him to Washington to defend the Field Foundation against charges of anti-American subversion. When his newspapers endorsed the Republican Dwight D. Eisenhower for president in 1952, he wrote a letter to the editor disagreeing, but didn't interfere. His company was large and successful, and he let his managers run it. In the fall of 1956, he died of brain cancer. His estate was thought to total $150 million. His last wife, who was left $1.1 million and the family homes, quickly sold the New York apartment to Cowles. "She didn't want to be in there anymore," says Marshall V. "She got a little ahead of herself and wanted to sell quickly and get the money."

Field also gave checks of $10,000 and $20,000 to his secretaries, valet, and chauffeur, a month's salary for every year of employment to sixty other employees, $100,000 each to eleven grandchildren, and $30 million to his foundation.

The Field family did not fare well after his death. Broken marriages and suicide were the norm. Marshall IV and his sister Barbara were both institutionalized repeatedly for mental problems. Marshall IV, who got the rest of his father's estate, drank heavily and was addicted to prescription drugs when he died nine years after his father in what a relative calls a "kind of sort of suicide." Their younger sister Bettine divorced her first husband, a doctor, and married a black man without telling her family, abandoning her own daughter in the process. That daughter, also named Bettine, married and divorced three times before she was shot by an unknown killer in her mansion in rural Arkansas. Henry Phipps, one of Field's stepsons, died of a heroin overdose. Both of his daughters by Ruth Pruyn committed suicide.

The family sold its stake in the Marshall Field stores in 1965 after Marshall IV's death. Today, the best-known members of the Field family are Ted and Marshall V, who liquidated Field Enterprises after a feud in 1984. Marshall, who has been divorced once, bought companies like Cabot, Cabot & Forbes, Muzak, *My Weekly Reader*, and Funk & Wagnalls. Ted, who has been divorced three times and has three children, became a film producer and music mogul. It's unlikely he'd ever be accepted to live at 740 Park.

IN THE EARLY 1930S, ALLENE, PRINCESS HENRY XXXIII OF REUSS, spent most of her time traveling through Europe with a retinue of servants and hangers-on that one observer described as "a veritable procession of magnificence in her wake." Her homes were magnificent, too. "She had very, very excellent taste and asked the most famous decorators to furnish her apartments," says Viktoria Schäfer, a grandchild from Henry's first marriage. As the years passed, whispers spread that Allene's prince was less than a presence in her splendid Parisian home on rue Barbet de Jouy. And when she returned to America for the fall 1934 season, she was alone. Henry "had been a flat failure as a husband, judged from all angles," reported Cholly Knickerbocker, "but Allene kept her nose tilted proudly—and declined to confirm stories of marital discord." She stayed away from New York after that, subletting her apartment at 71 East Seventy-first Street to Gayer Dominick, a stockbroker, former National City Bank director, and associate of Albert Wiggin's.

The deal breaker for the Reuss marriage turned out to be his politics, not his husbandly performance. Henry had aligned himself with the Nazis, and Allene became an outspoken anti-Nazi as her husband began spending more time in Germany. Eventually, the French government made it plain that it would prefer that the German prince stay in Berlin. Allene was about as welcome in Germany as her husband had made himself in France. "Which," wrote her faithful Cholly, "brought about a pretty kettle of fish." So in utmost secrecy, Allene went to court in France in June 1935 and won a divorce.[3] And less than a year after she shed her prince, she wed a count.

Paul de Kotzebue, a bachelor in his fifties, was a descendant of a German dramatist whose family were ennobled and given an estate in Estonia when it was part of the Russian empire. One of Paul's uncles had been a czarist aide, another the imperial Russian ambassador to Washington in 1895, and a great-uncle, Otto von Kotzebue, was an explorer—Kotzebue Sound, an indentation in the Arctic Ocean off Alaska, and an island in the Bering Sound were both named for him. Count Paul served as an officer in the czar's imperial guard before the Russian Revolution. Married in civil and Russian Orthodox ceremonies in Geneva in March 1936, he and Allene honeymooned in Italy before returning to New York to live.

Allene seems to have been more popular with her divorced prince's family than he was. Henry's son Henry visited America as a guest of the Kotzebues in 1936. And Allene played matchmaker at the 1936 Olympics in Bavaria for another of her husband's relatives, introducing Holland's future queen Juliana to the German prince Bernhard, also an anti-Nazi. They married in 1937 and Allene was soon made godmother of their daughter, now Queen Beatrix of the Netherlands. As war loomed over Europe, the Kotzebues began spending more time in America, moving into a much-larger apartment, 6/7B, at 740 Park. Though Kotzebue, like his predecessor, had no money, his title was negotiable currency, and the Kotzebues took their place on the international social scene, entertaining Dutch royals at their homes, playing a large role in the émigré community of Russian aristocrats, lunching at the River Club (where one day, the countess was bitten by a pet monkey named Chico after the little simian guzzled two glasses of vintage champagne chased with pieces of foie gras), and in 1940 buying Beechwood, an estate in Newport, Rhode Island, from Vincent Astor for a mere $49,500.

A few years later, Countess Kotzebue was in the papers again, threatening suit against a Tew cousin, who'd married a Georgian prince, George Dadiani, who lived in Paris. During World War II, the count and countess had left their Paris home in her care and moved full-time to America. Upon their return, they'd discovered precious furnishings and artworks had disappeared. It emerged that her cousin hadn't sold her things, but, rather, had allowed them to be stolen by the Nazis. When the Dadianis promised to reimburse her, the countess dropped the threat to sue.

Unfortunately for Allene, her wealth and title did not earn her the place she had long desired in American high society. The war had changed things: once-upon-a-time kingdoms seemed that much more like fairy tales to the dogfaces who'd saved the world and were its new princes. Like their friends the Duke and Duchess of Windsor, the Kotzebues were relics.

The count and countess returned to France after the war, shuttling between their three homes there. "I stayed with her as a baby, then I met her at the Ritz just after the war," remembers Anne Felkin Walton, a relative of Anson Burchard's who was ten at the time. "She told my mother I was very weedy. I was terribly insulted." Walton remembers the countess as "slightly intimidating, rather awe-inspiring," she says.

Allene died in 1955 at seventy-nine in Cap-d'Ail, where they'd spent the winter. Before her death, Prince Bernhard of the Netherlands drove to the south of France to say good-bye. "Though my wife seemed to be unconscious," Count Kotzebue said, "she recognized his horn in the courtyard and said, 'That's my Bernilo, come to see me.' "

Her will was read three weeks later, and a court battle over the $23.6 million estate—the largest ever adjudicated in Newport Probate Court—followed as surely as European titles did American money. She'd left the bulk of hers in three trusts to her last husband, to her late son's one-time fiancée (who also inherited the Château de Suisnes), and to the Stevens Institute of Technology in Hoboken, where Anson Wood Burchard had long ago studied engineering. The villa at Cap-d'Ail went back to the Reuss family. Allene's jewelry—a star-sapphire necklace and matching star-sapphire and diamond earrings, a three-strand diamond necklace, a diamond chain, long strands of pearls, an emerald ring, and more—and lots of cash went to relatives, friends, and the sister of Seth Rosewater Burchard, who'd changed his name to honor his uncle. But Seth himself was cut out of her will. "She fell out with him" when he remarried after his first wife died, says Anne Felkin Walton. "I remember some unpleasantness. There always is when money rears its ugly head."[4]

Six relatives—distant Tew cousins all—immediately gave notice that they would contest the will, written while she was in a New York hospital in 1952, claiming it had been signed under duress. An out-of-court deal—terms undisclosed—was reached a year later, but it still took seven more years before the estate was settled. The United States inherited more than any of Allene's heirs, almost $11 million. The Count de Kotzebue went on to head the Russian Nobility Association in America for years before dying in Paris in 1966. Walter Chrysler Jr., son of the Detroit automaker, took over the countess's apartment at 740 in 1956. But he didn't rent it. In the interim, the building had become a cooperative again—though not without a long struggle.

15

Aside from the odd domestic drama, the war years were quiet for John D. Rockefeller Jr., 740's ever-so-proper nine-thousand-pound whale. His son David had returned to New York from the London School of Economics in the fall of 1939 and the following June proposed marriage to his lifelong friend Peggy McGrath in the sitting room outside his bedroom on the sixteenth floor. "I asked her one evening, and I didn't hear until the next day," David says, still recalling his anticipation. The next year he got his Ph.D., married, went to work, and moved to his own apartment.

Battered by the Depression, war, and the costs of Rockefeller Center, Junior's investment income no longer met his living expenses. So he sent a note through his office to Abby's, asking about her spending. Abby's team refused to reply. Junior clarified: he needed to know what the apartment had cost because he was still fighting over the painting bill. There is no record of Abby's compliance. But she did worry, too, about things as small as electrical bills, enough so that Con Edison came to check the wiring for evidence someone was tapping their lines.

With his eye for detail, Junior surely noticed that his staid building was in constant flux, families moving in and out frequently. "Everyone was in the same boat," says Martha Farish Gerry, whose parents rented 4/5A in 1940. "With rationing, this, that, and the other, you didn't feel anyplace special at all. America was at war, and nobody was thinking about their apartments."

They paid rent, though, and that mattered. In early 1940, the apartment owners got refunds again for 1939. And Lee kept working to make profits: in September 1940, he got permission from the city to alter the D-line maisonette and turn the ground floor into a doctor's office. Anything to make those mortgage payments. In December 1940, Edward Brewster sent Junior a note to say that $1,214.10—their share of the surplus that year—would be credited to his next rent bill.

The renters were a varied but not at all motley crew. Most had a connection to somebody in the building. H. D. Campbell knew more than one somebody; he'd been named president of the Chase in 1934 when Winthrop Aldrich replaced Charles McCain as the chairman. Campbell lived in the top two floors of Captain Hanrahan's former apartment throughout the war. Sidney A. Mitchell, who rented apartment 8/9A from 1940 until 1942, was the son of the founder of the Bonbright-financed Electric Bond & Share Co.; he bought Bonbright from Landon Thorne and Alfred Loomis in 1933. Thorne was his son Alex's godfather.

"The apartments were perfectly huge," Alex Mitchell says. "We had four or five live-in servants, and this was perfectly normal." They moved out when Alex's father went to Washington after Pearl Harbor to run a section that financed war production, and their apartment was rented by Major William Ottman Jr., the great-grandson of the brewer George Ehret. Once the second-largest property owner in the city behind only the Astor estate, Ehret kept his fortune thanks to one of his son's future neighbors, Francis Patrick Garvan, sub-lessor of the Bouvier apartment.

Ehret had gone to his native Germany for his health in 1914, just before war was declared, and was stuck there until 1918. Garvan, as alien property custodian during the war, was required to hold all German assets. Garvan not only returned them to Ehret in 1918; he praised Ehret's loyalty and patriotism. Sadly, Ottman died young; he had a heart attack at age thirty-six after spending only five years in his apartment at 740.

William Stamps Farish, a grandnephew of the Confederate president, Jefferson Davis, was practicing law in Beaumont, Texas, when oil was discovered in nearby Spindletop and he went to work as a roughneck and well supervisor. After a stint with the committee that coordinated oil supplies for the Allies in World War I, working for Standard Oil's then-chairman, Alfred Bedford, Farish organized Humble Oil and, in 1927, be-came a director of Standard, which financed him in exchange for a large block of Humble stock. In 1933, Farish was named chairman of Stan-dard Oil and, in 1937, traded jobs with its president. Nearing retirement, he moved to 740, decided to go into horse breeding, and bought four fil-lies at the 1942 Saratoga yearling sale, which was held at Belmont Park on Long Island because of gas shortages.

Farish had married Libbie Randon Rice in Houston in 1911. On Thanksgiving Day, 1942, he dined with her and their children at 740, spent Friday at the office, and then went to Millbrook, New York, where he and a group of friends kept a hunting lodge, for a weekend of shoot-ing. But that Saturday night, he fell ill. The next morning he died of a heart attack.

His daughter Martha had just married Edward Gerry, a great-great-great-grandson of the signer of the Declaration of Independence after whom the word "gerrymander"—referring to an oddly shaped electoral district created to favor one or another political party—was named. Gerry was also a nephew of the Harrimans, who owned America's oldest and largest private bank, Brown Brothers Harriman & Co., and, through his paternal grandmother, a member of the Knickerbocker families, the Livingstons and the Goelets.

"When the war came, my husband and I were all over the place for a couple years," says Martha Gerry. "Then he went overseas, my father dropped dead, and I was at 740 with my mother and two children." Martha didn't know that the building was full of Standard Oil fami-lies—"no clue whatsoever," she says—although she did know that her husband's father had owned horses with Marshall Field. "I was a young mother!"

When the war ended, Libbie Farish, whose son had died four months after her husband, decided the apartment was too big for her. Undone by the two deaths, she moved back to Houston, where she died in 1978 at age ninety. Martha Gerry took her father's four fillies and went on to be-come one of the most important women in the history of Thoroughbred racing. Her career was topped by the legendary Forego, named Horse of the Year three times.

IN 1946, BARBARA AND WILLIAM R. KIRKLAND JR. TOOK APARTMENT 2/3A for two years, moving from the Beekman Hotel, where they'd lived with Barbara's father while Kirkland was in the Navy. Kirkland, who ran an insurance brokerage, knew several 740 families. He was a friend of William Hale Harkness's, and he and his wife also knew the Garvans, the Gerrys, and the Marshall Fields. Mrs. Kirkland was the former Barbara Stoddard, the granddaughter of a Pittsburgh coal- and iron-mine owner. Her father, Major Louis Stoddard, came from a Revolutionary-era family in Connecticut and had played polo with Watson Webb. She inherited $1.2 million when her mother died giving birth to Barbara's younger brother.

"It was a very, very big apartment, the fanciest in the building," says a relative who requests anonymity. "There were two huge living rooms facing Park Avenue, with unbelievable, spectacular views." The Kirklands' six-year-old son used one of the parlors as a huge playroom. Though they didn't stay long, their connection to 740 continued for decades. The Kirklands' son would marry one of Electra and Watson Webb's granddaughters. And their apartment would eventually be taken over by another friend of the family, Winston Lord, whom the Kirklands knew from summers on Fishers Island.

FRANK GOULD, A GRANDSON OF THE ROBBER BARON JAY GOULD, BRIEFLY sublet Lynde Selden's apartment. A Yale graduate, member of the Jekyll Island Club, philanthropist, and vice president of the St. Louis Southwestern Railroad, he lived most of the year in Oyster Bay, and spent summers at a camp in Maine, but rented pied-à-terres in town; a year earlier he'd leased the Sutton Place town house originally built for J. P. Morgan's daughter Anne. Gould died in 1945 at age forty-five after retiring from the Army Air Force.

That year the Seldens sublet again, to Arthur Amory Houghton Jr., the great-grandson of the founder of Corning Glass and a descendant of a general in the American Revolution. He'd just returned from three years in the Army Air Force and become president of Steuben Glass, a Corning subsidiary. In 1952, Houghton followed Frank Gould again, buying Anne Morgan's house on Sutton Place. He later bought 1 Sutton Place next door for $436,000 and (after failing to sell it for $1 million) donated it to the United Nations as the home of its secretary-general.

Generous though that was, Houghton had another side. Shortly after taking over Steuben in 1933, he is said to have smashed every item in its warehouse with a lead pipe, so much did he hate its merchandise. Houghton couldn't have been easy in love, either; he would eventually marry four times. "He was a dedicated, cruel son of a bitch, the bad seed of the family," says a nephew of John M. Gates, who ran Steuben with him. "He dumped girls, bullied people less rich than he, and stole my uncle's wife right in front of him. That's the kind of SOB he was."

But Houghton was also a member of over a hundred organizations engaged in education and the arts; served as board member, president, and chairman of the Metropolitan Museum of Art from 1952 to 1974, as chairman of the New York Philharmonic Symphony Society, and as an officer of the Morgan Library; and was a collector and curator of rare books and manuscripts, including a significant Keats collection that he gave to the Houghton Library at Harvard. He endowed that, too.

JOHN D. ROCKEFELLER JR.'S HAND WAS VISIBLE WHEN THOMAS S. Nichols, a chemical company executive, sublet Edith and Grace Scoville's apartment at 740 after they moved around the corner to 71. Nichols, back from the war, had just married his third wife, Theresa McConnell, the widow of David H. McConnell Jr., the son of the founder of Avon Products. McConnell's parents had been golfing partners of Junior's father during his retirement years in Ormond Beach, Florida. The McConnells were also much married. Nichols would be Theresa's fourth husband.

David McConnell was a magnet for trouble: his first wife had died in a bizarre accident, getting stuck between her running car and the door of their garage and asphyxiating. He then married and divorced Muriel Dodge, the ex-wife of the heir to the Dodge Motors fortune, within two years.

"I don't know how anybody stayed married with all those houses they had," says Nichols's daughter, Judy Nichols Joyce. "They were never together." When Nichols was offered the presidency of a chemical company in his native Maryland, he bought a home nearby originally built for Alfred Vanderbilt, fell in love again, and got divorced again. "I don't think he could have affairs," says his daughter. "If something happened, he had to marry the person!" In all, Nichols would have seven wives before his death.

Nichols moved out of 740 before his divorce, and his apartment next went to Frederic and Alida Camp. Camp was the dean of the Stevens Institute of Technology, recipient of millions from the estate of Countess Kotzebue's third husband. Camp had more going for him than that relationship. In 1931, he'd married Alida Milliken, one of Dr. Seth Minot Milliken's daughters. The doctor was a renowned surgeon and a son of the founder of the Milliken textile dynasty who lived in three combined town houses a block away at 723 Park. Alida's brother was a financial backer of the far-right-wing John Birch Society, and her mother played cards with Birch Society playing cards, but Alida was a rebel whom one family member derides as "a fierce, I hate to use the word, liberal, a strong-minded woman, a real individualist." Camp's father had founded two lead companies, a railroad, and a bank in Missouri. John D. Rockefeller III was an usher at their wedding. The Millikens liked Frederic's politics more than his wife's. "Fred was a good conservative," says the Milliken relative.

Not everyone was socially connected. Hazel and George V. McLaughlin moved into Sherburn Becker Jr.'s apartment in 1943 and stayed five years. McLaughlin, Clarence Shearn, and Francis Patrick Garvan were the exceptions to the building's social rule. A former police commissioner, a former judge, and a former assistant district attorney, respectively, they were Irish politicians all. If blood and money were two legs of 740's tripod, they represented the third: political power.

McLaughlin was the son of an immigrant ferryboat captain who plied the waters between Staten Island and Brooklyn. He'd graduated from public high school and worked as a bank messenger and assistant cashier while studying accounting at night school, then taught accounting by day while earning a law degree at night. From 1911 to 1925, he worked for the state banking department, rising from examiner to super-intendent and coming to the attention of Governor Alfred E. Smith. It was Smith who urged New York's mayor in the Roaring Twenties, James J. Walker, to appoint an honest Irishman police commissioner to counter charges that the notoriously corrupt Prohibition-era force was, well, corrupt.

In his first year in office, the tall, husky, gruff-voiced McLaughlin re-organized the department, drove robberies down 44 percent, and organized a special squad to squash illegal gambling. It proved his undoing. When the squad raided gambling halls and clubhouses run by Tammany Hall, the city's Democratic political leadership, he butted heads with Walker and resigned a mere fifteen months into the job. He would later describe himself as "the best Police Commissioner the city ever had."

McLaughlin had a soft landing as executive vice president of a tele-graph and cable company and then as president of the Brooklyn Trust Company, a job that gave him control of the Brooklyn Dodgers after the bank was named trustee for the baseball team's owner. In 1934, he joined the Triborough Bridge Authority, and in 1946, when it took over more ar-teries and was renamed the Triborough Bridge and Tunnel Authority, he was its vice chairman, staying until 1967, when he lost an epic battle with the urban planner Robert Moses, who nonetheless turned up at his funeral.

McLaughlin always carried a fat roll of bills in his pocket and gave away dollars the same way John D. Rockefeller gave away dimes. "He wasn't as well-to-do as you'd imagine," says his grandson John Dobson Jeffords, an architect. "Business put him in places of power."

"He was a wonderful, warm guy," says his granddaughter Sarah Jef-fords, a lawyer. She says he did have some money at the end, and several camps in the Adirondacks. "He fit in everywhere because he knew every-body. When I was in law school, professors came up to me; when I first went to court, lawyers would say, 'I knew your grandpa, George V.' " Jef-fords thinks he got wind of 740's troubles and got a good deal on an apartment. "As a banker, he knew these things," she says. "My parents got their first co-op because he knew of a building in trouble."

·   ·   ·

THANKS TO JAMES T. LEE, IT WAS FAIRLY EASY TO BE IRISH AT 740.
Jewish was a different story. Back in December 1939, Robert Gumbel, Junior's chief cook and bottle washer, had sent the boss a note. Douglas
Gibbons had called that day to report that a broker had approached him,
asking about showing a client the empty apartment 10/11A, "the client
being a Jewess," Gumbel wrote. "Mr. Gibbons wonders if you would care
to express an opinion. He has in mind that there are now no other Jewish families in the apartment; there were none when you went in."

Gibbons immediately told the broker what he'd probably always told
brokers, that "some restriction about tenancies" applied at 740, but he
was called up short when the broker advised him that the client was Mrs.
Jerome Hanauer, the recent widow of a partner at the investment bank
Kuhn, Loeb. This "puts a different complexion on the matter," Gumbel
thought. She was as socially acceptable as a Jew could be in New York.

The world had changed perceptibly now that England and France
were at war with openly anti-Semitic Nazi Germany, so Gibbons punted.
"He felt he should speak to several of the tenants," Gumbel reported:
Beekman Hoppin had an open mind. What of Rockefeller? Gibbons
hoped for a fast answer.

According to Rockefeller Center's biographer Daniel Okrent, Junior
was a product of his times. He was capable of referring to a real estate
operator as a "slippery Jew" and was surrounded by advisers who were
skeptical of Jews. He ate lunch most days in a private club at Rockefeller
Center where Jewish membership was capped at 3.5 percent, equal to the
percentage of Jews in America's total population. But his wife was firmly
and vocally opposed to the social anti-Semitism that helped New York society define itself, and Junior had always done business with Jews, so it is
not surprising that New York real estate lore also credits his family with
"integrating" Jews into 740 Park relatively early. The truth is only somewhat less clear-cut.

Junior kept virtually every letter he ever sent and often jotted his reactions to requests right on them. But there was no reply to Gumbel's letter, and it contains no hint of what Junior might have said to Gibbons, or
if he reacted at all. "Father would have been staunchly opposed to taking action based on opposition to the Jews," says his son David. "It was a
strong belief. He would have insisted that that consideration be ruled out.

And I'm sure he would have said, if they're nice people, let them in, and if they're not, don't." But Mrs. Hanauer went to 998 Fifth Avenue instead, where she got sixteen rooms and five baths.

It would be another nine years before a Jew signed a lease at 740. But he was masquerading as an Episcopalian. "He wasn't Jewish!" insists Colonel William Schiff's stepdaughter Alice T. Blue. "He was a pillar of the Episcopal Church." Schiff certainly looked the part, dressed up in his riding clothes, polo mallet lifted high.

"He knew he was Jewish, but he wasn't happy to be," his son Frank said shortly before his death in 2004.

"He didn't admit it," says Andy Marks, who worked for Schiff. "Knowing him, he knew what it meant socially, and it was important to him. I guarantee [740's management] didn't know it. He would have denied it. He was very, very proper. He looked like an English lord, right out of central casting. You would never have known you got a Jew."

Though he was German, Schiff wasn't even one of the right Schiffs, the "Our Crowd" Schiffs of Kuhn, Loeb. William Schiff's family was from Newark, where he was called a dirty kike as a boy. His father, Simon, formerly a furrier, had founded an insurance brokerage, Schiff Terhune, in 1906. His partner, TenBroeck M. Terhune, came from a colonial Dutch family and sometimes turned up in social columns playing golf in Hot Springs, Arkansas, and Palm Beach before he retired in 1917. Schiff had meanwhile married Eugenie Steiner. Unlike most at 740, their wedding announcement was brief and gave no clubs or school affiliations. Schiff had gone straight to work as a young man and had never attended college.

Schiff Terhune specialized in commercial insurance. The colonel's clients were retailers like Gimbels and B. Altman, tobacco manufacturers like Philip Morris, and liquor companies like Schenley. He also did business with Lehman Brothers, the Jewish investment bank, but "they kept the name Terhune because it was WASPy," says David Schiff, a grandson who runs an insurance business newsletter. "But a lot of the companies that were clients were run by Jews."

In 1924, William's older brother Herbert, a lieutenant in the Naval Reserve, was doing his two weeks when suction from a propeller sucked him into the blades and he was killed on the spot. The next year William created and endowed the Herbert Schiff Memorial Trophy for the flier with the best safety record. In coming years, William would regularly turn up in the dapper suit, homburg, and white brush mustache that marked him as an Anglophile at the White House as Calvin Coolidge, Herbert Hoover, and Franklin Roosevelt presented the cup.

Schiff was known for his elegance. "Everyone loved Popsy," says a daughter-in-law, Margot Gordon. "He was debonair, charming, hand-some." He was also fussy; his tables were usually covered with plastic.

Schiff sailed through the Depression, riding horses and keeping ser-vants. "The insurance business wasn't that affected," says his grandson David. "If you had a decent income, you were richer than before." In 1941, Schiff, then fifty-four and a longtime Army reservist and military buff, became the fiscal director of the Army's Second Service Command, which made him one of World War II's top paymasters. On VE Day, the monthly payroll he supervised from his office on Governors Island topped $670 million. He called himself Colonel Schiff ever after.

Schiff and his wife lived on a sprawling Tudor-style horse farm in Mount Kisco, where he played polo and went foxhunting, and at the Plaza Hotel during the war. Mrs. Schiff, a captain in the Red Cross, died at fifty in 1943 after a lengthy illness.

"I think he did have social ambitions, if not for himself, then for his business," says Margot Gordon. "He moved in mixed circles." Those am-bitions were realized two years later when Colonel Schiff married his second wife, Alice T. Blue, the widow of a naval lieutenant commander. Years later, Schiff wrote an autobiographical sketch that noted his new wife's membership in the National Society of the Colonial Dames and the Daughters of the Barons of Runnemede.

"He'd lived in the country before that and kept a small apartment in the city," said his son Frank. Alice came to the marriage with two chil-dren, and Schiff still had a boy at home, so they needed a large apart-ment. Luckily, the former Gerry apartment had just turned over again.

Colonel Schiff and his new family moved in and became part of Manhattan's elite social scene. "My reaction was amazement," recalled Schiff's son Frank. "It was so big, and I don't know why he wanted an apartment like that." He thinks Schiff's wife, who had social ambitions, wanted to live there. And Schiff did what she wanted. "He did go to the

Episcopal church," says Frank, "but he never converted. He really wasn't religious." But he had his youngest son, Herbert, baptized, according to Herbert's widow, who still recalls her husband's dislike of his stepmother. "We used to laugh," says Margot Gordon. "She showed us a picture of a castle and said it was the family seat. She was awful, bitchy, none of us liked her at all."

The Schiffs had definitely arrived. Schiff's stepdaughter Alice, a graduate of the Madeira School, came out as a debutante at the New York Infirmary's annual Christmas Cotillion in 1949 while a freshman at Vassar. Before the dance, the Schiffs gave a party for 250 in their salon with entertainment by the Lester Lanin Orchestra. After transferring to the Katharine Gibbs secretarial school, Alice married the son of the superintendent of West Point in 1952 at St. Bartholomew's, the grand Episcopal church on Park Avenue, and had a reception at the Colony Club. Two years later, Schiff's son Frank, who'd become president of Schiff Terhune, married Gloria O'Connor, a former model and debutante. Her sister Consuelo was married to the Italian count Rodolfo Crespi. They'd appeared together as the Toni Twins in advertising for a home-permanent hair product.

But by then, the Schiffs had left 740, moving into a smaller apartment in the mid-1950s after Mrs. Schiff's younger daughter went away to boarding school. They eventually divorced, and Schiff, who never retired, died of a heart attack in a restaurant in 1964 while entertaining a client from Philip Morris.

16

Seven forty Park has been home to many widows, often quite merry ones with enough cash to afford their rambling apartments. The first to arrive as a renter was the most remarkable of all. Blanche Brownell Grant leased 71 East Seventy-first Street's two-bedroom penthouse, 17D, in 1933. The Brownell family had come from England in 1638 and landed in Vermont in the late eighteenth century. Samuel Aaron Brownell II, Blanche's father, ran a store and a lumber mill, opened Vermont's first electric power plant, and founded a bank. He was, needless to say, the most prominent man in his town. Brownell's second child, Lena Blanche, was born in 1875. She'd become a teacher by the time she met William Thomas Grant, a buyer and floorwalker in a department store in Salem, Massachusetts, through her brother-in-law, who was helping the high-school dropout put together a plan for a chain of five-, ten-, and twenty-five-cent stores. "Follow me and you'll wear diamonds," Grant told his first employees.

Grant, thirty, opened his first W. T. Grant store in 1906 and married Blanche, thirty-one, who hated her first name and never used it, the next year. By 1910, Grant had three stores, one rented from Lizzie Borden, before the murder that made her a legend. Grant and Blanche's brother-in-law eventually opened hundreds of stores based on Grant's theory that selling a lot of things at low prices could be hugely profitable.

They all moved to New York, where the Grants lived in Westchester with two adopted girls, and socialized with other budget retailers like the Penneys and Kresges. But they didn't enjoy their $40 million fortune. Grant was "busy all the time," says his granddaughter Deborah Lobmeyer. And Blanche "was the kind of mother who didn't have anything to do with her children; they didn't have much family life," says her granddaughter Marion Nelson. "They were both very, very strong personalities, they were not social at all, and I'm sure they clashed at many points."

Then Grant fell in love with his secretary and left their rented pied-à-terre on lower Park Avenue, bought a yacht, the *Marlen* (named for daughters Marion and Helen), anchored it off City Island, and made it his home. Luckily, Blanche already had a life and a mind of her own. But she also had those daughters, eight and sixteen years old. So it appears she did the sensible thing. On July 9, 1920, she and her elder daughter boarded the *Aquitania* for France, seen off by her husband "in the friendliest humor and filling her suite with gay flowers," according to the *Herald Tribune*. He followed twelve hours later on the *France*. Their younger daughter, who was horse-crazy, had been sent to a Wyoming dude ranch.

"It was said," the newspaper continued, "there would be no difficulties over financial arrangements." Grant was "very, very generous with her," their granddaughter Marion Nelson confirms. The Brownells were shocked, but took things in stride. "It was much discussed," says a cousin, Lincoln Brownell, who still lives in Vermont. "Divorce was not yet fashionable. One way to make it fashionable was to go to Paris."

Blanche began calling herself Mrs. Brownell Grant. After her daughters were married, she moved into her 740 penthouse. Aside from the typical Candela touches, the apartment wasn't lavish, and neither were her furnishings—mostly heavy Italian castoffs from the house in Pelham—but physically, it was breathtaking, with light and windows facing four directions. Blanche chose it because of the address, which was full of sevens and ones. She'd never say aloud that she also occupied the eighteenth floor. "I'd ask why, and she'd never tell me," says Nelson. "It had to do with Gurdjieff."

In the 1920s, Blanche Grant fell under the spell of an esoteric meta-physical philosopher, occultist, and mystic, George I. Gurdjieff. Gurdjieff's teachings, focused on helping followers find the real "I," could be odd and off-putting. "He'd find the sorest corn on your foot and stomp as hard as he could on it," says Benjamin Moore, a disciple. Gurdjieff also believed in numerological divination and claimed that the number seven had special mystical properties (represented by the seven notes, do, re, mi, fa, so, la, and ti), that man had seven centers of psychic functioning, and that there were seven types of men. Blanche felt living on the seventeenth floor of 71 East Seventy-first Street was very auspicious.

Grant started sponsoring Gurdjieff's Russian disciples when they fled the Bolsheviks for America. She hoped, says her granddaughter Marion Nelson, to become a high priestess in the Gurdjieff cult. But her interests were many: she was also passionate about the arts, ran something called the Women's New Economic Committee, and, sometime in the 1930s, began seeing a Columbia University neurology professor, the Russian-born Joshua Rosett.

Rosett was, as *The New York Times* put it in 1914, "a radical Socialist physician" who'd been divorced once and lost custody of his children. A Sephardic Jew with a pronounced accent, he'd studied medicine in czarist Russia but run away to avoid conscription, landing in Maryland. Tall, with piercing eyes, the thirty-nine-year-old became a local character in Baltimore. While working as a public health officer, he edited a socialist newspaper and wrote political plays and novels. He met Louise Carey, the daughter of, as *The Times* wrote, "leaders in the most exclusive circles of Baltimore society," at a garden party, where they bonded discussing women's suffrage and social problems. After studying at Bryn Mawr, Louise had given up the debutante whirl to become a settlement worker.

They met in the spring and were separated all summer; in December they were engaged. She was doing good, he was up to no good, or at least that's what the papers intimated. "That the two should meet while engaged in work among the downtrodden and that both should care so little for the aristocratic and exclusive things of social life seem quite without the pale of prosaic everyday happenings," said *The Baltimore Evening Sun.*

The *Sun* seemed more amused than perturbed by the idea that a pretty, well-dressed society girl would fall for Rosett's likes, and continued to cover the bribes offered and pleas made to break up the couple. A family member reported from Hot Springs, West Virginia, that Louise had had a nervous breakdown and the wedding was postponed indefinitely. Louise responded with special-delivery letters to editors insisting the wedding was *on!* Then, in February, Rosett turned up at the Greenbriar Hotel and snatched her—along with her nurse.

But eloping didn't prove easy. After arguing about marriage law with a court clerk who insisted they had to see a minister, the couple were turned away by four rural clergymen until they found one who consented to perform the ceremony. It wasn't their political or class or age difference—Louise was twenty-six—that caused the clergy to balk; it was the fact that Rosett had been divorced.

"Society," the *Sun* said, was "agog."

Rumors the newlyweds would go abroad or to New York proved untrue, and they settled into a three-room, one-bath apartment while Rosett studied psychiatry at Johns Hopkins. The thoroughly modern couple also launched a column, Life as It Is by Louise and Joshua Rosett, in the *Sun*, full of parables, reportage (sometimes from a fictional character they named Ebenezer Z. Snotley), and diatribes against public schools and John D. Rockefeller Jr.'s war against the Ludlow miners. In 1919, Rosett went to Siberia on a specially outfitted train with a team of medical volunteers to fight a typhus epidemic. Back home, he got a job teaching neuroanatomy at the College of Physicians and Surgeons at Columbia University. He sired a daughter and built by hand a home and cabin on forty acres he'd bought atop Ohayo Mountain in Woodstock, New York. There he foraged for mushrooms, another of his passions, and ran a self-styled Brain Institute. He stayed out of the newspapers for fifteen years, only to pop up again in Reno in 1934, establishing residency to divorce his wife, charging her with desertion.

She may have deserted him, but as locals tell the story, the suave and elegant Rosett was having an affair himself, with his next-door neighbor in Woodstock, a Columbia psychiatric researcher named Nina Bull. A specialist in the organic sources of emotions, she was also a society girl, the niece of Henry Adsit Bull, the editor of *Town & Country* magazine, and a friend of the Renaissance woman Blanche Grant, who rented a cottage on Rosett's property as a summer retreat. Blanche promptly beau-snatched Rosett.

Woodstock's arts colony had been formed three decades earlier by a group of freethinkers who promoted arts and crafts as an antidote to the ills of the Industrial Revolution. Blanche Grant fit in better than Rosett—like 740, Woodstock didn't have a lot of Jews. Its arts colony consisted of "very rich, very oddball, very free-living revolutionists, swingers," claims Stanley Banks, who now owns Rosett's Woodstock house. "Lots of sex, booze, big-time four-day parties. They were all screwing around, especially among that class. They had no rules. They had money when other people didn't, and so they did what they wanted. The doctor was her girlfriend's boyfriend and she stole him." Blanche hesitated when he proposed because he was Jewish, "but she did go ahead, and she was happy she did," says Marion Nelson. "They had a meeting of the minds."

If anyone at 740 objected to Mrs. Grant's new sleepover guest, or even picked him out of the Gurdjieff crowd, there is no record of it. But the Rosetts became, briefly, a power couple in Woodstock. Blanche opened a gallery, dabbled in interior design, sponsored the local crafts guild. They also ran a salon, sponsoring lectures and recitals, held in a small circular building with a big open fireplace on their manicured property. It was called the Shell Cabin, because Rosett built cases there for his impressive collection of seashells. "He had ideas about shells as natural forms," says Alf Evers, the town historian. "She had a good deal of money."

In April 1940, the Rosetts flew to the Yucatán to visit Mayan ruins. Dr. Rosett had a hemorrhage while they were touring Chichén Itzá and was rushed to Mérida, the nearest city for blood transfusions, but died there at age sixty-four. Blanche inherited the Woodstock property and spent summers there for the rest of her life, ferried between Seventy-first Street and upstate in a limousine driven by her caretaker. When Marion Nelson's father went off to World War II, she and her mother moved into Blanche's apartment, staying in the study on a pullout sofa.

"I adored her, even though she was very proper," says Nelson. "Not the sort of grandmother you would hug. But she paid an awful lot of attention to me," taking Nelson to museums and the movies, when she wasn't off at Gurdjieff House doing her spiritual "exercises, as they called them." Nelson was looking out the window on a morning in 1945 when a B-25 bomber flying in dense fog smashed into the seventy-ninth floor of the Empire State Building.

W. T. Grant set up trusts for his children in the 1940s, but most of the proceeds went to a foundation he created, and the small payments provided to his offspring began shrinking after he suffered a stroke in 1952 and became incapacitated. "We never saw anything, because the company went kaput," says Nelson. "Grandmother was well provided for. She had all this income, but she was embarrassed by it and gave it all away. There was nothing in the estate at the end."

A few years before she died, Blanche gave her granddaughter a tapestry embroidered with zodiac signs around an image of the devil in a sailboat. "I'd ask her the meaning of it," says Nelson. "She'd just smile and not tell me."

Blanche Rosett died in her apartment in June 1967 at age ninety-two, almost twenty years after George Gurdjieff but a few years before William Grant. Her daughter Marion had long since moved to California, where she married a doctor. The Grants' younger daughter, Helen, lived a more tragic life. "She was a tall, thin flapper, a party girl from the word 'go,' " says Marion. "It's a sad story. She had too much money."

Helen's first marriage broke up quickly, and then her second husband, a Virginia horseman who married her for that money, wrapped his Packard around a post on the Fifty-ninth Street Bridge just after their daughter was born. Helen moved into her mother's apartment. "Blanche was trying to keep her on the straight and narrow, but she was inclined to alcohol," says cousin Lincoln Brownell. Helen married three more times, the last to her British chauffeur. "The family looked down on him, but he was very good to her in her last years," says Nelson. "That meant everything."

HARRIET PULLMAN SCHERMERHORN, WHO RENTED BERTRAM BORDEN'S apartment in 1935 and stayed in it twenty-two years, wasn't burdened with children, adoptive or otherwise. But she did carry the weight of two extraordinary American family names. The Schermerhorns were very old; the Pullmans were very rich.

George Pullman, the inventor of the Pullman railroad car, was one of the richest men in Chicago. He'd fought and beaten Seward Webb in the battle of private railcars, eventually taking over the Vanderbilts' company. He even had a town, Pullman, Illinois, named after him. When she was twenty-one in 1892, Harriet, his prettiest daughter, married a San Francisco society man whose occupation was given as going to clubs and playing polo. Harriet already had a fortune of $500,000, thanks in part to her father's habit of paying her $100 each time she named one of his railcars. Then the Pullman name lost some of its luster when workers living in its company town struck and rioted. Half the U.S. Army was called in to stop a national railroad workers' boycott.

George Pullman never recovered, and three years later he died, leaving a $7.5 million estate. Harriet and her sister each got $1 million outright; the rest was left in trust. Their two brothers were disinherited for bad judgment and irresponsibility. In 1912, Harriet hired a French architect to build the finest home in California on one thousand acres she owned just south of San Francisco. Six years later, she was the victim of a $30,000 jewel theft while at the St. Regis in New York—and ended up suing the hotel. By 1919, she was living in New York alone. The childless couple had separated by the time Harriet's mother died and she inherited a couple million more; her mother had given the bulk of her fortune, about $12 million, to charity.

Her husband died, and within two years Harriet was engaged to Colonel Arthur Frederic Schermerhorn, a widower, the ninth in line in a family of Dutch tradesmen who'd risen into the landowning upper class by the early nineteenth century. Loyalists to the Crown, they'd left the country during the Revolution but returned in time to give Caroline Schermerhorn in marriage to William Astor. The Astor fortune had gone to his older brother; William's consolation prize was Caroline, who became known as "The" Mrs. Astor, the one with the ballroom that could only hold the Four Hundred families she deemed acceptable in 1880s society. Arthur Schermerhorn's genealogical credits also included a Revolutionary general, whom he emulated; he'd seen action in the Spanish-American War and in World War I.

Shortly after her second marriage, Harriet sued the estate of her late husband, claiming all his assets—about $1.3 million—were actually hers, and won a share of them. Then, in 1933, Colonel Schermerhorn died of a stroke and left her everything—the papers said it was another million or so. But in 1934, it emerged that Schermerhorn had died flat broke, owing his wife $106,445. The following year she moved into 740 and, other than real estate transactions, selling and donating buildings to charity, never got her name in the newspaper again until she died in 1956. The sole professional activity mentioned in her obituary was her service as honorary president of something called the Outdoor Cleanliness Association, where she presided over an annual flower show and won praise and prizes for her floral arrangements. Her French furniture and collections of Americana and first editions were auctioned off in 1957 for more than $300,000.

FLORA WHITING, ANOTHER WIDOW AND COLLECTOR, WOULD HAVE BEEN the first Jewish tenant in 740 had anyone, herself included, known she was Jewish. But that was a deep, dark secret. "Our family was very closed-mouthed," says Whiting's surviving granddaughter, who requests anonymity. "It was like they had a lot to hide."

One secret, at least, was revealed when a great-niece, Barbara Sirna, opened a sealed envelope passed down to her by her parents—her father was Whiting's nephew—and discovered that Louis and Henrietta Ettlinger, Flora's parents and Sirna's great-grandparents, had been married twice, but only acknowledged their civil ceremony, not the Jewish one that had preceded it. "No one knew," says Sirna. "We were raised Presbyterian and had no idea."

"We never discussed religion," confirms Whiting's granddaughter, who was raised Episcopalian. "Back in that society, you couldn't be Jewish and social, I guess."

Louis Ettlinger, Flora's father, had come to New York from Germany in 1866. After a brief spell as a greengrocer, Ettlinger switched to printing and had an immediate success printing labels for cigars. In 1879, he merged with eight other printing firms to form American Lithographic, which controlled 90 percent of the printing business in America. Ettlinger was treasurer of the company that eventually became Crowell-Collier, a major publisher of books and magazines.

His hazel-eyed daughter stood about five feet five inches. An art student, Flora married Giles Whiting, an architect, in 1899. It's unclear if Giles had much success, but since Flora loved to travel and shop for antiques, Ettlinger backed Whiting in the Persian rug business and was chairman of his company. Even before 1927, when Ettlinger died, leaving just under $5 million to his two daughters, the Whitings were living large in a house on East Eighty-first Street and on a hundred-acre working farm on the Hudson River. They had a Greek Revival mansion there full of antiques, and everything they ate—vegetables, fruit, Black Angus beef, and game—was raised on the estate. In 1933, the Whitings were in town at the Hotel Pierre when their adopted daughter, a Sarah Lawrence student, ran off with a salesman from Macy's and her mother stopped speaking to her. "How dare she run off and elope!" says Whiting's granddaughter. "She felt this was beneath her family. Flora could be very snobby."

Giles Whiting died of heart disease in 1937, and three years later Flora rented the until-then-empty apartment 10/11A at 740 Park, ironically, the very one that Jerome Hanauer's widow, the Jewess, had decided not to rent a few years earlier. From then until her death, Whiting stayed single, quiet, and reclusive, say the few who knew her. "She didn't do much in her lifetime," says Robert Pennoyer, a trustee of the foundation she established in 1963. "But she was a very astute investor, she lived well, and she collected beautiful things."

How astute she was is evident in an anecdote Pennoyer tells. "She sat next to a man named Thomas Watson at a dinner in the 1920s," Pennoyer says. "He said he had a little company; this was before it was named IBM [that is, before 1924, when Watson's Computing-Tabulating-Recording Company merged with International Business Machines]. When she died, a significant part of her wealth was in IBM stock."

Flora's financial adviser was the former president Herbert Hoover.' It was Hoover's wife, Lou Henry, who focused Flora's philanthropy on young girls. The Hoovers were regulars at Whiting's canasta games. "She loved canasta, but she cheated," says her granddaughter. But her business acumen was great—she was a devotee of the stock market. "You could ask her about any stock, and she could tell you what it was trading for today, what it traded for yesterday. She knew exactly what she was doing." And kept her business to herself.

Eventually, her grandchildren were cut off like their mother was, but before that they stayed with Whiting when their mother fell ill in the late 1940s. At the farm, they and a governess had their own house, only going to the big house for dinner with Flora. "She was very prim and proper," says the granddaughter. "Women never wore slacks or shorts. You dressed for dinner. You had a drink before and one glass of wine at dinner, which was served by a butler on sterling silver. Children were seen and not heard. I was never allowed in the servants' quarters. But I'd sneak in."

Whiting kept her passion for collecting, also inherited from her father, as quiet as she did her fortune. The size of the latter only became known after her death at ninety-three in 1971, when her will was filed and it was revealed that she'd left about $25 million. The extent of the former was made manifest a year later, when Parke-Bernet concluded a five-day sale of her belongings to benefit the Girls Clubs, earning her a full-page article in *The New York Times*.

It described her as "publicity-shy and reserved . . . a movie buff . . . a dedicated world traveler . . . But above all, she was a pioneer among collectors of American decorative arts who began buying, with her father's encouragement, at the age of 9 and never stopped."

Her first purchases were several candle stands. In 1929, she and Lou Henry Hoover and the wives of five former presidents, Grover Cleveland, Theodore Roosevelt, William Howard Taft, Woodrow Wilson, and Calvin Coolidge, set up the first serious exhibition ever of American antiques, the Girl Scouts Loan Exhibition. So her sofa, saucers, clocks, and quilts all sold well above their estimates, and the Girls Clubs of America, another of her quiet interests, netted nearly $500,000. Though most of her money went to charities and her foundation, she did set up trusts for her daughter and her children, having softened toward them when her first great-grandchild was born.

But still the distance persisted, whether caused by secrets, class, or the unfathomable chasms that can divide families. "She was not about to confide in me," the granddaughter says when asked what Whiting was really like. "She was of the old school."

. . .

SAMUEL SLOAN COLT, THE PRESIDENT OF BANKERS TRUST, MARRIED FOR a second time in September 1945, five days after his first wife divorced him (Reno, cruelty), and immediately rented apartment 2/3B at 740 Park, the top two floors of a maisonette chopped up by James T. Lee.

Colt was part of the matrix: a *Mayflower* descendant, a graduate of Groton and Yale. His grandfather had been president of the Delaware, Lackawanna & Western Railroad, financed by Mary Moulton Hanrahan's great-grandfather. Colt spent his life as a banker, except for a stint as an officer in World War I. He was still in the Army in 1917 when he married Margaret van Buren Mason, whose father, another Yale man, was working on a Midwestern railroad in 1907 when he inherited one of America's great fortunes.

It had been made by a Scot named George Smith, who speculated in Chicago and Milwaukee real estate in the 1830s and put his profits into banking, insurance, and railroads. When Smith retired to London, he turned his interests over to a nephew, James Henry Smith, a reclusive figure who was known on Wall Street, if at all, as "Silent" Smith. But his silence was relative; he soon inherited his uncle's fortune and entered New York society, buying a grand house, hobnobbing with Vanderbilts and Astors, and marrying Mrs. William Rhinelander Stewart a mere twenty-four days after she divorced her husband. But then "Silent" Smith died in Kyoto on their around-the-world honeymoon cruise.

As his body sailed back to New York from Japan, and his will came the other way from Scotland, newspapers tracked their daily progress—then played his bequests as front-page news when he left his wife a mere $3 million and an unknown nephew from Aberdeen, South Dakota, $12 million. George Grant Mason's windfall—a reward for his devotion to his uncle's railroad—and his immediate elevation into the pantheon of society, were tracked with similar intensity. He and his wife soon bought a Manhattan mansion and built another in Tuxedo Park.

The Colts' daughters both married just before the war. Shortly after it began, Colt's wife left for England, where she volunteered for the Red Cross and fell in love with a brigadier general. "It was a perfectly good arrangement," says their daughter Cathy Yandell, because the Colts were desperately unhappy. "Mother thought bankers were boring," she says, and Colt, who cared as much for her passion, horses, as she did for his, was already seeing the woman who became his second wife, the twice-divorced Anne King Weld, also from Tuxedo, the daughter of a former president of the New York Stock Exchange.

At war's end, Colt sent his wife to Reno "and we all supported them," says Yandell of her siblings. "We felt he'd have a much happier life. It was not only civilized; we each wrote letters to both of them saying it was the right thing to do."

It wasn't right for Bill Crawford, a child of Weld's first marriage, then in boarding school. "It was not a particularly pleasant time in my life," he says, recalling that his mother and Colt were both alcoholics. Colt later stopped cold turkey, and won his stepson's affections during summers spent in Westhampton on Long Island, where they often saw the former Janet Lee, a friend of his mother's, and the Garvans, who knew Colt. "But they were hugely self-centered and disinterested in their kids," says a cousin. "Anne preferred her dogs to her children because they didn't talk back. She was awful, just a terrible woman."

In 1948, when the couple moved to Candela's 19 East Seventy-second Street, they'd still never gotten around to decorating their huge corner parlor at 740. "They never used it," says Crawford. "It was closed off." Closed off, too, were conversations of family finances, so Crawford has no idea why his mother and stepfather moved. But it made sense that the apartment next went to C. Ledyard Blair and his second wife, Harriet, the daughter of a founder of Alexander Brown & Sons, the banking house that became part of Brown Brothers Harriman & Co. Blair's grandfather, John Insley Blair, had also been in business with Mary Hanrahan's grandfather.

Though he lived in the same simple farmhouse most of his life, John Insley Blair was, like Moses Taylor and George Mason, one of the richest men in America. The unschooled child of Scottish immigrants, he opened a general store in New Jersey when he was eighteen, owned five stores and four flour mills before he turned thirty, and then began building railroads. He organized the Delaware, Lackawanna & Western (financed by Taylor), co-founded the Union Pacific, and became the president of sixteen different lines and the largest owner of railroad miles (and land abutting them) in the world.

Asked before his death to comment on the discrepancy between his life and his grandson's, John Insley Blair said, "There's a huge difference: he has a rich grandfather and I didn't." But the Ledyard Blairs were downsizing when they moved into 2/3B in 1947.

Harriet Blair's parents had given her and her first husband, a securities dealer and social figure named T. Suffern Tailer, thirteen dozen sets of silver and a check for $1 million upon their marriage in 1909, and the groom gave her a fully furnished town house and a fistful of diamonds. Six years later, Harriet's second husband inherited half of his father DeWitt Clinton Blair's $50 million estate. Blair spent some of it on a house on the corner of Seventieth Street and Fifth Avenue. But he spent most of his time at Blairsden, the $2 million, 423-acre estate he'd built around 1900 in New Jersey hunt country. It had a sixty-two-thousand-square-foot Carrère & Hastings mansion with a three-hundred-foot-long reflecting pool lined with maple trees and busts of Roman emperors leading to its front door. He loved it so much he divested his town house in 1927, and a new Candela apartment building rose in its place. Blair also built a twenty-eight-room house on ten acres in Bermuda in 1929.

"No house will ever be too big for me," he said. A staff of about sixty servants ran them. "He was a bit of a financial wild man," says his grandson Anthony Gambrill Villa. "He spent money like water, much to the regret of his great-grandchildren."

Blair's first wife had died in 1931, and he married Harriet Tailer in 1936 at her summer home, Honeysuckle Lodge, in Newport. They moved to 740 a few years later because she "did not like the country one bit," says Anne van den Bergh, a granddaughter. But Blair had also suffered the last in a lifetime of financial reverses and quite likely wanted to get as far away from New Jersey as he could. Though his four daughters had married well—one, Marie Louise, married and divorced Pierpont Hamilton, a great-great-grandson of Alexander Hamilton and grandson of J. P. Morgan—they'd suddenly woken up to their father's wild spending and demanded their share of his dwindling fortune.

When Blair graduated from Princeton in 1890, he'd joined his father and grandfather in setting up Blair & Co., a private investment bank. "His grandfather either gave him the money or put it into the company and had him start to run it," says his granddaughter Anne Martindell. "He went on his yacht for six months, and when he came back, his partners had lost the money." He lost more, "a huge amount," in the early 1920s, causing "a huge family row," Martindell continues, "a great deal of irritation."

Irritation was nothing new to Blair, even though he retired in 1921 and spent the rest of his life flaunting his wealth. He hated taxes and duties with a passion, and relatives say he smuggled things past customs on his yacht *Diana*, a 254-foot steel-hulled craft; imported French wines during Prohibition; and kept millions in cash stashed in safe-deposit boxes. "Of course, he had a girlfriend, too," says a female descendant who does not approve.

Martindell, a lifelong Democrat, former state legislator, and Jimmy Carter's ambassador to New Zealand, admits she didn't like her grandfather, either. "He was the last of the Bourbons," she says, "very, very right-wing." She remembers a dinner conversation in which he placed Woodrow Wilson second only to the devil on his list of most-hated figures in history. Wilson's sin? Creating the income tax.

"By 1947, he'd run through all his money, and he was entirely dependent on his daughters," says his great-grandson James Rivington "Riv" Pyne. "He'd lived extremely well and squandered a lot of money on Blairsden and that damned yacht." So when his daughters and their husbands staged an intervention, Blair reluctantly agreed to put what was left in a corporation owned by his heirs and live on the interest. He also sold his Bermuda estate.

The apartment at 740 "was referred to as hers," Harriet's, says Martindell. "She had a lot of money, and it saved him and allowed him to continue his lifestyle." Blair's descendants aren't sure when the decision was made to sell Blairsden; some think it was put on the market before Blair's death but failed to sell because "it defined white elephant," says Riv Pyne. "Who was gonna buy it?"

They still had Newport. "They went every weekend with their butler and two of their girls," says the elevator man Patrick O'Connor. In the summer of 1948, Blair had a heart attack there and never recovered. He died the following February in his apartment. Harriet Blair moved out of 740 soon afterward. "I was married about that time," says their granddaughter Harriet Tailer Reed, who'd lived at 740 while attending Barnard. "I wasn't going to be with her anymore; she wanted a smaller apartment."

In June 1950, Parke-Bernet auctioned off Blair's collection of jewelry and the better contents of Blairsden—including Louis XV furniture, Beauvais tapestries, and a pair of Tiepolo murals—by order of his executors. A year later, after it failed to sell for the asking price of $250,000, the $2 million main house at Blairsden, as well as fifty acres, was sold to an order of Catholic nuns for $60,000—"a pittance," in the words of Riv Pyne. By the fall of 1951, eight more land sales had been made, including several to family members.

The family's resentment at Blair's profligacy continues to this day. "Money really is a source of a lot of evil," says Fern Tailer de Navarez, Harriet Blair's sister-in-law. "Money corrupts. People go nuts. That's why Jesus talked more about money than anything else."

17

THE CLOCK WAS RUNNING OUT ON 740 PARK AVENUE'S MORTGAGE. THE
principal was due in December 1949. The constant churn of tenants
around the remaining owners was, for those paying attention, a reminder
of the shaky foundation the grand palace rested upon.

James T. Lee had a big problem. The sensitive, headache-prone John
D. Rockefeller Jr. had two. Not only was his lease due to expire that fall,
but a sharp Irish blade named Clarence J. Shearn was hanging over his
head.

Shearn had rented apartment 17B starting in 1933. It was small by
740 standards but well situated on the corner of Park and Seventy-first,
with a typical Candela layout of huge public rooms, a thirty-four-by-
twenty-foot living room with two exposures, a twenty-by-twenty-four-
foot library, three terraces, a twenty-by-twenty-seven-foot dining room,
servants' quarters with three maids' rooms behind, and two quiet bedrooms high above Seventy-first Street.

A small, balding, dapper man who wore wire-rim glasses over a
pinched Dickensian face, Shearn was an aggressive lawyer from western
Massachusetts. He'd gone to Cornell and New York Law School while
moonlighting as a newspaper reporter, then become an investigative

lawyer. A brawler, he spent his early career railing against "almost everything available on Manhattan Island from Tammany to the beef trust," *The New York Times* said.

Shearn got involved in Democratic Party politics and gained enough clout to be appointed a receiver for bankrupt companies. Then he went to work for William Randolph Hearst. Hearst's father, George, had owned the Anaconda copper mine before selling it to his old friend Marcus Daly and becoming immensely rich in the process. William Randolph Hearst used his inheritance to take over *The San Francisco Examiner*, transforming it into a pro-labor, anticapitalist, antitrust newspaper for readers sure they were getting screwed by the rich. By the turn of the century, Hearst owned coast-to-coast newspapers, including the *New York Journal*, and his crusades had made him a force in politics, a champion of immigrants and workers, a demagogue in the making.

Hearst put Shearn on retainer in 1896 to investigate evildoers and sue to force government to respond. Hearst inveighed against the trusts that had control of vital city services like gas and oil mains and delighted in exposing crooked politicians. He would call Shearn to talk tactics at 2:00 A.M. Soon Shearn was working for the publisher full-time. Hearst hailed his efforts, which saved the city's taxpayers millions, in the *New York Journal*, reporting Shearn's first injunction against New York City with the headline WHILE OTHERS TALK THE JOURNAL *ACTS!*

By 1903, Hearst had entered Congress—a reward from the Democrats of Tammany Hall for his support—and Shearn was doing his research and drafting bills aimed at breaking up monopolies. Shearn had become "the crusading attorney who led most of Hearst's battles," says David Nasaw, a Hearst biographer. "Day after day, Shearn goes after corruption, writes position papers, goes to court, becomes one of the great radical progressives." One day, he charged that the American Ice Company was an illegal trust. The next, he rode shotgun on Hearst's crusade against monopolistic coal, gas, and electric light companies. In 1905, he represented Hearst when he was sued for libel by *The New York Times*, after Hearst's *American* and *Journal* both claimed, in overtly anti-Semitic editorials, that the *Times* and its owner Adolph Ochs were secretly controlled by August Belmont.

Another Hearst target, the Republican president, Teddy Roosevelt, coined the term "muckraker" for Hearst. After he decided that the Tammany Democrats were as much in thrall to the trusts as the Republicans, Hearst ran for mayor of New York on the ticket of a party he financed. Shearn joined the ticket as a candidate for district attorney, running against the incumbent, William Travers Jerome, a regular at a Bible class taught by John D. Rockefeller Jr.

Hearst and Shearn went down to a narrow defeat in an election stolen by Tammany. Unbowed, Hearst ran for governor the next year as a Democrat; that party had seen the errors of its ways and had suddenly become reform-friendly. Hearst and Shearn, his chief mouthpiece, traveled the state, trawling for votes, vilifying their opponents as "servile lickspittles," rats, and cockroaches, hoping wildly for a win that would propel him into the White House.

In his stump speeches, Shearn pointed at the people's enemies: the shipbuilding trust, the typewriter trust, Rockefeller, and Morgan—740 types, all. Hearst singled out financiers, calling them "Captain Kidds of industry" and "wary old rats of Wall Street" who were "more responsible for corruption in our public life than all the other evil influences in politics."

The counterattacks were as nasty. Forced to defend himself against the White House and a charge that his recklessness had caused the assassination of President William McKinley, Hearst was soundly defeated, but hardly silenced. That's when John D. Rockefeller Jr. came into his sights.

In December 1908, Hearst's *New York American* ran a front-page story accusing Junior of personally ordering the creation of a "peonage stockade," a plank-fenced box topped by barbed wire guarded by armed sentries. According to a labor leader, it was built to "keep hobo laborers" at the Standard Oil–controlled Corn Products Refining Company from running away from their jobs. In other words, they called Junior a slave master. And predictably, he wasn't thrilled.

Junior sued the newspaper and its bosses that very day for libel and gave a statement explaining why. "The press of this country has come to believe that it can ruin a man's reputation or forever soil his good name for the purpose of extending their circulation, with absolute impunity," he said. The time had come, he continued, for self-respecting citizens to "arise in the dignity of their wrath" and insist on "decent censorship of the press" via "the enactment of proper and adequate libel laws" to protect them against "such infamous onslaughts." He concluded by promising "a fight to the finish."

Though the paper published a front-page correction immediately, Junior pursued his case in court, and the newspaper's top officers were arrested. Both lawyers in the matter would, thirty years later, be Rockefeller's neighbors at 740 Park. The assistant district attorney fighting for Junior was Francis Garvan, Janet Bouvier's subtenant. The lawyer for the Hearst side was Clarence J. Shearn, who would take apartment 17B.

A month later, Junior, accompanied by Garvan, testified before a grand jury. That spring, despite agreeing that the *Journal* had printed "a gross and vicious libel," a judge upheld Shearn's argument: the officers were not responsible for what the newspaper printed. Rockefeller appealed, faced Shearn in court, and won. The publisher was fined $500. But Shearn would have the last laugh. Six months later, the United States Circuit Court of Appeals upheld a lower court's dissolution of Standard Oil as a monopoly that restrained interstate trade, a decision that would be upheld by the Supreme Court in 1911.'

Meanwhile, in 1908, Hearst's Independence Party nominated a kerosene and axle grease dealer to run for president. Shearn was the party's nominee for governor of New York, and once again ran against the rich and the railroads and the politicians who supported them. Though colorful (he called the leader of Tammany Hall a "vulgar fathead"), his run was an exercise in futility, and he was soundly defeated by the incumbent Republican. In 1909, when Hearst ran for mayor again, and in 1910, when he ran for lieutenant governor, Shearn tagged along as his attorney and shill. Hearst, defeated both times, ended his political career, but not his muckraking.

Shearn remained a controversial public figure, too, trying high-profile cases for Hearst and representing French aviators in a suit against the American heroes Orville and Wilbur Wright. He kept fighting Tammany, too. In 1911, Shearn ran for the state supreme court on an anti-Tammany fusion ticket with several Republicans. He lost, but in 1914 was appointed to the bench to fill a vacant seat, and the next year, when

Hearst and Tammany shared a distaste for Woodrow Wilson, Shearn was nominated by both parties to retain his judgeship. Some thought it a Tammany concession to Hearst. Yet Hearst then turned right-wing and isolationist. It suddenly "made sense for Shearn to distance himself," says Nasaw.

Shearn stayed on the bench until 1919, deciding, among other cases, one in which an old English law that subjugated wives to their husbands was overturned. Mankind, he ruled, had "emerged from the dark ages when women were the same as slaves." That ruling helped win him promotion to the appellate division, but after five years on the bench he returned to private practice.

Shearn finally declared his independence from Hearst when he was named special counsel for the Transit Commission and tangled with Hearst-owned officeholders. His former boss had turned right, but Shearn remained a committed progressive, investigating corruption in the subways, criminal waste and political corruption in the construction of sewers, overbilling by Edison Electric, and legal misconduct. He made some money, too, and moved from the unfashionable West Side to Fifth Avenue.

Eva Petty Shearn, the Southern belle he'd married at the turn of the century, died in 1929, and Shearn's law partner died in 1931. In 1932, Shearn married the widow of a pharmaceutical executive. "The marriage will come as a surprise to many in society and in legal circles," *The New York Times* noted succinctly. The newlyweds were off to Europe indefinitely. Shearn's sudden marriage caused a breach with his two children by his first wife. "My mother objected," says his grandson Tony Kerrigan.

An aunt explained: "He's a highly sexed man. What does she expect?"

On their return months later, Shearn rented the empty seventeenth-floor apartment at 740 and Spy Rock Farm, a fifty-one-acre estate in Mount Kisco, a hilltop used as a lookout post during the Revolutionary War. No longer a rabble-rouser, Shearn had reinvented himself, winning election to the vice presidency of the New York County Lawyers' Association and the presidency of the city's bar association.

Shearn's second wife fell ill early in 1938, just as Junior was moving into 740. She died in the apartment that Halloween. Shearn inherited the bulk of her estate, almost $100,000 ($1.333 million in 2004 dollars). Then, in 1939, fate threw him a curve: Dorothea Quigley Troyte-Bullock. Shearn was sixty-nine years old. Dorothea, a friend of his late wife's, was forty years younger.

"WHERE DO I START?" DOROTHEA'S CLOSEST LIVING RELATIVE, HER niece Margaret Graubard, e-mails from her home in the English countryside. "Briefly, my mother was born in Greenville, Texas. Her father was a very refined, gentlemanly drunk who drank himself to an early grave. Her grandfather was founder of the Greenville National Bank and a prosperous businessman who would have nothing to do with her while she was living a life of hell with the drunk. Once he was dead he took in the family of three girls and his daughter. But my grandmother had big ideas and Texas was too small for her. My aunt was a great beauty and started a lengthy romance with [Charles] Haskell, governor of Oklahoma and quite a character in his own right. They moved to New York when he went there. There was a move for him to be a presidential candidate on the oil ticket. Oil men felt they should run the country since they represented the wealth of America. So they had to get his young girlfriend well out of the way. Hearst was determined to destroy Haskell and would certainly have ammunition if he discovered dear Aunty. So where better to deposit her but the Ritz in Paris? And that is how it all began."

It actually began with a child of farmers, William A. Williams, a Texan who'd fought with the Confederacy, married a grocer's daughter, become a county clerk, and then organized two banks. Cotton farming had made Greenville prosperous and proud. "Welcome to Greenville, Blackest Land, Whitest People," read a sign in town.

Williams ran the Greenville National Bank until his death in 1908. He lived in a white frame house with a wide front porch and rooms with twelve-foot ceilings. His daughter Margaruite, known as Maggie, was a bookish, French-speaking loner with highfalutin tastes. She bought by mail order from New York stores. She was stubborn, too. When Williams forbade her to cut her hair, she did it anyway, and then claimed a thief had cut it off, looking for diamonds he insisted were hidden in there.

In 1895, at twenty-three, Maggie married Kentucky-born James Bruce Quigley, a tall, handsome redheaded Confederate veteran. He'd hit Greenville six months earlier behind a fine set of trotters. A traveling salesman for a Connecticut shoe maker, he opened a shoe store in Greenville with his younger brother, but that didn't carry much weight with Williams, who refused to attend their wedding and cut off his daughter. For the next nine years, she bore Quigley children while he was on the road, selling shoes by day, drinking by night, and declining, steadily, into debt and incoherence.

Dorothea, the eldest, was born in 1895, Clothilde in 1898. Willabeth, who followed in 1902, would die in her teens. Even as the town's fortunes rose following the discovery of nearby oil fields, the Quigleys remained mired in poverty, living in rooming houses. Williams wouldn't give his daughter an ounce of help so long as she stayed with her husband. Finally, Margaruite had enough and moved back to her father's house. In thanks, Williams got Andrew Carnegie to donate $15,000 to build a library in Greenville and put his daughter in charge. Shortly after it opened, Quigley died in San Antonio and was buried in a pauper's grave.

Living in her grandparents' house, Dorothea grew beautiful but spoiled, a show-off and bully with a fervent desire to seem sophisticated, a hot temper, and a tendency to boss the black servants. Clothilde preferred playing with them. After Quigley's death, their mother began taking long trips to get away from small-town gossip, then moved to Los Angeles. "She always felt certain something wonderful would happen—a sentiment she never abandoned and passed on to her daughters," writes Graubard, in an unpublished memoir in progress about this extraordinary family.

Los Angeles wasn't wonderful, so in 1907, when Dorothea was twelve, Margaruite moved to Oklahoma, which was about to attain statehood, at the behest of a brother who was the secretary of the local Democratic Party. Again taking a job as a librarian, she remained there eleven years—and put her daughter Dorothea at the center of a scandal stirred up by William Randolph Hearst and his henchman, Dorothea's future husband, Clarence J. Shearn.

· · ·

THE FORMER OKLAHOMA AND INDIAN TERRITORIES WERE COMBINED AND admitted to the Union as the forty-sixth state in 1907, and Charles N. Haskell, a wealthy railroad promoter who'd spearheaded the drive for statehood, was elected Oklahoma's first governor. He beat a crony of President Teddy Roosevelt, who became a powerful enemy. Haskell was named treasurer of the Democratic National Committee in 1908, when William Jennings Bryan ran for president. A powerful man, Haskell harbored passions that would destroy him—and add a bit of intrigue to life at 740 Park.

Haskell took a subtle approach to the oil and gas companies that hoped to make fortunes in his state. When a Kansas-based firm tried to build a pipeline out of Oklahoma shortly before it gained statehood, Haskell had himself sworn into office early and ordered the National Guard to stop construction. Then he authorized an Oklahoma-based subsidiary of Standard Oil to build a pipeline to the gulf, which led to a political power struggle with the state's trust-busting attorney general.

That was all William Randolph Hearst needed. Trying to drum up publicity for Thomas Hisgen, his Independence Party's axle-grease-dealer-for-president, he went after Haskell, claiming to have purloined letters proving that Standard Oil had bribed him. When Haskell responded that it was "another Haskell"—not he—who was in bed with Standard Oil, the story metastasized into a full-blown scandal, with Hearst, his newspapers, and Republicans and their papers, too, pounding Haskell daily. Even Teddy Roosevelt got a few shots in.

At the state convention for Hearst's Independence Party, Shearn was nominated as candidate for governor, and Hearst charged that the Democrats had rewarded Haskell for being "a Standard tool, a promoter of crooked railroads . . . an organizer of trusts." In his acceptance speech, Shearn piled on, too. "There is today but one issue before the people," he said. "That issue is treason against our country—treason committed by millionaire outlaws who purchase public men and corrupt political parties to serve their law-defying corporations."

Haskell was forced to resign his party treasurer's post. But he also served Hearst with a $600,000 slander and libel suit and had a legal associate of Shearn's arrested, charging he paid people to lie.

Haskell left office in 1911 and, after failing in a bid for the Senate, went back into the railroad and oil businesses with Harry Sinclair, a former traveling salesman who'd made millions exploiting Oklahoma's oil deposits. To give an idea of the company Haskell was keeping: Sinclair later set off the Teapot Dome scandal.

Haskell was married twice, and during his reign as governor the second Mrs. Haskell had been renowned for sitting outside her husband's office, knitting and listening, and later offering up opinions her husband tended to follow. A handsome man of forty-seven when he took office, Haskell stood five feet ten inches tall, with friendly brown eyes and thick brown hair dappled with gray. "He was a terrific speaker, a terrific personality, a huge, great, bluff man," says Graubard.

IN HER POOR FRONTIER TOWN, REDHEADED DOROTHEA QUIGLEY, POPULAR and athletic, with her button nose and bright blue eyes, blossomed into a performer—always the center of attention and "much given to hysterics and tantrums when thwarted," writes Graubard.

In 1911, Dorothea, aged sixteen, won a United Daughters of the Confederacy scholarship and went away to college. She graduated in 1916 after becoming her sorority's president and starring in the senior class play. Then she embarked on the Oklahoma version of a debutante year, going to lunches and dinners and dances like the Daughters' annual Grand March and ball, where she was guest of honor, in clothes sewn by her mother. She dated, but, thanks to Margaruite, her sights were set above the field before her.

In 1917, Dorothea went to work as a high-school teacher. By then, she was smoking and drinking and dating soldiers. When her baby sister died in 1918, life in Oklahoma lost its luster, and the family moved to New York City, where Margaruite, a lover of romantic poetry, could indulge herself in the arts and where the family's star, Dorothea, might marry the right sort of man.

It was 1920. Charles Haskell had opened an office in New York three years earlier and begun amassing a great fortune, buying and developing oil fields, when he got a letter from Margaruite Quigley, enclosing a letter of introduction from her brother, who'd worked for Haskell. She hoped he'd help her find a job. He came to their tiny apartment on West

Fifty-ninth Street for tea. Dorothea donned a pink chiffon dance dress and joined him when Haskell poured some whiskey from a flask into his teacup.

Haskell's wife and children were back in Oklahoma—and soon the inevitable occurred. When Dorothea complained about the cigar taste in his mouth, her sister and mother realized it was an affair. They moved to a better apartment, where a photo of Haskell held pride of place on the piano. Dorothea called him her Fairy Prince; he granted her every wish—except Margaruite's wish to become part of society. Society wasn't interested in vulgar Westerners like Haskell—only in their money.

"But Dorothea relished this new order and could not have cared less that she was not meeting the elite," her niece writes. The Roaring Twenties "was a dance-mad world and Dorothea loved to dance . . . New York was as exuberant as the Champagne that poured all too freely during Prohibition, and Dorothea was intoxicated." Even more so because, every time he did a deal, Haskell would give her and her mother a taste. In 1922, Dorothea estimated their safe-deposit box contained $15 million in stocks. "He poured millions into her pocket," says Graubard. "He actually was a very shady character."

Luckily for Haskell, even though he was cheating on his wife with a woman a third his age, he only made the papers when he bought something: a railroad in 1922, an estate in Glen Cove on Long Island's North Shore in 1923. Pembroke had belonged to a Captain De Lamar, the Nickel Trust King, who'd left it to his daughter, who'd sold it to Haskell for $2 million.

Then Haskell's fortunes took a bad turn. Competitors had it in for him. Graubard thinks he was considering a run for president and Hearst was lying in wait. In the months after he bought Pembroke, Haskell was sued, hauled before a grand jury, and forced out of his oil company, which went broke. He was charged with fraud, mismanagement, and manipulation of the price of its stock, and he lost Pembroke in a foreclosure. In court, it emerged that, just as his troubles became known, Haskell had sent the oil company's books to Paris in fourteen large cases.

Oddly enough, that's where Dorothea was.

. . .

THE QUIGLEY WOMEN HAD SAILED FOR EUROPE IN THE FALL OF 1922. Their first stop was Claridge's in London, but England depressed Dorothea, so within days they were off to the Ritz in Paris, all expenses paid by Charles N. Haskell. So besotted was he that they had dozens of telegrams—all from him—awaiting them on arrival. "Soon the girls began to appear dressed in the latest creations of Worth and Poiret," writes Clothilde's daughter. Parisian society noticed. "If you were a pretty woman and you sat in the entrance hall, well, people got to know you," Clothilde said.

Charles Mendl, the British embassy's press attaché, who frequented the Ritz, made a point of chatting them up and became their sponsor. He introduced them to an embassy colleague, Victor Frederick William Cavendish-Bentinck, known as Bill, who fell for Clothilde's dark, slim looks and proposed to her a mere two weeks later.

The Cavendish-Bentinck family had been aristocrats for five centuries, moving from Holland to England when one of their number was a page for William of Orange, who married King James II's daughter Mary, overthrew his father-in-law, and was crowned king of England. In thanks, William made his page the Earl of Portland. Bill Cavendish-Bentinck would eventually inherit that title. In 2004, the Cavendish-Bentinck family fortune was estimated to be a bit more than $700 million. Bill's mother decided Clothilde was an adventuress.

Dorothea was having an affair in Paris, too, with Paul Morand, a diplomat and novelist friend of Mendl's. She managed to keep her lovers apart the one time Haskell came to see her. Those boxes of corporate records followed, but Dorothea was having too good a time to worry about them, dining with aristocrats and artists like Jean Cocteau, taking her Pomeranian, Chick, for walks on the rue St.-Honoré, constantly fussed over by maids paid for by Haskell, driving around in a car he'd provided after he'd asked if she needed anything. Soon she was tooling around in a Hispano-Suiza with a uniformed chauffeur, making "something of an impact in certain circles in Paris," wrote Cavendish-Bentinck's biographer, Patrick Howarth.

After Dorothea took a long tour of Italy, Haskell cabled, begging her to come home, and, though she'd fallen in love with Morand, back she sailed. During her visit, Haskell learned of Morand. "She killed the goose that laid the golden egg," says her niece.

Haskell moved on. In 1927, he moved to Mexico, where he built a toll road, and later went to Texas, where he dealt in oil. He returned to New York to fight off a shareholder suit seeking money he'd diverted into his own accounts, and finally went back to Oklahoma, where he died in 1933—amazingly enough, with his wife by his side.

Clothilde Quigley married Cavendish-Bentinck on Valentine's Day in 1924—but only after his father sicced detectives on the Quigleys and learned about Haskell. Margaruite, in turn, had her lawyer draw up a marital contract, and kept negotiating until moments before the ceremony. Behind many an adventuress stands a mother of invention. But if Margaruite thought her prayers had been answered, she was wrong. Clothilde "probably was a fortune hunter," says Howarth, "but he didn't have a fortune. The name was very distinguished. Bill wasn't."

WHEN BILL CAVENDISH-BENTINCK WAS TRANSFERRED TO THE HAGUE, Margaruite and Dorothea returned to New York, where they took an apartment on Park Avenue. Though she was twenty-nine, Dorothea still needed a husband, so she carved a decade off her age and joined the debutante circuit, rubbing shoulders with eligible men, enjoying the revels of the flapper era, and getting her name and photograph in the social columns. Clothilde, meanwhile, had joined British society; when her first child, a son, was born, the Duchess of York was made his godmother.

Once, when Dorothea was visiting London, Clothilde introduced her to George Victor Troyte-Bullock, a minor aristocrat and aide to a British general. His family owned an estate in Wiltshire, and in the spring of 1927 they got married. Engagement and wedding portraits of Dorothea were cabled to *The New York Times*. "The marriage lasted about three months, I believe," says Margaret Graubard. "They just didn't get along. At the end, she'd had enough and moved out."

After that, Dorothea "traveled from rich boyfriend to richer," says Graubard. "There is a letter from my grandma in which she says you cannot drop him just after he has given you that diamond necklace you wanted. Then there was another admirer who rode his white stallion into the lobby of some hotel."

Her sporadic visits to Clothilde inevitably caused trouble. Clothilde didn't get along with other diplomatic wives, and so in 1932 Cavendish-Bentinck was punished with a posting to the embassy in Athens, where their marriage began to slide into acrimony. When Dorothea visited from Paris, she paraded through the halls of the embassy in nothing but high heels as guests were arriving for a party. "An old bachelor and his sister were sitting there," says Graubard, and when Clothilde apologized, the sister said, "Don't worry. He thought it was rejuvenating."

Dorothea commenced an affair with a Greek, says Graubard, "and somehow Mumsie got involved and the Greek tabloids had Mumsie yachting alone with the gentleman. Somehow, the foreign office in London got wind of the scandal. Absolutely delightful!" Though not for Cavendish-Bentinck, who was punished and transferred again—this time, alone, to Santiago, Chile. With their marriage "clearly doomed," in his words, Clothilde stayed behind in London. Her husband started calling her "The Clot."

A regular in the newspapers in the 1920s, Dorothea dropped from view after her divorce from Troyte-Bullock. "She meandered around like a lost lamb and finally settled in New York," says Graubard, whose parents separated after Cavendish-Bentinck fell in love with a younger woman. Press reports later said they'd both been cheating for years, and court records show that in Athens they'd wife-swapped with a Spanish diplomatic couple. Finally, Clothilde simply left, taking their children with her to New York in 1939. But when she realized process servers were hunting for her with divorce papers, she dropped the kids with Aunt Dossie—Dorothea—and went into hiding. Dossie, still single, lived with her mother in a bare apartment. "There seemed to be a shortage of furniture and it then appeared that there was also a shortage of food," Graubard writes.

When Clothilde made it clear she wouldn't give him a divorce, Cavendish-Bentinck agreed to pay for boarding school for the kids, and she began looking for a job. But then, in a development as stupefying as it was sudden, Dorothea eloped to Baltimore and married Clarence J. Shearn, the man who'd tried to ruin her beau Haskell. They'd just met.

Shearn looked like a catch: he was a powerful and newly wealthy widower, lived above a Rockefeller, and went around in a chauffeured Rolls-Royce. In 1938, he'd been named trustee for the profligate William

Randolph Hearst and given the task of reorganizing all of his holdings. It was his downfall. Hearst owed millions, no one would refinance his debt, and though he approved Shearn because he thought he could trust and control him, the former bankruptcy receiver was defying him, selling his holdings. John D. Rockefeller Jr. bought $100,000 worth of Hearst's silver collection. Shearn also worked with Milbank, Tweed, the lawyers for the Chase, one of Hearst's largest creditors; during the years of untangling and reorganizing, the law firm sold off half his art collection.

"Shearn didn't do a very good job," says the publisher's biographer David Nasaw, who wonders if Hearst's trustee wasn't losing his grip. Hearst considered Shearn a schemer, grew to detest him, and finally raised the money to pay off his own debts and retake control in 1943. "Shearn acted without loyalty to the man to whom he owed everything," says Nasaw. His career never recovered. His earnings dropped rapidly to zero.

At first, Dorothea lived high and rubbed her younger sister's face in it. "My mother and my aunt fought the whole time," says Graubard. "Like cats, absolutely black and blue, about everything." So Shearn and Margaruite slipped Clothilde money, and she decided to get out of town. Clothilde asked her mother to broker a loan so she could buy a Los Angeles house. Instead, Dorothea bought the house and let her sister live there. Collecting real estate had become Dorothea's passion. Torturing Clothilde was merely a hobby.

It was clear, even to a child, that Dorothea had some issues. When she came to California with Shearn and Mrs. Quigley, she stole a blanket from her sleeper car. In restaurants, she would linger behind and snatch tips off the table. And she once tried to bean her sister with a milk bottle. "I proudly believed I saved my mother's life," Graubard says.

Back in New York, Dorothea decided it was her niece that needed saving. "We were happily living in California when my aunt told my mother that I was growing up like a weed with no manners and she would put me in a private school to meet the right sort of girls," Graubard says. "I came east, she never put me in a school, and I was a prisoner at 740"— never allowed to leave the building for fear she might be kidnapped. Despite the staff's love of children, they were not allowed to take her downstairs.

Graubard's new home was a supermodern apartment with the odd antique slipped in by Aunt Dossie. "The rooms were huge and rather barren," she writes, and the balconies "were grimy and much too windy for any use. The most fascinating thing in the apartment was Auntie's huge round bed with an enormous oval mirror as the bed head. Auntie lay there most of the day twisting her hair with her fingers and talking on the telephone, wrapped in a vast faux leopard-skin bedcover." Margaruite shared the round bed with Dorothea while Shearn was exiled to the smaller room next door, dominated by a model of a yacht he'd once owned.

Shearn's staff of five shrank over the years as Dorothea "managed to get rid of all, one at a time," writes Graubard—even Finch, his faithful British chauffeur with a waxed mustache who'd driven General Pershing. Dorothea accused Finch of sending her threatening letters and replaced them all with Amy, "a black girl of uncertain habits," says Graubard, who would disappear for days on end. Shearn's kitchen produced mostly starch and vitamin pills, Dorothea's version of health food.

"I was a girl of eleven and I wasn't allowed to [call my mother] and my mother was calling me all the time and they never put me through," says Graubard. Finally, she snuck down the service stairs and telegrammed her mother, who arrived to save her. "This may have been the time that dear Dossie dug her nails so deeply into my mother's face that the hall porters took her into their own sitting room so that she might wipe off the blood before she could go out on the street." Clothilde tried once more to reconcile with her sister, accepting an invitation to the Shearns' country house for Christmas, 1940. But when they arrived, the place was empty, save for the deserted wife of another employee, living in a stable with her infant son. Christmas dinner was Spam from a can. Clothilde stopped speaking to her sister.[2]

IN 1936, JUST AFTER HE RENTED HIS APARTMENT, JOHN D. ROCKEFELLER Jr. started making discreet inquiries to Douglas Gibbons, the managing agent, about renting Shearn's place as well. Thus began a long, twisty saga marked by cloudy motives, feints, and dodges as Shearn apparently sought to profit from Junior's desire for his apartment and Junior did his

best to downplay his interest while working assiduously to rid the building of his onetime antagonist. Whether Junior was seeking revenge or
simply to rid himself of a painful reminder, it would be a dish served
stone-cold.

In January 1937, Gibbons sent him a floor plan for 17B along with a
fervent note of apology; he'd told Junior that Shearn was below, not
above. This appeared to be a point of concern. "I can well imagine that
if the people above him were people that he didn't like the sound of, he
therefore would have wanted the apartment," says Junior's son David.
"He didn't really need it for his own use; he probably wanted to get rid
of neighbors he didn't think of so well. I think it's as simple as that."

But he didn't want to appear eager. So, even though Junior wrote back
immediately, asking how much Shearn's apartment rented for, he said
there was no rush because "there is not one chance in a thousand that I
would be interested in taking this additional apartment." But clearly
there was a chance, for Gibbons kept him updated regularly. And in June
1937, when Junior contracted with Otis to install a small elevator with a
cabin of brass and straight-grained American walnut to run between
floors within his apartment, he insisted that it be built so that it could, if
necessary, rise to the seventeenth floor.

Rockefeller called Shearn on New Year's Day, 1938, and followed up
with a letter ten days later, apologizing for the construction racket his
renovations were causing (the summer-only work rules having obviously
been waived). "I cannot tell you how distressed Mrs. Rockefeller and I
are to make so unfavorable an impression upon our new neighbors," he
wrote, adding "the hope that Mrs. Rockefeller and I may before long
have the pleasure of receiving you in the finished apartment and of voic-
ing our regrets in person."

Shearn wrote back two days later, attempting humor but revealing
annoyance. "I hope that you do not think us captious or unreasonable,"
he said. "You can hardly imagine what the daily hammering was for over
six months. I realized that it was unavoidable over a considerable period,
but as winter drew on we became restive in spite of the fact that it is good
for one to get up early in the morning. My repugnance to the emblem of
the hammer and sickle has become greatly intensified." This from the
champion of the peons.

Junior and Gibbons returned to the subject of Shearn often. Gibbons thought that Shearn might abandon his apartment for his country house; he had the right to cancel his lease on October 1, 1938, and again in 1939. In November 1938, Junior wrote to Captain Byron Long, who'd taken over daily management for Gibbons, and noted the death of Shearn's second wife. Junior said that Alfred Caspary, a wealthy acquaintance who had no family, needed a winter apartment where he could display his porcelain collection. Long wrote back that nothing was definite with Shearn. "As you realize, the situation is a little delicate." A few days later, Shearn announced that he was staying. "He planned to build a house in Bedford, but he never did," says his grandson Kerrigan. "He had a garage with an apartment over it where he lived."

Shearn became an issue again in 1940 when his shower started leaking into Junior's study, ruining the paneling on the walls. It would take three years for Captain Long to find the leak's source, so it wasn't repaired until 1943.

Then, in the summer of 1942, Shearn called Junior's assistant. His lease was coming due again, he said, and the last time he'd renewed, in 1939, his rent had been raised a couple thousand dollars, supposedly because Junior wanted the apartment. Shearn hoped to avoid a repeat, so he wanted to know if Junior was still interested. "Because of the war and the uncertainties of the time," Junior replied, he wasn't. Shearn negotiated his rent down to $6,500 a year.

Junior was worried about *his* lease, too, and all through 1944 pressed to change it. He'd been paying that extra $15,000 a year to the Brewsters and wanted to take over the lease. But Edward Brewster, the son who controlled it, was with the Navy in the South Pacific.

Early in May 1944, Douglas Gibbons was summoned by Junior's lawyers and presented with a gentle ultimatum. Junior's rent was way too high and he wanted it lowered. Gibbons explained that the war had changed everything; the building was no longer making profits, so the base rent of $25,000 was not negotiable. But he offered to speak to Eleanor Brewster and see if she would reduce the additional $15,000 a year she was charging Junior. When Gibbons came back with the news that the Brewsters were "not disposed to suggest any modification," Vanderbilt Webb upped the ante, hinting that Junior might move out and throw the dilemma of renewing the underlying lease (set to expire in September 1945) back in the lap of the Brewsters. Webb also brought up Junior's "substantial investment in the apartment" and his desire to see a return on it.

The ploy worked, and in July the Brewsters offered a $7,500-per-year rent reduction effective in 1945. Junior gently asked for $10,000 but said he'd accept the $7,500 reduction if it was made effective immediately. Two months later, there was still no reply, and Junior nudged Gibbons, who came back with a response that Webb found "entirely unsatisfactory"—the same one the Brewsters had made in July.

Gibbons asked to meet with Junior to discuss "this whole situation," Webb wrote, "including the prospects of the building at 740 Park Avenue and the possibilities as to other apartments elsewhere in the city." Though he was clearly in no mood to move, neither would Junior yield, so he replied that yes, he'd like to stop by Gibbons's office and look over plans of available apartments elsewhere. That did the trick.

Gibbons proposed an alternative: Rockefeller would continue to pay $40,000 a year through 1945, when he would sign a new four-year lease as the primary tenant for only $25,000 a year. He would also have to pay the Brewsters $5,000 a year, making his total outlay the $30,000 originally offered. If, as still seemed possible, MetLife foreclosed the mortgage, Rockefeller would no longer pay the Brewsters. In order to keep him as a tenant, the building (i.e., James T. Lee) would pay an additional $2,000 a year to the Brewsters. But Junior balked at one condition, that he promise to pay to restore the original mantels, remove the security features he'd added to the windows and terraces, and restore the stone to its original condition if he left. He proposed instead that he pay the Brewsters $6,000 a year, but be relieved of any obligation to restore the apartment. The Brewsters agreed, papers were drawn up and forwarded to James T. Lee, but again nothing happened.

Finally, early in March 1945, as he was about to leave for Williamsburg and Maine, Junior issued an ultimatum. "If the 740 Park Avenue Corporation is no longer desirous of having me continue on as a tenant," he wrote to Gibbons, "I shall appreciate your so advising me without further delay." Otherwise, he wanted a signed lease within a week.

Suddenly James T. Lee (who had left the Chase in 1943 to become president of the Central Savings Bank and was no longer Junior's employee) leaped into the fray. In a letter to Gibbons that was passed on to Junior, Lee said the corporation was "extremely desirous of retaining him as a tenant for so long as he is willing to live in the building." So much so, in fact, that he would reluctantly agree to let Junior off the hook over his alterations, even though he found that demand "a little strong in favor of the tenant." Lee also revealed, if obliquely, just how tenuous 740's finances had again become when he added that "the situation with the mortgage" meant the building was again operating at a loss. Making matters worse, all but two of the directors had resigned, and the leasing committee had vanished, but Lee assured Gibbons that he would approve the Brewster deal "and I am sure that that is all that is necessary." It took a bit longer than the week Junior allowed, but Junior did finally get his lease in exchange for a payment to the Brewsters of $31,500. Junior's rent dropped from $3,333.34 to $2,083.34 a month.

In April 1945, with his lease up for renewal again, Shearn again raised Junior's hopes that he might be willing to move out. The former jurist and his new wife had been busily acquiring real estate in the beaten-down wartime market. He'd increased his holdings in Westchester, buying more acreage in Katonah from the estate of the stockbroker William Fahnestock in 1941. In May 1944, Dorothea bought a town house at 131 East Seventy-first Street, a block away from 740. Elsie de Wolfe, the society decorator who'd married Dorothea's old friend Charles Mendl in 1926, had lived there from 1915 until 1921. The *Times* said that the Shearns planned to live there. But in November 1944, Shearn bought another nearby house, 13 East Sixty-ninth Street, which had been rented for years by Harry K. Thaw's nephew Lawrence Copley Thaw. Dorothea negotiated the purchase for $50,000.

Shearn moved his office into that house and contacted both Gibbons and Junior, again offering to give up his lease if he got a "speedy decision" and, presumably, a Rockefeller-sized payoff for the apartment. But Junior declined, and once again Shearn remained, a constant, nagging irritant to his dyspeptic downstairs neighbor.

ABBY AND JUNIOR CELEBRATED THEIR FORTY-FIFTH WEDDING ANNIVERsary in 1946. They now had seventeen grandchildren. But their joy in watching them grow up was tempered by her failing health. In early 1947, it was concern for her, not Junior, that led them to Arizona. Back in New York that April, there was a weekend-long family reunion in Pocantico. Junior was in the process of transferring ownership of Rockefeller Center to his sons (he'd also give them Pocantico), and Abby was overheard to say that she'd never been happier in her whole life. A day later, back at 740, she woke up with an upset stomach, and a doctor was summoned. As she was telling him her symptoms, she fell back and died of a heart attack.

Junior was devastated—and spent the next summer working in her garden in Seal Harbor. But he was also lonely. So three years later, he married Martha Baird Allen, a concert pianist and the widow of one of his old friends from Brown. She was almost twenty years younger than he. Shortly afterward, he created a new series of trusts and transferred more than $50 million to his sons and his new wife. At the same time, he gave more millions to the Museum of Modern Art in honor of Abby.

Junior renewed his lease at 740 for another two years early in 1947. But back in New York in the fall of 1948, well aware that the building's mortgage would shortly come due, he huddled with Gibbons and cooked up a plan to make it a cooperative again. By late November, Gibbons had the paperwork ready to create the new Park–Seventy-first Street Corporation. Tenants who wished to remain would have to pay $13 per share. So Rockefeller, who owned the largest apartment, would be charged $32,500, and Clinton Black, a former Yale football All-American who worked as an insurance broker and had just rented one of the smallest, 2/3C, would have to pony up $9,360. On average, Gibbons felt, the apartments would go for a third of their current market value. The remaining owners, who'd bought when the building was new, would get just over $200,000; $320,000 more would go toward reducing the mortgage; and MetLife agreed to knock another $200,000 off the loan. After minor adjustments, the proposal went to all the tenants in the spring of 1949.

Five immediately told Gibbons they would leave the building when their leases ran out that fall. Gibbons wrote all to say he'd found buyers for two of those apartments and was optimistic he could sell the others. Galvanized, the tenants all began maneuvering, hiring lawyers, chattering with each other. The ailing Belle Ledyard put a nephew in charge, who said she'd go along if her friends did. The French government, then looking for a home for its ambassador, said it would buy Ledyard Blair's apartment. Watson Webb told Junior he'd "rather rent than buy" but would also rather "remain . . . than move." Still, the number of tenants who signed the subscription agreement was insufficient: in June, Gibbons warned them all that if six or more refused to go along, the co-op plan would have to be abandoned.

By August, it had become obvious that the plan was failing. Too many tenants were balking. After gaining Gibbons's assurances that regardless of what happened, he wouldn't be evicted, Junior wrote the holdouts letters as polite and reticent as their author. He told them that he, too, would have preferred not to buy, but had gone along because the deal seemed as solid as the building they all shared. "What the position of all of us who are present tenants of the building will be if the scheme fails to go through, I do not know and dislike to conjecture," he said, concluding with an apology for the intrusion.

Junior's letter convinced no one. Rejection after rejection came in response, so Rockefeller wrote Gibbons again, asking his aid in finding "some other adequate apartment" he could move into. In reply, Gibbons reminded him his lease still had a year to run and added that James T. Lee wanted to meet with Junior "and talk with you about the whole matter." Junior responded with a list of requirements for a new apartment. Three days later, Lee blinked and offered all the tenants new three-year leases running through the fall of 1952.

ON DECEMBER 28, 1951, LANDON KETCHUM THORNE'S OLD HOLDING company American Superpower was back in the headlines. Superpower was buying Webb & Knapp, a real estate company founded in 1922 by Watson and Van Webb's brother Seward, James T. Lee's old partner Eliot Cross, and others. Webb & Knapp had developed the New York Central Railroad's properties on Park Avenue and "the society colony in Sutton Place" on Manhattan's East Side. In 1936, Webb retired, and two years later William Zeckendorf, an ambitious young real estate man, became a partner, helping manage and broker buildings around New York.

Zeckendorf, paunchy and balding with a round, open face, was a natural entrepreneur and quickly took over. "I became aware of a Depression market of sellers," he would write years later in his autobiography, "who would sell property at tremendous discounts if they could get cash. At the same time, partly because Depression-caused retrenchments had left various institutions with idle cash, one could get some quite extraordinary low-cost, long-term loans and mortgages from banks and insurance companies—if these lenders saw a 'safe' investment. Moreover, if you could provide them with a 'market rationale,' the value these mortgagers put on a property could be quite high . . . This made me keenly aware that it paid to look at the real-estate business not as an end in itself but as a device for bridging gaps between the needs of disparate groups. The greater the number of separate groups (or their needs) that one could interconnect (or satisfy), the greater the profit to the innovator-entrepreneur."

THE DEALS THAT FOLLOWED WERE A TEXTBOOK CASE OF ZECKENDORF'S formula at work. He was the grandson of a German-Jewish merchant who came to the American Southwest after the Civil War and opened a store. Zeckendorf's father co-owned a shoe company. William grew up in a Long Island suburb, then moved to the West Side of Manhattan during World War I. Bored by school, he dropped out and went to work as a broker of office space. During the Depression, as building values plummeted, Zeckendorf made part of his living renegotiating mortgages for property owners. Bankers often were willing to change terms for a smart operator who could make money. "I don't care what you paid for it," James T. Lee would later say to Zeckendorf, explaining his philosophy of loans. "What matters is the value of the building now."

After joining Webb & Knapp, Zeckendorf turned it into a powerhouse, buying buildings and land on which he could build cheap, refinancing mortgages, selling properties at a profit, and moving on. At the end of 1942, the company controlled assets worth about $2 million when it was hired to manage the real estate holdings of John Jacob Astor's great-grandson Vincent while he went to war. After the war, Zeckendorf lost the Astor holdings, but he also lost his partners, who cashed out and retired, leaving him in control of Webb & Knapp. The pace of business picked up, as did the quality and wealth of those Zeckendorf dealt with—aristocrats and investment bankers.

In 1946, the energetic dynamo, whose imperial ambitions were surpassed only by those of the urban planner Robert Moses (whom he considered a competitor as well as a megalomaniac), acquired a swath of land on the East River that had been occupied by slaughterhouses for decades. He paid $6.5 million, bought more land around it, and decided to build a seven-block-long, two-block-wide platform, atop which he would erect a city within New York City—the greatest development since Rockefeller Center. He even hired Wallace Harrison, the Rockefellers' chief architect, to design it. But the immense project was quixotic, and Zeckendorf's hold on the property was tenuous. Fortunately, at that very moment, the new United Nations was looking for a home, and Zeckendorf saw an opportunity and offered the UN the slaughterhouse parcel. But the UN had no way to pay for it.

John D. Rockefeller Jr. had dinner alone with his next-door neighbor, Belle Ledyard, once every few weeks "because she was absolutely fascinating," says Jarden Guenther, the husband of one of her granddaughters. Belle's brother Dave Hennen Morris had been Franklin Roosevelt's ambassador to Belgium before the war. When a Belgian banker, Noël Monod, was named treasurer of the UN in 1946, he needed a place to stay in New York, and Belle took him in. Monod joined his hostess and Junior at one of their dinners. After Belle went to bed, Monod told Rockefeller that unless the UN could raise the money for the land within forty-eight hours, the international body would take the second-best offer and move from its temporary quarters on Long Island to San Francisco.

"Let me see what I can do," Junior told him. The next day Nelson Rockefeller, a member of the city's UN-site committee, sent the family's architect, Wallace Harrison, to Zeckendorf, and a few nights later, sitting in a nightclub, Zeckendorf drew a boundary on a map and signed a thirty-day option giving the United Nations the right to buy the land within the line for $8.5 million.

The next morning Nelson told Zeckendorf that his father was going to donate the purchase price. Ten days after Zeckendorf's brainstorm, the General Assembly approved the purchase. It was the sort of transaction Zeckendorf was proudest of. It not only gave the UN a home; it also increased the value of Zeckendorf's holdings on surrounding streets. He put not only the city in his debt but the Rockefellers, too, for along with the publicity bonanza for the family, they'd eliminated a potential competitive threat and brought new business to the city, which would benefit Rockefeller Center. And atop all that, Zeckendorf made a fast $2 million profit.

The UN deal was the first of many encounters Zeckendorf was to have with the Rockefellers. He became a consultant to Nelson, who handled many of the family's business affairs, and they saw each other often in coming years. Zeckendorf also got involved in solving a little problem of Junior's.

In 1948, Zeckendorf bought out his remaining Webb & Knapp partners. The company's assets were worth $25 million. Its net worth was $5.6 million. Still, Zeckendorf had to sell buildings to pay for it; he even sold Webb & Knapp's headquarters to Metropolitan Life. "I was able to arrange a great series of sales, leasebacks and loans" from Frederick Ecker and James T. Lee, among others, Zeckendorf wrote. The three of them were tight as ticks. Lee, while still at the Chase during the Depression, had been one of Zeckendorf's mentors. And Zeckendorf and his wife traveled with the Eckers. "But I was still dissatisfied. I wanted to do more, and decided to acquire superpower—American Superpower," Zeckendorf wrote. "That takeover provided the basis for some grand adventures."

Zeckendorf heard about Landon Thorne's company in 1951 from the president of Pepsi-Cola, one of his investors. Zeckendorf learned that Superpower had "limped along" before the war "gave it a boost by which it was able to clear up some of its back debt." But it still owed $114.50 on each of its outstanding sixty-three thousand preferred shares, so Thorne and his remaining preferred shareholders had decided to liquidate the company and wash their hands of it.

The transaction was structured as a reverse merger. Superpower changed its name in Delaware to Webb & Knapp and absorbed Zeckendorf's New York company. Zeckendorf exchanged his shares of the latter, worth $42 million, for a million shares of junior preferred stock and millions of shares of common stock in the Delaware company. In return, Superpower's senior preferred shareholders—that is, Thorne and the others—were given first claim to $13.2 million in assets of the new, merged Webb & Knapp, and its remaining common shares, which had been worthless, were suddenly worth sixty cents apiece. Zeckendorf figured the deal cost him $10 million, but in return he had a publicly traded company, its valuable tax credits, and access to an additional $9 million in capital once its last utility holdings were sold off. "One more deal where all involved ended up better off than when they started," Zeckendorf crowed. But he wasn't through. He was about to buy another of Landon Thorne's devalued assets.

18

Part Two of Zeckendorf's eponymous autobiography opens in about 1950, when the developer realized he'd become an inhabitant of "the greatest peaks" of American society, a lofty zone where social and business eminences were all "readily accessible, each one to the other," he wrote. "The importance to me of being on the heights was that in an hour I could achieve what previously would have taken a year or more." Despite "some quite precipitous slopes and occasional ice slides on the various routes to and about the heights," he continued, "I found it possible to join their ranks without discommoding or unsettling them, for one way to succeed is by aiding and supporting the position of others through new or ingenious ideas."

The last, without question, he provided to all with a stake in 740 Park. What's not entirely clear is how he came to be involved at all. Zeckendorf himself would later hint that the odd sequence of events that followed was actually set off by Thelma Chrysler Foy, the daughter of the automaker Walter Chrysler. Foy, a lacquered socialite with black hair pulled back to show her widow's peak, wanted an apartment at 740, wanted it bad. She'd signed an agreement with Clarence Shearn to take over his in exchange for what amounted to key money—a cash payment for him to leave. No. 17B was smaller than most 740 apartments, because it had lost rooms to the Webbs' penthouse, but Foy still loved its grace, scale, and views. Getting it proved complicated, though. Her desire for Shearn's apartment lit the fuse that led to a series of larger real estate deals, culminating in Zeckendorf's headline-grabbing simultaneous purchase of several landmark buildings near Grand Central Station, one of them the giddiest star of the New York skyline, Walter Chrysler's silver-topped, gargoyle-studded Art Deco masterpiece, the Chrysler Building.

Thelma Irene Chrysler was born in 1902, the first child of the foreman of a railroad repair shop in Salt Lake City. Another daughter and two sons, Walter junior and Jack, followed. After buying his first automobile and taking it apart to see how it worked, Chrysler moved to Michigan and got work running a Buick plant. He introduced the first Chrysler car in 1924. That year he sold $50 million worth, and his daughter married Byron C. Foy, a car salesman who'd become president of the Reo Motor Car Company, maker of the iconic Reo Speed Wagon truck. Foy soon moved to Chrysler, where he was made a vice president and board member, and then president of the DeSoto division. After serving as an officer in the Army Air Force in World War II (he'd been a naval ensign in the first war), he took over a Cleveland company that made aircraft components while remaining on the board of Chrysler.

By that time, his wife, Thelma, had been named America's best-dressed woman—a designation she'd hang on to for twenty years and would more than earn due to her heavy expenditures on Paris couture. Living in a town house built for a Vanderbilt and an estate in Locust Valley, she shuttled between them in a Chrysler driven by, as Cholly Knickerbocker put it, "her colored chauffeur, who's been with the family for 20 years [and] does the better part of her incidental buying, such as bags, sweaters, accessories." According to Knickerbocker, Foy was an intellectual who detested shopping and champagne but drank old-fashioneds, hated rich food but loved foie gras and gooey desserts, and had "a shyness about her that is often mistaken for snobbishness, but she's one of the kindest women I know."

That was her public image. Privately, she was an angry, entitled woman with "a total temper," says a daughter, Joan French, who recalls a privileged childhood ("I had a governess and my sister had a nurse in the same apartment") and tells of her mother pushing to the front of a line in Bloomingdale's, because, "She didn't get it, you know?" Once French asked her father why he didn't fight back. "I never argued with my mother," he told her, "and I won't argue with yours."

"The whole family was insane," says Thelma's niece Helen Chrysler. "The genes were programmed for huge tempers, very intense, and the most intense of all was Thelma. She was absolutely bizarre, self-absorbed, and fashion-conscious." Once, annoyed at one of the hands at Hattie Carnegie's dress shop, Thelma grabbed a pair of scissors and tried to stab her. "She drove couturiers insane if things were not exactly as she wanted," says Vincent Curcio, her father's biographer. "She was a *very* fastidious person."

Kindness was certainly not in evidence late in the fall of 1951, when Foy began negotiating with the Shearns just as Zeckendorf was buying Superpower from Thorne. Though there's no direct evidence, the two deals were likely connected. "It isn't a coincidence, obviously," says Landon Thorne's lawyer, Emerson Markham. "He and Zeckendorf were luncheon buddies. I have no doubt he said, 'Let's get this straightened out. Rockefeller is making noises, Lee can't run it.' That was the way they operated."

The Foys and the Shearns had been socializing for years. Both couples were charter subscribers to the New Opera Company, formed in the spring of 1941, rubbed shoulders at the opera's premier performance of *Così fan tutte*, and shared an intimate supper at the Plaza Hotel after the opening of Verdi's *Macbeth* that fall. Thelma Foy and Zeckendorf's wife knew each other, too; they served on charity committees together.

Clarence Shearn was a sitting duck, and these were big-game hunters. Shearn's health was declining, and that allowed Dorothea to isolate him. His two children "kept their distance," says his grandson Tony Kerrigan. "My mother was very distraught." By 1951, Shearn "was, if not fully senile, then not 100 percent," thinks his step-grandson Peter Pruyn.

Dorothea wasn't at her best, either. The quirks in her character had finally overwhelmed her flapper-era charms. She'd taken to using other names, most often Sondra, for reasons unknown. "I'm sure the wife was Sondra," says Pruyn. But she was sometimes Alexandra and sometimes Sondra Sheram. "She changed her name by the hour," says Graubard.

"She had about sixteen she used. She was crazy, badly crazy. I never felt he got a square deal. She dominated him. And bullied, bullied, bullied. If he didn't do what she told him to, she would hide his glasses. And he would be quite desperate because he couldn't do anything, he couldn't even look for his glasses."

Early in 1952, as Zeckendorf's takeover of Superpower was approved by the SEC, the latest lease-renewal deadline confronted the residents of 740 Park. Three years earlier, along with his last lease, Junior had gotten a blunt assessment of James T. Lee's situation from Gibbons: "The landlord has no income and no hope." Although Junior's arrival in 1938 had helped Lee put 740 back on an even keel financially, the war had knocked it off kilter again, and it was still losing money.

Now Gibbons was back to say that he was trying to talk to Lee about the building and its future. He promised to update Junior as soon as he had any news. But aside from an exchange about a new steam pipe in Junior's bathroom ("I am most appreciative and should continue to thank you every time I go into this bathroom, warmed instead of chilly"), and another about a fireman who came to his service entrance selling raffle tickets ("If a fireman can come to one's door in this way, why not policemen and other people? I am not criticizing. I am merely telling you of a situation . . ."), Junior heard not a peep from Gibbons until May 1952, when Lee offered a two-year lease renewal with two strings attached. The rent was going up 15 percent, and there would be no option to renew.

Rockefeller agreed to Lee's terms. But not all the tenants followed suit. Clarence Shearn, for one, was still trying to get paid to leave his apartment. And it seemed he was finally on the verge of succeeding. On January 30, 1952, he signed a document giving the Foys the right to take over his lease on its expiration on March 4, 1952. But a month later, Shearn's attorney canceled the agreement and returned a check for $250 that Thelma had written to him—announcing to both Mrs. Foy and the 740 corporation that Shearn would not be moving out.

Shearn would later claim that Mrs. Foy had "intruded" into his home while he was ill and "hysterically" hectored and "extorted" him into signing the agreement, causing him to faint twice in the process.

The weirdness had only begun.

Into the breach rode Zeckendorf. That July, seemingly out of the blue, Webb & Knapp bought the 740 Park Avenue Corporation from Lee and Ecker, who effectively controlled it. Lee "absolutely admired Zeckendorf to the *n*th degree," says his granddaughter LeeLee Brown. "He thought Zeckendorf was the most amazing person, the only man he knew who could raise millions on the phone with no plans or meetings. He got what he wanted." And he wanted 740 Park. Almost immediately Webb & Knapp began negotiating to acquire both the Chrysler and the Graybar buildings and the leaseholds under them.'

News accounts of the connection between the two deals seem calculated to obscure rather than shed light on them. After the $52 million sale of the two office buildings closed on October 9, 1953, Zeckendorf told reporters it was a result of a chance remark Byron Foy had made that May, about his wife's desire to live in 740. "Mr. Zeckendorf said he replied that he was not really interested in apartment buildings but in commercial properties," the *Times* reported. Then Zeckendorf supposedly added, "I want you to sell us the Chrysler Building."

The problem is, at the time Webb & Knapp already owned 740.

The Foys, of course, had been trying to get the Shearn apartment for at least six months before Zeckendorf bought 740.

A different version of the same story appeared the same day in the *Herald Tribune*. It said Foy approached Zeckendorf for an apartment during the brief period that Webb & Knapp owned 740. A few days later, they met again, and, just like that, Zeckendorf told Foy he could have an apartment. "And then the idea came into my mind," said Zeckendorf, "that here was the man I needed and I told him, 'Now that I have done something for you, you can do something for me. How about selling the Chrysler Building to us?' And that's how it happened."

Or maybe it's not.

※

As Zeckendorf swallowed his building whole, 740's nine-thousand-pound whale must have been napping. As the Jack Chryslers were moving into one of the largest and prettiest apartments in the D line, overlooking St. James Church, John D. Rockefeller Jr. was writing a letter to Douglas Gibbons, asking what the purchase of the building, which he'd read about in the paper in Maine, meant.

"Have you any idea what they propose to do with the property?" Junior asked. "Will it in any way affect the occupancy of the present tenants? I know Mr. Z of the firm and would, of course, write him about the matter but thought it best not to do so until I heard from you."

Gibbons replied immediately: "He told me I was to continue as managing agent and I believe it will go along just as it has in the past. What his plans are for the future, he hasn't told me because I don't think he has made up his mind as to that. However, if the building had to be sold, I am glad it is in his hands. I have known him for a long time and I know that you know him too."

Junior wrote to Zeckendorf to say he was gratified by the sale, express his love for his home ("there is no other apartment in New York so much like a private house or so completely adapted to our purposes and needs"), offer to show it to his new landlord, and then bluntly state his concern: "I hope you are not planning to alter it or tear it down."

Zeckendorf assured Junior that his plan was to hold 740 as an investment or else sell it, and he promised he'd do neither without letting Junior know first. A month later, a deal was struck: Junior paid $3.7 million for the building, putting $750,000 down and taking over the mortgage, as renegotiated by Zeckendorf, who'd bargained the principal down from $3.5 million to $2.95 million and the interest rate to 3.5 percent, with the principal due in 1972. Junior planned to quickly sell the property to its tenants and make it a cooperative again.

Their deal closed in mid-December 1952. But just before it did, the Shearn apartment was in play again. Either the Shearns had stopped paying rent or Zeckendorf had refused their rent checks, and they were sued for eviction by Gibbons. Shearn thought Thelma Foy was behind the suit, which claimed that they'd refused to permit an inspection of the apartment. Dorothea said the lawsuit had made her husband ill.

Tony Kerrigan had last seen his grandfather in the winter of 1951. "He was not ill; he was in relatively good shape," he says. "Dorothea disappeared so we could talk, but there was rustling behind the curtains. He didn't look ill to me, but my father thought Sondra had him popped up with something." After that, whenever Shearn's children called, they couldn't reach him. "I tried to see him again when I was shipping out [to Korea] but I couldn't get through," Kerrigan says. "I asked my father,

'Why not force the issue?' He didn't want anybody in our family to look money-hungry."

Shearn, they were sure, was quite rich.

"He was senile at the end," thinks his step-grandson Peter Pruyn, whose mother and father, Clarence junior, wanted nothing to do with Shearn in his last years. "Dorothea had him change his will two or three times. Because of his position, people didn't want to get involved. He was a man of eminence. And he was afraid of his wife. She was totally irresponsible, never paid taxes, got her hands on everything she possibly could."

By the fall of 1952, Shearn, eighty-three, was in decline—and the evidence of it was in front of his door, "mail piled four feet high," says Kerrigan. "All kinds of lawsuits. I think Mrs. Rockefeller sued them [when their terrace leaked into her dressing room below]. The building tried to get them out. Everyone in the building was in great horror."

One day in October, Dorothea bumped into Junior's secretary in the elevator, told her they'd decided to vacate at the end of November, and asked if Junior still wanted their apartment. She also complained that Zeckendorf was suing them to force them out. On November 1, a note was hand-delivered to Shearn, saying that in fact Junior did want the place. Dorothea was delighted. She said she'd make arrangements and be in touch in two weeks.

Simultaneously, the negotiations to sell 740 to Rockefeller were coming to a head, and Junior was again immersed in the minutiae of his latest real estate deal: Which leases were still in effect? Were the rents Lee was charging legal? Would Zeckendorf paint apartments that had not seen a brush in years? Could the State Rent Commission enforce rent reductions if he refused? Who owned the mantels and grates and electrical fixtures in the apartments, and if they'd been changed or removed, who was to pay to reinstall them? How had the Webbs come to rent their space on the nineteenth floor for just $1 a year? Especially considering that, formally speaking under the city's rules, it could only be used for service or storage purposes, not for living.

Gibbons, meanwhile, was stirring up interest in advance of expected vacancies. He told Junior that the Foys, the Milbank, Tweed partner John McCloy, Mrs. Simon Guggenheim, and Bobby Lehman of the banking family all wanted apartments. Junior wrote back to say that he hoped McCloy, especially, would get one.[2]

Zeckendorf was also making it clear that he attached "very great importance" to his desire to occupy the first vacant apartment in the building. He also wanted the Shearn apartment—presumably for Mrs. Foy. In months to come, Dorothea would write a series of increasingly hysterical letters to the Rockefellers, giving her take on what was happening above their heads. Zeckendorf, she claimed, had offered to drop the eviction litigation (a trial was set for January 5, 1953) if they gave him their apartment before the sale to Rockefeller closed. He'd first offered them $10,000 on the Foys' behalf, but then, once he saw it, decided he wanted it for himself, she claimed.

"What will you take?" Zeckendorf asked, according to Dorothea. They could name their price. "This is beautiful! It's just what I want for my family! If I can square myself with Mrs. Foy, I will take it for myself. I will take it whether I can square myself or not! What will you take from me for immediate possession? And will you let Mrs. Zeckendorf come to see your apartment tomorrow morning?"

On November 12, Dorothea called Junior's office, begging him to intervene with Zeckendorf, whose wife had called, demanding to see the place. Unspecified others had offered them money for the lease, she said, but they wanted Rockefeller to have it. She seemed to be negotiating, pointedly mentioning that Shearn had spent $55,000 decorating the apartment.

A week later, referring to the "delicate situation in connection with the Shearns," Rockefeller told Debevoise he was surprised by Zeckendorf's sudden desire to occupy their apartment but added that, as far as he knew, Zeckendorf had backed off on his demand to see it.

At the end of December, Junior closed the deal, bought 740 Park, and formally took title. Almost immediately, on December 28, Dorothea cabled him, begging him, in language as colorful as one of Shearn's old campaign speeches, to intervene and stop "THE CAMPAIGN PUT ON BY MR Z . . . THE FOMENTING OF GROUNDLESS LITIGATION, SUBJECTING US TO THE INDIGNITY OF HAVING TO DEFEND OURSELF AGAINST A BASELESS SUIT FOR EVICTION . . . WHILE WE KNOW OF COURSE THAT THESE ACTS ARE WITHOUT YOUR KNOWLEDGE OR APPROVAL, WE SHOULD LIKE TO HAVE YOUR DISAVOWAL OF THEM . . . I NEED YOUR ACTIVE HELP."

She didn't get it. On the advice of Thomas Debevoise, Rockefeller sent Shearn to Gibbons, who was prepared to argue that a previous rent reduction offset his expenditures on the apartment. "Mr. Shearn evidently believes he can be bought off," Debevoise said. "Shearn will have no choice if he is dealt with firmly from the start." Unaware of the forces arrayed against him, Shearn was sure Rockefeller never got his telegraph and blamed only "the Machiavellian influence of Gibbons."

Then Shearn fell ill and failed to pay his rent in January 1953. On February 3, Gibbons sent a dunning letter. It was ignored. Four nights later, Dorothea telephoned Junior in Tucson, begging for "a continuation of the status quo." But when the February rent went unpaid as well, Gibbons kept after them. On February 9, he left what Dorothea called "an ominous message" to say they'd be getting a letter from Junior's lawyer. That letter, sent on February 11 by Milbank, Tweed, demanded payment. It crossed in the mail with one to Junior handwritten and signed by Sandra Shearn, with accompanying photos of the apartment.

"It has been my felicity to have the close association of this great man, and to become a recluse with him," she wrote. "To have had fourteen years of close association with his great mind and character, his well-known sweetness, goodness and strength, as the quiet years came along has been a privilege which you will understand."

Right after she wrote it, Shearn died in his apartment of a cerebral hemorrhage.

AT AGE TWENTY-SIX, PATRICK O'CONNOR WAS HIRED BY 740 PARK ON November 13, 1948, to run the manual elevators on the Park Avenue side of the building. Today, retired at eighty-two, he lives in a small apartment near Prospect Park in Brooklyn and moves around with a walker. Remembered fondly by many of the building's residents, the bluff Irish immigrant remembers them, too.

"There was an old gentleman, a sharp little man by the name of Lee, that owned the building," he says. "Ernest Waldron [the hall captain] told me his granddaughters were full of hell, always playing tricks on him. They were little rascals. I'd see Lee once or twice when he came to pick out slipcovers. In Lee's day the lobby furniture had to be covered.

Next thing we heard there were negotiations between him and old man Rockefeller. We never knew the details, but they took away the big couches and chairs and put in leatherette so we wouldn't have to bother with covers in the summertime."

Even though he worked a six-day week, O'Connor liked his job fine, except in the summer, when it was stifling hot, the doors were left open, and the lobby filled with noise. Asked whom he remembers from his first days on the job, he mentions Watson Webb. "He'd call one of the help upstairs to get his bags when he was going shooting in Scotland," O'Connor says. "He had a couple of guns, of course. They all did that."

Then there was Rockefeller. "The super explained to me. He married his second wife, a widow." Every Sunday, he went to Riverside Church. "He'd ring the [elevator] bell just once, never rung it a second time. He was a real gentleman. 'Good morning to you,' he'd say. His Swedish butler went with him. His chauffeur would be outside. He'd have a light overcoat on him and another one over his arm. I'm sure they cost him plenty."

Clarence and Dorothea Shearn come up next. "He was not well," O'Connor says. "His wife was there—it was Sondra, I think—and his mother-in-law lived with them. I remember taking them down in the elevator, acting strange, all right. I used to hear the superintendent, John Andrews, a Scotsman, talking about it. They'd say they'd lost their key, trying to find out if somebody else had a key. He got the handyman to break the lock. 'No, no, we'll find it.' They were kind of peculiar people. A nuisance, troublesome. Not Shearn himself—the woman. I never had any trouble, but I was careful with them. Then again, we were told to be careful with them all. Give them service and security. That's what we were there for."

One day O'Connor was summoned to 17 to pick up Shearn, and then descended to 15, "and who steps in?" he says. "John D. He turns to Clarence Shearn and says, 'So what do you think of the United Nations?' Shearn said, 'I don't believe in it. It will be as big a flop as the League of Nations.' That impressed me, but it didn't go down good with John D."

Elevator men like O'Connor were privy to a lot—even last exits. O'Connor was driving the car the day Marshall Field "came down in a silver coffin right into the lobby," he says. But by the time Shearn died,

O'Connor had been transferred to the quieter Seventy-first Street elevators, so he missed the scene when Dorothea Shearn pushed her husband's
corpse out into a winter night, propped up in a wheelchair and wrapped
in a blanket.

"I think he died from neglect," says Dorothea's niece Margaret
Graubard. "She had him taken out in a wheelchair and pretended he
wasn't dead. The porters knew he was. Such a cruel fate. The poor man."
Shearn's grandson Tony Kerrigan thinks Dorothea took the body to the
house they owned up the block. Graubard doesn't. "I don't know where
it went. I imagine the funeral home."[5]

"The only way we knew was the doorman at 740 called Clarence
junior to say the judge has died," says Shearn's step-grandson Peter
Pruyn. "My understanding is, she spirited his remains out the back door.
She made a lot of trouble for a lot of people."

That didn't keep the American legal establishment from his funeral.
Supreme Court justices, law school deans, leading politicians, and Frederick Ecker were there, but were likely unaware of the family drama that
played out before them. "We all went," says Kerrigan. "Sondra grabbed
me and said I should sit in the front pew with her. That horrified the
family, my mother especially. Afterwards, there was a hearse and one
limo and Sondra jumped in it and took off. I never knew where he was
buried."

19

DOROTHEA SHEARN JUMPED THE RAILS AFTER HER HUSBAND'S DEATH. Junior, who was in Tucson at the time, sent her a condolence letter on February 15. "May the Great Comforter sustain and strengthen you in this dark hour," he wrote. It crossed in the mail a half-typed, half-handwritten unsigned letter from Dorothea, saying again that they'd only been trying to give Rockefeller their apartment. "Then came death," she wrote. "Judge Shearn served Mr. Rockefeller with his last heartbeat."

Unmoved, Junior wrote back in late March. Milbank, Tweed vetted the chilly hand-delivered letter that pointedly noted that the Shearns had not vacated in November 1952, as promised, and asked her to leave 740 as soon as possible. Dorothea didn't respond for two months, then called Junior's office to say that she'd had a nervous breakdown and high fever, had only just found Rockefeller's letter in "a great quantity of mail," and would respond when "she could get herself together."

On June 17, she followed with a nine-page typed letter addressed to Mrs. Rockefeller, signed Dorothea Alexandra Shearn. "May I trespass on your time and enlist your aid?" it began. Describing herself as "defenseless, ill and distraught," "far from recovery," and "also trying to nurse my mother through a similar case of distress, strain and shock which has resulted in her invalidism and relegated her to a wheelchair indefinitely," she called Junior's letter urging her out "incredible to my feverished [*sic*] brain."

Upping the ante of what had been spent on the apartment to $75,000, she spoke of how Shearn's decor had attracted "many contenders ... accompanied by substantial pecuniary offers to vacate in their favor." She accused Gibbons ("who is well known as 'The little friend to the rich' ") of malice and Thelma Foy of "high pressure methods and gross misrepresentations" and repeated how they'd held out for Rockefeller even after Zeckendorf had made his "tempting" offer.

Dorothea quoted a letter she said Shearn had written but never sent to Junior, in which he claimed he'd been made ill "by the chicanery, deceit and indignities to which I have been subjected," all because he wanted the Rockefellers to take his apartment. He also claimed that he'd represented Standard Oil in several lawsuits and that Thelma Foy had circulated "libels about me and my loyal wife." As a result of the litigation, Dorothea said she'd ended up "far from provided for." The letter ended with a not-very-veiled plea that she be paid off to vacate.

Junior then signed a letter written by Debevoise to Dorothea, saying that as of April, he'd sold the building to the new cooperative corporation and Dorothea would have to take it up with them. Thelma and Byron Foy had already bought the apartment from that corporation. That was clearly part of the price Junior paid for the building. It was Foy who'd brought the last dispossess proceeding that ended with a court order that Dorothea move out by the end of July.

Even that didn't stop her. She threatened suit against Gibbons, and Milbank, Tweed considered suing her for the back rent, but Junior said he'd waive the debt if she just left. The move took several days, but Dorothea Shearn finally left the building on August 3.

Gibbons was droll in private but "a pretty tough SOB in business," says Osborn Elliott, whose mother, Audrey, was one of Gibbons's top brokers. And he was still afraid Dorothea might sue him. So at his request, as she moved out, Junior sent a letter to Debevoise from Seal Harbor, summing up, as he put it, "the facts as I remember them."

Junior's memory was either shaky or convenient.

"Except for the fact that I sometimes met Judge Shearn in the elevator at 740 Park Avenue," he began, "his tenancy in the building, or which apartment he occupied, meant nothing to me until two or three years ago." Only then did he ask Gibbons about buying the apartment to display his art and a new collection of Chinese porcelains he was considering buying. "Only at that time," he continued, did he become "conscious of the fact that the apartment immediately above us was occupied by the Shearns. Which apartment the Shearns had occupied in the building prior to that time, and when they moved to the 17th floor, I do not know."

Later that month, one last exchange of letters ended the chapter for Junior and Gibbons. Confirming that Dorothea had indeed departed, Gibbons wrote, "The new owner will immediately decorate and I think we will all be considerably better off."

Junior's response was swift. "Good news! May I also tell you how much I have been impressed with your patience, wisdom and tact in the handling of this difficult matter."

THELMA FOY EXTINGUISHED THE SHEARNS FROM HER NEW APARTMENT as surely as Gibbons and Rockefeller had erased their sixteen-year battle for it from their memories. But she also treated Junior (during the few months he owned 740) and his manager just as she did her couturiers, complaining about the condition of the floors, the bathroom tiles, unsanitary plumbing, and unsatisfactory fixtures.

After a long renovation that caused Junior some alarm when they installed an air-conditioning system, the Foys moved in in 1954 and, early the next year, announced their takeover with a five-page spread of photos in *Vogue*, headlined THE FINEST FRENCH HOUSE IN NEW YORK. "Everything reflects Mrs. Foy's unerring collector's eye, her unswerving taste, and her talent for making a house gay and livable, as well as visually lovely," the magazine rhapsodized. She'd installed Louis XV boiserie in the library, Louis XVI gold paneling in the dining room, Regency gold and white boiserie in the drawing room that had been Shearn's library, Louis XV and Louis XVI furniture, "much of it signed," and new-old parquet floors, topped by a Persian silk carpet once owned by the king of Spain, "all looking as though they had always been here."

Artists, politicians, and socialites clamored for invitations to the Foys' frequent dinner parties, where a servant stood behind every chair and the tables would be pushed back afterward for dancing on the marble floors. Between spins on the floor, guests could admire the Foys' eight Renoirs, two Degas ballet pastels, Toulouse-Lautrec's *Femme rousse dans le jardin*, a Boldini, a Winslow Homer, a Vuillard, a statue of Aphrodite by Giovanni da Bologna, two white marble sphinxes with women's heads made for Marie Antoinette, a chandelier from a Russian palace, plenty of porcelains, terra-cotta nymphs and cherubs, and an Oriental clock from an Italian royal palace.

Sadly, Thelma Foy hardly got to enjoy it. "She was pretty sick those years," says her daughter Cynthia Rupp. "Trips to Europe were canceled, but these things weren't discussed." Dressmakers kept visiting her in the hospital in the weeks before she succumbed, in August 1957, to a long battle with leukemia.

Byron Foy lived on at 740 for a few months, but early in January 1958 he let Gibbons know he wanted to sell. Although he said he and his late wife had spent $341,000 on the apartment, he accepted Junior's offer of $300,000 in cash—"not just because it is such a showplace," Cholly Knickerbocker reported, "but because he occupies the apartment below and doesn't like the noise from parties taking place in the marble-floored premises above." Or the lingering memories of battles past. "I remember him buying it, and being pleased to have it," says David Rockefeller.

THEIR LONG CAMPAIGN TO ENTER NOTWITHSTANDING, FOY'S BROTHERS remained at 740 only slightly longer than she did. Jack Chrysler "never seemed to find his way," wrote his father's biographer Vincent Curcio. After attending prep school, he'd worked briefly as an apprentice machinist at Chrysler, become a vice president, and in 1941, just before Pearl Harbor, married Edith Backus, a John Robert Powers model who'd been born "dirt-poor," says their daughter Helen. The next year Jack went to war as a Navy lieutenant and, on his return, joined the stock exchange and several charity and corporate boards (including Chrysler's) and formed a venture capital company that operated out of the Chrysler Building.

But Jack's wife was, in Curcio's words, "extremely difficult," and their life was miserable, even though their apartment was "absolutely beautiful," says Helen. "Extraordinarily beautiful." Jack was plagued by weight problems all his life, but Helen believes his unhappy marriage was the cause of his sudden death at forty-six in 1958. "All the Chryslers despised her, and she couldn't handle it," says their daughter, who was fourteen when her father died. "They thought she was a whore. She became an introvert, and my father got fatter and fatter. She was perfectly horrible and a terrible alcoholic. I have nothing good to say about my mother. It was just terrible."

The year after Jack Chrysler died, Edith got married again to a man who, her daughter says, had been in the oil business with Chrysler. "They had an affair before my father died, and I always felt Father was so upset it caused him to go downhill. My poor father, I guess, wasn't so bright. He should have shot this man."

Edith and her second husband remained at 71 East Seventy-first Street until 1973.

By the time Walter Chrysler Jr. bought his apartment from the estate of Countess Kotzebue, he was already a well-known art collector. He'd bought his first Renoir while in prep school and started an art magazine with Nelson Rockefeller when they were students at Dartmouth. At twenty-one, Chrysler started a publishing company to republish classics and sell them by subscription. His schoolmate Rockefeller was a charter subscriber. Four years later, Chrysler formed an air-conditioning company and a year after that quit to become president of the Chrysler Building Corporation.

Though he was gay, Walter junior married a stockbroker's daughter in 1938; she went to Reno and divorced him a year later, charging, as always, cruelty. Six years later, just after leaving the Navy steps ahead of a homosexual scandal, Walter married again, to a librarian in Norfolk, Virginia, right near the thousand-acre estate where he bred horses and cattle and lived in a seventy-two-room mansion.

Mostly, Chrysler devoted himself to art, buying and selling twenty-five thousand works before his death in 1988, sending his pictures on museum tours, even opening his own museum. His cache of old masters was considered one of the finest in American hands. But just after he moved out of 740 in 1959, his collection and his reputation were tarnished when he was accused of knowingly buying forgeries. An open season of criticism followed, with artists and dealers calling him arrogant and cheap. Pablo Picasso scrawled "faux" on photos of two alleged Picassos in his collection. Of 180 paintings Chrysler showed at a Canadian museum, half, including works purported to be by van Gogh, Matisse, Bonnard, and Klee, were deemed forgeries.

WHAT DID WILLIAM ZECKENDORF REALLY WANT? *NOT* AN APARTMENT at 740, says his grandson Will Zeckendorf, who co-owns the company that manages the building today. "He was a modernist," says Zeckendorf. "He only would have wanted a modern building." Two letters in Zeckendorf's files refer to his sale of 740 to, as he put it, "old Mr. Rockefeller," according to young Zeckendorf, and neither refers to the Foys or his own desire for an apartment in the building. Rather, he speaks of "working very closely with the [Rockefeller] clan" on "large-scale . . . joint activities."

Zeckendorf was at "the apex of his career," says his grandson. "This was his glory period. He wants 740 like a hole in his head. It was one of eighteen conversions he had that day." Society "was not a life he wanted or aspired to," either. "But he would certainly want to ingratiate himself with John D. Rockefeller."[1]

Zeckendorf knew, as he wrote in his autobiography, that "a Jewish realtor" could cause great "resentment and unease" among "top families . . . welded together by time and social contact, where not knitted together by intermarriage." Yet just weeks before the sale of 740 to Rockefeller closed, Thomas Debevoise still thought Zeckendorf wanted an apartment for himself—specifically, 2/3B, which had been rented to the French government for its UN representative after the 1949 co-op conversion attempt failed, but without a renewal option. "This is a matter to which Mr. Zeckendorf attaches very great importance," another lawyer reported, adding that Zeckendorf believed Junior had promised him "the first apartment that he might wish."

Debevoise advised Junior that "the approval of any new tenant—which would include Mr. Zeckendorf—had to be obtained." But Junior had already given Zeckendorf a qualified assurance that he would be considered "a satisfactory tenant and would be given preference on the first vacant apartment he might wish."

Just before the sale closed, Zeckendorf turned down one vacated apartment, telling Gibbons it was too large, but he remained first on the priority list. And Junior kept reassuring him, even signing a letter written by Debevoise, promising him the French apartment. When Junior took title, the issue remained unresolved.

Zeckendorf, the Chryslers, and the Shearns aside, Junior and Gibbons had lots to do to make the building a cooperative again. In January 1953, Junior authorized repairs to the facade and replacement of elevator cables. He induced his neighbor Morris Hadley of Milbank, Tweed to accept the presidency of a new 740 Corporation. In the first draft of the latest offering plan, Gibbons noted that Junior would make a small profit, but when Rockefeller objected, the phrase was deleted.

The first week in February they sent out a revised plan showing that Junior was selling apartments for just enough to recoup his investment, "but in order to make the terms as favorable as possible," Gibbons explained, Rockefeller was also going to finance a second mortgage, at 3.5 percent interest, which would self-liquidate in ten years, giving the building an extra $365,000. To gild the lily, Gibbons reminded the tenants that as owners they would be allowed to deduct their share of the building's real estate taxes and mortgage interest from their income taxes, and added that the doctors' offices and servants' rooms would remain income-producing rentals, lowering the maintenance bills. Two of the doctors' offices rented for $5,000 a year, two for $3,000. A servant's room went for between $300 and $400. One of the doctors had attached four of them to his seven-room suite of offices. Countess Kotzebue had three, Marshall Field five, the Webbs and Jack Chrysler two each. More income came from Lewis Brothers, a dry-cleaning service headquartered in the basement, which paid $75 a month.

The new plan reapportioned the shares for all the apartments, reflecting changes made to the building since 1929. More important, the apartments were offered to the residents for a tiny fraction of their original prices; to keep his own home, and ensure they all bought theirs and made the plan effective, Junior was being astonishingly generous to his neighbors.

The small C-line apartments, which had cost $72,000 to $111,000 in 1929, were priced at $10,800 to $16,080. The larger A- and D-line apartments, originally $130,000 to $185,000, were selling for $14,640 to $24,600. Lee's old apartment had dropped from $185,000 in 1929 to the $20,400 asked of Belle Ledyard. The Webbs, who'd already paid more than $205,000, only had to kick in another $24,720. Blanche Rosett's penthouse, originally $120,000, was going for $16,560. The two fourteenth-floor simplexes, originally $185,000 and $130,000, were priced to sell at $22,200 and $15,600. And Rockefeller's grand domain, which was valued at $250,000 when the Brewsters moved in, remained the most expensive apartment but cost a mere $38,160.

Monthly charges ranged from $616 for the smallest duplex on the second and third floors to the $2,512 Rockefeller would pay, which worked out to just $146.40 a year more than he'd paid when he took over the lease in 1945. Annual operating expenses, which had been estimated at about $83,000 in the 1929 offering, were now running $134,000. But gross expenses, thanks to the renegotiated mortgage, had dropped about $14,000, and Gibbons promised they would fall another $43,000 when the second mortgage held by Junior was paid off.

Many families had left during the uncertain period between Junior's attempts to co-op the building, among them the Kirklands, who were replaced by a public-works builder and equestrian named Anthony Del Balso; the Ottmans, who gave way to the Bartholomew Barrys (he was a textile broker, she the daughter of the Coal King of Brooklyn); the Lloyd-Smiths, whose apartment went to the mining potentate Solomon R. Guggenheim's widow, Irene; the George McLaughlins, replaced by R. Sterling Clark, a racehorse owner and Singer Sewing Machine heir; and the Farrar Batesons, replaced by the Greek shipping magnate George Embiricos. All the newcomers bought their apartments. This time it took only five weeks before 80 percent of the tenants agreed to buy, and the co-op plan was declared effective. The sole holdout was Mrs. Bliss, and Gibbons eventually talked her into buying, too. With Clarence Shearn's widow having a nervous breakdown above him, one can only hope Junior got a good laugh when Mrs. William Randolph Hearst, whose husband had died two years earlier, inquired about buying the only remaining vacant apartment.

Then Junior got his reward, the extra space he'd been denied by the Foys. As she'd always predicted, Belle Ledyard had lived into her nineties. "She lived too long," says Jarden Guenther. "The heirs were wringing their hands." But she was clever and entertaining to the end. "She looked like an incompetent old lady, but boy, her mind was sharp," says her granddaughter Frances Ferry Dennison. At least it was until she suffered a stroke in 1953. Belle was "lying there, gaga, with the shades drawn," says her grandson John Ferry. "She was hopelessly out of it." Relatives and lawyers decided to buy the apartment anyway, but only if Junior agreed to take it off her estate's hands when she died at the same price she paid.

When Belle died in February 1955, Junior bought it, annexed a bedroom suite, and attached it to his apartment. Then he flipped the place to Margaret Bedford Bancroft, better known as Peggy, a newlywed Standard Oil heiress, selling the nibbled-down duplex for $60,000—making back the price of his own apartment plus $840 for his trouble. His father would have approved.

On March 4, 1953, J. Watson Webb's diary mentions a meeting on 740's return to cooperative status. The sale to the 740 Corporation closed on March 31, and on June 3 Webb made another notation. "Meeting at 5 at Doug Gibbons office re: 740 Corporation (our apartment has been made a coop again)," Webb wrote. "I am a director." After Junior declined a seat on the board, the others went to Hadley, Landon Thorne (who was also made treasurer of the corporation), Marshall Field, Robert Vanderbilt, and Langbourne Williams, who'd rented Beekman Hoppin's apartment when he left during the war. A nickel-mine owner whose family had known the Founding Fathers in colonial Virginia, Williams was also elected vice president.

In 1955, just after John D. Rockefeller Jr. made 740 Park a cooperative again, Frederick Ecker was given an honorary Doctor of Letters degree by Long Island University in Brooklyn, where William Zeckendorf was president and chairman of the board of trustees. The next year James T. Lee got an LIU doctorate, too. Lee retired in 1961 and died seven years later.

A decade earlier, Lee's last home, J. E. R. Carpenter's 580 Park, had been converted into a cooperative. The tenants were offered their apartments for $5,000. "Grampy Lee didn't want to do it," says his granddaughter Mimi Cecil. "He paid his rent and wanted them to disappear. They finally said, 'Move out or pay.' He huffed and he puffed and he paid up. It was the worst day of his life."

2 0

"THEY DIDN'T WANT HIM IN THERE," SAYS THE ELEVATOR MAN PATRICK O'Connor. So William Zeckendorf never did get into 740 Park, though he kept trying. The day Belle Ledyard's obituary appeared in the *Times*, Gibbons called the new board president, Morris Hadley, taking "a very strong line to the effect that you promised this to Mrs. Zeckendorf and that the directors of the corporation have no choice as to whether or not they regard him as a satisfactory tenant," said a letter Junior got from Debevoise.

Advised that Junior "very carefully never made any commitment" about how the co-op board would feel about Zeckendorf, Gibbons back-tracked and sent him a letter, which Debevoise paraphrased to Junior, again in Tucson for the winter. "Any lease application he may make will rest entirely with the committee appointed by the Cooperative Owners," he wrote. "Your name is not mentioned in the letter."

And with that, William Zeckendorf rode off into the sunset. In-formed that Junior was buying the Ledyard apartment, 740's unloved savior "was very contented about it," Gibbons wrote. "No feeling at all was left. I think that everybody seems happy."

Just to be sure, Junior wrote both Debevoise and Gibbons. "The committee appointed by the cooperative owners has sole jurisdiction and authority—I have none," he informed his lawyer, who certainly already knew that. To Gibbons he sent thanks, again: "That Mr. Zeckendorf is entirely happy about the way things have turned out is . . . gratifying. As always, you have handled this situation with great tact, consideration and skill."

It turned out the board was wise in rejecting Zeckendorf, who continued wheeling and dealing on borrowed funds, going deeper and deeper into debt. Webb & Knapp, the former American Superpower, was forced into bankruptcy by creditors in 1965, and after declaring personal bankruptcy as well, he worked as a consultant for the successor corporation run by his son William junior into the 1970s, when he began suffering a series of strokes. Just before his death in 1976, he was indicted for failure to file state income taxes in 1972 and 1973. He denied the charges that could have sent him to jail, and then died in his sleep. The wife of one board member says he continued trying to buy apartments at 740 Park into the 1960s, but finally gave up and began telling people he wouldn't live there if they asked him to.

They weren't about to do that. "He was a brilliant genius," says the realtor Alice Mason, "but he never had liquid money."

DOROTHEA TROYTE-BULLOCK SHEARN, AS SHE WAS CALLED IN ONE OF her husband's obituaries, lived another fourteen years, making trouble every inch of the way. Her husband's will, written in 1941, left his law library to his son; his personal effects and their mother's to his children; his half share of a California beach property to his sister, the widow of the actor who'd played Charlie Chan in the movies. Half the remainder and the Katonah estate went to Dorothea and the other half to his children. But they didn't know that. Through the long months of Dorothea's nervous breakdown, they were kept in the dark; she claimed she couldn't find Shearn's will.

In it, Dorothea and George Warren, a former vice president of the Chase, were named co-executors. Warren had known Shearn since 1920, but hadn't seen him in years, when Dorothea called and invited him to her husband's funeral. A few days later, he went to 740 and saw the will along with Dorothea's lawyer, an old friend of Shearn's named J. Carlisle Swaim. In coming years, Swaim would be the one constant in her life. "He was the prototype expedient lawyer," says a daughter-in-law, Claudette Hollenbeck. "He skated the edge, which made him perfect for Dorothea. The other big element was, he was a sexaholic. He had sex with anyone who was willing, and I suspect Dorothea used that method on him. If you went to bed with him, he'd do anything. Their eccentricities crossed."

Warren was leaving for Europe, but Swaim and Dorothea assured him they'd handle everything. They didn't do anything. After she moved out of 740, Warren tried to get her attention again and failed. Then he filed a motion demanding she submit the will for probate.

Dorothea finally produced it in August after she moved to her house on Seventy-first Street. To an untrained eye, Shearn's signature on it looks very much like her handwriting, as does the one on a letter dated seven days before Shearn died, stating that he'd borrowed more than $100,000 from her and promising to repay it out of the proceeds of a sale of his town house on East Sixty-ninth Street.

Dorothea finally began dealing with estate matters in December. The estate owed several default judgments on lawsuits, $6,525 in arrears to 740, and other debts. Shearn had earned nothing since 1945, Dorothea said, and had lived on loans from her. To raise some cash now, she netted $18,000 by selling an empty co-op apartment he'd bought for a dollar. But then she turned around and bought another house near Shearn's Westchester estate.

Saying she refused to cooperate and promptly liquidate the estate's assets, Shearn's children petitioned the court in April 1954 to remove her as "unfit" to be an executor. They believed the house on Sixty-ninth Street was Shearn's major asset, and she owed $14,000 in back taxes on it. They said she'd refused to pay for their father's funeral or the judgments and hadn't given them their inherited property, which was locked in a warehouse. Warren filed his accounting over her objections. One day she answered her door to find a process server trying to hand her a petition asking her to resign, but Dorothea claimed to be a housekeeper. The second time the server came, a man answered the door and slammed it shut before the papers could be served.

For the next six years, Dorothea stalled and evaded and pleaded illness, infuriating all around her. She ran through fifteen lawyers while three co-executors came and went, each eventually begging the court to release him from his responsibilities. When any of them sought to be paid for his time, she said she was "determined to put them through the wringer and make them sweat." When one of her lawyers died, his wife blamed Dorothea.

She refused to sell the house on Sixty-ninth Street, claiming at various times that Shearn had wanted to give it to her, that she'd been showing it to buyers, and that she was using it for storage of Shearn's records, records she'd later claim were stolen by a drunken caretaker. Meanwhile, the Internal Revenue Service was dunning her for years of unpaid back taxes, estate taxes, and gift taxes. Hauled into court, Dorothea condemned what she called a "vicious proceeding."

A year after the will was filed, her husband's children sued to take the estate away from her, and she hired William Zeckendorf's law firm to defend her. When the court ordered a co-executor be named to help settle the estate, she refused to sign the stipulation. Meanwhile, the tax bills against the estate kept growing, more lawyers came and went, and after the children blocked her attempt to put the Sixty-ninth Street house in her name alone, Dorothea abandoned Manhattan for Westchester. In June 1956, she appeared in court, pleading her case. Her husband had been ill for years, she said, and she'd cared for him night and day. Was it any wonder that after his death, she'd lost his will and had a breakdown? Finally the children gave up and sold her their interest in the town house; they received $25,000 and the personal effects Shearn had left to them. Nine months later, Dorothea's latest lawyer suggested she be examined by a psychiatrist in order to explain her continuing failure to pay taxes.

In the spring of 1957, the latest co-executor petitioned the court to replace her, pointing out that money was owed to many parties, among them Shearn's sister. In response, Dorothea sued him and Shearn's kids, and then refused to cooperate with her latest lawyer, who, of course, resigned. Shearn's sister, meanwhile, was threatening to sue for the money owed to her. Dorothea demanded a jury trial. Summoned to court, she failed to show, claiming again to be ill.

In May 1958, the judge overseeing the estate finally turned it over to a referee. For the next two years, he held hearings that Dorothea skipped, either because she'd changed lawyers again or because she had a convenient and newly discovered heart ailment. By the fall of 1960, despite all her stalling, the referee filed his accounting. Two months later, Dorothea filed a motion to reject it, charging that he'd caused her to succumb again to nervous exhaustion. The motion was denied, as was another requesting that she be relieved of paying both the referee's "confiscatory fee" and the bills submitted by court stenographers. Then the surrogate directed her to sell both the Sixty-ninth Street house and the Katonah property to pay the estate's debts. His decision memorandum began with a reference to "prolonged and wasting" litigation that "calls to mind Jarndyce v. Jarndyce" in Charles Dickens's *Bleak House*.

"It is time that the executrix faces reality," the judge said.

The next accounting of the estate took another two years—and only then did Dorothea finally give in to the inevitable and sell Shearn's two properties, as well as the house she'd bought in Bedford. She ran ads for the vacant Manhattan town house, which was in total disrepair, calling the place palatial. When she got an offer, she refused it and raised the price. Years later, a neighbor would describe the house as a shambles, full of old books and garbage, damaged pipes and plaster, and pigeon droppings. "Mrs. Shearn, who had a fondness for birds, left the skylight open for the benefit of the pigeons, and they made themselves at home," *The New York Times* reported. "She was possessed of the idea that the house was being burglarized, although there was no furniture in it."

In June 1964, she disposed of the neglected, overgrown, and dilapidated estate in Katonah. Over the years it would pass through many hands; it is now part of a huge property owned by the fashion designer Ralph Lauren.

In the end, after paying all her bills, Dorothea was left with nothing but the two Manhattan town houses. "Money was hidden or stolen and property was sold far below market value," says a great-nephew, William Georgiades. Years later, relatives hired private investigators to try to learn where it had all gone. Shearn's daughter, too, "was interested in delving into it," says Tony Kerrigan, "but my father put the kibosh on it. He didn't want to scare up gossip. He said, 'I don't want my wife's picture in the *Journal-American.*' He felt Dorothea had it sewn up. Whatever money he had went to her."

Peter Pruyn last saw Dorothea at the funeral of his stepfather, Clarence Shearn Jr., in 1961, "wearing black from head to foot, a black broad-brimmed hat, like she was in a stage role," he says. "She was the last person on earth who should have been there."

Clothilde Cavendish-Bentinck tried to be a good sister again. "My mother would go around and she wouldn't let her in," says Graubard. "She was fed up with my mother and wouldn't speak to her. And my mother was sort of worried about her."

A former secretary would stop by now and then to check in on her. But one day, in 1967, Dorothea didn't answer, and the housekeeper told him that her boss had become so paranoid, withdrawn, and abusive that she refused to speak to her anymore. When Dorothea's doorman said he hadn't seen her in some time, the secretary called the police, who broke down the door and found her dead in her bathtub. The coroner estimated she'd been there five days.

21

JOHN D. ROCKEFELLER JR.'S LAST YEARS AT 740 PARK WERE JUST WHAT he deserved: quiet and dignified. With the tenants back in charge, the ship was run tightly. A new president at Douglas Gibbons who also served as secretary of the 740 Corporation even asked tenants to ensure that their maids stopped shaking their mops out of windows or in the service stairwells.

Junior remained attentive. In November 1955, a small piece of stone dropped off the tenth-floor facade, ripping through the Park Avenue canopy. "The incident will undoubtedly reach Mr. Rockefeller and, I am afraid, by that time the size of the piece of stone may have increased considerably," a vice president of Hegeman-Harris, the original builders, wrote to a Rockefeller factotum, to assure him that the occurrence was neither unusual for a limestone building nor a cause for alarm.

Junior initially planned to connect his apartment with the one above that he'd bought from Thelma Foy's estate, even filing plans to do so, to create the fabled triplex the newspapers would speak of ever after. But he never completed the job, using 17B as an attic instead for excess furniture and central-air-conditioning equipment. Like Clarence Shearn, Junior was isolated by his last wife, Martha, toward the end of his life. They were rarely in New York, spending the winter in Tucson and the spring and fall in Williamsburg. In 1952, he sold his Pocantico estate to his children; five years later, he donated $1 million to Colonial Williamsburg to open a folk art center named for Abby. He was slowing, declining, in 1959, suffering from chronic bronchitis and a prostate condition. "When he came in, the heat was turned on, even in summer," says Charles Cowles, who arrived at 740 as a teenage tenant.

Junior had just had prostate surgery, but kept the results secret from his family and left for Tucson that winter, supposedly to recuperate. Soon, though, he was back in the hospital, and remained there almost five months; his children only knew because his nurse kept them informed. When David insisted that his father get a second opinion, he got back a letter expressing fury over his second-guessing of Martha and demanding that his children refrain from intervening in matters of his health. It was cold, hostile, and signed with a shaky hand. David later learned it had been written by Martha. Junior had refused to sign it several times, but she sent it anyway.

When David finally showed up unannounced in Tucson, he learned that Martha had been bedridden for weeks herself and hadn't seen her husband. David was shocked at his father's weakened condition. Nonetheless, Junior begged his youngest son to take care of his widow. Junior was eighty-six years old when he died on May 11, 1960. The cause of death was given as pneumonia and heart strain. His body was brought back to Pocantico by his sons Laurance and Nelson, who'd arrived just before he died. Nelson was already in the day's headlines; it was rumored he'd be Richard Nixon's Republican running mate for the upcoming presidential race. John F. Kennedy, the husband of 740's Jacqueline Bouvier, was running hard for the Democratic nomination.

Back in New York, Junior was cremated and his ashes interred next to Abby's in the family cemetery. His widow did not attend the private family service, nor is she mentioned in press accounts of the public memorial at Riverside Church. Junior's $160 million estate was split between Martha (who received more than $50 million tax-free) and the Rockefeller Brothers Fund, a philanthropic foundation created twenty years earlier. Martha got the apartment and the right to dispose of the principal in the trust Junior left her. Thanks to Milbank, Tweed's work, the estate only paid $3 million in taxes, while the law firm's fees totaled about $1 million.

In September 1960, John D. Rockefeller Jr.'s 740 lease was transferred into the name of his widow, Martha Baird Rockefeller. A month later, she jotted a note to herself, summarizing vital facts about her new apartment. She owned 4,815 shares of the 740 Corporation, appraised at $350,000. The market value of the apartment was estimated to be $378,800. Her maintenance was going to rise forty-eight cents a share the following June, an annual increase of $2,311. As the years passed, she would jot one more thing down, that "my apartment," as she put it, encompassed thirty-four rooms and seventeen baths on three floors. She wrote it again and again, as if she didn't quite believe it.

"We used to go and see her," says David Rockefeller. "She lived a . . . very secluded life and saw very few people, almost no one. She did very little entertaining and went out very little."

Even though Martha Rockefeller played no official role in the building's governance, Douglas Gibbons would dutifully keep her informed about 740, providing her with copies of the monthly rent rolls, first typed, then eventually computerized.

She kept the first set, sent to her in 1961, and annotated it over the years. When someone sold, the name of the buyer was penciled in and underlined in red, a blue slash meant "have met or know," and there were penciled notes on when and where she'd met her neighbors, whether they were listed in *WW* (*Who's Who*) or the *SR* (*Social Register*), what number spouse they were on, whether they had mutual friends ("friends of W. Aldrich," she noted of the Hills), and sometimes their religions, physical descriptions ("tall, blond, slight English accent and very nice," she wrote of one new tenant), and even the names of their servants (Mrs. Garvan's chauffeur was Willy).

Many apartments had changed hands in the years since her late husband had made them co-ops again, so a crib sheet was probably useful. Junior's widow could still rest easy that most of her neighbors were, as the saying goes, "people like us." But that didn't quite mean "social." Seven forty "was really known for money," says the realtor Alice Mason, who has sold apartments there since the 1960s, "it really was never known as a *Social Register* building. It was always a money building." Or, more precisely, as James T. Lee envisioned it, a building where the meritocracy met the Episcocracy for the common good of both.

The Rockefellers were the thread that tied the two groups together. Langbourne Meade Williams Jr. and his wife, Elizabeth, had rented Beek Hoppin's apartment in 1944, long before Rockefeller bought 740 and made it a co-op again. She was a Stillman and a niece of several Rockefellers, as well as a *Mayflower* descendant in the line of the first governor of the Plymouth Colony. He came from the actual colonial Williamsburg, a descendant of one of the governing Randolphs of Virginia and of Martha Washington's brother.

A nephew of the controller of the currency in the Wilson administration, a controversial Democrat who'd charged big banks with usury, Langbourne junior joined the family investment bank in Richmond, Virginia, in the late 1920s. He was soon sued for libel for $1 million, after he accused executives of a sulfur firm—his family had a stake in the company—of self-dealing. He ended up replacing them, moving to New York to run the company under John Hay Whitney until 1957, then succeeding Whitney as chairman until 1967.

Williams had married Elizabeth Stillman in 1930. Resettled at 740, she led a busy and respectable life as treasurer and then president of the Junior League, president of the Colony Club, the first female trustee of the Children's Aid Society, and a trustee of her alma mater, Vassar, of the Community Service Society, and of the Association for Improving the Condition of the Poor. She was childless when she died in 1956. Three years later, Williams married Frances Pinckney Breckenridge, the niece of a Richmond newspaper publisher. Martha Baird carefully noted it when the second Mrs. Williams was elected to the Opera Association in 1964. The Williamses sold their apartment and moved to a town house nearby the following year.

Alfred Caspary, the porcelain collector Junior had tried to slide into Clarence Shearn's apartment, finally did move into 740 several years later. Caspary's father, a cloak manufacturer and importer, had gone insane in 1904 and been committed to an asylum. The family, trying to economize, sold its house on Seventy-first Street. Alfred became a stockbroker at the age of twenty-one and amassed a fortune of almost $15 million, but he hardly left a mark until his death, when he was revealed to be one of the world's greatest stamp collectors. Caspary's true worth was revealed, too, when he donated millions, including the proceeds of the sale of his stamps, and his porcelain collection, to hospitals, art museums, and the Rockefeller Institute. His was the largest donation ever made to that school by a non-Rockefeller.

Other tenants boasted Rockefeller-sized fortunes without Rockefeller connections. George Embiricos, the ship owner, had rented a small C-line apartment from James T. Lee in 1950, when many of the rich Greeks in New York lived at 998 Fifth. "We were staying at the Savoy Plaza, and somehow he found this as a rental, which was strange," says Doda Goulandris, his ex-wife, also from a Greek shipping clan. "Rockefeller was a gentleman and sold it for a very, very low price," she continues. "I don't know why he did that.

"It was nothing, empty," when the Embiricoses rented it, she continues. "I made it very pretty with M. Samuel, the Paris decorator. We put green velvet walls and red silk in the dining room, very pretty doors, and we had a lot of pictures." Especially Impressionists, like a version of Cézanne's *Cardplayers*, the only one in a private collection, estimated to be worth $100 million by *ARTnews* magazine.

Irene Guggenheim rented the same year Embiricos did, though the lease was in the name of one of her late husband's partners, a onetime office boy named Albert Thiele. Irene was one of five children of V. Henry Rothschild, a German shirtmaker so successful that in 1892 he erected one of New York's first modern office buildings and employed seven thousand people. In 1895, she'd married Solomon R. Guggenheim, one of the five surviving children of Meyer, all of them descended from one of the first Jewish families in Switzerland. Meyer was a lace importer turned silver miner whose empire eventually included the mining and smelting of precious metals all around the world.

In 1937, Solomon Guggenheim, an heir to that business, created an art fund to augment his collection of what was called nonobjectivist art. Like Abby Rockefeller, he was a modernist, his walls thickly hung with abstract paintings by Kandinsky, Modigliani, Chagall, Picasso, and Léger. He died at eighty-eight in 1949 and left $8 million to pay for the

Solomon R. Guggenheim Museum on Fifth Avenue. He donated the land it stands on, too. Just after buying her apartment, Irene Guggenheim died there in 1954 at age eighty-five. "She was lying there two, three days," remembers Patrick O'Connor. "One of the butlers said, 'Come see Mrs. laid out.' "

FREDERIC AND ALIDA CAMP WERE EAGER TO DOWNSIZE, SO THEY grabbed the Guggenheim apartment when Irene's estate sold it and put the larger 4/5B on the market at $65,000. They quickly found a buyer, but, in a first since the building had gone co-op again, the applicant was turned down by the board. A cryptic note in John D. Rockefeller's files indicates the buyer was likely the actress Joan Crawford.

The Camps were friends of Junior's eldest, John D. Rockefeller III, who named one of his children after Alida. They lived at 71 East Seventy-first Street for fifteen years. But one day not long after their move, Frederic found that he couldn't get up from a restaurant table. He was diagnosed with multiple sclerosis and died in 1963.

"The building was full of little old ladies" like Alida, who lived on in her splendid apartment, says a family friend who requests anonymity. In the summer of 1964, Alida and Martha Rockefeller formed a committee of two to redecorate the lobby at Mrs. Rockefeller's expense because the "worn-out" furniture was "no longer suitable in the entrance of a building of this quality." It finally cost Martha $5,100 ($30,000 in 2004 dollars).

Unlike her right-wing family members, Alida "never talked politics. She was too much of a lady." She had moved to Florida during her husband's illness, but kept the apartment and sometimes lent it out. "A German cook and an Irish maid waited on me every day except Thursday, when they were off," says a guest who lived in Frederic's bedroom for a year, enjoying the view from his balcony, which looked downtown to the RCA tower.

"You'd have thought, 'That poor old lady,' " he says of Alida. "She did not live fancy." She drove a 1958 Mercedes coupe, smoked Philip Morris cigarettes, and had an angular, weather-beaten face like Katharine Hepburn. Alida had four adopted children but didn't get along with them.

"She wasn't warm," says the friend. "They'd be rude to her at the dinner table and she'd ignore them. She'd fire any nanny they got close to."

When she put the apartment on the market in 1971, it, like the Rocke-feller duplex, had few takers. Times were tough; few wanted expensive apartments like these. When she finally found buyers, they were turned down by the board—the second time that happened to her. But she should have known better; inexplicably, Alida had tried to sell to an ac-tress again, only this time the applicant was also a singer and a leftist. Barbra Streisand, just hitting the peak of her fame, getting divorced from her first husband, Elliott Gould, and still living in a six-room apart-ment on the West Side, wanted the place and came to see it in her chauf-feured Bentley. "We all heard about that," says Patrick O'Connor. "They were worried about parties. And she was a Democratic fund-raiser, so the Republicans didn't want her."

THERE WERE SOME SERIOUS REPUBLICANS AT 740 PARK. TWO OF THE most serious were Preston and May Davie, who'd arrived in 1953. "My family is very interesting, extremely strange, a very odd group of people with huge egos," says their granddaughter Deirdre Davie, an administra-tor at the University of Virginia. "It's a lot of dysfunctional people, and it goes back generations. When I was very young, I decided they were way too strange for me and I would just go off and live my own life. There was so much money, it brought out the worst in people. There was a huge tendency to manipulate people. They could get away with it. Money perpetuates madness." Preston Davie was a descendant of a Rev-olutionary War general who went on to found the University of North Carolina and serve as that state's governor and America's minister to France. Davie's grandfather was in the Confederate army and the U.S. Congress and served as an American minister to Spain. Born in Louisville, Davie graduated from Harvard Law School and worked as a partner in his father's Kentucky law firm, then joined a New York firm in 1907. He'd met Emily Bedford, an equestrian, at that year's Louisville Horse Show, and she was no doubt part of the lure of the city. She was the daughter of Edward T. Bedford, a director of Standard Oil and the president of the Corn Products Refining Company, the very same company where, the Hearst newspapers had just falsely claimed, Junior built a stockade for his hobo slave laborers.

The son of a wood-carver from England, Edward Bedford was educated in public schools and had worked as a flour salesman before getting into his family's lubricating-oil business. When Standard Oil bought it, the mutton-chopped, two-hundred-pound businessman's fortunes rose, as did he through the ranks of the Rockefellers' trust to director in 1903. His brother Frederick, a cousin, Alfred, and son, C. E. Bedford, all worked for Standard, too. After forming a company with them and other top Standard men in 1900 to refine sweeteners and starches from corn, Bedford began a trade war against the Glucose Trust, the giant in the field, an $80 million company. It ended up merging with his, and he became president of Corn Products.

The Bedfords could afford to be a part of New York society but kept their distance, living in a town house in Brooklyn, on their farm in Connecticut (where Edward raised flowers and horses), and on a winter estate in Florida. "He had the simplest, most homely life you can imagine," says Preston and May's son Bedford Davie. "He would get up at 4:30, have his breakfast and a cold bath, walk down his pier [his farm sat on Long Island Sound], then jump on the train and go to work. If it wasn't for him, none of us would have a plug nickel."

Preston Davie married Emily Bedford in 1910, a year before her father quit Standard Oil. Edward Bedford remained a major stockholder—holdings that made him a multimillionaire. His cousin Alfred became Standard Oil's president in 1916 and, following its reorganization in 1917, its chairman.

The Davies traveled in nice circles; Preston was friends with Alfred Vanderbilt, and one of Emily's nephews married one of Mrs. Seward Webb Jr.'s sisters. They moved to Tuxedo Park, and Preston went to work as the head of the legal department at Corn Products Refining. "But he never bothered to show up for work," says his grandson. "He was busy being a Kentucky colonel. There was this whole litigation about glucose and fructose and whether it should be regulated, and this was the lifeblood of the company, but he was too busy. He dropped the ball, and he was fired when they divorced. After you divorce the favorite daughter, you're not going to be staying with the company very long."

That was in April 1929, when, finding themselves "temperamentally different," as Preston put it, Emily moved into the Savoy Plaza in New York while he took an apartment at 920 Fifth. "He got caught practicing black arts with another woman," says Bedford Davie. "That's the quote that was handed down in the family. He and May [Ladenburg, who would become his second wife] were dallying around because Emily was not exactly on fire in bed."

Early in 1930, Emily Davie took the inevitable trip to Reno, charging constant and marked neglect over three years. "He would absent himself from home for long periods, take his vacations alone, take her to no places of entertainment nor social affairs, but go alone, and he would take no interest in anything in which she was interested," said the *Times*. "The conduct made her ill, nervous and unhappy." Mrs. Davie won custody of their children, a sixteen-year-old son and a fourteen-year-old daughter, and though there was no indication of who got what, their property settlement was said to be "unusually large."[2]

Preston Davie moved fast, remarrying almost immediately and ending up at least as well-off. His bride, Eugenie May Ladenburg, was a descendant of Ebenezer Stevens, who fought under George Washington and was a founder of Tammany Hall, the headquarters of the New York Democratic Party. She was a great-great-granddaughter of Thomas Jefferson's treasury secretary; the granddaughter of the president of the Sixth National Bank; a cousin of the historian Samuel Eliot Morison; and the daughter of the investment banker Adolf Ladenburg, who suffered a painful malady for which he was taking morphine. He disappeared from the steamer *Niagara* as it left the Bahamas in a furious gale and was presumed to have fallen overboard. May, as she'd be called, was eleven months old at the time. At twenty-one, she'd inherited $10 million.

After Ladenburg's death, May's mother was reported engaged at least four times, but remained single and the mistress of the Oasis, her estate in Westbury, Connecticut, where Preston and May took up residence as well. May, until then known mostly for her skill with a gun (she was a champion trapshooter as a girl and hunted all around the world), immediately became active—despite her family history—in Republican politics, named finance chairman of the party's state committee just after Franklin Roosevelt's election in 1932. Though her husband had once been friendly with FDR, "her zeal grew in proportion to New Deal proposals," the *Times* would later say.

While May played politics, her husband retreated into history. He collected a library on the history of North Carolina; Americana, including Gilbert Stuart and Rembrandt Peale portraits; manuscripts and autographs; and even suits of armor. "The stuff he had was not to be believed," says his grandson. "He just wanted to know about his family, but he kept acquiring all this stuff, more and more history. He did nothing but history."

May was a delegate to the Republican Party convention for the 1936 presidential election, and then took up arms for the candidate, Alfred M. Landon, writing daily columns for the *New York Herald Tribune*. She said Roosevelt's reelection would threaten the American way of life. After doing volunteer work during World War II, she became chairman of the New York County Republican Committee's women's auxiliary in 1946 and worked for Robert Taft until he was defeated for the Republican nomination by Dwight D. Eisenhower in 1952.

The Davies moved to apartment 4/5D at 71 East Seventy-first Street the next year, and in 1958 May emerged from the shadows when she tried to take over the New York County Republican Committee. She was described by a party operative as having "the best two-fisted brain of any girl I've ever dealt with." She was sixty-three years old at the time. Her husband could not have cared less. "Patrick," he'd tell the elevator man O'Connor, "I understand May is going to have some politicians upstairs. Don't take them to 5. I don't want to see them."

Republican candidates made the Davie home one of their first stops on any visit to New York. "A big dinner in the biggest dining room anyone has ever seen," Bedford Davie recalls. Richard Nixon came in 1960 (May was a convention delegate again that year) and again in 1969. "I was marched downstairs in my pj's, terrified, to meet Nixon," says Bedford Davie. "I would not get out of bed," boasts his sister, Deirdre. "May was Lady Bountiful, name-dropping all over the place. I guess she was important, but she made sure you knew it. She wasn't humble."

Just before Nixon's run for a second term as president, Preston Davie died in the apartment at age eighty-six. Bedford connects his widowed grandmother's demise with Nixon's subsequent downfall in the Watergate scandal. "Her biggest disappointment was when Nixon turned out to be guilty," he says. "My God, that was a catastrophe. She was so undone about that, I can't tell you. Just beside herself. She sort of lost interest in everything, had sort of a very small stroke, then she slipped in the bathtub and broke her hip and her arm. She never recovered, really." Though she tried physical therapy, squeezing a ball of putty, "she was gripping it harder and harder every time she thought about [Watergate]," says Davie. "She had a very moral character. She took the whole thing quite personally. She couldn't believe she'd been hoodwinked by this man."

May Davie, who'd helped develop the New York Heart Association and was its honorary chairman, died of heart failure at her home on September 19, 1975, thirteen months after Richard Nixon resigned.

ISABEL "MISSY" LEIB SEATED JUNIOR NEXT TO HER ONE NIGHT AT DINNER—the Leibs and the Rockefellers were old friends—and when he called her Mrs. Leib (which rhymes with "imbibe"), as he always did, she asked him to please call her Isabel. "Mrs. Leib," he replied, "when I married Abby, I promised her I'd never call another woman by her first name."

George and Isabel Leib were more social than the Rockefellers. Leib, an investment banker, was tall and taciturn, a slow-talking storyteller. Missy was a short, freckled Southern sparkplug who couldn't shut up. "Oh, you must have more enthusiasm!" she would tell her grandchildren. Their friends in the building included the Foys and May Davie; George worked with May as the chairman of the Republican National Finance Committee. The Duke and Duchess of Windsor (he the former king of England, she the American divorcée he'd abdicated to marry), Millicent Rogers, the granddaughter of another Standard Oil founder, and the Gilbert Millers (she was the daughter of the financier Jules Bache) were typical guests in what had once been Bayard Hoppin's sprawling apartment, 12/13D.

Isabel Leib was related to James Buchanan, the fifteenth American president, and was the granddaughter of the founder of *The Louisville Courier-Journal* and the daughter of its editor. During the Civil War, her grandfather evaded arrest by Union troops and published the paper from behind Confederate lines. When he ran out of newsprint, he published on wallpaper. He also founded Naples, Florida, before he was hit by a streetcar and died in 1902. George Carr Leib's family was from Cologne, Germany. En route to a German settlement in Ohio, his grandfather stopped in Louisville, where he ran a meatpacking factory. His son George was always "slightly ashamed of his roots," says his grandson Barclay. George went to San Francisco as a teenager and was there when the San Francisco earthquake struck in 1906. Afterward, with no more than a high-school education, he found work selling municipal bonds. When his boss announced his retirement a few years later and offered his salesmen the furniture, they pooled their resources and founded the first investment bank on the West Coast, Blyth, Witter & Co., in 1914. Leib, the junior-most partner, invested $2,000 for one-fifth of the firm. He had to sell a fur coat to raise it. After an argument with Blyth ten years later, Witter left the partnership (and went on to found Dean Witter, since absorbed into Morgan Stanley).

Leib opened branches of Blyth & Co. in Chicago, New York, and Paris, where his future wife was told to look him up. Married not long afterward in the American Cathedral, they moved back to California, where their three boys were born. In 1933, Leib moved to New York to save that office, which had ballooned with the stock market and had 170 employees. "Charley Blyth asked my grandfather to shrink it to seven," says Barclay Leib. "He almost missed the payroll a couple times." J. P. Morgan helped him out, and the firm survived and prospered, floating bonds for, among others, South American governments, the Golden Gate Bridge, and the Ford Motor Company.

The Leibs lived at 625 Park, where their landlords were the cosmetics queen Helena Rubinstein and her husband, Artchil Gourielli-Tchkonia, a Georgian prince. In 1955, when Leib was named vice chairman of Blyth & Co., he moved to 740 Park with his wife, sons, the English couple who worked as their butler and maid, and a cook. "It was the first house he ever owned," says his son Bruce. "My father hated to be tied down. Obviously, the price was right." He was one of the first "outside" purchasers after the building went co-op again, buying from Alfred Caspary's estate in 1955. The estate lawyer, who knew Leib, alerted him to the good deal.

They paid about $150,000, their son Bruce thinks. "They were beloved and got in quite easily," says their daughter-in-law.

Isabel Leib, a little superstitious, had the signs changed on their landing to call the thirteenth floor 12A. The apartment was basic when they moved in, although the library was paneled. Family portraits filled the walls in the living room. The upstairs hallways were hung with Missy's own photographs. The Leibs slept in separate bedrooms. "He was a snorer, and my mother couldn't stand that," says Bruce Leib.

Leib and Frederic Camp replaced Robert Vanderbilt and Marshall Field on the board in the mid-1950s. Leib would serve as a director for the next decade and help set standards that would last for decades more. Though in years to come, there would be "some pretty cruddy people in the building," as his daughter-in-law puts it, during Leib's reign, says his son Bruce, "it was a pretty tight ship; you had to mind your p's and q's and be thought fitting."

As the years went by, and Leib had less to do, he began walking to work on Wall Street every morning. The two-hour stroll was his daily exercise. But he also exercised his will on the board, where he tried to be a restraining influence, the presence of Colonel Schiff and Mrs. Guggenheim notwithstanding, "I think there was some anti-Semitism on the board," says Bruce Leib. "It was practically 100 percent Christian. There weren't any Jews, I'm sure of that. The Jewish-versus-Christian feeling was quite strong, although not overwhelming. My father wasn't [anti-Semitic]; it was the person that counted. Mr. Rockefeller was like my father, but there had to be some agreement, and the conservative wing would overrule them and say, 'Let's wait.' If the tide was against him, he wouldn't step up unless he knew the person and wanted to go to bat for them."

THE CO-OP BOARD'S TONE WAS SET BY ITS CHAIRMAN, MORRIS HADLEY, who, like Leib and Rockefeller, might be best described as a progressive conservative. Hadley's wife, Kay, was not only chairman of the board at that bastion of upper-class feminism, Vassar, she was also on the executive committee of the Planned Parenthood Federation, promoting birth control. But behind closed doors, the Hadleys expected their children to adhere to old-fashioned standards of behavior and sat on the fence about the era's subtle, lingering anti-Semitism. Several of their offspring ended up estranged as a result.

The Hadleys' private attitudes, though kept out of the workplace, were reflected in the posture of 740's co-op board, where anti-Semitism or the appearance of it was often explained away as mere social strictness. "The Hadleys get to the crux of the story," says a New Yorker whose family was close to them. "It underscores how high anti-Semitism ran. Jews were considered an alien race by the WASP aristocracy of New York."

"My mother was a Scot," says Arthur Hadley, who enlisted in the Army on his eighteenth birthday "to get away from my family and what they wanted me to be. My mother's slogan was, 'Marry a rich woman and put that money to work.' The Army took me out of the WASP world and made me realize what real people were. If you worked hard you got ahead. They were parents who'd beat up on you if you weren't 100 percent successful and yet were in competition with you. It instills a basic lack of confidence."

Like her mother and her grandmother before her, the Hadleys' elder daughter, Katherine, who called Winky, went to Vassar. All well and good. But while there, she converted to Judaism. "That caused a problem," says a relative. "She was a black sheep, a rebel. Her mother was angrier than her father. She expected everyone to toe the line and [Winky] didn't. It was more about her being a rebel than about anti-Semitism."

Then, in 1952, Winky married. A friend of the elder Hadleys was told that Kay Hadley objected to her new son-in-law's profession, gardening. But actually, he was a chiropractor, much older than Winky, and a Jew, albeit a nonobservant one.

Kay Hadley was known to joke that people thought her husband, Morris, was Jewish because of his first name. Morris Hadley, tall and jolly, with blue eyes and gray hair and a cigar or a pipe in his mouth, "was not anti-Semitic," says his then-daughter-in-law, Leila Luce, at least not in the way many of his class were at the time. "I grew up hearing my father say ghastly things," Luce continues. "In the twenties and thirties, there was a tremendous amount of anti-Semitism, but that was the norm at that point. Then things changed."

Hadley was a brilliant lawyer, and he and Kay were "very good at the business part of business relationships," says Arthur. "He entertained the whole firm, seventy-five people, at 71 East Seventy-first Street," recalls Alexander Forger, a partner. "It astounded my wife. Kay had arrived twenty minutes before the guests."

Their family ran less smoothly than Morris's career. The Hadleys were neither warm nor open people. The children were raised by nannies. "They weren't hug, kiss, slobber, take-you-to-the-kitchen-for-a-meal kind of parents," says the relative. "They were not good at the personal part," Arthur confirms. "They were a closefisted couple. They never had small dinners for one or two friends; they always had dinner dances. My father was very secretive. A lot of his standards were hidden. Sex, power, and money were never discussed at the dinner table. Never. Taboo!"

So it isn't unnatural that family members disagree about the Hadleys' attitude toward the society they were part of. Since she came from newer money, Kay Hadley was more concerned about appearances than her husband. "I don't think Father ever thought much about society," says Arthur. "He knew he was from a good family. They got into all the good dances, but it was just assumed." The elder Hadleys had always "put a lot of time and effort into maintaining their social status," thinks the relative, who is younger and knew them later in life, after they and Arthur were estranged. "Clearly, that stuff mattered a lot."

The relative insists the Hadleys were more concerned with their social standing than religious matters. "They didn't spend much time discriminating religiously; they were religious about martinis," he says. "If the gin kissed the ice for more than fifteen seconds, you dumped the jigger out and started over."

Winky did the same with her husband. Her marriage was annulled after a year, and a "get" was issued by a rabbi dissolving the union. "She didn't talk much about it," says her relative, nor does her first husband, Dr. Manus Maltz, though he confirms both the marriage and its end. "There was no problem with her parents for me," he says. "We got along fine. With her, I'm not sure." Winky promptly married another older Jewish man, a motel owner from Poughkeepsie. Ironically, her second husband, a summa cum laude Yale graduate, had spent his life trying to pass as a gentile, the relative says.

Kay was angrier than Morris—or at least made her feelings known. She stopped speaking to her daughter, and although they kept a good front up at family events, Winky was disinherited. "She wasn't left high and dry," says the relative, who explains that she remained the beneficiary of family trusts. But it wasn't only Winky and Kay. Morris disinherited his son Arthur, too, when he left his wife. "He said, 'If you leave Mary, I will never see you again,' " Arthur recalls. "I said the only thing a man could say. 'Good-bye.' " They later relented and lunched occasionally, but Arthur was never reinstated in his father's will and remains estranged from his family.

MORRIS HADLEY'S CAREER HIGH POINT WAS PROBABLY THE 1955 merger of the Chase National Bank and the Bank of Manhattan, which he engineered with John McCloy, the Milbank, Tweed partner Junior had hoped would move into 740. Frederic W. Ecker, a relative of the chairman of Metropolitan Life, was elected to the newly merged bank's board along with Hadley.

That year Hadley interviewed Isaac "Ike" Shapiro, who became Milbank, Tweed's first openly Jewish partner. Hadley and his partners were "really superb, patrician, noblesse oblige people who didn't regard law as a business; it was a profession," Shapiro says. He was soon dining at 740. Hadley "loved to tell stories and was very sociable," says Shapiro, "but he was extremely discreet, never spoke about his childhood, his upbringing, his father. He told professional anecdotes. He was friendly without letting his guard down." His wife, Kay, on the other hand, was "independent and outgoing" and "made no bones about how upset they were that their daughter had married a Jewish man."

Milbank, Tweed had hired Jewish lawyers since 1922. An Irish Catholic made partner in 1957, the same year Shapiro arrived fresh from law school. There was one Jewish partner before him, but like Colonel Schiff he was passing. "With a name like Isaac Shapiro," Shapiro says, "there's no doubt. There was [anti-Semitism] as far as their daughter's marriage but not insofar as employing and promoting a Jewish lawyer. Professionally, Morris Hadley was an open, decent person who never exhibited either directly or indirectly any sort of prejudice. He would never show it in public. Kay shared some of her prejudice, if you will, trying to come to grips with the loss of her daughter."

Winky Hadley's second husband died in 1970. Winky was murdered four years later, en route home with her youngest child from Israel, where she was chairman of the board of the American College in Jerusalem. Her TWA flight was bombed by the Abu Nidal Palestinian terrorist faction over the Aegean Sea, killing all eighty-eight people aboard. Almost to the end of his life, Morris Hadley continued going to work in the financial district downtown, often walking there from 740. He died in 1979 in his apartment. Kay followed her husband in 1980.

22

As in the days of James T. Lee, a few 740 families lived apart from, even unaware of, the building's influential web. Bartholomew Barry was a textile broker from a humble Boston Irish background. His wife, Lillian, was the daughter of the Coal King of Brooklyn, Michael Francis Burns. Married in 1908, they had a house in Rumson and in 1948, before the co-op conversion, rented an A-line apartment at 740.

The Barrys were fortunate. Burns sold his company just before the crash, so his fortune was liquid and largely unaffected. Cotton brokerage was flourishing, and Barry sold cotton canvas to tire and sneaker makers. "He knew the Keds family," says his granddaughter Sandy Packard. "He provided the uppers." He had a yacht and a house on Shelter Island and gave enough to the church that he had his own pew at St. Patrick's Cathedral. But after the war, Barry retired, and then died in 1951.

When Lillian Barry died, the apartment was sold, but not before two turndowns. Sandy Packard's mother and her sister, who had inherited it, were told the purchasers were rejected because they were Jewish. "That's what we thought," Packard says. "They were very annoyed."

. . .

LIKE THE MEN WHO PUT ROSARIO CANDELA IN BUSINESS, MICHAEL DEL Balso was an immigrant from Italy who struck it rich doing heavy construction in New York. The Del Balso Construction Company built roads and bridges, not luxury apartment buildings, but it made Del Balso's son, Anthony, rich enough to live like a Rockefeller—and free enough to become 740 Park's first wife-swapper.

Michael Del Balso came to America from Italy in 1902 and by the time he died in 1947 had built structures worth $200 million, including parts of the East River Drive, several subway lines, the Triborough and George Washington bridges, a steel plant, and storm sewers in Washington, D.C. Just after Anthony took over his father's company, he won a contract to connect the Bronx River and Cross County parkways. Jobs like that made it easy for him to afford the $647 monthly rent for apartment 2/3A (the equivalent of $5,000 a month in 2004), and a few years later, the $12,000 purchase price (about $93,000 today).

In 1938, Del Balso had married Mary Therese Perrotty, a girl from the New York suburb Yonkers. By the time they moved to 740 twelve years later, they'd had two children and become leading figures in New York's equestrian world. Anthony had long been a foxhunter, and together they took riding lessons at the Ox Ridge Hunt Club in Darien, Connecticut, and Secor Farms Riding Club in White Plains, New York, both among the finest riding and training stables in the Northeast.

"Most of us good riders started taking lessons with Gordon Wright, the premier riding teacher," says one of their equestrian friends. "He produced all the great riders of his day. Somehow the Del Balsos hooked in with him and became very good clients."

Secor Farms "was a bit of a Peyton Place," says the horseman. "There was a lot of socializing." Wright loved the ladies, as did many in their circle. "There was a lot of sleeping with this one, sleeping with that one," says the equestrian. "I had a girlfriend who took lessons from Gordon, and at one point she stayed with him a few days. He was fat, older, and bald, but I'm positive they slept together. He was the vortex."

Into that vortex rode two more of Wright's students, Emile Albert Berol and his wife Suzanne. Albert Berol's great-grandfather, Daniel

Berolzheimer, had founded the Eagle Pencil Company before the Civil War. After graduating from Harvard and Cambridge, Berol had joined the family firm, married in 1945, and had two children. "The Berols lived on a wonderful estate in Bedford Village," says the equestrian. "They were old money. Very, very horsey, very aristocratic, very intelligent, very wealthy, Jewish blue bloods."

The Berols also took lessons at Secor Farms, and they "ended up going on weekend hunts together" with the Del Balsos, says the equestrian. Mary Del Balso and Suzanne Berol were even photographed in a stable together for *Town & Country*, promoting a 1955 horse show they helped run, and toiled together on horse show committees through the end of the 1950s. They and their children all rode and competed alongside each other. "It was almost incestuous," says the equestrian. "We were this tight little clique, all of us so close. We rode, took lessons, hunted, and ate together."

Anthony Del Balso soon became a top rider, competing with professionals. But his wife, Mary, though "very, very attractive" and "a social type," was "a low-level rider," says their equestrian friend. Suzanne Berol, on the other hand, was "not as attractive, but she was more a horse person than Mary. Her horsiness and intellect attracted Tony." Though he rode, too, Albert Berol was "never like Del Balso on a horse," so "he was left out."

"Then they swapped," the equestrian says. "It was a scandal!"

It wasn't quite that simple. By about 1962, Suzanne Berol and Anthony Del Balso had fallen in love. The two couples divorced, and the newlywed Del Balsos moved to Unionville, Pennsylvania, another equestrian center, leaving Mary Del Balso behind at 740. "I'd raised a family there and was very happy up to a point," she says of her husband's departure. "A year and a half later, Mr. Berol appeared in my life. I'd known him twenty-five or thirty years." She'd also known Suzanne, but didn't consider her a friend. "We may have been photographed together because we were in the same area at the same time, but that doesn't mean we were bosom buddies," she says.

"Mary bounced to a very rich situation," the equestrian says, laughing. "They found each other on the rebound, and Albert got a very pretty wife." The two new marriages were both happy and lasted longer than those that preceded them. Albert Berol died in 1993, and Suzanne and Tony Del Balso died within two weeks of each other in 1997. Mary Berol sold her apartment for just over $100,000 to the German government for its local consul general and moved to Bedford, where she is considered a local grande dame.

23

SOCIALLY EXPLOSIVE AS THE DEL BALSO–BEROL *MÉNAGE* WAS, IT WAS nothing compared with the impact Peggy Bancroft, born Margaret Wright Bedford, would have on 740 Park.

She was the daughter of Frederick H. Bedford Jr. The first Mrs. Preston Davie, Emily, was her second cousin, Robert Thurlow Vanderbilt's wife her aunt. The Rockefellers, of course, were her family's longtime business partners. So Peggy Bedford was a natural fit with 740 even before she married Thomas Moore Bancroft Jr., a grandson of Elsie Woodward. Elsie was one of the Cryder triplets, who took fin-de-siècle New York by storm. After marrying William Woodward, the head of Central Hanover Bank (later, Manufacturers Hanover) and the owner of Maryland's Belair Stud farm, Elsie became a social eminence, a late-model version of "The" Mrs. Astor.

Peggy was a friend of the Bancrofts from Long Island. Lilly Pulitzer was an old friend, too. She grew up down the street from Bancroft and attended Chapin with Peggy, who then went on to Miss Porter's School, where she met Jacqueline and Lee Bouvier. Peggy was "the prettiest thing you've ever seen," says Pulitzer. But she didn't quite manage to graduate with her class in 1949 (she finished up with the class of 1950) and was introduced to society in June 1950 at a dance given by her parents, Margaret, known as Mugsy, and Frederick Henry "Fritz" Bedford Jr., at the Creek Club in Locust Valley, overlooking Long Island Sound. Eight months later, the eighteen-year-old violet-eyed blonde was engaged to Tommy Bancroft, twenty-one, a golden boy and amateur tennis champion finishing his senior year at Princeton. The wedding took place in April 1951 at St. James Episcopal Church, next door to 740 Park. A party followed in the ballroom of the Colony Club.

Two months before the young couple had a daughter they named Muffie, Peggy's father died. Six days later, she turned twenty. The first few years of the Bancrofts' marriage were spent in temporary homes. Tommy had joined the Navy and was stationed in La Jolla, California, in Korea, and in the Mediterranean. Back in New York when he was at sea, Peggy and Muffie would stay with the Bancrofts at their apartment in the Hotel Pierre.

After Tommy returned to New York and joined his father's textile company, Mount Vernon Mills, Peggy bought apartment 15/16D from her old family friend Junior. She could afford it; she'd come into her share of her grandfather's trust. Friends believe she had $5 million (equivalent to $35 million today), although a published report pegged it at $3 million. Tommy begged her not to buy the apartment; it was too big, too expensive, too grown-up, but she insisted, and the deal closed on October 10, 1955, eight days before her twenty-third birthday. Eleven days after that, Tommy's uncle Billy Woodward was shot and killed by his wife, Ann, a former actress. Billy's mother, Elsie, considered Ann a fortune hunter, so Ann had already been ostracized by society long before what she said was an accident.

"Nothing like a murder in the country to cure what ails you," the Duchess of Windsor supposedly said, summing up the prevailing attitude toward the deed.

Peggy quickly replaced Ann as New York society's girl of the moment. "She wasn't a super-refined, uptight Newport lady going on all guns," says a family friend, Geoffrey Gates. "She was a huge flirt but not a vamp, gay, sexy, and cutesy-pie."

Seven forty Park was Peggy's stage. The society photographer Slim Aarons says, "There was always a leading hostess, and she'd decided to take over. I photographed her because she became the hostess with the mostes'.' "

Peggy was the full flowering of the Rockefeller era at 740 Park. She filled the apartment with French furniture and turned James T. Lee's former sunroom into a card room "that seems suspended over the rooftops like a tiny cage," a reporter said. "You can't help wondering how Peggy and her pals keep their minds on bridge or canasta with the panorama around them." A bedroom suite was turned into a nursery for Muffie, painted by Peggy's friend Bea Dabney with scenes from Little Boy Blue and Cinderella. The models were former beaux of Peggy's and Bea's, George Plimpton among them. "I would paint all day, then come back at night for dinner parties," says Dabney.

"People would come to see it when I was in bed," says Muffie Bancroft Murray. " 'Oh, are you awake?' 'I am now.' "

The New York social season ran from October through December. "Only the hoi polloi traveled at Christmastime," says Reinaldo Herrera, a handsome, young Venezuelan friend of the Foys, heir to a marquess, and descendant of two popes. "Everybody stayed in their own houses and gave dinners and balls." From the end of the war until the mid-1950s, Herrera's friends the Foys had been the only truly social couple in 740— a building designed for, but seriously lacking in, grand entertaining. Peggy immediately set about letting 740 be 740.

"Peggy launched herself on a social career," Cholly Knickerbocker would soon write, and she became "one of the most active Jet Set hostesses in the New York-Newport-Nassau-Palm Beach-Rome-Paris-London-Cannes-Jaipur and El Morocco axis. Peggy, who became a formidable rival of veteran Elsa Maxwell as a party-giver, is a blonde, wasp-waisted beauty."

"It came naturally to her," says Herrera. "She came from a very proper family. She was married to the grandson of one of the great hostesses of New York. She liked giving parties, and she was the best catalyst I have ever known. The three greatest were Steve Rubell, Peggy, and Elsa Maxwell. Fantastic with people. The right people, the wrong people, and everyone thought they were in the right room. She was also a person who had great fun. You could bring anyone you wanted for a drink."

Geoffrey Gates, who was a bit younger, calls himself Peggy's "giggling buddy, much as I tried to change that," he says. "She said, 'You must come to dinner.' " He'd never experienced a guest list quite like hers. "It was the early jet set. She loved the fancy, the cultivated, the rich, the poor Euro swine. There was always someone known, always some sputtering Spanish grandee."

"She loved the Europeans," agrees Letitia Gates, who married Geoffrey's cousin Demi, another old friend of Peggy's. "She loved attractive people, older people. They were the cream of the crop in New York." And the world. Aly Khan, Princess Astrid of Norway, and the Sicilian princesses Mita and Mimi di Niscemi were part of Peggy's set. But she also invited Tommy's buddies from Locust Valley, "busloads of them," says Geoffrey Gates. "Peggy gave people a chance to whoopee who weren't loose guys. She never neglected old pals; she didn't replace them. They could hold their own against the freeloaders."

The parties had a pattern. Peggy was always the last to arrive, her husband the first to leave, if he bothered coming at all. "We'd all hunker around, eat caviar, drink champagne, and see our buddies," says Geoffrey Gates. Meanwhile, Muffie would lie in Peggy's bed, watching as her mother tried on dress after dress, throwing them off in every direction. If anyone came upstairs looking for her, "Peggy was not there," says Herrera. "She was in another room, trying on the fiftieth dress." Finally she would emerge, float down the grand Candela staircase past "all the beautiful people in New York," and join the fun, says Pulitzer. "She'd come downstairs dripping borrowed jewels from Harry Winston," says Muffie, "because most of hers had been stolen at various times."

Peggy was "a great entertainer," says the bandleader Peter Duchin, "always buzzing around, introducing people, people gathered around the piano, a card game in a corner, great food, superb wine." The seating was calculated for maximum effect. "I always had a brain-dead heiress on one side and a pretty babe on the other," says Gates. And the parties never—ever—ended early. "They were incredible parties, extremely eclectic, everyone attractive, and they went very, very late," says Duchin. "Now everybody goes to bed at eleven. You're talking about a time when people actually stayed up."

All except Tommy Bancroft. He'd sometimes come back from a golf game, bag over his shoulder, while a party was in full swing. "Grumpy, handsome Tommy would be in a snit upstairs," says Gates. "He'd come downstairs and give us all shit. He didn't cotton to this. He hated the simpering people who came to dinner. He hated non-WASPs, thought they were all white trash. Once in a while he'd give a witty, sardonic toast." Sometimes he was inspired by the unctuous praise poured over his wife. "They would all be saying, 'Oh, Peggy, this is so wonderful, we toast you,' " Letitia Gates remembers. At one dinner for twenty-four, Tommy finally had enough. He stood up at his end of the long table and announced, "I'm Tommy Bancroft and I want you to know that *I'm* your host." Then he dropped his napkin and went upstairs to bed. "He had to get up in the morning," his daughter explains, "and all-night parties were not conducive to a good night's rest."

"He was known to us all as Tommy *Who?*" says Herrera. "One of the great gentlemen of New York. But Tommy was never social. Hated going out. Really hated going out."

"Peggy couldn't have cared less if he was there or not," says Joan Whiteman, a frequent guest whose in-laws also lived in the building. "She had *lots* of admirers."

Even Tommy had to admit that his wife knew her stuff. "Eat, drink, and be merry was her whole attitude," Geoffrey Gates says. "Make people happy." One party turned into an elaborate spoof that many recall to this day. "It was done at the spur of the moment," says Herrera. The guest of honor was a Michel La Rivière, who'd never been in New York. Mutual friends—he was related to a number of social families—had written to ask that Peggy receive him. The Bancrofts and friends all came as servants. One, dressed as a butler, spilled food in La Rivière's lap; Peggy acted like a Texas heiress, with badly applied false eyelashes she made sure to drop in the poor fellow's soup. Before dinner began, she insisted an empty chair at her table be filled by the elevator operator, and in walked Tommy in the liftman's uniform. Then someone took La Rivière for a tour. Behind a curtain in the library, there were Peggy and Reinaldo Herrera "in a clinch," he says. "It was very amusing. The butlers kept giving the names of terrible wines. Michel hadn't a clue what was going on."

Gates recalls a party for Juan Carlos, the future king of Spain. "I'd get there right on time, and there would be a huge bowl of caviar," he says. " 'Get Gates away from the caviar.' The party was black tie as always, and she had the waiters in black tie. Not a great idea. After dinner, I was working on a pretty lady and we needed drinks. I tugged the dinner jacket of a man and asked for a drink. He said, 'I don't know where to get them.' I realized it was the king of Spain. He laughed. She had the damnedest people."

Another night, even though she had a live-in cook, Peggy simply forgot dinner. "She quickly picked up the phone, called a hotel, and ordered dinner for thirty," says Letitia Gates. "We were all wondering what was taking so long. It was so typical of her. She was so openhearted and generous. She was a very unusual woman."

Peggy used the apartment's marble-checkerboard-floor entrance gallery as a dance floor. "She'd have flamenco dancers," says Muffie. "Those poor people who lived beneath her! They were never invited, of course, so the police were called. Then she had her Indian period. She brought up an elephant and it broke the elevator. You can imagine how that went down. The complaints were constant, the parties went on for hours." The co-op board president, Morris Hadley, reportedly griped, "They behaved badly—they gave dinner dances."

No doubt he heard that from the downstairs neighbors, the Santrys, who controlled a company called Combustion Engineering. "There was much more combustion upstairs," says Herrera. The police were called so often that finally Peggy took to putting food out in the servants' dining room so that when the cops arrived, they'd be "ushered in to have a snack and a chat with the cute waitresses," Muffie says, "and that was the end of the complaints."

Sometimes the joke was on Peggy. One night Muffie and Herrera snuck into Peggy's bedroom and completely filled it with draped toilet paper. "We were all really *very* young," Herrera says.

Years later, Muffie and her first husband were photographed at a costume ball while trying to win approval from a co-op board. When they were turned down, her father declared it no surprise. "They probably felt you would park a camel in the lobby," Tommy said. " 'God, don't let *them* in,' " Muffie confirms with a laugh. "But eventually we did get in, and now I'm one of the oldest tenants."

• • •

IN 1958, UPON PEGGY'S RETURN FROM A WINTER LEARNING TO SKI IN St. Moritz, she was anointed when she was photographed by Vittorio De Sica for a *Vogue* feature on good looks—her pouty picture filled a full page—and named to the best-dressed list for the first time. "Pretty Peggy," the fashion columnist Eugenia Sheppard rhapsodized, "dresses in Paris, where she goes every fall and spring. She is famous as a hostess of the young crowd, goes to all the charity parties and is most often seen in Desses evening gowns." She'd buy half the couturier's collection, then give the dresses away to friends like Sunny Crawford (who would later marry Claus von Bülow).

"She was extremely kind and generous," says Herrera. "Generous to a fault, always. She'd take her shirt off her back and give it away." She once gave an unprepared visitor to Paris a dress she'd bought that very day to wear the same night. But she also shopped the bargain basement at Bloomingdale's and wore her finds "ad nauseam to all the great balls in Paris," says Herrera. Her generosity extended to her apartment. For some, the party there literally never ended. "She had friends who were out of money staying there ad infinitum," says Muffie. "She really was a good sport."

She needed to have a sense of humor when dealing with her mother. Mugsy and Peggy never got along. "Peggy was her daddy's little girl," Geoffrey Gates says. "There was animosity, and her mother had the money." Angry that she was neglecting Muffie and furious at her wanton spending, Margaret Bedford was always cutting Peggy off. "She was obsessed with Muffie," says Gates. "There were terrific explosions." "Mrs. Bedford behaved terribly," says another of Peggy's best friends. "It was all jealousy. She was jealous of anyone who was near Peggy. She wouldn't give her a cent. Which in a way was good, because she saved a vast fortune. Peggy spent everything she had, everything."

"There were constant disappointments," says Lilly Pulitzer, "about Muffie, about life in general. She was crazy mad for Peggy's child and wanted to take control." In fact, another pal adds, "she had a case that Peggy was not a great mother. She was always downstairs at dinner. She shouldn't have had a child."

Muffie Murray, now married with children of her own, seems not at all unhappy to recount that "a lot of people remember me sitting, legs dangling from the top of the stairs," during parties, she says. "I had so much fun watching."

It wasn't long before Peggy blew through whatever part of her inheritance was outside her mother's control. Geoffrey Gates, who'd become her stockbroker, was ordered to "sell one hundred shares of Jersey"—Standard Oil of New Jersey, that is—whenever she needed to pay for another batch of couture clothes or a lavish party.

If the party wasn't at 740, Peggy would find it. When she wasn't giving one at home, she was at one somewhere, or chairing a dinner or a dance for the Police Athletic League, the Fresh Air Fund, the March of Dimes, Lenox Hill Hospital, and the New York Infirmary. One newspaper described her as "New York's busiest and most popular hostess," one who called benefit balls "the thing I know most about."

Because Tommy so hated the social scene, Gates or Herrera would often escort her. "She'd have some slob on her other side, trying to feel her up," Gates says. But once they were seated with Jack and Jackie Kennedy at an April in Paris Ball. Afterward, Peggy called Kennedy "a most amusing senator."

But all the partying was taking its toll. People whispered that Peggy was having affairs and Tommy was picking up one-night flings in nightclubs. "In recent seasons she was often linked by Society gossip with a well-known and wealthy Venezuelan playboy, a French prince and with the late Ali Khan," wrote Cholly Knickerbocker, referring to Herrera's father and Charles d'Arenberg, a French descendant of German royals.

By the end of the decade, the seams of Peggy and Tommy's marriage were not just showing but set to burst. In the winter of 1959, Peggy went without him to Nepal, which she declared "the dream place of the world—everybody should go." En route home, she brought a suitcase full of saris to Paris to have them altered into evening clothes. "Peggy also bought the jewels to go with—dangling sapphire earrings and a bracelet," wrote Sheppard.

"I declared everything, so I don't mind telling," Bancroft quipped.

"Get ready for an American invasion, Nepal. Follow-the-leader is a fun game and Peggy, herself, plans to go back," Sheppard ended ominously, "as soon as she can convince her husband to make the trip, too." Some couples went on like the Bancrofts for years, husbands and wives living separate lives in peaceful coexistence. Tommy "was not very happy in that life, the limelight didn't appeal to him," says a friend. "He was a guy guy."

In the spring of 1960, just after Peggy made the best-dressed list for the third year in a row, she quietly divorced Tommy in Alabama, then hightailed it to Paris, where she'd already begun a new romance. She'd been reintroduced to Charles-Auguste Armand, the third Prince and Duc d'Arenberg and prince and duke of the Holy Roman Empire, that winter in St. Moritz. He was twenty-seven years older than Peggy and was a small, wizened man with an egg-shaped head and a mousy demeanor. But he was also friends of many of her friends, and Peggy's mother had once dated Charles's father. "Mummy would have known the whole circle," says Muffie. "She loved the whole idea that he was older. She'd adored her father, she was very spoiled, still very much a little girl. She thought it was a fairy tale. She loved the idea of being a princess."

"We weren't all that surprised when she disappeared," says her friend Bea Dabney Adams. "I had the feeling things weren't as compatible as they might have been. People have different paces to their lives." Geoffrey Gates felt Europe beckoned her. "She loved the life there," he says. "Nobody on the WASP horizon was gonna give her a thrill. It was a naive search for the exotic. More class, more romance." And there were other signs, too. A few days before she left New York, Peggy purged her closets. "Friends descended on her Park Avenue apartment like a locust storm," a gossip column revealed, "and carried off ball gowns and suits." A resale shop got the rest: forty-eight cashmere sweaters, twenty-six bathing suits, and seventy-two waist cinchers, some with the price tags still on them. Only then did Cholly Knickerbocker reveal the divorce in his column.

Come the season, Peggy returned to New York after a tiff with the prince. Her path was cleared by Eugenia Sheppard, who wrote a column on the void where the grandes dames used to be in New York society. "School-girlish as she looks, Peggy was a lion-hearted hostess who thought nothing of putting out curry for ninety or tossing a party for hundreds when a visiting celebrity came to town," Sheppard wrote. "But it's my guess, Peggy finally saw through the plot and ducked out of becoming a Grande Dame." It wasn't clear what she wanted. Gossip had it she wanted Tommy back. She announced a plan to only date men her own age. Then she dated older men like the portly Earl of Dudley and Serge Obolensky, a Russian prince turned hotel executive and P.R. man.

In December, Peggy was back in the papers, confirming "pleasantly" and "without a tremor of regret" that her ex-husband, Tommy, had suddenly and without fanfare married Melissa "Missy" Weston, a model, minor society girl, and divorcée, in a quiet Connecticut ceremony. Peggy sent them a gift, and then, to show how little she cared, gave a party for friends like Prince Francesco Borghese, Dickie Fellowes-Gordon, and Viscount Villa Miranda in El Morocco's Champagne Room.

Maybe she did care, though. Their tiff forgotten, Peggy finally married Charles, precisely one week later in Massachusetts, though the American ceremony was kept secret for more than a month. Apologizing that the announcement was held up by the "administrative complications" of arranging a civil ceremony in France, Peggy finally cabled her good news to Cholly Knickerbocker in February.

Peggy initially won custody of Muffie, but the little girl spent the summer of the divorce in her grandmother Mugsy's summerhouse. Then she moved in with her father when he remarried. And in the summer of 1961, she became a pawn when Peggy sued Tommy, claiming he'd kidnapped the child while on a visit to Paris. He countersued, offering secret reasons to a judge why he should get custody. Pleading pregnancy, Peggy didn't come to court from Paris. Tommy's lawyer pointed out that she'd managed to rouse herself for the Paris fashion shows and a jaunt to Deauville. Peggy *was* pregnant and bore Charles a son, Pierre-Frédérick Henri Charles Bernard William, that fall, but the court ordered that Muffie remain in New York.

A new Cholly Knickerbocker wannabe, calling herself Suzy, reported in the *New York Mirror* that Peggy wanted it all hushed up, but "when you were once supposed to be the chief aspirant for the New York social throne left vacant by the late Mrs. Cornelius Vanderbilt, when you are one of the world's best-dressed and most photographed women, when you're young and rich and blonde and beautiful and married to a very important prince and all," she wrote to the woman she called Madame la Princesse, that "ain't exactly realistic."

One of Suzy's competitors, Nancy Randolph of the *Daily News*, was scoring regular scoops at Peggy's expense. In March 1962, Randolph had the princess back in Paris after a visit in Palm Beach with Muffie, by then nine and a fourth grader at Spence. Randolph revealed that Peggy had not only lost custody of the child but quietly settled for a one-week visitation during spring vacation and two weeks in summer, limited to the United States and only with a third party present.

Four months later, like clockwork, Randolph covered Peggy's return, adding fresh tidbits about her ruptured family. Though Peggy's mother sided with Tommy in the custody battle, she'd also bought the 740 apartment from her daughter for $240,000. She did it "just to help her out," confirms Muffie Murray, then sold it about a year later. But clearly that didn't mend the rift in their relationship. According to Randolph, Peggy "sent up a deputy sheriff to demand 14 pairs of sconces (wall lights) and the marble mantels. This caused a terrible uproar . . . Now, there's a report that Mrs. Bedford is suing Peggy for money paid into her daughter's bank account, while Peggy claims she gave too much cash to her mother." Denials were promptly issued from Peggy's camp, but Randolph stood by her story.

"Mugsy came down against Peggy in the custody case," says a member of their set. "Peggy felt very strongly that was not right." They rarely spoke again.

By then, Peggy had run out of money. There was no more stock to sell, and the trust was gone. An apocryphal version of Peggy's story was told to one future banker as a child, "as an example of imprudence and foolhardiness," he says. "Peggy had a huge trust, but she sold it to the Jews in Philadelphia. They were always called that, in the charming way that WASPs have. They were a group in Philadelphia you could sell your trust to, sell the right to the principal or your lifetime income for a discounted value, and get a lump sum of cash up front."

She started borrowing from friends. "She was always borrowing to live," says Geoffrey Gates, who loaned her $5,000. She wrote him an IOU and said if anything ever happened to her, he should call her lawyer in France. "I called him after her death, and he said there were many letters like mine," says Gates.

That didn't stop Peggy from hiring Baron Frédéric de Cabrol to organize her new home in Paris (the d'Arenbergs lived at the Ritz while it was readied, when they weren't in their château near Bourges, that is) or from laying on a dinner for seventy at Maxim's at the end of the spring 1964 social season. Although she was, typically, an hour late, it led *The New York Times* to declare that she remained "one of the world's great hostesses." And a year later, at the château outside Paris of the Mexican millionaire Carlos de Beistegui, Peggy told Charlotte Curtis of the *Times* that she'd upgraded her wardrobe as well. "Always Balenciaga," she said.

That fall she was back in New York. "Like a soignée homing pigeon, Peggy always touches down . . . in our town on her myriad peregrinations," wrote the *World-Telegram & Sun*. She was also back in Eugenia Sheppard's column, seeking to clear up some misconceptions spread by detractors "since she pulled up stakes and went to Europe," Sheppard wrote. She did not refer to her prince as mousy, she said, nor did she spend her life in airplanes. Yes, she'd been in Capri, St. Moritz, Salzburg, and Deauville that summer and Fiji, Bali, Tahiti, and Rio the winter before, but on a boat! In between were a trip to Palm Beach to see Lilly Pulitzer, another to Tokyo with Vicomtesse Jacqueline de Ribes for the Olympics, and the three nights she never slept as she shuttled between parties. "But don't say that," Peggy warned Sheppard, who printed it anyway. "It makes me sound so frivolous."

Before heading off for game shooting in Austria, Spain, and England and several visits to India, she went to a party in her honor hosted by Geoffrey Gates and his cousin, and tossed another at El Morocco for Ira Fürstenberg, flying a chef in from Paris to cook for her hundred guests. "It sounds like old times," Sheppard wrote. The *Telegram* knew better. "Things have never been as gay since Peggy went away," it wrote.

It turned out things were really not so gay for Peggy, either. Just before Halloween, 1966, she filed for divorce. Her next husband was apparently waiting in the wings, although Peggy declined to identify him for the indefatigable Nancy Randolph. "I cannot tell you who it is, or his nationality—it might affect the present legal proceedings," she said, adding that she and d'Arenberg still lived together in his grand manse. "We are on excellent terms—so why not?" she said. In fact, it emerged, she'd been ordered to remain under d'Arenberg's roof and not remove their five-year-old son after an official conciliation procedure in a Paris court failed. Two weeks later, d'Arenberg charged her with adultery, which, under French law, would make it difficult for Peggy to collect alimony.

Fighting back against Nancy Randolph, the pseudonymous Suzy (actually Aileen Mehle, a woman eleven years older than Peggy who'd moved to the *Journal-American* and been rechristened Suzy Knickerbocker) reported that Charles had charged that his wife had four lovers and claimed he had letters to prove it—which was "tacky," said Suzy. As a result, she went on, Peggy planned to skip Christmas in New York to fight for custody of her young son. But she came to New York after all, for who could miss Truman Capote's Black & White Ball for Katharine Graham (Geoff Gates was enlisted as her escort) and Tommy Tailer's party for Count and Countess Crespi (Tailer was, of course, the child of Mrs. Ledyard Blair's first husband and Countess Crespi, Colonel William Schiff's sister-in-law).

Just before Peggy went back to Paris in December, Suzy reported she'd won custody of her son, Pierre, but that proved premature. In May 1967, she was still not divorced, and Charles was still fighting her. He requested that sealed files from Peggy's custody fight with Tommy Bancroft over Muffie be opened for the French court. But Charles died five weeks later, at age sixty-two. Suzy was soon back on the ball, reporting that his estate had reached a settlement with Peggy, leaving "everything" to her and her son, though the fine print added that she would only get an allowance and only on the condition that she vacate the prince's house. Peggy was apparently claiming that she and her husband had reconciled before his death.

If so, she didn't mourn long, for in the summer of 1968 in Marrakech she married Emmanuel Jacques Géraud de Crussol, the Duc d'Uzès, known as Manu, a handsome forty-one-year-old chemical engineer with bushy eyebrows and two children (his first marriage had been annulled, and his wife went on to marry a grandson of J. E. R. Carpenter's). Peggy's third husband was a member of several of the oldest aristocratic families in France, and though officially he had no standing in its society, he was still known as its highest-ranking nobleman and premier duke. In other words, she'd traded up again and would henceforth have not only a thousand-year-old château and a four-bedroom apartment in Paris but another home in Rabat, Morocco. Manu had met his future duchess the previous November, and it all happened so fast that when Peggy called the *Times* to announce her engagement, the paper said that "she knew the highlights but not the specifics" of who her husband-to-be was. The maharaja of Jaipur served as witness at a ceremony conducted by the pasha of Marrakech.

D'Uzès was "handsome and obviously a bad boy," thought Peggy's old friend Geoff Gates. Though he was a step up in rank from a prince, "he was not a step up in class," says Gates. "He was a broken-down duke, a real smoothy. You enjoyed him right away. He had the charm, but you always watched your pocket."

A year later, a column now called "Suzy Says," for she'd dropped the Knickerbocker surname, announced Peggy's third pregnancy, but it would never be mentioned again, nor would a child be born. On a visit to New York a few months later, when Manu was profiled by the *Times* ("Privileged classes have a tendency to get rotten, don't you think?" he mused, a perfect sentiment for 1969), the paper noted that the people of Uzès were concerned about his failure to produce an heir.

But the d'Uzèses were too busy partying to propagate. They returned to New York regularly. The following spring they gave a dance for 250 friends at the St. Regis Roof, friends with names like Astor, Hearst, Van Alen, Baker, Biddle, and Gould. Preparations were under way for Muffie's debut a few months hence, and Peggy escorted her to a tea for the debs. A year later, Muffie got married. A few nights before the wedding, Peggy and Manu gave another party in New York, then headed to Locust Valley for the nuptials and a party at the Bancrofts' in Old Westbury. It was all very civilized. Pierre d'Arenberg, nine, was a page, and Tommy's kids served as flower girl and ring bearer.

By the mid-1970s, Tommy and Muffie were both divorced. Tommy remarried in 1977. A month and a half later, tragedy. Geoffrey Gates had sensed trouble coming. Peggy and the duke had been estranged for a year; her son, Pierre, had been in boarding school for four years. "She was probably aware that the money was running out," Gates says. "I don't know where she was going the year she was killed."

At five o'clock one morning, en route home from a party for seven hundred at a castle outside Paris in thick fog, Peggy was in a car that crashed into a parapet six miles west of Versailles and rolled over five times. Three others in the car, a driver and two passengers, were slightly injured. Peggy lived well and died young, killed in the accident the night before her forty-fifth birthday.

"She died coming home from a party," says Lilly Pulitzer. "Whoopee! We all thought that was the way to go." Several of Peggy's friends refused to speak to her mother at her funeral.

Many are those who remember Peggy Bancroft. Her family, unlike so many at 740, lived long and continued to prosper. Her mother, Mugsy Bedford, outlived her by nine years. The Duc d'Uzès lived until 1999. In 2005, Tommy Bancroft Jr., the retired chairman of the New York Racing Association, was still alive and well. Prince Pierre d'Arenberg, sixteen when his mother died, is today considered a great host and quite a charmer. Muffie Bancroft Murray is happily remarried and a mother. "It's not a sin to be rich, it's a miracle," she says, quoting a pillow in her house.

Peggy Bancroft was a shooting star in New York, here and gone. Today's Bright Young Things know her name barely, if at all, but among the social set of a certain age it still excites a certain wistful, slightly naughty nostalgia. Even now, people tell Muffie how much fun they had in Peggy's apartment. "It was a time they all missed when it was over," she says. "I'm so lucky to have been there," says Gates. "Peggy was wonderful, so generous and sparkling, like a bubbling glass of champagne," says Bea Dabney Adams. "We didn't think very much about things; we just danced away the night. It's different now."

24

ONLY ONE OF PEGGY BANCROFT'S 740 NEIGHBORS HAD ANYTHING approaching her pedigree, youth, and chic: Angier Biddle Duke Jr. The buyer of Edith and Grace Scoville's cavernous B-line apartment was the standout in the building's freshman class of 1956 arrivals, which also included Walter and Maud Aldridge and Richard Hallam Grant Jr. and his wife, Helen. Aldridge was the stone-faced chairman of Texas Gulf Sulphur, a mining engineer made good. Grant, a retired General Motors executive and former president of Chevrolet and Frigidaire, lived mostly in Dayton, Ohio, where he had a Norman estate and dairy farm. The bridge-playing couple bought Robert Thurlow Vanderbilt's apartment as a pied-à-terre because they had lots of friends in the building.

Angie Duke was born ten months to the day after his parents married in 1915. "The youth and beauty of the bride—she is only 17 and possesses far more than the average share of good looks—together with the attractive vivacity of manner, the wealth of the young bridegroom, and the fact that one of the oldest and richest Philadelphia families was united with one of the richest families of the South combined to make today's ceremony one of the most notable in this city in recent years," *The New York Times* said.

Angie's maternal grandfather was Anthony J. Drexel Biddle, whose Drexel ancestors were present at the founding of the investment banks that became J. P. Morgan & Co., Morgan Stanley, and Drexel Burnham Lambert. Five generations earlier, his ancestor Nicholas Biddle had served as president of the Bank of the United States. On his father's side, he descended from Washington Duke, the founder of the American Tobacco Company, and was a grandson of the founder of Duke University and a cousin of the famous tobacco heiress Doris. When their father drowned in a yachting accident in Long Island Sound in 1923, Angie and his younger brother, Anthony Drexel, split a $10 million inheritance ($108 million today).

The summer before Angie started college in 1934, he and Anthony visited their uncle Tony Biddle, a career diplomat then posted in Norway, and afterward drove through Austria, where they stumbled into a pro-Nazi uprising. "We heard on the radio that the chancellor had been murdered in Vienna," Tony Duke recalls. "There was going to be a funeral three days later, and we decided to go, because history was happening. We heard on the radio that the uprising had been put down, but it hadn't been."

Driving across a river, they were set upon by a band of armed men hardly older than themselves. A bullet smashed their windshield. Pulled from the car, Tony understood when the Nazi band's leader said in German, "If they're Jewish, kill them." After hours in a makeshift jail cell beneath a bakery, they were rescued by Austrian troops. "We're going to have another world war," Angie said as they headed for Vienna.

"That set him on the course of his life," says Tony Duke. By the time war broke out in Europe, both brothers had become Democrats and considered Franklin Roosevelt "our statesman leader," Duke says.

A Yale dropout, Angie Duke married at twenty-two; his bride, Priscilla St. George of Tuxedo Park, was related to FDR and the banking Bakers. After a yearlong around-the-world honeymoon, they stayed married for another two years; they settled in Tuxedo, and Angie "made an effort to get into business," says his brother, Tony. "He invested in a few companies. It was a detour. He was getting serious and Priscilla was not as serious. When he decided to go into the Army"—he enlisted in 1940—"I don't think she liked it."

Duke got a Reno divorce in 1940 and married his second wife, Margaret Screven White Tuck, an older woman, hours after she followed suit (it was her second divorce). A descendant of a signer of the Declaration of Independence, she was the great-granddaughter of the commander of the *Merrimac*, the famous ironclad Civil War battleship.

Duke rose from private to major during his five-year stint in uniform. Afterward, he started a trading corporation dealing mostly in Latin America, "but his heart was not in it," says his brother. "It was a stopgap between the military and what he really wanted, diplomacy. He always had his eye on our uncle," even emulating Tony Biddle's dress.

In 1949, Angie joined the Foreign Service as an assistant to the ambassador to Argentina, then moved with him to another posting in Madrid. In 1952, Duke was named ambassador to El Salvador by Harry Truman, the youngest American ever to head a foreign embassy. Earlier that year, his second marriage had failed after he met and fell in love with Maria Luisa de Arana, the granddaughter of the Marqués de Campo Real, a Basque nobleman. Duke converted to Roman Catholicism just before they married in December in Mexico City, then moved to El Salvador. When Tony, his best man, couldn't find an open florist, he visited funeral parlors and filled a taxi with wreaths.

Dwight D. Eisenhower took office a month later, and a heartbroken Duke was certain he would be fired but won a six-month reprieve thanks to his brother, who'd met Eisenhower in London just before D-day and prevailed upon him to let Angie stay in El Salvador. "Eventually, he had to give in to the political pressure," Tony says, but Angie had time to arrange another job that let him stay in the diplomatic arena, president of the International Rescue Committee.

Founded in 1933 at the suggestion of Albert Einstein to help refugees from Nazi Germany, and later Mussolini's Italy and Franco's Spain, the IRC had, by the 1950s, turned its attention to refugees from the Soviet Union and Communist regimes in Southeast Asia. Duke came on board just before the Soviets crushed the Hungarian revolution in 1956 and began bringing doctors, scientists, and dissidents to safety in the West. "He turned an excellent but not very well known organization into something five times better," says his brother. "It was dying on the vine, and he had benefits and dinner parties for top-ranking citizens in political and social life and shined a light on it." Seven forty Park was his venue.

Duke had lived his life in apartments full of Georgian consoles, Aubusson rugs, and checkered-marble entry halls. He was at 1 Sutton Place when his son A. St. George Biddle Duke, who is known as Pony, was born, then moved to 410 Park and Riverview Terrace off Sutton Place. "He was the most unsuccessful real estate person ever known," says Pony. "He always bought and sold just before a boom." But when he moved to 740, he was looking for a bargain. "Neither of us had the money people thought we had," says his brother. "He had a great social position but not the dollar worth automatically assumed because of our name. We had one-one-thousandth what Doris Duke had, or less."

But Duke needed room for entertaining; he'd become a social star, and, says Pony Duke, he "entertained lavishly, seated thirty, forty for dinner." Though he was a Democrat, he got along with Republicans like his mother's friend May Davie. He also knew Bruce Leib and the Bancrofts, all of which, along with his middle and last names, no doubt eased his way into 740. "He was very much in demand," says his brother.

Angie had by then lived down a youthful reputation as a party boy, created mostly at one of his properties in Southampton, a remodeled stable known as the Duke Box, where wellborn bachelors, young and not so, Bruce Leib among them, cavorted in a grown-up Neverland, moving in and out between marriages. Peggy Bancroft was a regular visitor in the mid-1950s. One of her alleged beaux, Serge Obolensky, was a resident. "But Angie was much more serious than Cholly Knickerbocker recognized," says Tony Duke. Unlike his friend Tommy Bancroft, "Angie went with the flow," says his brother. "But if you started talking politics, you'd know where he stood. I don't think he ever took his eye off the ball. He'd found his way and pushed it to the end."

The end of Duke's reign at 740 was sudden and tragic. In 1960, after Duke had headed the candidate's state committee, President-elect John F. Kennedy asked him to come to Washington as his chief of protocol. Duke agreed on condition he have the title and rank of ambassador. As one of his first official acts, he resigned from Washington's Metropolitan Club to protest its policy of refusing admission to nonwhite diplomats.

A mere six months after Kennedy's inauguration, the Dukes flew home from a visit at Vice President Lyndon Baines Johnson's LBJ Ranch in Texas to Washington, and stopped in New York so Angie could bid farewell to the visiting president of Pakistan. He then flew on to Washington, while Lulu, as his wife was known, hopped on a chartered single-engine Beechcraft airplane with two friends and took off for Southampton, where she was planning a seventh birthday party for their daughter. Moments later, the little plane crashed and all aboard were killed. "I got a message Mrs. Duke had been killed," says Tony, "but they didn't know which Mrs. Duke." Angie was still on Air Force One en route to Washington. "I had to call him. It was a terrible thing."

A year later, in Washington, Duke married Robin Chandler Lynn, a former model who'd gone to work at the State Department. "We weren't going to move back to New York," she says, "because we presumed JFK would be president for eight years." After subletting to the Turkish government for a year, they put the apartment on the market and sold it to the Japanese government as a residence for its UN representative. "It went for peanuts," Robin says, "a couple hundred thousand, that's all."

Angie Duke later became Lyndon Johnson's Spanish and Danish ambassador and continued to work in various political, international, and philanthropic pursuits until he was seventy-nine, when he was struck by a car and killed near his Southampton home. He was Rollerblading at the time. Robin Duke still lives in the River House apartment they'd bought for $250,000. Too late, Angie had finally made a good deal. "It's now worth $6 million or $7 million," says Pony Duke.

GARDNER "MIKE" COWLES JR. WAS THE KIND OF PUBLISHER JOURNALists love: despite the potential for embarrassment, each of his divorces was announced on the front page of the hometown newspaper his father bought and built into a heartland power, *The Des Moines Register and Tribune*, the cornerstone of a media empire that Mike Cowles then expanded into radio, television, magazines, and books. It was after the third divorce that Cowles, a tall, lean, blandly handsome gray-haired, blue-eyed man who favored thick-framed spectacles and bow ties, bought Marshall Field's apartment at 740 Park from his fellow publisher's widow.

Born in 1903 in Algona, Iowa, Cowles (pronounced *Coles*) was the grandson of a Methodist minister. His father began his career as a schoolteacher and superintendent while moonlighting as a newspaper editor, but soon went into business, managing and investing in real estate, then segued into banking, beginning with a one-room bank but eventually taking over nine more. After a four-year stint in state politics, he sold his banks and, the same year Mike was born, bought a tiny newspaper that was deep in debt. Within three years, he'd made it a success and begun taking over its rivals. By 1927, when Mike, who'd graduated from Phillips Exeter and Harvard, became president of the company at twenty-four, the *Register and Tribune* was Iowa's leading newspaper.

Mike, who got his nickname because his father thought he looked Irish and thought the name sounded Irish, along with his brother John, began expanding the company, buying radio stations (he gave Ronald Reagan his first radio-announcing job in Des Moines), then more newspapers in Minneapolis (which John ran), and, after consulting polls conducted by George Gallup, a graduate student he'd hired, decided to launch a national picture magazine. Although Henry Luce, the publisher of *Time*, announced a similar venture, *Life*, after *Look* was conceived, he got it to newsstands first in 1936. Cowles's creation, *Look*, followed in January 1937 and was successful enough that Luce bought stock in it. Though he was a liberal Republican who, like Landon Thorne, had grown close to Wendell Wilkie in the 1940s, Mike accepted Franklin Roosevelt's invitation to become deputy director of the Office of War Information in World War II. There he "learned there was more to life than Des Moines," says Charles Cowles, the son of his last wife. So he moved to New York just after he was divorced by his wife of thirteen years, a former *Des Moines Tribune* reporter. His second spouse (a first marriage had only lasted a few weeks), she'd charged him with cruel and inhuman treatment, the legal euphemism for adultery. Within days, the gossip columnist Hedda Hopper announced Cowles's plan to marry a divorcée named Fleur Fenton, a former newspaper columnist and, with her ex-husband, the head of a New York advertising agency. Clients like Helena Rubinstein and Van Heusen shirts advertised in Cowles-owned publications. Cowles backed Fleur in launching *Flair*, a brief-lived but influential fashion magazine.

One of Hopper's competitors, Dorothy Kilgallen, broke the story of the breakup of that marriage in July 1955. Fleur had moved out of their

East Sixty-eighth Street town house and Connecticut home two months earlier, but the split was described as amicable, and she signed a three-year contract to continue working for her ex-husband's magazine. That arrangement lasted three months. By November, Fleur had gotten a divorce in Juárez, Mexico, and within days married a British timber magnate in a ceremony attended only by Mr. and Mrs. Cary Grant and the president of Rexall Drugs and his wife. Though she'd never used Cowles's name during the marriage, she insisted on the right to use it for the rest of her life—and did. Hedda Hopper revealed that Fleur had met her new husband two years earlier on a trip to Asia. Five months after Fleur's latest marriage, Mike remarried, too. Jan Hochstraser Streate Cox, his new bride, had just divorced her second husband, the publisher of *The Miami News*, where she worked as the interior design editor, when she met Mike and married him in the space of a month. After a honeymoon in Europe and the Soviet Union, they returned to his bachelor apartment on East Sixty-sixth Street.

They were still there when the new Mrs. Cowles gave birth to her second child, a daughter named Virginia, in 1957. But shortly after she was born, they and Jan's son, Charles, moved into 740 Park. The last Mrs. Field was already gone when they came to see it. "It was broom clean," Jan Cowles recalls, "except for the library. They'd never cleaned behind their books." Charles Cowles, who adopted his stepfather's name, thinks they paid $120,000 for it.

Jan hired several decorators and Edward Wormley, a noted modernist furniture designer who'd gotten his start working for Marshall Field & Co., to redo the apartment. They combined two bedrooms into a master suite for the couple and filled the place with custom-designed furniture, including a twisting white sectional sofa big enough to seat one hundred. It was so big, Charles remembers, "it had to come in by crane." The Cowleses kept the moldings and fireplace surrounds left behind by the Fields and their exquisite, minimal Art Deco library paneling. The closets all had built-in cabinetry. But even though Cowles let her buy and hang the modern art she loved, a Roy Lichtenstein painting, some Jasper Johns prints, Jan Cowles never warmed up to the place.

"It was a really gloomy apartment," she says. "It just had four or five rooms facing Park Avenue and the rest on the side street. I was from

Florida, and I was used to more air." In her ten years there, Cowles raised her two children "and entertained a lot," she says. "It was a great apartment to entertain in. We had big parties." The dining room seated thirty-two for dinner, and they used it once a week. They would hire a piano player, Bill Harrington, who'd play in the entrance gallery.

Half the guests were friends, half businesspeople. "It was very seldom pure business," says Charles. "They were very close to John Loeb and the Kempners [partners at Loeb, Rhoades], the [William F.] Buckleys, Bill Blass. Mike was pretty open. If he liked someone, they were invited." They knew the Thornes and several of the Rockefeller children, too, but though they sometimes met in the elevator, they were of a different generation and didn't socialize.

Charles Cowles, then a teenager at boarding school, found the building intimidating. "I felt I had to wear a coat and tie to walk through the lobby," he says. "I would put on a raincoat to hide the fact that I sometimes wore jeans." He preferred their many weekend houses in Connecticut, East Hampton, and Mount Kisco. In winter, they went to Indian Creek Island off Miami, where Jan Cowles kept a house.

Cowles, though nearing sixty, was still quite active in his business, flying off somewhere "almost every week," says Charles, who remembers his stepfather eating breakfast in a coat and tie every morning then, when the weather was good, walking twenty blocks south to his office on Madison Avenue. When it was cold or rainy, the family's longtime "retainer," Olson, who'd been General Patton's chauffeur during the war, drove him in a Cadillac limousine Cowles kept in a local garage. There were also upstairs and downstairs maids, a cook, and a kitchen helper, nothing like Marshall Field's staff of thirty-two, but enough to keep them more than comfortable. Several of the six servants' bedrooms sat unused.

Not only was it intimidating; it was also lonely. "Some people wouldn't allow the elevator to stop at another floor," Charles Cowles says. "It would pass me by and I'd think, what's going on here? I didn't chat with the doormen; I'd never see the staff. You never saw anybody in the building." Cowles did find one friend in the basement, where the Lewis Brothers dry-cleaning service had an outpost. It and its successor, George Torpe, Inc., were not only rent-paying tenants; they also provided a range of valet services exclusively to the residents of 740 and neighboring buildings (and their staffs—those uniforms had to be crisp). The valets would shine shoes, sponge-clean and press clothes, and even handle alterations out of a small office directly beneath the Park Avenue entrance. "The rich and famous would come down and chew the fat," says Jim Torpe, who still runs the business from another location. "They'd walk down past the garbage. It was a secret privilege. They got a kick out of it." And at least one of their children considered it a refuge. "An older black gentleman ran it," says Charles Cowles. "He was one of the few people in the building who was friendly."

HARRIET PULLMAN SCHERMERHORN'S EXECUTORS PUT HER APARTMENT on the market in January 1957, and Douglas Gibbons sent out a letter to all the owners. "In view of the scarcity of apartments," he wondered if they knew anyone who wanted one. By fall, Mary Hayward Weir had bought and moved into 4/5C. Her husband, Ernest T. Weir, had died that June at eighty-one. His widow was forty-two years old.

Ernest Weir "was a classic embodiment of the rugged individualist," *The New York Times* said in his obituary. Chief executive of the National Steel Corporation, the founder of Weirton, West Virginia, and a bitter enemy of Franklin Roosevelt's (he refused to drive through Grosvenor Square in London because a statue of FDR stood there), Weir had risen from being a $3-a-week office boy to heading the nation's fifth-largest steel producer. Though he considered himself a commoner, he was virulently opposed to labor unions, married three times, and had three homes, in Pittsburgh, in Hobe Sound, and on Park Avenue.

He had the last at the insistence of his third wife, Mary, whom he'd married at age sixty-six in 1941 when she was only twenty-six. Their affair had not only broken up her first marriage to a journalist but also drawn the scrutiny of the FBI; in the run-up to war, the mistress of a corporate chief who'd appeared on the cover of *Life* magazine in 1937 was a subject of some concern. Mary Weir hated Pittsburgh, so Weir allowed her to keep a New York pied-à-terre, first at 300 Park, then at 521. Even after he suffered a heart attack in January 1957, followed by a massive cerebral hemorrhage, and was hospitalized in Philadelphia, she spent most of her time in New York. Within a month of her husband's death, she was preparing to move permanently from the town she called Shitts-burgh.

Four years later, Mary Weir, then forty-six, married a Polish émigré eighteen years her junior, a doctoral candidate at Columbia University who would soon become a notorious novelist. His name was Jerzy Kosinski.

Later, Kosinski would claim he met his future wife when she wrote him a fan letter, praising a collection of anti-Communist essays, *The Future Is Ours, Comrade*, he'd written under a pen name, Joseph Novak. Kosinski would variously say that he used the pseudonym because his English wasn't good, "to prevent myself becoming involved in controversies which might have led to the interruption of my academic work," and to prevent his professors from knowing he was moonlighting. Weir's son says the story Kosinski told of meeting his mother was just as dicey. "He made it up," says David Manson Weir. "Just about everything he ever said was made up."

Kosinski claimed Weir offered him the use of her library in researching an upcoming book. "When Kosinski stopped by her lavish triplex in New York," *The Washington Post* would report in a 1982 profile,

> he assumed the wife of the 82-year-old
> steel baron would be in her late seventies.
> Instead, he was confronted by a thirty-ish
> woman he assumed was Mrs. Weir's nurse.
> Kosinski liked her and invited her out to
> dinner. After dinner that night, he took
> her to bed. She was seven years older than
> he, not particularly attractive. But she had
> beautiful skin, a good mouth, a narrow
> waist, "and there was something girlish
> about her, very innocent." As it turned out,
> she was not Mrs. Weir's nurse, but Mrs.
> Weir herself. Two years later, they were
> married.

That same year another version of the "meet cute" appeared in a *New York Times* profile. "Kosinski envisioned her as a frail, elderly widow and she, aware of his error, impersonated her own secretary during their first meeting. A woman who could play a trick like that was, of course, a woman Kosinski couldn't resist."

The *Times*, which said Mary was thirty-one at the time, also quoted a passage from a Kosinski novel that seemed to give a third version of the scene: "Long ago . . . when I had received enough fan letters to know how similar they all were, I received one unusual one. The writer, a woman, said she knew me only from my work . . . but her analysis . . . was so acute, as were her perceptions of . . . the undercurrents of my life . . . that I was flat-out enthralled."

In those two profiles, Kosinski's enviable life with Weir is described. She'd been left the income from her late husband's $10.5 million trust, they said, and kept homes in Pittsburgh, Hobe Sound, and Southampton, a permanently reserved floor at the Ritz in Paris, a suite at the Connaught, a villa in Florence, a corporate plane, a 148-foot yacht with seventeen in crew, four cars, and a huge staff.

Some of that, at least, was true. David Weir says Kosinski had been living in a foreigner's residence on a student visa and wanted to stay in America. No fan letter preceded his meeting his future wife, though. David's godmother, a board member of an international educational institute at Columbia, ran a salon for young intellectuals, introducing them around, and, David thinks, vetting them, seeking foreign "assets" for the American government. Mary Weir had met her Ernest when she was hired to catalog and shelve his library. Now she mentioned to her friend that she needed someone to do the same for her, and her friend knew just the right young man. "Jerzy Kosinski showed up," says David Weir, "and I guess he liked what he saw. He hung around and eventually got into a thing with my mother. Of course [he married her for her money]."

Mary Weir was "periodically alcoholic," says her son. "She'd be fine for a while, and then she'd have a drink and be off again, and they'd come in a big black car and take her to the institute in Philadelphia, where there should be a Weir Wing. My mother didn't understand you don't marry somebody like Kosinski. But he was very bright, a breath of fresh air in a funny way. She'd hung out with WASP businessmen."

Things weren't quite the way Kosinski described them, either. The Weirs' home in Pittsburgh was gone by the time they began their affair,

as was the corporate jet. There was one car, not four—a Continental
Mark II she gave him before he moved in with her—and no yacht. Weir
hated boats and after one trip on an ocean liner refused to ever step foot
on one again, says her son. The floor at the Ritz and the permanent suite
at the Connaught were also fictions, though Weir did stay at both hotels.
There was no Weir villa in Florence, either. And the houses in
Southampton and Hobe Sound had been sold. Kosinski knew that, because she'd hired him to incorporate the libraries from those houses into
the one at 740. The elevator man Patrick O'Connor remembers him
"rushing in and out, always rushing. Her housekeeper, a blond lassie
from Czechoslovakia, told us her husband was a very wealthy old man
and she'd inherited all his money."

At first Kosinski kept his own apartment near Columbia, but then
they eloped and were married in a civil ceremony in Birmingham, Alabama, in January 1962. "I didn't want to get married," Kosinski "confessed" to one of the credulous reporters. "It was Mary's idea that we
should marry, because she was, after all, a socially prominent widow and
I was a writer with my own career and reputation, and there would be
gossip." Depending on the source, Kosinski was already making $250,000
a year on his political essays (which is highly unlikely), or earning a modest living, or else she'd given him a dowry, a trust fund of his own, of several hundred thousand dollars. Either way, he claimed he contributed to
expenses by carrying an attaché case full of small bills and tipping everyone around them. He also loved to dress up, sometimes wearing a red
tuxedo and faux military uniforms he designed himself so he could pose
as a dashing officer. He dropped many of his old friends and, within the
bubble of her wealth, wrote the book that made his reputation, *The
Painted Bird*, a fictionalized account of his boyhood in Nazi-occupied
Poland.

"During my marriage, I had often thought that it was Stendhal or
F. Scott Fitzgerald, both preoccupied with wealth they did not have, who
deserved to have had my experience," he told a reporter after Weir's
death. "I wanted to start writing fiction and, frankly, was tempted to begin with a novel that . . . would utilize my immediate experience, the di-
mension of wealth, power and high society that surrounded me, not the
poverty I had seen and experienced so shortly before. But during my

marriage I was too much a part of Mary's world to extract from it the nucleus of what I saw, of what I felt. And as a writer, I perceived fiction as the art of imaginative extraction. So instead, I decided to write my first novel, *The Painted Bird*, about a homeless boy in the war-torn Eastern Europe, an existence I've known but also one that was shared by millions of Europeans, yet was foreign to Mary and our American friends. The novel was my gift to Mary, and to her world." In future novels, many of them about the rich, he would take as much as he'd given.

According to Kosinski's version of events, he lived the life of a kept man. "She would say things like, 'Tomorrow, let's fly to Greece,' " Kosinski told a reporter, recalling tables appearing at restaurants like "21" and customs officials disappearing upon their arrival at airports. In that interview, Kosinski admitted that his wife's friends thought him an interloper. "And I was, to a large degree," he said. "Do you think I would have married Mary if she really had been a nurse? Of course not. The sexual attractiveness is increased by what a person represents. Ours was the stuff of romantic fiction. She became a princess and I was the vagrant knight." He insisted the marriage was "profoundly satisfying" until, just after the publication of *The Painted Bird*, which he'd dedicated to her, she started falling backward and losing her balance and was diagnosed with brain cancer. "Yes, when she was dying, it was difficult," he said. "But I'm not affected by illness."

"I never knew it was fatal and neither did she," Kosinski claimed in another interview. "She was concerned she'd be ill that way for years to come, and that I would be imprisoned by it." They split up. She left him nothing, he said; her trust went back to her husband's estate. "And I was broke from spending all my own money on tips," he complained. Luckily for him, his novel, published in the fall of 1965, was a huge success and launched his career.

He'd found another lover by then, too, Katherina von Fraunhofer, known as Kiki, whom he'd eventually marry. She says Kosinski played up Mary's brain cancer because he didn't want to reveal the truth, that his wife was "a major mental case . . . a raving alcoholic . . . in rehab here and in Europe." Mary, she continues, had been confined not to a hospital but to a mental institution, and the couple "were well separated before I met him. The divorce was going on." All Kiki knows about their life at 740 is that Kosinski wrote *The Painted Bird* "in one tiny room" there.

"He couldn't stand the rest of the apartment. He was fed on huge trays at his desk, flushed the food down the john, and the cook quit."

David Weir and Andrew Heineman, who was both Kosinski's and Mary Weir's lawyer, tell a different story. Weir takes issue with Kosinski's claim that he and Mary had married for form's sake because, in her world, they'd have been better off without the certificate. "Cholly Knickerbocker published something adverse," Weir says. "Her friends were horrified, too. My mother liked intellectuals. Some of her friends were not very bright. Kosinski was Jewish. He never admitted it, but a lot of my mother's friends didn't like him for that reason. They felt, 'We don't go to their clubs, they shouldn't go to ours.' " Not only that, Mary had made herself unwelcome in some of them. After the wedding, the summer edition of the *Social Register* "ignored the marriage," *The Washington Post* reported, even as it added Robin Duke to the listing of her new husband, Angie. "This is considered an indication that [Weir] will be dropped from the . . . winter edition."

David Weir says Kosinski slowly took over their household. His old governess, Mamzelle, who'd stayed with Mary (along with three or four other servants), "figured him out and left," he says. When she did, Kosinski annexed her bedroom as an office. Then, when David began college in 1962, Kosinski suggested he get his own apartment. "My conjecture is he liked having the place to himself," says David, "so he could operate without interference. I was quite young, and there were a lot of secrets."

One was that Kosinski was "endlessly unfaithful," Weir says, with Kiki, among others, he alleges, and she was the actual trigger of the separation. Mary Weir had just sold the apartment at 740 for a little over $100,000 and moved to a smaller one on Sutton Place. There, she had a phone installed in Kosinski's room that did not allow outgoing calls. "I was told she walked in on him with a man," says Weir. "He played with men and women. His affair with Kiki was one reason my mother divorced him. She didn't understand. She was from Indianapolis." Heineman also says Kiki was the other woman.

In the summer of 1965, Weir threw her husband out. He did not go quietly. "He tried to drive her to distraction," says Heineman, who'd first been Kosinski's lawyer. "He kept trying to rule the roost. He'd make plots out of her life to use in his books. He liked seeing how people reacted."

So, early in 1966, Mary went to Mexico and divorced Kosinski. She died that summer, but not from brain cancer, as the Kosinskis claim, or suicide, as her son believes. She'd just returned from a rare visit to London and was ecstatic with happiness, says Heineman. He confirms her alcoholism but adds that though she had deep depressions, he did not believe she was mentally ill. "She did kill herself," he continues, but accidentally, by drinking on top of prescribed barbiturates. She sent her maid home one night and lay down in Kosinski's room, where the phone did not dial out. Her housekeeper found her body the next morning. Ironically, it was Kosinski who actually committed suicide; despondent over a heart condition, he was found in a half-filled bathtub in 1991 with a plastic bag twisted over his head.

PART THREE

NEW MONEY

Edgar and Ann Loeb Bronfman's dining room, eighteenth floor (1961–79)

(Photograph by Edward Lee Cave, courtesy Albert Hadley Collection)

25

"I'm probably a little naive," says Barbara Gimbel. "It wasn't anything that ever entered my thinking." But when she and her husband, Bruce, bought Colonel William Schiff's apartment in 1957, they were the first to participate in what would become one of 740 Park's most secret traditions, for theirs was the first turnover of a "Jewish" apartment from one member of that faith (albeit one posing as an Episcopalian) to another.

As far as his family knows, Schiff's religion had never come up with the building; by the time he rented, the leasing committee had fallen by the wayside. Though he was upset by the Rockefeller conversion, he bought his apartment and made a little money when he sold it to the Gimbels, a family he'd known for years both as clients and as friends. They knew he was Jewish, and so did others around town. The wall barring Jews from the fortress, if there ever really was one, was down.

The Jewish apartment can't be called an institution at 740, because it was never formally instituted, nor written down, nor even discussed. And if there was a single person responsible for it, or for consciously letting the first openly Jewish person into the building for that matter, it was left unrecorded. Building legend, which has it that the Rockefeller family decided to lift a ban on Jews when Junior's son Nelson began considering a run against Averell Harriman for governor of New York in 1957, may be true. Even if few knew Schiff was Jewish, everyone knew who the Gimbels were, one of the most prominent carriage-trade families in New York; they owned Saks Fifth Avenue as well as Gimbels. And they did buy Schiff's apartment in 1957 as Rockefeller began considering the race.'

"The Rockefellers controlled the buildings they lived in and would tolerate no discrimination," one retired broker believes. "You can credit 740 and 834 Fifth, where Laurance Rockefeller lived. They were the first wonderful buildings to take Jewish people. Because they approved, it became chic, and it was only Miss Prissy Smith in a side-street building paying $500 maintenance who tried to impose her standards on her little world."

Regardless, Mr. and Mrs. Bruce A. Gimbel were the perfect couple to play the part. Like Schiff, the ersatz English colonel, they fit in beautifully. Bruce was the great-grandson of Adam Gimbel, an immigrant peddler who founded a dynasty, and the son of Bernard Gimbel, who won the backing of Lehman Brothers, took the company public, and bought Saks before it was built in 1924. One of Bruce's brothers was married to a granddaughter of Mrs. C. Ledyard Blair and the George Bakers. A Yale graduate, then a captain in the Army Air Force, Bruce Gimbel had made the first successful flight around South America in a non-amphibious plane in 1939 and won an Air Medal in the war. He and Barbara Ann Poulson Caton, a California girl, had both previously been divorced when they wed at the end of World War II. The couple had three children, all raised in the Episcopal Church and confirmed at St. James. "It wasn't religion" that led them to St. James, says Barbara Gimbel, leaving unsaid what it was. Proximity, perhaps.

Bruce had joined the family firm after college. Tough, even ruthless in business, he rose from merchandise manager to president of Saks in twenty years and moved to 740 shortly after taking that title. Barbara Gimbel can't remember an admissions interview. But the family was known, which is a station stop en route to arrival. "I didn't think of us as social, but we were young and went out a lot," she says. They soon made lots of friends in the building, particularly with the few other couples who had children. They shared a landing with the Dukes; when the Gimbels' daughter had her deb party in the apartment, the Dukes stored their furniture. Later, when Lulu Duke was killed, her young children spent that night with the Gimbels. Barbara Gimbel started a group called Women for Rockefeller supporting Nelson when he ran for governor of New York, but not because they'd been admitted, she says. Rather, the Republican big shot May Davie had waggled her finger at Barbara in the lobby one day and scolded, "You have to get involved in politics."

Gimbel remains very fond of the doormen at 740, who kept track of her children. In 1959, when Fidel Castro came to New York and visited the Russian embassy two blocks away, "there were Secret Service men in great numbers on our roof. Well armed, I might add," she says.

"I bet you can't guess where your son is?" the doorman asked. Up on the roof, of course. How'd he get up there? "He's very resourceful," said the doorman. It was all about the children for the Gimbels, so when their youngest went away to school, the apartment suddenly seemed too big. "We were rattling around" by 1965, says Barbara. "It was time to move on"—back to Beekman Place. They sold to Martin and Janet Coleman, another Jewish couple; she was the Mosler Safe heiress. They didn't get much for it, about $100,000, Gimbel thinks. "Too bad we didn't keep it."[2]

MAURICE E. OLEN MAY NOT HAVE BEEN THE FIRST CROOK TO LIVE AT 740 Park, but he was the first to get caught. "They bought and sold before we ever moved in," says his son, Steve Olen. "My mother won't talk about it."

Maurice Olen was an ambitious young man from Mobile, Alabama, where his father, H. E. Olen (born Olinsky, Steve believes), started a chain with two five-and-ten-cent retail stores. Maurice joined his father's company at age twenty-three and over ten years grew it to 107 stores, with more under construction, when he decided to sell stock to the public. In 1957, Olen opened a full-time buying office in New York and started spending a week a month in the city, living in the Hotel Pierre. A believer in scientific merchandising and personnel policies, he bragged to *The New York Times* that year that he'd installed an IBM computer, applied inventory and quality control, opened a plant to make his own store fixtures, and instituted a novel policy for handling executives who failed to measure up. He'd give a man a raise to force him either onto "his mettle" or into resignation. He wanted Olen Stores to become the First National City Bank of retailing.

In April 1958, Olen went public. That fall it merged with a retail chain called H. L. Green, and Maurice Olen took over its presidency for $49,600 a year ($318,000 in 2004 dollars). He also received $3 million worth of stock in the merged company. Big ambitions apparently required a big apartment to contain them. So Olen decided to move his young family (he had children aged seven and five) to New York and in February 1959 bought apartment 12/13A.

Unfortunately for Olen, his good times were gone by the time he closed on the apartment. All that winter, he'd failed to respond to repeated requests from H. L. Green for an audited balance sheet for his stores, finally submitting an unaudited one in January 1959. Olen was brazen. The day after he bought the apartment, he announced that his company was merging with another, which controlled two other variety-store chains, McCrory and McLellan. The deal would make H. L. Green the second-largest chain in America after F. W. Woolworth, with 859 stores. But in March, Olen abruptly resigned an hour before the directors called a highly unusual press conference to reveal they'd found "an apparent deficiency approaching $3 million" on the Olen chain's balance sheet.

The merger was delayed, and the Securities and Exchange Commission began investigating. Olen immediately deposited $1 million in cash and more in stock from his personal holdings in an account with Green while the mysterious matter, described as an overstatement of inventory and an understatement of liabilities, was investigated. Green's board met a few days later at Milbank, Tweed to replace Olen as president and in mid-April sued Olen for $3.3 million for deception and fraud, charging he'd misrepresented his company's finances before the merger. In May, after Green said the missing sum was actually $6 million, Olen put his apartment on the market.

By December, Olen had agreed to settle Green's suit against him for another $1.6 million—all his assets and then some. Some of that money came from the sale of the apartment, more from the sale of his 123,000 remaining shares of Green; among the group of buyers was one Raymond G. Perelman, whose son Ronald Owen Perelman would later buy an apartment at 740 Park.

But Olen's troubles had just begun. A day after the settlement, he was indicted for fraud by a federal grand jury, charged with violating the Securities Act of 1933 and the Securities Exchange Act of 1934, misstating his company's financial condition by claiming net profits of nearly $500,000 when it was actually operating at a loss, then continuing to doctor his books through the merger with Green. His accountants were also charged with certifying his false statements. After pleading not guilty, he was released on bail and in 1961 made a bargain to change his plea to no contest and pay a $2,500 fine, over the objection of the U.S. attorney. Five years later, the SEC adopted stricter rules for policing certified public accountants after issuing a staff report on the Olen fraud.

Olen, astonishingly, remained in the retail business, working with a network of retailers in the East and the South, several of which ended up bankrupt. In 1967, he was indicted again for mail and securities fraud, again plea-bargained the charges away, and was placed on federal probation and barred from the securities business and from accepting funds for investment or receiving any fees or commissions. He promptly violated those terms, moving to New York again alone (he and his wife had divorced). There he advised, bought, and sold troubled stores under a variety of corporate names.

When that came to light in 1973, while he was still under probation, Olen found himself in hot water again and never recovered. He died, unnoticed and unmourned, in 1977 at age fifty-three.

WHEN OLEN'S APARTMENT WENT ON THE MARKET, THE FRENCH WERE trying to sell 2/3B, Walter Chrysler was moving from 6/7B, and the Preston Davies had decided to sell as well. Early in 1960, the Scoville apartment went on the market, too, and stayed there two years. After an early burst of enthusiasm for the "Rockefeller" co-op, the apartments had again become hard sells, a decade's growth in the economy notwithstanding. They were too expensive, too costly to run. Now they were glutting the market.

But newly wealthy, ambitious outsiders and Hollywood types, the very types buildings such as 740 had long disdained, were at the bronze doors, gazing in longingly, and they were the only types who could still afford them. How to tell the good guys from the bad when they weren't in your families, your clubs, your stud book (the *Social Register*)? Somehow, 740 got lucky.

Henry David Epstein paid market rates—about $200,000—when he bought apartment 12/13A from Olen on July 10, 1959. He'd not only acquired a "Jewish" apartment; he became 740's equivalent of the court Jews who appeared in Europe during the Renaissance and played roles of significance in the Austrian and German empires. Cultivated, highly adaptable businessmen, they held positions of influence within the courts of nobles, serving as agents and financiers (Christians never lent money), positions that, at least when they were in favor, allowed them to be representatives of their people. "They were permitted to stay wherever the emperor held his court, and to live anywhere in the German empire, even in places where no other Jews were allowed," says the *Jewish Encyclopedia.*

Twinkle-eyed and wry, if a bit owlish to some, the bespectacled Epstein was a self-made man. In 1954, at age thirty-two, he was the subject of a lengthy profile in *The Saturday Evening Post* titled "The Man Who Buys Whole Towns." The son of a family that lost its home in the Depression, Epstein dropped out of college at nineteen in 1941 to go to work hustling magazine subscriptions door-to-door to support his widowed mother and younger sister. By 1943, when he was drafted, he'd paid his family's debts and bought them a house. After serving in the Philippines, he returned to a booming real estate market, full of discharged GIs looking to start families in an America that, though still a class-based society, would no longer tolerate unquestioned rule by the hereditary elite listed in the *Social Register.*

Borrowing $2,000 from his mother, Epstein started buying and selling houses, then whole blocks of them. At twenty-six, he made $200,000 buying a housing project outside Philadelphia and selling the homes to individuals. Then he bought an entire town in Tennessee from the oil company that owned it; that time he made almost $500,000. In 1952, he bought thousands of homes in Levittown, New York, built as rentals by the famous brothers William and Alfred Levitt. At thirty-one, Epstein broke records, paying $32 million for four thousand Cape Cod–style tract houses, then another $10 million for fourteen hundred more, then turned around and sold them for a $4 million profit (veterans were offered a special deal and could buy a house for a down payment of $340). *The Saturday Evening Post* deemed him "the most remarkable thing that has happened to real estate since the Louisiana Purchase."

Three years later, Epstein was engaged to Dasha Amsterdam, a Barnard College graduate thirteen years his junior who was working in the theater as a gofer for Lillian Hellman and an assistant to the producer Jules Styne. She was the granddaughter of Isidor Leviton, a Russian immigrant who founded Leviton Manufacturing, America's largest producer of electrical wiring equipment, sockets, and switches. Leviton, it was said, exaggerating only slightly, made money every time an American turned on a light.

When the Epsteins moved into 740 a year and a half after their wedding, Dasha was twenty-one and had just had their first child, a son named Robert. The Epsteins were sure they were, by far, the youngest owners in the building. And though they were not the first Jews, their arrival at 740 came as a shock to some. "He wasn't passing," says a realtor. "He was a card-carrying member of the synagogue." And so it was that not long after they moved in, the Epsteins attended a dinner party where someone asked Henry where they lived and was shocked by his reply. "Your name is Epstein?" he said. "And you live at 740? No, impossible. You *can't* live there." Their entry had been smoothed, says a relative, by references from both Christians and Jews. "They were very low profile. That's one of the reasons they got in."

They still had a lot to learn. When their son, Bobby, was three, he insisted on going trick-or-treating one Halloween. His German governess took him around, and when he came back, the Epsteins were floored by the bounty he'd collected. Not candy corn, but caviar, pâté, and salmon canapés.

A few months after they moved in, Epstein, who normally worked twelve-hour days, came home early one night, smiling broadly. He'd gotten a call from a lawyer that day and been summoned to a meeting with Electra Webb and Martha Rockefeller. "The first thing they said to me," he recounted to his wife, "was: we know Jews are very smart and we want you to be the building's treasurer." He accepted on the spot.

He was quickly accepted in return. "He was a very personable guy," says his son, now a police officer in Florida. "He could talk to anybody, from a street sweeper to a king of industry. He treated them with equal dignity." He was also dignified himself. His daughter, Danielle, who was born in 1963 and now works as a designer and builder of homes, says, "They entertained a lot and went out a lot, but it was my mother who liked that. My father did not. He'd sit in a corner with the most interesting person in the room. He had a dry sense of humor, but he wasn't a party boy by any stretch of the imagination."

Epstein became the trusted go-to guy whenever another Jew wanted to buy an apartment. "Henry said that if we ever had Jews interested in buying to give the name to him and he'd let us know if we wanted them," says Ronald Jeançon, a board member who became president in the mid-1970s. "He said, 'I know every Jew who has enough money.'"

In many of the better buildings, "Jewish people would get in and slam the door so it wouldn't become a Jewish building," says a top-flight realtor. Adds another, "You want to see intense discrimination? Some German Jews would throw up at the thought of a Russian Jew moving in."

Epstein didn't operate that way. "Henry was an activist," says Alexander Mellon Laughlin, who would become president of the co-op board. "He was willing to dig into people and others weren't." Epstein agreed with the board's basic criteria. "The building was still very quiet, very private," his relative says. "No ostentation was allowed."

"It was still a conservative board," says Bruce Leib, "until Mr. Epstein got on as a point man. He could shepherd nice people through. The barrier wasn't removed, but it dropped a bit for someone with the balance sheet who fit the mold. They certainly wouldn't have wanted a boxer or a movie star."

While at 740, Epstein did a little business with Albert Selden, Lynde Selden's son. Selden produced musicals, mostly disasters. Then he asked Epstein to put up the front money for a new one, about Don Quixote, promising he'd return it within four years, win or lose. Epstein read the script for *Man of La Mancha* and pronounced it Selden's worst idea in a career full of them. To stop him, he decided to deny Selden the money and blame it on his accountant. The musical went on to be a huge hit, and Selden nonetheless gave Epstein a small percentage.

The Epsteins remained in the building until 1976, when they sold to the German government so its consul could move upstairs. The Germans paid $500,000. "I still think, why did they ever sell?" says Danielle Epstein. "It was beautiful, so incredibly elegant. When I walk by, I wish I could go back."[3]

THE NEXT ARRIVAL WAS A DEVELOPER, TOO. LEWIS LEADER, A YOUNG man from Florida, worked as a United Press International reporter in Italy before World War II, then got rich building apartment houses and shopping centers in Memphis and New Orleans. In the 1950s, after his company was threatened by federal housing officials and accused of making improper windfall profits on government-sponsored housing projects, he and a partner split up, and he moved with his family to Venezuela. Then, as the decade changed, he pulled up roots again for New York in 1960, taking over R. P. Farnsworth, a major international contracting company that developed everything from office buildings to a Titan missile base to the Kabul-Kandahar Highway in Afghanistan.

Leader had been living in the Hotel Pierre for six months when he heard about Walter Chrysler's apartment through a broker and went to see it with one of his sons, Michael. They were most impressed by Chrysler's ballroom, which contained a grand piano, on which sat a Rodin sculpture of a pair of hands.

"We had to be approved by a committee, which was Mr. Rockefeller," the elderly and ailing Leader says in a brief telephone conversation. "He pretty much called the tune of who he preferred in the building and that worked out okay. It was all handled by letter. I didn't know anyone." (Junior was actually ailing and in Arizona when Leader came on the scene.)

Michael Leader says that the actress Elizabeth Taylor was also vying for the apartment. "We're not going to allow an actress," a board member told his father. The fact that they were Jewish—Lena Leader was a first-generation immigrant from Eastern Europe—didn't appear to matter. "It was a choice between a Jew and an actress," says their son.

Leader says that he paid "more than" $125,000 for the apartment. Its walls were all painted eggshell white, since Chrysler had used the apartment to show his art. He offered to sell some of it to Leader, along with his furniture. The Leaders did buy Chrysler's piano—Lena was a concert-trained pianist—and also two murals that couldn't be removed. And when Lena began redecorating, she discovered they'd gotten a bonus: when they stripped off paint prior to redecorating, they discovered a cherry-paneled living room and a library paneled in pegged oak with floral borders, likely installed by Countess Kotzebue. They never did decorate the big room they called the ballroom. "My mother was the opposite of social," says Michael. "We never entertained; we were very family-oriented. We used it as a storeroom for antiques."

Unfortunately, the painter they hired left open containers of turpentine around, and when he yanked an electrical cord from the wall, a spark set off the fumes, and the doors were blown off the living room, which was engulfed in flames. "He was so frightened he was seen running away down the street," says Michael, who was in a bedroom upstairs at the time. "I woke up to a thump, leaned over the rail, and got hit with smoke in the face. It's a credit to the builder, the walls and glass in the building were of such high quality" that the fire didn't spread. But when Michael grabbed a fire hose from the service staircase, ran it into the apartment, and turned on the water, the old linen hoses split. Luckily, firemen arrived, led him out, knocked down Mabel Garvan's door, and knocked out all the windows. Water from their hoses also inundated the Dukes' and the French ambassador's apartments. Many insurance claims followed.

Outside, the evacuated residents eyed each other curiously. One noted that all Martha Rockefeller had carried downstairs were two small bars of soap.

The next day was John F. Kennedy's inauguration as president. "We watched in our coats because the windows were all broken," says Michael Leader. The youngest child of the family, Michael spent the most time at 740 and in many ways got the most out of it. "That apartment helped my standing immeasurably," he said. "We'd get invitations and have no earthly idea who the people were." In seventh grade, he attended a ball for the Daughters of the American Revolution. "I wore out a set of tails and two tuxes," he says. "Going to the Plaza was old hat."

Young Leader, now a practicing Orthodox Jew, takes a philosophical view of his years at 740. "Moses was raised in the palace of the Pharaoh and when he fled became a shepherd in circumstances less than regal. The question is, why was he raised there? So he should not be awed when God sent him back to the palace. My sister went to Brearley, my brothers to Yale, Williams, Edinburgh, and Oxford. We are blessed with not being turned by wealth. Power is a transitory thing. What affected me was to see what really rich people are like. I respect wealthy people, but I also find, in my religious bent now, that God tests one with wealth—a lot or a lack. Seven forty was one of the serious clubs for the rich, and I found it to be underwhelming. It was a magnificent place to live, but I was never taken with my neighbors. It certainly helped me in dealing with power: it doesn't matter to me at all."

Their tenure was brief. Lewis Leader had suffered from ulcers all his life. "He had a thousand, two thousand men reporting to him," his son continues, "and it became too much and his ulcers popped and the doctor said, 'You have two choices: take your stomach out and keep doing what you're doing and you might die before the stitches heal, or you can quit right now and live a long, long time.' My mother said, 'I know how I vote.' And that was flat-out it. That day he fired his staff and began to wind it down. Shutting down an active business is a problem. It was a nightmare. He sustained serious financial damage." In 1967, a downsizing Leader sold his apartment and moved to a smaller one before abruptly leaving America altogether, first for South Africa, then London, where he now lives.

Business associates were shocked. "One day he was here, the next he was gone," says one of them, Peter Brown. "We never knew what happened. His children don't, either." Michael Leader knows one thing. "Seven forty was too much financially," he says; the maintenance had risen to about $2,000 a month. And Leader could no longer afford it. He'd borrowed $7 million from a commercial finance company; they'd foreclosed on the loan and seized a long list of assets belonging to Leader, his wife, and several dozen companies. All of it was sold to pay his debt in the fall of 1968.

26

JAMES WATSON WEBB DIED IN HIS APARTMENT AT 740 IN MARCH 1960.
Elinor Dorrance Hill replaced him on the co-op board at the May 1960
annual meeting. Electra Webb followed her husband to the hereafter that
November. Nine months later, Edgar Miles Bronfman, a member of
Canada's wealthiest family, paid $235,000 for the penthouse. His broker,
Evelin Corsey, believes it was the highest price ever paid in the building.

There was resistance to his purchase. "He was a *likker* salesman,"
says Elinor Hill's daughter Dorrance. The real estate department of the
Webbs' bank was handling the sale and was concerned that Bronfman
would be rejected. The bank called Corsey and in essence asked her if she
was crazy. They were under the impression that Bronfman would never
get past the board.

Bronfman's last name means "whiskey man" in Yiddish. He was,
says one former neighbor, the first "rough Jew" to buy an apartment
at 740, the son of a rumrunner and nephew of another who was shot-
gunned to death. Another uncle had gone to jail for attempting to
bribe a customs officer. The Bronfmans made their fortune supplying
American bootleggers during Prohibition. They were responsible for
"about half the liquor that poured into the United States" in those years,

according to Peter C. Newman, the biographer of the patriarch, Sam Bronfman.

Edgar, born toward the end of the Prohibition era in 1929, was the great-grandson of a Russian tobacco farmer who'd come to Canada to escape anti-Semitism. The family owned hotels and stores in Canada's west. When loophole-ridden Prohibition laws were enacted there, the Bronfmans moved into the narrow spaces where whiskey was still legal—selling it through drugstores and mail order while learning to distill the stuff themselves. By the time America enacted Prohibition in 1919, they'd made connections with its bootleggers.

As the illicit booze trade exploded in the Roaring Twenties, the Bronfmans raked in profits and prepared for the day when the unenforceable law was repealed. They'd merged their distilleries with Joseph E. Seagram and Sons, Ltd., and cut a licensing deal with the Distillers Company Limited in Scotland, which controlled more than half the world's Scotch as well as Gordon's and Tanqueray gin. But when the aristocratic Scots declined the Bronfmans' suggestion that they enter the American market together once Prohibition was repealed (as it was in December 1933), Edgar's father bought them out and opened an American office in the Chrysler Building. By the end of 1934, their Five Crown whiskey was the best-selling brand in a thirsty America.

Edgar Bronfman attended a private school in Ontario where he and his brother were the only Jews. He went on to Williams College, majoring in sports cars and pretty women, then finished his education at Canada's McGill and went to work for the family firm in 1951. He and his brother Charles divided their inheritance the next year: Edgar took New York. One of his first acts was to set in motion the construction of the Seagram Building at 375 Park Avenue (his sister Phyllis planned it and hired Mies van der Rohe to design it). The landmark opened in 1957.

Meanwhile, the twenty-three-year-old heir fell in love. On a weekend trip to New York, his brother set him up with Ann Margaret Loeb, a catch, even for a Bronfman. Edgar's father, Sam, had spent his life with his nose pressed against the window of society. Rebuffed by Canada's establishment, he became one of the world's most generous contributors to Jewish causes. Edgar became "a man who has so much he thinks he should have everything," the family biographer Newman wrote, adding, he "generally lives on a scale that Sam's conscience could not have afforded."

Ann Loeb represented a step up from that; she was as high society as a Jewish girl could be, the daughter of John Langeloth Loeb, senior partner in Loeb, Rhoades, one of Wall Street's richest investment banks, founded by her German-born grandfather, Carl M. Loeb. She was also a granddaughter of Arthur Lehman, a great-granddaughter of the mining magnate Adolph Lewisohn, and, through another great-grandfather, Alfred Huger Moses of Charleston, a member of the Daughters of the American Revolution. Carl Loeb was not one of the Loebs of Kuhn, Loeb, but his family were best friends and relations by marriage with the Lehmans of Lehman Brothers. So their investment bank, which had merged with an older, impecunious WASP firm to form Loeb, Rhoades, had power far beyond its size. Founding fathers of Wall Street, the Kuhns, Loebs, and Lehmans were "more Yankee than the Yankees, more Protestant than the Protestants," John Brooks wrote. "Many of their partners and some of their senior partners were Protestants, not by conversion but by birth."

Ann Loeb had grown up at 730 Park Avenue (where the Bronfmans were married by the rabbi of Temple Emanu-El) and attended Bennington College. In *"Our Crowd,"* his book on New York's great Jewish families, Stephen Birmingham wrote that at his daughter's wedding, John Loeb quipped, "Now I know what it feels like to be the poor relation."

The Bronfmans' first child, a son named Samuel II, was born nine months after the wedding. Edgar junior, Holly, and Matthew followed in 1955, 1956, and 1959. Edgar built a Westchester home, applied for American citizenship, and began to assert himself at Seagram. After demanding the title of president in 1957, he finally got it from his father in 1962. By 1965, Seagram's sales had surpassed $1 billion a year.

In May 1961, Douglas Gibbons had sent the board (and, of course, Martha Rockefeller) a list of the Bronfmans' references. Thomas L. Kempner, a Loeb, Rhoades partner and one of Ann's cousins, certified that their portfolio was worth in excess of $2 million. Edgar's accountant added that his net worth exceeded $5 million. An assistant vice president at Bankers Trust told the board his bank loved Edgar so much they gave him unsecured loans, and Horace C. Flanagan, the chairman of Manufacturers Trust and a next-door neighbor of Ann's grandmother in Purchase, added

that the couple were "cultured and attractive in every way." Ann's grandmother gave them a reference, too, as did Walter N. Thayer of Whitney
Communications, who spoke of their "great sense of responsibility."

The director of the New York Philharmonic was out of town, but his
secretary said she was sure he would recommend the Bronfmans. So
did the 740 owners Bruce Gimbel and Gardner Cowles, who considered the couple highly desirable. John T. Cahill, who'd just bought Mrs.
Bliss's apartment, said he couldn't "commend them to you too highly"
and looked "forward with pleasure to having the Bronfmans for neighbors." That was really saying something, because, early in his career, the
corporate lawyer had been the U.S. attorney who prosecuted the
Prohibition-era gangsters Jack "Legs" Diamond and Johnny Torrio, a
partner of Al Capone's. The Bronfmans' broker had not only put together
a persuasive package; she'd also had a chat with Gibbons. "She told them
it was about time," says the person involved with the sale. "They lived in
a cosmopolitan city and they should behave as if they did." Despite his
background, Edgar was accepted without an interview. "The Bronfmans
really broke the ice," she continues. "You did not have to be 'Our Crowd'
any longer."

In mid-January 1962, the Bronfmans asked the co-op board and New
York City's Department of Buildings for permission to make structural
changes. The board said yes at the end of February, but the city dragged its
heels, so Bronfman threw his weight around. On March 1, he wrote the
city's superintendent of buildings that he was "in a great hurry" because he
wanted to move to the city permanently and enroll his children in school.
Apparently assuming he could treat a city official like a Seagram employee,
he asked the superintendent to "instruct" a subordinate to "take up the
matter as quickly as possible so that we may get started early."

Two weeks later, he pressed harder, this time writing to the commissioner of buildings to express the "imperative" that work begin in April,
even though he'd been informed that "following normal procedure, it
will be at least three months before the plans can be reviewed." That, he
continued, "would obviously present me with considerable hardship," so
he asked again that the approvals be expedited.

Two days after that, a local lawyer called a friend, the city's labor
commissioner, to ask him to intervene. "I know nothing of the facts, nor

do I know the tenant," the labor boss noted to his counterpart at Buildings, who did finally expedite the request, although not until mid-April.

According to Martha Rockefeller's notes, Bronfman ignored the need for permits and simply went ahead with his renovations. The Bronfmans had hired a society architect, Jack Pickens Coble, and the society decorator Sister Parish to redo the apartment, which had been stripped to bare walls and studs when the interiors were sent to the Shelburne Museum.

Albert Hadley, a young decorator, was supposed to begin a job in the Parish office on January 2, 1962, but the morning before, Sister called to ask that he meet her at 740 Park. "No 'Happy New Year,' " Hadley recalls, "but 'I thought we might get a head start.' I pulled myself together and met her at noon. Mrs. Webb had wrecked the place, I must say." After walking him around, explaining that there had once been paneling here, a chandelier there, Sister hied off to lunch.

Several meetings with Ann and Edgar later, it was decided they would create a traditional apartment within Candela's "nicely laid-out" spaces, Hadley continues. "Then they went to Mexico, and while they were away, Sister got a telegram." "STOP ALL WORK," it said. "WE WANT A FLOATING APARTMENT."

"What in God's name do they mean?" Sister asked.

Hadley explained: they wanted a modern apartment in which walls, stairs, and fixtures all seem to fly, unsupported. His new boss said, "Awwgh."

But then she and Coble "got kind of excited," says Hadley. "This was right up my alley, a modern apartment in a traditional configuration with floating fireplaces. We opened it up, took walls out." They were replaced with new walls that stopped short of the ceiling. They put a dome in the ceiling of the dining room; replaced Candela's staircase with one made of steel and blocks of travertine marble; installed wall-to-wall beige marble floors, slablike green-lacquered doors, and a fireplace made of more travertine; and closed small windows and opened up big ones—two huge expanses of glass running floor to ceiling replacing the original limestone exterior. The children's bedrooms, done in modular 1960s style, were in the back of the U-shaped eighteenth floor, and a master suite was created on the roof with fifteen-foot ceilings and a sitting room cantilevered over the terrace (to avoid a restriction on building on the roof). Ann, of course, got an elaborate dressing room as well as a tub carved from a single slab of marble.

Everything was clean and sleek—one broker described it as the brightest prewar apartment on Park Avenue—and Hadley had no hesitation about making such a radical change. "It was not a very distinguished apartment," he says. With its additions above and below, Hadley adds, the Webbs' apartment "had no merit at all. There was nothing left of Candela at the end." Hadley brought back that Candela feeling, though, at least in the eyes of Mark Hampton, another new hire in Sister's shop. "Albert wanted it to reflect the sort of thirties atmosphere of the building," Hampton told the authors of *Sister*, an oral history of the decorator's life, "and that was not the sort of territory that Sister wanted to wade into. It turned out to be a marvelous combination of the two . . . this wonderful kind of Fred Astaire and Ginger Rogers background. It was a real New York penthouse for the thirties."

It was also a nightmare for Martha Rockefeller. Between March and November, the vibrations from the demolition cracked a washstand in her apartment, an air-conditioning system went on the fritz, she was forced to remove some of Junior's precious porcelain collection from the cabinets where it was displayed, plaster dust spewed from a duct onto her secretary, and her terraces were covered with debris.

"Above everything else has been the almost unbearable noise," Donald Macdonald, who'd become president of Gibbons in 1953, wrote to Edgar in November. He'd just been summoned by Martha, who was still in ill health. "She has been most patient but events of the last two days have just been the last straw," Macdonald continued. After workmen began using electric hammers, Coble agreed to stop using them, but the very next day they were in use again, leaving Mrs. Rockefeller "completely at her wits end."

Not only that; she saw no relief on the horizon. "Mrs. Rockefeller is also conscious of the present condition of your apartment and went so far as to hazard a guess that it might take a year to complete," Macdonald said. She'd sent him upstairs to take a look and he'd had to agree. "Mrs. Rockefeller expressed herself as being pleased when she was advised that you . . . were purchasing the apartment . . . I know that you want this feeling to continue." So do whatever is necessary "to eliminate these disturbances," he continued. "May I repeat that I regret the necessity of writing you and I am certain that were you aware of the situation, it would not have continued this long."

Macdonald had the deft Gibbons touch. But he'd made it abundantly clear that the nine-thousand-pound whale's widow was not to be trifled with. Nine days later Martha got a handwritten letter from Ann Bronfman. She'd just heard about "the ghastly things that have been happening to you," Ann wrote. "I cannot tell you how sorry I am at these indignities you have been subjected to . . . I know how disturbing, distasteful and irritating it must be for you." She promised that work would be concluded "as quickly but as quietly as possible" and asked to be informed if her neighbor was ever disturbed again.

"Quickly," of course, is a relative term. Late the next February, the apartment was still unfinished when Coble filed an amendment with the city, requesting permission to alter the placement of windows and doors, demolish servants' rooms to enlarge the kitchen, move bathroom walls, relocate fixtures, and add an extra bathroom to the new master suite on the roof. The approvals were finally issued in July 1963, and only then did the additional work commence.

Meanwhile, the Bronfmans had stayed in Westchester; Ann had gotten pregnant again and had her fifth and last child, another son, Adam, in 1963. Only then did she and Sister Parish begin shopping for furniture. They came back with mostly traditional pieces—sofas, chairs, ottomans, and a piano—that, Hadley felt, worked quite well in the huge living room. For the master bedroom, Parish and Hadley created a canopy bed, split in the middle so that each Bronfman could have a separate mattress. In the zebrawood library, a wall of books framed a fireplace with pictures leaned on its mantel. "I remember Mrs. Parish saying that all this money had come from liquor, so why don't we paint it the color of whisky?" said Mark Hampton. "And they did. They painted this wonderful glazed cognac color."

"LIKE ANNE MORROW LINDBERGH, ANOTHER WOMAN OF PRIVILEGE AND position with a literary bent, Ann Bronfman chose to remain home with her family," says the citation naming her Rosemary Hall's 1999 Alumnae

Award winner, "as Lindbergh put it in her book *Gift from the Sea*, 'to be the still axis within the revolving wheel of relationships, obligations, and activities.' Like Lindbergh, she was eager 'to still the soul in the midst of activities.' "

For a few years after Ann and Edgar moved into 740 Park, she stilled her soul by raising her children and serving on a variety of hospital and school boards while Edgar built up Seagram and, still waiting for his father to retire, dabbled in the movie business, buying voting control of Metro-Goldwyn-Mayer. When Sam accused him of doing it for sex, he answered, "Oh no, Pop, it doesn't cost $40 million to get laid." But he did get screwed, losing millions for Seagram, just as his son Edgar junior would do years later, when he bought control of MCA-Universal (Edgar senior at least made a personal profit).

Bronfman was great friends with Henry Epstein, who had an office in the Seagram Building; the two would sometimes walk home from work together. One night, as they approached the building, they saw a pack of police outside. It turned out they were waiting for Bronfman and Epstein. Edgar's son Matthew and Henry's son Robert had spent the afternoon practicing for a baseball game by tossing batteries out the Epsteins' window, trying to hit the narrow island that ran down the center of Park Avenue.

After his father's death in 1971, Edgar finally took over Seagram. But just then Ann suddenly left him. *Time* magazine thought the divorce was caused by Edgar's "open involvement with young models and society girls." But according to some, there was another reason: Ann had decided to live as a lesbian and had taken up residence with one of the children's babysitters in what had, until then, been the family's house in Westchester. "It was well known to anyone who knew the Bronfmans or Loebs," says a banker who did. "She loved women," says Tova Leidesdorf, a friend who'd moved into 740 in 1967. "What can we do? Everybody has their own, you know? Their life together was probably not so satisfying."

Ann dropped from public view after she divorced Edgar in 1973. In a brief conversation in which she declines to be interviewed, she says she's never heard of the Watson Webbs and has no idea how she and Edgar came to buy their apartment at 740. "It was just a great big ugly apartment," she concludes, "and that's all I'm going to say."

Edgar was about to embark on a new career on the gossip pages. The next December he married Lady Carolyn Elizabeth Townshend, who, at thirty, was fourteen years his junior. She was a descendant of the man who created the tax on tea that sparked the American Revolution. Bronfman had met the blue-eyed blond beauty ten years after she was named London's Deb of the Year in 1958. Separated from an Italian patrician with whom she'd had a child, she was dabbling in social journalism and running a P.R. firm that had her showing Hollywood stars around London.

After getting a divorce, Carolyn joined Seagram's public-relations staff in London, and two years later, on a trip to Paris, Edgar proposed. He gave her a generous prenuptial agreement: a cash payment of $1 million and the deed to a Tudor-style mansion on a 174-acre estate in Yorktown Heights that Bronfman had bought for $750,000 after Ann left him. The granite house at the end of a half-mile-long driveway was secluded but chic, right next door to Averell and Pamela Harriman's home. Edgar also promised Carolyn he'd sell his 740 penthouse, which reminded her of his ex-wife. He soon bought another penthouse at 960 Fifth Avenue, but remained at 740 during another set of years-long renovations.

Things went awry right from the start of the marriage. On their wedding night, Lady Carolyn refused to have sex with Edgar in their nuptial suite at the St. Regis Hotel and made him go uptown to sleep at 740. Carolyn later insisted the marriage was consummated on their honeymoon in Acapulco, but Edgar denied it. He accused her of having a "hang-up" about sex, albeit one that only manifested itself after their marriage.

In March 1974, Edgar filed suit in New York seeking to freeze the assets he'd given to his bride and annul the marriage. The $1 million was placed in escrow, with the interest going to Carolyn for spending money, and a trial was set for that fall. There, she denied Edgar's claim that they'd not had sex since their wedding, claiming that on their wedding night she'd been menstruating, was put off by his unromantic advances, but was nonetheless shocked when he left the hotel. They did make love a few nights later after a party, she continued. That time, even though she was suffering from the flu, she felt so low and unloved, she said, that she seduced him. She also denied having an affair with a Manhattan doctor, claiming she'd only called him from Acapulco for medical advice. But a friend of the bride's testified that she'd actually spent most of her wedding night with the doctor and that she'd also boasted that since Edgar "had screwed so many people, it gives me a lot of satisfaction to screw him without delivering."

Within days, the marriage was annulled. The judge ruled that Carolyn's testimony was "not credible," while Edgar's version of the story was corroborated by others. Carolyn walked away with $40,000 a year for eleven years and got to keep $115,000 worth of jewelry and furs he'd given her, but agreed to never use the Bronfman name. "It was simply a matter of pride," Edgar told Peter Newman. "I hate to be taken."

Shortly afterward, Dasha and Henry Epstein introduced him to Georgiana Eileen Webb, the daughter of a retired architect who ran a pub called Ye Olde Nosebag in Essex, outside London. They knew Georgy, twenty-five, from Marbella, where she was dating "a title who was horrid to her," says a friend. She was in New York visiting the Epsteins when Matthew, Edgar's son, came to visit Robert Epstein. Dasha suggested that Matthew take Georgy upstairs to see the view. The moment Edgar saw her, he was smitten; she was only four years older than Edgar's oldest son, Samuel II, who was about to graduate from Williams. The age difference notwithstanding, Bronfman soon proposed, and a small, private wedding was scheduled for a Saturday in mid-August 1975. But a week before the wedding, the Bronfmans' lives took an even more baroque turn.

Sam telephoned his father collect that night at about 2:00 A.M. and blurted out that he'd been kidnapped and blindfolded by three men who would contact Bronfman later. Then Sam hung up. His car, a green 1973 BMW, was soon found in the garage at his mother's house, twenty miles away in Purchase. She was out of town.

In the week that followed, as friends like the Epsteins kept vigil with the Bronfmans, America obsessively followed the case. Sam was the third scion of wealth kidnapped in two years (J. Paul Getty III and Patricia Hearst had been snatched before him) and the second member of the Bronfman family to be abducted. His grandfather Sam's older brother had been kidnapped in the 1930s. Newspapers reported that no one had told Sam's next-youngest brother, Edgar junior, twenty, about the kidnapping; he'd learned about it from a reporter. Much was made of the fact that Edgar junior, who'd inherited his father's yen for show business, had recently optioned a potboiler novel about the kidnapping of a wealthy businessman's son.

Tall and husky, Sam wore glasses and had a mustache and long, curly dark hair; he was described by friends as athletic and unpretentious. He'd just left a summer job with a state senator to join the staff of *Sports Illustrated*.

Two mornings after the initial call, a family spokesman held a press conference outside the gates of Bronfman's estate, where Sam and Ann Bronfman, Georgy Webb, family, and friends had gathered. Two armed guards watched. The spokesman announced that a ransom demand (later revealed to have been for $4.5 million in $20 bills and signed "The Raven") had been mailed to 740 Park Avenue. Although it contained no evidence that the author actually had Sam, the family would proceed under the assumption the kidnapping was real. The special-delivery letter implied that Sam's life would be in danger if the ransom wasn't paid within a week. Rumors were already circulating that Sam himself was perpetuating a hoax, but the spokesman denied that. He did admit, however, that the party Sam had supposedly gone to the night he was kidnapped was a fiction.

"I'm the one that received the kidnap note," says John Hughes, who'd just replaced William White as the superintendent of 740 Park. "The kidnapper apparently realized it was a safe place to send the note, and Bronfman still used that as an address, even though he lived over on Fifth Avenue. The press was vicious, because obviously Edgar Bronfman was a big name."

After four days of sometimes tortured negotiations, futile searches for Sam, the delivery of a tape recording with the heir's voice on it, and a reduction in the ransom demand, Edgar (tailed by FBI agents) handed over $2.3 million, the ransom note, and the tape, stuffed into two garbage bags in the middle of the night. But still Sam was not returned. A day later, he was found by police and FBI agents, bound and gagged in the Brooklyn apartment of Mel Lynch, a New York fireman. The ransom money was stuffed under a bed in the apartment of a neighbor who was in the hospital. Lynch's alleged accomplice, Dominic Byrne, an elfin limousine driver, had gotten nervous when he saw FBI agents staked out near Lynch's house and sent his own daughter to the police with a note saying where Sam was being held. The two Irishmen, both naturalized citizens, were neighbors and friends. And not terribly bright; the ransom note had been mailed with ten cents postage due, and it later emerged that it was actually Lynch who'd led the police to his house after he picked up the ransom in his own car.

Shortly after the call announcing Sam's release, one of his friends spoke to him by phone. "You'll do anything for publicity," the friend joked. "And I don't think you're worth $4.5 million." When Sam was helicoptered back to Yorktown Heights, champagne corks popped and the whole family celebrated. Subsequent press reports said the kidnappers had decided to nab a Bronfman after reading press accounts of Edgar's court battle with Lady Carolyn and detailed three separate attempts by an agonized Edgar to pay the ransom, including one in which he cut off another car and ended up in an argument with its driver.

At various points after their arrest, the two kidnappers claimed they'd been abducted and forced into the crime and separately confessed to aspects of it. Byrne's lawyer said he'd been duped by Lynch. One of Lynch's lawyers called the snatch an aberrant act, if it happened at all. Another claimed that Sam had masterminded the whole thing. Newspapers reported rumors that Sam knew his kidnappers.

As if that weren't enough to keep the family in the public eye, three days after Sam's rescue Edgar remarried; a photo of Sam, Edgar, and Georgy drinking Perrier Jouët, a Seagram-owned champagne, ran on the front page of *The New York Times*. Ann Loeb Bronfman was among the guests. To some, that seemed civilized; to others, it was just another bizarre twist in a story full of them. And more were yet to come. A month later, unnamed federal law enforcement sources "revealed" to reporters that Lynch and Byrne were habitués of gay bars. Then, the following March, Sam married his college sweetheart. Cynics would connect those two facts when Lynch, who is described by someone who knew him as "very, very, very" clever, claimed in court that he and Sam had been lovers and that Sam had blackmailed him into participating in the hoax by threatening to tell the fire department that Lynch was gay.

The trial, which began in the fall of 1976, was just as confusing and farcical. Witnesses for the prosecution repeatedly contradicted each other. In a tape recording of a phone call to his father that was played to the jury, Sam appeared to be in league with the kidnappers. Although Lynch changed his story several times, and had apparently cased Ann

Bronfman's house in Purchase repeatedly for two years before the kidnapping, the lawyers did a good job of convincing the jury that there was reasonable doubt of Lynch's guilt.

Sam's testimony didn't change that. On the stand, he was at last confronted with the specifics behind the gay whispers. Lynch's attorney brandished two affidavits. One was signed by an old friend of one of Ann Loeb Bronfman's brothers, a man who'd been convicted for both forgery and taking a stolen vehicle across state lines, and who'd also been arrested for endangering the morals of minors. He claimed Sam had once come to him with a scheme to make a gay porn movie and use it to shake down his father for money. It had already been established that Sam's income from his family trusts was relatively small and would stay so for years.

The second affidavit had been written by a man who'd once been arrested for extorting money from homosexuals (and who'd offered to sell his story to newspapers before his testimony); he claimed he'd had sex with Sam after meeting him at Uncle Charlie's, a Greenwich Village gay bar. Neither of these men would ever testify, but Sam, understandably upset when he left the stand, angrily banged his hand against a bench in the corridor afterward.

Eight days later, Sam's new stepmother, Georgiana Bronfman, gave birth to a daughter. A few days after that, the defense let Lynch repeat his charges, and then, during final arguments, a defense lawyer wondered aloud whether it was really coincidental that the alleged kidnapping was preceded by Edgar's remarriage and the trial by Sam's first venture into matrimony. The implication was that Sam had staged the kidnapping with his gay lover to punish his father, then staged his own wedding to inoculate himself from Lynch's claim he was gay. Unfortunately for Sam, the family's behavior, though relatively normal for the upper classes, didn't make them very sympathetic.

Three days after beginning deliberations, the jury found Lynch and Byrne guilty of extortion but innocent of kidnapping. Two members of the panel said they believed Sam had staged the snatch himself. A third said that many jurors felt Sam and the defendants were all lying. Sam said he was "shocked and stunned." Thirty years later, doubts persist about what really happened. "I was told it was a setup by Sam's friends," says a 740 teenager who knew the Bronfman kids well but had no idea if Sam was gay or not. "I wouldn't have known the difference," he says, "but if he was, his father would not have let him come out; he had a certain image to uphold."

At their sentencing a few months after the trial, Byrne and Lynch were given minimum jail terms, and then faded into obscurity. Sam, who works in the wine business in California, did not respond to a request for comment. He had two children with his college sweetheart before she died in 1992, then remarried and had two more children. Edgar and Georgy had two daughters before divorcing in 1983, remarrying in 1984, and then divorcing again. In the interim, late in 1979 Edgar finally sold his long-empty 740 penthouse for $600,000 to Steven J. Ross, the head of Warner Communications. But before that, in the mid-1970s, he tried to get rid of it in what would have been the most unique deal in the history of 740 Park.

Bronfman agreed to a trade with Ben Heller, a real estate developer and art collector. Edgar would receive five Pompeian paintings worth several million dollars in exchange for the penthouse. "I wanted to be a private dealer in art," Heller says, "so I said to Eddie, I don't want to be told I can't deal." Bronfman went to the board and got an informal assurance that Heller would be allowed to sell art out of the penthouse. With that in hand, he flew to Zurich, where the paintings had just been shown, to see them with an expert.

Bronfman then gave Heller a ride to London on his airplane and remained in Europe while Heller returned to New York to begin the formal admissions process. Unfortunately for all, the board promptly changed its mind. "They were really pissy," says the spouse of a board member. Some realtors think Heller had been, as one put it, "japped," turned down for being Jewish. But Heller doesn't think so. "It was legitimate," he says, "and I do not feel resentful, though I probably have less traffic in my home than some people at 740 do socially." And 740 didn't keep him out permanently after all; early in 2005, he went there to sell some Rothkos to a resident.

Edgar Bronfman married his last wife, the artist Jan Aronson, in 1993, and they still live at 960 Fifth. His secretary says that recalling his years at 740 "isn't really something he wants to do."

27

THE PLUTOCRAT PALACE, WHERE WIDOWS AND DIVORCÉES HAD ALWAYS seemed to outnumber out-of-sight children, was turning into a building full of young families. Jan Cowles remembers sharing the elevator with Ann Bronfman, both of them pushing baby carriages. The Gimbels and Epsteins also had small children, as did many of those who bought apartments in the 1960s. Though they were a less homogeneous lot than in years past, they still had much in common. They may not have belonged to the same clubs, gone to the same churches, engaged in the same forms of ancestor worship, or been listed in the same social directories, but their kids still went to the same schools, and, most crucial of all, they could afford to live with children in one of New York's most expensive buildings.

Jack Danglade, a chemical engineer, had bounced around Texas in the 1920s, looking for work in the oil business before landing in Lovington, New Mexico, a ranching town without paved roads, a bank, or a railroad, but near a town called Hobbs, where a wildcat oil well was operating. Danglade spent the rest of his career buying and selling oil and raising his daughter, June, after his wife died in 1941. Just after June married Randolph Speight in 1952, Danglade was elected to the New Mexico legislature, where he served as a senator until his death.

Speight, a North Carolina–born investment banker, made partner at Shearson, Hammill & Co. in 1959. "He was a real bounder," says a woman who knew him. "Handsome and charming and always after women, living on *her* daddy's money." He had his admirers, too. "He was wonderful, elegant," says one. "Right out of a book." Otherwise he hardly made a mark on the world, so dedicated was he to his privacy, says his widow, who otherwise declines comment. But Speight's outline is discernible; he, like May Davie, sat on the board of the Pioneer Fund, founded in 1937 by an advocate of restrictive immigration and forced sterilization to study heredity and, as its literature puts it, "human difference."

A controversial group, the Pioneer Fund is decried by its critics as a band of extremist neo-Nazi racists promoting eugenics, the study of behavioral genetics, how genes affect ability and intelligence. At its edges, eugenics asks whether the human race can be improved by selective breeding. Eugenics was discredited after its use by Germany's Nazis to justify their murderous racial policies, but in America its appeal persisted, particularly among WASPs who feared that their northern European culture was being overrun by genetically inferior blacks, Irish, Italians, and Jews. Speight was known to spend long liquid lunches at the exclusive "21" Club in midtown Manhattan, inveighing against just such people. Says a woman who knew him, "He would talk out against the Jews after a few drinks."

In a possibly coincidental juxtaposition, four years after he joined the Pioneer board in 1975, Speight was elected president of the 740 co-op board, a job he would hold for more than twenty years, even though, according to the super John Hughes, he and his wife were living on the edge of poverty, 740-style. "The money was hers," says Hughes. "And they could not handle money. They used to get in debt so badly that the paper would not be delivered. Then the check would come from New Mexico. Pay all the bills, everything's hunky-dory again."

ROBERT LIVINGSTON "TIM" IRELAND III AND ALEXANDER MELLON Laughlin preceded Speight onto the board, though they followed him into 71 East Seventy-first. Both arrived in 1962, when Ireland bought the former Scoville apartment, and Laughlin, Mrs. Langbourne Williams's sprawling home on the tenth and eleventh floors overlooking St. James Church. Both were from families any eugenics fan would have approved of, but Ireland's family history, at least, was quite colorful.

The Irelands were from Knickerbocker stock, descended from Robert Livingston; James Duane, an early New York mayor; General William Floyd and Stephen Hopkins, both signers of the Declaration of Independence; and Robert Livingston Pell. Landowners with towns (Pelham Manor) and streets (Duane Street) named for them, they controlled city properties and vast country estates along the Hudson River when Pell's sole heir, a daughter, married an Ireland and inherited her father's properties.

The first Robert Livingston Ireland was a shipping executive when he married Kate Hanna, the daughter of H. M. Hanna, a Cleveland mining magnate, in 1894 and went to work for her father. But in 1928, he shot himself four times with a revolver, and his wife discovered his body in their apartment. A few months later, it was revealed that he'd died broke; though he owned shares in fifty mining companies, they were worthless. His wife inherited a bit less than $3,500. Then, in 1946, she killed herself, too, at age fifty-seven, tying a nylon stocking around her throat and strangling.

Robert L. Ireland Jr. recovered financially, working for Hanna in Cleveland and running a coal company in Pittsburgh. When his first wife died, he married a cousin. Ireland's son, called Tim, was a Yale and Yale Law School graduate and former flier with the Army Air Corps. He sat on the board of Hanna Mining and worked as a banker at New York Trust. Tim married a Jacqueline Kennedy look-alike named Jacqueline Mayhew Ellis in 1952 and made partner at Brown Brothers Harriman in 1960. Two years later, one of their four children, Tom, eleven, went off to summer camp from 1107 Park Avenue and came home to 71 East Seventy-first Street. They'd paid the Scoville estate $90,000 for the privilege of living in an apartment big enough for a family of six.

A year later, Jacqueline Ireland provoked a firestorm when, without telling her husband first, she posed for *Vogue*, along with their two daughters, in their new apartment. "Dad's mother had a maxim," says Tom. " 'Fools' names and fools' faces appear in public places.' Dad had a fit."

Tom, who'd just entered Buckley, thought the new building was "a big step up," he says. "It felt like a fortress." They decorated the place with overstuffed furniture, antiques, muted chintz, and sporting art.

There was only one drawback as far as Tom Ireland was concerned. At 1107, he'd had a courtyard to play stickball in. At 740, the courtyard was narrow, so he played in the street, "which would drive the doormen crazy, worrying we'd get hit by cars," he says. But mostly the staff were co-conspirators, not monitors. "My parents were quite strict," says Tom. His sisters, in particular, "didn't like the dress code." In eighth grade, barred from wearing stockings, one of them would hide them and put them on in the elevator. "The elevator man was sworn to secrecy." The late-night doorman, named Frank, became a friend, too, because after midnight the Seventy-first Street door was locked, and Tom and his older brother, Will, would have to ring the bell to be let into the building. "We'd have a giggle about where we'd been. Then we'd have to get into our bedrooms without waking up Mom and Dad."

In 1965, Tim Ireland got into a scrape that almost killed him—and kept his whole family up late. On a freezing night in Columbus, Ohio, where he'd gone for a board meeting, he was mugged, stripped, and left unconscious in an alley, wearing nothing but an overcoat. He'd last been seen after midnight leaving a bar near, as *The New York Times* put it, "a predominately Negro neighborhood" in the company of "a Negro man and woman." After sharing a cab to a nearby apartment, Ireland was beaten to a pulp, his skull fractured, and he was dragged to the alley where he was found. A former convict was arrested for nearly killing him. "That was scary," says Tom. "They picked him clean and left him for dead, but he lived. He was in the hospital for weeks."

The Irelands were social but rarely socialized; they had a family to raise—and it grew larger two years later when they had a fifth child, Bob. But times had changed; in the Ireland household, family outnumbered staff. Aside from a nanny for the girls and, later, an au pair for the baby, the family made do with a couple who lived off the pantry and a single maid. When all but their last child left, they decided to downsize and sold the apartment in 1976, buying something smaller on Seventy-second Street. But then their buyers changed their minds, abandoning a hefty deposit. "Dad said he had a reputation to protect and wouldn't back out" of his purchase, says Tom. So Tim bought the second apartment and listed both, determined to sell whichever he could. He got $165,000 for the one at 740 from an Oriental-art dealer named Alan Hartman the next year, and moved after all.

TIM IRELAND WAS NAMED TO THE 740 CO-OP BOARD SHORTLY AFTER HE moved in. The board remained all-gentile into the mid-1960s (consisting of Ireland, Alida Camp, Julia Thorne, Elinor Dorrance Hill, Morris Hadley, and George Leib), but it became more active after Ireland joined in 1963 and began having regular meetings for the first time that May. A few months later, residents received a letter reminding them that the front elevators were not to be used for deliveries. Then, early in 1964, the board commissioned a security survey that discovered that the back doors of eleven apartments had been left unlocked. From 1969 to 1972, Ireland was the board president, succeeding the elderly Hadley. Then, in 1972, Ireland stepped down to vice president, and Alexander Laughlin, a brokerage executive and grandson of William Larimer Mellon, a co-founder of Gulf Oil, took over. The Laughlins had moved to 740 "because they had children," says Barbara Gimbel. But they also had many connections to the building's past.

Laughlin's mother's second husband was Tommy Hitchcock, Watson Webb's polo teammate. Judy Laughlin, née Walker, had known the Lees and Bouviers as a girl spending summers in East Hampton. "Mr. Lee would say, 'Tell Mrs. Lee to pass the salt,' " she recalls. She also grew up with Thelma Foy's daughter Joan. "Thelma wasn't very motherly," she says. "I went to visit once and I wanted to go home." Her sister later married Carroll Wainwright, the Rockefeller family lawyer from Milbank, Tweed. When she and Laughlin married in 1947, 740's Charles S. McCain and David H. McConnell were ushers.

The Laughlins lived in Locust Valley but wanted to move to the city and heard about a vacancy at 740 from Ireland. "I would buy it, but I have one," he told them. "I wish I'd waited." The D-line apartments were so much bigger than their neighbors. So the Laughlins bought late in 1962, redecorated for months, and finally moved in in the fall of 1963.

They thought they'd landed in paradise. "I could float in the bathtub," Judy Laughlin says. "We had the best wine cellar. Mr. White was a marvelous super." Adds her husband, "When you lay in bed, you looked at the cross of St. James." The servants' quarters were smaller but shared the same view. "It was pretty smart," says Judy. "It seemed like a house. Light is very important. The marble floors and bronze windows you could open with one finger, they could not be replaced now."

Their sons, David and Sandy, loved it, too. "I was a male Eloise," David says, and 740 was his Plaza Hotel. "I spent lots of time roaming around." He kept his bicycle in their storage cage in the basement and would accompany his father when he went to the long hallway lined with the tenants' walk-in vaults. "You didn't have to worry about your wine and cigars being stolen."

Because he walked dogs and kept his bike in the basement, David got to know the staff well. Patrick O'Connor was "quintessential," he says. William White, the super from 1959 through 1976, was a trained engineer. (O'Connor calls him "a top-class man.") But when White wasn't fixing everything in sight—he could even repair the elevators himself— he would sit at his desk in his office in a white dress shirt, the overhead lights off, illuminated by a brass lamp with a green shade "like an accountant," David Laughlin says. "To me, he was a grump."

David also loved the fact that 740 was in many ways two separate buildings. The front apartments were showier. The side-street address seemed to attract a distinct type, more family-oriented, more Old Crowd. "If you saw 740, you'd know it was a good address," says Tom Ireland. "What appealed to my dad was, you had to know that 71 was a good address. It felt lower-key. I don't know whether to call it reverse snobbism, but he got a kick out of it." For David Laughlin, the distinction was in the class difference. "We were on the poor side," he says. "When you walked the corridor between them and down the steps to 740, it was like going to another world. I knew nobody over there." Happily, perhaps, for the Laughlins and Irelands, the poor folks controlled the board. "It just happened to suit us perfectly," says Alex Laughlin.

"You have to be pretty sure of yourself to be in 71," says Edward Lee Cave, one of New York's top real estate brokers.

There was only one problem: when it stormed, the Laughlins' terrace drains clogged with debris. Edith Chrysler, who'd remarried and was now Edith Carr, called one day. "I could have killed her," says Judy. "She'd had too much to drink, I think. It was coming into their bedroom, so she sued us."

"Only time we've been sued," her husband adds.

"Not a very nice lady, to say the least," Judy concludes, dispensing with Edith. Then Alex takes on the rest of the neighbors. "We saw very few people," he says. "I was working pretty hard. But it wasn't a friendly building." Besides the Irelands, they knew only their D-line cohort, the Hadleys, Davies, and Leibs, "although they were all old enough to be our parents," says Judy. "We went to dinner at the Leibs quite a bit because she liked younger people."

Nonetheless, when Tim Ireland asked, Laughlin took over the board presidency for the next six years. The Camps, Thornes, and Hills had quit. Most of the other members were also from the back of the building, and Laughlin allows that they were, for the most part, what is described as Old Guard. The Hadleys and Leibs were elderly and less than active, though, so Ireland, Laughlin, and their A-line neighbor Epstein (who'd replaced Morris Hadley on the board) did the heavy lifting.

One of Laughlin's first jobs was to renegotiate the building's first mortgage, which was set to run out in 1972. The cooperative still owed principal on the 1929 loan of about $1.4 million. Laughlin arranged a new second mortgage (the Rockefeller loan had been paid off) for just under $500,000 from the Dollar Savings Bank, then consolidated it with the existing one, to give the corporation a cash infusion and a debt of $1.9 million. Luckily for the owners, mortgage interest rates had been dropping for two years and were hovering just over 7 percent, but this time the mortgage would come due in a mere ten years.

There wasn't a lot of owner turnover during Ireland's and Laughlin's years at 740. The economy had soured after the stock market plunged in the spring of 1962 following President Kennedy's confrontation with U.S. Steel over a price increase. That May 28, known as Blue Monday, the market plummeted in its largest drop since 1929. Things had improved by 1964, but then the markets turned rocky through the end of the decade and finally headed inexorably south. By the time Ireland handed off his board job to Laughlin in the early 1970s, the economy was in the pits again, and so was New York City. After the exuberance of the mid-1960s, when Mayor John Lindsay declared New York to be Fun City and the Dow Jones average briefly flirted with the 1,000-point mark, it began to seem as if New York were Rome and its decline and fall had begun. In

1964, a crime wave had led the board to strengthen the building's security. And in 1966, after Donald Macdonald of Gibbons wrote to Martha Rockefeller urging her to oppose an increase in real estate taxes (suggested by her stepson's government), a family retainer wrote back to ask sharply how Macdonald expected the city to solve its "very substantial financial problem" without more revenue.

When prices dropped, tenants were disinclined to sell unless they had to. Though Laughlin concedes that "there's probably some truth" to reports that Henry Epstein vetted Jews, he adds in the same breath that religion wasn't the board's litmus test. "I can tell you what we looked at very thoroughly," he says. "Number one, can they afford it? We also looked at the family; the interviews became thorough. We required letters, suitable letters." And it mattered who wrote them because "in most cases one or two of us knew them." Brokers knew there was "no point submitting people with no chance" of getting in, he continues. But that was "not about whether they were black or Jews or Greek, but whether they were nice people." Or at least knew a few. But they didn't have to be in the Old Crowd anymore. Indeed, its loss of influence was a defining sign of the times. Chewed up by taxes, old money had begun to crumble into the middle class. And many of its children had turned their backs on its fondest traditions; captivated by the vibrant and vibrantly democratic youth culture of the times, they wanted to go to Doors concerts, not deb balls. They worshipped Andy Warhol, not Vanderbilts or Whitneys.

The building's "restricted" reputation notwithstanding, its standard of admittance really was loosening as the connections between residents grew more tenuous, so it was important, in order to maintain a veneer of cooperation in the cooperative, to enforce some standards. They just weren't about religion. Though Bartholomew Barry's family believe their first two attempts to sell his apartment in the early 1960s were foiled because the applicants were Jewish, so were six of the next seven apartment buyers. And a Jew eventually bought Barry's. Emanuel Terner, who had begun making beer and soda bottles in 1929, had already bought the New Jersey estate of Rudolf Pabst, a brewer. When Terner's company, Metro Glass, was sold to National Dairy (now Kraft Foods) for over $9 million, Terner (whose wife, an avid golfer, sometimes played with 740's Mrs. William Kirkland) got even richer.

Money mattered. Members of the Lucky Sperm Club, who stayed lucky by practicing discretion and frugality, would keep their toehold at 740 into the next millennium, but their position was eroding in direct correlation to the rising cost of living there. Monthly maintenance bills at 740, already extravagant, were becoming prohibitive: in 1970, the smallest apartment cost, in 2005 dollars, almost $4,700 a month to maintain, and the Bronfmans' penthouse, about $12,000 per month. Social credentials would continue to matter, but only if they had cash behind them.

LYDIA O'LEARY WAS BORN WITH NEITHER WEALTH NOR LINEAGE, BUT with a red-wine-colored birthmark covering her face from her chin to her forehead. After graduating from college in 1921, she'd moved to New York and tried to get a job as a salesgirl in a department store, finally settling for one painting signs in a back room when she came to understand that although she was quite beautiful, her blemish disqualified her from a sales job. One day, while painting an iris on a card, she made it too dark, covered it with a lighter shade, and wondered if she could do the same with her birthmark.

O'Leary began experimenting with ingredients she bought from a drugstore. Determined to succeed, she teamed up with a chemist and invented Covermark, a foundation makeup. She couldn't win a patent for it at first, but finally did after she demonstrated its effectiveness by removing the makeup in front of a federal judge in 1932. Thirteen years later, she married James Reeves, a widower who'd just merged a chain of groceries he'd started into the Safeway stores. Seven years after Reeves died in 1957, his widow, in ill health herself, sold Covermark, and with the proceeds bought the twelve-room fourteenth-floor simplex at 71 East Seventy-first Street from the estate of Joseph Santry.

The accomplished O'Leary had an active life, even in retirement, traveling extensively between homes in Southampton, Palm Beach, and more exotic ports of call. In the early 1970s, she met Leonard Sills, a property owner whose wife, a member of the Rudin real estate clan, had just died; they became a couple and got engaged. Then, tragically, O'Leary had a stroke and spent her last decade under round-the-clock care. She died in 1985, and her apartment was sold to pay estate taxes.

Spyros Niarchos, a son of the Greek shipping tycoon Stavros Niarchos, bought it and has owned it ever since.

Doris Vidor, who bought 6/7C from George Embiricos the same year the Irelands and Laughlins arrived, was the first Hollywood type admitted into 740, a daughter of Harry M. Warner, one of the Warner brothers. In the 1950s, long before Irving "Swifty" Lazar, *Vanity Fair*, and Dani Janssen, Vidor inaugurated the custom of Oscar night parties at her home in Beverly Hills. She had a colorful marital history as well. Her first husband, Mervyn LeRoy, had already directed ten movies, including *Little Caesar*, when they hooked up. Together, they produced two children before she divorced him in Reno in 1945. A few months later, she married another producer-director, Charles Vidor, then making *Gilda*, starring Rita Hayworth.

Harry Warner died in 1958, leaving his two daughters $750,000 each (about $5 million today). Charles Vidor died a year later; he was only fifty-eight. His widow went to work in the movies. This was nothing new for her; in 1932, she'd backed a play, *Men in White*, that won a Pulitzer Prize and a few years later asked her father to option a novel she'd just read. He turned her down and likely lived to regret it; it was called *Gone With the Wind*. After a similar frustration with another novel, Edna Ferber's *Giant*, and a foiled bid to produce television commercials following her divorce from LeRoy, Doris retreated into motherhood (her two children by LeRoy were grown, but she'd had two more boys with Vidor). She finally cracked the ranks of Hollywood executives in 1960, when she got a job at United Artists. Not long afterward, though, she decided to move to New York to be nearer to her older children. A son, Warner, was trying to launch a career in theater and would later become one of New York's great restaurateurs (Tavern on the Green was his greatest success). Her daughter Linda, just out of college, had married a lawyer named Morton Janklow.

"The Internal Revenue Service had a new ruling requiring nonresident aliens to disclose their sources of income," recalls Janklow, who later became a top literary agent. "I called her and said, 'Rich foreigners will flee.' " Indeed they did. "All the Greeks fled," says Linda Janklow. "And they all had big apartments. My mother called me one day and said she was looking at one and would I come over? We fell in love." It had room for her boys, as well as for entertaining. Vidor's new son-in-law, then working as a real estate lawyer, negotiated the sale for a mere $91,000 (Embiricos had originally asked $150,000). As far as the Janklows know, Vidor's religion never came up.

"She would not have gone if it had," Linda says.

The decorator Renny Saltzman spruced the place up a bit, adding California touches to lighten it but leaving Embiricos's velvet on the living room walls. "European splendor!" Linda Janklow says, laughing. "Paintings looked great on it." Soon the apartment was full of Vidor's wide mix of friends, "everybody from the Leonard Bernsteins to Sinatra to political people," says Linda. "God, she knew everybody."

Just after she moved in, another of her friends, a decorator named Melanie Kahane, introduced Doris to Billy Rose, sixty-three, when they were all in Montego Bay. Rose was a character, a slum kid who'd become a multimillionaire songwriter ("Me and My Shadow," "It's Only a Paper Moon"), nightclub owner, Broadway producer, and investor. He'd been married four times before, to the Broadway comedienne Fanny Brice, the swimmer Eleanor Holm, and the actress Joyce Mathews, whom he married twice. But in 1963, shortly after he divorced Mathews the second time, he was alone and lonely, just like forty-eight-year-old Vidor. A few months later, she became wife No. 5. "He romanced her like mad," says Linda Janklow. "They laughed. They had a good time. He was fascinating, odd, brilliant.

"She thought it would be happy companionship; it was a disaster." They moved into 740 while she renovated his town house twenty blocks north. "By the time it was getting to a place where a couple could live there, it was over. She realized it was not for her. He smoked all the time and it drove her crazy. That sounds frivolous, but there were ashes everywhere."

"He was a little bit of a man," Patrick O'Connor recalls, "who'd tip the doormen a quarter when they opened his car doors for him. Wouldn't buy a newspaper now."

Four months after the wedding, the gossip columnist Hedda Hopper revealed that Doris was divorcing Billy and he wanted back some gifts he'd given her. Linda and her mother were in Lake Tahoe, Nevada, establishing residency when Rose celebrated his sixty-fifth birthday. "My main interest in life now is to keep breathing," he told Hopper's competitor Louella Parsons. Rose died seventeen months later. In 1967, Doris Vidor—she'd kept that last name—moved to Sutton Place and made a nice profit, selling her apartment for $240,000. "Doris was ecstatic," says Janklow, who once again handled the deal.' For the moment at least, prices were rising.

The buyers were Ronald Jeançon and his wife, Sally McConnell Faile, a granddaughter of the founder of Avon Products, then the biggest cosmetics company in the world. Avon's high-priced stock was one of the so-called Nifty Fifty securities of the go-go 1960s. The rise in the market was a contributing factor to the rise in real estate values.

David H. McConnell, Faile's grandfather, had been a friend of the senior John D. Rockefeller, and 740's much-married Mrs. Thomas Nichols was the last wife of Sally's (also much-married) uncle, David McConnell Jr. Not only that, but the family was worth hundreds of millions, a Rockefeller-sized fortune; they were a slam dunk with the co-op board. "I never had to go in front of a board," says Sally Faile, now living in Reno and Paris. "If you knew the right people, you didn't have to."

Sally Faile's father had died in 1947, a year before his daughter debuted in Connecticut. Three years later, she married a law student she'd met at the University of Florida. She married her second husband, Jeançon, a divorced stockbroker, in 1961. Vidor's apartment at 71 "was in the right place, the building looked good from the outside, the non-Park address was a very good idea," says Jeançon. "We didn't want people to know we lived on Park—the old family thing." They bought it on the spot—or rather, Sally did—and gutted the place, putting in both modern central air-conditioning and, as Jeançon puts it, "flooring out of some schloss in Paris, installed at great cost. The Greek had put in lots of marble, and the walls were all marbleized." They kept that and the green velvet in the thirty-six-foot-long living room, re-covering Sally's French antiques in gold velvet to go with the walls.

When Alex Laughlin put his apartment up for sale in 1975, he resigned the presidency of 740's co-op board, and the job was turned over to Jeançon, who held the post for four or five years and considered it easy. Only one owner ever caused Jeançon's board problems: Enid Haupt, who bought the seven-room penthouse 17D from Blanche Rosett's estate in 1967. Haupt was one of the children of Moses Annenberg. After starting his career as a circulation executive for the Hearst newspapers, Annenberg became the country's leading purveyor of racetrack results. He published the *Morning Telegraph* and the *Daily Racing Form*, as well as *The Philadelphia Inquirer*, and controlled the news service that sent race results over telephone and telegraph wires to illegal bookie joints around the country. That made him rich but also won him a jail term in 1940 for income-tax evasion. He died shortly after his release from prison in 1942, and his son Walter took over the business, legitimizing it and turning it into a media powerhouse. Annenberg also scrubbed the family name clean with generous donations to high-visibility causes.

Enid, one of Moe Annenberg's seven daughters, married twice. Her first husband, Norman Bensinger, owned the Room, a Chicago billiard parlor he called the nation's oldest. The most she would ever say about him was that she never talked about him. She later married a commodities broker, Ira Haupt, who died just before his company collapsed in a swindle in 1963. The year before, Enid had been named editor in chief of her family's *Seventeen* magazine. Evelin Corsey, her broker, believes that Haupt paid a record-setting $350,000 for the apartment and considered it well worth the money. "This was one of a kind and she knew it," Corsey says.

By the time she got to 71 East Seventy-first Street, driven there, of course, in her Rolls-Royce, Enid Haupt was already famous for her extensive art collection (Monet, Tiepolo, Giacometti, Gauguin, Cézanne, Toulouse-Lautrec, Renoir, van Gogh, Rothko), her books on etiquette, her position on the best-dressed list, and especially her green thumb and her devotion to garden-related institutions like the New York Botanical Garden. Haupt retired from *Seventeen* shortly after moving into her apartment full of eighteenth-century French antiques and dedicated the next twenty-seven years to philanthropy, horticulture, and socializing. A perfectionist, whose orchid arrangements always perfectly matched the paintings they sat beneath, she herself rarely entertained yet was considered the epitome of elegance.

Haupt was constantly pulling up in front of the building with a station wagon full of flowers. "The elevator was always full of flowers," says

Judy Laughlin. But the street was often clogged with limousines, which made it difficult for Haupt to get them inside. "She was a complainer," says Ronald Jeançon. "I never paid much attention to her. She had a small apartment. I'd refer her to the super."

"She was hell on wheels," says John Hughes. "I have been dressed down by some of the best in my lifetime, okay? But she would be at the top of the list. She would call me up in the morning. 'Mr. Hughes, I want to talk to you now.' I'd come upstairs. They'd send me up into her bedroom, where she was sitting in bed with her tray and she had her newspaper. She'd fold the newspaper down, and she'd say, 'I have lived with leaks in this apartment just a little bit too long, and the day has come when if the leaks don't go, you're going to go.' And she folded the paper back up. 'Our conversation is now complete.' "

Haupt had also objected to a plan to replace the manual elevators with self-service ones at the same time the building was repointed. She told the staff that all her sisters had elevator operators in their buildings, and she was afraid of taking the elevator by herself. "We'd always assure her," says O'Connor. But then the work on the building began, and Haupt's fears were realized. She was robbed.

There were scaffolds outside Haupt's windows. The staff assumed someone went in that way, then just rode the elevator down. When Haupt got home that night, she called the lobby on the house phone. "Patrick, I've been robbed," she said. "The FBI came, the police," says O'Connor. "It was a mystery. That's the bad thing about self-service elevators, you see?"

"A lot of jewelry was stolen," says Hughes. "And when the Nineteenth Precinct came over, we went into her bedroom, into this area where she had her safe. The detective says, 'What's this? It looks like the combination to the safe.' She said, 'It is.' He says, 'Why do you have the combination to the safe here? The safe is right there.' She says, 'I didn't want to forget the combination.' They later found out. You know the old story the butler did it? I think it really was the butler in this case. Because there was no evidence whatsoever of a break-in. She owned two maids' rooms on the first floor. Mysteriously, like about three months after all of this, the butler moves back to South America."

Haupt suffered a stroke in the mid-1990s and has spent the last eight years under twenty-four-hour care. No one has lived in her penthouse for years; her family put it on the market for a moment in 2000—realtors assume they did so to get a sense of its worth—then promptly snatched it off once they learned it could fetch $18 million. Though small, the apartment has lordly views that ensure it will be much coveted when it is finally sold.

THE BOARD'S MOST IMPORTANT JOB WAS ADMISSIONS. AND JEANÇON SAYS he came up with a perfect, and easy, way to deal with that sticky subject. "I told the board no turndowns, no shows of prejudice. If we thought somebody wouldn't work, we'd tell the broker, 'We think we may have a little problem, and the best thing would be for you to find somebody else.' " He says he came up with that after one unwanted applicant "kept coming back." Jeançon remembers him not by name but rather by his "peroxided hair" and "pushy sort" of manner. "His father was of the same ilk," Jeançon says. "I didn't want it hanging over me or the building that we were snobbish."

Barbra Streisand had gotten the treatment when she tried to buy the Camps' apartment. "We thought the kind of people she would attract would not work out with the kind of unassuming people we had in the building," Jeançon says. But the turndown was unofficial. "She would have raised hell. It was done diplomatically. We checked into that. I don't believe she felt put out about it." Her broker, Evelin Corsey, confirms that "she came to realize she would never be approved."

Jeançon doesn't say how the board reacted to the news that the former secretary of state Henry Kissinger was looking at the French government's apartment before it sold in 1979. "He'd heard our security was the best in New York," the board president says, "but he never applied."

"Henry came and wanted to purchase an apartment," says John Hughes. "He looked very closely at it. It's not a bad apartment. But I don't think Kissinger was really in the league with the other people there at that point."

28

"THEY WOULD NEVER HAVE MOVED THERE IF THERE HAD BEEN PROBLEMS; that's not them," says Nancy Coleman Mintzis, the daughter of Janet and Martin Coleman, who bought the Gimbel apartment in 1964. "We had an uncle who was a lot showier; my father was very low-key. Marrying a Mosler was not a big deal to him." Janet Mosler Coleman is a member of the fourth generation of the Austrian family that founded the Mosler Safe Company in 1848. Janet's father was responsible for installing America's gold vault at Fort Knox; a bank vault in Hiroshima, Japan, that withstood the atomic blast there; the vault in the National Archives Building in Washington that held the original Declaration of Independence, the Bill of Rights, and the Constitution; and the basement vaults at 740 Park. Though their business was in Ohio, the Moslers lived in New York.

Janet married Martin Coleman in 1939 at the Mosler summerhouse in Deal, a predominantly Jewish resort on the New Jersey shore. They lived on East Eighty-eighth Street, had three children in nine years, and moved to 740 Park shortly after the kids were grown. Coleman was named president of Mosler in 1966, when Janet's elder brother retired and her younger one succeeded him as chairman. A year later, the family sold

Mosler to American Standard, the bathroom-fixture maker. Just under half of the $86 million sale price went to the family, and Coleman retired.

Nancy Coleman was in high school when her parents moved to 740—and she doesn't have good memories. She and a younger brother fought over who got which bedroom, and Nancy was thrilled to leave for college a few years later. She'd hated having dates pick her up there. Coleman had gone to school on the unfashionable West Side, and her fondest recollections are of dismounting motorcycles at the Seventy-first Street door. "I woke a few people up," she says. "I didn't want people to know I lived in a fancy apartment. I was embarrassed by it."

She can't confirm what her parents paid for the apartment. "Those were things parents didn't discuss with kids," she says. "I never saw my mother write a check." Martin Coleman died in 2000 after sixty-one years of marriage. Janet Mosler Coleman lives on alone at 740, accompanied only by round-the-clock help. She dines with her daughter weekly.

NANCY COLEMAN REMEMBERS HER MOTORCYCLE ARRIVALS. MILTON AND Elinor Gordon's kids, Stephen and Leslie, remember the bullets. Stephen found two, lodged in the floor and covered with a carpet that was ripped up when they began renovating apartment 15/16D. A rancher and gun enthusiast, Stephen is pretty sure they were .38s, though "they could have been .357s." And he's certain they were fired intentionally. "Someone could have pulled the trigger to be sure there was nothing in the chamber, but then there would be only one hole," he says. "There were two." How two bullets got in the floor of Leslie's bedroom, neither knows.

Who did it? Presumably, the James T. Lees, Belle Ledyard, or one of the Bancrofts. The first two don't get a lot of votes. "I guess it was the people before us," says Stephen Gordon. "Somebody else would have fixed it." "It sounds like Tommy Bancroft to me," says one of the Bancrofts' friends. "He would have been mad enough, I'll tell you. He was so mad at Peggy, furious." But a relative of hers suggests that if a gun was indeed fired, it was just as likely Peggy who pulled the trigger. "She was the one with a temper." Through his daughter Muffie, Tommy Bancroft says he's dumbfounded by the bullets. Regardless, it was a dramatic beginning to the Gordons' tenure at 740 Park.

They were just settling in as Lyndon Baines Johnson took over the presidency. It was the dawn of the Great Society, and the Gordons were major players. Elinor was from a middle-class Chicago family. Milton had grown up poor in a steel town in Indiana where his family ran a dry goods store. After attending the University of Chicago and its law school on scholarship, he rented a desk from a friend who ran a troubled ladies' pocketbook business. When the friend died and left the company to Gordon, he retooled its factories to make canvas duffel bags for World War II, then sold it and went to work for a factoring company, Walter Heller, in 1947. Factors financed small businesses with loans secured by accounts receivable.

Gordon set his sights higher. After he put together the international package of funding and tax breaks that paid for *The African Queen*, starring Humphrey Bogart and Katharine Hepburn, Gordon was assigned to reorganize a troubled movie studio, United Artists, and engineered its purchase from its surviving owners, Charlie Chaplin and Mary Pickford. Two film executives, Arthur Krim and Robert Benjamin, were the front men, but Gordon stood right behind them holding the pocketbook. He was building a new home on Lake Michigan when he was asked to run the company, but his wife put her foot down. "She said she'd rather be dead than live in California," says her daughter. "The story is, they flipped a coin and Arthur got to go."

When his bosses at Heller denied him the firm's presidency, Gordon retired with $250,000 in his bank account, moved to Paris to figure out what to do next, and returned to found Television Programs of America with Edward Small, a movie producer, investing $125,000 each. Two years later, it was producing *Lassie, Fury, Stage 7, Star Showcase, Ramar of the Jungle, Adventures of Ellery Queen*, and *The Adventures of Tugboat Annie*. The company was grossing $10 million a year with profits of nearly $1 million when Gordon bought out his partner for $2 million. In 1958, with network power growing and that of independent producers shrinking, Gordon sold the company for $13.5 million.

The Gordons had since moved to Riverdale, a bucolic slice of the Bronx perched on the Hudson River (the television business was based in New York in those days). But they yearned for the bright lights of Manhattan. So with their children nearly grown up (Leslie in her last year of high school, Stephen already in college), they went looking for a city home. "My mother wanted the best of everything," says Leslie Gordon Glass. "She looked for a long time. She knew every building, and she wanted a town house or one of the two or three top buildings with cachet and services." Elinor found a house on Sutton Place, but its kitchen was belowground and inelegant, so in 1962 they paid $250,000 to Peggy Bancroft's mother for James T. Lee's shrunken duplex. "They bought it to be the place where they could operate," Glass says. Simultaneously, Gordon bought a house on Martha's Vineyard (now owned by Mike Nichols and Diane Sawyer).

"My father had made a lot of money and he bought her the best," says Stephen.

Elinor knew the building; Marshall Field's widow, Ruth, was her closest friend. The Gordons also knew the Bronfmans. "They were very, very well connected," says Glass. Still, says Stephen, "it was not easy getting in. It was run by the Old Crowd." If anything could have hurt them, it would have been their politics, not their religion. "My mother used to say she wouldn't have a Republican at her table," says Stephen. "She wouldn't have me now."

Elinor had been raised by Nebraskan fundamentalists. Milton, though a child of Orthodox Jews, "grew up without shoes, with a sense of anger at Judaism," says Glass. "My mother repudiated extremes. My father repudiated Judaism." Still, the only country club they'd been able to join in Chicago was a Jewish one. "That was another motivation to move to New York," says Stephen. "They wanted diversity." The children got their spiritual education at the humanist Society for Ethical Culture.

Their apartment sat unoccupied for months while Elinor had second thoughts about leaving Riverdale. She was afraid of 740—its size, its formality, the attendant loss of privacy. Then one of her closest friends, the playwright Lillian Hellman, offered to have the apartment decorated by a set designer she knew, but only on condition the Gordons couldn't see it until it was done. When they did, they were overwhelmed, literally. The Gordons were small people. "He designed it like a set with throne-like chairs and dramatic drapes," says Glass. Though suitable for the scale of the place, "it was seriously awful. The next day everything was ripped out, and she called in the traditionalists" Sister Parish and Albert Hadley. Hellman was furious for years.

Finally the apartment was done with light walls, yellow rugs, lots of chintz, bright colors, and Gordon's modern art collection, including a de Kooning of Marilyn Monroe. One of the first visitors was Chubby Checker, who gave the kids twist lessons. Joe Pilates, the exercise guru, came to give the family workouts in their new exercise room. Glass thought they might have been the first family in New York with a personal trainer. "Whatever was in was us," she says.

Gordon formed his own investment bank and consulting firm, set up a venture capital business, and became an early proponent of leveraged buyouts, debt-financed deals to buy troubled companies and turn them around. But it was his position in television—he kept his hand in by financing early efforts in cable television—that made their apartment a magnet, so "mother followed in Peggy Bancroft's footsteps," says her daughter. Like her predecessor, Elinor knew an invitation to 740 Park was irresistible. But she entertained a different crowd.

"My parents only liked people of accomplishment," says Stephen. "People who did something, who stood for something. They were highly motivated and wanted to be around people like that. If you only had money or were social, they didn't want to know you. You were what you did, and if you didn't do anything, you were a bum." The meritocracy was replacing the aristocracy at 740 Park.

"She had a vision of bringing together the various groups they knew," says Glass, "and combined literary people, TV people, news people, university people with social people with money who could help their causes. There was always a dual purpose." Elinor Gordon was "socially schizophrenic," says her daughter. "She went to Paris twice a year to buy clothes, but she was devoted to social causes. She marched in Selma." The Gordons' presence, like Angie Duke's, helped alter the building's prevailing political conservatism. A protégée of Eleanor Roosevelt's, Elinor was involved in civil rights and the United Nations, ran the Citizens' Committee for Children of New York, worked for the New School for Social Research, organized a conference on racism for President Johnson, and took her children on outings to prisons and mental hospitals.

"They were players in the days when it was about ideas and achievement and not just money," says Glass. "She was very effective." At her parties, one would bump into General Omar Bradley, the authors John

Hersey and William Styron, the publishers Katharine Graham (*The Washington Post*) and Robert Bernstein (Random House), the New York mayors John Lindsay and Robert Wagner, Vernon Jordan of the Urban League, and H. Carl McCall, a protégé of Elinor's, who became an important city politician. Governor Nelson Rockefeller was another regular, "always in his rumpled suit," says Glass. May Davie, on the other hand, was never invited.

Elinor was superstitious. There were always fourteen for dinner, "black-tie dinners to which I was dragged whenever a husband couldn't make it and there were only thirteen," says Stephen, then in law school in Manhattan. "I'd get a swell dinner, but basically I hated sitting with a bunch of old people." It wasn't always that bad. The Gordons gave a ball for Walter Cronkite when he was named the anchor of *CBS News.* "You don't meet many people whose apartments are big enough to have an orchestra under the stairwell," Cronkite told Stephen.

Ironically, having absorbed her parents' politics, Leslie, like Nancy Coleman, was ashamed of living there. "I would tell taxi drivers I was the super's daughter," she says. Glass also caught glimpses of the other 740. "I knew there were unfriendly faces in the building," she says. "Republicans. Anti-Semites."

"You didn't feel comfortable going in and out in jeans," adds her brother. "It was a very formal place." Yet it could be vastly amusing. The Gordons' cook, Jai Feh Weh, and his wife, who'd fled Communists in Shanghai in 1949, would bring them back-elevator gossip. Martha Rockefeller, Weh revealed, had ten in staff, one of whom did nothing but clean chandeliers.

Glass married a British aristocrat in the apartment in June 1966, but the union didn't last. "My parents wanted to raise a socialite," she says. "They failed. They didn't want me to work. They wanted me to be the people I loathe." Instead, she went to work for an advertising agency and eventually became a mystery novelist.

In 1970, Gordon, sixty-two, got his fondest desire when he bought Hall & Steigliz, a nineteenth-century brokerage house, and merged it with an investment research firm to create his own investment bank. Unfortunately, for once his timing was terrible. He'd invested his whole fortune in the purchase, but the market was sagging, the company didn't have enough volume to support its operations, and Gordon was forced to sell. "He always found a way out," says his daughter. "And he always went his own way." In the 1980s, he bought a conglomerate that made seat belts, parachutes, and steel beams, recovering the family's wealth. But in the meantime, he'd had to abandon 740 Park.

"Everything happened at once," says Glass. In 1972, Gordon merged his firm with a rival's under a cloud of, as the *Wall Street Journal* headline put it, "money woes." Simultaneously, his wife was diagnosed with brain cancer. Overwhelmed, Gordon decided to downsize, put the apartment on the market, quickly sold it for $575,000—a record, thinks Stephen, who handled the sale—and moved into a nearby rental, where he nursed his wife until her death.

IF DORIS VIDOR AND THE GORDONS WEREN'T ENOUGH TO WAKE UP 740, then the man who bought apartment 2/3C in 1966 was. "It was a miracle they got into the building," says Jacqueline Everly, the stepdaughter of Archie Bleyer. Though he had the money and was Episcopalian, Bleyer was barely acceptable; he owned Cadence Records, one of the earliest pop music labels, which had hits like the Chordettes' "Mr. Sandman" and the Everly Brothers' string of chart toppers. Then, in 1962, Bleyer bought *The First Family*, a comedy record by Vaughn Meader, an impressionist who did an uncanny imitation of John Fitzgerald Kennedy. Released that fall, just after the Cuban missile crisis, it was, until the Beatles came along, the fastest-selling record of all time. In 1963, a follow-up was released just before Kennedy was assassinated, and it was an understandable flop. Two years later, Bleyer retired, and Andy Williams, another Cadence artist, bought the company's master tapes.

The son of a Prussian-born classical trumpet player and a half-German, half-British mother, Bleyer first gained fame as the on-screen music director for *Arthur Godfrey and His Friends*, the televised variety show, where he met his wife, Janet Ertel, who sang with the Chordettes. They married in 1954 and lived in Freeport, on the unfashionable south shore of Long Island. Instead of yachts, Bleyer took the Long Island Rail Road to work. In 1956, he decided to get into country music, went to Nashville, and signed the Everly Brothers. Seven years later, Phil Everly would marry Bleyer's stepdaughter, Jacqueline.

After Cadence shut down, Bleyer started looking for a place to live in

New York, lost a town house to Gloria Vanderbilt ("my mother was heartbroken," says Jacqueline), and then bought at 740, paying just over $100,000 to the estate of Clinton Black (who'd paid a bit more than $9,000 ten years before his 1963 death). Though he'd segued from pop to opera by that time, Bleyer was not an easy sell to the board. Everly credits Bleyer's "socially connected" secretary with getting him into 740.

"Old Mrs. Rockefeller kind of controlled things," says that secretary, Betty Gautier Smith. "It was extremely selective." Alan Jay Lerner, the Broadway composer, had "tried and tried to get in there and couldn't," she says. Bleyer was "rather naive," Smith continues, and "thought if you paid for something, you got it. It all went over his head like a tent." Bleyer's realtor tried to discourage him from making an offer. "Lots of luck," he was told. But Smith's father knew a Japanese-art collector named Louis Ledoux, who knew Martha Rockefeller and put in a good word, "and the Bleyers got in," Smith says. "Lerner got so mad. He said, 'I don't see how in the world *you* got in when we couldn't.' "

Smith, who "ran the family, too," she says, moved in first and set up a little apartment for herself in the third-floor servants' quarters (the Finnish cook and maid lived on 2), even fitting a Pullman kitchen into a broom closet. She says the Bleyers went unnoticed because they were polite and quiet and, despite their pop provenance, never had loud parties. "We only had ladies and gentlemen," says Smith, though she adds that Bleyer's opera arrangements, attempts to truncate long works so they could be televised and taught to schoolchildren, "were ghastly to listen to."

The only neighbor Jacqueline Everly ever met was Mrs. Griggs, next door, whose estrangement from her husband was clear; she called herself Auchincloss, her first husband's name. "I never talked to a soul that lived there," Jacqueline says. "We were told they didn't like show-business people. I just got in and out of cabs and put money into everyone's hands on the way."

Tova Dreiman Tabor was a nineteen-year-old from Haifa when she was named Miss Israel and came to America, sponsored by a second cousin, the movie producer Sam Spiegel. Seeking a film career, she made personal appearances across America and one dreary afternoon in 1964 gave a speech at a United Jewish Appeal luncheon, where her life was turned on its head. Sitting on the dais was Arthur Leidesdorf, the son of the UJA's founder. Though he was married, he was floored by the dark-haired beauty queen and demanded to escort her home. The result was one ruptured family, one new one, and two new tenants at 740 Park.

Arthur was the son of Samuel Leidesdorf, a friend of Winthrop Rockefeller, Junior's second-youngest son. The son of a yeast maker, "Uncle Sam" Leidesdorf, as he was known, ran errands for a malt and hops shop in Brooklyn as a boy to support his widowed mother, and rose to bookkeeper and then credit manager before he quit his job to study accounting. In 1904, he became the youngest certified public accountant in New York. The next year he founded S. D. Leidesdorf & Co. Though he was hurt by the Depression—even losing a building he'd bought at Park Avenue and Fortieth Street to his mortgage lender—he persevered and built the world's ninth-largest accounting firm.

Uncle Sam was perhaps even better known for his philanthropy, raising millions for Jewish causes and running several of the largest, as well as the Red Cross, the Boy Scouts, the United Negro College Fund, and the Young Women's Christian Association. "I'm the best *schnorrer* in town," he'd boast, using the Yiddish word for "beggar." He was also instrumental in founding the Institute for Advanced Study at Princeton, New Jersey (where he met and became financial adviser to Albert Einstein), and creating New York University Medical Center (he'd wanted to be a doctor as a child but lacked the funds). He proudly told the story of how he thought it was a hoax the day the elder John D. Rockefeller called to ask advice on how to give away money. He became friends with the family, though he was not, as Tova likes to boast, the godfather of Junior's children.

Sam's son Arthur married his first wife, Joan Rose Wheeler, in 1939 while attending NYU. After serving as a first lieutenant in the Army, he went to work for his father's firm and spent his entire professional life there. Like his father, Arthur invested in real estate and Jewish philanthropy. In the mid-1950s, he was a partner in the slum-clearance project that created Washington Square Village. In 1958, he and two neighbors bought their home at 1125 Park and turned it into a cooperative. He was elected president of the 92nd Street Y shortly after his fateful meeting with Tova.

In the mid-1960s, Leidesdorf and his wife were living in a smallish apartment in the Madison Hotel, which he co-owned, and Leidesdorf, an inveterate collector of art, Chippendale furniture, and Fabergé eggs, was frustrated because much of what he'd acquired was in storage. "He'd collected for thirty years," says Tova. "Years before, he'd seen Rockefeller's apartment, and he visualized his antiques at 740."

"He'd been dreaming of this place for ten, twenty years," confirms Leidesdorf's son Samuel. "Our mother was somewhat impossible. She would not move there. There are lots of dysfunctional families. Put it this way: ours was not healthy."

Though his dreams helped doom his marriage, Joan Leidesdorf's successor says she was right. "At that time, it was impossible to get help, so running an apartment like that was a full-time job and she was fragile," says Tova. "She couldn't handle it. It was just too much for her. She lived in a hotel. She said, 'I have all the comforts. I will not be a slave to an apartment.' " Years later, Tova adds, the truth of her predecessor's words came home to her when she hired an English butler and maid and discovered they were running a ring of prostitutes from the Leidesdorf apartment.

When Arthur and Tova met, Leidesdorf and his first wife were fighting; 740 was a point of contention. "They divorced over the apartment," Tova thinks. "She said if he wanted 740, she would leave. He said, 'Leave!' " She sued for divorce instead. "He was in the middle of a very bitter divorce," says Tova, who was a replacement speaker at that UJA luncheon. Once he saw her, she says, Arthur, then forty-five, changed place cards to sit near her. Arthur "was bugging me," she says, "but he was so thin and gorgeous; I thought he was thirty! He started criticizing my dress. I was upset by this SOB. What am I going to do? Then he introduced me."

After her speech, she resisted his attempt to take her back to her hotel room, but he made it as far as the bar, and the next day filled her room with flowers. She called the UJA to complain and found out who he was. He showed up that night, demanding to see her. She put a coat on over her flannel pajamas and went downstairs to talk to him in his antique Rolls-Royce—"He had forty of them, magnificent!" He drove her to the

Battery and, while his two standard poodles listened, told her he was getting divorced; he'd been unhappy for years. Then he proposed. She told
him he was crazy. "You are the woman of my dreams," he said. "Then,"
she continues, "the whole tragedy started."

When Leidesdorf's wife learned what he was up to, she tried to withdraw the divorce action, Tova says. And Samuel Leidesdorf, still feisty at
eighty-three, was dead set against the marriage, insisting Miss Israel was
a gold digger. Uncle Sam made Arthur choose between the firm and the
woman of his dreams. "Arthur said, 'I have $200 million in receivables,' "
Tova continues. "He chose me. He gave a big chunk to marry me. He'd
had a lot of girlfriends. He wanted a normal life. We suited each other
very well." Finally Sam came around, Tova continues, and she married
Arthur the day after his divorce.

Leidesdorf didn't own Lewis Leader's apartment yet; the newlyweds
lived in a hotel, and Tova was pregnant when "Arthur schleps me to 740,"
Tova says. The apartment was empty. "We could put an army in here,"
she told him. But he'd been planning this moment for years. "My furniture will fill every corner," he told her, smiling broadly.

Tova Leidesdorf calls the next fifteen years the happiest of her life.
But she didn't enjoy the apartment as much as her husband did. "In the
beginning, it was wonderful," she remembers. "Martha Rockefeller
would come for tea. I had to have tea with her every afternoon." Friends
like those got them into 740, Tova thinks. "It was not for Jews," she believes. "But you must understand, Leidesdorf was bipartisan. He was accepted. Cardinal Spellman was his friend. He could get into the White
House. It was no problem to get into 740 Park."

After rejecting some of Arthur's masculine decorating ideas and fir-
ing a decorator, they went to Colonial Williamsburg for inspiration and
came back to knock down a few walls and fill their library and living
room with English antiques. "We had a curator coming daily!" Martha
Rockefeller's curator only visited once a month. They put in a gym with
a whirlpool, too. "You name it, we got it," says Tova. "We slept in a
queen's bed; I can't tell you who, if it was Sheba. Canopied and curtained.
We had another bedroom, very modern."

At their big party in 1973 for the naming of a plaza on First Avenue
for Uncle Sam, they had forty-two guests at one table, "only billionaires,"
she continues. They socialized with Saul and Barbara Steinberg and the

Bronfmans. "We had the same problems," says Tova. "To run an apartment like that took a lot of people. I loved it. It was too big. I couldn't make myself at home. It's tough to live with other people and their problems. We had seven sleep-in servants. We had an Italian chef. We called her Caterina the Great. The English butler took a knife to her. He was impossible. They stole from us, and you cannot accuse. Ann and I talked about it. She lost a maid, I lost a maid. Impossible! Take it from me."

Tova cried. She told Arthur the apartment was killing her. "My parents called it a golden cage," she says. "I ran out in the morning to a coffee shop on Madison, and I would have coffee and a bagel and go back to the apartment. I did not go for that coffee-in-bed baloney." They had two children, and she wanted to raise them simply. He told her he'd been born with "a silver spoon in his mouth, and a gold spoon," she says. She wouldn't give him an ultimatum, but she wanted out.

They'd vacationed in Palm Beach for years and in the mid-1970s began spending most of their time there. Tova agreed to make it their home, and Arthur bought an estate from the Dodge family with a four-hundred-year-old pagoda in its Japanese garden and began a gut renovation. Then, in 1978, his doctors discovered a throat tumor. "Twenty-seven operations," says Tova. "He survived twelve years. Arthur wanted to keep the apartment, but we had small children, and we couldn't come to New York that often." Finally they put the apartment on the market. Among the tire-kickers was John DeLorean, the automaker, then riding high. The eventual buyer would prove even more colorful.

It was October 1969. After a decade at 740, Mike and Jan Cowles, whose children had all left, decided that apartment 12/13B was just too big. "It was so beautiful, so grand, so spacious, I can't imagine why anybody would want to move out," says her son, Charles. "If I was there, I'd just lock a couple bedrooms and pretend they didn't exist. But she thought it would be easier to move than redecorate" and bought a smaller but still lavish place nearby.

In truth, Cowles was downsizing more than his room count. The financial markets had peaked in November 1968, and then turned downward after a twenty-year bull market; the Dow Jones Industrial Average had been dropping all year, and Cowles started selling off properties. The same week his apartment went on the market, Mike was forced to shut down the *Suffolk Sun*, a three-year-old daily newspaper he'd started on Long Island; it had lost $7 million. *Look* was losing money, too; despite a circulation of nearly 8 million, advertising revenues were declining. Cowles cut back there, too, slashing his print run to 6.5 million to save money, but the magazine would fold in 1971.

Three 740 apartments were on the market simultaneously, but theirs was the biggest; the other sellers, Northam Griggs and Edith Chrysler Carr, lived in the C line. Would it sell? When a realtor brought Keith and Ann Barish to see it, Jan had cause for optimism. It had only been on the market for four days—and they loved it. She found them "quite attractive," she says. Ann was a pretty, bubbly blonde. He was a preppy, with reddish blond hair and a boyish appeal. "Her mother and father had lived across the street, and they were very anxious for her to have that apartment," says Cowles. Best of all, Barish "came with a check in his hand," says Charles Cowles.

Barish, who was staying at the Hotel Carlyle, seemed to have come out of nowhere when he made his offer, and Cowles accepted it on the spot. He was a young man in a hurry, the head of a faddish, fast-money mutual fund. Born in Los Angeles, Barish had moved to Miami at age three, when his parents divorced. As a teenager, he'd developed a passion for politics, volunteering in local campaigns, then serving as an intern in the Johnson White House, where he was inspired to study business because rich politicians could afford to be independent. As a student at the University of Miami, Barish co-founded the Manufacturers National Bank of Hialeah and built a housing project in Mexico. He was too young to take a seat on the bank's board, so his mother became a director in his stead. He has said he was a millionaire at twenty-three.

Florida was in the midst of a real estate boom, and Barish saw the potential for profit. He and Rafael Navarro, a thirty-year-old Cuban diplomat who'd fled his country after Fidel Castro's overthrow of the Batista government and gone to work for a mutual fund, founded the Great American Management and Research Company International in 1966. Barish had decided to open a mutual fund that invested in U.S. real estate, not stocks, and sell shares only overseas, avoiding taxes and government regulators. In the fall of 1968, Gramco, as it was called, announced that Pierre Salinger, previously the Kennedy White House's press secretary, would become one of its top executives. Ten other Kennedy and Johnson administration aides signed on, too, giving the company a precious aura of New Frontier association. Gramco, based in the Bahamas, where it wouldn't be bothered by taxes or regulations, and using Panama, Curaçao, and Luxembourg as tax shelters, was in the midst of a two-year buying spree, acquiring $185 million worth of income-producing American real estate—office buildings, apartment complexes, a science center, fifty-five properties in all in fifteen states.

The properties, all in America, were placed in the United States Investment Fund, a Gramco-managed mutual fund that began selling shares to foreign investors—mostly Central and South American businessmen—in 1967. Navarro and Barish had opened sales offices in fifty countries and recruited four hundred salesmen who promised 12 percent returns. Several other financiers were selling similar funds at the time, all of them carefully structured so that foreign investors could make money in American real estate without having to pay taxes on their gains. Bernard Cornfeld, who'd pioneered offshore mutual funds, was Barish's idol: his Investors Overseas Services had $1.6 billion in annual sales. When Gramco took over Cornfeld's Latin American sales force after he had a dispute with the Brazilian government, Barish's personal fortune hit $10 million. He seemed well on his way to his stated ambition of beating Cornfeld at his own game.

Pierre Salinger's well-known face soon popped up in articles in the American press and advertisements in European newspapers (in Europe, IOS was still the market leader), touting Gramco's fund, which claimed net earnings of $4 million on a volume of $45 million that year. "Stocks go up and down," the ads said. "Prime U.S. real estate goes up and up." Early in 1969, Barish announced plans to spend another $700 million on properties, $100 million of that in New York City alone, and boasted that fund sales would soon hit $150 million. That May, Gramco sold a million shares of stock to the public on the Luxembourg stock exchange; Navarro and Barish made another $10 million. "The sky is the limit," Barish said. That was certainly true for the young entrepreneur, who was about to use some of his profits to buy a palace in the sky.

Keith Barish and Edith Ann Schwartz, the daughter of a knitwear manufacturer, got married that August and immediately went looking for an apartment. Within a month, they'd found one. Eugenia Sheppard, the fashion columnist, broke the news. "The most romantic young couple" had "met only nine weeks ago and been married for six," she wrote. "He's the 28-year-old board chairman of Gramco and she's a 23-year-old graduate of Brearley and Finch. They already have homes in Miami and London, but the Cowles apartment is a birthday present from Keith Barish to his wife. It will make her feel at home, since she grew up next door at 730 Park."

Douglas Gibbons had merged with another patrician realtor in 1957, and Gibbons himself died in 1962; the firm was now called Douglas Gibbons–Hollyday & Ives, and its tone had become more businesslike. An executive vice president forwarded Barish's references to the board and to Martha Rockefeller under cover of a letter giving the barest biographical details and five references that spoke of Keith's "substantial means," "extraordinary business success," and support of "a whole spectrum of philanthropic enterprises."

Until then, diplomats had been the only problems in the building. Or rather, the French had been (nobody noticed the Germans and the Japanese, who rarely entertained, and the Turks were long gone). "What parties they used to have!" says Patrick O'Connor, who'd become a doorman when automatic elevators were installed. "Oh, my God. All the Secret Service men!" Governments were generally reliable and willing to pay for grand entertaining space, but "we all felt there was too much entertaining, too many limousines double- and triple-parked outside," says Barbara Gimbel. "The French entertained all the time." The doors were sometimes blocked. One night Edgar Bronfman was told he couldn't enter his own building.

Complaints finally crescendoed in 1966, and the embassies were asked to limit their parties to fewer than eighty guests. At the same time, the board barred tenants from letting charities sell tickets to groups touring apartments. Still, the city's coordinator for the United Nations would call all the time, "and they all wanted the big A- and B-line apartments for entertaining, so people on that side really got upset," Alex Laughlin says. "They tied up the elevators and the staff, and there were always cars outside jamming up the place." There was also a question about whether a New York corporation could sue someone with diplomatic immunity if it had to. Informally, a decision was made: no more governments. The Finns, the first to be rejected, would keep trying, and failing, to get in.

Diplomats were a long-term problem. Keith Barish was causing immediate alarm. Laughlin, the board president, wrote the directors to say that he and Henry Epstein considered it "unusual" that Barish's references came only from employees and banks where he did business. "Historically this type of reference does not hold much water," he went on. Barish had made his money "rather rapidly," and coincidentally the current issue of *Barron's* contained what could only be called an exposé of his business, questioning its "morality and financial stability." It was high time, Laughlin concluded, that the citizens of 740 establish some procedures to "check applicants for these apartments." In the meantime, Laughlin hoped everyone would do that on an ad hoc basis. Barish would have to be carefully vetted.

"We should tighten up our screening procedures," Laughlin wrote separately to Mrs. Rockefeller. "I agree," she jotted on her letter. And at the bottom, she wrote one more word: "Appalling."

The *Barron's* article was certainly that. Funds like Gramco's (Barish had inspired dozens) were illegal in both the United States and Great Britain, it said, but by setting up offshore, Barish had avoided those laws and, using creative financing, also avoided income, withholding, and capital gains taxes. Worst of all, it paid itself quite well for its cleverness. *Barron's* revealed that Gramco was claiming one-tenth of the money invested in its fund as net profit and raking off another $1 million a year in fees to a subsidiary. And its fees were based on the fully realized value of its real estate holdings, not its actual equity, which was substantially lower, since its properties were all mortgaged to the hilt. As a result, it sometimes pocketed 20 percent of the money it got from investors. The magazine called it a pyramid scheme, dependent on continuing infusions of fresh cash, and predicted its eventual collapse.

The board did its due diligence—barely. Though he was still only twenty-five, Barish walked the walk in his three-piece suits and fob watch and talked the talk, regularly declaring himself an "eight-figure millionaire." He was summoned for an interview. "I never met the full board," he says. "I met some guy and had lunch. It was not probing or invasive or in any way intimidating. It was nothing memorable. I can't get into Costco as easily." The only question he remembers being asked was whether they would have late parties. "Keith was working 24-7," says Ann Barish, "so they didn't need to worry about that."

More important perhaps, the board member George Leib paid a call to one of their references, Jane Salomon Bernheim, Ann's mother's best friend and the daughter of the founder of the Salomon Brothers investment bank. "And all of a sudden we were in," Ann Barish says.

"They couldn't find facts to back up the *Barron's* article," says someone privy to the board's decision making on Barish. "A lot of phone calls went back and forth. The story had no legs. He made a concerted effort to schmooze the right people. His wife was polished, so was their application, and he did write the full check immediately."

"Seven forty," a realtor says, "had truly become a building where money talked more than anything. That's why Barish got in. They harrumphed, but he had $10 million, which was big stuff in those days."

Today, Barish brushes off the charges leveled at Gramco. Had he done anything illegal, he would have had legal problems, he says. The public censure didn't bother him in the slightest. "I'm so oblivious," he says. "I never read the good or the bad. It comes with the territory. I'm sure I'm appalling to a lot of people. Whatever went on went on, and the forces of good triumphed over evil." He also denies that he flourished a check to preempt the apartment. "I don't carry checks for $500,000 with me, although I had it," he says, adding that neither did he pay the full asking price. "I got them to throw in the furniture. We wanted to move in right away."

Although he'd bought it, Barish got rid of a lot of the built-in furniture—particularly the Dunbar sectional seating. "It wasn't particularly distinguished then," he says. "Now it's collectible." "Barish got a chain saw, cut it up, and threw it out," says Charles Cowles. They also knocked down the wall between two bedrooms on the thirteenth floor and created a screening room. Working with the decorator Arthur Smith, they filled the living and sitting rooms with upholstered furniture and a geometric-patterned rug; mirrored the fireplace; installed a canopied bed, a wicker chaise, bedside tables made from Chinese coromandel screens, and Lucite lamps; and painted the walls in light colors that would set off their collection in progress of contemporary art. As time went by, they would fill those walls with works by Roy Lichtenstein, Robert Motherwell, Kenneth Noland, and Ed Ruscha, and one whole wing would be turned into a spa.

Almost immediately, a bear bit Barish—or at least his investors. Though it wasn't 1929 again, the slow collapse of the stock market that caused Cowles to sell in 1969 accelerated in 1970. In just three months that spring, the Dow plunged 235 points below the high set in late 1968, and the Nifty Fifty stocks plunged from their peaks, their values cut by as much as 90 percent. Interest rates were soaring, the dollar was shaky, brokerage houses were failing, industrial expansion and the housing market were stumbling, and unemployment was rising. The market had lost 35 percent of its value in eighteen months. "This was vintage 1929 stuff, and the prospect of another great depression," wrote John Brooks, the financial journalist, "was a real one." Gramco was one of the casualties. "Gramco didn't end; it just ceased," Barish claims, showing a talent for splitting hairs equal to his financial legerdemain.

Early in 1970, before Barish had even moved into 740, the anti-Gramco forces were in full cry, pointing out that its investments were illiquid and hard to value and might be difficult to sell, which was why Gramco's prospectus gave it the right to refuse investors seeking to cash out in a crisis. Critics accused companies like Gramco of inflating real estate prices, creating, as one accountant put it, "a pretty flimsy bubble," and repeated the charge that Gramco's fees were eating up a huge percentage of the money it took from gullible investors. A sudden rush of redemptions after accusations of mismanagement had already caused a crisis at Cornfeld's IOS. Foreign governments were also growing concerned about the flight of capital from their countries.

Gramco not only didn't flinch, it kept buying, making deals large and small. It made a play for IOS and picked up James T. Lee's Shelton Hotel, which it said it would replace with an office tower. Barish told *The Wall Street Journal* he planned to create $1 billion in new residential housing and become "the largest developer in the world." But that fall, when the German government began investigating Gramco, it abruptly stopped selling shares in Germany. Five days later, it was banned there and within a week so many investors were trying to cash out that the company began frantically selling property. Its share price had already plunged from $38 to $1.50 before the problems in Germany became known. In early October, it stopped redeeming shares. It would later emerge that about $275 million was locked into the fund and twenty-three thousand investors were locked out, unable to get at their money.

Gramco's liquidity reserves had sunk beneath the legal minimum. It had made loans financed by borrowing, secured by stock with no value. The copycat funds were having troubles, too, threatening to swamp the market with properties, driving values down. Then Gramco belatedly released results that showed its income dropping and expenses doubling. Salinger announced that it was going to switch to selling development bonds in concert with Aristotle Onassis, who'd recently married Salinger's old boss's widow, 740-bred Jackie Kennedy. The former press secretary promised returns of 17.5 percent, which proved to be as fictional as the bonds themselves. In January 1971, *Barron's* called Gramco's shares worthless. The real estate portfolio would have to be sold before shareholders saw any money.

"The banks took over and we said adieu," Barish says. But before that, in 1973, two shareholders filed a $40 million class-action lawsuit against Barish and company, who began negotiating a merger with Robert Vesco, who'd acquired IOS from Cornfeld. When those talks collapsed, they went looking for another merger partner.[2] Finally, in 1974, the banks did take over and arranged a merger with a solvent real estate company that eventually began repaying the investors.

Meanwhile, bodyguards were stationed on Barish's landing, greatly upsetting his new neighbors. "This was a building where doors were always open," one says. By 1977, Barish had tired of real estate, he later claimed. "It does not require a great deal of foresight and I didn't particularly find it challenging anymore," he told *The Washington Post.* "I woke up one day and said: Look, I can't do this for the rest of my life. I'd hate to see my obituary with nothing but my net worth." Or worse, an obituary explaining the way his net worth had been achieved. So he spent two years studying for a career change.

"Keith Barish pretty much went broke," John Hughes, the super, thinks. "When he sold the apartment [in 1978], he moved to a rental unit and called me and asked if I would be interested in remodeling it for him. I knew that he was a bit shaky financially at that juncture, so I diplomatically got out of it." Barish wasn't that shaky. He'd hired Alice Mason as his broker, and she sold his 740 apartment for $600,000 to the French government, whose UN representative finally got his wish to move upstairs to a light-filled apartment. And in 1979 Barish reemerged as a force in Hollywood. He bought the film rights for great novels like

William Styron's *Sophie's Choice* and D. M. Thomas's *White Hotel*, hired
top writers and directors to make them, and produced a raft of highbrow
movies. Later, he became a partner in the Planet Hollywood chain, another company whose stock price soared then sank to nearly nothing, inspiring lawsuits from Sylvester Stallone, among others. Whenever he was
profiled in the press, he would repeat his denials that he'd done anything
wrong at Gramco and describe himself vaguely as a Florida real estate
developer.[5]

Barish maintained that he made his real fortune in Florida land
deals, not at Gramco. If that's so, then his next-door neighbor Henry
David Epstein helped, at least a little. One day Barish asked Epstein
about the viability of Florida land deals. Epstein told the younger man
about a parcel he was considering, and how you had to be patient to make
money, but eventually you could. Two days later, Epstein's broker called
him with the news that the orange groves he'd been eyeing had suddenly
been sold to someone named Keith Barish. In 1976, the Epsteins paid
Barish back when they sold their apartment to the very entity he often
blamed for bringing Gramco crashing down, the German government,
for about $275,000.

The collapse of Gramco reflected a broader malaise that affected the
entire country, New York City and its real estate market, and, despite the
vast and seemingly unassailable wealth of its tenants, 740 Park, too. By
the end of 1970, even the wealthiest were feeling the pinch. John Brooks
wrote of empty limousines, seats at the opera going begging, luxury
stores without customers. Republicans were furious over the economy,
Democrats over Nixon in the White House, the young seethed over the
Vietnam War, and crime and racial tension were undermining all large
urban areas.

You had to look hard to find good in it all, but you could: Gramco had
planned to knock the Shelton Hotel down, but the same economy that
felled Gardner Cowles put an end to those plans, and James T. Lee's landmark still stands.

So does 740 Park, although after Barish it would be a very different
building.

PART FOUR

BORROWED MONEY

John H. and Sally French's living room, sixth floor (1980–87)

(Photograph courtesy John H. French II)

29

SAUL STEINBERG WAS BORN IN A FOUR-FAMILY HOUSE IN BROOKLYN IN August 1939. But during the war, his father, Julius, moved up in the world, making enough money recapping old tires to open Ideal Rubber Products, a small plant manufacturing rubber kitchen and bathroom objects. He soon moved his family to Lawrence, a prosperous suburb of New York City. Saul worked summers in the factory and became obsessed with business; by the time he hit thirteen, bar mitzvah age, he was a regular reader of *The Wall Street Journal.* "He wasn't the kid who was playing kickball on the street—ever," says someone who has known him more than forty years.

Saul graduated from high school in three years and was accepted at the Wharton School of Finance at the University of Pennsylvania in 1956. His senior year there, he woke his brother Bobby in the bedroom they shared and announced, "We're driving to Virginia." He'd read about a badly managed company that made rubber soles and heels for shoes. Though still a teenager, Saul decided to take it over and waged a proxy fight. The company bought back the 3 percent stake he'd acquired at three times the price he'd paid for it.

Saul finished Wharton in three years, too. Years later, he'd explain that he'd run out of tuition money and asked permission to cram two years' worth of classes into one. One of his teachers suggested he write a senior thesis called "The Decline and Fall of IBM," but Saul refused after he decided his professor's take on the subject was wrong.

He didn't let his research go to waste, though. After two years of working for his father—while moonlighting as the boss of a chain of forty-six newsstands he'd leased with borrowed money—Steinberg opened a computer-leasing company, using a $25,000 stake he'd gotten from his father. He worked out of the Ideal Rubber factory and at first called his company Ideal Leasing because his aunt Dottie worked as the receptionist and answered the phone, "Ideal."

Saul's business concept was to speculate on the shelf life of computers, buying them and then leasing them to companies for less than the price IBM charged. Saul demanded leases long enough to let him make back his costs; he figured he'd then either sell the used machines or lease them out again, earning profits until they died. "It took me three months to get my first lease, and I had to come back from my honeymoon to sign it," he said.

After their wedding, Saul and Barbara Steinberg moved into an apartment in Forest Hills, a white-collar community in central Queens County—the perfect place for a middle-class couple to start a family. It wasn't long before Saul convinced his father to sell his rubber company and invest the proceeds (along with an equal stake from one of Saul's uncles) in the computer-leasing business, renamed Leasco. It quickly became IBM's biggest customer. In 1965, Saul sold stock to the public at $5 a share. By 1968, when Saul turned twenty-nine, Leasco had $74 million in assets, and the stock was at $180. After a second stock offering that year, Saul was a millionaire many times over.

The Steinbergs had moved to another of the Five Towns, Woodmere. Then, after the money started pouring in, Saul moved his company to ritzy Great Neck, Long Island, and his family to a waterfront estate in Hewlett Harbor, where they had twenty-nine rooms, a tennis court, and two saunas. Urged to collect by Barbara, an art student, Saul spent $160,000 on what he later deemed a "bad" Picasso and a "fabulous" Giacometti, but Steinberg's business, social, and residential ambitions had not been fulfilled. Hewlett Harbor, like Julius Steinberg's home in

Lawrence, was a Jewish enclave tucked into Long Island's southwest corner, not like Locust Valley or Lloyd's Neck on the north shore where the
WASP elite lived. "I relax by thinking," Saul told *The New York Times*
the first time it wrote him up in 1968. He was already thinking about
where he was going next, "looking to ease out of computer leasing," he
would say, and find a field "for the rest of my business life . . . One of the
things you got at Wharton was that everything is possible. Don't worry
about your background or where you come from."

That same attitude motivated Carter, Berlind & Weill, a maverick
brokerage firm that was touting the idea that by taking over an insurance
company, a diversified holding company could gain access to a huge stash
of cash and use it as a deal-making war chest. Saul figured he had the paper wherewithal to skip the step of building a diversified holding company. Thanks to the high price of Leasco's stock, Steinberg was able to
use it to take over a much larger company, an old-fashioned firm called
Reliance Insurance. To keep his moves secret, he nicknamed Reliance
"Raquel," after the actress Raquel Welch, because it was so well endowed. After he took over Reliance that fall using so-called Chinese paper, corporate securities of fluctuating value, to pay for it, *Forbes* hailed
him for having made more money on his own—more than $50 mil-
lion—than any other American aged thirty or under. His father, uncle,
and brother were rich, too. His company was worth $400 million. And
he'd only just begun to think.

Why couldn't a diversified holding company that owned an insurance
company use its leverage to buy a bank and recast itself as a diversified
financial corporation offering one-stop shopping for money? Saul decided
to take over the 150-year-old Chemical Bank New York Trust Company,
the sixth-largest commercial bank in America, with $9 billion in assets.
While planning his run at Chemical, he referred to the bank as Faye, after Faye Dunaway, for its icy allure.

Saul saw himself as a rebel, just like all those other kids his age who
were in the streets, protesting war and oppression. The directors of the
great bank, snugly ensconced in the ruling class, were horrified that this
kid, this nobody, this little Jew from Brooklyn, would have the audacity
to dare a takeover. So the bank, backed up by the blue-blooded financial,
legal, and political communities it was linked to, ganged up on Steinberg

and savagely beat him off. "There was a sense of backs to the wall, of the barbarians at the gates, of time running out," the financial historian John Brooks wrote of the battle.

The press could never prove that Chemical's board illegally inspired a steep sell-off of Leasco stock, but most of the rest of what they did to thwart Saul is public record—and the source of his roguish reputation. The bank even drafted legislation to bar the takeover; the final straw came when Junior's son Governor Nelson Rockefeller lobbied the New York legislature to pass just such a law, giving the state the right to stop a nonbank from taking over a bank. On Valentine's Day, 1969, Saul lost his heart's desire, and within days he surrendered.

He sold his Chemical stock for a $36 million profit, but still, it was a humiliating defeat. The vanquished Steinberg reacted with bewilderment and humor. "We'd touched some kind of a nerve center," he said. Though he didn't think the reaction to him was anti-Semitic, he volunteered, he did find the emotion "rancid."

"I always knew there was an Establishment," he also said. "I just used to think I was a part of it."

WHEN STEINBERG BOUGHT THE BREWSTER/ROCKEFELLER APARTMENT, it was the nadir of 740's once-great fortunes. Just after Saul's feint at Chemical, stocks went into a slow free fall. By 1971, the market had lost $300 billion in equity—and the apartment was, unbelievably, worth less than its 1929 asking price.

It was Barbara Steinberg who demanded they move to Manhattan. Saul's dark-haired, dark-eyed pixieish wife "hated being in the suburbs," says an intimate friend of hers who requests anonymity, as did others close to Steinberg. "Not that Saul was against it. He had a long ride to the city every day and it was a waste of time. And then Saul took charge. He wanted the biggest. No matter what he saw, nothing was big enough, not even a double town house with a pool." Despite his failed bid for Chemical, he was in the big leagues—working with the Rothschilds, for instance, in 1969 and 1970 in a similarly unsuccessful attempt to take over a London publishing house—and he wanted a home that fit his new self-image.

Then he found an apartment that, in the words of a lifelong friend, "was totally compatible with his ego." Junior's widow had just died. The apartment was empty, and the estate was desperate to get rid of it. "It was a buy," Saul's friend chortles. "It had been sitting on the market forever. It was called the White Elephant."

The $225,000 price Saul negotiated wasn't a problem, though the monthly costs were high and Barbara thought thirty-four rooms were a bit much. But Saul got what he wanted. He'd sometimes referred to himself as a lost child of the Rockefellers. "There's no question that Saul was very proud of the fact that he'd bought Rockefeller's apartment," says his friend. "He was ecstatic."

When Saul came before the board, its chairman, Ronald Jeançon, already knew him as a brokerage client. "I interviewed him alone; no one else was there, and I told the board, 'Let 'em in,' " Jeançon says. Holding their noses, the directors agreed.

"There was a lot of talk about Steinberg," Laughlin says. "Everybody knew what he wanted. We weren't sure we wanted him. But he wasn't a crook. He had some beautiful paintings. He seemed like somebody we could live with. There wasn't anybody who objected. And it was not easy to get somebody to buy in those days. We had a hell of a time when we sold ours." Even with all his losses, Saul had the $10 million in liquid cash ($58 million in 2004 dollars) the board required in those days.

Yet it was a watershed and everyone knew it. Henceforth, just as Junior had done, Steinberg would set the building's tone. "Saul didn't have the warts on him then," says Laughlin's son David. "Nobody really knew who he was, how he would mature. But when my dad let Saul Steinberg in, that was the end. The building was changing hands."

AFTER THE CLOSING, SAUL, WHO WAS THEN ONLY THIRTY-THREE, SAvored his first walk through his magnificent new home with the interior decorator Albert Hadley. Hadley was pointing out things he wanted to change, including some faux-antique paneling, when Steinberg stopped him. "If it was good enough for John D. Rockefeller Jr.," Saul said, "isn't it good for us?"

Hadley quickly convinced him that the apartment did indeed need updating and met with Barbara once a week to go shopping. They decorated quickly—"whatever Barbara wanted"—and moved in, "and then Saul changed," says Barbara's intimate. "That's when everything went haywire. All the things he was exposed to! It's an open field in Manhattan. It's not the apartment that changes you, it's you, but it creates a greater monster."

Saul's once-high-flying business was in the dumps; it lost $45 million in 1974. His personal stock holdings had sunk, too, from $90 million to $8 million. And he was being sued by the Long Island private school his children attended for failure to pay part of a pledge to build a Barbara Steinberg Library and Computer Center.

That was the first of several legal battles he'd have in the 1970s, including another against *Barron's*, which accused him of questionable accounting, and a third with the Securities and Exchange Commission, which said he illegally manipulated a stock he was speculating in (Steinberg signed a consent decree without admitting or denying wrongdoing).

At the same time, thanks to a young investment banker named Michael Milken at the firm Drexel Burnham Lambert, Saul found his way back to the cutting edge of finance. Saul's specialty wasn't really computers; it was investing. He was always on the hunt for new opportunities. In 1973, Milken had begun touting non-investment-grade bonds, also known as high-yield bonds, and later junk bonds, that paid exorbitant interest on what most investors saw as huge risks. Saul's holding company, now called Reliance Group, became one of Milken's first buyers—and a borrower, too. By 1975, Reliance was taking huge tax write-offs on its obsolete computers and had canceled dividend payments for two years. It owed $500 million, and its stock price had fallen from $100 to $10 a share. Saul didn't let that get him down; he used corporate funds to buy back the newly cheap shares, strengthening his control, and then reorganized, adding his father and brother, among others, to the Reliance board.

Saul traveled all the time while Barbara stayed home with their children. Their oldest was nine, the youngest was two; Barbara didn't believe in nannies and raised them herself. When she did join him on trips, they went their separate ways in two chauffeured cars. "So Saul suddenly is alone a lot, and, remember, in Manhattan you can be sexy without good looks if you have money," says Barbara's friend. "Women came on to him, and at some point, obviously, he said, 'Why not?' and started to fool around."

One night late in 1975, Steinberg came home and announced he'd been having an affair. He didn't say with whom, but it was Laura (pronounced *LAU*-ra) Bordoni Sconocchia Fisher, the daughter of an Italian foreign-service officer who worked in the public-relations business. He'd met the stunning Italian in Los Angeles the year before. She, too, was married, but, later press reports said, he pursued her across two continents. "He chased her all over the Mediterranean on yachts, planes, and God knows what else," says John Hughes, then 740's resident superintendent. "He had to have her. Forbidden fruit tastes best."

"I'm sorry," Saul told Barbara. "It doesn't mean anything."

But it did. "It was the end of several things," says her friend. Saul was "using something," as the friend puts it—drugs—"and he became enraged, physically abusive. He weighed 250 pounds, and Barbara was five feet four inches and weighed ninety. He beat her up badly. She said, 'I want out.' "

Their divorce seemed straightforward and was filed and concluded in 1977. But the maneuvering started that night, and to Laura it seemed to go on forever. Told she would win a lot of money if she let her children testify in court, Barbara refused and "got almost nothing, peanuts," says her friend. She kept the kids; he kept the money, a house in the Hamptons, the butler, and even Brutus, their two-hundred-pound Great Dane (who had his own room in the apartment with a telephone and a fake tree to pee on).

If anything, Barbara lost money. Saul owed her. "During the marriage," her pal continues, "Saul had ups and downs, and a year before the divorce he had a down and needed money." Reliance's stock price had plummeted in 1974, when it had a $6.60 per share loss versus 1973's $2.55 profit, and the computer-leasing business, hobbled by obsolete equipment, was losing millions, too. "And since the family had been living on the dividends," says Saul's old friend, "this was a big hit." For a time, Steinberg even stopped paying maintenance; the board discussed seizing the apartment and auctioning it, but worried no one would want it.

Saul's wife rescued him. "Barbara gave him a Harry Winston sapphire," says her friend. "Saul said she'd get it back. She cashed her grandfather's bonds out and gave the money to Saul, too. All gone."

So Laura was certainly a distraction, and quite possibly a welcome one. Saul moved out and shacked up with his Italian lover in a town house floor-through apartment on East Sixty-seventh Street. "He wouldn't pay the maintenance at 740," Barbara's friend says. Alone with three children in the echoing apartment, Barbara sold their wine cellar and returned silver to antiques shops to pay the bills. At one point, the utilities were cut off. "She made one mistake and didn't change the locks," says her intimate. "She came home one day and all the art was gone from the walls."

Steinberg decided to put the place on the market, and he asked the board president, Ronald Jeançon, to take a look at the warren of servants' rooms on the mezzanine, and see what could be done with it. "I had architects come up," Jeançon says. "We thought we'd take the whole floor out, but nothing came of it."

"A Rare Offering" was the title of the unprecedented ten-page brochure produced by an international marketing firm to sell the apartment. It called the Steinbergs' home "uniquely spacious even by Park Avenue's demanding standards," and, of course, it was within "one of the 20 best addresses in Manhattan," offering "impeccable service and impregnable security . . . In fact, there are enough Captains of American Commerce among the residents to make this building a financial community in and of itself." The missing art had been replaced by posters; the brokers claimed Saul was "a poster buff."

In pricing the apartment, Saul had seen the future, but it was still a way off. He asked an outrageous $13 million; the apartment next door, only slightly smaller, would sell for just $500,000 the next year. "Nobody wanted it," says Barbara's pal. When the divorce was finalized, an angry Barbara showed up at a Fifty-seventh Street antique furniture store, wanting to sell everything she and Saul owned. Told that her furniture was irreplaceable, she changed her mind and moved to a rental, taking everything that wasn't nailed down, "even the doorknobs," says a decorator who also advised her to keep her antiques. Saul immediately moved back in—with Laura Sconocchia. By February 1978, she was pregnant.

"There's no question in my mind that the best times for Saul and Laura were before they got married," Saul's close friend says. "I've always felt they loved each other very much and they were very well suited, unlike Saul and Barbara, who never should have gotten married in the first place." But once they moved into 740 together, the friend continues, "their relationship became turbulent, lots of fighting."

In May 1978, Laura and Saul reconciled after one of those fights, and Saul signed an agreement to support the child she was carrying, a son they named Julian when he was born that October. Two months and ten days after that, they were married by a rabbi at 740.

AFTER A BRIEF CONVERSATION, IN WHICH SHE SAYS THAT THE STORY OF what followed is "better than you think," Laura Steinberg changes her mind about telling it. Friends say that despite Saul's troubles, and his parsimony toward the mother of his first three children, Steinberg continues to provide some financial support to his second ex-wife. Their child and Gayfryd Steinberg's son co-own an apartment, so the ties still bind.

The newspapers told a lot of the tale that Laura decided not to tell about the dissolution of their marriage. But they hardly told all of it. Steinberg's second breakup actually began months before the first lawsuits were filed, nine months before word leaked into the press. In 1979, Saul had a summerhouse on Beaver Dam River in the bucolic Westchester village of Bedford Hills. "Mirrors on the bedroom ceiling, porn on the shelves, guns in the room," says Martha Noakes, then his next-door neighbor in Bedford, who was shown the room by one of Saul's employees. "It was a little play nest," says another neighbor.

Despite Saul's love for Laura and their son, the marriage was "not in great shape," this neighbor continues. "Saul was known to spend money on women not related to him. Wifey sniffed this out, came at an inopportune time, and found him in the sack with a woman." One of Laura's several divorce lawyers says the same. "The girl was in bed with Saul, Laura comes in, pulls a rifle out of the closet, and pulls the trigger. The gun's not loaded. The girl jumps out of the window naked and runs into the woods."

Martha Noakes heard the story, too. "You mean the time the woman ran naked to Bedford Village? Everyone in Bedford heard this."

"There were multiple weapons," the Bedford resident clarifies. Luckily for Saul and his lady friend, Laura grabbed one that wasn't loaded. "Click, click, click. Stark naked, out the window, from the second floor. She runs to Route 22, where she gets picked up and taken to a shelter. Members of the police force were hired to sit there 24-7 to be sure the wife didn't come back."

The Bedford police "don't know anything, won't remember anything, and there's no record," predicts Laura's divorce lawyer. And sure enough, Knut Johannessen, then Bedford's police chief, recalls nothing of the incident or of his officers being hired as private guards by Steinberg. But twenty-five years later, the story *is* remembered by Steinberg's Bedford neighbors. "I had heard this," says Beazy Durfee, laughing. "A parade of cop cars chasing a buck-naked woman."

Saul's close friend confirms the story, too. "It was just this big, messy evening," she says. "They must have been separated. Saul was in the house with another woman. Laura pulled the gun, but nobody was shot or hurt or anything. And the girl definitely jumped out the window." Saul's friend isn't sure if drugs were involved—that night at least. "I would never deny that Saul and Laura were drug users. My memory is hazy, but my instinct tells me they probably were [high that night]."

The divorce lawyer says that afterward, Laura swore out a complaint against Saul. "He was arrested in a bar and handcuffed. But he got out pretty quick." Raoul Lionel Felder, another of Laura's lawyers, confirms it. "He was arrested," Felder says. "Didn't somebody jump out a window?"

After that, Laura "was very vindictive," says Saul's friend. "They were terrible to each other. It was rocky, turbulent. She filed lots of litigation against him."

"We actually had [Saul] thrown out of the building," Felder says. "A judge signed an order and put him out. It was a unique proceeding." Though Laura had won exclusive possession of the apartment and had Saul barred, both orders lapsed when they got back together in September, after Saul agreed to pay $120,000 a year to Laura if they separated again. Saul also gave her $600,000 worth of Reliance shares. Subsequently, he upped that to $1 million.

That bought Saul five months before the marriage was rocked again. Late in January 1980, Laura left 740 and checked into the $1,000-a-night Presidential Suite in the nearby Hotel Pierre with their son, Julian. This time Steinberg got a restraining order that barred her from the apartment. She vowed to return.

"I decided to move out because we were fighting, not because it was meant to be forever," Laura explains in that one brief conversation. "When I moved out, Saul had bodyguards in the house. Armed guards. There were twenty of them around the Pierre, 'guarding' me and seeing what I would do next. And he changed the locks."

In mid-March, Laura went to court, represented by Felder, seeking to receive support and to overturn the order barring her from the apartment—and the *New York Post* was there. Wrapped in a mink, Laura testified that her standard of living was "extraordinarily high. I have been accustomed to some things that, under this agreement—even if it would be a lot of money for a normal person—I couldn't possibly afford." Her son, she said, couldn't stand the hotel's food and was vomiting.

"My husband is a cocaine addict," she charged, "and he's been on the drug off and on for 2½ years, and at times he gets very violent and very dangerous." She'd tried to get him psychiatric help, but he'd told a psychiatrist "he did not want to change his ways of life . . . and that *I* should be helped to cope with *him.*"

Steinberg's lawyer claimed Saul was afraid of *her.* "Her emotions are obviously out of control." She'd threatened her husband's life. A lawyer even intimated that Saul had broken Laura's jaw and she'd broken his arm.

"That was a very dark time," says Saul's friend. "Cocaine was the drug. Saul was doing it, Laura was doing it, everyone was doing it."

Where had all the good times gone? "I just wanted to go back home," Laura says now. "So I went to a judge. I asked for a protective order so his bodyguards couldn't come near me. And I said, 'I want to go home.' " Felder says he won Laura the right to return. Though their separation was unofficial and no one had sued for divorce, Felder continues, "we also tried to get exclusive occupancy." That was denied. Saul sought exclusive occupancy, too. "The judge told him if he wanted relief to sue for divorce," Felder says. A protective order was issued barring Steinberg and his agents from "assaulting, harassing, annoying, menacing, or intimidating" Laura. Then she fired Felder. "He said, 'Pay me!' " recalls another of her many lawyers. "She gave him a diamond earring."

Two and a half weeks later, Saul was in Hawaii when Laura suddenly appeared at 740 on a Friday night. The staff of 740 had taken to locking the big front doors at night. "You'd see hoodlums going by," says the doorman Patrick O'Connor. "You open the door, they could hit you on the head."

Sal Ingenita was on the door when the mink-clad Laura, accompanied by two cops and two lawyers, demanded to be let in. The super told Ingenita not to open the door, but the cops insisted.

Saul had indeed hired bodyguards—retired and off-duty policemen—to guard his apartment and drive him around town. "She'd threatened him, she'd tried to have him arrested," says one, Dominic Abatiello, who was hired, as he puts it, "to ride shotgun. I worked for him about a month. He was on vacation. I was guarding the premises. She'd threatened to enter and cut up all his paintings. That's what everyone was worried about." Saul had traded in his modern art for German Expressionists, a Schiele, five Klees, a few Rodins, and two Frances Bacon triptychs.

Laura and her posse got off the elevator outside the reinforced steel gate. "The first door had a two-way mirror," Abatiello recalls. "You could see who was ringing the bell. I seen who it was. She came with a nanny, a bodyguard, a locksmith, a lawyer, the police. They destroyed the locks and came in. The locksmith got paid off and ran." The police left, too. Laura sent Julian to bed with his nanny, then locked herself in her bedroom. "You guys goofed," Abatiello told Laura's crew, demanding their names. "She has no right. Get her out of here."

In an affirmation filed in court a few days later, Mark Denbeaux, a law professor, told Laura's side of the story. She'd left 740 "as a temporary measure" to protect her "from various violent acts which she had reason to fear her husband was about to inflict upon her," Denbeaux swore. After the scene at the front door of 740, they went upstairs, and Laura "directed the locksmith to take the steps necessary for her to enter her home." Once inside, she "went about her business . . . arranged for the child to be fed" and put to bed in his room, then "retired to her own bedroom." The policemen left, feeling matters were under control.

Abatiello thinks Laura called the *Post* while another Steinberg body-guard called Saul's lawyer Buddy Monasch, who quickly joined the party, along with another lawyer, "several security guards who may or may not have been armed, their own locksmith . . . several unidentified individuals," and "several police officers," said Denbeaux. A well-wired lawyer, Monasch didn't need court orders to make things happen fast.

Julian was sleeping and Laura resting, Denbeaux said, when he let Saul's team in, and "several hours of telephone calls, discussion and deliberation ensued." Monasch wanted Laura arrested. The police refused. The decision came from the top: not only were a sergeant and a captain on the scene, they consulted police lawyers. Monasch insisted they process a citizen's arrest for trespassing: it was Saul's name on the lease. They telephoned Laura in the bedroom and asked her to open the door. She taped the call.

Standing outside the locked door, Monasch and his associate announced they were arresting her. Asked if he was acting on Saul's order, Monasch wouldn't reply and ordered his locksmith to open the door. "When the door was unlocked, the horde of agents under Mr. Steinberg's employ . . . burst into the room," Denbeaux said, but Laura had vanished. They quickly realized she'd locked herself in the bathroom. "This is my home," she pleaded through the door. "I will honor any police orders. I do not recognize any other authority in my own home. I am committing no crime and I have no intention of committing any crime. *Please* leave me alone."

Monasch called out that the cops were there to take her. A police captain gently reminded him this was his show, not theirs. Just then, Laura opened the bathroom door and began pleading with the captain that she'd only left the first time for fear of Saul.

The cops had had enough and were walking out when the telephone rang and Saul asked to speak with them. Told Laura had been granted an order of protection against him, he ordered Monasch to put her under citizen's arrest. Abatiello did the honors, accusing her of criminal trespass. City cops walked her out of the building, grimly determined but still lovely in her full-length mink. A squad car took her to central book-ing. The *Post* picked up the story from there under the headline POOR LIT-TLE RICH GIRL IN A BIND IS DRAGGED AWAY BY COPS:

> Although a sympathetic cop ignored police
> regulations and did not handcuff her, she
> was treated to all the other indignities of
> the booking process . . . With tears in her
> eyes, Mrs. Steinberg stood in a dirty corner
> formed by bars and a brick wall before
> being searched, fingerprinted and
> photographed . . . "I'm flabbergasted," a
> sobbing Mrs. Steinberg told The Post as
> police brought her out of the building at
> 740 Park Av. . . . "My husband has too
> much power and too much money. He is
> a very sick man. He has a very large
> police force. He is trying to scare me and
> intimidate me."

"The Night of the Dueling Locksmiths," as Steinberg's neighbors later called it, was the beginning of an epic battle that raged on for the next three years, filling the newspapers with embarrassing tales of life at 740.

Directed to stay away from the apartment, Laura changed lawyers twice more within a few weeks, ending up with the famous pit bull Roy Cohn. Cohn rattled his saber at Steinberg, trying to take a deposition from Saul's personal bookkeeper, claiming that Saul was "a habitual user of expensive narcotics" and had been misappropriating corporate funds to pay for them. Following Cohn's lead, Laura's latest divorce lawyer, Robert Stephan Cohen, raised the notion that she might report her husband to the Securities and Exchange Commission.

Laura was fishing for a payoff. She wanted Saul to buy back her Reliance stock for $1 million. Cohn wrote Monasch that Laura had been hearing things about Saul, things "of an abusive and threatening nature . . . particularly to the effect that he was not going to complete the arrangement we had discussed." Cohn gave Monasch a week, warning of dire consequences if the "arrangement" wasn't completed.

It actually took nine days before Laura dropped her bomb: a twenty-one-page complaint opening a class-action suit on behalf of Laura and all the insurance company's shareholders that targeted Saul, his lawyer, family and Reliance board members, and even the comptroller of the city of New York. Throwing a ton of mud, she hoped some of it would stick. The inevitable headline—STEINBERG SAGA OF COKE AND CASH—appeared the same day the papers were filed, making it clear Cohn was pursuing his case in public as well as in court.

Laura charged a vast conspiracy to use Reliance assets for personal advantage at the expense of shareholders. She claimed Saul had used illegal campaign contributions to get a contract to build New York City bus shelters; that he'd created a private security force that, among other things, interfered with the investigation of the bus shelter mess; and that he'd used corporate funds to make cash contributions to politicians, to furnish the 740 apartment and buy art and a sophisticated security system for it, and to buy a private plane "utilized exclusively by Steinberg and his friends for their personal use and enjoyment." She also claimed Saul spent $190,000 in Reliance money "to purchase illegal drugs, including but not limited to . . . cocaine." Saul, she alleged, "was and still is a heavy user of and, in fact, psychologically dependent upon narcotics and, consequently, was not and is presently not capable of carrying out the duties and obligations" for which Reliance paid him $500,000 a year. ("Everything she has said so far is a goddam lie," said Saul, calling his wife "outraged and vengeful.")'

A few days later, one of Cohn's associates, Tom Andrews, told Monasch that she was going to take her story to the FBI and the U.S. attorney. Then, in June, she sued Saul, Monasch, and New York City for false arrest. The bickering and maneuvering wouldn't end until December 1983, when Laura finally settled for a reported $10,000 a month and a trust fund for Julian. "I'm relieved," she told the *New York Post.* "It's like pulling a tooth. You miss the tooth but you feel relieved the pain is over."

By that time, Saul had finessed a $550 million leveraged buyout of Reliance, swapping its stock for more than $500 million in junk-bond debt, taking it off the public market and out of range of complaints by shareholders and regulators. He also put his apartment on the market again, this time for a more reasonable $10.6 million, and then changed his mind again. He started buying stock in Twentieth Century Fox, the New York Times, Filmways, Flying Tiger airlines, an insurance competitor called Republic Financial, Paine Webber, and the utility that owned the Three Mile Island nuclear reactor, but took none of them over; formed an investment partnership with Michael Milken that, *Barron's* would say four years later, "has been a corporate whirling dervish, acquiring businesses, making leveraged buyouts and then spinning off pieces of its repackaged holdings to a pliant public"; bought himself a forty-first birthday party featuring a sit-down dinner for two hundred and songs by Broadway's Evita, Patti LuPone; slept his way through several more women (he even moved out of 740 at the request of one of them, the Lancôme cosmetics model Nancy Dutiel); snorted a bunch more cocaine; and finally settled down for the long run. According to the *Post*'s Page Six, after the board rejected three buyers, including the shah of Iran's sister, Princess Ashraf, Saul reconsidered. His German Expressionists were sold, and the apartment was taken off the market. The woman he'd shortly make wife No. 3, Gayfryd Johnson, a New Orleans socialite, was already in residence and embarking on a total makeover of it—and him. She planned to turn her new honey and their home into symbols of wealth for the next generation.

30

As 740 Park entered its fiftieth year, it still attracted a mostly traditional cast. Charles Dyson, a friend of George Leib's, who bought his apartment for $375,000 from Archie Bleyer in 1979, could easily have lived there in the building's earliest days. The public-school-educated son of a carpenter, he was a trained accountant who began doing leveraged buyouts in 1954 with an initial investment of $10,000 and quietly built a conglomerate that made unglamorous things like engine parts and plumbing and heating products into a $200 million fortune.

Though Dyson came from nowhere, he ended up a philanthropist at the pinnacle of American society—the equivalent of the Chase men who built 740 and spent weekends in Tuxedo Park. Though not from old money, Dyson was certainly old-school, so he was inevitably invited onto the co-op board and eventually followed Randolph Speight as its president.

Dyson played a vital role in the building's history as its vice president in the late 1980s and president through the 1990s. In 1978, Alex Laughlin and Henry Epstein had renegotiated the original mortgage, moving it away from MetLife and to a new bank. They also increased 740's debt by $400,000—to $2.3 million—to pay for those new automatic elevators and the building's conversion from steam to oil heat. In 1981, when the 1971 mortgage came due, a new chairman of the Federal Reserve System, Paul Volcker, was attempting to rein in inflation and had begun raising interest rates. Another new apartment owner, Steven J. Ross, the chairman of Warner Communications, advised the board to "get a mortgage at any price," says Jeançon, "before the rates went up." In June 1981, a new mortgage was signed, leaving the building owing $2.26 million at 8.5 percent. Soon a flip tax of 3 percent, essentially a fee paid to the building every time an apartment was sold, was imposed to give the building more cash.

Then, in 1987, when Dyson was vice president, the board paid down more than half the principal it owed by selling the two doctors' offices the building still owned (two other doctors were shareholders) to their tenants. It was a brief respite. The board had known of a serious defect in the building's original design ever since the facade was cleaned in 1963: the steel lintels above all the windows were rusting. The building needed to be scaffolded, and sections of limestone above each window cut out to allow replacement of the steel. New, matching limestone then had to be installed. The work, which commenced in the spring of 1990, cost more than $10 million. The board raised about half that with an assessment (in essence, a demand for immediate cash from shareholders) against every owner, averaging $258,000 per apartment, and then financed the rest by increasing its mortgage by a whopping $4.5 million to $5.5 million.' "They want everything perfect, and it's not such a negative," says one owner who took a deep breath and paid. Others sold as quickly as they could.

Dyson was also on the co-op board as the building filled with the new-money stars of the decade's so-called Nouvelle Society, but his role in that story must remain untold. "I really have nothing to say to you," sniffs his widow, June, who was the ex-wife of Randolph Marston, a descendant of colonial-era settlers who managed the interests of Laurance Rockefeller for thirty years. She married Dyson when he was eighty and she seventy-two, after their respective spouses had died. "We're a quiet little building."

The staff at 740 knows that following her lead is a requirement for keeping your job. "They're not too keen," the doorman Billy Connors reported back after he was asked for an interview. Current staff members won't speak about the building. And most of them work their whole lives on the job. "These are really private people," says Connors. "They want to be low-profile. I got thirty-four bosses. They're all my bosses." Patrick O'Connor is one of the few surviving building employees, perhaps the only one, who remembers John D. Rockefeller Jr. He worked there six days a week at first, when he arrived in 1948, then after a few years got a half day off on Saturdays. He worked from 7:00 A.M. to 3:00 P.M. with a half-hour lunch until the citywide building workers union won a half-hour reduction. Afterward, he worked from 8:00 A.M. to 4:00 P.M. with an hour off. "Nobody should have to work six days a week in this day and age," George Leib announced one day. He couldn't do anything about it, but he did manage to convince the board to replace the mean little staff benches in the lobby with comfortable chairs.

Until he retired in the mid-1980s, the only times O'Connor wasn't at his post were on those rare occasions when Local 32B-32J of the Service Employees International Union called a strike. Neither the regular threat of them (staff contracts were renegotiated every three years) nor the sporadic appearance of picket lines rippled the implacable surface of 740 Park. In Junior's day, whenever the union went out on strike, the 740 staff would post a sign in the door saying they'd made a deal with an independent owner and would go along with whatever agreement was made. But twice in O'Connor's tenure, the staff walked out.

In 1978, they picketed for forty-eight days. Mabel Garvan sent her maid and cook out with coffee and sandwiches for the workers. "It was terrible for the old folks that was there," says O'Connor. "Strikes are no good. You settle for a few dollars and never make back what you lose." O'Connor was paid $48 a week in 1948 and $300 when he retired.

The building and its staff were run by the superintendent, who lived in a small first-floor apartment and reported to a manager at Gibbons, then Elliman, and now Brown Harris Stevens. One superintendent was ex-OSS and ex-FBI, says O'Connor. "A legend." Another was hit on the head by a falling brick at another building and never recovered. More recently, a manager is said to have committed suicide.

The super in the late 1970s was John Hughes. The son of a contractor, he was a builder himself, "an attractive young fellow who was interested in what was going on and had his eyes and ears on everything. He told me about a problem in the D line," says Ronald Jeançon. "A husband was out of town and the wife had taken up with the leader of a black orchestra, and Hughes didn't think it was right. How he did it, I don't know, but the black gentleman didn't come around anymore."

Hughes was an operator, a dapper man with a country house who drove a white Cadillac. He renovated the super's apartment, incorporating several maids' rooms to expand it to a four-bedroom apartment for himself. Over the years, he furnished it with castoffs from some of the residents. Barbara Steinberg "threw all kinds of things of value away," he says. "Some of that garbage hangs in my apartment today." Another resident, Kay Gilman, whose family co-owned the New York Jets, threw away two LeRoy Neiman charcoals. "I happen to be a Jet fan, so they're hanging in my den," says Hughes. "I have a small child's antique baby carriage, all handmade, has to be eighteenth century. That came out of the Rockefeller apartment. We recently sold a four-poster bed that came out of the [home of] the one who used to have tea for every president who had been in office, Davie. I was paid to take it downstairs, all wrapped up, because Mr. Davie died in that bed, and she didn't want it in the apartment anymore. We sold it to an antiques dealer just recently for $3,000."

Hughes was controversial throughout his tenure. "There was a big uprising right before I came there, and that's how I might have got the job," he says. "There was a super who was a drunkard, and he'd been there for years. The building was going downhill. Downstairs was a pigsty. And the exec on that building said, 'If you can go in there and bring this building up and shape up the help, make the building crispy-clean, you've got a job for life.' In those days, you could have walked into any of the apartments you wanted to go to. There was, like, zero security. So I made the place secure, got rid of all the garbage, fired about half of the staff. Most of them had alcohol problems. I cleaned the whole place up."

Before he sold, Archie Bleyer accused Hughes of stealing. "He claimed that we had stolen all his stuff out of his bin downstairs, and I hadn't the foggiest idea what he was talking about. I got more gifts there. I didn't have to steal anything. I used to get paid to take stuff out."

Getting paid is important to Hughes. "He was terrible," says one owner. "All he ever wanted was money. He ruined my life there. Nothing was made easy unless money was involved." "I was at his mercy," says another. "Some people were able to get things done. I couldn't cross his palm."

Indeed, after an hour of reminiscing about 740, promising all sorts of juicy stories, Hughes demanded payment to continue. But some of his subsequent career is a matter of public record and sheds light on his character. Hughes left 740 after a dispute with members of the board and the management at Douglas Elliman and went to work for the developer Donald Trump. But in the mid-1980s, he returned to Elliman and, briefly, to 740 as the building's executive manager. In 1988, Elliman's whole management team left en masse to join an aggressive rival, Brown Harris Stevens, controlled by the real estate operator Harry Helmsley, because it was a more modern operation that wasn't mired in carriage-trade traditions like Elliman was. They took many of their buildings, including 740 Park, with them.

Six years later, in 1994, the Manhattan district attorney announced the results of a three-year investigation into bribery and systematic payoffs to apartment managers by contractors. More than eighty managers and management companies pleaded guilty. Hughes was one of them. He pleaded guilty to receiving commercial bribes after being charged with twenty-nine counts of receiving bribes, fraud, coercion, grand larceny, and commercial solicitation and was placed on probation and required to pay $100,000 (later bargained down to $80,000) to a victim restitution fund. But Hughes, who now lives in Florida, where he buys and rents out condominium units, is unapologetic. "Gratuities are a way of life in New York City," he says. "I never crossed the line. They made me a felon because I couldn't afford to fight it."

Though he had friends (mostly among those who tipped him generously and used the contractors he steered them to), many in the building were glad to see Hughes gone. "They're all alike," says Tova Leidesdorf. "He was, after all, the super of the super people."

Under Hughes was a hall captain who handled the payroll, helped with the mail, and ran the elevator during breaks. Aside from the six men who worked the two lobbies and elevators, two handymen and several porters were also always on duty, fourteen men per shift.

O'Connor's day was a regular routine that began with dog walkers. "Get them down and out as fast as we could," he says, "then sort the mail." Mail sorting was how the workers learned everyone's name. Husbands would leave for work and children for school. "The ladies would go shopping." Deliverymen were never allowed upstairs. "There was a package man in the basement." The resident diplomats always came home for lunch. "They were very particular about their health." In mid-afternoon, "the young children would come home from school; most of the time there would be a girl with them; they weren't left out wandering the streets like poor people. The most pressure is people on the Park Avenue side having big parties." When they did, one elevator would be switched to manual and someone would have to man it. "That's no fun; crowds of people in the lobby," O'Connor says. "Other owners would always get angry about having to wait."

He'd long since met and married Margaret O'Brien, a maid who worked for Northam Griggs. "She was general help, a waitress," he says of his late wife. "We met in the building, went on a date, and that was it. A year later, we were married. I was tired of living in room and board. She left. They understood. Sent us gifts."

The building and apartment staffs mixed in the basement; maids and butlers would have to use the service elevators and service entrance, next to St. James Church, unless they were walking the owners' dogs, in which case they got to use the front elevators. By the 1970s, chauffeurs, who'd once had a waiting room of their own, had to sit outside, idling in their cars; their waiting room had been incorporated into one of the doctors' offices. The era of the large and pampered staff was past. "In days gone by, ohmigod, the help they had," says O'Connor. "Nowadays, it's one or two at the most. They were treated good, and they knew a lot of things we didn't know."

The building always had a bunch of rich widows. "A lot of them, their husbands were dead," says O'Connor. "These enormous apartments! The living rooms on the Park Avenue side are something ferocious. My God, the closets was bigger than my rooms. I'd sometimes get a call to go upstairs and get clothes for them. They would have their chauffeurs pick them up. They all had chauffeurs." Saul Steinberg's driver would pick O'Connor up when he spotted him walking to work. " 'Jump in, Patrick,' he'd say. I'd sit up front with the driver, of course."

In order to spare the owners the embarrassment of dealing with tips, the building had an automatic bonus system, giving each man $50 every three months and at Christmas, minus withholding taxes. "Some of them were good" and tipped more, says O'Connor. "They had some murderous bags sometimes." One doorman would complain that with all their money, they should just buy more suitcases instead of "packing in so much they break your back," O'Connor recalls.

BY THE TIME CHARLES DYSON TOOK OVER THE BOARD, 740 WAS A VASTLY different sort of building from what it had been. The co-op boards had, throughout the years, done their best to adhere to the original ideal of the cooperative apartment house as a place for "gentlemen of congenial tastes . . . occupying the same social positions in life." Compatibility was an ideal not always achieved (as the tenancy of Lee's fellow Irishman Clarence Shearn demonstrated), but it was always sought after—even in wartime.

Ronald Jeançon, Alexander Laughlin, and Randolph Speight, the three men who headed the board in the 1970s and 1980s, were of the same ilk. Like every board president before and after them, they lived at 71, not 740, but they didn't occupy quite the same rung on the social ladder as their predecessors. Though they had jobs, Jeançon and Speight were seen as gentlemen of leisure, not accomplishment. "Those guys lived on their wives' money," says a realtor who has known the building for decades. "They didn't do anything. They were on the board because they had nothing else to do and it was the only power they ever had. And nobody else wanted the job."

Mrs. Astor's New York had been so small and homogeneous that neighbors called on each other unannounced. But though they still share wealth and proximity, today's 740 residents are atomized, separate, and don't generally know or care to know each other. Jeançon and Speight were the unconscious midwives of the birth of this new ecosystem, the one that changed the building from a shrine to family accomplishment over generations into one that respected and honored only one accomplishment: the individual accumulation of cash money.

What changed can be captured in a single question: Who on earth would want a white-elephant apartment, especially in the depths of a recession and in a city generally seen to be going straight to hell? "Saul Steinberg was the first of those," Alex Laughlin says carefully of the sort of people who began buying into 740 after Keith Barish. They were the kind who thought Candela apartments were feathers and who had the cash to stick one in their caps. But the survival of the co-op depended on attracting and approving such buyers, which required a new kind of board, one that could adapt to the changing seasons of American wealth.

Judy Laughlin recalls that her brother-in-law Carroll Wainwright, the Rockefeller family lawyer, told the board how badly the Rockefeller office, which managed Martha's affairs, wanted to sell the apartment. It had sat on the market for months with no takers, says David Laughlin. "There was no great pressure to unload it," Wainwright insists. "It was not an estate that could not afford that maintenance. Like any estate, they all want to sell." Finally there was a nibble. The French government had long wanted to move its diplomatic apartment to a higher floor. It offered $175,000, and although it was far less than the apartment's value, the offer was accepted. But then Steinberg offered $50,000 more and snatched the place away.

So "people like us" gave way to people with all kinds of likes and dislikes. Yet there remained coherent solar systems in 740's chaotic constellation of households. The first to form clustered around a mysterious businessman named Donald Rynne, who bought Landon Ketchum Thorne's fourteenth-floor simplex in 1975.

The money to pay for it came from Rynne's wife, Trinka Davis. She was the granddaughter of an executive at Goodyear Tire & Rubber Company and the daughter of an inner-tube manufacturer, Poncet Davis, of Akron, Ohio. In 1952, Poncet Davis was convicted in one of the largest income-tax-evasion cases in Ohio history, charged with evading more than $730,000 in taxes, and was sentenced to five years in prison. Trinka Rynne still runs the successor to the family business, which now makes small rubber wheels.

Donald and Trinka had both been divorced from others when they married in the mid-1970s. Rynne has had a mysterious career that has left more speculation than facts in its wake. Not even his wife knew much about him. "He was very quiet about what he did and where he was from," she says.

"I don't care to comment on anything," Rynne says. "Do whatever you please, but just count me out." One explanation for his reticence may be his purported links to the Central Intelligence Agency. Born in 1923, Rynne went to Columbia University, and then served in the military in World War II. Stationed overseas, he met Mohammed Abdel Rahman, a Palestinian who would soon become a founding investor in Intra Bank, which would become one of the two largest banks in the Middle East.

Through his new friend, he met a number of Arab princes and "became an agent for them," says a friend of Trinka's. "He sold planes, became an importer and exporter. They used him to procure things, airplanes, Rolls-Royces. He was a small-time Adnan Khasshoggi." Every once in a while, he broke surface. In 1964, Rynne was president of Admiralty Line, Ltd., a new shipping company running express coffee ships between the Gulf of Mexico and Kenya and Tanganyika, two African nations that had just won their independence. It went into involuntary bankruptcy two years later. In the years that followed, his wife and her friend say, Rynne traveled to the Middle East frequently.

Rynne next pops up in the press almost thirty years later as the chairman of Donald G. Rynne & Co., an international maritime trading and consulting company specializing in the Middle East and dealing mostly in oil and the equipment used to find, refine, and transport it. He also had ties to two shipping and trading companies and worked as a consultant for major corporations like Borden, Uniroyal, and Archer Daniels Midland. In 1992, he was named to the board of directors of the American International Petroleum Company, which explored, refined, and sold oil and natural gas. By that point, he'd been on the 740 co-op board for seventeen years.

Shortly after that 1992 appointment, *Platts Oilgram News*, an industry publication, identified Rynne as "a long-time close acquaintance" of William Casey, the CIA director in the Reagan administration. Years before, *Platts* said, Casey had also been Rynne's personal attorney. The implication was obvious, and for good reason, says James Norman, a *Platts* reporter. "He's a spook, I'm sure," says Norman. "Rynne's profile fits the clandestine, cowboy-CIA-Terry-and-the-Pirates type."[2] Rynne certainly was in a lot of hot spots as their temperature peaked.

"That story has gone around forever," says Trinka. "He had nothing to do with that as far as I know." She allows, however, that the Caseys were frequent dinner guests.

Rynne found their apartment and liked it right away. "We'd been looking a very long time," says Trinka, "and I didn't like it at first. It had a very strange layout, and it had been untouched for many years, but actually it was perfect." "Untouched" is an understatement; the apartment still had the original 1930 wiring and fixtures in it. "I'd never seen anything like that before," says a realtor who showed it.

First National City Bank had put the apartment on the market in May 1974 for $260,000. The Rynnes paid $225,000 (the maintenance was $2,883 a month). Despite the low price (which still horrifies Thorne's grandchildren), the Thornes' attorney was so pleased to sell it that he told the Rynnes' broker they could take any two items in it that they wanted. The Rynnes let their realtor decide, says a friend, and she chose a chandelier and two half-moon tables. Trinka Rynne thought the latter ugly and was planning to sell them until a curator from Versailles asked to buy them. "Needless to say, she didn't throw them out," says the friend. "They were worth more than the apartment." Trinka also loved the Thornes' French paneling. "It was magnificent," she says.

Rynne installed a gym in the servants' quarters and an office in one of the four bedrooms and filled it with pictures of himself with his many powerful friends in the Arab world. "He sold things there," a New York friend says vaguely. "I think it was automobiles. I don't know if he was important, but he was more than a guy with a rich wife. He loved to go to the Middle East for a month to get away from her."

"He was mysterious," says the building's super John Hughes, who considered Rynne a friend. "It was always a mystery to me [what he did], and I never pried. We would go out and have a couple of drinks and sing around the piano over at the hotel across the way. He loved to sing. He was not social with that many people. He was very standoffish. Do you recall back when they did the Gucci Cadillac? Well, he thought that this would be a great deal in Saudi Arabia. He thought that this would really fly well with them. He bought like twenty or twenty-five and got stuck with about eighteen of them."

Trinka found it hard to tell one of his business associates from the next. "You'd meet so many of them, and their names are difficult," she says. "I would practice all day long, and the minute they opened the door, the names flew out of your mind." Still, says an old friend of hers, "the Arabs would give her diamonds and emeralds and she loved it." This friend scoffs at the claim that Rynne was involved in espionage. "He was just an operator," he says, but adds that he believes Rynne was quite anti-Semitic. "He wouldn't let me go to their wedding because I was a Jew," he says. Rynne was also considered one of the most intransigent members of the co-op board.

When Keith Barish decided to sell, he hired Alice Mason as his broker; she was still hoping to move the French to a higher floor in the building. Though he was the champion of Arabs, Rynne was thought to be the board member most opposed to making concessions to the resident diplomats. So Mason advised the French to spend a few months making friends by inviting every board member except Rynne to their parties. Then she waited for Rynne to leave town before proposing the sale at a breakfast meeting with the rest of the board. "And that's how I made that deal," she says. Not long afterward, Rynne heard about the role she'd played and invited her for a drink. "We became very good pals instead of adversaries," Mason says. "I always looked for a friend on every board."

Rynne may have heard about the Thorne apartment through an old friend of his, Homer Langdon. Langdon had bought 17B, the former home of Clarence Shearn and Thelma Foy, from Martha Rockefeller's estate shortly before Saul Steinberg bought his duplex right below. Langdon's mother had made a fortune in IBM stock, which was convenient because both Homer and his wife, Vicki, loved to spend. After the Rynnes moved in and introduced them to the Jeançons and the Speights, they formed a clique. And then Rynne took a seat on the board and became an activist like Henry Epstein, but different.

Saul Steinberg's modern renovation of the apartment between them horrified both the Rynnes and the Langdons. "The noise was horrendous," says Trinka Rynne. "He was always putting in new marble bathrooms. Bang bang bang bang bang." That bothered her more than

Steinberg's disputes with his second wife, Laura. "I knew there was trouble," says Trinka. "We didn't pay attention." Then Homer suffered "reverses" and had to move. "There was nobody more chic than Vicki Langdon," explains a realtor who was close to them, "but she burned money like a pro and they lost it all."

Luckily for the Langdons, Donald Rynne knew just the man to take the place off their hands. "A good friend of mine" is all Rynne will say. Fascinating, charismatic, and brilliant, say others. "He was a great man, yes, I will certify that," says Bill Haddad of his old friend Kamel Abdel Rahman, the brother of Rynne's old friend Mohammed. Kar, as he was known, was not an obvious choice for 740, even though he was one of the world's richest Palestinians, a retired construction mogul whose influence stretched from the palaces of Baghdad to those of Houston, Texas. A political moderate, at least in Palestinian terms, he was also a lifelong friend, adviser, and financial backer of Yasser Arafat.

Kar was born in Haifa, in the British protectorate of Palestine, and started Contracting and Trading, a construction company, working primarily for the Iraq Petroleum Company. In 1948, many Palestinians fled Haifa when the first Arab-Israeli War began. Kamel and Mohammed Abdel Rahman were taken to Beirut on a British boat. Among the refugees were the founders of a competitor, the Consolidated Contractors Company, formed in 1945 to build apartments for Jewish British army veterans. CCC, as it is known, also did work for Iraq Petroleum. In 1950, Kar joined a CCC regrouped in Syria and then moved to Aden, now South Yemen, to build the largest refinery on the gulf.

CCC next moved to Beirut and, thanks to subcontracts from the Bechtel Group of Texas, rode the postwar Arabian oil boom to become one of the largest contracting companies in the Middle East. Today it's a billion-dollar concern with forty thousand employees in sixty nations, building oil pipelines, refineries, and highways, even the Saudi port of Jubail, and providing offshore services to the oil and gas industries of the Arabian Gulf.

Abdel Rahman's role is minimized in CCC's official history. "I do not like the way they treat Kamel's name and memory," says Said Aburish, the author of biographies of the Egyptian president Gamal Abdel Nasser, Arafat, and Saddam Hussein. Aburish met Kar in 1949. "He started CCC, and if they don't like it, they can stuff it. He cut a swath, this guy."

Kar was also in banking—and, peripherally, in a banking scandal. In 1948, he and Mohammed were founding investors in Intra Bank. Bloated with oil revenues, it became one of the Middle East's largest banks before it collapsed in 1966, when interest rates rose in America and the oil sheiks who were Intra's best customers pulled their money out. A year later, the head of the bank was arrested on a fugitive warrant with a fake passport, $37,000, and a bunch of safe-deposit-box keys. The canny, ambitious Abdel Rahman brothers had overreached. They'd tried to use the bank as a tool to give the whole Middle East a Palestinian face.

In 1974, at the beginning of the OPEC-fueled oil boom, Abdel Rahman & Co. aided Iraq's effort to gain nuclear and unconventional weapons and military parity with Israel, a drive headed by Iraq's then vice president Saddam Hussein. Hussein hired Beirut-based Arab Projects and Development, a nonprofit organization funded by Abdel Rahman and a partner to repatriate Arab scientists scattered around the world. But in 1975, when civil war broke out in Lebanon, CCC, by then earning $100 million a year, left Beirut to move to Athens and APD was dissolved. A year later, Abdel Rahman sold his share of CCC and retired.

KAR'S PRIVATE LIFE WAS AS TUMULTUOUS AS HIS CAREER. A GRADUATE OF the American University of Beirut, he had three daughters, Ghana, Nadia, and Ferial, and a son, Aboudi, by his first wife, a Christian Palestinian he married in 1949. While in Aden, Kar married again. Abla Rbeuz was an extremely beautiful older woman from an old Lebanese family who had been the secretary of an Iraq Petroleum executive in the 1940s, when it controlled the second-largest refinery in the Middle East. "Smart, very thoughtful, very strong," says Aboudi. "She was living fifty years ahead of her time." Adds Haddad, "She was behind Kar's success."

It's unclear if Kar ever divorced his first wife. "Kamel had a very, very strange habit," says Said Aburish, who worked for APD. "He married his first wife at least three times, back and forth. Islamically, he would have to marry somebody in between. He married so many times people who knew him lost count." A nephew, Mohamed Habbal, says that on the contrary, Kar never divorced the mother of his children, but took two additional wives in succession.

Abla's contacts with Western oil companies were a cornerstone of CCC's growth, and she owned a quarter of its stock. She also raised Kar's children. Aboudi took after Kar, who was tall and slender with jet-black hair and rakish good looks. Aboudi, even more handsome, was "a likable devil," but also a problem and a troublemaker, says Bill Haddad.

Before South Yemen gained independence in 1967, Kar moved to Beirut, where Abla's influence wasn't as strong and her usefulness to him diminished. One of Kar's partners helped him out by convincing Abla to sell Kar her shares. "Once she'd sold, he kicked her out," says Haddad. After that, Kar became CCC's majority stockholder; his partners held 25 percent each.

But Kar was "getting on in age," Haddad says, intimating that he was having a midlife crisis when, in June 1973, he married a Syrian named Clothilde Chabenne, who was younger than his eldest daughter. "A little chubby, but terribly decorative," says Aburish. "That's the way Arabs like them. But she didn't measure up to Abla, who would have been high society anywhere."

"His daughters were very, very upset," says Mohamed Habbal. "She was Christian. It didn't sit well among the relatives." Aboudi, "a miserable fellow, a wretched guy," slapped his father in public and was disinherited, says Aburish. His daughter Ghana was disinherited, too, says Habbal. "We heard one daughter sided with Aboudi," says Leila Kubba, whose husband worked at CCC.

Rumors began to circulate that Kar had married a prostitute. "Her past was very well known," Aboudi says. "My father used to bring her to his house, the most beautiful house in Lebanon, eighteen thousand square meters overlooking the airport and the sea. He had a 270-degree view at about a hundred feet of elevation in the mountains. And he was living alone there. You get your experience when you are young, right? But if you don't go out when you are young?"

Not everyone around Kar agreed about Claudia, as she was known in the family. "Aboudi thought every woman who approached his father was a prostitute, so I would take that with a pinch of salt," says Haddad.

Others say she merely worked in a cosmetics shop, a less-than-respectable profession, perhaps, but not prostitution. "My understanding was that she was married to another person, a Christian, when she married my uncle," says Habbal. "Their church forbids divorce." Aboudi explains: "She was married before to a Maronite, I think. According to the Muslim religion, you cannot remarry before three months to be sure you are not pregnant. It seems that he married her before that time. That is unlawful, but not in Jersey."

Not long after he retired, Kar, who'd increased his fortune through investments in silver, set up a trust on Jersey Island, a tax haven in the English Channel. He promised to pay Claudia $500,000 from the trust on his death. Kar "had cash, a lot of land, assets all over the place," says Aburish. Aboudi thinks his father's trust totaled $160 million.

So Kar could well afford it in 1978, when Rynne told him there was a great apartment available at 740. "It was suggested that he should acquire it" in Claudia's name, but he refused, according to a decision in one of the multitude of lawsuits that would shortly become part of the paper trail of their marriage. He finally agreed to put it in Claudia's name in exchange for her signature on an interest-free note saying that she'd borrowed $850,000 from his trust to pay for the apartment and furnishings and would repay it on demand.

Ronald Jeançon was delighted about 740's latest shareholder. "We were very proud we had Arabs and Jews," he says. "We were very open, no restrictions whatsoever." But not everyone agreed. The Steinbergs, for instance, had entertained the Israeli leaders Moshe Dayan and Golda Meir in the apartment beneath Kar's. "A lot of people who are very prominent in business today, young Jewish fellows, okay? They could not stand Kamel," says John Hughes. "One day, he said to me, 'My good friend Arafat is coming to the UN, and I'm going to bring him to my apartment.' I said, 'Kamel, you're going to start World War III. You cannot do this!' Donald Rynne and I both talked to him." Kar understood. "He would never be a terrorist," says Aburish. "If he'd had a needy Jewish neighbor, he would have helped. He grew up in an atmosphere of tolerance."

Arafat wasn't the only recipient of Kar's generosity. "He was like my grandfather; he couldn't have been nicer," says Hughes, who claims

Abdel Rahman promised to buy a Connecticut estate and put it in his name. "He gave me a brand-new Lincoln, too, because he couldn't find a garage for it. There was a gas crunch on, so I sold it." When Hughes told him he'd gotten $10,000 for it, Abdel Rahman mocked him. "I paid $19,000," he said. "You didn't do very well." In return, Hughes built Kar a snooker room in the basement. "He used to go down there and pop the pool balls around, always in his stocking feet. Hated to wear shoes."

Claudia, who'd returned to her formal name, Clothilde, and converted to Islam ("to inherit, of course," snipes Aboudi), made out best of all. "We visited their beautiful home on a hill," says Leila Kubba. "His family saw her as a money-grubber. Anybody could see that's what she was interested in. I will never forget, the whole lunch she talked about Jackie and Onassis and how generous he was with her. The comparison was obvious. Kar turned a deaf ear. He was annoyed by it."

Claudia had already done quite well. If she stayed with him until he died, she'd keep the apartment and furniture, though he changed his mind often—once after writing her another six-figure check—about how much of the "debt" she'd have to repay on his death. By 1979, he'd instructed his trust to "loan" her a total of $1.05 million.

"He gave her an extraordinary amount of money one day to go out and buy some jewelry, and he says, 'Watch when she gets back. She doesn't do smart things. If she were smart, she'd buy one piece which would be an investment piece,' " says John Hughes. "She came back with small pieces." According to Hughes, his best friend on the staff, Kar was no longer in love with Claudia. Hughes didn't think much of her and "neither did he," Hughes says.

Kar never got the chance to make much of an impression on his other neighbors at 740. In 1979, the couple were in Cleveland visiting Claudia's brother, a doctor, when Kar complained of chest pains and ended up in heart-valve-replacement surgery. That fall, as part of his recovery, he took to exercising in the lobby, walking from 740 to 71, "apologizing for being a nuisance," says O'Connor. Hughes recalls laughing at him "because he used to walk in his stocking feet, and we used to say, 'Here's a man with all this money and he has holes in his socks.' " At Thanksgiving, Abdel Rahman had dinner with the Rynnes before flying to his penthouse apartment on the French Riviera.

What happened there on December 5, 1980, is a matter of dispute. "I heard from Donald Rynne that he slipped and fell in the shower," says Hughes. But most agree that Kar was puttering around the roof garden of his Riviera home when something happened. "Some people say he fell seven stories," says Hadi Abdel Rahman. "It's hard to believe he had a heart attack and fell."

Trinka Rynne's version: "He had a garden on his roof. He loved his flowers and plants and trees. He went up on the roof and just fell over and died. He hadn't taken his blood thinner. He was very well monitored, but it had been snowing in New York, and he didn't know that climate change" affected the medication. "There was no hanky-panky. [Claudia] loved him very much. She's a lovely woman. It was just ludicrous what they were trying to say."

Aboudi Abdel Rahman comes out and says it. "He died, yes, in Monte Carlo. And she was with him. He was taking pills to liquefy his blood. And I think he had an overdose. He took more than the required pills, got dizzy, and fell through the skylight. I don't know who gave it to him. It was mysterious." By the time Aboudi reached Monte Carlo, his father's blood was normal. Still, Aboudi believes Claudia fed him an overdose. "I do," he says, "but we couldn't prove it. I am telling you the truth. I have nothing to hide."

Trinka Rynne calls Aboudi's charge "very strange."

"What happened after [Kar] died was just pathetic; it's a soap opera, basically," says Mohamed Habbal, who says that Kar's body was flown out of France and buried in Beirut without an autopsy. "It was a huge topic of conversation. There were so many rumors." But there is no record of any criminal proceedings against anyone. And then the civil lawsuits began.

The first, brought by Claudia in Jersey the year after her husband's death, was an assault on his estate and his bequest to her of a mere $1 million. She wanted to be declared Abdel Rahman's legal widow and have Lebanon declared his legal domicile. She also wanted the trust invalidated and his English will revoked. Then, under Lebanese law, she would inherit everything. The main defendants, Kar's children, responded that it was the marriage to Claudia that was invalid. Later, more defendants were added to the suit, including Chase Bank, as his trustee, Kar's education charity (which was left $70 million, according to Said

Aburish), and relatives of Kar's mother, who'd outlived him by a year; they were entitled to one-sixth of the estate under Lebanese law. The issue of the validity of the marriage was settled first, in Lebanon, and Clothilde was declared a legal wife and widow in 1987. The trust was declared a sham in 1991, because of the way Abdel Rahman used it like a piggy bank; so officially, Kar had died intestate, and the question became how his estate would be divided: under British, Jersey, American, or Sharia law. That's when Clothilde settled with the children, but the litigation lingered on into 1994 as the education fund fought for its share and lawyers for their fees.

Finally the money was handed out. "They split the estate five ways," says one of the countless lawyers who worked on the case. "Clothilde got the biggest share, like $25 million, the son got $25 million, the daughters got about $20 million each. We wanted $6 million. They said, bugger off. We settled for a substantial slice. Clothilde may have given a small sum to his education trust, but in the end they didn't get what they thought." More went to the Palestine Liberation Organization, but "never hit the books," Aburish claims. Hadi Abdel Rahman, a nephew, says Kar's fund got its bequest ("I made sure") but vehemently denies that the PLO got a penny. "Baloney!" he says. "Absolutely not. I think they hated him."

Though he got money, Aboudi Abdel Rahman never got satisfaction. Said Aburish tells more about that. "The Palestine Liberation Organization was based in Tunisia when Kar died," he says, "and Aboudi went and asked for a meeting with the fuzzy-bearded monster [Yasser Arafat]. Arafat had very bad manners. A dozen people were sitting in a room, and Aboudi was supposed to sit and say why he was there. Arafat grabs him and hugs him, and says, 'Your father was my brother; I loved him. Sit here next to me.' Aboudi says, 'I want you to know my father did not fall. Claudia pushed him.' Arafat said, 'You don't think I have enough to do? You want me to be a detective? Please! I'm a very busy man.' And that was the end of it."

But it wasn't. Aboudi Abdel Rahman continues to believe that his stepmother killed his father. Others have their doubts as well. "None of my family are on talking terms with her," says Mohammed Abdel Rahman's son, Hadi.

"You're talking about the race of the conspiracy theory," says Abur-ish. "In Arab legend, when you have this kind of money, nothing hap-pens naturally. But having lived through many conspiracies, I am terribly dismissive of them. They were married for a long time. She was better off with him alive."

Clothilde had long since sold her apartment at 740 Park—and made a considerable profit. Times had changed since 1978, when New York's economic comeback had barely begun. Clarence Shearn's old $10,000-per-year digs went on the market in 1984 for $4.5 million (maintenance on it had reached $44,220 a year) and were snapped up immediately for just a bit less by a venture capitalist.

Clothilde moved to the Brompton Road in London, a neighborhood fashionable among wealthy Middle Easterners, established a *société anonyme* called François 1er Investment & Property S.A. in Luxembourg, and dropped from sight. Though she'd pursued her fortune in public courts for fourteen years, Clothilde Abdel Rahman says, through one of her former lawyers, she "has no interest in being involved in any way" in telling her story and "is well aware that others may speak about her [and] that they will say whatever they wish. She is an extremely private person and wishes to remain so."

The two families that have occupied Thelma Foy's apartment since have been far less dramatic. The first was John Foster, who specialized in health care for both humans and pets, and his wife, Lynn, a financial an-alyst. Initially, they found the apartment stylistically schizophrenic, with its formal living room and contemporary touches, and too small for their family (they had four children between them from previous marriages). And Clothilde Abdel Rahman insisted on being present whenever the place was shown. So they kept looking. But everything else they saw, Lynn Foster says, "was dark, not elegant, not gracious, not detailed, so we kept coming back." When they decided to buy, the board, still run by Randolph Speight, called them in for an interview.

"It was quite formal," Foster recalls. They entered the Speight apart-ment and were ushered to two chairs facing two semicircles of inquisi-tors. But despite the formal setting, the interview was easy. All the board wanted to know was whether they had enough money, and what they planned to do with the apartment. How did they plan to fit a family of six in? That proved tricky. A butler's room and two maids' rooms became bedrooms for the children. "They loved it because they were away from us," Lynn says. But it was a tight fit, and though the public spaces were elegant and the building well managed, they didn't stay long, moving with Foster's job. They put the apartment on the market for $7.5 million in 1993 and dropped their price steadily until it sold in May 1994 for about $6.3 million.

The buyer, Gregory Fischbach, was a computer games manufacturer. Once an entertainment lawyer and record executive, he'd founded Acclaim Entertainment in 1987 to develop games for Nintendo and Game Boy. Its most famous product was Mortal Kombat, featuring gory decapitations and bloody dismembering. Though it had $600 million in sales in 1996, it lost money through the 1990s, lost the rights to Mortal Kombat, and went bankrupt in 2004. Fischbach seems not to have suffered, though; he's held on to his 740 digs.

31

THE WORD MOST OFTEN INVOKED TO DESCRIBE DAVID J. MAHONEY, early in his career, was "maverick." Born in the Bronx, the son of a construction worker, educated on a basketball scholarship at Wharton and as a World War II infantry captain, Mahoney began his career in an ad agency mail room but by twenty-five had become the youngest vice president on Madison Avenue. In the era of the Organization Man, the blue-eyed, imposingly handsome executive was a standout: unabashedly ambitious, restless, and high-profile, another Landon Thorne. In 1951, at twenty-eight, he formed his own ad agency, then sold it to become chairman of a client, Good Humor, the ice cream company whose jingling trucks were a fixture in the suburbs built by another young maverick, Henry David Epstein.

Though he now ran a great American brand, Mahoney was just getting started. When Good Humor was sold in 1961, he leaped to Colgate-Palmolive, gearing up for an all-out war with Procter & Gamble. Five years later, he was on the fly to Canada Dry, where he was named president. Then, in 1969, he made his boldest move, presiding over the merger of drink (Canada Dry), food (Hunt's Tomato Sauce), and publishing (*McCall's* magazine) companies to form one of the newly fashionable conglomerates (collections of diversified companies), Norton Simon Inc. It was named for its backer, a California corporate takeover artist and art collector, who immediately left. Promoted to chairman in 1970, Mahoney, who'd lived on Park before moving to California to run Norton Simon, relocated the company to New York and bought apartment 8/9B at 740 Park, from the lawyer John T. Cahill. Listed at $525,000, it sold for $485,000 in 1972.

Mahoney built Norton Simon into one of the most high-profile companies in America, adding Max Factor, Halston, United Can, and Avis Rent A Car to its $3 billion portfolio and earning almost $1 million a year in the mid-1970s, to the dismay of some stockholders. That helped him move in the highest circles of American society, even advising presidents. But his family life was disintegrating: his first wife was an alcoholic. In 1973, he was separated, moving first to the Waldorf Towers, then to a rental on Fifth Avenue. When his wife threw his children out of the house, the spouses swapped apartments, and Mahoney returned to 740. "David, being a big, tall man, always loved his high ceilings and big rooms," says Hildegard "Hillie" Merrill, who would shortly become his second wife.

The Mahoneys were divorced, and his ex moved to Florida, where she died soon afterward. In the interim, he'd met Merrill, a Miss Rheingold who'd become a spokeswoman for Kodak and New York Telephone. "It was love at first sight, but it was a very sad period in our lives," she says, so they waited years to marry. "His children had been traumatized. You had to be sensitive." Hillie had a family, too, so she kept her own apartment during their long engagement but spent enough time at 740 to know one thing. "David," she told him, "I love you, but not this unhappy apartment."

Real estate had yet to emerge from its 1970s swoon, though, and Mahoney was a smart enough businessman to realize that. So when James T. Lee's old apartment came on the market, in what was, effectively a distress sale, he moved quickly.

The seller, Stan Zimmerman, a department store executive who'd lost his job, had already suffered through one board turndown. Nelson Peltz was a Wharton business school dropout who'd gone into his family's frozen-food business in 1963, the same year he married the daughter of the president of Emerson Radio and Phonograph. Peltz, who would eventually accumulate a fortune in the hundreds of millions as chairman of Triarc (which owns Arby's), was still a small-timer when he tried to buy Zimmerman's apartment, though he'd begun acquiring companies like Coffee-Mat, which sold candy and coffee vending machines. A great pal of Saul Steinberg's, he'd been divorced in 1981 and lived large; he was notorious in New York for throwing wild parties. Worse, as far as the board was concerned, after Peltz had renamed and sold his company, leaving him only with Coffee-Mat, it went south, from $1.1 million in earnings in 1976 to a $2.3 million loss in 1978. (Peltz didn't return repeated calls for comment.) Mahoney, who'd joined the co-op board, knew of the turndown, of course, and snapped the place up. Mark Hampton was already decorating, painting the dining room claret and the living room pale yellow and installing dark brown velvet furniture in the library, when the busy couple finally found time to scoot off to Haiti and marry.

Mahoney was clever enough to come up with an alluring buyer for his first 740 apartment. His Royal Highness Nawwaf bin Abd al-Aziz bin Abd al-Rahman Al Saud, one of the forty-three sons of Saudi Arabia's King Abdul Aziz bin Abdul al-Rahman Al Saud (known as Ibn Saud), and a brother of the late King Fahd and his successor, King Abdullah, was as unlikely as they come to subject himself to the scrutiny of a co-op board. But thanks to Donald Rynne, 740 Park had become "a haven for the disparate rich from all over the world," says Alice Mason, the realtor. Rynne didn't know the prince, "but he was anxious to have him," says someone involved in the deal.

He wasn't alone. With OPEC always in the news, the board members were all eager to meet a Saudi prince. But getting Prince Nawwaf to attend an admissions interview was a hurdle. He was not used to being judged, let alone by a bunch of white guys living off their wives' fortunes. So Mason told Mahoney to gently suggest to Nawwaf that he might want to meet some people who would be his neighbors—in effect, interview them to be sure he wanted to live so near them—and Mason escorted him to the meeting, where the prince, who "hardly spoke English," says a witness, "thought he was interviewing them and they were all so pleased to meet him." For $500,000, he had himself a New York pied-à-terre.

Prince Nawwaf's résumé is sketchy, but his wealth is obvious. He commanded the Saudi National Guard at a very young age, served as a royal court chief under the late king Saud (who reigned from 1953 to 1964), was a special adviser to King Faisal, and often accompanied the King's brother, Crown Prince Abdullah, who would become the kingdom's de facto ruler in the 1990s when King Fahd was incapacitated by strokes. But in the 1980s, Prince Nawwaf was just another Saudi prince, albeit one of the most powerful. A founder of the Saudi–New Zealand Bank, he owned and developed real estate.

Nawwaf came to his interview from the Waldorf Towers, where he stayed at Christmas with his wife and children. It was, in part, his promise to be an absentee owner, and come to the building no more than a few times a year, that helped win the co-op board's approval. "They said, he won't be around that much, why not let him in?" says Hillie Mahoney. He was good as his word. Nawwaf would visit his apartment, decorated with a tented room and a fountain in the entrance, only two or three times a year. "The secret police, this and that," says the doorman Patrick O'Connor. "They'd be on the back stairs, oh yes. They were worried about the back elevators." Nawwaf would "come and go like a thief in the night," says John Hughes, always with an escort and usually through the discreet Seventy-first Street door, then down the hallway to 740. "We'd be told in advance we'd be questioned by them," says O'Connor.

Nawwaf didn't have parties, and no family was ever in evidence. Indeed, most of his fellow owners say they weren't even aware of him. "But he had plenty of females coming in to see him," O'Connor recalls. "Right through the front door," adds Guy Salvadore, head of transportation for Warner Communications, who sometimes stayed in an apartment owned by his boss, Warner's chairman Steve Ross. "They were coming in by the fucking truckload. You'd know he was there because you'd see the women." Mrs. Prince Nawwaf was nowhere to be seen.'

Nawwaf listed the apartment in 1987 then again in 1992, when it sold for $8 million to Wolfgang Flottl, a thirty-six-year-old Austrian financier and art collector who, a few years earlier, had married Anne Eisenhower, President Dwight D. Eisenhower's granddaughter. They owned the apartment for eight years but never moved in. "The reality was, we were not living in the United States," Anne says, "so we never actually lived there. It was too big for me. If you wanted to hit the refrigerator in the middle of the night, it was a long way. We were going to renovate, we had plans done, but we ended up not doing it because the building was redoing its elevators, and then they banned construction for one or two years, and we truly lost steam. I was ambivalent anyway. It didn't end up all bad. Real estate climbed substantially, so it was a good investment."

The Flottls signed a confidentiality agreement with the prince when they bought, so she won't confirm any details of their purchase. They put it on the market for $15 million in January 2000, and it was sold the very same day to fifty-year-old Thomas J. Tisch, a private investor. Tisch works through a firm called Four Partners (also known as FLF, for four lucky fellows), an investment partnership with three brothers whose fortunes were inherited from their father, Laurence Tisch, the chairman of Loews Corporation, which owned Loews Hotels, Lorillard Tobacco, and CNA Financial. The son of a Seventh Avenue garment businessman, Larry Tisch parlayed a 1946 loan of $125,000 from his parents into a fortune in the billions. When Tommy, his wife, and four children moved into their mansion in the sky at 740 Park, his parents lived eight blocks north in the same, far more modest postwar apartment they'd occupied for many years.

Tisch is a quiet, funny, modest, and overtly Jewish man. So, ironically, is the man who now lives in Donald Rynne's apartment. Right around the time that their friend Kamel Abdel Rahman died, things had started going downhill for Trinka and Donald Rynne. "It was disgusting, horrible," says Hadi Abdel Rahman, who sided with Trinka, whom he considers "like my godmother." Finally they got divorced. And only then did Trinka discover she didn't own the apartment she'd paid for. "I thought it was in my name, but it wasn't," she says. Rynne agreed to forsake a claim on her tire company if she gave him the apartment, she says.

"He put it in his name," says an old friend of Trinka's. "He got the shares. She hates him."

The apartment went on the market in March 1998 and sold a year later for $13 million. Though it was $1 million less than the asking price, it was nonetheless one of the highest prices ever paid for a Park Avenue cooperative.[2] The right to pay $10,892 a month in maintenance was won in the spring of 1999 by Steven Rales, a grandson of Russian immigrants and son of a once-penniless home-improvement millionaire. A member of the Forbes 400, with an estimated $2 billion fortune, Rales, with a brother, set up Danaher Corporation in 1984 and began taking over companies. Among their acquisitions were Craftsman tools, considerable real estate, and about three dozen companies making everything from barcode readers to heart-pump motors. Rales and his first wife, Christine, were on the cusp of a long, contentious divorce. "She had nothing to do with it," says someone close to her. "He was making a New York play. It was Ozzie buying and Harriet not knowing about it. It might've been the beginning of the end of their relationship."

Though they later bought another New York apartment, the Raleses would soon make the papers for other reasons. After their separation in 2001, with Christine charging Steven with "persistent abusive behavior," Rales removed a $50 million art collection from their home, replacing the originals with posters, and she filed for divorce in early 2003, amid charges that he had engaged in "dangerous and threatening conduct," specifically, driving his car straight at hers. Asked why he'd done it, Rales allegedly replied, "To get your attention."

In March 2000, Rales sold the old Thorne apartment, without ever moving in, to Israel "Izzy" Englander, a self-described "yeshiva kid from Brooklyn" whose father, Moses, ran a wine store and whose mother, Roza, ran a clothing store. After starting his career as a floor broker on the American Stock Exchange, Englander, a pale, sandy-haired fifty-five-year-old typically clad in steel-rim glasses, a dark gray suit, black knit tie, and white shirt (and, when at home, a yarmulke), founded his own brokerage in 1977, then formed Jamie Securities in 1984 with another trader, John A. Mulheren ("Jamie" was an acronym of their names), working for clients like the Tisch and Belzberg families. Mulheren, a generous, gregarious, and brilliant manic-depressive, would be jailed four years later after he threatened to kill the arbitrageur Ivan F. Boesky for implicating him in an insider-trader scandal. He was arrested near Boesky's home carrying a semiautomatic rifle.[3]

Arbitrage and hedge funds are related Wall Street specialities. In the first, securities are bought and sold simultaneously in order to take advantage of tiny technical price differences. Hedge funds are unregulated private mutual funds for a limited number of extremely wealthy investors that use a laundry list of sophisticated techniques—including options, short selling, and leverage, futures, swaps, and arbitrage strategies—to minimize risk and maximize returns. Englander, who was untouched by the Boesky scandal, ran the business and managed his partner's erratic moods while Mulheren concentrated in investments. In awe of his partner yet also keenly aware of his flaws, Englander loved to quote Mulheren confronting a group of besuited management consultants in a Hawaiian shirt. "I'm a revolutionary," he told them. "I liberate money from second-generation WASPs. Yours came on the *Mayflower?* Mine flew the Concorde."

Englander started his hedge fund, Millennium Partners, in 1990, backed by the Belzbergs (another Canadian dynasty like the Bronfmans), and averaged annual returns of 18 percent. He did even better in 2000, giving his investors a return of over 30 percent. Managers of hedge funds, which typically begin with $500 million, charge management fees of 1 or 2 percent (or $5 to $10 million a year), plus 20 percent of all profits, so the apartment was likely not a stretch for Englander, even when Millennium's returns fell over the next few years. *Institutional Investor* magazine reported that he earned $99 million in 2002 and $128 million in 2003.

Englander refuses to discuss his apartment, and the reason why became apparent in 2004. One of Millennium's traders pleaded guilty, the previous October, to placing after-hours trades that allowed him to make profits when normal investors could not, and investors began pulling their money from Millennium. The fund's assets slid from $4 billion to $3.2 billion. The Web site TheStreet.com also alleged that Millennium was under an investigation by New York's crusading attorney general Eliot Spitzer. A few months later, a similar story appeared on the front page of the business section of *The New York Times.* But it added that in the months since the story first emerged, Englander had raised hundreds of millions more from investors. And the *Times* ended its story with praise quite at odds with its drift: an ex-employee was quoted saying that Englander "is an honorable guy. You don't often see that on Wall Street."

DAVID AND HILLIE MAHONEY REMAINED AT 71 EAST SEVENTY-FIRST Street until 1981, when all their children were gone. "David and I traveled so much," says Hillie. "We had houses in Beverly Hills and Jamaica, and we were hardly ever there. It didn't make sense to stay, so we went to the Waldorf Towers."

One of Norton Simon's businesses was cosmetics, so the Mahoneys were naturally friendly with Estée Lauder, the queen of that business, and knew that she was not only a canny real estate investor but interested in their apartment in particular. "She believed in buying and never selling real estate," says Mahoney. "She'd said that if we ever wanted to sell, we should let her know because she might want it for Ronald," one of her sons. The Lauders often worked with the Mahoneys' broker, Alice Mason, and so a deal was quietly arranged. "Jo Carole and Ronald bought it," says Mahoney, who adds that though she has no memory of what they paid, "it was a pretty big number, up there in the millions."[4]

RONALD LAUDER IS "NOT KEEN ON ANYONE KNOWING WHAT HE DOES with his life," says a woman who identifies herself as his executive assistant. "He gets hounded all the time." Oddly, then, he's chosen to pursue highly public activities, particularly in the years since he took over James T. Lee's old apartment, stripped it of all its original fixtures, and turned it into a boxy, white-walled museum of art. The indulged younger son of Estée and Joseph Lauder, Ronald was born in 1943, shortly after his parents married each other a second time. The wedding took place four years after their divorce.

After attending Wharton and the Sorbonne, Lauder went to work for the family firm but was overshadowed by his older brother Leonard. Ronald eventually became the head of Lauder Investments, Inc., and maintains a sideline as an active art collector. But his unrequited love was public policy. In 1975, he was named to an economic policy board by New York's Governor Hugh Carey, a Democrat. Then, in 1980, just as he was moving to 71 East Seventy-first Street, he became head of the finance committee for New York's Republican Party, after contributing large sums to Republican candidates. He began lobbying for a job in the new Reagan administration immediately, and his mother's friendship with First Lady Nancy Reagan was said to have given him an edge, though he had few credentials aside from speaking several languages and having experience in international business. When it was revealed that he had declined an offer to become ambassador to Jamaica and wanted to go to work for the Defense Department, one wag joked to *The New York Times* that the department should adopt the slogan "Keep your powder dry." Shortly after that, Lauder was named deputy assistant secretary of defense for European and NATO affairs. His experience as an armor and armaments collector would serve him well, he told a reporter. It was generally thought that he'd bought the job by raising $4 million for the Reagan campaign. He soon made an enemy of the Canadian prime minister, Pierre Trudeau, who dismissed him as "a Pentagon pipsqueak." In 1985, Reagan took him out of the line of fire, appointing him ambassador to Austria.

When Lauder left that post in 1987, the Austrian government launched an investigation to determine if he'd broken laws when he left the country with a cache of Austrian paintings, furniture, and objets d'art. Lauder said the "scurrilous, malevolent" campaign against him was begun by anti-Semites who objected to his attitude toward the Austrian president, Kurt Waldheim, a former Nazi. Regardless, the incident was considered less than diplomatic, as were later disclosures that one of his deputies was under investigation as a Soviet spy. But it was a perfect prelude to his next endeavor, a fruitless 1989 primary run against the former federal prosecutor Rudolph Giuliani to be the Republican nominee for mayor of New York City.

By that July, he'd spent $8 million of his own money in his bid for public office (the total would eventually hit $14.4 million). He'd also been forced to reveal his net worth of $227 million (the equivalent of $342 million today). Lauder claimed he'd worked hard for his money and led a "very simple lifestyle," despite his art collection, six classic cars, and three homes, among them an eighteenth-century saltbox he'd moved two miles to his property on the ocean in Bridgehampton, New York. The very private public man had allowed *Architectural Digest* to publish photos of the William and Mary antiques-stuffed house, albeit anonymously, that June. He would publish photos of the house again after a redecoration seven years later.

Lauder's mayoral campaign was rocked by charges that he'd been "impetuous and incompetent" in Vienna, in the words of *The New York*

Times. He lost to Giuliani by a 2–1 margin. Staying in the race as the Conservative candidate, Lauder polled about 9,000 votes, versus 800,000-plus for David Dinkins, the Democrat who won, and Giuliani, who would succeed him four years later. Having spent about $1,425 for each of those votes, Lauder wisely retired from politics. But not from public life. He invested in a Hungarian bank and a Budapest restaurant and bought the privatized holdings of eastern European governments and by 1996, at fifty-one, was a factor in the television and telecommunications industries there. Sometimes that caused more embarrassment, as when *The Wall Street Journal* profiled him on its front page in 1995, just before Estée Lauder offered its stock to the public, and revealed that Lauder owed the family firm and its bankers over $200 million. But he was a good credit risk: he took home an average $11 million a year and earned about $192 million from the public offering.

Lauder's greatest success has been in the world of art. He'd joined the board of trustees of the Museum of Modern Art in 1977, and in 1995, after making a large financial pledge, he was named its chairman (his brother is chairman of the Whitney Museum) and began repositioning himself as an art mogul and impresario. His huge personal collection includes old-master drawings, arms and armor, medieval art, a $50 million Cézanne, and works by German artists like Anselm Kiefer and Gerhard Richter and Austrians like Gustav Klimt and Egon Schiele. Much of the art is in storage because it won't fit in his Park Avenue aerie, where one room alone contains seven Brancusi sculptures.

His collection of Austrian art, including at least twenty Schieles, formed the basis of the most successful venture of his life, the Neue Galerie. Named for an avant-garde Viennese gallery of the 1920s, it was opened by Lauder and an art dealer in a 1914 mansion once owned by Mrs. Cornelius Vanderbilt at Eighty-sixth Street and Fifth Avenue and proved an immediate sensation, finally giving Lauder the public respect he'd wanted for so long. And now, at last, the public pays to see what he has wrought.

32

IN THE EARLY 1970S, IT BEGAN TO SEEM AS IF NO ONE WAS WATCHING the bronze doors of 740 Park. Even people with Mafia and show business ties were getting in. In 1973, Michael and Caryl Palin purchased Flora Whiting's apartment, 10/11A. Caryl had been born Caryl Entratter, the daughter of "Smilin' " Jack Entratter, who'd begun his career as a bouncer in a tavern owned by Billy LaHiff, New York's most famous restaurateur in the 1920s and 1930s. LaHiff's place was one of those watering holes where show business, the Mob, the media, and the men who ran New York all drank together. From there, Entratter moved to the Stork Club, the famous crucible of café society, and then the Copacabana, the East Sixtieth Street nightclub, where he rose from manager to partner.

The Copa was officially owned by Monte Prosser, a Mob-connected P.R. man and booking agent, but in 1944 the reformist mayor Fiorello La Guardia began making what the *Times* called "thinly veiled accusations" that racketeers controlled the place, particularly the colorfully named Joe Adonis, Mush Trackiner, and Mob boss Frank Costello. Entratter's influence extended to Saratoga Springs, New York, where he was said to control the door at the Piping Rock restaurant, which boasted an illegal casino in the rear. In 1949, Clendenin Ryan, the grandson of a financier and a former La Guardia aide, ran for mayor, and made lots of noise about how Costello was the "real boss" of New York and of the Copa, even though Prosser, his brother, and Entratter were the owners of record. According to some accounts, by then Entratter owned the controlling interest.

Three years later, at age thirty-eight, Smilin' Jack moved his family to Las Vegas, where he'd been named vice president of the Sands, a new hotel casino. "The Sands Hotel is owned by Hoodlums," an FBI report would later say. It was semi-secretly controlled by various mobsters from across the country, including Meyer Lansky, Longy Zwillman, and Sam Giancana, as well as the singer Frank Sinatra. Entratter was allegedly there to watch over Frank Costello's interests in the joint, assumed to be part of Smilin' Jack's 12 percent share. But Jack was really the key man in the mix: entertainers like Dean Martin, Jerry Lewis, and Frank Sinatra would follow him anywhere, and the public followed them. In 1958, Entratter became the Sands' president.

In 1960, Entratter achieved showbiz nirvana and began booking the legendary Rat Pack appearances at the Sands during the filming of the original *Ocean's 11.* That same year, his daughter, Caryl, married Michael Palin of Brooklyn, who'd been working since he was nine years old and would eventually become a significant industrial developer and New Jersey property owner.

Jack Entratter remained in the Rat Pack's nest until his death in 1971: serving as Sinatra's spokesman when his son, Frank junior, was kidnapped, giving away Mia Farrow in marriage to Sinatra in 1966, and selling his interest in the Sands for more than $1.8 million ($8.3 million in 2004 dollars) when Howard Hughes bought the casino for $14.6 million in 1967. Whether he'd shared in the Mob's infamous skimming operations at the Sands is undocumented.

Entratter's Vegas was over anyway. According to Dean Martin's biographer Nick Tosches, when he'd been introduced to Wayne Newton in the hotel coffee shop one day, Smilin' Jack snarled, "Get that fag out of here." Shortly after Entratter's death, a deputy mayor of Jerusalem was forced to concede that he'd done business with mobsters he met through Entratter. Small wonder that the Palins are among the lowest-profile residents of 740 Park.

Not so low-profile were another group of residents in the 1980s, most of whom revolved around another Sinatra associate with links to both the Mafia and the music industry, Steven J. Ross, the charismatic chairman of Warner Communications. Ross was not, however, the first person in his orbit to move into 740 Park. "I believe I was the poorest person to ever live in that building," says William Goldman, the Academy Award–winning screenwriter, then best known for his script for 1969's *Butch Cassidy and the Sundance Kid*, which starred Paul Newman and Goldman's friend Robert Redford.

Goldman's wife, Ilene, had always wanted to buy a co-op—and with New York on the skids in 1972, the time was right. Their only requirement was a room large enough to hold a pool table. After losing John Cahill's apartment to the Mahoneys, they took a look at Walter Aldridge's even larger A-line apartment on the same day the wheelchair-bound mining magnate was taken to a nursing home. "The size of the fucking place!" Goldman remembers. "I thought I'd never be able to furnish it." Goldman believes he was only allowed in the building because two factors converged to his benefit—the economy and the board's growing disdain for diplomats. Goldman was initially rejected in favor of the Finns, but then all three resident diplomats had parties on the same night. The poor Finns were rejected again.

"So we got it," Goldman believes, for $225,000.

The Goldmans were in abject terror before their admissions interview at the Speights' apartment. "For the most part, they don't want people in the arts," Bill knew. "People who will disappear to Mexico or give drug parties. But they were actually very nice." Bill and Ilene were interviewed separately by the board. After the ordeal, the Goldmans went to a Mexican restaurant and argued over margaritas. "I can't live with those people," said Bill, who hated being scrutinized.

"You'll never see them; it's New York," Ilene assured him. And time would prove her right. "I could go a year and not ride the elevator with anybody," she says. "I had more interaction with the super and the doormen."

The apartment still had all its original fixtures—all they did was paint, update the kitchen, and add bookcases. When a contractor asked Ilene if she wanted the servant call buttons put back into operation, she replied, "That's silly; I'd have to answer them myself." She wasn't used to this style of life. "I was very glad for the Seventy-first Street entrance," she says. "I was a painter and a photographer. I simply didn't dress every day." The one day she did, the super John Hughes commented, "Now, *that's* Madison Avenue."

Goldman was the first owner to attract a hard-core celebrity contingent to the building. "Bill Bradley would come to see him, Archie Bunker, Redford," says Patrick O'Connor. At forty and thirty-four, the Goldmans were also, they believed, the youngest couple in the building. But in fact, one couple was younger, "very young," says Ilene Goldman, "and gorgeous!"

ALEX AND JUDY LAUGHLIN HAD DECIDED TO SELL THEIR APARTMENT IN 1975 after their youngest, David, went off to boarding school. "We were rattling around in it," says Judy. They quickly went into contract with Joseph Cullman III, the longtime head of Philip Morris, the cigarette executive who had famously denied to Congress that smoking was bad for you. But Cullman, suspended between two wives, walked away from the deal—and a $35,000 deposit—on the day of his closing, and later moved into a penthouse at 19 East Seventy-second Street. He'd divorced his first wife, Susan Lehman, a grandniece of the New York governor Herbert Lehman in 1974, then married Joan Paley Straus, although they almost immediately divorced. The couple later lived together for ten years before remarrying in 1988, but it was during those peregrinations—"he was living alone at the Carlyle, and he didn't know which woman to go to," says a relative—that Cullman crossed paths unhappily with the Laughlins.

"It was inexcusable," Judy says of Cullman's withdrawal from the deal. Instead of moving to their new digs at 960 Fifth that day, as they'd planned, they put all their belongings into storage and moved in with Laughlin's mother at 10 Gracie Square. "The place looked like hell," she continues, one of the reasons it didn't sell for nine more months. The ultimate buyer, Kenneth Rosen, paid far less than their original price.

Rosen was the son of the youngest judge in the history of New York and grew up on Manhattan's East Side. After graduating from Middlebury College, the handsome, ambitious young man was debating attending law school (New York's attorney general, Louis Lefkowitz, was his father's best friend) when a family friend, Morton Rosenthal, sent him to chat about his future with Steven J. Ross. Ross was married to Rosenthal's niece Carol and was running the family company. He'd expanded it from its origins in the mortuary business by combining it with Kinney, a parking lot company with ties to the Newark, New Jersey, mob; according to *Master of the Game*, Connie Bruck's definitive biography of Ross, the father of Kinney's founder was an intimate associate of the very same mobsters who secretly owned the Copacabana and the Sands in Las Vegas.

Ross took Kinney public in 1961, and it remained his power base for the rest of his life. Two years later, Ross convinced young Ken Rosen to defy his parents and skip law school—he'd already bought books for his first term—and become his assistant. A year after that, Ross sent Rosen, along with a bunch of Kinney rental limousines, to the Democratic Convention in Atlantic City, where Lyndon Johnson was being nominated to run for president. There Rosen met Lou Hill, a graduate of Texas Christian University and a former Watermelon Thump Queen of Lockhart, Texas ("You thump 'em to see if they're ripe," they'd say). The blue-eyed blonde worked for Vice President Johnson in Washington while in college.

Lou was in Atlantic City working for the treasurer of the Democratic National Committee's President's Club for big donors. "We locked eyes at an orange juice fountain," says Lou, "and I guess he inquired about who I was. I fell hard. He was very persistent, and he had a charismatic personality." They met in August and were married in December. "He took me to meet Steve before his parents," she says. She was immediately aware that her fiancé had a complex relationship with his boss. "No question, Steve was Ken's mentor," she says, "but it wasn't black-and-white. Ken was like a younger brother."

Ross paid for their wedding and honeymoon with a loan, then Ken almost immediately left his job. "He wanted more business experience," says Lou, and also to make progress and money on his own. After a short stint at an ad agency, Rosen was introduced to Ted Ashley, the founder of Ashley Famous, a talent agency, and in 1967 got a job scouting new businesses for him. Ashley was a restless businessman seeking new challenges, and Ross wanted the same—he was on an acquisition binge and was planning a move into the entertainment business. So Rosen put them together, and Kinney soon bought Ashley Famous and went on the hunt for a movie studio to buy.

Rosen still wanted his freedom, so Ross called Arthur Carter, a partner in a Wall Street brokerage he'd worked with—the same one that inspired Saul Steinberg's bid for Reliance Insurance—to set his protégé up with a job. "He wanted to be on Wall Street and we were an up-and-coming bunch of guys," says Carter, "although not as young as he was." When Carter, Cogan, Berlind & Weill broke up not long afterward, Rosen followed to the new Arthur Carter Group, where he helped Carter do deals and run a water utility holding company and investment bank the company had bought.

"He was very, very ambitious and also very, very attractive," says Carter. "I thought he'd be a doer, and he did very well with me. They became the 'It' couple, very wired in socially, politically, in business, every which way." By the early 1970s, the Rosens had adopted two kids (the first, tellingly, named Ross), had bought an estate in Bedford, and had moved into their first apartment at 1130 Park. In 1974, Ken was named to the board of Coca-Cola. After leaving Carter, he worked as a merchant banker and deal broker with another young financier, Henry Silverman, and Fred Carr, one of the mutual fund cowboys of the 1960s; among his clients was Warner Communications. "He was just a kid, but he was a major risk taker; it reminded me of Texas in the wildcat era," Lou says. "They were doing things that hadn't been done."

Ken was the driving force behind the move to the Laughlins' apartment—and although he'd become rich, it was still beyond their means. "Ken had the most developed sense of panache," says Lou. "He was extraordinary in his concept of who he was going to be when he grew up. He definitely had Gatsby DNA in him." Lou doesn't know how he found it, but does recall his bringing her there for the first time. "I was just aghast," she says. "I couldn't appreciate it the way he did. It was cavernous, but he was the ultimate salesman. He said we'd make it cozy."

A British friend, recruited to reassure Lou, told her that once it was decorated, it would be an English stately home in the middle of Manhattan. Only then did Lou begin to appreciate the magnificence, the orangey pink, rose, and deep green marble mantels, the paneled library, the intricate moldings on the living room ceiling. "Everything was original," she says with a sigh, "every fixture. The soap dishes were ridged glass, pedestal sinks, marble floors. It was like living at the Connaught." Before they'd even closed, an investment banker named George Ohrstrom tried to buy it from them at a profit.

"The admissions meeting was in our apartment," remembers Sally Faile. "She was from Texas. The husband was an attractive Jewish man. They had some money. There was some question. I was appalled. I said, 'He's one of the most attractive people here.'" The Rosens were accepted. "But it was one of the few times Ken was ever nervous," says Lou. "We were so young." Mark Hampton, the Parish-Hadley veteran, decorated the apartment in formal Georgian style with comfortable Adam-style chairs, large nineteenth-century paintings, and Frederic Remington sculptures. The dining room was formal, the library dark, masculine, and equestrian, the bedroom pretty, with floral-printed-cotton walls.

Just as the Rosens were settling in, Steve Ross succeeded in taking over Warner Brothers–Seven Arts, and renamed the company Warner Communications. He promptly shed his past by selling the Rosenthals' funeral business, and left his wife Carol as well, replacing her with several girlfriends, one of whom, Courtney Sale, the granddaughter of a Coca-Cola bottler and a recent Skidmore graduate, was a Texas girl just like Lou Rosen. The two couples sometimes socialized and traveled together frequently—at least until Ross traded up to a tonier lover.

In 1975, William vanden Heuvel, a former diplomat who served on a corporate board with Ken, suggested that he set up Ross with a friend of his, Amanda Jay Mortimer Burden, the just-divorced daughter of the socialite Barbara "Babe" Paley and Stanley G. Mortimer and the stepdaughter of the CBS chairman William Paley, one of Ross's idols. Rosen booked a dinner at "21," vanden Heuvel brought Burden, and it was love at first sight.

They were an imaginative match. Ross, in the process of becoming a major media figure much like Burden's stepfather, was rich and strong enough to care for her and her two children—no small thing. Her 1964 marriage to and 1972 divorce from the city councilman Carter Burden, a descendant of Commodore Vanderbilt, had played out in the painful glare of public attention: they were leaders of the city's beautiful people. And the auburn-haired, hazel-eyed Amanda, smart, beautiful, wellborn, and best-dressed, was a marvelous reflection of Ross's view of himself, what he'd achieved, and where he was headed. The couple immediately began traveling and living together in Burden's apartment on Gracie Square. Courtney Sale, who'd met Ross after getting a job at a Warner subsidiary, did not take the news well—and could not have enjoyed the concentrated burst of attention the new lovers attracted, their every move covered by society publications like *W*, which ran photos of Burden and her "show biz beau" whenever it could.

Lou and Ken Rosen adopted their third child, and at Lou's urging, shortly after they moved into 740, Ken agreed to go back to work for his mentor. In October 1976, at age thirty-five, Ken was named one of four executive vice presidents and directors of Warner Communications; he, three colleagues, and Ross would manage the company. People around Ross assumed that Rosen's job would be to serve as Ross's alter ego, doing deals, cutting corners, and operating in the shadows in ways that Ross no longer could. "It was like a secret pact they had," says Jay Emmett, the only Warner executive as close to Ross as Rosen. "Nobody knew what was going on. [Ken] was a deal maker and a good one and people liked him, but when you got to know him, you were a little wary. There was secret stuff between the two of them. He was an operator. He'd rather take a buck under the table than two dollars over it." But he never got the chance again.

Early in April 1977, just after his contract to rejoin Warner was signed, Rosen went to ride the horse he kept at a stable near Central Park. "It was Palm Sunday," says Lou. "We'd had a Seder the night before, and we were having another that night. I get a call. 'Is this the home of Kenneth Rosen? Come to Saint Luke's. There's been an accident.' " When she got to the hospital and asked for her husband, someone said, "Oh yeah, the DOA." Only, in fact, things were worse. Rosen had either been thrown from his horse and hit a tree or ridden into a low branch. He wasn't dead, but he was in surgery for hours, and then spent weeks in a coma.

Ross was there when Lou arrived and remained at Ken's side constantly, arranging for the best doctors and care, but to no avail. When Rosen woke up three weeks later, he remembered nothing and was, at best, "sort of ambulatory." He was placed in a locked-ward rehabilitation center, then returned to the apartment and the house in Bedford, "but it was just a nightmare, even with nurses," says Lou. "There was a sort of fantasy that maybe it was like amnesia, and by bringing him home and showing him pictures, we'd trigger something and he'd come back." He even returned to work in the care of an aide. "But it became clear he was not going to be a viable person again," says Lou. He had irreversible brain damage.

His friends were bereft. "Ken was literally gone," says Arthur Carter. "He couldn't recognize people. It was so very, very sad." Ken would eventually be placed in a home for the disabled. (He remains there, content and well cared for to this day, his bills covered by Warner. Lou, though she later remarried, still visits him.)

Through the spring and summer of 1977, "Steve was amazing," Lou says. "He hung in there as long as he could and remained a support system always." Lou even took a house at the beach close to one where Ross and Burden were staying. By the fall, Amanda Burden had had enough; according to Ross's biographer, Connie Bruck, she began to suspect that the Ross-Rosen relationship had taken on an even odder cast and that Steve and Lou were having an affair. "I don't think it was sexual, but Amanda was offended," says Jay Emmett. And that September, when Ross gave himself a fiftieth birthday party at the Waldorf-Astoria and brought both Lou and Amanda, things came to a head, Burden issued an ultimatum, and Ross stopped visiting Lou.

"I found reality sooner than everyone else," says Lou, who had to deal with Ken's reality moment by moment. "It was harder for Steve." Ross, as he would later admit, had seen Rosen as his successor. He clung to the hope Rosen would recover. But now that was not to be. Years later, Lou would look at photos of that night at the Waldorf and think only about how young they all seemed, and how kind Ross and Burden were to her that night. But still, she was confused by the abrupt way Ross cut the cord afterward.

"Yeah, what was that about?" she asks today, before suggesting an answer: "As beautiful and wealthy as Amanda is, there were insecurities there, and Steve's emotional well was being drained by the needy wife and children of his best friend, Ken. She'd not known Ken, so it must have confused her that he had so much invested in the situation. The situation just took so much out of her time with Steve. I can empathize with that. But I wouldn't say I was a threat. It was surreal."

Lou had an eight-year-old, a six-year-old, and a six-month-old, and had never been an independent person. "But I wasn't going to become a fatality with Ken," she says. She's never spoken to Burden since, and she "pretty much" lost touch with Ross after that night, she reports. "Everyone was trying to think fast and make the best of it. But deal makers make things happen. Coming to grips with the fact that you couldn't fix it had to be hard for Steve to accept. He needed a break. I'm sure it was hard for him." It would be years before Ross and Rosen were in touch again.

BRIEFLY, AS THE 1970S ENDED, 740 PARK WAS AGAIN A BUILDING FULL of young children. So, a year after Ken's accident, when Lou Rosen's younger brother Rocky ("who was working for Warner, dontcha know?" she says) was caught in a hotel fire in Boston and spent seven weeks in the burn unit there, dying, Lou left her infant daughter with another young 740 mother, Jane Foster Lorber, whom she'd met right after Ken's accident. Lorber and her husband, Martin, had just bought apartment 2/3D, in what Lorber jokingly called "the back of the bus," the genteel 71 East Seventy-first Street.

That apartment had changed hands twice in three years. Northam Griggs's widow had finally left in 1973, after twenty-five years of acute unhappiness. The Griggses had both had curious marital careers. After graduating from Yale in 1927, Northam married three times. His last wife, Eleanor Grant (Elisabeth Harkness's sister), was a divorcée when they wed. And probably would have been better off had she divorced again. "They didn't speak to each other," says Judy Laughlin, "but they lived together; they led separate lives in a big apartment." He would use the service stairs, she the Candela stairs. They did their best to never see each other. And fate seemed to want them locked into that dysfunctional relationship. When they'd first put the apartment on the market in the fall of 1969 for $325,000 (the maintenance was then $866 monthly), it failed to sell. Two years before Northam died in March 1975, and Eleanor married F. Warren Pershing (the Laughlins' doctor), they finally managed to dump it for about $170,000 in the depths of the city's financial crisis.

The buyer, the socially registered T. Kirk Parrish, was the general manager of Beech-Nut–Life Savers and would shortly be named secretary of the co-op board. But in 1977 he got a new job and put the apartment back on the market. His first two buyers were rejected. One, a music publisher, "had earrings and was socially unacceptable," a board member recalls. The second, a senior executive at a cosmetics company and his wife, were turned down, the board member believes, because of 740's informal Jewish quota. Parrish's apartment was not a Jewish apartment, and the two Jewish members of the board at the time, Henry David Epstein and Kenneth Rosen, "thought there were too many Jews in the building," the board member asserts.

"I knew that and I know that," says the executive's wife, who knew many of the Jewish families in the building and "didn't think it was going to be a problem, or we wouldn't have applied." Though she confirms that the board never even met them, she asks not to be identified, arguing that although co-op board anti-Semitism "was and perhaps still is rampant in most" New York co-ops, openly discussing it will only "do more damage."

The third time around, Parrish was more careful. Jane and Martin Lorber both had the sorts of family backgrounds that were once the rule but were increasingly the exception at 740. Martin descended from Whitehead Hicks, New York's last royal mayor from 1766 to 1776. His great-great-great-great-great-great-great-great-grandfather had held the royal land grant for Flushing in the years shortly after Landon Thorne's ancestors signed the Flushing Remonstrance. The family of Lorber's wife, Jane de Moret Foster, came to America in its own ship in the 1680s, the recipients of a Dutch land grant. She descends from Philip Hone, who was mayor in 1826 and 1827. The former house of her grandfather Giraud Foster is now the Canyon Ranch spa in Lenox, Massachusetts. "I'm American pie," the pretty plantation-raised blonde says with a tinkling laugh.

After attending Finch College alongside Richard Nixon's daughter Tricia, Jane Foster went to work at Sotheby's (she was among the workers who dismantled Martha Baird Rockefeller's apartment after her death) and married Lorber, one of its Oriental-art experts. When they were expecting their second child, "I called my father and said I needed a larger apartment," she recalls, "just a little larger. He said, 'Ridiculous, get a big one. I don't want to pay for all this moving around.'" Foster had always used the high-society decorator Mario Buatta, and her father, weary of repeatedly paying for his services, agreed to pay $245,000 for the apartment. Their admissions interview was held in Donald Rynne's apartment. "It was just like having cocktails," Jane says. "We talked about people we knew."

As soon as they were in, Buatta returned, hanging their family portraits and mirrors and adding zigzag stains and mosaics to the floors, decorative painting to the entry hall, red walls to the library, an eighteenth-century Scottish mantel inset with seashells in the bedroom, and a Georgian mantel and a jukebox tucked behind a screen in the living room ("We used to dance wildly"). "Mario was the best partner to guide me," Jane says. "There wasn't a lot you wanted to change. It was perfection, with marvelous proportions and moldings and the old pantries with warming ovens and stainless steel counters. But he got me the best painters and the best furniture; I have it still." Over the years, she acquired some of the contiguous second-floor servants' rooms ("for the same price I paid for the apartment") and expanded.

The Lorbers' son was a year old. Their daughter came home from the hospital to the new apartment. And they considered it a family building, "cozy and nice," Jane says, remembering countless children's parties and reeling off the names of neighbors' children. Martin recalls his daughter playing with the Rosen kids one day and assigning roles: "You're the daddy and I'm the mommy, but who's the nurse?"

But it wasn't all sunshine and gentility. They would soon call their elevator bank the "D-as-in-divorce line," Jane says, "because eventually we all did." Foster and Lorber had a fairly amicable divorce in the late 1980s ("I absolutely adore her," he says; "He is one of the dearest," says she), and she remained in the apartment. After remarrying briefly and unhappily in 1989, Jane put the apartment on the market for $9.5 million in

1990, dropped the price to $7.8 million in 1995, and finally sold it for $5.5 million in March 1997 after the board rejected her first prospective buyer.

The next, Kent Swig, should have been a slam-dunk acceptance; a son of the wealthy San Francisco family that owns the Fairmont Hotels chain, he'd bought Brown Harris Stevens after the 1994 managing agent scandal, along with two grandsons of William Zeckendorf and another partner. Brown Harris Stevens, of course, had been managing 740 since 1988. But in fact "Kent had a hard time getting in," says Brian Marlowe, chairman emeritus of Remco, a building maintenance company. Word spread that Swig and his wife, Elizabeth (whose father is the rough-and-tumble real estate developer Harry Macklowe), had been rejected by a nearby building, and it was only after 740's manager, who conveniently worked for Swig, spoke up for him that he was admitted. Management, apparently, has its privileges.

STEVE ROSS AND HIS FIRST WIFE WERE FINALLY DIVORCED IN 1979, AND that fall he married Amanda Burden. Shortly afterward, right around the time they were dubbed "the most glittering of the party people" by *WWD* in front-page coverage of a state dinner at the Carter White House, Ross bought Edgar Bronfman's triplex atop 740 Park for about $600,000. It had "stayed vacant for many, many years," says John Hughes. "He wasn't really trying very hard to sell it." But one neighbor thinks differently. "Bronfman almost gave his apartment away," says Samuel Leidesdorf, whose father was a family friend. "It took years. There were no buyers."

Ross, whose broker was Alice Mason, passed the board, but not easily. "People were concerned," says a board member. "But Ross came across more as a businessman than a show person." One person, at least, was shocked when she heard he'd been approved. Lou Rosen hadn't even known that her husband's mentor was considering a move. "I remember being stunned," she says, and thinking it was yet another reflection of the complex interplay between her husband and his mentor. "I often felt," says Lou, "that Ken got a blonde from Texas, then there's Courtney. Ken moved to 740 and ... well, somebody could draw a pattern there.

The younger brother taking the risks. Sometimes Steve had the advantage, but sometimes Ken did. They were both salesmen. They sold themselves to each other. They loved each other. They filled in the gaps of each other. I think they adored each other. So you can make it complex and weird, but what's on the surface was probably what it was about: it was a fabulous apartment and a great deal."

Thirty years after he'd first decorated the penthouse, Albert Hadley got a call from Amanda Burden, who asked him to come take a look at it again. "Curtains we'd made years before were still hanging," says Hadley. "Everything was in good condition. But it was not what they wanted, of course. Amanda was very traditional and cozy. But not that traditional." They added a screening room and decided to expand the master bedroom on the roof (much to Enid Haupt's distress: the proposed work altered her view, and she insisted Ross change his plans). In its April 1981 proxy statement, Warner Communications revealed that it had kicked in $450,000 to pay for the screening room, furnishings, and equipment, which it would own. Ross would be responsible for its maintenance and promised the company a cut of the proceeds of any eventual sale. (Not that Ross needed the money; his 1980 salary was $350,000, and he received a cash bonus of just under $1 million.) "Then they got married and divorced and the new wife came in and that was the end of us," says Hadley.

It did happen almost that fast. Ross's fiftieth birthday party was, in some ways, the end of an era, celebrating not just a personal milestone but the arrival of Warner Communications at the top of the heap in both television and music, which made its chairman one of the most glamorous figures in the entertainment business, a true successor to William Paley. Yet just when he stood at the pinnacle, his fortunes took a turn. As he was celebrating with Lou and Amanda, the FBI was beginning an investigation into Warner's involvement in a racketeering, fraud, skimming, and kickback scandal at the Westchester Premier Theater, part-owned by Warner. While Frank Sinatra's involvement in the story gave it a certain dark glamour, Ross couldn't have been pleased to see his name linked in news reports with those of Jimmy "The Weasel" Fratianno and the Mafia chief Carlo Gambino. Ross biographer Connie Bruck believes that the stress of the investigation, which would result in racketeering indictments against two Warner executives in September 1980, helped trigger the heart attack Ross suffered three months earlier.

That fall he and Amanda went on a cruise that was part honeymoon, part recuperation and, when they returned, moved straight into 740. But their relationship had changed. "He wanted to be Bill Paley, and I'm not sure Amanda wanted him to be," says the Warner executive Jay Emmett. "Amanda had her feet on the ground. The cruise was a disaster. He was playing king of the world, and she was offended by a lot of it."

Burden not only hated the cruise, but she'd shaken off her father-figure fantasies about Ross—and realized she'd made an awful mistake in marrying him. This wasn't the life she wanted—chatelaine of a media mogul, presiding over a grand apartment and staff. Having studied and worked in urban planning, she realized she wanted a career, not a protector. She was starting out and Steve was winding down. "Amanda really didn't care for him," thinks a society woman who was close to them all. "Steve was very kind. He was without subterfuge. But he was very crude and uncultured."

"It was very sad," says Hillie Mahoney, a friend. "They spent a lot of time fixing up the apartment to live in happily, and then, sadly, they got divorced. She walked in and said, 'I can't do this. I don't want to live here.' " She departed so quickly she left her furniture behind and never got it back. "I only lived there two weeks," Amanda Burden affirms. "It's long ago and too personal." Asked if she takes issue with any previously published accounts of those last few days with Ross, she says, "I've never heard anything said about it that was grossly untrue."

"Amanda was overwhelmed," says Guy Salvadore, Warner's head of transportation and an old friend, who briefly moved in to keep Ross company after Amanda left. "She was trying to grow up." In anguish over the breakup, Ross renewed his friendship with Lou Rosen. In the interim, though she remained married to her husband, she'd begun seeing Ralph Davidson, a longtime publisher of *Time* magazine who'd just been named chairman of Time, Inc. Davidson, a divorcée who'd been introduced to Lou by good friends of Ken's, was also chairman of the Business Committee for the Arts, vice chairman of the World Wildlife Fund, a director of the New York City Ballet, and a trustee of the National Urban League. She would marry him in 1983 and four years later, when

Davidson was named head of the John F. Kennedy Center for the Performing Arts, sell the apartment and move to Washington. But Ross beat them to the altar.

Davidson was there the night a "clearly suffering" Ross came to visit, Lou says, and a plot was hatched to mend his broken heart. "I probably suggested calling Courtney. I knew her a little bit. After Ken's accident, she'd made quite a few overtures of kindness to me. He hesitated. He thought she wouldn't respond," but Sale, who'd become a documentary filmmaker, "was delighted."

Society was again agog. "First he fell in love with Amanda and dumped Courtney," says the society woman who was close to them all. "Then Amanda dumped him, he goes back to Courtney, and they're getting married." But not until, at Courtney's understandable insistence, they moved out of the love nest he'd built for himself and Amanda.

33

Even though New York's economy had turned around by 1978, Bruce Leib still found his late father's apartment, 12/13D, hard to sell. "The maintenance was very high," says Leib, who'd watched, aghast, as the $6,000 monthly payments drained his father's estate after his 1974 death. His mother remained for a year while Leib's lawyers tried to sell it, then moved out and died, too, in 1976. George Leib had paid about $150,000 for it. His estate finally sold it in 1978 for about $200,000. "You'd think it would have appreciated more after forty-eight years, but we were not disappointed," says Bruce Leib. "We wanted to get out from under that maintenance."

The buyers were both divorced and had just gotten engaged. Although they likely weren't the first unmarried couple to dally at 740 Park, Richard Hogeland and Kay Iselin were the first duo living "in sin" to officially cohabit there. The times, they really were a-changing.

Richard W. Hogeland, yet another mining executive, had just been made the head of the Gulf & Western conglomerate's Natural Resources Group, which had interests in coal, zinc, and titanium. His family traced back to the turn of the sixteenth century, when they were among the earliest settlers in New Amsterdam and ran a ferry service in New York harbor. Hogeland also had a Jewish grandmother, "which would have been catastrophic for me if any of my colleagues had known it," he says.

Kay Iselin's father, Philip, was a co-owner of the New York Jets and of Monmouth Park Racetrack in New Jersey. After a troubled first marriage that produced two sons, Kay became a reporter and in the 1970s was the first female sportswriter at New York's *Daily News*. She found the apartment and fell in love with its original details, all dating back to Bayard Hoppin. "It was faded wealth—and I mean faded," says Hogeland. "I bought most of the furniture. The curtains were lovely, but if I'd touched them, they would have disintegrated."

After a $750,000 six-month renovation, including a total rewiring, installation of central air-conditioning, a new kitchen and laundry, and redecoration by Sister Parish and Albert Hadley, Hogeland and Iselin moved in. They had many friends in the building, including the Rosens, the Mahoneys, Steve Ross, and Enid Haupt. They met their next-door neighbors, the Goldmans, through their maids, who were friends. Not long after they arrived, they got a taste of what made the building special when their doorbell rang one night and they found Robert Redford outside. Looking for the Mahoneys, he'd gotten off the elevator at the wrong floor.

Three years later, in November 1980, the couple had broken up when Hogeland, who'd left Gulf & Western and was trying to acquire companies on his own, found himself in a cash-flow crunch and put the apartment on the market for $3 million (the maintenance had risen to $3,750 monthly) to raise cash. Hogeland soon discovered his troubles had just begun—and eight months later declared war on the co-op board. "I caused a total revolt," he says proudly from his current home in the English countryside.

Hogeland listed the apartment and quickly found an eager buyer, then another, then another, six in all, each of whom, Hogeland was advised, "could not be approved by the board." Inexplicably, one of them was Edgar Bronfman's sister Minda, who'd become the Baroness de Gunzburg after marrying Alain de Gunzburg. One of the most aristocratic Jews in Europe, he was the managing director of the Banque Louis-Dreyfus, then France's third-largest merchant bank, and an intimate of the Rothschilds.

Another prospective buyer, the Daimler-Benz heir Friedrich Christian "Mick" Flick, was flicked off for more obvious reasons: not only was he an international playboy; he was a grandson and heir of the German industrialist Friedrich Flick, who'd manufactured arms for the Nazis during World War II, run his factories largely with forced labor, and been jailed by the Nuremberg war crimes tribunal. Unlike other German industrial families of the era, the Flicks were notorious for their longtime refusal to show remorse, compensate former slave laborers, or open their archives to the public.

Then, in March 1981, Hogeland went into contract to sell his apartment for the asking price to Carlos Hank Rhon, the elder of two sons of Carlos Hank González, one of the most powerful politicians and wealthiest businessmen in Mexico. Hank, as he was called, ran the Institutional Revolutionary Party, which ruled Mexico for seventy years, served as the mayor of Mexico City and the country's secretary of agriculture, and became known as the Mexican Rockefeller as well as a symbol of the corruption of Mexico's politics by wealth. Over the years, his family would be accused of drug trafficking and money laundering, but their notoriety was still in the future when Rhon and his wife submitted a package to 740's well-wired board. "There were questions about how he'd gotten his money," says a board member.

"Six weeks went by without hearing from the board about a meeting," Hogeland would later complain in a letter to the board vice president, Charles Dyson. "By that time, the Hanks were embarrassed and upset and withdrew their offer." The board did in fact schedule an interview, but Hank did not appear. Hogeland believes Rhon's father induced him to walk away from his deposit because "his father was afraid of a turndown." Through a spokesman, Rhon says he "just doesn't recall." Not long afterward, Hogeland let *Fortune* photograph the apartment for a story on real estate selling for over $1.5 million. It ran in May 1981, and almost immediately Hogeland went into contract again. This time his buyer seemed unassailable. Alice Mason had brought Ted Ashley, who'd just resigned as chairman of the Warner Brothers movie studio to become vice chairman of Warner Communications, to see the apartment with his third wife (he'd eventually have four), Joyce Easton, an actress.

Ashley's references were extraordinary. Letters came in from Peter G.

Peterson, the chairman of the board of Lehman Brothers Kuhn Loeb; from the future chairman of the Federal Reserve Alan Greenspan; from Blanchette Rockefeller; from the chairman of United Brands, who was president of the cooperative at the Sherry-Netherland on Fifth Avenue, where the Ashleys lived; and from Deane Johnson, a lawyer whose clients included William Paley, James Stewart, Bing Crosby, and Shirley Temple. But Mason failed to crack the 740 fortress. After three separate discussions, the board signaled that the Ashleys would not be admitted.

Ashley and his family were led to believe that he was rejected because the board feared that with Ross and Rosen already in residence—Rosen's disability notwithstanding—a Warner takeover was in the offing. "The Warner group was just a little bit too brash and ha-ha-ha and ho-ho-ho for them," says John Hughes. "It takes very few apartments to gain control," says a member of the co-op board at the time. "There was a fear, mainly on the part of Randy Speight." But a source who claims knowledge of the board's deliberations insists that the truth was more mundane. Joyce Easton Ashley, according to this version of events, "was rude to the doorman" when she came to see the apartment, and on learning that, Dyson and Speight were outraged. "Never happened," Joyce Easton insists. "It's totally unlike me."

Hogeland believed none of those theories. "No one ever said, 'He's Jewish,'" he says, "but the building had its quota at the time, and it was not a Jewish apartment." Hogeland singled out Randy Speight for his ire. "He was beyond the pale," Hogeland says, "living in one of the smallest apartments, pushing his authority."

So Hogeland went on the warpath. "According to the bylaws, you could override the board," he says, if you collected the signatures of a majority of shareholders. "So I knocked on every door in the place," he continues, handing out the Ashley application package. "Ted Ashley was a fine, fine man. I went to bat for him because I felt, how could I get anyone better than this man?"

Many of his neighbors had signed his petition, Hogeland continues, when, on July 1, 1981, the board sent a memo to shareholders over Dyson's signature, spelling out its admissions process and restating "the high standards of this building, one of the finest in the country." The board described itself as "fair, considerate . . . deliberative," and "careful

not to embarrass any applicant in any way." Then the directors bluntly
threatened to resign, en masse, if a majority signed Hogeland's petition.
The letter went on to discuss "annoying communications" from an unnamed realtor "relative to a recent unfavorable decision ... on an applicant." Three unfavorable decisions in a row, in fact. "This is the first time
any real estate agent has undertaken annoying residents and we regret
the embarrassment this agent must be causing to the applicant. YOUR
BOARD RECOMMENDS YOUR NOT SIGNING ANY PETITION."

Hogeland responded the next day with a lengthy letter to Dyson,
copied to all. "The Board would not even meet and interview the Ashleys," he wrote.

> Is this what you in your letter call fair,
> considerate, deliberate? In my opinion the
> Board was arbitrary and capricious in their
> action when dealing with my property
> rights ... When you are given the respon-
> sibility to exercise some control over other
> people's property you have a great burden;
> one that must be exercised properly.

A few days later, Charles Dyson wrote to the shareholders again, calling
Hogeland's letter "grossly misleading" and declaring the whole affair
"most distressing since it has damaged the traditional serenity and civil-
ity that has always typified our building's affairs."

Though he was flying in the face of Gold Coast co-op tradition,
Hogeland was hardly alone in his outrage. "As far as I'm concerned, that
building can burn to the ground," says someone close to Ashley, who believes the anti-Warner theory. "It was a shock," admits Mason, who categorically denies she was the annoying realtor. And indeed, though she
won't discuss it, she appears to have defused the crisis. Hogeland ended
up selling to a Warner executive after all—Steve Ross, who'd just been
issued orders to find a new apartment by his lover, Courtney Sale.

When Ross told Mason, his broker, that he would buy the apartment,
"the board grabbed hold of that," Hogeland says. Since Ross was already
in the building, there was no need to approve him, and the board would

be off the hook, but it still flexed its muscles, forcing Ross to give up the right to vote the shares for the penthouse until he sold it.

Ross neglected to tell Lou Rosen that he was moving to her elevator line, and though she was invited to the wedding to Courtney that followed, they never had much contact again. "I'd see him in passing," Lou says. "He was always cordial and most generous," never mean or thoughtless, but he did not stay a friend. "There were no acts of commission," says Lou, "but there were acts of omission."

Ross put his penthouse on the market, asking $9 million, in December 1981, dropped the price to $7.5 million in 1982, and finally sold it in June 1983 to Luis Noboa, the Ecuadorian banana king, and his wife, Mercedes, for $4.1 million. They would use it as a pied-à-terre for a few months a year, spending the rest of their time traveling in Europe or at their other homes in Lyford Cay, Southampton, and Ecuador.

"I knew the building was tops," says Noboa's widow, Mercedes, seventy-two, who found the apartment after rejecting another on a lower floor of 740 as too dark. "I liked the space. It was my husband who flipped because of the media room" and the rooftop master-bedroom suite. A previous buyer had been rejected by the board, says Mrs. Noboa, and Ross, "frankly, wanted to get rid of it."

"They were wealthy like Croesus," says someone close to the Noboas. "But even with wealth and power, they had sleepless nights before passing the board. It was very important for them. For her. He loved to talk about his beginnings, and she always tried to change the subject. It's a world of its own. They entertained, but not as much as you'd think. They want better names and better connections, even at that level. People look at the address and think it's wealth and happiness, but everyone struggles."

Mercedes Santistevan de Noboa did—first when Noboa had an affair with the daughter of one of her best friends, then battling with the children of his first wife over his estate after Luis died in 1994 and left control of his company to her. Hours before his will was to be read, *Forbes* reported, three armed Colombians stormed the Ecuadorian consulate in New York; Noboa's daughters' lawyer later speculated in a London court that they'd been hired by Noboa's son (who was left a relative pittance) to steal the will. By the time that son won a controlling interest in the family's business, Mercedes had sold her shares to the children for $300 million. The $25 million more that she got for the apartment in 2004 was icing on the cake, a reward for her patience and persistence, a dish of sweet, if cold, revenge.

Meanwhile, Ross and Courtney Sale planned their wedding for the fall of 1982. Sale went to Martha, a couture salon on Park Avenue, to buy a wedding dress. "The way she treated help was dreadful," says someone who was there that day. "She was so rude to everyone, so antagonistic, you could see the heat. She was getting even. I think she hated Ross. When he threw her over the first time, she never let him forget it. And she was going to let everyone know she was number one."

Ross, on the other hand, "was a dream," says someone involved in the wedding planning. "He wanted perfection. It was the most expensive wedding for the most obnoxious woman." They had a religious ceremony first in Ross's apartment, where a chuppah, or altar, was set up in front of a wedge of chairs with potted flowers between them and candles in rows. Steven Spielberg, Ross's great friend and protégé, took one look at the room and called it "a hot set, ready to be shot." The wedding cost $50,000, and Ross paid it, even though Atari's sinking earnings were wreaking havoc on Warner's stock price, and on Ross's reputation as a corporate Midas. "He didn't flinch," says a friend. "He was thrilled. She criticized everything." (Through her lawyer, Courtney Ross denies that she was angry with her husband.)

"She came from nowhere," says a neighbor, and "became very full of herself." No wonder, when her wedding guests included Spielberg, Frank Sinatra, Cary Grant, Beverly Sills, Clint Eastwood, Charlotte Ford, Helen Gurley and David Brown, Pelé (whose Cosmos soccer team was owned by Warner), the New York governor Hugh Carey, and Barbara Walters.

Unlike Amanda Burden, Courtney was new to wealth and gloried in it, just like Ross did. They were renowned for sending a private jet ahead of them on trips so their luggage would be waiting for them on arrival and booking whole floors at the best hotels so they could bring friends, servants, and bodyguards with them. "The lifestyle became something I would hear about," says Lou Rosen, who'd become Lou Davidson. "It was so far over the top it was beyond me. I would have thought Courtney and

I had more in common, but I was a provincial little girl and she was a very smart cookie."

ALTHOUGH WILLIAM GOLDMAN HAD WRITTEN THE SCRIPT AND WON AN Academy Award for the film version of *All the President's Men* for Warner Brothers (the film was also nominated for Best Picture), he'd never met Steve Ross. "The idea of somebody with my job title talking to somebody with his is just inconceivable," Goldman says. But their paths finally crossed in 1987. Despite embarrassments like convictions of top Warner executives in the Westchester Premier Theater scandal and severe business reverses that forced Ross to sell large chunks of Warner, he'd remained the nation's highest-paid CEO, and a figure of great glamour, in the mid-1980s. He deserved a home equal to his stature.

Goldman and his wife, Ilene, had decided to get a friendly divorce. "They still met and went to dinner," says the doorman Patrick O'Connor. "Usually, you'd know something was going on, and the next thing the man or the woman would be gone and they'd be selling the apartment." But real estate was in another of its periodic slumps after the stock market crash that fall, so Goldman and his divorce lawyer, Robert Stephan Cohen, had a meeting about how to dispose of the apartment. Cohen was a canny operator with a keen sense of New York. "Who are your contiguous neighbors?" he asked. When the screenwriter mentioned Ross, Cohen called him. "How would you like the largest apartment in the whole world?" he asked the mogul. Ross said he already owned one. "No, bigger," Cohen said.

Courtney Ross "was desperate to have the biggest apartment in the building," says an owner. (She denies that and says that in fact she asked Ross to sell the penthouse because she wanted a *smaller* apartment. They bought the second apartment, she continues, because he wanted a screening room.) Then Ross called Goldman. "I hear you're selling your apartment," he said. "I'd like to buy it."

"My mother didn't raise children dumb enough to negotiate a deal with Steve Ross," Goldman replied. "Call my accountant."

The deal was quickly concluded. Ross agreed to pay $4.95 million. When the board heard that he planned to combine the two apartments, they threatened to scuttle the deal. But after much discussion, the directors backed down. Still, the Rosses needed to get their plans approved, and carried the two apartments separately for a very long time before they got permission. "They joined our fourteen rooms to their eighteen," says Ilene Goldman. "Our dining room and kitchen were made into a children's dining room, our living room into a screening room. They sueded our bedroom." Ilene heard about it all from one of the neighbors. "We were never invited," she says.

Ross barely got to enjoy it. Shortly after the sale, he immersed himself in planning the biggest deal of his life, the merger of Warner with Time, Inc. Ross closed that deal in 1990—and Time Warner's stock promptly plunged. So did Ross's health. He'd had surgery for prostate cancer in 1985, and in the early 1990s he relapsed. Ross died in December 1992, and Courtney inherited the apartments, "packed with museum-quality collections of fine and decorative arts," according to *W* magazine, as well as Ross's estate in East Hampton and close to $1 billion in Time Warner stock options. By the end of the decade, she was sharing it all with a new man, Anders Holst, a Swedish management consultant, whom she married in Florence, Italy, in May 2000. Approximately three hundred guests flew in from all over the world. The Reverend Jesse Jackson performed the ceremony, Steven Spielberg was a witness, Deepak Chopra read a poem, Andrea Bocelli sang, and Quincy Jones was a guest.

Until spring 2005, when the gossip columnist Liz Smith announced that they were getting a divorce, Courtney and Holst, his three children, and her daughter by Ross spent most of their time in East Hampton, where she founded the experimental Ross School for her daughter in 1991 and is said to surround herself with artists, intellectuals, and academics. She uses her spread at 740 as a pied-à-terre and crash pad for the kids, and she's been advised to hang on to it because it's so valuable and will only get more so. Neighbors say the two-pack apartment remains fully staffed.

In 2002 the city of New York challenged Courtney's claim to be a legal resident of the east end of Long Island and demanded almost a million dollars in back taxes from her. A judge reviewed her diary, her voting records, the location of her nine cars and her $68 million art collection, and even an affidavit from her butler before determining, in January 2003, that she spent at least half her time at 71 East Seventy-first

Street and owed the city a small fortune—a two-year tax bill for 1993 and 1994 of $521,000 plus $159,000 in interest and a $165,000 penalty. That likely pinched even more given that, as the *Daily News* gleefully pointed out, after the ill-fated merger of Time Warner and America Online, her stock holdings had lost 75 percent of their value in the previous eighteen months.

REJECTION. THE 740 CO-OP BOARD TRIED TO HIDE BEHIND OBFUSCATING language, but the agreements and understandings underlying the admissions process were communicated anyway, with telling silences, nudges, and winks. Self-image is at stake for the buyer: Will they let me in? And for the seller, too: They wouldn't dare reject my buyer, would they? Much is unspoken, or whispered only behind the pillars, because in a litigious society, boards have found it better to operate in utter secrecy. No matter, their decisions can sting.

Richard Hogeland's saga was almost certainly one of the worst cases in the building's history, but it was hardly the only one. Many refuse to even acknowledge that they engaged in the tango of desire and acceptance and hoped for an approval that was withheld. Nelson Peltz, for example, did not respond to repeated requests for comment on his attempt to buy the James T. Lee apartment. The same is true of Kenneth Rosen's onetime partner Henry Silverman, who was also an associate of Saul Steinberg's and is now chairman of the Cendant Corporation. He also failed to enter 740.

While people still talk about religious differences causing turndowns, that isn't often the case anymore. "WASPs haven't been turning down Jews for fifty years," insists the realtor Alice Mason. "Now it's Jews turning down Jews. Sometimes, they don't want another powerful Jew in the building. Every time I get someone in, I hope they'll get on the board and help me get someone else in, and it's just the opposite. Most often, it's just a power play."

Brian Marlowe, the ex-chairman of Remco, was rejected, too, when he tried to buy Arthur Leidesdorf's apartment in the late 1970s, at least according to the ex-super John Hughes. "Every time there would be a listing, he'd come and want to see the apartment," says Hughes. "I said, 'You're beating a dead horse; you're not going to get in here.' " Marlowe insists he *was* approved—without an interview—but rejected 740. "I ended up in Olympic Towers," he claims by phone from his yacht, *Perfect Persuasion*, anchored in Monte Carlo. Perhaps, but apartments at Olympic Towers, a Fifth Avenue condo overlooking St. Patrick's Cathedral, while expensive, are a large step down from 740.

Perhaps it's her self-confidence that lets Barbra Streisand not only confirm her 740 rejection but admit to her disappointment, "because she loved the [Camps'] seventeen-room duplex," she says through a spokesman. "One of the ironies is that she was not one to have parties or play loud music that might disturb her neighbors, which seemed to be their expectation."

Neil and Leba Sedaka, too, still feel visceral hurt from their 740 rejection. Though they live in a sprawling, beautiful Park Avenue apartment, the memory of losing out on one at 740 still chafes. In 1982, the Sedakas had just moved home from England, where Neil had enjoyed a huge comeback, reviving a career that began in the late 1950s with pop hits like "Oh, Carol" and "Breaking Up Is Hard to Do." Living in a rental, they spent a year looking for the perfect place to buy, and when a realtor brought them to the late Elinor Dorrance and Admiral Stuart Ingersoll's apartment, 10/11B, says Leba, "I thought I'd died and gone to heaven."

"We said, we'll take it," Neil remembers, "and we put down 10 percent on the spot. Leba was already decorating in her mind." She brought a decorator, Robert Metzger, to see the place and began making a checklist of things to do. "They let us come in whenever we wanted," says Leba, who decided to remove the servants' quarters and renovate a kitchen that, in her words, "was untouched for a hundred and five years."

The Sedakas were gathering references when they got a call from their broker two weeks later: the board had turned them down. "But they haven't even met us!" Neil cried, shocked. "You have to understand how naive we were," says Leba. "We had no idea about co-op boards. It was quite enlightening. It introduced us to the real world of Manhattan."

Neil sniffs. "I'm not exactly Mick Jagger," he says. "I have a reputation as a family man. I'm not controversial, no paparazzi, no crazy parties. We had two small children. We thought, because of the Palins and Steinberg, religion wouldn't be an issue. Poor Leba was devastated."

"I went into shock," she confirms. "I didn't understand. They won't meet with you? They never gave us an explanation! It's all such a sore point to me. I still remember the apartment. But 740 might have done us a favor." She finally smiles. "We had fifteen wonderful years at 1021 Park," another Candela building—and made a $5 million profit when they sold their apartment there.

PART FIVE

OTHER PEOPLE'S MONEY

Saul and Gayfryd Steinberg in their living room, fifteenth floor (1971–2000, photographed June 13, 1985) *(Photograph by Arnold Newman/Getty Images)*

34

In 1980, Rand V. Araskog and his wife, Jessie, bought what had been Black Jack Bouvier's A-line apartment. Its owner, Mabel Brady Garvan, had died in 1979. Her Roslyn estate had already been sold and razed in 1974, its one hundred acres subdivided into two-acre plots. The apartment went on the market, but the first potential purchaser, an investment banker, was turned down. "I got a call before the meeting was over, and the apartment went back on the market," says Marcia Garvan Coyle. "He said he was a friend of Saul Steinberg's. That was the kiss of death." It was finally sold to ITT, the former International Telephone and Telegraph, for the use of its just-promoted chairman and chief executive officer, Rand V. Araskog. "He had the company buy the apartment," says Coyle. "We left the fixtures. I wonder if they kept them? Americans are terrible about that sort of thing. They should keep things from the past. It's really foolish."

Araskog had just been named chairman of ITT, a communications company that had been turned into a conglomerate by Harold Geneen, who became its president in 1960. A hundred mergers later, he'd transformed it into a woolly mammoth with $4 billion in assets, one of America's largest corporations. Unfortunately, when Republicans took over the

White House in 1969, Geneen seemed to link a contribution to the party to a favorable settlement in an antitrust case, and then made matters worse by plotting against a newly elected Socialist president of Chile. ITT's reputation suffered, and by 1978 Geneen had retired. Eighteen months later, Araskog got the job after Geneen's handpicked successor was fired.

A grandson of Swedish immigrants, Araskog was the son of a dairyman and tax assessor in a small western Minnesota town. A West Point graduate, the six-foot-one Araskog had worked at the Pentagon, joined the aerospace division of Honeywell as a marketing man in 1960, jumped to ITT in 1966 as the head of its Defense-Space Group's marketing division, and then risen through its executive ranks in the 1970s to take over the company in 1979. He promptly became the next decade's symbol of corporate greed.

"ITT bought the apartment for Araskog," a member of the co-op board at the time agrees. In fact, it's unclear whether ITT paid for the apartment, but it did announce, in its April 1980 proxy statement, that it would pay the interest on the loan that had allowed its new chairman to buy and renovate it, explaining that it had "requested" him to find a place near its Park Avenue headquarters. Apparently, Araskog's home, thirty miles away in New Jersey, wasn't close enough (even though neighbors say he would continue to sleep there most nights throughout his tenure at ITT). Aside from interest costs of up to $950,000 a year (mortgage rates were hovering at 17 percent), the company also agreed to pay the portion of his maintenance attributable to real estate taxes and the building's underlying mortgage. Araskog, who'd been paid $694,917 in 1979, and another $98,000 in benefits and other remuneration, agreed to pay off the principal on the loan within fifteen years. By 1990, according to the *Chicago Tribune*, Araskog would be earning $21.69 a minute, every minute of every day, whether working, playing, or sleeping and had already paid off his loan.

Years earlier, though, when that loan was revealed by the press (along with other juicy details like the $1,000 Araskog was paid every time he attended a meeting of his board, and the $750 he got for showing up at committee meetings), the co-op board was outraged, says John Hughes. "The board did not want Rand Araskog in that building," Hughes claims. "They said, 'John, make him jump through hoops, make him toe the mark.' And I did. He found out, and he always held this against me. Later, he got on the board, and his first order of business was to see how quickly he could get me out of there."

Some of the neighbors didn't approve of the Araskogs' renovations, either. "It was decorated like a hotel," says one. "They were very grand." Jane Foster felt that, too, and began to worry that 740 wasn't a family building anymore. "It got grander and grander, not so old-shoe-ish," she says.'

But the Araskogs were exemplars of good taste and good behavior compared with some of the other new arrivals at 740 Park. One of the first to raise hackles was Ronald Owen Perelman, the businessman from Philadelphia who'd bought Arthur Leidesdorf's "Jewish" apartment on the sixth and seventh floors of the B line for about $300,000 in 1978.²

Perelman was the son of a millionaire who owned a metal-fabricating company, bought and sold other small companies (like Maurice Olen's H. L. Green stores), and instilled in Ronald an unquenchable thirst for moneymaking; he even attended board meetings as a youngster. "When Ronnie was a boy," his father once said, "whenever I was thinking of making an acquisition, we would drive out to look at the company and discuss the pluses and minuses together." Tough and savvy, Raymond Perelman taught his son well and sent him to good schools, where he grew up conservative, self-assured, focused, and ambitious.

While earning a master's degree in business administration at Wharton, Perelman met Faith Golding, eighteen, a blond-bobbed Park Avenue princess whose grandfather Samuel Golding founded New York's Sterling National Bank in 1929 and had been its chairman ever since; Sterling specialized in bankrolling garment manufacturers in New York's fashion district. Golding, a devout Orthodox Jew like Perelman, also owned high-end real estate, including the Essex House on Central Park.

Faith and Ronald married in 1965 and moved into a house near his parents outside Philadelphia, and Ronald went to work as vice president of his father's ironworks. Together, Ronald and his father acquired more companies while Faith raised a family, adopting three children and having a fourth of her own. After Faith's father died at age fifty in 1967, the family, hit by estate taxes, began selling its assets. The Essex House went for $26 million, and the family sold 44 percent of Sterling for almost $19 million in 1968. Around that time, Perelman began visiting New York to oversee Faith's complex business affairs; she retained an interest in the bank and in 1981 raised her personal stake to 9.9 percent.

In mid-1978, after a bored and restless Ronald realized his father wasn't going to step back and let him run the family business (among other things, Raymond didn't approve of his son's taste for debt), he went out on his own, buying control of a chain of jewelry stores with $1,939,734 borrowed from Faith and from Bankers Trust, which loaned him money on her guarantee. After selling the stores and liquidating the inventory, he ended up with $15 million. Using that grubstake as collateral, Perelman began building a pyramid of acquisitions, all neatly balanced on the money he'd borrowed on his wife's guarantee. He and his father didn't speak for six years.

At the end of 1979, Perelman took over MacAndrews and Forbes, a publicly traded candy and flavoring company, and repaid the loan that had paid for the purchase with a then-novel financial instrument, junk bonds. With junk in his pocket and MacAndrews and Forbes as his base, the thirty-six-year-old Perelman emerged as a Wall Street player and embarked on one of the most colorful careers in financial history, one that would eventually make him richer than his new neighbor and fellow Wharton grad, Saul Steinberg. By 1985, through trial and error, buying marginal companies and selling their marginal operations to finance subsequent purchases, he'd build a nine-figure fortune.

While making his initial moves in New York, Perelman lived at the Sherry-Netherland Hotel, but he wanted and soon found a home of his own. Again, Faith's fortune came in handy. "He had money," says someone privy to the deal, "but not the kind that she had." Indeed, although the total amount of Faith's loan to her husband is blacked out in the copy of Perelman's promissory note on file with the Securities and Exchange Commission, it also included the money to pay for the apartment.

Though it would prove to be a very good investment, Perelman wouldn't be around long enough to cash in on it. All his deal making had obviously caused other juices to start flowing in Perelman's loins. He'd begun an affair with Susan Kasen, the owner of Green Thumb Flowers, a florist shop a few blocks from 740. It was in full swing by the winter of 1981, when the heat in 740 went off for ten days and the owners held a meeting in the Perelmans' apartment. "We were all frozen, all in fur coats, surrounded by glorious flowers," says one attendee. "They were done by the mistress, though we didn't know that at the time."

The building staff may have been the first to learn of the affair, and some of them later came to believe that a scene in the film based on Tom Wolfe's novel *The Bonfire of the Vanities*, in which the protagonist Sherman McCoy calls his mistress from a pay phone right outside his building, was based on Perelman and Kasen. "He had that reputation," Patrick O'Connor says carefully. "He was a strange character. Not very polite. A double life is bound to catch up with you."

Perelman's double life caught up with him when the luxury jeweler Bulgari accidentally sent a pair of blue-sapphire-and-diamond earrings meant for Kasen to Faith. "It was a repair, not something bought," says a former executive of Bulgari. "Then the wife called, saying it was not hers, it was a mistake." The salesperson corrected her, saying Perelman had purchased it, so it had to be hers. "She'd had some suspicions, but there was no proof," says the executive. "Then she had proof."

Faith hired several lawyers, including Stanley S. Arkin, a specialist in white-collar crime, and a divorce lawyer, Stanley Plesant, and the latter hired private detectives to tail her wayward spouse and investigate his paramour. The detectives soon discovered that Kasen, a forty-something blond divorcée with a teenage daughter, had opened Green Thumb Flowers in 1979 with money "that came from nowhere," says someone close to the matter, leading them to wonder if Perelman had paid for it and been seeing her for years.

Their surveillance began in November 1982, and over the next month they would watch as Perelman met Kasen at various Madison Avenue coffee shops, a restaurant in Little Italy, and several hotels, often brazenly dropping her off at her home and office, sometimes kissing, sometimes fighting, as couples having an affair will do.

Tailing him all over the city, they got to know his routine. Ronald would be picked up by a black limousine owned by MacAndrews and Forbes every morning at 8:30 and come home around eleven hours later. Investigating the cars he used, they came to believe he'd given Kasen a

Mercedes by buying cars on Faith's tab to chauffeur her and the kids around—and overcharging her $12,000 per vehicle.

Faith asked for a bodyguard in December 1982. That may have been wise. On December 10, Perelman "went berserk" outside Green Thumb, according to one of the investigators' reports, storming up to Kasen's car and demanding she get out. When she refused and ordered her driver to pull away, Perelman blocked the car, then tried to open its door. The game of cat and mouse continued as the chauffeur kept trying to drive away and Perelman repeatedly leaped in front of the car.

Finally Kasen opened her window a crack, and he grabbed the pane of glass, "shaking it like a crazy man," according to a witness, until it broke and shattered, cutting his face. As a passerby tried to restrain him and a small crowd gathered to watch, Kasen leaped from her car, picked him up, and kissed and hugged him as she brushed pieces of shattered glass off of him. "It appeared Ms. Kasen was also wiping tears from Mr. Perelman's face" as the car drove off, one of the investigators reported.

Two days later, Kasen sued Perelman. Her charges were later revealed by the *New York Post*, which reported that she'd sued for $30 million, alleging that he beat her when she declined his marriage proposal in September 1983. But their lovers' spat was apparently short-lived, because eight days later Perelman and Kasen flew to Paris together. Investigators went ahead of them while others followed them to the airport, where Perelman and Kasen were taking the Concorde. She wore a white sweater, white pants, and a brown scarf and carried a fur coat. He was in a blue blazer and gray slacks. They had three suitcases. As they left their car, a hidden photographer snapped them walking hand in hand to the Air France check-in desk. The detectives noted that Perelman lit up a cigar in the Concorde lounge, made a phone call ("I'll see you Thursday," he said. "Be good"), then acted uncomfortable when a European man walked over and struck up a conversation. Kasen retreated, and once an agitated Ronald ended his chat, he joined her in the farthest corner of the lounge.

The couple reached Paris around 10:30 that night and were picked up in a light rain by a maroon Mercedes. They kissed passionately in the back of the car, which took them to the Plaza Athénée hotel, where Ronald had made a reservation under the name Parsons, a name he also used on bank accounts. Arriving at 11:48, they went to their one-bedroom suite on the fourth floor, then left for an hour. Back at 1:00 A.M., Perelman put his shoes outside the door and didn't emerge until noon the next day. Some of Faith's neighbors heard that by the time Perelman returned to New York a few days later, all of his clothes had been packed and were waiting for him. When that got around, another 740 wife grabbed Faith to say, "You're my hero." Ronald moved into a town house on East Sixty-third Street, where MacAndrews and Forbes had its headquarters. Until 1983, it had rented the place from Faith, but following their breakup Perelman bought it from her.

On January 5, detectives followed Perelman and Kasen separately to the town house office of the lawyer Roy Cohn. But their alliance would soon shatter. Months later, more details emerged in Manhattan Supreme Court, when Perelman sued Kasen for the return of $500,000 he'd paid her and she sued the so-called Southampton Diet doctor, Stuart Berger, for the return of $30,000 she'd paid him. It turned out that the lovers had met in Barbados in 1975 and started seeing each other a few months later. When Kasen agreed to leave her husband, they'd made a pact in May 1982, allegedly brokered by Dr. Berger, in which Perelman agreed to give Kasen a lump sum of $1 million tax-free plus $60,000 a year for five years, pay off the principal due on the Mercedes, buy her an apartment, and name her beneficiary of a $1 million life insurance policy. He'd agreed, a judge said in court, "to protect himself and his family from [her] threats to reveal intimate details" of their affair—that is, blackmail. Perelman, Berger alleged, paid Kasen to keep those same matters out of her divorce action.

For his part, Berger described Kasen as "seductive and mysterious" but also greedy. "Miss Kasen is almost always in financial difficulty," said his sworn statement. "She lives in a very high style, spends compulsively and has little control over her finances." He alleged that she was torn between Perelman and a music business executive, Robert Summer, and that Perelman, upset by this rival, had had Kasen followed and personally threatened her. Berger even said he'd served Perelman with a summons in the criminal action Kasen brought against him after the car window incident. Then she turned around and sued Berger!

Kasen replied that the $30,000 was a loan, that Berger's accusations were "unfounded and scurrilous," and that she and Perelman and Summer all had children who should be spared from "the wild fabrications of a completely desperate man" trying to duck repaying a loan. "Ms. Kasen left her children when she left her husband and moved into an apartment for which Mr. Perelman paid," Berger spat back.

What happened next is a mystery; although these were all civil actions, Perelman and Cohn managed to get them sealed from prying eyes. Berger, the diet guru, died in 1994 of heart problems exacerbated by obesity and cocaine. Kasen married Robert Summer, and together they became major collectors of contemporary British art and founded a 3-D optical imagery company.

Faith sued Perelman, too, for divorce on grounds of adultery, charging, among other things, that her husband had spent "at least $100,000" on Kasen, on a Mercedes and jewelry, and on taking her not just to Paris but also to London, Amsterdam, Rome, Geneva, and Zagreb, all paid for with money "wrongly diverted from First Sterling Corporation—an entity" owned by Faith. Ronald denied all, to no avail. Faith filed a statement with the Securities and Exchange Commission in June 1983, asserting that Perelman had falsely claimed to own the shares in MacAndrews and Forbes that her money had paid for. Three weeks later, her husband (who'd just announced plans to convert MacAndrews and Forbes into a private—that is, less-regulated—corporation) settled, paying Faith $3.8 million in cash (and, according to some, as much as $6.2 million more) in exchange for her relinquishing her claim to the shares. She also got the apartment. And Perelman had to explain himself to the MacAndrews and Forbes board. "He laid out the facts and that Faith, never mentioned by name, had been fully repaid and compensated," a board member recalls. "No question in my mind that Ronald used her money."

Despite the embarrassment, Perelman walked away financially intact and by 1990, says *Forbes*, the third-richest man in America. Arkin, who said the settlement was "a complete vindication of all of Mrs. Perelman's claims," later defended Perelman in a lawsuit in which it was alleged that he made sexual boasts during business meetings.

These petty annoyances apparently came with the territory. Perelman went on to take MacAndrews and Forbes private and acquire Revlon, Marvel Comics, New World Entertainment, five savings banks, estates in Palm Beach and East Hampton, and three more wives: Claudia

Cohen, another wealthy Park Avenue girl (who'd worked as a gossip columnist); Patricia Duff, a blond beauty who left the Hollywood mogul Mike Medavoy for him; and Ellen Barkin, the actress, his (as of now) last wife. In the process, he was also famously rejected by the co-op board at 820 Fifth Avenue, "a process that was devastating to my ego," he told the writer Craig Horowitz.

Faith dropped Perelman's name, but stayed in 740 until she married plastic surgeon Peter Linden in 1994. The rich get richer; she made about $11 million on her $300,000 investment. The buyer, Ezra Merkin, was the son of Hermann Merkin, the child of a family of furriers who'd escaped from Nazi Germany. Hermann became an American intelligence officer, a private investor, and one of the philanthropic elder statesmen of New York's Jewish community. Like his father before him, Ezra is president of the Orthodox Jewish Fifth Avenue Synagogue, where Faith worshipped. Like Israel Englander, he's a principal in a hedge fund.

Unlike his sister Daphne, a writer who publicized her rejection by the co-op board at 1075 Park Avenue (she claimed her essay on sado-masochism in a book titled *Dreaming of Hitler* inspired the turndown), Ezra Merkin is an intensely private man. Aside from one 1991 tantrum against what he deemed Steve Ross's mismanagement of Time Warner, neither he nor his Gabriel Capital Corporation is much in the public eye. Some in the building even believe he is a rabbi. Which may explain why, when he appeared in a yarmulke for his admissions interview at 740 Park, Donald Rynne later told a realtor, board members thought he was a rabbi and were so afraid of offending him they hardly asked a question before accepting him.[3]

STANLEY ARKIN, THE CRIMINAL LAWYER, NEXT APPEARED IN THE LIFE OF 740 on the losing side of a criminal matter; for the first time, a member of the community was about to go to jail. Antonio Gebauer had lived a quiet life in apartment 10/11C at 71 East Seventy-first Street ever since he bought it from Alida Camp in 1973, following the board's rejection of Streisand. Gebauer didn't carry the burden of fame, and he certainly had the funds to buy the apartment, one of the smallest in the building, for $157,000. Indeed, he proved likable and trustworthy enough that, after

Ken Rosen's accident, Gebauer was asked to replace him on a co-op board that was changing as rapidly as the building was. All the Old Guard types were leaving, replaced by a former fashion model, Sandra Ohrstrom, Martin Coleman, David Mahoney, Donald Rynne, and Gebauer.

Antonio Gebauer was born in Bogotá in 1940 and grew up in Caracas, Venezuela, the son of a German beer maker who sent his son to good schools where he mingled with members of Venezuela's ruling class. In 1957, while he was in New York learning English, antigovernment riots broke out in Venezuela, and Gebauer decided to stay in New York and enrolled at Columbia College to study business.

There he met his first wife, a daughter of a socially prominent family of coffee growers, who would later help him network his way to the highest echelons of Brazilian society. He also met a Morgan Guaranty Trust banker who helped him win a job in the elite bank's tiny Latin American office in 1963. Within a few years, the sandy-haired banker in horn-rim glasses and power suits was a rising star at Morgan—and in Brazil. Brazil became his specialty right around the time a military dictatorship took over its government. Gebauer was in charge of loans, among other things, and the men running Brazil were hungry for them. The more they borrowed, the more they needed to service their debt.

With the suave Gebauer in the lead, Morgan became a key lender to state-run companies, and Gebauer became a popular figure in South America, "attractive, intelligent, hard-working, thoroughly professional—one of the really great performers," according to a fellow banker quoted in *The Blood Bankers*, James S. Henry's book that chronicles his rise and fall. At age thirty-two, Gebauer was named a vice president of Morgan, overseeing loans worth more than $1 billion by the end of the 1970s as Brazil became the world's largest debtor nation. "Tony Gebauer," wrote Ron Chernow in *The House of Morgan*,

> socialized in elite circles and was probably
> on a first-name basis with every Latin
> finance minister and central banker. In the
> heady world of petrodollar recycling in the
> 1970s, Gebauer was a jet-setting star, a
> frequent guest at Brazilian coffee

plantations, his doings covered by Rio de
Janeiro gossip columnists. He appeared on
Brazilian television, landed on the cover
of the country's top new magazine, *Veja*,
and became president of the Brazilian-
American Chamber of Commerce. It was
highly unusual for the Morgan bank to
tolerate such a high-profile approach to
banking.

By 1984, when he married Aurelia Reinhardt, the daughter of a former
American ambassador to Vietnam and Italy, Gebauer had become a superstar, the man who'd led an international consortium of banks in raising a
$4.4 billion loan to keep the near-bankrupt Brazil afloat. But doubts about
him were growing inside Morgan, where his role was drawing attention to,
as Chernow put it, "the bank's embarrassingly huge Latin American expo-
sure." Only then did Morgan learn it had a serious problem.

Gebauer's lifestyle had changed. In 1971, he'd had a house in East
Hampton and a Manhattan co-op. When he traded up to 740, people be-
gan to notice his wealth. "He lived like a king," says Patrick O'Connor.
"His butler would tell us."

In the years that followed, even though he had to pay enormous alimony after he was divorced in 1981, Gebauer bought a share in a coffee
ranch in Bahia and began acquiring art, first editions, jade, and other
trappings of wealth: a Louis XVI desk, two Mercedeses, a sailboat, and
memberships at elite clubs like the Union and the Knickerbocker. According to Henry, he was spending far more than he made.

How was he paying for it? Henry alleges that Gebauer's crimes went beyond those he was eventually charged with. "From August 1976 to July
1983," he writes, "Gebauer siphoned $1,750 to $75,000 every other week
from six [clients'] accounts under his control," cutting checks to himself,
family members, even art dealers, 210 in all, including 116 payable to his own
bank account—stealing more than $4 million. When he drained an account
dry, he arranged loans from Morgan to replenish them. Someone close to
Gebauer describes that all as inaccurate and exaggerated. "The loans were
not related to the funds that were diverted. They were bona fide loans."

Henry says more in an interview. "Morgan accused him of being a bad apple, but other people in the bank knew," he charges. "He was taking private commissions on dubious loans." In layman's terms, Gebauer's so-called diversions were, Henry says, "kickbacks from the recipients," commissions he was splitting with clients getting "bogus loans." But since Gebauer was also laundering the commissions in banks outside Brazil for clients who "were really his partners," Henry writes, "he had virtually unlimited discretion" over the accounts, "and he was helping himself to a little on the side." At least until "someone lost his temper" and raised an alarm, Henry says.

"Nonsense," says Gebauer's advocate. "To the extent that accounts abroad were flight capital, then yes. But the loans were legitimate."

By then, Gebauer was gone. In the summer of 1985, he'd joined the less-prestigious Drexel Burnham Lambert, with a brief to expand the firm's junk-bond business into Latin America. Some at 740 claim, in hindsight, that they thought the move significant. "I knew he was in trouble," says one.

"Why would you leave the bank?" another asked him.

"You don't know anything about business," Gebauer snapped.

Less than a year later, Gebauer resigned from Drexel the same day he was confronted with the results of a just-concluded internal investigation at Morgan. In the context of the ongoing debt crisis in Latin America, Gebauer's "impropriety" had international repercussions, and so it made headlines for weeks that spring. Initially, Morgan said that some $6 million in unauthorized withdrawals had been made from fewer than six accounts, but no clients had suffered any "ultimate loss," implying that all the diverted money had been returned and Morgan had had nothing to do with it. The bank also announced that it had referred the matter to the U.S. attorney for possible criminal investigation. Within days, though, *The New York Times* was reporting that the diversions "may not have been as clear-cut as Morgan Guaranty has implied" and that the accounts Gebauer had plundered may have contained "flight capital," funds illegally deposited outside of Brazil.

"Absolute nonsense," says Gebauer's advocate. "Totally erroneous. Pure conjecture. If they converted dollars loaned for business purposes, the bank did not know anything about it."

"That was embarrassing," says Ronald Jeançon, "but it didn't reflect on the building." His neighbors liked the charming, suave Gebauer (who immediately quit the co-op board); they were sympathetic. "Tony's in trouble" was all they said. Dyson told the staff that Gebauer was the last person in the building he figured as a crook.

At first, Gebauer's lawyer, Arkin, said he would contest the charges. But after seventeen months, a plea bargain was struck that avoided a charge of embezzlement and conveniently kept many of the details of Gebauer's crimes out of the public record. "Nobody had an interest in pressing it," James Henry says. So in October 1986, Gebauer pleaded guilty to one count of bank fraud, one count of evading $3.4 million in taxes, and two counts of creating false reports by making unauthorized loans to cover up his withdrawals. He was released on a $2 million bond secured by his 740 apartment to await sentencing.

A few months later, after repaying another $4.4 million, Gebauer went to court and said he took the money "because I was weak, because I had bad judgment and my life got out of control . . . I feel grief, sorrow, pain and mostly a sense of shame," he continued. "In spite of what I have done, I know there's some good in me." He was sentenced to three and a half years in prison and heard himself described by the judge as "a lucifer, a fallen angel of the banking world," who, though paid "a princely income . . . spent like an emperor . . . to maintain an extraordinarily lavish lifestyle."[4]

Gebauer eventually made good and now lives a quiet life in upstate New York, where he is considered a decent, if chastened, man. "Tony Gebauer made full restitution," says the person close to him. "Every penny Morgan and the account holders claimed he owed was paid back with interest. Whatever was left over went to the IRS. Nobody ever mentions that. People try to find mysterious accounts and funny transactions, but he did a lot of very, very good business for Morgan. People talk about what you did wrong, not what you did well, unfortunately."

Luckily for Gebauer, while he was in jail—he ultimately served a year two months in 1987 and 1988—his case was forgotten, lost in a wave of late-1980s financial scandals as bigger fish like Dennis Levine and Ivan Boesky were arrested, indicted, and in some cases convicted of financial crimes, elbowing Gebauer out of the news.

But his trials weren't over. Gebauer still owed $6.9 million in back taxes, penalties, and interest, and though he'd put his apartment on the market immediately for $5.8 million, it didn't sell, and several potential buyers, including the newscaster Barbara Walters, were discouraged from trying to buy it. (Walters says she never made an offer.) Finally, after the price was knocked down to $4.3 million, it was sold to Lewis van Amerongen, a forty-nine-year-old partner in a leveraged buyout firm.

A descendant of an old Dutch family that still owns castles (although "they live in them like they're condos," says his wife, Diane), van Amerongen had no trouble with the board. "Nobody hates the Dutch, I guess," Diane says. They knew Rand Araskog's wife. And the Princeton graduate could afford it. Over the years, his firm had bought others like Budget Rent A Car and Kash n' Karry Food Stores. "It wasn't as much an interview as it was like joining a club," Diane says. "It was pretty obvious they couldn't have been more thrilled to see a cute blond couple with three towheaded children and no pets. We're pretty serious white bread."

But van Amerongen hated living in the "new" 740. "He felt it was too high-profile," says Diane. "The Lauders would receive guests in the lobby, and he hated the kids seeing limos parked three deep when they were catching the school bus for Spence. We had someone to drive us, so it was a little hypocritical, but it bothered him that it was not discreet. And he wanted to live in a house." So a mere three years later, they put the place on the market for $7.5 million and sold it in 1994 for just over $7 million to the current occupants, Miranda and Hamburg Tang, the Hong Kong Chinese founder of Alloys Unlimited, a semiconductor and holding company. But only after Tang brought in a feng shui expert to approve the purchase.

Tang wasn't the first Chinese owner in the building. Elinor Dorrance Ingersoll's estate had sold her apartment to Cheng Ching and Florence Wang, the parents of the fashion designer Vera Wang, for $350,000. A quiet, cultured, unassuming family man, a child of wealth and influence who ran a trading company, Wang was "more WASP than the WASPs," says a relative. His father had been a general under Chiang Kai-shek, for fifty years the leader of Nationalist China. Florence Wang's father was a Chinese warlord.

Peter Huang bought the former Preston Davie apartment in the mid-1970s for $145,000. Born in Shanghai the son and heir of a 1930s finance minister of Nationalist China, Huang—pronounced *Wong*—attended Stanford University, began his career as an engineer for Bechtel, then went back to school for an MBA. He briefly worked for William Zeckendorf before joining City Investing, a real estate company that had decided to leverage its assets and become a conglomerate. Huang was hired as its chief executive's assistant just as that process began. Within two years, City Investing was a billion-dollar company.

Though he was described as "a swinger" in "groovy ties" and "out of sight" suits who spent his nights at Le Club, Raffles, and Elaine's in a *New York Times* profile in 1970, a year later he settled down. Huang married his second wife, Nancy Stoddart, the granddaughter of the composer of the battle song "The Caissons Go Rolling Along," the daughter of a steel man, and a former girlfriend of David Thorne's. Though Stoddart was from Main Line Philadelphia, they'd met in Paris a year earlier, where she was making clothes for rich socialites. She would joke that she married Huang because she was desperate. No more. Huang was making $230,000 a year, so when she went looking for a new apartment, she started at the very top of the market and almost immediately found one being sold by a couple on the verge of divorce.

C. Channing Blake and his wife, Jill, had bought Edith Chrysler Carr's apartment in 1972. "It all came from ice cream cones originally," says Curtis Blake, Channing's father, who founded Friendly Ice Cream Corporation in 1935 with his brother Prestley on a $547.50 loan from their father. They made their first ice cream in the back of a store in Springfield, Massachusetts. By 1960, they had 70 Friendly's Ice Cream stores, and seven years later, when Channing turned twenty-one, they had 170, making $1.7 million a year. When they sold stock to the public in 1968, they walked away with $7 million while holding on to another million shares, worth $50 million at the end of the first day of trading. "That gave him a lot of liquidity," Curtis Blake says.

A year later, Chan Blake, as he was known, by then a graduate student at Columbia University (where he'd eventually earn a master's degree in architectural restoration and preservation and a doctorate in architectural history), proposed to Jill Sloan Kogan, who was going to its sister school, Barnard. They'd met in a medieval-architecture class and courted in the Frick and the Metropolitan Museum, where they flirted among the seventeenth- and eighteenth-century paintings and sneaked sandwiches in Egyptian tombs.

An Upper East Sider, Jill was the daughter of a Madison Avenue jeweler and, compared with Chan, a free spirit. "I was a liberal, left-leaning gypsy, in bright-colored clothes and jewelry everywhere, a strong, exotic creature to him," she says. "He was a very conservative preppy, clean-cut Brooks Brothers New England snob, seemingly at times, to me, a spoiled brat. I was fascinated that he could be so clueless, literally not knowing that there was a war in Vietnam. But he looked like an angel with rosy cheeks, and he could be sweet and so open to learning about art. We were both very attracted to and loved each other, but being young and inexperienced, we both felt that we could tame and change each other. He lived by schedule and routine. I stayed up both day and a lot of the night. I kept him up some nights, sitting for me while I drew him. Other than our mutual love of art and architecture—a glue that provided much shared delight over the six and a half years that we were together—it was a case of opposites attracting."

"Jill embodied everything my brother was rebelling against: everything my parents were about," says Chan's sister Susan Blake. "He didn't fit with my father."

Chan and Jill married in 1969 and moved into an apartment on Central Park West. While getting his degrees, Chan worked for a sculpture dealer. After their son Noah was born, they decided they needed a bigger apartment. "He wanted a library," says Jill. "I needed a place to paint." So they went looking and quickly found the former Jack Chrysler apartment, with its immense living room paneled in eighteenth-century boiserie, a forty-foot dining room, a paneled library, marble fireplaces, a shower with twenty gold-plated heads, and a small terrace. "After two months of making Channing look at other apartments after he had fallen in love with the Chrysler duplex, I said okay, if it didn't change our lives," says Jill. Chan promised. "Which was insane."

They paid about $275,000, redid the ancient kitchen, and then moved in, planning to decorate slowly. After interviewing every top decorator in town, Chan decided that Jill should do it, "and stupidly, I said yes," she recalls.

Later, she would decide that he'd bought the apartment to outdo his father in taste and style. "He wasn't the son Curtis wanted," she says. "They were interested in completely different things from the day Channing was born. Channing was not interested in sports or cars or becoming a part of the family business. And Curt's take on aesthetics and art was, Art who?"

One night, after a dinner at the Metropolitan Museum with Henry Ford and Jayne Wrightsman, Jill realized Chan longed to be in museum society. "He'd watched those movies about the sophisticated New York cognoscenti," Jill says, "and he wanted that life." But he was also full of contradictions, spending copiously on antiques, objects, and paintings while turning off lights for fear of wasting pennies on electricity and fighting with Jill over their three servants' salaries and the cost of food and window and paint treatments and the new kitchen that he'd asked for.

"Then he'd say we're having forty people over for supper tomorrow night," she says. "It was very confusing. I wanted to be the good wife, but I wanted to have time for my child and time to make art. I wanted my life back the way it was before we moved. I wanted to be in the creating world. He wanted to be in the owning world. It seemed like a put-on, bought life. I wanted a sense of personal achievement as a mother and an artist."

Meanwhile, unbeknownst to Jill, while she raised Noah and did the house, faux-marbling the walls, draping windows in Scalamandré fabric, and filling the vast rooms with antiques Chan chose, her husband was embarking on a second, secret life. He'd met Everett Fahy, a European paintings curator at the Metropolitan, before they bought the apartment. "There's no doubt Everett broke up the marriage," says Susan Blake. His wife didn't yet know, but Chan had decided he was gay, and by the spring of 1973 they were talking divorce. "He was trying to be straight and have a family," Jill thinks. "He said he wished he wasn't gay."

"Being born a gay man has been a heavy burden for me," Chan agreed in words composed years later for his funeral. "The gift of irony that goes along with it does not compensate for the separation that being gay causes. It is not a unifying force. If I had the choice, I would not choose it for the next go-round."

The next year was long and hard as their lawyers fought it out. "Nobody would move out and relinquish the apartment," says Susan Blake. "Those were dark days." Jill hunkered down on the ninth floor with her son and their maid while Chan lived on 8. Finally an agreement was signed. Jill gave up money to win the right to leave New York with Noah and eventually moved to California. Chan went to Idaho to ski while she moved out, then returned and moved his lover Fahy in. "I lived with him there at least a year," says Fahy. "I didn't feel at all odd there. I knew many people in the building. Enid Haupt came to dinner."

Blake sold the apartment in 1975—although not to the Huangs—and moved to upstate New York, where he became a noted landscape architect. A few years later, he met Roger Ferri, an architect, and they lived together for fourteen years before Ferri's death from AIDS in 1991. Chan Blake died, also from AIDS, in 1995.[5] "I have two main regrets in life," his last words continued, "that I did not have more children, and that I never wept enough tears. Too much sorrow and depression, not enough tears. I am at peace with my life."

AN APARTMENT AT 740 PARK WOULD NOT BRING PEACE TO THE LIVES OF Peter and Nancy Huang, either. Though Huang wouldn't spend the $325,000 Blake was asking, he agreed to buy the cheaper Davie apartment four floors below for $145,000. They were interviewed in the Irelands' apartment. "They were all much older," says Nancy. "You went, you behaved properly, and they said, 'Fine.' "

While Peter worked at City Investing, Nancy Huang went to college at Sarah Lawrence, and then got a job as a stockbroker. The more independent she was, the more unhappy their marriage became, or so it appeared to her. Clearly, it was disintegrating. Peter often traveled without her. Nancy complained to Amanda Burden, who'd attended Sarah Lawrence the same years she did, "and we went out to dinner with Steve Ross one night when Peter was away on another ski trip, and Steve said, 'Come to work at my company.' " Ross induced Ahmet Ertegun, the son of a Turkish diplomat who headed Atlantic Records, a Warner subsidiary, to give Nancy a job. Soon she "went from being scared of my own shadow to saying 'Fuck it,' " she recalls.

From insecure mouse, she became a social lioness, giving parties that people still talk about a quarter century later. "Any excuse," she says. "It's Easter! After we got divorced, he began to learn how many people admired his fabulous apartment." They included Mariel Hemingway, Robert De Niro, musicians like Debbie Harry and Kid Creole, early hip-hop artists like Fab Five Freddy Braithwaite, artists like Jean-Michel Basquiat, the man-about-town Jean Pigozzi, and members of the Andy Warhol Factory set. One of the bands Nancy worked with was Chic, and Nile Rodgers, its front man, became a close friend and the black "orchestra leader" Ronald Jeançon complained to John Hughes about. Jane Foster would sometimes complain when Rodgers and his friend Herbie Hancock came over and played the Huangs' Steinway piano. Seven forty had never seen anything like it. Nancy would bribe the Chinese houseman to keep her husband in the dark about her parties. The doormen, too. When Huang called, everyone had to shut up. "The whole town was in on the joke," she says. "Nobody would tell him." But inevitably Peter "began to see the writing on the wall." So Nancy finally "dropped the bomb" and asked for a divorce in the fall of 1981.

Peter Huang doesn't want to discuss it. "My ex-wife is extremely . . . eccentric," he allows. The only thing he will say "is that she was having these parties," he continues. "She got involved with a lot of black people in the music business, and she threw parties. All blacks, which I'm sure was pretty unusual for this building. It is very, very unusual to have parties in this building where all the guests are black. Certainly, that was a cause for the divorce.

"Divorces," he adds, "are very complicated."

The Huangs agree that the end wasn't pretty. After many disagreements and an intense three-month negotiation, Nancy got $515,000 to leave, and on New Year's Eve, 1982, she moved out. She would later have a ten-year affair with Nile Rodgers and move to Los Angeles, where she became a decorator and screenwriter. Huang remarried and remains in the apartment. In 1985, he resigned from City Investing shortly before it was liquidated by its partners—an event that triggered a termination payment to Huang of $12.7 million. His shares in the company were worth another $2.5 million. He spent some of it in 1987, buying a controlling interest in American Global, a shipping company that owned American Hawaii Cruises. The company was sold in 1993 and went bankrupt shortly after September 11, 2001.

35

Channing Blake's apartment was finally sold to George Ohrstrom Junior, a private-equity investor, and his wife, Sandra, the former fashion model who was soon named to the co-op board. Ohrstrom's father had made his fortune like Landon Thorne, financing public utilities and heading holding companies that did the same. In the 1930s, he got in trouble with the new Securities and Exchange Commission, which charged him with fraudulent dealing, and his brokerage registrations were revoked but were reinstated during World War II over the objections of a commissioner. The elder Ohrstrom died in 1955, and his firm was taken over by George junior. In 1968, he bought Clarence Dillon's Georgian town house on East Eightieth Street. When he married the former Sandra Wright, both of them had previously been divorced.

Ohrstrom sold his town house to the Iraqi government in 1974 for $1.3 million and shortly afterward paid $325,000 for the Blake apartment. Aside from Sandra's beauty and her unusual interest in shamanism, gurus, and esoteric sciences, the Ohrstroms didn't make much of an impression on anyone but the Lorbers, who wanted to buy a maid's room from them. When Sandra insisted she used it all the time, they thought otherwise and, as a test, dropped a match into the toilet. Months later, it was still floating there.

Steeplechasers, the Ohrstroms spent most weekends in Virginia until 1983, when Sandra sued for divorce. After a year of Sandra's living alone in the apartment, her husband "wanted to sell it, so I had to move out," she says. "It was very painful." The Lorbers got their maid's room.

Ohrstrom listed the apartment in the summer of 1985 at $5.5 million (the maintenance was $4,535 a month). Prices had increased in just a few years, and between New York's recovery and the Reagan-era economy 740 apartments had finally begun appreciating the way they'd always been meant to. So once again, it took a special kind of person to get in. Henry Kravis looked like one of those.

The son of Raymond Kravis, a petroleum engineer from England who became a self-made millionaire working for the likes of Joseph P. Kennedy and the Chase Bank, Henry Kravis was born in Tulsa, Oklahoma, attended eastern prep schools, studied business at Columbia, interned at Goldman Sachs, worked briefly for the company that owned the Missouri-Kansas-Texas Railroad, and ended up at the Bear Stearns investment bank in 1969, the same year he married Helene Diane Shulman, who was known as Hedi, the petite, dark-haired daughter of a psychiatrist.

In 1976, Kravis, a cousin named George Roberts, and their boss, Jerome Kohlberg, who specialized in what would become known as leveraged buyouts, left to form their own merchant banking firm, Kohlberg, Kravis & Roberts. Starting slowly and conservatively, only buying companies where management welcomed them, they did good but not spectacular business into the early 1980s. Then, in 1984, Kravis agreed to side with Gulf Oil management in its war with a takeover artist, T. Boone Pickens, and KKR, as it was known, emerged as a major player on the corporate battlefield. Kravis's fortune was then estimated at $300 million.

At the time, Kravis, a wiry man with the face of a pugilist, divorced his first wife, the mother of his three children, and began stepping out with a lanky fashion designer named Carolyne Jayne Smith Roehm. They'd met at a holiday cocktail party in 1981, when she was just divorced after an unhappy two-year marriage to Axel Roehm, a member of a German chemical dynasty, and Henry had just separated from his wife. Her mother chaperoned them on their first two dates that Christmas, when they were both in Vail, Colorado. She was seeing the Kansas oil tycoon David Koch at the same time, and it was said that she arranged to have the two men cross paths in her apartment building's elevator, just to keep the competition heated.

By the mid-1980s, Kravis was in the catbird seat with Carolyne. Though at five feet ten inches, the size-four Roehm was more than an inch taller than he, wags joked that when he stood on his wallet, they were a perfectly balanced couple. Late in 1984, that wallet got a little thinner when Kravis, forty-five, provided the money for Roehm, then thirty-eight, to launch her own line of goddess gowns for her friends in the new society set. Roehm, a St. Louis native whose parents were teachers, had started her career designing polyester dresses for Sears and worked as an assistant to Oscar de la Renta for nine years. Kravis not only attended her shows; he reportedly shed tears of happiness at the end of the first one and was said to keep close tabs on her books.

The following July, Kravis signed a contract to buy the Ohrstrom apartment with its views over the spires of St. James Church. But even though he'd only just begun to emerge as a public figure, getting into the building didn't prove easy. After Steinberg and Perelman, there was a feeling on the board that they'd had enough of, "well, they said Wall Street guys, they didn't say Jewish, but it was understood what they meant," says a realtor. "Kravis came at that moment." And though he would later prove to be the best of the bunch, a public-minded, quiet citizen ideal for 71 East Seventy-first Street, he almost paid for his predecessors' bad behavior.

John French "got Kravis in," says a resident of the building at the time. French was an investor from a Southern family that had had its ups and downs since arriving in America in colonial days. In their heyday, they'd owned a plantation with twenty-five slaves.

French had made a small fortune as an early venture capitalist, providing seed money for electronics ventures in the 1960s and, in the late 1970s, an Australian oil shale operation. He was married to his second wife, Sally Phelps, a retired banker who chose the former Morris Hadley apartment, 6/7D, just below the Ohrstroms and bought it in her name.

They paid $1.1 million in 1980 and were interviewed by Tony Gebauer. They had Robert Denning decorate the place in 1930s style and moved in a year later. "No sooner did we move in than the hot water quit and the boiler broke down," says French's then-wife, Sally Phelps. "They parked a boiler in the street like in Harlem, chugging all winter. Rand Araskog was all upset. He said maybe he'd run too tight a ship and not spent enough."

Kravis knew the Frenches; like him, they were major supporters of Ronald Reagan. Kravis also likely knew he was going to have trouble getting into the building. "Henry wouldn't have gotten in," says a neighbor. "They were trying to keep a balance. Araskog, Speight, Dyson, and Rynne didn't want it to get too Jewish. It wasn't anti-Semitic. They felt it would detract from the value of the building. Carolyne being a dress designer might have had some impact, too."

"Henry courted us assiduously," says Sally Phelps, who was invited to Roehm's first fashion shows. Then the Frenches arranged a dinner for twenty people to introduce Kravis to the Araskogs and the Rynnes, and the Kravises were approved.

"I didn't know who he was," says a board member. "I asked a good friend and was told he was very able and very fine." Kravis renovated the apartment, partly furnished it, and moved in two days before he and Carolyne were married there in November 1985. One neighbor recalls that a string quartet played Bach as they took their vows in front of a marble fireplace. A sit-down dinner for 101 guests followed, overflowing their apricot and gold damask dining room, where an American Empire table with thirteen leaves was topped with George II silver, and spreading out into the burgundy and apple green brocaded living room, the Louis XV sitting room, and the peach-lit, Georgian-paneled library dotted with equestrian art.

The Frenches were not invited to the wedding they'd facilitated, but the Araskogs were. Jessie Araskog still remembers live doves being released at the wedding.

Working with the design firm of Denning & Fourcade, Roehm turned the apartment into an overstuffed (and some thought overdecorated) showcase, filled the faux-marble walls with art—ancestor portraits, a Sargent, a Winterhalter, a Monet, a Tissot, a Sisley, a Pissarro, and what Roehm described to a visitor as "my little Renoir"—and then used it as a stage set, tended by a staff of six, for the burst of publicity that launched her design career.

"Henry led a very different life," says Reinaldo Herrera. "He is a tiger in the boardroom, but he is a very quiet man, a gent. She was the one who made all the noise, not him. Even now, he's as quiet as quiet can be."

Yet their show of wealth and conspicuous lifestyle—in 1988, they rented the Temple of Dendur at the Metropolitan Museum for a private dinner party—rankled some, including Raymond Kravis, who looked at the Sargent portrait of the sixth Marquess of Londonderry and asked his son, "Which one of our relatives is this?"

Manhattan, Inc., a feisty business magazine, repeated a conversation in which a friend admired some of Roehm's emeralds and she announced, "I found them under my pillow."

"Where have you been sleeping?" the friend asked.

"In the right bed," she shot back.

After one particularly revealing story, "The Rich Life of Carolyne & Henry," appeared in *W* at the same time his business exploded (in 1985 and 1986, KKR took part in takeovers of Union Texas Petroleum, Pace Industries, Motel 6, Red Lion Inns, Amstar, and Lorimar-Telepictures, as well as the $6.2 billion leveraged buyout of the Beatrice Companies, the largest ever attempted), an embarrassed Kravis vowed to never speak to the press about his private life again. Though his fame would only grow, particularly after KKR's hard-fought $25 billion takeover of RJR Nabisco in 1989, he has stuck to that vow, even as he continued to be a very public figure, donating $10 million to the Met and to Mount Sinai Medical Center, which named a wing and a medical center, respectively, for him. Magazines and newspapers continued covering them, too. Roehm soon appeared on the cover of an issue of *Fortune* as the embodiment of a story on trophy wives called "The CEO's Second Wife."

In July 1991, the Kravises were stunned when one of his sons by Hedi, nineteen-year-old Harrison, died in a car crash. Inexorably, their lives changed. A few weeks later, though she'd just announced expansion plans and hired a high-profile executive to run it, Roehm abruptly shut down her fashion label. The RJR Nabisco deal proved a tough Oreo for KKR to swallow. Early in 1993, Henry and Carolyne embarked on a trial separation, announced with appropriate fanfare in several social gossip columns. Liz Smith even reported that Kravis was keeping the apartment while Roehm would get their house in Connecticut. What wasn't revealed was the complex deal that led to that arrangement.

Kravis insisted that his surviving children needed the security of remaining in a familiar place. Friends say that Roehm's settlement included a provision that she'd have to give up her home, and considerable income, if she ever remarried. Kravis, on the other hand, was well on the way to his third wedding. In July, Liz Smith reported that Henry was squiring a French-Canadian economist, Marie-Josée Drouin, around the Hamptons. She'd been separated for six months from her husband, a Canadian conductor. In February 1994, Kravis married her. That same year he bought a new apartment, a twenty-six-room triplex penthouse palace, complete with a sixty-eight-foot-long ballroom, formerly owned by the cosmetics queen Helena Rubinstein, and then by Princess Ashraf Pahlavi, the twin sister of the late shah of Iran, at J. E. R. Carpenter's 625 Park Avenue. He paid $15 million for his new abode.

Once his new home was ready, Kravis put the apartment at 71 East Seventy-first Street on the market for $9 million in January 1995. By spring, it had been sold. But two months later, the former Lynde Selden apartment came back on the market.

Kravis's buyer had been turned away by the board.

Some of those who knew the buyer scratched their heads at that, for he was as perfect a purchaser as 740 Park could hope for. Others, who knew a bit about his complex personal life, nodded sagely, and told their friends they knew exactly why he was turned down. They were wrong.

Charles Porter Stevenson Jr.'s family owned the Eastman Machine Company in Buffalo, New York. It was founded by the inventor of a machine that cut cloth, who sold it to Stevenson's great-grandfather, one of the original investors, in 1901. The youngest of his three sons left Harvard to run the business (many years later, Randy Speight would work for another of the brothers). "The business prospered," says a family member. "The sewing machine had just been invented, and one cloth-cutting machine would keep fifty sewing machines going. It was the dawn of mass-produced clothing, and big orders of military uniforms helped, too." Charles Stevenson Sr. sold the company to three of his sons in 1988. The fourth, Charles junior, had long since made his own fortune.

Charles junior was born with social as well as business advantages. His mother, Mary-Louise "Cissie" Lord, was the child of Louise Stephanie Stewart Trevor Lord and, through her, a descendant of the Schieffelin, Lawrence, Delaplaine, Lispenard, and Stewart families of old New York. Lewis Morris, Louise's second husband, was a descendant of a signer of the Declaration of Independence, as well as a lawyer and chairman of a trust company. Her third husband, Charles Mellon, was an investment banker from the Pittsburgh family. On her father's side, Cissie was a granddaughter of Mrs. Thomas Fortune Ryan. The Stevensons were longtime residents of Southampton, and Charles senior, who'd graduated from St. Paul's and Yale, was a member of Skull and Bones.

Cissie Lord was suffering from polio when she married Stevenson senior. Stricken in 1936, she'd spent months in one of the only iron lungs in New York—brought to her on a private train owned by a Groton schoolmate of her father's, Franklin Delano Roosevelt—before improving sufficiently to make her debut in 1938. Her 1945 wedding was considered enough of a triumph that it earned headlines in several New York newspapers.

"It made for an unusual home growing up," says a friend. "Charles went out and made his own money very young." After graduating from Yale in 1969, Stevenson started painting apartments, sleeping in them when he could to save money on rent. With a nest egg of $18,000, he started a hedge fund, Zebra Associates, in the early 1970s and made a fortune. A childhood friend who gave him $10,000 when he started got back $1.6 million in 1980. Charles commuted to work on the subway wearing a backpack.

In the 1980s, Stevenson teamed up briefly with Asher Edelman, an arbitrageur often described as a "feared corporate raider" in reports of his battles to wrest control of companies he'd invested in from entrenched management. But Edelman retired to run an art museum in Switzerland; newspapers speculated that one reason for his retreat was increasing government scrutiny of corporate raiders in the late 1980s. Stevenson lowered his profile, too, but continued working as a private investor and head of two hedge funds, Navigator Partners Fund and Navigator Diversified Strategies Fund. One friend describes him as "a WASP who thinks more like a Jew than any Jew you ever met." Another calls him "a traditional cut of suit, kind of conservative in his thinking." But not when it comes to women.

In 1974, Stevenson married Suzanne Guerlac, whose family line boasted a poet, an appeals court judge, and a dean and several professors at Cornell University. "He and I spent about eight years together when we were very young," says Guerlac, now a professor of French at the University of California at Berkeley. "We were only married for a couple of those years. We were growing up. To me he was an artist. He wrote fiction beautifully. When he decided to make his fortune, I went on to study Baudelaire. He likes bright women—always a good trait in a man!" She sued for divorce in 1979.

Stevenson next married Susan Reis, one of the first women to graduate from Yale, and with her had four children and lived at 720 Park Avenue and in Southampton. But it became a loveless marriage, says a friend. So they split up, and Stevenson bought and moved into a second apartment at 720 Park. "The marriage had been over for many years," says the friend, who goes on to catalog a variety of entanglements not conducive to matrimony. "There was lots of activity," he continues. "They were not as conventional as they appeared to be. He's oversexed. At least that's what I hear. And I know a lot of girls he's gone out with."

"Everyone liked Susan," adds a Southampton neighbor. "She's very bright, very well educated. It's terrible what happened to her. It's not exactly attractive."

In the late 1980s, Stevenson met a beautiful personal trainer and nutritionist named Loriann Berge through a mutual friend. She would become his third wife. She also became a very controversial addition on the Southampton social scene. Part-Jewish, part-Filipino, and part-Chinese, she "was smart—very smart," says a friend of hers. Both friends and acquaintances wondered about her sexuality. "In a different world, she'd be a lesbian, but she's not comfortable with it," says her friend. Her tendencies did allow for "wild moments," he continues. "They had a very hot relationship."

That, it was said, was what it was all about for quiet, diminutive Charles Stevenson. A boyish man whose age—he's in his late fifties—

shows only on his hands, he is handsome if, on first impression, a bit neb-bishy. Friends describe him as a brilliant, solitary man, mesmerized by his work, but also an avid fitness buff, squash player, golfer, and reader who would rather quote poetry than stock prices.

Loriann Stevenson says that after their initial meeting, several months passed before Stevenson called her while visiting Los Angeles. "I started training him," she continues. "We started corresponding. He was getting divorced. He was cool, fit, and funny. I don't think he planned on meeting somebody so quickly."

She moved to New York to live with him, and they got married after she got pregnant and he was divorced in 1992. At first, they stayed in 720 Park so Stevenson's children would understand "he wasn't divorcing them," Loriann says. But when they had their first child, "it was not nice for Susan," she continues. "It was only right that we move." She found a new apartment in a Candela building, 1021 Park, but Stevenson didn't like the neighborhood, and it was too far away from his Rockefeller Center office for him to walk to work. "We started looking," Loriann says, and almost bought Jacqueline Onassis's apartment at 1040 Fifth, but they were "way outbid" by Carolyne Roehm's former suitor David Koch, who would later become their neighbor at 740.

Then they found the Kravis apartment. But the board never responded to their application. Though he wasn't turned down, Stevenson was not approved, because a director "had a vendetta" against him, says a broker privy to the incident.

That director was Rand Araskog, who, though not the chairman of the 740 co-op board, was the most powerful person on it. Many who heard the story thought Loriann was the problem. Loriann's lifestyle— she was thought to be bisexual and a drug user—could very well have offended the former West Pointer. Loriann "was not exactly a class act," says a New York neighbor. "She was coaching Olympic tennis and staying in his house, preaching about food and exercise, then eating chocolate chip cookies." She "could ruffle feathers," says another acquaintance. A third calls her "bizarre, hostile, always stoned out of her mind, with a body of death."

But Charles was in love with her. While still married to Susan, he bought a second piece of Southampton property and built Loriann and his five children a multimillion-dollar gym with a rock-climbing wall and a lap pool next to it. Stories soon spread around the insular summer community that one end of the pool had a glass wall, which allowed anyone in the gym to watch swimmers underwater. Skinny-dipping girls, it was said, were always encouraged by the Stevensons. Not quite the sort of entertainment the sentinels of 740 Park were likely to appreciate.

The truth lay elsewhere, though. After Stevenson had filed his plans to build the gym with the town of Southampton, several of his neighbors, led by the head of the Lazard Frères investment bank, Felix Rohatyn, were outraged and launched a campaign to stop the gym. "We did everything we could to dissuade him," Rohatyn confirms. Unaware that Rohatyn was living in a small cottage on the edge of his property, Stevenson had planned the gym so it blocked the view from what, it turned out, was Rohatyn's bedroom. When he did realize that, Charles walked next door, knocked on the door, and quickly reached an accommodation with Rohatyn, changing the shape and position of his planned gym.

After two months in which the board still declined to consider him, Stevenson asked Kravis for his deposit back and said he'd find another apartment. "Hang in there," Kravis advised him.

Only then did Stevenson recall that Rohatyn had been Rand Araskog's mentor for years, and decided that this might be the source of his 740 problem. "Yes, it's possible," says Rohatyn. "Not only did we not make it a secret; we tried to broaden it." So back next door Stevenson went. "Rand probably figured he was being a loyal friend," says another source close to Stevenson. "Charles told Felix he respected that." He also said he respected Rohatyn for protecting his view. And then he told Rohatyn that he feared Araskog wouldn't budge on the apartment unless given Rohatyn's explicit permission. "He asked Felix to talk to Rand."

Other calls were made on Stevenson's behalf, too. He was a proprietary member of the Shinnecock Hills Golf Club, one of the oldest and most exclusive private golf courses in the country. The course president pointed out to Araskog that when his son had applied for membership, Stevenson was among those who approved him. And just like that, the co-op board reversed itself. In November 1995, Charles and Loriann closed on their new apartment, conveniently only a block away from the one in which his children lived. She soon bore him another child, a daughter.

A year later, with the co-op board shrunk to three directors—Rynne, Speight, and Araskog—the latter took Stevenson to lunch at the Racquet Club and asked him to join. Stevenson tried to beg off, but Araskog insisted, telling him it was his civic responsibility. Three years after that, when Speight died, Araskog suggested that Stevenson take over as president. All was forgiven. The reject was now the ruler.

In the meantime, Loriann had departed. Again there is dispute about what happened. Many people in Southampton were left with the impression that Loriann, fed up with Stevenson's alleged priapism, took a powder—an impression they say they got from her. "It ended for a variety of reasons," says a friend of hers. "You can't assign it all to Loriann. She was very difficult, very temperamental. She wanted to divorce him. At the end, she was a nightmare, but she had every reason to be unhappy. It was a very volatile marriage, but it takes two to tango."

But someone close to Stevenson's fourth and current wife, the writer Alex Kuczynski, insists that Stevenson threw her out. "He'd had enough after a couple of rehabs and multiple transgressions against marriage and told her to hit the road," this person says.

Loriann denies nothing. "Whatever anybody says about me that's nice is wonderful," she says. "Whatever is not nice, I don't care. I was thirty-six when the marriage ended. Nobody wants that to happen when they have a baby." So what happened? "I was in love," she says. "What happened was sad. You can only close your eyes so tight. Gowns, cars, and jewels are enough for some. I had no choice but to leave. I was not doing well. And I have no problem saying I'm a sober addict now. We all have our faults and our issues. All I care about is that he's happy and he's getting laid on a regular basis."

Stevenson won't comment. But someone very close to him says, "Loriann is not a saint, but she isn't the devil, either. She was very unhappy in New York and they separated." And it was he who sued for divorce in 1998.

Charles is most likely getting laid regularly these days. Kuczynski, a five-foot-ten-inch brassy, whip-smart, and ambitious blonde, makes no bones about being a sexy woman—and she's outspoken about it, too. At

her first meeting with a fellow journalist several years before her marriage, she shocked him by announcing, apropos of nothing and long before it became a fashion, that she'd had what's called a Brazilian,
removing her pubic hair to improve her sex life with an earlier lover, a
TV newscaster. The daughter of a Peruvian economist and banker, she
began seeing Stevenson in 2000. Engaged a year later, they were married
in November 2002. Soon after that, Kuczynski left her full-time job at
The New York Times to write a book. She was overheard not long ago
while on the treadmill in the small gym in 740's basement discussing her
desire to follow the book with a baby. Stevenson is no doubt pleased. "He
likes 'em pregnant," says his friend.

A MEMBER OF 740'S CO-OP BOARD RECALLS THAT AFTER CHARLES DYSON
died in 1997 and Donald Rynne sold his apartment in 1999, "that left
Rand Araskog and Charles Stevenson looking at each other" at meetings,
wondering what to do next. Stevenson had had an encounter with Rynne
the day he quit the building for good that left the board president shaking his head in disbelief, says a witness. They were standing together under the awning when Rynne offered up his final words.

"You have to protect our building," he said. "Keep it Christian."

Then Rynne left and Stevenson was in charge. Rynne couldn't have
liked what happened next. After a brief real estate recession in the early
1990s, the Bill Clinton boom years began, and the prices of apartments
at 740 Park resumed their climb into the stratosphere. The sort of people who could afford and, more important, wanted to pay for them were
not the sort Rynne approved of. One of the so-called Jewish apartments
offers a unique perspective on the rise in 740's real estate values.

There is no record of how much Emanuel Terner paid for 8/9A
when he bought it from Bartholomew Barry in the early 1960s, and all
his descendants refuse to discuss it, perhaps because the apartment has
remained in his family ever since. But apartments in the A line were not
selling for much in those days. Mary Berol sold hers for under $100,000
the next year. Barbara and Bruce Gimbel's went for about the same in
1965. After adding 740 to his real estate portfolio, Terner got even richer
when he quit his bottle company, formed a competitor in the late 1960s,

took it public in 1972 and made millions, and finally sold out in 1983 for another $39 million.

In 1979, Terner moved to Palm Beach and sold the apartment to his daughter, Carol, and her husband of twelve years, Mark Lederman, a garment center heir. The Ledermans raised two daughters there before putting it on the market in 1999. In 2000, they sold it to one of Carol's nephews, Steven Mnuchin, for $10.5 million. Just because you're selling to a relative doesn't mean you can't make a couple bucks.

Mnuchin probably didn't blink. A Yale graduate, he'd joined Goldman Sachs out of college; his father, Robert Mnuchin, was a partner and head of its equity trading business. Beginning in the mortgage department, Steven rose to partner himself in 1994. Just before he bought the apartment, he'd married Heather deForest Crosby. In the ultimate modern 740 Park merger, the dark-haired child of a self-made Jewish philanthropist had married a stunningly beautiful, blond-haired descendant of several colonial families, including that of William Floyd, a signer of the Declaration of Independence. Heather Mnuchin's family tree also included a Supreme Court justice and Francis Scott Key, author of "The Star-Spangled Banner." In 2002, Mnuchin retired from Goldman Sachs with $46 million worth of its stock and another $12.6 million he'd cashed out in the preceding months. Today he works as CEO of a branch of the $12 billion hedge fund run by George Soros, mostly making investment loans to troubled companies.

Mnuchin, like half of his neighbors, is Jewish; the building's balance tipped in 2005, when the Araskogs sold for about $20 million to yet another hedge fund executive, David Ganek. But far more interesting is the waning of the sorts of families that once provided a certain social security to their neighbors. Wizards of Wall Street now dominate the building. "It's finance central," says Dana Stone, the wife of Andrew Stone, forty-eight, who bought the former Sloan Colt apartment for about $6 million in 1996.

One of the only remaining owners who resembles the patricians who once ruled 740 is Winston Lord, who, like Steven Mnuchin, is married to someone from a different world, the Chinese-born novelist Bette Bao Lord. They bought their second-floor apartment from the German government in 1977, several years after the Germans moved upstairs. Lord, a lifetime diplomat who'd worked in the State Department under Henry Kissinger and had just been hired to run the Council on Foreign Relations, considers the apartment the single best investment he's made in his life. En route to a family vacation in Africa, the Lords spent two days in New York that August looking at fifty apartments. The one at 740 was the last they saw, and, aware how long it had been on the market, Winston made a quick lowball offer of just over $200,000. Seven forty's social-cachet history "was totally lost on us," Winston says. "It was just a beautiful place at a good price."

Invited for tea and an interview at the Dysons', the Lords thought it was a social call and initially declined. After they realized their error ("We were quite innocent," Winston says), they showed up and were easily accepted.

Aside from its diplomats and the Chinese contingent, 740 Park has several other foreign residents. Spyros Niarchos, the middle son of Stavros Niarchos and heir to about an eighth of his father's $10 billion fortune, bought Lydia O'Leary's apartment for $4.25 million in 1986. He has owned it ever since, although, like his South American neighbors the Noboas, he rarely uses it. Niarchos, forty-nine, also has homes in Paris and St. Moritz and a 379-foot 7-inch superyacht, *Atlantis II*, based in Monte Carlo. He married Daphne Guinness, of the British brewing family, in 1987, and they had three children before divorcing in 1999 on the grounds of unreasonable behavior: reportedly, Niarchos had a security fetish she found confining. She got $40 million for her trouble, according to the *Daily Mail* columnist Nigel Dempster. Niarchos kept the apartment.

The most social couple in the building are the only South Americans who live there full-time. Julio Mario Santo Domingo and his second wife, Beatrice, bought Lou Rosen Davidson's apartment in June 1988 for $6.5 million. Alice Mason, their broker, called Rosen moments after it was listed. "I'm sure she'd been waiting for me," says Lou. "She's so smart. She named a price and that was it."

Through his holding company, Bavaria, Santo Domingo, a graduate of Phillips Academy Andover, owns more than one hundred companies worth billions of dollars in his native Colombia, including the world's fifth-largest beer brewery, the airline Avianca, newspapers, and media outlets of all sorts. But to the distress of some of their countrymen, they spend most of their time in New York. And why not? Their apartment, decorated by the Parisian François Catroux, is like a private museum full of Dutch landscapes; Italian architectural paintings; surrealist canvases by Dalí, Magritte, and Wifredo Lam and abstracts by Léger and Picasso; Greek vases and Etruscan jars; French Empire, English Regency, and Portuguese chinoiserie furniture; eighteenth-century porcelain, Georgian silver, and fantastic faux-painted trompe l'oeil friezes. A complete antique English pine library was imported. An eighteenth-century bust of Louis XVI sits beside the Candela stairs. "He is without scandal or compromise," says his biographer, Gerardo Reyes. "They are fabulous," says a neighbor, "the perfect couple."

At the opposite extreme is Giovanna Bongiasca, whose husband, Mario, bought Sally Faile's apartment for $3.5 million in 1985. Faile had long since grown tired of her husband, Ronald Jeançon. "She had a great habit of writing down incidents she didn't like," he recalls. "She kept notes on me." But the first hint he had that things were going wrong was when she told him that he ought to consider finding a farm of his own. She'd bought one in both their names in Old Chatham, so he wasn't sure what she meant. "When I throw you out, you won't be able to afford it," she told him. When they separated in 1981, Jeançon handed the board presidency to Randolph Speight, despite his antediluvian attitudes. "Nobody paid much attention to his snobbery," Jeançon says. "Speight didn't work," so he had time to do the job.

After she divorced Jeançon, Faile followed in Countess Kotzebue's wake, went up the Nile, and fell in love again, according to her ex. She briefly became Mrs. Mohsen Lolti El-Sayed. "He was an Egyptian she met on an excursion boat," says Jeançon. "He was giving lectures on Europe. He had two things he lived for, French food and French wine. Sally had no interest in that, but he had an apartment in Paris, and she bought it and all the furnishings from him. He moved to New York and lived in the apartment [at 740, but only for a short time]. She divorced him after she got the Paris apartment, I think." His departure was noisier than most. "She told him to hit the road and he didn't like that," says the doorman Patrick O'Connor.

When Bongiasca bought the Faile apartment, he was in the process of getting divorced from Giovanna, but they played the happy couple in front of the co-op board so that she could get into 740. The apartment still has the green velvet walls first installed by Doda Embiricos. "Everyone says it's beautiful," says Bongiasca, who is now married to an American. "They don't make apartments like this anymore. New apartments have low ceilings. Old apartments are all chopped up." Not long ago, Clarissa Bronfman, whose husband is Edgar Bronfman Jr., called and asked to buy it. Bongiasca said no.

SEVEN FORTY PARK APARTMENTS JUST KEEP APPRECIATING. THE ONE Angie Duke sold in 1965 for no more than $200,000 went for $17 million in 2004, when the Japanese government sold it to the oilman David Koch, of Koch Industries, and his wife, Julia. Koch got lots of media attention in 1995 when he bought the late Jacqueline Onassis's apartment at 1040 Fifth Avenue, snatching it away from Charles Stevenson.² He used a similar modus operandi to get into 740 Park when he decided he needed a larger apartment. This time the loser was Leonard Blavatnik, a man used to winning. Blavatnik left the Soviet Union for America in 1978 and is a skilled financial operator. In partnership with Viktor Vekselberg, he profited from Russian privatization and, even if he isn't one himself, consorted with his nation's oligarchs. He's being sued by NoreX Petroleum of Canada, which claims in filings that it has "irrefutable proof" of "profit diversion, money-laundering and tax evasion" and accuses Blavatnik's company of engaging in "Corrupt Privatization," "Corrupt Takeover," and "Corrupt Bankruptcy."

"That was unfortunate," says a realtor who knows of Blavatnik's bid for the Japanese apartment. Blavatnik had collected "really nice letters," but "they [the co-op board] didn't want him," so when Koch, who knew four of the six directors personally, came along with a competitive bid, he got the apartment.

"The Russian, as I understand it, had a contract but sat on it, it was never executed," says Koch. "I took it out from under his nose. I'm sure they preferred me. Obviously, the devil you know is better than the devil you don't. It's nice to be wanted. That's not always the case in my life."

Mercedes Noboa made a profit of just under $21 million when she sold 740's penthouse triplex to George A. David. The redheaded, steel-eyed son of a Rhodes scholar, history professor, and director of libraries at the University of Pennsylvania, David graduated from Harvard after he took a year off to indulge his passion for motorcycles. He began his career as a teacher at the University of Virginia, where he'd picked up both an MBA and married his first wife, his high-school sweetheart. In 1968, he joined the Boston Consulting Group, which advised clients of a Boston bank on business strategy.

In 1975, a frustrated David left, seeking hands-on management experience, and joined Otis Elevators as the executive assistant of its president. He'd been in the job a mere four months when Otis was acquired in a hostile takeover by United Technologies, a conglomerate centered on aerospace businesses. "I was terrified," he later told the *Hartford Courant*. "I was overpaid and overtitled." Though he was sure he'd be fired, a dozen years later, after a lengthy spell as president of Otis, he became a top executive, later the president, and finally, in 1997, the chairman of United Technologies. In that job, he took home $3.9 million and $70 million in stock options in 2003, atop $327 million in stock options in the preceding ten years.

"I love my work," he's said. "I have no regrets." Even though along the way, the personable, scholarly, but hard-charging and intimidating executive infuriated employees, who gathered outside his home to sing nasty rewrites of Christmas carols (while his three children were inside). He also lost his wife of thirty years in a 1997 divorce.

David, sixty-three, is not without outside interests. An avid sailor, he led the United States team that competed for the Admiral's Cup in 1999. And three years later, he revealed a new romantic interest when he began making public appearances with the lanky blond beauty who would become his third wife and the latest titled lady at 740 Park. Marie Douglas David didn't have to marry to become a countess; she was born one.

She is a descendant, albeit an illegitimate one, of Ludwig I, the ruling Grand Duke of Baden, and his mistress Catharina Werner. Through their daughter and the family of her father, Count Philip Douglas, a descendant of the Scottish nobleman who was a British envoy to Copenhagen in the seventeenth century, she is related by marriage to England's Cavendish-Bentincks and Winston Churchill, Prince Max of Bavaria, the Crown Prince of Liechtenstein, the heads of Sotheby's in Germany and France, and Walburga von Habsburg, the granddaughter of the last emperor of Austria. The Douglases are also members in good standing of Swedish nobility and own castles in Sweden and Germany.

36

George and Marie Douglas David live above all their neighbors at 740 Park and stand above them, too, at least in the circles where things like titles still count. But in the rest of the world, particularly those corners where he who dies with the most square footage wins, it is the occupant of the apartment built for George Brewster, and then occupied by John D. Rockefeller Jr., who rules the roost. Even if it is no longer the most expensive co-op apartment in New York, 15/16B is the gold ring, the ultimate prize in a city full of them.

After the Night of the Dueling Locksmiths, the board was "dying to get Saul Steinberg out, but there was no way they could," says a realtor. Even when Saul put the apartment on the market, "he didn't really," the realtor says. "He put it on to make the wife think he was selling, but it was just a ploy. He would never sell it."

The modern apartment by Albert Hadley that he'd shared with Barbara was redone post-Laura by Kevin McNamara, who was working on two other 740 apartments at the same time. Three weeks after Saul met his latest girlfriend, Gayfryd Johnson, she told one of McNamara's assistants two things. "I've sold $40 million in oil pipelines," she said. "I'm also a decorator." The assistant turned to McNamara. "She'll marry Saul," he said. "He's met his match."

In short order, Gayfryd did marry Saul and divorced her decorators—several times in fact—first doing the place up in chintz by Stuart Greet, then having it redone by Tom Collum, a decorator from New Orleans. Finally, it was tweaked by Mark Hampton.

While she redecorated, Saul returned to work, greenmailing Quaker State and Walt Disney (his Drexel-financed raid, launched on Donald Duck's fiftieth birthday, inspired the *Philadelphia Daily News* to warn: "Run for the hills, Bambi!"). He also took over the Days Inn motel chain and the Grand Hotel in Cap-Ferrat; bought a controlling interest in a retail chain and smaller interests in the company that made Rolls-Royce automobiles and a Texas airline holding company; and attempted to oust the board of directors of Flying Tiger, an airline Reliance had invested in (Saul wanted four board seats and got two).

Saul also sought to redecorate his image, cooperating with *Manhattan, Inc.*, a new business magazine, when it profiled him in the fall of 1985. The story, of course, opened at a party at 740 Park. And its point was that "one of the most villainous financiers in the country . . . the ultimate corporate renegade" had not only arrived but been domesticated. "I'm an investor, not a raider," Saul told the magazine. "I'm not out for the fast buck." Instead, he was out to give money away and remake himself as a public man. Recent recipients of Steinberg's charity were listed along with the wide range of new acquaintances—all with boldfaced names—who'd begun attending his and Gayfryd's frequent dinner parties. "He is, in fact, in many respects a different man," Hope Lampert wrote, "more controlled . . . more poised . . . more mature."

Much of the credit for the new Saul was given to the third Mrs. Steinberg. Gayfryd locked the refrigerator so he couldn't raid it, put him on a diet and exercise regimen, enforced new priorities that gave his children precedence over eighteen-hour workdays, and made it clear that she'd leave him if he ever took cocaine again. "Gayfryd is an unbelievable woman with great values, and she just cleans house," says Saul's lifelong friend. "Saul's second childhood stops abruptly with Gayfryd." After meeting her when Gayfryd was recruited to raise money for PEN, the international writers' group, Tina Brown, the editor of *Vanity Fair*, was so impressed she wrote a glowing profile and predicted a glorious future: "Hallowed benefactress, *grande dame*...the year 2025's Brooke Astor."

GAYFRYD AND SAUL HAD MET IN THE FALL OF 1982 AT A DINNER AT THE home of Saul's art dealer, Richard Feigen, and then again a few weeks later, when Feigen brought her to dinner at Saul's apartment. "Saul took one look at Gayfryd and switched place cards and put her next to him at the table," says his friend.

"I was looking for someone to be bad with that night," Gayfryd later admitted.

"Had he been one of the lamb chops we were serving for dinner, she would have devoured him in a single bite," Saul's butler, Desmond Atholl, later wrote in a tell-all. They left the table and the other guests mid-meal and never returned.

Gayfryd was from Vancouver, Canada, the daughter of a clerk and a mother with aspirations. She left when she married an engineer who took her to South Africa, where she finished college. The couple moved to New Orleans, where she worked with troubled adolescents in a psychiatric ward and met Norman Johnson, a wealthy oilman. They both divorced to marry each other in 1976. They remarried in 1977, when Gayfryd's Dominican Republic divorce proved insufficient for Louisiana authorities, and then had a son who was later adopted by Steinberg.

The Johnsons lived in the biggest house in New Orleans, but, considered climbers, they were ostracized by society. Though he was secure enough to encourage Gayfryd to start her own oil-pipeline business, Johnson was also troubled, as was their marriage, and things got worse in 1982, when he pleaded guilty to tax fraud. Their home and possessions were seized by the Internal Revenue Service that fall.

In response, Johnson got a face-lift and Gayfryd began thinking divorce. That same season she met Steinberg, and the following spring she filed for divorce just before her husband was sentenced to prison. In the summer of 1983, she moved into 740 with her son. By winter, she'd converted to Judaism, divorced, and within hours married Saul. Six months later, Norman Johnson, recently released from prison, jumped to his death from the fourteenth floor of a Houston hotel. According to a family friend, Saul and Gayfryd signed a prenuptial agreement that gave her $1 million a year for every year they stay married.

In New York, Gayfryd was considered baldly ambitious, but also likable and intelligent, especially compared with her peers—the first generation of wealthy wives since the 1960s to embrace the old forms of social life. Their generosity and hospitality won the Steinbergs notice and friends. Gayfryd grew close to her new stepchildren, joined the board of the New York Public Library (even though Saul was continually rebuffed by the Metropolitan Museum, where his long-ago raid on Chemical was still held against him), and arranged for their redecorated apartment to be featured in *Town & Country* magazine.

"If it wasn't gold, the Steinbergs didn't own it," *The New York Times* would later quip of what *Town & Country* called their "barony on Park Avenue." The living room walls were covered in scarlet and gold Fortuny fabric. A George III four-poster bed dominated the master bedroom. Throughout, Rodin, Hepworth, and Manzù sculptures guarded Chinese porcelains, Titian's *Salome with the Head of John the Baptist*, Rubens's *Death of Adonis*, and more paintings by Brueghel, Boucher, and Moroni. A ladies' powder room boasted Louis XVI wallpaper, a Renoir landscape, and Scalamandré silks. Saul's billiard room had gray flannel walls. A massive rococo ormolu-mounted gilded bronze and mahogany writing commode and Francis Bacon paintings dominated the entry foyer. The more formal of two dining rooms was furnished with a twenty-one foot George III table and twenty-three mahogany chairs. And everywhere you looked, there were Dutch and Flemish paintings, Regency silver, George II armchairs, a nineteenth-century harp, and more mid-eighteenth-century British antiques. "What nouveau riche would buy . . . regilded," the dealer who sold them later sniped to *New York* magazine—after the Steinbergs' fall, of course.

Even bad luck was good for Saul. In 1986, he decided to sell Reliance stock to the public again to raise money to pay down debt (he personally owed Reliance almost $47 million). But before he could do that, the Securities and Exchange Commission accused Dennis Levine, an investment banker at Drexel Burnham Lambert, of illegal inside trading—opening a scandal that would eventually send Levine and the speculator Ivan Boesky to prison, tarnish several other Wall Street firms, and bring down Drexel and its junk-bond prodigy, Michael Milken.

Junk accounted for almost half of Reliance's bond portfolio. So Steinberg raised less than half the money he expected, but nonetheless his remaining shares, representing 77 percent ownership, were worth $580 million, just under four times their 1982 value. Saul and Gayfryd may have lived in Junior's apartment, but Saul wheeled and dealed like Landon Ketchum Thorne and partied like him, too. There were dinners for causes like PEN (which brought Jerzy Kosinski back to 740 Park) and private parties, several of which became, like Saul and Gayfryd, symbols of their extravagant era.

Along with their new neighbors Henry Kravis and Carolyne Roehm, the Steinbergs were leading lights of what *W* magazine dubbed Nouvelle Society. In April 1987, *W* crowned her Queen Gayfryd after her social debut, her first big gala for PEN, two years after she'd decided to make it her cause. Photos of Donald Trump, Arnold Scaasi, Georgette Mosbacher, and Brooke Astor at the Metropolitan Club party illustrated a story in which Gayfryd earnestly set about positioning herself. "I find it difficult to walk a block in New York without being passionate about something, without seeing a homeless person," she said. "I feel lucky every day. I am married to a very rich and powerful person who does good things."

In the fall of 1987, Saul and Barbara Steinberg's daughter, Laura, was engaged to Jon Tisch, the son of the U.S. postmaster general Robert Preston Tisch, from the family that controlled Loews and Lorillard Tobacco. Even though the stock market had just crashed, the Steinbergs' partying went on unabated. Gayfryd took over the wedding planning, and Laura's mother "was really, really hurt," says a friend. "She felt like a guest at her daughter's wedding." But Barbara Steinberg may have been better off. Held in April 1988, the party attracted scorn from around the world. Even *W*, which approved, covered the fete in a story headlined LET 'EM EAT CAKES.

The ceremony took place at Central Synagogue beneath antique brass palm fronds from the apartment. Gayfryd had obsessed over every detail of the $3 million French Directoire-themed dinner for five hundred that followed in the Metropolitan Museum of Art, rented for the evening for $30,000. There were a hundred French roses for every guest and twelve thousand white tulips besides. Arnold Scaasi, Nouvelle Society's dressmaker, whipped up the wedding gown and nine bridesmaids' dresses, and the Kravises, the Mahoneys, Lord Weidenfeld, Norman Mailer, Barbara Walters, Donald Trump, and Vernon Jordan toasted the newlyweds with 1982 Roederer Cristal and 1973 Chateau Latour and dined on poached coho salmon with champagne aspic and a trio of veal, lamb, and chicken. Gayfryd called it "very much a family party."

There was another PEN gala in April 1989, and that August, Gayfryd gave Saul a $1 million fiftieth birthday party at his beach house in Quogue that featured *tableaux vivants* of his favorite old masters—one of them, a living nude in an oversized frame. There were also identical twins dressed as mermaids in the pool, dancers and heralds in seventeenth-century costumes, and everyone from cabinet secretaries to fashion photographers (as well as the Kravises, the Araskogs, Ronald Perelman, and Steve and Courtney Ross) in attendance. The press was supposedly barred, but the gossip columnist Liz Smith attended, as did journalists from *Vanity Fair*, so details made their way out. "Honey, if this moment were a stock, I'd short it," Saul toasted his wife. The party was "appropriate," he said. "Maybe it's a little understated."

In the aftermath, the newspaper columnist Ken Auletta called Saul "sleazy" and complained that the Steinbergs were trying to buy respectability through PEN by making writers "pets." When comparisons to Marie Antoinette replaced references to her queenliness, Gayfryd quit the organization's board. *W* soon announced the advent of a social recession and Nouvelle Society went underground.

Nonetheless, Saul believed that he had changed the face of American wealth, just as they'd taught him he could at Wharton. *The Philadelphia Inquirer*'s Joseph DiStefano quotes Saul telling an unnamed business partner at the time, "You'd be a billionaire, too, if you were Jewish."

IN FACT, STEINBERG'S GLORY DAYS WERE ALMOST OVER. WITH HIS JUNK-bond buddies in jail, the high-yield bond market collapsing, and new regulations making takeovers harder, Saul had decided to dedicate himself to the insurance business. He began reorganizing Reliance and developed risky new products like nuclear plant insurance to raise revenues. But by the summer of 1990, regulators were trying to tame Reliance, too. Saul fought back. Former Steinberg employees somehow happened to be appointed insurance watchdogs by the governors of New York (George Pataki) and Pennsylvania (Tom Ridge), both of whom had, no doubt coincidentally, received campaign donations from Steinberg and his Reliance cabal. But even well-placed friends couldn't help Saul solve his larger problems, a mountain of debt "without a huge amount of equity or net worth to support operations," as *Barron's* put it, and a stock selling for less than $5 a share.

"Then Saul had his stroke," says his intimate, "and he was no longer at the helm of the company. He just couldn't be. He was recuperating, and he put his brother at the helm, and clearly the company wasn't being run as tightly as it should have been."

Gayfryd promptly proved her mettle, not as Brooke Astor, but as her husband's best asset, nursing him back, if not into perfect health, then at least into dinner jackets and out to black-tie benefits. She couldn't fix the problems at Reliance, though; despite some canny investments and Saul's plans to sell insurance on the Internet, the losses kept mounting and the debt didn't shrink. And then the Steinbergs started in on each other.

"Everything falls apart," says Saul's friend, "and it couldn't be a bigger mess. The company falls apart, Saul's two sisters are angry at the brothers because they know they'll no longer have money; they only had money because of the brothers. Bobby is angry at Saul because he fired Bobby. It was just a total circus. The boys had borrowed some money from their mother—all of the money that she had was from them, and she was going to forgive the loan—and the sisters made her call in the loan [and sue when he didn't pay up]. She still had an apartment in Palm Beach, an apartment and driver in New York, her lifestyle hadn't changed one iota, but I guess they needed some cash. That was all about the girls being furious at the brothers. Money is the root of all family dissension. And theirs was a particularly bad story."

But thanks to his wife, the denouement of Saul's own story turned out far better than it might have. "I started with a very, very, very special and good guy," Gayfryd says of her decision to stand by her man in sickness as well as health. "I signed on for both ways."

In January 2000, with Reliance's vital credit rating in doubt, Gayfryd called Saul's former sister-in-law Kathy Steinberg, a realtor. After assuring Gayfryd that she could change her mind at any time, Kathy started marketing the apartment, according to *The New York Observer*'s Manhattan Transfers columnist, Deborah Schoeneman, by "indiscreetly . . . floating the idea that he had set his price: $40 million." But Kathy Steinberg was actually incredibly discreet. According to Schoeneman, the apartment never formally went on the market, and it was never listed in Realtor Plus, the computer system brokers use to share "official" listings.

"Saul was resistant—understandably so," says the intimate. "It was very, very difficult for Saul; it had all sorts of psychological ramifications. This was a big let-go." But things moved quite quickly. Within a week, three serious buyers were circling. Rumor had it that one was Leon Black, a former executive of Drexel Burnham Lambert. "Leon was in heat," someone told Schoeneman. Also named were Gary Winnick, the then-billionaire owner of Global Crossing (and another Drexel alum), and, according to the *New York Post*, an investment banker, Martin Gruss. But sources say none of them were finalists.

One of those was Steve Schwarzman, an investment banker and chief executive of the Blackstone Group, a buyout firm. And the other was J. Christopher Burch, a newcomer to the New York scene. A graduate of Ithaca College, Burch was the son of a New Jersey distributor of mining equipment. While still in school, he and his family had started Eagle's Eye, a preppy sportswear line, with a $2,000 investment and built it into a company that claimed $46 million worth of annual retail sales through department stores and fifteen boutiques. In 1989, they sold 70 percent of the company to a Hong Kong conglomerate. Ten years later, the Burch brothers sold their remaining interest for $18 million. Chris, already an investor in real estate and movies, announced plans to open a venture capital operation.

In the meantime, Burch had divorced his wife of more than a decade and hooked up with Tory Robinson, a fashion publicity woman who'd just ended a brief marriage to the real estate mogul Harry Macklowe's son, William. She and Chris married in 1996, and Tory promptly got pregnant, adding twins to Chris's brood of three girls. They bought an apartment in the Hotel Pierre and began making their move in New

York society, volunteering for the right charities, appearing in the right clothes, and enrolling their son in the same $9,800-a-year preschool as Ronald Perelman's children.

In February 2000, Schwarzman made an offer—of about $30 million—on the Steinbergs' apartment, and after several days passed without an answer from Saul, Kathy Steinberg told him he had to decide. Though the Burches were still interested—indeed, Chris later sent Saul a letter "offering sizably more" than Schwarzman, says Saul's intimate— Kathy urged him to sign a contract with Schwarzman, both wanting the ordeal to end and fearing that Burch would not be accepted by the board.

Steinberg agreed to sell to Schwarzman, "and of course, it was very, very difficult, but it turned out to be a very, very important financial decision for them because shortly thereafter, it was very clear that—excuse the expression—the shit had really hit the fan with Reliance," says Saul's friend. "Reliance was going under. And Saul had a major asset that was not sold under fire-sale conditions. And that was a billion percent Gayfryd. Gayfryd was very attached to this apartment, too, let's not forget. It was her home. She had decorated it and lived there and loved it. She didn't drag Saul kicking and screaming to the lawyer's table, but it was all Gayfryd."

Clearly, though, Saul knew what was coming. As he dickered with regulators over the impending bankruptcy of Reliance, girded for legal battles to come, and prepared to pack up and move out of 740, he transferred his beach house in Quogue to Gayfryd in April 2000. Less than two years later, she sold it for $7 million (a lot of money, but $9 million less than it was reportedly listed for). Saul and Gayfryd had moved from 740 into a hotel in May 2000, but after disposing of Quogue, Gayfryd bought a town house two blocks from their former home from Donald and Mera Rubell, the art-collecting brother and sister-in-law of Studio 54's co-founder Steve Rubell.

WHATEVER IS LEFT OF SAUL'S FORTUNE, IT NOW SEEMS RELATIVELY SAFE. Lawsuits lingered (including the one filed by Saul's eighty-three-year-old mother; it was eventually settled), lenders had their hands out, and regulators were swarming, but finally Steinberg walked away from the wreckage. Insurance rates and taxes—that is, the rest of us—will eventually cover Reliance's losses. Saul was sued personally, of course, both by the state of Pennsylvania and by angry shareholders, who claimed he'd sucked Reliance dry to maintain his lavish lifestyle. But he denied he'd done anything of the sort, blaming "market forces" instead. And anyway, he had insurance policies that indemnified him from civil judgments— and attorneys' fees.

By 2003, though still infirm, he was going out to parties again—even as the cleanup of the Reliance mess proceeded. In 2004, the state of Pennsylvania began liquidating Reliance and started settlement talks with its, and Saul's, insurance companies. But most shareholders knew what those talks were worth. "Peanuts without the shells," one worker grumbled. Finally, early in 2005, Pennsylvania settled for a meager $51 million.

"There is an ongoing [criminal] investigation," the state's insurance commissioner said in February 2005—and then refused to elaborate.

37

"A MAN OF RECOGNIZED TALENT AND CHARM," IN THE WORDS OF THE AU-
thor Ken Auletta, Stephen A. Schwarzman looks more like a borscht-belt
second banana than, as *Fortune* once called him, "Wall Street's hottest
hand," but the steel in his blue eyes is the window onto his soul.

He grew up in Philadelphia, the son of the owner of Schwarzman's
Curtain and Linen Store. At Yale the same years as Charles Stevenson, he
majored in behavioral studies and was tapped for Skull and Bones, an
honor that eluded his future neighbor. A born entrepreneur, Schwarzman induced the school to finance his senior thesis, paying some students
to take a survey and others to tabulate the results. He claims it helped
students abolish the parietals rules that made dormitory sexual encounters illegal, and organized a series of ballets—to meet girls, he says, since
Yale was then an all-male school. While earning an MBA at Harvard, he
married Ellen Jane Philips, a course assistant who graded papers at the
business school. That wasn't her only attractive attribute. Her father had
made millions from Jalousie Windows of Ohio, which manufactured
windows and doors for mobile homes.

After getting his degree in June 1972, Schwarzman passed through
Donaldson, Lufkin & Jenrette (where he was hired by a Bonesman) and

joined Lehman Brothers, where his drive and salesmanship helped lift him to the rank of managing director in a mere six years. He worked on mergers for Bendix, Chrysler, Litton, and RCA and became the head of Lehman's mergers and acquisitions committee, where he set in motion a deal to sell Lehman (at that point, Lehman Brothers Kuhn Loeb) to Shearson/American Express, effectively ending its reign as Wall Street's oldest investment bank. Schwarzman took home $7 million.

One of the consequences of that transaction was the formation of the Blackstone Group in 1985, with Peter G. Peterson, Schwarzman's long-time boss at Lehman, as chairman and his thirty-eight-year-old protégé as president and chief executive. Prior to the Shearson deal, Peterson had been forced out of Lehman after losing a leadership struggle. Their small investment house, named for the German root of Schwarzman (black) and the Greek equivalent of Peterson (*petros,* or stone), turned into a powerhouse. They were soon representing Sony in its takeover of CBS Records, and Nestlé in its takeover of Westin Hotels. Once Blackstone gained a reputation, it began raising millions for a buyout fund and went on to bigger deals. Today, it's a leader in corporate restructuring and runs multibillion-dollar hedge, private-equity, real estate, and mezzanine funds. With an income far in excess of $50 million a year, Schwarzman is an eminence of finance.

Six years after Blackstone began, Ellen Schwarzman sued her husband for divorce and walked away with half his net worth—almost $20 million. In financial circles, the story is told that Steve had used the family travel agent to book a room at the Plaza Athénée in Paris, the same hotel where Ronald Perelman had had his tryst with Susan Kasen. When the unknowing agent asked the unknowing Ellen how she'd liked Paris, the marriage ended.

After a few years on the dating circuit, Schwarzman began seeing a blond lawyer named Christine Hearst. Five years Schwarzman's junior, she was the daughter of Peter Mularchuk, a retired lieutenant in the New York City Fire Department, and was twice divorced. Her second husband and the father of her two children, Austin Chilton Hearst, was a grandson of the late William Randolph Hearst, the newspaper publisher. When she married Hearst in 1984, she worked as a salesperson for a Teletype company and a director of the Videotape Producers Association.

Although she'd sued Hearst for divorce a year before her first appearance with Schwarzman in *The New York Times*'s Evening Hours column in 1994, Christine continued using Hearst's name, a fact that some catty types say helped attract the status-conscious Schwarzman. But in the meantime, she'd also enhanced her lot in life, graduating from New York University Law School and becoming an associate in a New York law firm, specializing in intellectual property law. In their November 1995 marriage announcement, in which she was called simply Christine Hearst, her father's fire department career went unmentioned.

Besides a husband, Christine Hearst Schwarzman, as she now calls herself, got a new career after her marriage. Several months before the purchase of Steinberg's apartment, she founded and named herself chairman of a new business, IPnetwork.com, which described itself as "the premier licensing and event sponsorship Website" and "the online leader in transaction, management and information services for the licensing, event sponsorship and intellectual property communities." Just as the Internet bubble was poised to pop, she raised $20 million in financing for the venture, which she promised would, among other things, help Web site owners avoid copyright-infringement litigation.

"All of Schwarzman's friends invested, but it went *pfft* in the bubble," says an observer of the financial world. The Web site is not currently operational. But Schwarzman and his wife began operating furiously once they were able to occupy their new apartment—tossing large parties for society high and low.

Schwarzman was asked to join the co-op board as soon as they moved in. He'd made a good impression when he was told he couldn't continue renovating after the summer of 2000 (summer work rules were back in effect), and would not be able to move in until the fall of 2001. "He was angry for a moment but calmed down and was a gentleman about it," says a board member. "He didn't get his nose out of joint and we liked that."[1] His neighbors, many of whom now drink and nibble beneath the $5 million Cy Twombly painting in his living room, probably also liked the fact that it was reported that he paid as much as $37 million for the apartment, for that false claim likely enhanced the value of theirs.

Schwarzman's ambitions became even clearer late in 2004, when he moved up to chairman of Blackstone shortly after being named chairman of the Kennedy Center in Washington. To celebrate his new status, Schwarzman sat for a revealing, possibly too revealing, profile for the front page of the *New York Times* Sunday Business section, part of what the newspaper described as "a campaign to rise above his status as just another fabulously rich deal maker and to achieve renown on the larger, more alluring public stage of the arts—and Washington politics." Schwarzman's lust for a seat in the Bush cabinet had been a topic of press speculation for months, but the smart money said he just wanted his name out there, floating around alongside the $37 million he didn't pay for his apartment. Branding!

The *Times* estimated Schwarzman's worth at near $1 billion, cataloged his real estate holdings (he also has a summerhouse in St.-Tropez, an estate in East Hampton, a mansion in Palm Beach), his perks (use of a corporate jet and a Sikorsky helicopter), his art (that Twombly and several Monets), and his board seats (the New York Public Library, the Frick Collection, and the New York City Ballet), made prominent mention of his "striving for more," and portrayed him as something of a name-dropping braggart, desperate to continue his upward trajectory but unclear on where he's heading. Despite his professional accomplishments, his self-absorbed description of a lunch at the White House—complete with a cake bearing his name in frosting—showed a man more interested in surface than substance. "There's no offending these types of people," says the financial observer. "It's all about the publicity."

But the publicity begs the question. Is there anything uplifting about living at the top of a heap of your own kind? "What clubs is Steve Schwarzman in?" an Upper East Side wag asks. "If you look at 740 as a club, then he's in the best apartment club, and if Blackstone is a club, then he's in the best firm club, but he has no shot at all at joining the right clubs"—that is, the Brook, the Union, or any of their ilk. "And my guess is he cares."

"What's amusing is that Steve Schwarzman's $30-odd million apartment was 'the Steinberg apartment' for thirty years," notes the author and acerbic observer of Manhattan moguls Michael M. Thomas. "Now it's once again the old Rockefeller apartment. Clearly kinship of residency with the moguls of more recent vintage—products of the essentially seamless big-money continuum that began back in 1982—isn't what was paid for. One wants fancier antecedents. That's the kicker: when the doors are thrown open, who do you find, whose company have you forked over thirty big ones to be in? People rather like yourself: a dreadful outcome! Much better to console yourself with Rockefeller ghosts. Ah, well, time marches on—which is the tragedy of riches, or should I say, the hazard of new fortunes."

By laying bets on brands like Rockefeller, 740, and Hearst, instead of family and friends, the Schwarzmans of the world risk eroding the power of real belonging. They've become the proprietors of the clubs they wanted to join but, having arrived, discover the ultimate (Groucho) Marxian irony, that they are nowhere. For so many years, from the 1930s through the 1970s, 740 Park was an impregnable fortress from without, while, within, its empty, echoing unsold and unwanted rooms, built to stand for something, stood only for folly. It was an emptied ballroom after a raucous but forgettable party. Now, a building imagined as F. Scott Fitzgerald has instead, in middle age, morphed into Jay McInerney, yearning for Daisy Buchanan but settling for Carrie Bradshaw.

Ultimately, his mere residence at 740 will not be the yardstick by which Schwarzman will be judged. People will look at his legacy. John D. Rockefeller Jr. left a long record of good works, albeit one financed by his father, and a pack of children who went on to do wonderful things in the world. Schwarzman's life thus far is about calculation and accumulation. And his family has yet to make a mark.

Friends think he will. "Steve has the integrity and brains to do anything he wants to do," says a Washington hostess who has known him for years. "He's made a success of everything he's ever done, including friendship. He's already contributed—but not visibly. He would give anonymously and ask that his name not be used. He didn't want the notoriety. Yes, he wanted a big apartment—but not a Rockefeller apartment, just a big one—and he had the perspicacity to buy one that's already worth far more than he paid and to restore it to its former glory. The restoration of a grand apartment is in itself a good act. He's not out to prove anything. He's a really decent guy." So why buy such a totemic apartment? "He likes to be amused," his friend says. "Think of him as a theater producer. Now, he's got a great stage on which to produce whatever amuses him."

Certainly, real estate is a way of keeping score. "It matters to people," says the gadfly Michael M. Thomas. "Addresses matter. It's a way, particularly in co-ops, to gain two kinds of validity. You've paid a lot of cash, so you're rich. And you've passed a co-op controlled by the *oldveau* crowd, which means you're acceptable. So you get double bang for your buck."

A co-op at 740 Park, then, is the ultimate sign of arrival: gilt by association with an address that's now more elevated than most of its residents. Spending $20 million on one of its apartments, rather than on a tacky yacht, an ugly McMansion, or a glass-walled condo, demonstrates not only wealth but taste and readiness (as opposed to willingness) to take a place in the highest echelons of the plutocracy. It's as refined a form of ostentation as buying a van Gogh at auction, guaranteed to enhance one's brand and ensure it never loses its desirability.

If the cast of characters at 740 Park today seems less colorful than the ones who preceded it, it's because the residents are types now, not sui generis, life-size, not larger-than. A few diplomats, a few princelings of wealth, a lot of money manipulators of one sort or another, a slurry of foreign rich folk (usually more there than here), one computer-gaming mogul, and a lucky few who bought in when apartment prices were low and then hung on. There is no Countess Kotzebue, let alone a John D. Rockefeller Jr., among them.

And although he's trying, hard, Steve Schwarzman is no Junior, not even a Saul Steinberg. He has climbed the status ladder to perch on its highest rung. But when he stops to survey the view, all he can see are others just like himself. Sure, he's finished decorating, and his art and books-by-the-yard are installed, but Schwarzman, having only just arrived, still has a very big pair of floors to fill.

ACKNOWLEDGMENTS
AND SOURCES

I chose 740 as a subject with the guidance of the late George Trescher, who was not only New York's greatest fund-raiser but also a social observer nonpareil, and also several of the city's top high-end real estate brokers, including A. Laurance Kaiser IV of Key Ventures, Wendy Sarasohn of Corcoran, Martha Kramer of Fox Residential, Patricia Burnham of P. S. Burnham, and Kirk Henckels of Stribling Private Brokerage. None of them knew why I was asking about New York's best apartment buildings back in the spring of 2003. I wasn't entirely sure myself. But they helped me narrow my list, even though they had to know I was not rich enough to live in such buildings.

I was greatly aided by a few writers who are steeped in the lore of New York real estate. I am particularly grateful to Andrew Alpern, who has been a vital source of information, encouragement, and inspiration; to Christopher Gray of the Office of Metropolitan History; and to Donald Wrobleski, a Chicago architect who shared the fruits of his long research on Rosario Candela's buildings.

I was fortunate enough to begin researching this book while people who grew up at 740 during the Depression are still alive. Their generation is fading fast, but thanks to them the story of 740 Park Avenue could be told from the beginning. The end of the story turned out to be more difficult. The majority of the building's recent and current residents are among the most powerful people in the world, people whose names regularly appear in the press. Their building is also constantly in the public eye through everything from items in the rapidly multiplying real estate columns of local newspapers to glossy, semi-anonymous spreads in upscale shelter magazines. But the idea that their lives might be discussed in a context they do not control is sometimes upsetting to them. Approached for interviews for this book, many, unsurprisingly, declined. The co-op's directors and management also refused to help in any way.

Concerned about the approbation of their neighbors, many current residents of 740 Park and 71 East Seventy-first Street who did help me, inviting me into their homes, granting interviews, or fact-checking what I learned elsewhere, asked not to be acknowledged. They nonetheless have my gratitude, and I hope they will feel their faith in me was not misplaced. Similarly, a handful of sources offered to speak about living 740 tenants, but only under the cloak of anonymity. Sometimes that's the price of incisive opinions and revealing facts about the powerful, so when I thought such requests were justified, I accepted those terms. I thank all of them, too.

The first great hurdle in researching this book was learning who had lived at 740 Park in its seventy-five years. Secrecy, it turns out, is another advantage of cooperatives. Because owners buy and sell shares of stock, not real property, there are no official records of co-op sales and purchases. And all-cash-purchase buildings like 740 do not allow mortgages, so there are no public loan records, either. However, the names of tenants were often in the press, at least in the building's early years. When the building opened, the names of prominent buyers were used to lure others in. And until World War II, *The New York Times* ran regular columns titled Manhattan Transfers and Apartment Rentals that were lists of who had bought, sold, and rented apartments.

Some tenants, like John D. Rockefeller Jr., made news simply by moving in. But others were not prominent enough to get such attention. Luckily, then, the New York Public Library and the New-York Historical Society maintain archives of reverse telephone directories, organized by address, that give the names of everyone in the city with a listed telephone number. Even Rockefeller briefly appeared in one of those directories.

The Rockefeller family also deserves particular thanks, because they kept a treasure trove of documents about 740 Park that was a source of many more names. The Rockefellers seem to have been trained from the cradle to keep and file every single piece of paper that passed before them, and they employed a private archivist to organize and preserve them. Then the family, along with Rockefeller University, the Rockefeller Brothers Fund, and the Rockefeller Foundation, founded the Rockefeller Archive Center, which they maintain in Sleepy Hollow, New York, in a home originally built for John D. Rockefeller Jr.'s widow, Martha Baird Rockefeller, adjacent to the family's vast properties there. At the archive, I thank Ken Rose, Darwin Stapleton, Michele Hiltzik, and particularly Thomas Rosenbaum. I'm also especially indebted to Peter J. Johnson in the Office of the Messrs. Rockefeller.

The Webb family also endowed two great institutions in Vermont where I did research. At the Shelburne Museum, I thank Polly Darnell, and at Shelburne Farms, my thanks to Julie Eldridge Edwards and Marcia Hawkins, who read through twenty years of James Watson Webb's diaries on my behalf.

I am particularly indebted to Sy Bram of New York City's Department of Buildings for his awesome ability to cut through red tape and find hidden treasures in his department's archival records, to Terry Goyette of the New York Department of State, and to Charlie Scott of the Westchester Surrogate Court.

Many authors have walked this way before me. Although there has never been a book on 740 Park, many of its residents have been the subjects of books. All those works are mentioned in the bibliography that follows. I would like to single out Jan Pottker, the author of *Janet and Jackie*, a dual biography of Janet Lee Bouvier Auchincloss and her daughter Jacqueline Bouvier Kennedy Onassis, and Ed Klein, the author of several books on the Kennedy family, for their generosity.

I also want to single out a number of fellow authors and journalists and thank them for their aid: my sister Jane Gross, Barbara Graustark, Linda Lee, and Michael Cannell of *The New York Times*; Paige Rense of *Architectural Digest*; Ed Nardoza, Delano Knox, and Merle Thomason of Fairchild Publications; Jennet Conant, Connie Bruck, Christopher Byron, Daniel Okrent, Ron Chernow, Jared Paul Stern, Liz Smith, Deborah Schoeneman, Gerardo Reyes, Ellen Pollock, Phoebe Eaton, Suzanne O'Malley, and Miles Chapman; Sandy Levy and David Ettlin at *The Baltimore Sun*; Nancy Burris at *The New Orleans Times-Picayune*; and Debby at *The Lovington Leader*.

Other research assistance was provided by Melinda Bowers at the Museum of the City of New York; Cressie Taylor-Scott at Milbank,

Tweed; Elliott Meisel of Brill & Meisel; Daniel May, Karen Eldred, and Holly Sheffer at MetLife; Amey Hutchins at the University of Pennsylvania; Carol Taylor, the librarian for genealogy and local history at the W. Walworth Harrison Public Library in Greenville, Texas; Tessa Veazey at the Smithsonian Archives of American Art; James O'Connor and Lara Berdine at Douglas Elliman; Martha Noblick at Historic Deerfield; Dan Castleman at the office of the New York City district attorney; Jeff Brown of General Property Management; James Quigel and Jackie Esposito at Penn State University; Martyn Henderson of the Wiltshire and Swindon Record Office; and Cindy Cathcart of the Condé Nast archives.

I have been lucky enough to have worked on this book with a number of interns, most of them journalism students, whose enthusiasm and doggedness made my life far easier. Thanks to Asli Pelit, Radhika Mitra, Shannon Resnick, Rebecca Hessel, Chris Walker, Mackenzie Dawson Parks, Cynthia Kane, Aida Baligh Mahmood, and Whitney West. Research assistance was also provided by Meena Hartenstein, Chrissy Shackle, Stephen Bryant, Lisette Johnson, Stephen Bowles, Lauren Marcus, Kara Clark, and Charlene Kwan. Most of the interns came through New York University's Ellen Walterscheid. Ted Panken provided expert transcriptions.

I was inspired to write *740 Park* by Christine Mortimer Biddle and Cathy Hemming. I am grateful to both of them. The book is a reality thanks to my agent, Dan Strone, of Trident Media Group, and my editor and friend, Peter Gethers, and his colleagues Stephen Rubin and Bill Thomas of the Doubleday Broadway Publishing Group, whose sage advice sharpened the book immeasurably. I am thrilled to have had the opportunity to work with each of them. At Doubleday Broadway, I also thank Claudia Herr, Frieda Duggan, Ingrid Sterner, and Maria Carella, and at Trident Media Group, Kimberly Whalen, Hilary Rubin, Sara Roby, and Lily Kosner.

And personal thanks to Roy and Mallory Kean, Stephen Demorest, Mary Ann Page, Mary Michele Rutherfurd, Michael Millius, Nancy Burges, Jay Mulvaney, Jill Brooke, Janis Kaye, Robert Pounder, Vincent Giroud, Gene Gutowski, Daisy Corsini, Denise Hale, Alexandra Marshall, Nancy Novogrod, Laura Begley, Arthur Altschul, Victoria Leacock,

Nancy Gillon, Lisa and Julian Niccolini, Alex von Bidder, Keith Fleer, and Edward Hayes.

Most of my sources are cited in the text in a way that makes clear where the information came from. Quotations attributed in the present tense (for example, followed by "she says") were spoken directly to me in interviews. Quotations from previously published sources are attributed in the past tense (for example, "he said"). In general, newspaper and magazine articles are not cited in the text. The most frequently consulted sources were *The New York Times* and *The Wall Street Journal*, but my researchers and I searched the world for references to 740 Park and its residents. Other publications that printed multiple stories that proved uniquely valuable were *Fortune*, *Forbes*, *BusinessWeek*, *Barron's*, *Vanity Fair*, and *New York*.

In our digital age, newspaper morgues are sometimes forgotten repositories of invaluable information. I'd like to single out the *New York Post*, where the morgue is run by Laura Harris; the *Daily News*, run by the indomitable Faigi Rosenthal; and the Center for American History at the University of Texas at Austin, where Evan Hocker presides over the preserved clipping libraries of the *New York Herald Tribune* and the *New York Journal-American*. As newspapers are the first draft of history, whenever possible I have tried to confirm, correct, or clarify information gleaned from them elsewhere.

Last but hardly least, I would like to thank each of the following, who either gave an interview, gave me information, or helped lead me to others who did. This list is both necessarily and accidentally incomplete. Those who spoke anonymously, as described above, have my thanks, and to those who have been left out inadvertently, my apologies. Many of those listed below lived at 740, come from families that did, or were close friends of residents. Most 740 tenants are neither brash show-offs nor the querulous sort who quake at the thought that, as Alice said, a cat may look at a king. Though many were brought up to believe that one's name should only appear in print three times, when you're born, when you marry, and when you die, dozens of them nonetheless revealed their quiet pride in the lives and accomplishments that brought them, their families, and their friends to the most distinguished apartment building in New York. And courageously, they also spoke of the unavoidable unhappiness and sorrows that marked those lives as well. Their voices, and those of the many others who helped me, make this story come alive.

Thanks to Slim Aarons, Dominic Abatiello, Aboudi Abdel Rahman, Hadi Abdel Rahman, Said Aburish, Bea Dabney Adams, Joan Adler, Jessie Araskog, Steven M. L. Aronson, Lloyd Aspinwall III, Verne S. Atwater, David Auchincloss, Judy Auchincloss, Louis Auchincloss, Yusha Auchincloss, Muriel "Muggins" Badgley, Polly Baldwin, Muffie Bancroft Murray, Mrs. Stanley Banks, Stanley Banks, Boris Baranovich, Keith and Ann Barish, Michael Barker, David Barrett, Marion Becker, Tim Bentinck (the Earl of Portland), Lara Berdine, Michael Berg, Mary Berol, Mrs. Loren C. Berry, Paul Birdsall, Curtis Blake, Jill Kogan Blake, Noah Blake, Susan Blake, Jacqueline Bleyer Everly, James Boisi, Christina Bonn, Kathleen Bouvier, Melanie Bower, Joe Braswell, Edward and Robert Braverman, Jeff Brink, Peter Bronstein, the two LeeLee Browns, Peter Brown, Lincoln Brownell, Mario Buatta, Joseph Buffum, Moya Bullis, Christopher and Tory Burch, Amanda Burden, Dominic Byrne, Carolina Ryan Camperio, Gertrude Candela, Steve Candela, Patricia Candela MacLeod, Leighton Candler, Isabel Cardin, Bliss Carnochan, Arthur Carter, Dundeen Bostwick Catlin, Edward Lee Cave, Mimi Cecil, Count Nikita Cheremeteff, Jack Chrysler Jr., Jack Chrysler III, Helen Chrysler Greene, Teresa Collins, Evelin Corsey, Carolyn Cowan, Charles Cowles, Jan Cowles, Virginia Cowles, Mabel Coyle, Marcia Coyle, Aileen Cramer, Bill Crawford, Frank Crocitto, Vincent Curcio, Marcus Daly IV, Sally D'Arcy, Lou Rosen Davidson, Bedford Davie, Deirdre Davie, John Davis, Maud Davis, Samuel Riker Davis, Peter De Blasio, Robert Denning, Mrs. Frances Ferry Dennison, Paul Di Lisio, Gilly Drummond, Maldwin Drummond, Peter Duchin, A. St. George Biddle "Pony" Duke, Robin Duke, Tony Drexel Duke, Beazy Durfee, Debbie Ecker, Karen Eldred, Osborn Elliott, Diana Emmet, Jay Emmett, Danielle and Robert Epstein, Roger Erickson, Irv Ettinger, Betty Evans, Alf Evers, Everett Fahy, Sally Faile, Christine and Chris Farrington, Raoul Lionel Felder, John Ferry, Bob Ficarola, Marshall Field V, Tom Fleming, Anne Eisenhower Flottl, John Foreman, Alexander Forger, Jane Foster, Lynn Foster, Frank Fox, Alan Freer, Joan Foy French, John H. French II, John and Marina French, S. Donald Friedman, Elizabeth Fry, Brenda Fuller, David Ganek, Beatrice Garvan, Geoffrey Gates, William

Georgiades, James Gerard, Sumner Gerard, Cristine Gerry, Martha Far-
ish Gerry, Wendy Gifford, Kay Gilman, Barbara Gimbel, Leslie Glass,
Ilene Goldman, William A. Goldman, Margot Gordon, Stephen Gordon,
Carl Gortzig, Doda Voridis Goulandris, Darlene Gould, Margaret
Graubard, J. Jarden Guenther, Suzanne Guerlac, Dick Gutman, Christopher Haan, Mohamed Habbal, Frederic Hack Jr., Richard Hack, Bill
Haddad, Albert Hadley, Arthur Hadley, David Hamer, Dorrance Hamil-
ton, Mrs. John D. Hannum, Kate "Kitty" Harris, Charles N. Haskell III,
Ed Haskell, Robert Haskell, Margaret Haskell Potter, William J. Haus-
man, Harry Havemeyer, William Heckeroth, Grace (McCain) Heidt, An-
drew Heineman, Ben Heller, Mary Hellerstein, Clifford Hendrix Jr.,
James Henry, Reinaldo Herrera, Joel Hirschtritt, Anna Elizabeth Clai-
borne Hogeland, Richard Wright Hogeland, Claudette Hollenbeck,
Mary-Cay Hollenbeck, Frederick Hoppin, May Hoppin, Nancy Hoppin,
Chuck Houghton, Doug Houghton, Patrick Howarth, Deering Howe, Pe-
ter Huang, Lee Hudson, John Webster Hughes, Mitchell Hurley, Tony
Ingrao, Judy Insle, Bob Ireland, Tom Ireland, Alice T. Blue Irving,
Donna Italiano, Linda Janklow, Mort Janklow, Michael Javelos, Ronald
D. Jeançon, John Dobson Jeffords, Sarah Jeffords, Robert Jewell, Glenn
Jewison, Knut Johannessen, Rhonda Johnson, Orrin Judd, David Kahn,
Betsy Kaiser, Tony Kerrigan, Marty Kimmelman, David S. Kirkland,
Stephen Kirschenbaum, John Knott, David Koch, Kiki Kosinski, Ed
Kotite, Robert Kraus, Louis Kruh, Leila Kubba, Alex and Judy Laughlin,
David Laughlin, Sandy Laughlin, Jenny Lawrence, Peter Lawson-John-
ston, Lewis Leader, Michael Leader, Sheldon Leader, Michael M. Led-
yard, Barclay Leib, Bruce Leib, Samuel Leidesdorf, Tova Dreiman
Leidesdorf, William Leidesdorf, Jerry Levy, Joanie Linclau, Diane Lloyd-
Smith, Deborah Lobmeyer, Howard Lorber, Martin Lorber, Winston and
Bette Lord, Leila Luce, Hillie Mahoney, Dr. Manus Maltz, Emerson
Markham, Andy Marks, Brian Marlowe, Anne Martindell, Alice Mason,
Joan Matthews, Daniel May, Michael May, Charles McCain, Larry Mc-
Donald, Janet McGannon, Linda McKean, Harry McRandle, Alex
Mitchell, Candace Mohr, Robin Mohr, Juan Pablo Molyneux, Anne
Harkness Mooney, Benjamin Moore, Ernesto Mora, Penelope Straus
More, Bill Morse, Mrs. Tim Morse, Virginia Lea Mulligan, Louis de
L'Aigle Munds Jr., Scott Munds, Peter Murphy, David Nasaw, Marion

Grant Nelson, David Netto, Martha Noakes, Mercedes Noboa, James Norman, Bob Notti, Donald O'Brien, Jim O'Connor, Patrick O'Connor, Sandra Wright Ohrstrom, Wright Ohrstrom, Raymond O'Keefe Jr., Steve Olen, Doris Oliver, Richard Ortoli, Carly Barry McDonnell Otoshi, Lilias Outerbridge, Sandy Grove Packard, Mimi Paris, Melissa Peacock, Gabrielle Pearce, Rob Pearson, Robert Pennoyer, Joan Perkins, Elizabeth Perry, Sally Phelps, Robert Phipps, Sumner Pingree, Peter Pruyn, Lilly Pulitzer, Russell Bradhurst Pyne, Taylor Pyne, Diana Quasha, Lee Radziwill, Susan Reeves, John Renwick Sr., Jeri Reyhold, Frank Rhodes, Alexandra L. Robbins, Bill Roberts, Keith Roberts, David Rockefeller, Felix Rohatyn, Joanna Rose, Lynn Royden, Cynthia Foy Rupp, Marina Rust, John Ryan III, Trinka Rynne, Guy Salvadore, Irina San Filipo, Viktoria Sibylle Theisen Schäfer, Wolfgang Schäfer, David Schiff, Frank Schiff, William Schiff III, Dr. Werner Schmidt, Ann Scoville, Charles Scribner Jr., Richard C. Sears, Tony Sears, Neil and Leba Sedaka, Paul Selden, Isaac Shapiro, David Shulman, Robert Siegfried, Rafael de la Sierra, John L. Sills, Kelly Simpson, Barbara Sirna, Gail K. Grant Slingluff, Betty Gautier Smith, Loraine Smith, Presley Smith, Toni Smith, Flo Snyder, Laura Steinberg, Loriann Stevenson, John Stockbridge, Nancy Stoddart, Dana Stone, Kip Stratton, Barnard Straus, Donald B. Straus, John Wendell Straus, Thomas Strauss, Mimi Strong, David Styles, Ken Sunshine, Kathy Swain, Jan Sweet, Stephen Swid, Jean Tailer, J. D. Tew III, Mrs. John (Valerie) Tew, Paul Theroff, Roger H. Thiele, Michael M. Thomas, Barry Thomson, David Thorne, Ed Thorne, Francis Thorne, Julia Stimson Thorne, Landon Thorne, Peter Thorne, Cari Tio, Carlo Toresani, Jim Torpe, Bob Torre, Yvonne and Alberto Uribe, Diane van Amerongen, Hope van Beueren, Joan van Clefe, Anne van den Bergh, William vanden Heuvel, Anthony Gambrill Villa, Peter Villa, Elliott Vose, Carroll Wainwright, Anne Walton, Marshall Webb, David Weir, Catherine Whalen, Katharine Brewster Whipple, Joan Whiteman, Sue Wild, John Wilmerding, John Winslow, Barbara Swain Wittman, Cathy Yandell, Will Zeckendorf, William Zeckendorf Jr., Martin Zimet, Stanford and Eve Zimmerman, and Harvey Zimond.

NOTES

INTRODUCTION

1. Steinberg wasn't the only original greenmailer. In the 1980s, T. Boone Pickens Jr., Irwin Jacobs, and Carl Icahn were also credited with initiating the hardball tactic.

2. The cooperative corporation owns the property, takes out a mortgage on the building, and pays the taxes, but the tenant-shareholders get the tax deductions for interest payments on the mortgage, again, proportional to the number of shares they hold.

CHAPTER 1

1. A few of these one-family homes still stand, converted for use as consulates and museums. Almost none remain in private hands.

2. The first cooperative, the Albany, in London's Piccadilly, was created in 1804 in a mansion originally occupied by one Baron Melbourne of Kilmore, then sold to a son of King George III. As a co-op, it was the home of William Gladstone, Lord Byron, Aldous Huxley, and Graham Greene, according to *Luxury Apartment Houses of Manhattan* by Andrew Alpern.

CHAPTER 2

1. The Shelton is now the Marriott East Side Hotel.

2. Brewster's brother, Robert, vice president of the Metropolitan Opera, was a block south in a Delano & Aldrich mansion completed in 1907.

CHAPTER 3

1. When it was vacated at the end of the fifteen-year lease, the Hutton triplex penthouse stood empty for ten years, and then was split up into six separate apartments.

CHAPTER 4

1. John D. Rockefeller Sr.'s brother William and an associate, James Stillman, were central figures in the National City Bank, New York's largest, which is now known as Citicorp. John D. Rockefeller Jr. briefly joined that bank's board of directors in 1901, but left it within a year. Though Senior had a small stake in the bank (as he did in the First National Bank, controlled by an ally of J. P. Morgan's, and in New

York Trust, which was dominated by the Harknesses, another Standard Oil family), his major banking interest, later inherited by Junior, was in Equitable.

2. The rest of the Presbyterian Hospital land was filled by 33 East Seventieth Street, which occupied the entire Madison Avenue block front, and, between the three giant apartment houses, two rows of private homes, many of which were also purchased by Jews, among them the chairman of the Abraham & Straus stores and several relatives of the family that founded Lehman Brothers, the banking concern.

CHAPTER 5

1. Gertrude Candela, who was married to Candela's son Joseph, then an OSS officer, thinks that her father-in-law may have broken a German code as well.

2. His brother Jonathon, who never married, became mayor of Buffalo and died in 1891.

3. When Michel Bouvier died, William Fahnestock, founder of Fahnestock & Co., became the dean of Wall Street, the longest-tenured holder of a seat on the New York Stock Exchange. John D. Rockefeller, at age ninety-six, placed second. Continuing the It's-a-Small-World theme, a great nephew of Fahnestock's would later marry Mimi Beardsley, one of President John F. Kennedy's White House mistresses.

CHAPTER 6

1. Polo was brought to America by James Gordon Bennett Jr., publisher of *The New York Herald*, in 1876. Five years later, the Meadow Brook Club was formed in Old Westbury. Aficionados had to be rich, because they needed a stable of specialized ponies to play the sport. A standardized set of rules rated players from one to ten goals, with a ten-goal rating reserved for the best players, like Webb, a member of Meadow Brook.

CHAPTER 7

1. Wiggin offered $2 million in 1937 to settle the suits.

2. The Seldens also had a son, Albert Wiggin Selden, who grew up to produce *Man of La Mancha* on Broadway.

3. The SEC's first chairman was Joseph P. Kennedy, the father of Jacqueline Bouvier's future husband.

4. Glass-Steagall was repealed in 1999, allowing commercial banks back into the underwriting business.

5. Even foes of Prohibition like Mrs. George Brewster hated Roosevelt enough that when an advocacy group they'd formed to protest the dry laws endorsed FDR, they protested vehemently. Other signers of the protest were future 740 tenants Mrs. Marshall Field, Mrs. Deering Howe, and Mrs. Preston Davie.

CHAPTER 8

1. Ironically, David Thorne has spent the last thirty years advising John F. Kerry, whose first wife, Julia Thorne, is the mother of Kerry's two daughters. Kerry, of course, ran against the Republican George W. Bush for the presidency in 2004. And David Thorne's wife, Rose, is a great-niece of Mrs. George Baker.

2. After Wilkie's defeat, Thorne and John Cowles, publisher of the *Minneapolis Star Tribune* (whose brother Gardner would later move into 740 Park), would join him on a 1941 fact-finding trip to England as America considered whether to get involved in World War II. Air travel across oceans was still so new that their return flight was the subject of moment-by-moment press coverage. It was the longest nonstop flight in history, and was the first time an American commercial aircraft ever landed on the African continent. Wilkie's conclusions, that America could avoid involvement in the war, proved incorrect.

CHAPTER 10

1. Katherine's matron of honor, Mrs. S. Sloan Colt, would move into 740 Park shortly after she did.

CHAPTER 11

1. The Met would not get a new home until 1966, when it moved to Lincoln Center. Its chairman at that point would be John D. Rockefeller III, Junior's eldest son.

2. Ecker actually paid out less than he committed. Between 1931 and 1935, Metropolitan Life's loans to build Rockefeller Center totaled $44.9 million.

3. Father and son's real estate was assessed at $1.6 million. The value of 740 Park was put at $4.75 million, down from $5 million the year before.

4. Besides David, they were Abby, John D. III, Nelson, Laurance, and Winthrop.

5. Between 1919 and 1960, Junior would give away $1.17 billion to charity and pay $317 million in taxes. He ended up with $200 million more to bequeath at his death in 1960. In his biography of Junior's father, *Titan*, Ron Chernow estimates that the Rockefeller descendants were worth $6.2 billion in 1996.

6. Between 1929 and 1941, MetLife foreclosed on 33,200 properties worth $390 million. Meanwhile, its urban mortgage lending dropped from $231 million in 1921, to $8 million.

CHAPTER 12

1. Field paid more taxes than Rockefeller, because he owned $40 million worth of real estate in the Chicago area.

CHAPTER 13

1. Unfortunately, like so much else in the legend of 740, that story may be apocryphal. Right from the beginning, the New York City directory listed both ad-

dresses. But it's also possible that Mrs. Ledyard simply wanted her friends to know *which* address was hers.

2. The depositions came into the possession of Jackie and Lee's cousin John Davis, via his mother, who was Black Jack's executor. "He got them from Mom's attic," says his sister, Maud. "He helped himself to everything." The books he wrote, based in part on that material, led to a split between the Davis family and Jackie and her surviving brother-in-law, Senator Edward M. Kennedy, Maud Davis says. Though Davis is still alive, neither his health nor his memory is very good, and he can no longer locate the original documents. Kathleen Bouvier, who was married to Black Jack's nephew, confirms that Davis's mother was the source of the documents.

3. Brendan Gill interview with Edward Klein. Date unknown. Courtesy Edward Klein.

CHAPTER 14

1. Requests to view Junior's art would be so frequent over the years that boilerplate answers were drawn up to respond to them. "To make an exception would be embarrassing," supplicants were told. "Mr. Rockefeller is hoping you will not press the request."

2. Some of the brown bricks from Rockefeller Sr.'s house were transported to Pocantico, where they were reused in a house built for David Milton, a Rockefeller in-law.

3. Prince Henry XXXIII died in 1942.

4. Seth Rosewater Burchard attended Harvard, his education paid for by Allene, then worked for General Electric his whole life, before ending his days as a volunteer in a library in Ithaca, New York. When he died, he left an estate of about $1 million to friends and to a local foundation. Friends also inherited a painting he owned of the Château des Suisnes.

CHAPTER 16

1. By the mid-1950s, Flora Whiting's holdings in her father's former company were small; she owned but 2.4 percent, but it was enough to give her a seat on the board of the publisher of *Collier's, Woman's Home Companion,* and *The American Magazine.* In 1960, Crowell-Collier bought the Macmillan Company, the fourth-largest book publisher in America.

CHAPTER 17

1. A number of major corporations emerged from the breakup, among them, Standard Oil of New Jersey, which became Esso; Standard Oil of Indiana, which became Amoco; Standard Oil of New York, which became Mobil; and Standard Oil of California, which became Chevron.

2. In the early 1950s, when she and Cavendish-Bentinck were finally divorced after a prolonged, divisive, tawdry, and very public battle that featured cross-accusations of multiple adulteries and even an appeal to England's House of Lords, Clothilde brought a lawsuit against her sister, attempting to recover money Dorothea had received from the prenuptial agreement with Cavendish-Bentinck. After Clothilde left him, his career recovered, and in 1939 Winston Churchill made him the chairman of the Joint Intelligence Committee, a position he held with distinction throughout World War II. After the war, he was named ambassador to Poland, but was dismissed from the post and deprived of his pension by the postwar Labour government, which used his divorce as an excuse to be rid of a political enemy. He became the ninth Duke of Portland in 1979, and when he died in 1990, the dukedom died with him. The remaining title, Earl of Portland, and the family fortune passed to other branches of the family. Several of his obituaries referred to what one called his "unfortunate marriage."

CHAPTER 18

1. Milbank, Tweed worked with Zeckendorf on the financing.

2. When McCloy served as Franklin Roosevelt's assistant secretary of war, he grew close to Nelson Rockefeller, who then ran the Office of Inter-American Affairs. Nelson helped him take over the World Bank after the war, and then arranged a partnership at Milbank, Tweed when he stepped down.

3. Oddly, another source claims that Dorothea later spirited her mother's body away in the same manner and disposed of the corpse. Claudette Hollenbeck says her father-in-law, Dorothea's lawyer J. Carlisle Swaim, "thought Dorothea dumped her in the river—there was no record of her death and her body was never found." Relatives admit they're not sure what happened to Margaruite Williams. "I am sure she died in New York," says Graubard, who thinks her grandmother died and was cremated, but isn't sure when. "The cremation occurred without my grandmother's knowledge," says William Georgiades, Clothilde's grandson. "She was informed after the fact. It is one of the mysteries of our family, precisely when she died or how she died. We simply don't know. I doubt there was anything sinister about it. Dorothea didn't have much to gain from her death, and she wasn't exactly the murdering type. It was, you know, her mother."

CHAPTER 19

1. In years to come, he'd work closely with Laurance and David, as well as Nelson, on a series of ventures, most notably the five-year "Wall Street Maneuver," as he called it, in which Webb & Knapp moved Chase Manhattan Bank (its name changed by further mergers) to a new headquarters, not incidentally making millions and keeping New York's fabled financial district in the Wall Street neighborhood.

CHAPTER 21

1. In 1950, Junior also set up trusts with Standard Oil stock for all his living grandchildren, each of whom got about $5 million.

2. Emily Bedford remarried soon after that, was divorced again quickly, and remarried again before she died in 1975.

CHAPTER 25

1. In 1963, a New York family that was very prominent in the real estate business made headlines when they filed a complaint with New York's Commission on Human Rights that they'd been rejected by 720 Park Avenue, the building constructed by Jesse Straus, because they were Jewish. They explained, on condition they not be identified, that upon hearing that the building barred Jews, Democrats, and nonwhite servants, they'd asked the co-op board to let them know if there was any point applying and were told they would be acceptable. They later learned that a Straus relative, who was Jewish and on the board but out of town when that assurance was given, overruled the board when he returned. As their complaint wended its way through official channels, the apartment sat empty for almost a year, and their family received anonymous threats, as well as offers to move into other top co-ops. Finally, when reporters again began asking questions, the board member withdrew his objection, and they were invited to move in, but declined. The man of the family went on to serve as the president of his co-op's board for thirty-five years, and 720 was eventually integrated.

2. Bruce Gimbel became chairman of Gimbel Brothers in 1973, presided over its sale to Brown & Williamson, and died in 1980.

3. Epstein spent the rest of his life building homes and planned communities in Florida. In 1968, he founded a development, construction, and building supply company there and was still its chairman when he died in 1980. He spent every other week there, though he always came home for weekends in Bedford. He also dabbled in Broadway theater with his wife, producing the hits *Same Time, Next Year, Ain't Misbehavin'*, and, just before his death, *Children of a Lesser God*. Dasha Epstein continued to produce on Broadway for many years.

CHAPTER 26

1. Dominic Byrne had often picked up customers in his limousine at Uncle Charlie's but didn't know they were homosexuals. "He said they were nice gentlemen," says someone who knew him. "He was in another world, a child." *Newsweek* described Byrne as "a man so thoroughly dominated that Lynch had only to ask to get him to heel." And Bronfman testified that he'd been kind and thoughtful and even seemed ready to turn him loose at one point.

CHAPTER 27

1. Doris Vidor died in 1978.

CHAPTER 28

1. Leaving 740 was the beginning of the end of Mike Cowles's glory years. Following the death of *Look*, he continued to shed properties and professional responsibilities, and in 1978 Cowles Communications was dissolved, its assets distributed to its stockholders, and Cowles devoted himself to philanthropy. The couple downsized again that year, moving to an even smaller apartment. With the sale of the Des Moines newspaper in 1985, all that remained was the Minneapolis newspapers. Cowles died after a long battle with cancer a week after that sale. First Lady Nancy Reagan led the mourners at his memorial service.

2. The Securities and Exchange Commission later accused Vesco and associates of looting IOS of $224 million, defrauding thousands of investors. In 1973, he was indicted for making illegal contributions to the reelection campaign of President Richard M. Nixon, and in 1976 he was indicted by a federal grand jury on charges relating to his fraudulent schemes in IOS. He fled the country and remains a fugitive to this day.

3. After Keith and Ann moved back to New York in the 1990s, one of Barish's best friends would be Sam Waksal, the head of the biotech company ImClone, convicted inside trader, and former best friend of the homemaking guru Martha Stewart.

CHAPTER 29

1. After their settlement, Laura Steinberg reportedly retracted many of her charges.

CHAPTER 30

1. After several renegotiations of the interest rate in the 1990s, that mortgage was to come due early in 2005, but was renewed at the end of 2003 by Randolph Speight's successor, who also borrowed an additional $500,000 to raise the building's debt to $6 million.

2. In a later article, Norman reported that in 1997 American International acquired control of oil and gas rights to a 4.7-million-acre parcel in the former Soviet republic of Kazakhstan, causing its stock price to triple in three days, just after Rynne and a fellow director, AIP's chairman, bought $1.2 million of shares between them at a price of just twenty-five cents each. Rynne resigned from AIP in 2002 in the midst of a financial restructuring.

CHAPTER 31

1. Nawwaf would be named head of Saudi foreign intelligence just after September 11, 2001, replacing his nephew Prince Turki. He had a stroke in 2002 at age seventy.

2. At the time, the record was held by Martin Zweig, a securities executive who'd paid $21.5 million for a triplex at the Hotel Pierre. In 2004, he put it on the market for $70 million.

3. Mulheren had been found guilty of conspiring with Boesky to manipulate stock prices. After an appeal, the case was thrown out of federal court in 1991. Englander was not charged.

4. In 1983, Mahoney attempted to take Norton Simon private, but lost the company to a rival called Esmark. He dedicated the rest of his life to the Charles A. Dana Foundation, which funds studies of the brain and its diseases. Mahoney died in 2000.

CHAPTER 34

1. Araskog retired from ITT in 1998 and began spending most of his time at his neo-classical mansion on Lake Worth in Palm Beach. His apartment went on the market in 2004 and was sold early in 2005 to a hedge fund manager.

2. Arthur spent his last years as an investor and died in Palm Beach in 1991. "My stepmother got everything," Samuel Leidesdorf says. "I did not go to the funeral."

3. The board had reason to be concerned about its image. Not long before, when a Jewish staff member's father died, the employee, who worked at the 740 Park entrance, began wearing a yarmulke to work—and was banished to the back of the building after residents deemed his attire inappropriate. The story quickly spread among New York's elite Jewish community.

4. Subsequently, another Morgan Guaranty Trust official was charged with aiding and abetting Gebauer and receiving $212,000 in kickbacks from consultants assisting in financial work for two of their clients. In that indictment, it was revealed that Gebauer received $300,000 in kickbacks as well.

5. Blake was a trustee of Historic Deerfield, in Massachusetts, where he went to prep school, and the Channing Blake Meadow Walk there is named for him. Paintings and sculptures he donated to the Museum of Fine Arts in Springfield, Massachusetts, form the basis of its Italian Baroque collection.

CHAPTER 35

1. "I do not like to talk about my personal life in the press or in books, which is all part of the times we live in," Kravis wrote in response to a request for an interview. Roehm declined comment, too. Friends say she is barred from discussing Kravis by the terms of their divorce agreement.

2. As this book goes to press, Koch still lives at 1040 Fifth. The "summer work rules"

in effect at 740 mean major renovations can only be done in summertime. He expects to move in in the fall of 2005.

CHAPTER 37
1. Stevenson had also added June Speight and June Dyson to the board "because he wanted history," says a board member. "They are people who have been here a long time and have a sense of how the building should be run."

BIBLIOGRAPHY

ALDRICH, NELSON W., JR. *Old Money: The Mythology of Wealth in America.* New York: Allworth Press, 1996.

ALPERN, ANDREW. *Historic Manhattan Apartment Houses.* New York: Dover, 1996.

———. *Luxury Apartment Houses of Manhattan.* New York: Dover, 1992.

———. *The New York Apartment Houses of Rosario Candela and James Carpenter.* New York: Acanthus Press, 2001.

AMORY, CLEVELAND. *The Last Resorts.* New York: Harper & Brothers, 1948.

———. *Who Killed Society?* New York: Harper & Brothers, 1960.

ANTHONY, CARL SFERRAZZA. *As We Remember Her.* New York: HarperCollins, 1997.

BENDER, MARYLIN. *At the Top.* Garden City, N.Y.: Doubleday, 1975.

———. *The Beautiful People.* New York: Coward-McCann, 1967.

BERGMAN, EDWARD F. *Woodlawn Remembers.* Utica, N.Y.: North Country Books, 1988.

BIRMINGHAM, STEPHEN. *America's Secret Aristocracy.* Boston: Little, Brown, 1987.

———. *"Our Crowd."* New York: Harper & Row, 1967.

BOUVIER, KATHLEEN. *Black Jack Bouvier.* New York: Pinnacle, 1979.

BRADFORD, SARAH. *America's Queen: The Life of Jacqueline Kennedy Onassis.* New York: Viking, 2000.

BRAUDY, SUSAN. *This Crazy Thing Called Love.* New York: Knopf, 1992.

BROOKS, JOHN. *The Go-Go Years.* New York: Weybright and Talley, 1973.

———. *Once in Golconda.* New York: W. W. Norton, 1969.

BRUCK, CONNIE. *Master of the Game.* New York: Simon and Schuster, 1994.

———. *The Predators' Ball.* New York: Simon and Schuster, 1988.

BYRON, CHRISTOPHER. *Testosterone, Inc.* Hoboken, N.J.: Wiley, 2004.

CARNOCHAN, W. B. *Momentary Bliss: An American Memoir.* Stanford, Calif.: Stanford University Libraries, 1999.

CHERNOW, RON. *The House of Morgan.* New York: Atlantic Monthly Press, 1990.

———. *Titan: The Life of John D. Rockefeller Sr.* New York: Random House, 1998.

CHORLEY, E. CLOWES. *The Centennial History of Saint Bartholomew's Church in the City of New York, 1835–1935.* New York, 1935.

COLLIER, PETER, and DAVID HOROWITZ. *The Rockefellers: An American Dynasty.* New York: Holt, Rinehart, and Winston, 1976.

CONANT, JENNET. *Tuxedo Park.* New York: Simon and Schuster, 2003.

CONRAD, EARL. *Billy Rose, Manhattan Primitive.* Cleveland: World, 1968.

CRATER, SUSAN BARTLETT, and APPLE PARISH BARTLETT. *Sister: The Life of Legendary American Interior Decorator Mrs. Henry Parish II.* New York: St. Martin's, 2000.

CURCIO, VINCENT. *Chrysler: The Life and Times of an Automotive Genius.* New York: Oxford University Press, 2000.

DAVIS, JOHN H. *The Bouviers.* New York: Farrar, Straus & Giroux, 1969.

———. *The Kennedys: Dynasty and Disaster.* New York: McGraw-Hill, 1984.

EHRLICH, JUDITH RAMSEY, and BARRY J. REHFELD. *The New Crowd: The Changing of the Jewish Guard on Wall Street.* Boston: Little, Brown, 1989.

EVERS, ALF. *Woodstock: History of an American Town.* Woodstock, N.Y.: Overlook Press, 1987.

FOREMAN, JOHN, and ROBBE PIERCE STIMSON. *The Vanderbilts and the Gilded Age.* New York: St. Martin's, 1991.

FOWLER, OSCAR PRESLEY. *The Haskell Regime.* Oklahoma City: Boles Printing Company, 1933.

GREER, MARGARET. *The Sands of Time: A History of Hilton Head Island.* Hilton Head Island, S.C.: SouthArt, 1989.

GROSSMAN, PETER Z. *American Express.* New York: Crown, 1987.

HACK, RICHARD. *When Money Is King.* Los Angeles: Dove Books, 1996.

HAVEMEYER, HARRY W. *Along the Great South Bay.* Mattituck, N.Y.: Amereon House, 1996.

HAWES, ELIZABETH. *New York, New York: How the Apartment House Transformed the Life of the City.* New York: Knopf, 1993.

HENRY, JAMES S. *The Blood Bankers: Tales from the Global Underground Economy.* New York: Four Walls Eight Windows, 2003.

HEWES, LAUREN B., and CELIA Y. OLIVER. *To Collect in Earnest: The Life and Work of Electra Havemeyer Webb.* Shelburne, Vt.: Shelburne Museum, 1997.

HEYMANN, C. DAVID. *A Woman Named Jackie.* New York: Lyle Stuart, 1989.

HOMBERGER, ERIC. *Mrs. Astor's New York.* New Haven, Conn.: Yale University Press, 2002.

HOYT, EDWIN P. *The Goulds.* New York: Weybright and Talley, 1969.

HURST, IRVIN. *The 46th Star.* Oklahoma City: Semco Color Press, 1957.

KELLEY, KITTY. *Jackie Oh!* New York: Lyle Stuart, 1978.

KLEIN, EDWARD. *All Too Human: The Love Story of Jack and Jackie Kennedy.* New York: Pocket Books, 1996.

KONOLIGE, KIT, and FREDERICA KONOLIGE. *The Power of Their Glory.* New York: Wyden Books, 1978.

MADSEN, AXEL. *The Marshall Fields.* Hoboken, N.J.: Wiley, 2002.

MANCHESTER, WILLIAM. *A Rockefeller Family Portrait.* Boston: Little, Brown, 1958.

MARQUIS, JAMES. *The Metropolitan Life.* New York: Viking, 1947.

MORRIS, CHARLES R. *Money, Greed, and Risk.* New York: Times Books, 1999.

MULVANEY, JAY. *Diana & Jackie: Maidens, Mothers, Myths*. New York: St. Martin's, 2003.

MUNSON, RICHARD. *The Power Makers*. Emmaus, Pa.: Rodale, 1985.

MURRAY, GEORGE WELWOOD. *Histories of the Predecessor Firms of Milbank, Tweed, Hope & Webb (Part 1)*. New York: Milbank, Tweed, Hope & Webb, 1937.

NASAW, DAVID. *The Chief: The Life of William Randolph Hearst*. New York: Houghton Mifflin, 2000.

NEWMAN, PETER C. *Bronfman Dynasty: The Rothschilds of the New World*. Toronto: McClelland and Stewart, 1978.

OKRENT, DANIEL. *Great Fortune: The Epic of Rockefeller Center*. New York: Viking, 2003.

PFEIFFER, TIMOTHY N. *Milbank, Tweed, Hadley & McCloy: Law Practice in a Turbulent World*. New York: Milbank, Tweed, Hadley & McCloy, 1965.

POLLOCK, ELLEN JOAN. *Turks and Brahmins: Upheaval at Milbank, Tweed: Wall Street's Gentlemen Take Off Their Gloves*. New York: Simon and Schuster, 1990.

POTTKER, JAN. *Janet and Jackie*. New York: St. Martin's, 2001.

ROCKEFELLER, DAVID. *Memoirs*. New York: Random House, 2002.

SCHNADELBACH, R. TERRY. *Ferruccio Vitale: Landscape Architect of the Country Place Era*. New York: Princeton Architectural Press, 2001.

SMITH, JAMES H. *History of Duchess* [sic] *County, New York*. Syracuse, N.Y.: D. Mason & Co., 1882.

STASZ, CLARICE. *The Rockefeller Women*. New York: St. Martin's, 1995.

STEWART, JAMES B. *Den of Thieves*. New York: Simon and Schuster, 1991.

———. *The Partners*. New York: Simon and Schuster, 1983.

SWANBERG, W. A. *Citizen Hearst*. New York: Scribner, 1961.

TOSCHES, NICK. *Dino: Living High in the Dirty Business of Dreams*. New York: Doubleday, 1992.

TRAGER, JAMES. *Park Avenue: Street of Dreams*. New York: Atheneum, 1990.

TWEED, KATHARINE. *The Finest Rooms by America's Great Decorators*. New York: Viking, 1964.

VANDERBILT, ARTHUR T., II. *Fortune's Children: The Fall of the House of Vanderbilt*. New York: Morrow, 1989.

VIDAL, GORE. *Palimpsest: A Memoir*. New York: Random House, 1995.

WILSON, JOHN DONALD. *The Chase: The Chase Manhattan Bank, N.A., 1945–1985*. Boston: Harvard Business School Press, 1986.

WORDEN, HELEN. *Society Circus*. New York: Covici, Friede, 1936.

ZECKENDORF, WILLIAM, with EDWARD McCREARY. *Zeckendorf*. Chicago: Plaza Press, 1987.

INDEX

© LINDSAY McCRUM

MICHAEL GROSS has written for the *New York Times*, *New York*, *Esquire*, *GQ*, *Vanity Fair*, *Town & Country*, and gawker.com. Currently a contributing editor at *Travel+Leisure*, he is the author of the bestselling exposés *Model: The Ugly Business of Beautiful Women*; *Genuine Authentic: The Real Life of Ralph Lauren*; and *My Generation: Fifty Years of Sex, Drugs, Rock, Revolution, Glamour, Greed, Valor, Faith, and Silicon Chips*. He lives in New York City, where he is president of his cooperative apartment building's board of directors.